Cooking Light

Holiday
Cookbook

Cooking Light.
Holiday
Cookbook

Compiled and Edited by
Heather Averett

Oxmoor
House.

ISBN: 0-8487-3004-6
Library of Congress Control Number:
2005925528

Printed in the United States of America
First printing 2005

Be sure to check with your health-care
provider before making any changes in
your diet.

Oxmoor House, Inc.
Editor in Chief: Nancy Fitzpatrick Wyatt
Executive Editor: Katherine M. Eakin
Art Director: Cynthia Rose Cooper
Copy Chief: Allison Long Lowery

Cooking Light® Holiday Cookbook
Editor: Heather Averett
Copy Editor: Diane Rose
Senior Designer: Emily Albright Parrish
Editorial Assistants: Shannon Friedmann,
    Terri Laschober
Senior Photographer: Jim Bathie
Senior Photo Stylist: Kay E. Clarke
Publishing Systems Administrator:
    Rick Tucker
Director of Production: Phillip Lee
Production Managers: Greg A. Amason,
    Amorice K. Nall
Production Assistant: Faye Porter Bonner

Contributors:
Indexer: Mary Ann Laurens
Editorial Intern: Julie Boston

To order additional publications, call 1-800-
765-6400, or visit **oxmoorhouse.com**

Cooking Light®
Editor in Chief: Mary Kay Culpepper
Executive Editor: Billy R. Sims
Art Director: Susan Waldrip Dendy
Managing Editor: Maelynn Cheung
Senior Food Editor: Alison Mann Ashton
Senior Editor: Anamary Pelayo
Projects Editor: Mary Simpson Creel, M.S., R.D.
Associate Food Editors: Ann Taylor Pittman;
    Joy E. Zacharia, R.D.
Associate Editor: Rachel Seligman
Assistant Editor: Cindy Hatcher
Contributing Beauty Editor: Lauren McCann
Test Kitchens Director: Vanessa Taylor Johnson
Food Stylist: Kellie Gerber Kelley
Assistant Food Stylist: M. Kathleen Kanen
Test Kitchens Staff: Sam Brannock,
    Kathryn Conrad, Mary H. Drennen,
    Jan Jacks Moon, Tiffany Vickers,
    Mike Wilson
Assistant Art Director: Maya Metz Logue
Senior Designer: Fernande Bondarenko
Designer: J. Shay McNamee
Assistant Designer: Brigette Mayer
Senior Photographers: Becky Luigart-Stayner,
    Randy Mayor
Senior Photo Stylist: Cindy Barr
Photo Stylists: Melanie J. Clarke, Jan Gautro
Digital Photo Stylist: Jan A. Smith
Studio Assistant: Celine Chenoweth
Copy Chief: Maria Parker Hopkins
Senior Copy Editor: Susan Roberts
Copy Editor: Tara Trenary
Copy Researcher: Johannah Paiva
Production Manager: Liz Rhoades
Production Editors: Joanne McCrary Brasseal,
    Hazel R. Eddins
Administrative Coordinator: Carol D. Johnson
Office Manager: Rita K. Jackson
Editorial Assistants: Melissa Hoover,
    Brandy Rushing
Correspondence Editor: Michelle Gibson
    Daniels

CookingLight.com
Editor: Jennifer Middleton
Online Producer: Abigail Masters

Cover: (clockwise from top left) Christmas Sugar Wafers with Vanilla Icing (page 111),
White Chocolate-Cashew Coffee Biscotti (page 114), Ginger Shortbread (page 109), and
Toasted Pecan Divinity (page 105)
Page 1: Tunisian-Spiced Turkey with Garlic Couscous and Harissa Gravy (page 266)
Page 5: Orange Marmalade Layer Cake (page 314)

Contents

Welcome

The holidays—that wonderfully special season from mid-November to January 1. What exactly does the holiday season mean to you?

Perhaps it evokes sentimental memories of a big family get-together with a fine china–laden table adorned with a juicy turkey and all of the tasty trimmings. Or perhaps it conjures up happy thoughts of hustle and bustle and all of the excitement associated with parties, trimming the tree, and gift-giving. Whatever the holiday season means to you, there's one thing for sure—food is definitely a huge part of it.

At *Cooking Light,* we recognize that in this season—crammed as it is with obligations and stress—what remains important isn't what blasts from TV screens, beckons from colorful store signs, or rings from cell phones. What truly is important and unique about this special time are the things that can't be bought—time with family and friends, good food, and things that speak to the heart and are soothing to the soul. The recollection of a special dish, the making of it, or the sharing of it can, like a certain aroma, open links to a time past and bring it to the present with breathtaking immediacy.

With that in mind, we've created a cookbook tailored especially for such a season—the *Cooking Light Holiday Cookbook.* Our holiday cookbook sets out to exemplify the *Cooking Light* motto: Eat Smart, Be Fit, Live Well. And everything within the pages of this treasure is designed to help you do just that. You'll discover over 500 delicious recipes that allow you to feast on fabulous holiday food but still keep a healthy lifestyle in mind. These recipes in no way deny or deprive. Instead, they simply delight!

But it's not just about the recipes themselves. After all, the holidays are about the occasion as a whole and creating memories with family and friends. That's why the *Cooking Light ® Holiday Cookbook* isn't just another cookbook—it's really a holiday handbook. In addition to terrific recipes and complete menu ideas, this compilation offers countless suggestions for make-ahead meals, table-decorating tips, and ingredient substitutions. It's also packed with how-to photos, a food and wine pairing chart, a party-planning guide, and gift-giving ideas.

This book features lightened versions of familiar favorites as well as exciting new recipes. Beautiful photography throughout illustrates many of the recipes, both to speed prep time and to reassure you that you're on the right track. We're so glad that this collection has made its way into your kitchen. Giving you fabulous recipes and entertaining ideas is our notion of a great way to celebrate the season. Here's wishing you a season of goodwill and good food. Happy holidays from all of us at *Cooking Light.*

Our Favorite Holiday Recipes

All Cooking Light recipes have to meet our high standards, but here are a select few that stand out above the rest. These delicious, memorable recipes are the ones that grace our editors' and kitchens staff's holiday tables.

◀ **Pear, Walnut, and Blue Cheese Salad with Cranberry Vinaigrette** *(page 194):*

The flavors of fruit, cheese, and nuts make this elegant salad the perfect complement to your turkey menu.

◀ **Apricot-Cream Cheese Braid** *(page 122):*

With a swirl of cream cheese and fruit throughout, this yeasty coffee bread is reminiscent of a Danish pastry minus the fat.

◀ **Vanilla Cheesecake with Cherry Topping** *(page 76):*

If you're not a cheesecake fan, the combination of the rich vanilla flavor and the luscious texture is guaranteed to win you over.

◀ **Macadamia Butter Cookies with Dried Cranberries** *(page 110):*

The macadamia nut butter is incredibly, fantastically, eat-it-with-a-spoon delicious. And the cranberries give these cookies the perfect holiday touch.

◀ **Potato-Gorgonzola Gratin** *(page 287):*

Just a bit of blue cheese goes a long way in this comforting, warming side, and Parmigiano-Reggiano sprinkled on top creates a nice brown crust.

◀ **Raspberry Strippers** *(page 110):*

It's hard to believe these bar cookies are light. They have all the flavor and texture of a traditional shortbread cookie.

◀ **Pennsylvania Dutch Tea Rolls** *(page 183):*

The height of these rolls when they come out of the oven will amaze you. It's virtually impossible to eat just one, as our staff discovered.

◄ *Cooking Light's* Ultimate Roasted Turkey *(page 264)*:

One taste and you'll agree: This is our best holiday turkey ever.

Herb-Roasted Turkey with Cheese Grits *(page 263)*:

This turkey is far more than just the usual holiday repeat; it's guaranteed to wow guests at any time of the year.

Asparagus, Ham, and Fontina Bread Puddings *(page 254)*:

Nutty, creamy fontina and savory ham yield a bona fide taste sensation.

◄ Persimmon and Fennel Salad *(page 196)*:

What a great way to use persimmons without cooking them to death! We prefer nonastringent Fuyu persimmons in this colorful salad.

◄ Stuffed French Toast *(page 166)*:

This recipe is so good and easy to pull together. It's ideal for overnight out-of-town trips with friends. You'll be amazed by how quickly it's gobbled up.

◄ Roasted-Poblano Guacamole with Garlic and Parsley *(page 129)*:

This spicy spread is always such a welcome change from the more traditional holiday fare.

◄ Clementine Salad with Spiced Walnuts and Pickled Onions *(page 193)*:

Other than eating clementines right out of the peel, this is one of our favorite ways to enjoy them.

◄ Old-Fashioned Caramel Layer Cake *(page 311)*:

Delicious! This cake is a keeper. It will impress even the pickiest sweet tooth. You'll want to keep this dessert around all year, not just during the holidays.

◄ Pecan Tassies in Cream Cheese Pastry *(page 333)*:

Packed with pecans, these miniature tarts have all the taste of a big pecan pie, but their small size makes them ideal for parties and buffets.

holiday menus

From classic Thanksgiving spreads to festive Christmas dinners, these unforgettable menus will quickly become integral parts of the ultimate memorable occasions.

Farmhouse Roast Turkey with Rosemary Gravy (recipe on page 24)

(clockwise from front) Lasagna with Fall Vegetables, Gruyère, and Sage Béchamel; Lemon-Poppy Seed Pan Rolls; Cranberry-Orange Compote with Port

Harvest Celebration

Usher in the holidays with nature's bounty of seasonal fruits and vegetables. All the recipes in this vegetarian menu are either make-ahead or have make-ahead components that save time for the busy cook during the holidays.

Menu

serves 8

*Crispy Butternut Won Tons with
Spicy Tomato Sauce*

Cauliflower-Leek Potage

*Lasagna with Fall Vegetables,
Gruyère, and Sage Béchamel*

Cranberry-Orange Compote with Port

*Green Apple and Celery Salad with
Mustard Vinaigrette*

Lemon-Poppy Seed Pan Rolls

Pear-Cranberry Crisp

Cranberry-Orange Compote with Port

```
1    cup port or other sweet red wine
½    cup honey
6    cups fresh cranberries
1    cup sugar
1    tablespoon grated orange rind
¼    teaspoon ground cinnamon
⅛    teaspoon ground cloves
⅛    teaspoon freshly ground black
     pepper
```

1. Combine port and honey in a large saucepan; bring to a boil. Add cranberries; cook 6 minutes or until cranberries begin to pop, stirring occasionally. Stir in sugar and remaining ingredients; cook 5 minutes or until sugar dissolves. Cover and chill. Yield: 4 cups (serving size: ¼ cup).

CALORIES 110 (1% from fat); FAT 0.1g (sat 0g, mono 0g, poly 0.1g); PROTEIN 0.2g; CARB 26.7g; FIBER 1.6g; CHOL 0mg; IRON 0.2mg; SODIUM 2mg; CALC 5mg

Cauliflower-Leek Potage

Puree in a blender for the smoothest, creamiest results. Make the soup up to a day ahead, and store in the refrigerator. Reheat over medium-low heat, stirring frequently.

```
4    quarts water
2    tablespoons fresh lemon juice
7    cups cauliflower florets (about
     2½ pounds)
1½   tablespoons butter, divided
     Cooking spray
3    cups thinly sliced leek (about
     2 large)
¼    teaspoon sea salt
2    (14-ounce) cans vegetable broth,
     divided
⅛    teaspoon white pepper
     Dash of ground nutmeg
4    teaspoons minced fresh chives
```

1. Bring 4 quarts water to a boil in a Dutch oven, and stir in juice. Add cauliflower, reduce heat, and simmer 15 minutes or until tender. Drain.
2. Melt 1½ teaspoons butter in a large nonstick skillet coated with cooking spray over medium heat. Add leek and salt; cover and cook 5 minutes, stirring occasionally. Reduce heat to medium-low; cook 5 minutes or until tender (do not brown), stirring occasionally. Combine leek and cauliflower.
3. Place half of cauliflower mixture and 1 cup broth in a blender; process until smooth. Pour pureed mixture into a large bowl. Repeat procedure with remaining cauliflower mixture and 1 cup broth.

4. Melt 1 tablespoon butter over medium heat in Dutch oven. Cook 3 minutes or until lightly browned, stirring occasionally. Add cauliflower puree and remaining broth. Simmer 5 minutes. Stir in pepper and nutmeg. Sprinkle each serving with ½ teaspoon chives. Yield: 8 servings (serving size: ¾ cup).

CALORIES 83 (33% from fat); FAT 3g (sat 1.4g, mono 0.6g, poly 0.3g); PROTEIN 4.2g; CARB 13.4g; FIBER 4.2g; CHOL 6mg; IRON 1.3mg; SODIUM 565mg; CALC 52mg

Green Apple and Celery Salad with Mustard Vinaigrette

```
3    tablespoons fresh lemon juice
3    tablespoons Dijon mustard
2    tablespoons honey
½    teaspoon sea salt
1½   teaspoons extravirgin olive oil
¼    teaspoon freshly ground black pepper
1    garlic clove, minced
6    cups sliced peeled Granny Smith
     apple (about 3 apples)
4    cups thinly sliced celery (about
     6 stalks)
¼    cup fresh flat-leaf parsley leaves
3    tablespoons coarsely chopped
     walnuts, toasted
```

1. Combine first 7 ingredients in a large bowl; stir well with a whisk. Add apple and remaining ingredients; toss well to combine. Yield: 8 servings (serving size: 1 cup).

CALORIES 108 (30% from fat); FAT 3.6g (sat 0.4g, mono 1.1g, poly 1.7g); PROTEIN 1.5g; CARB 20.6g; FIBER 3g; CHOL 0mg; IRON 0.7mg; SODIUM 340mg; CALC 42mg

Lasagna with Fall Vegetables, Gruyère, and Sage Béchamel

Although this hearty dish involves several steps, most can be done a couple of days in advance. Prepare and refrigerate the béchamel, covered, up to 2 days ahead. Refrigerate the mushroom-sweet potato mixture and the spinach mixture separately for up to 2 days.

Béchamel:
- ⅔ cup all-purpose flour
- 6 cups fat-free milk
- ½ cup finely chopped onion
- ¼ cup chopped fresh sage
- 2 tablespoons finely chopped shallots
- ½ teaspoon sea salt
- 1 bay leaf

Filling:
- 1 tablespoon olive oil, divided
- 2½ cups finely chopped onion
- 3 garlic cloves, minced
- 1 teaspoon sea salt, divided
- 1 (10-ounce) package fresh spinach
- 8 cups chopped portobello mushroom caps (about 1½ pounds)
- 6 cups (½-inch) cubed peeled sweet potato (about 2½ pounds)
- Cooking spray
- 1 cup (4 ounces) shredded Gruyère cheese
- ¾ cup (3 ounces) grated fresh Parmesan cheese

Noodles:
- 12 precooked lasagna noodles
- 2 cups warm water

1. Preheat oven to 450°.

2. To prepare béchamel, lightly spoon flour into dry measuring cups; level with a knife. Place flour in a Dutch oven, and gradually add milk, stirring with a whisk. Add ½ cup onion, sage, shallots, ½ teaspoon salt, and bay leaf. Bring the mixture to a boil; cook 1 minute or until thick. Strain béchamel through a sieve over a bowl, and discard solids. Set béchamel aside.

3. To prepare the filling, heat 1½ teaspoons olive oil in a large nonstick skillet over medium-high heat. Add 2½ cups onion and garlic; sauté 3 minutes. Add ½ teaspoon salt and spinach, and sauté 2 minutes or until spinach wilts. Set aside.

4. Combine 1½ teaspoons oil, ½ teaspoon salt, mushrooms, and sweet potato on a jelly-roll pan coated with cooking spray. Bake at 450° for 15 minutes.

5. Combine cheeses; set aside.

6. To prepare noodles, soak noodles in 2 cups warm water in a 13 x 9-inch baking dish 5 minutes. Drain.

7. Spread ¾ cup béchamel in bottom of a 13 x 9-inch baking dish coated with cooking spray. Arrange 3 noodles over béchamel; top with half of mushroom mixture, 1½ cups béchamel, and ⅓ cup cheese mixture. Top with 3 noodles, spinach mixture, 1½ cups béchamel, and ⅓ cup cheese mixture. Top with 3 noodles, remaining mushroom mixture, 1½ cups béchamel, and 3 noodles. Spread remaining béchamel over noodles. Bake at 450° for 20 minutes. Sprinkle with remaining cheese; bake an additional 10 minutes. Let stand 10 minutes before serving. Yield: 9 servings.

CALORIES 418 (20% from fat); FAT 9.5g (sat 4.5g, mono 3.2g, poly 1g); PROTEIN 22.3g; CARB 62.7g; FIBER 6.4g; CHOL 24mg; IRON 3.7mg; SODIUM 703mg; CALC 505mg

Crispy Butternut Won Tons with Spicy Tomato Sauce

You'll only use a cup of the cooked squash; mash the remaining squash with a little butter, salt, and pepper to serve another day. Prepare the won ton filling up to a day ahead, and make the sauce up to 2 days in advance.

Sauce:
- 1½ teaspoons olive oil
- 1½ cups thinly sliced leek (about 2 medium)
- 1 garlic clove, minced
- ¼ teaspoon crushed red pepper
- ⅛ teaspoon sea salt
- ⅛ teaspoon freshly ground black pepper
- 1 (14.5-ounce) can whole tomatoes, undrained and chopped
- 1 (3-inch) orange rind strip
- 1 bay leaf
- 1 fresh tarragon sprig

Won Tons:
- 1 small butternut squash (about 1½ pounds)
- ½ cup water
- ½ cup ricotta cheese
- 3 tablespoons grated fresh Parmesan cheese
- 2 tablespoons dry breadcrumbs
- ¼ teaspoon sea salt
- ¼ teaspoon freshly ground black pepper
- ⅛ teaspoon ground nutmeg
- 1 teaspoon water
- 1 large egg, lightly beaten
- 24 won ton wrappers
- Cooking spray

1. To prepare sauce, heat oil in a large nonstick skillet over medium heat. Add leek and garlic; cook 8 minutes or until tender (do not brown), stirring frequently. Increase heat to medium-high. Add red pepper and next 6 ingredients; bring to a boil. Reduce heat to low; simmer 15 minutes or until thick. Discard rind, bay leaf, and tarragon.

2. Preheat oven to 375°.

3. To prepare won tons, cut squash in half lengthwise; discard seeds and membrane. Place squash halves, cut sides down, in a 2-quart baking dish; add ½ cup water. Bake at 375° for 45 minutes or until squash is tender when pierced with a fork; cool. Scoop out pulp to measure 1 cup, and reserve remaining pulp for another use. Combine 1 cup pulp, ricotta, and next 5 ingredients, stirring until well combined.

4. Combine 1 teaspoon water and egg, stirring with a whisk. Working with 1 won ton wrapper at a time (cover remaining wrappers with a damp towel to keep from drying), spoon about 2 teaspoons squash mixture into center of each wrapper. Brush edges of dough with egg mixture; bring 2 opposite corners together. Press edges together to seal, forming a triangle. Repeat procedure with remaining won ton wrappers and squash mixture.

5. Place won tons on a large baking sheet coated with cooking spray, and brush lightly with remaining egg mixture. Bake at 375° for 17 minutes or until golden and crisp. Serve with sauce. Yield: 8 servings (serving size: 3 won tons and 3 tablespoons sauce).

CALORIES 157 (26% from fat); FAT 4.6g (sat 2.1g, mono 1.7g, poly 0.4g); PROTEIN 6.8g; CARB 22.3g; FIBER 2g; CHOL 38mg; IRON 1.8mg; SODIUM 385mg; CALC 100mg

Crispy Butternut Won Tons
with Spicy Tomato Sauce

Lemon-Poppy Seed Pan Rolls

If you can't find whole wheat pastry flour, substitute all-purpose flour. Make and freeze the bread up to a month ahead.

1½ cups warm 2% reduced-fat milk (100° to 110°)
1 tablespoon honey
1 package dry yeast (about 2¼ teaspoons)
3 cups all-purpose flour, divided
1 cup whole wheat pastry flour
2½ teaspoons poppy seeds, divided
1½ teaspoons salt
3 tablespoons butter, melted
4 teaspoons grated lemon rind
1 large egg, lightly beaten
Cooking spray
1 teaspoon water
1 large egg, lightly beaten

1. Combine first 3 ingredients in a large bowl, and let stand 5 minutes. Lightly spoon flours into dry measuring cups; level with a knife. Combine 2¾ cups all-purpose flour, pastry flour, 2 teaspoons poppy seeds, and salt; stir with a whisk. Add flour mixture to milk mixture; stir until a soft dough forms. Add butter, rind, and 1 egg. Turn dough out onto a lightly floured surface. Knead until smooth and elastic (about 10 minutes); add enough of remaining flour, 1 tablespoon at a time, to prevent dough from sticking to hands (dough will feel sticky).

2. Place dough in a large bowl coated with cooking spray, turning to coat top. Cover and let rise in a warm place (85°), free from drafts, 1 hour or until doubled in size. (Gently press 2 fingers into dough. If indentation remains, dough has risen enough.) Punch dough down; cover and let rise for 1 hour or until doubled in size.

3. Turn dough out onto a floured surface. Lightly dust dough with flour; pat into an 8 x 10-inch rectangle. Divide dough by making 3 lengthwise cuts and 4 crosswise cuts to form 20 equal pieces. Shape each piece into a ball, and arrange balls in a 13 x 9-inch baking pan coated with cooking spray. Combine water and 1 egg, stirring with a whisk. Lightly brush rolls with egg mixture; sprinkle with ½ teaspoon poppy seeds. Cover with plastic wrap, and let rise in a warm place (85°), free from drafts, 20 minutes.

4. Preheat oven to 400°.

5. Uncover dough. Bake at 400° for 20 minutes or until golden. Remove from heat; cool in pan 5 minutes. Serve warm, or cool completely on a wire rack. Yield: 20 servings (serving size: 1 roll).

CALORIES 127 (21% from fat); FAT 3g (sat 1.5g, mono 0.9g, poly 0.4g); PROTEIN 4.2g; CARB 20.8g; FIBER 1.4g; CHOL 27mg; IRON 1.3mg; SODIUM 210mg; CALC 36mg

The rustic, golden-hued colors of fall will highlight your table and create the perfect ambience for heralding you into the most wonderful time of the year.

Pear-Cranberry Crisp

This seasonal dessert doesn't take a lot of work. Prepare the topping earlier in the day, and refrigerate in a zip-top plastic bag.

Filling:
6 cups sliced peeled pear (about 3 pounds)
1 teaspoon cornstarch
½ cup fresh cranberries
½ cup apple juice
¼ cup maple syrup
1 teaspoon vanilla extract
¾ teaspoon ground ginger
⅛ teaspoon sea salt
Cooking spray

Topping:
¾ cup whole wheat pastry flour
¾ cup regular oats
¼ cup sugar
¼ cup chopped pecans
¼ cup butter, melted
1 teaspoon vanilla extract
¼ teaspoon sea salt

1. Preheat oven to 375°.

2. To prepare filling, place pears in a large bowl. Sprinkle with cornstarch; toss well to coat. Stir in cranberries and next 5 ingredients. Spoon pear mixture into a 2-quart baking dish coated with cooking spray.

3. To prepare topping, lightly spoon flour into a dry measuring cup; level with a knife. Combine flour and next 6 ingredients, tossing until moist. Sprinkle topping in an even layer over pear mixture. Cover with foil; bake at 375° for 40 minutes. Uncover and bake an additional 20 minutes or until topping is golden and fruit mixture is bubbly. Yield: 8 servings (serving size: about ¾ cup).

CALORIES 310 (30% from fat); FAT 10.2g (sat 3.9g, mono 3.4g, poly 1.3g); PROTEIN 4.2g; CARB 55.4g; FIBER 4.8g; CHOL 15mg; IRON 1.1mg; SODIUM 168mg; CALC 40mg

Pear-Cranberry
Crisp

Farmhouse Roast Turkey
with Rosemary Gravy

Thanksgiving Sampler

This assortment of classic recipes offers multiple options for your holiday meal. We don't expect you to prepare every dish. Instead, mix and match recipes to create your special menu to serve 12.

Menu Options

Creamy Salsa Dip

Sparkling White-Sangría Salad

Brined Maple Turkey with
Cream Gravy
or
Farmhouse Roast Turkey with
Rosemary Gravy

Sausage and Mushroom Stuffing
or
New England Sausage Stuffing
with Chestnuts

Gingered Cranberry Sauce
or
Cranberry-Fig Relish

Old-Fashioned Mashed Potatoes
or
Mashed Honey-Roasted Sweet Potatoes

Cider-Glazed Carrots
or
Broccoli and Carrots with
Toasted Almonds

Roasted Brussels Sprouts with
Ham and Garlic

Potato Rolls

Classic Pumpkin Pie
or
Pumpkin Cake with
Cream Cheese Glaze
or
Pecan and Date Pie

Creamy Salsa Dip

Make this spicy appetizer up to 2 days ahead, and sprinkle with cilantro right before serving. Serve the dip with baked tortilla chips.

- 2   teaspoons olive oil
- ½   cup finely chopped onion
- 2   garlic cloves, minced
- 1   finely chopped seeded jalapeño pepper
- 1   (14.5-ounce) can diced tomatoes, undrained
- 3   tablespoons chopped fresh cilantro, divided
- 1   teaspoon habanero hot pepper sauce or any hot pepper sauce
- 1   (16-ounce) carton low-fat sour cream

1. Heat oil in a large nonstick skillet over medium heat. Add onion, garlic, and jalapeño; cover and cook 3 minutes or until onion is tender. Add tomatoes; bring to a boil. Reduce heat, and simmer, uncovered, 5 minutes. Cool completely. Stir in 2 tablespoons cilantro, pepper sauce, and sour cream. Cover and chill. Sprinkle with 1 tablespoon cilantro. Yield: 16 servings (serving size: ¼ cup).

CALORIES 45 (48% from fat); FAT 2.4g (sat 1.5g, mono 0.4g, poly 0.1g); PROTEIN 1.2g; CARB 5.5g; FIBER 0.6g; CHOL 9mg; IRON 0.1mg; SODIUM 68mg; CALC 43mg

Sparkling White-Sangría Salad

Make up to a day ahead and refrigerate. Dip the covered mold into a bowl of warm water for 5 seconds to make the salad easier to unmold.

- 2   envelopes unflavored gelatin
- 1½   cups Riesling, divided
- 1½   cups white grape juice
- ¼   cup sugar
- 1½   cups orange sections
- 1   cup seedless green grapes, halved
- ¾   cup fresh raspberries

Cooking spray

1. Sprinkle gelatin over ½ cup wine, and let stand 5 minutes.

2. Combine 1 cup wine, juice, and sugar in a medium saucepan; bring to a boil over medium-high heat. Remove from heat; add gelatin mixture, stirring until gelatin dissolves. Place pan in a large ice-filled bowl; let stand 20 minutes or until thick but not set, stirring occasionally. Whisk gelatin mixture to form small bubbles; fold in orange sections, grapes, and raspberries. Spoon mixture into a 5-cup decorative mold coated with cooking spray. Cover; chill 4 hours. Place a plate upside down on top of mold; invert mold onto plate. Yield: 12 servings (serving size: 1 slice).

Note: For a nonalcoholic version, you may substitute sparkling white grape juice for the Riesling.

CALORIES 82 (2% from fat); FAT 0.2g (sat 0.1g, mono 0g, poly 0.1g); PROTEIN 1.5g; CARB 14.7g; FIBER 1.2g; CHOL 0mg; IRON 0.3mg; SODIUM 6mg; CALC 20mg

how to carve a turkey

1. Use a chef's knife to remove half of the breast by slicing along the breastbone's inside curve. Set each half-breast aside.

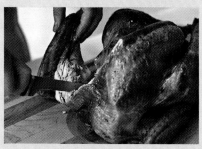

2. Pull back the wings and, using the knife, remove at the joint. Set aside.

3. Pull the leg and thigh back to expose the joint. Slice through the joint at its narrowest point . Separate the thighs from the legs in this same way.

4. Slice each half-breast on the diagonal into quarter-inch-thick pieces. Using the knife like a spatula, pick up each sliced breast half and place on a serving platter. Arrange the wings, thighs, and legs on the platter.

Brined Maple Turkey with Cream Gravy

The subtle flavors of the brine soak into the turkey, making it juicier. Kosher salt works well for the brine because it dissolves more easily than table salt.

Brine:
- 8 quarts water
- ¾ cup kosher salt
- ¾ cup maple syrup
- 3 tablespoons black peppercorns
- 8 garlic cloves, crushed
- 1 lemon, thinly sliced

Turkey:
- 1 (12-pound) fresh or frozen turkey, thawed
- 1 cup cola
- ½ cup maple syrup
- 2 tablespoons minced fresh thyme
- 1 tablespoon dried rubbed sage
- 1 tablespoon poultry seasoning
- ½ teaspoon black pepper
- 4 garlic cloves, chopped
- 2 onions, quartered

Cooking spray

Gravy:
- 1 (14-ounce) can fat-free, less-sodium chicken broth
- 1 cup whole milk
- 2 tablespoons cornstarch
- ¼ teaspoon salt
- ¼ teaspoon black pepper

1. To prepare brine, combine first 6 ingredients in a large stockpot, stirring until salt dissolves.

2. To prepare turkey, remove and reserve giblets and neck from turkey. Rinse thoroughly with cold water; pat dry. Trim excess fat. Add turkey to pot, turning to coat. Cover and refrigerate 24 hours, turning occasionally.

3. Preheat oven to 375°.

4. Bring cola and ½ cup syrup to a boil in a small saucepan; cook 1 minute.

5. Combine thyme, sage, seasoning, and ½ teaspoon black pepper. Remove turkey from brine; pat dry. Starting at neck cavity, loosen skin from breast and drumsticks by inserting fingers, gently pushing between skin and meat. Rub thyme mixture under skin; sprinkle inside body cavity. Place 4 garlic cloves and onions in body cavity. Tie legs together with twine. Lift wing tips up and over back; tuck under turkey.

6. Place turkey on a broiler pan coated with cooking spray. Insert a meat thermometer into meaty part of thigh, making sure not to touch bone. Bake at 375° for 45 minutes. Pour cola mixture over turkey; cover with foil. Bake 1 hour and 45 minutes or until thermometer registers 180°. Remove turkey from pan, reserving drippings for gravy. Place turkey on a platter. Cover loosely with foil; let stand 10 minutes. Remove twine. Discard skin.

7. To prepare gravy, while turkey bakes, combine reserved giblets and neck and the broth in a saucepan; bring to a boil. Cover, reduce heat, and simmer 45 minutes. Strain mixture through a colander into a bowl, discarding solids.

8. Place a zip-top bag inside a 2-cup glass measure. Pour pan drippings into bag; let stand 10 minutes (fat will rise to the top). Seal bag; snip off 1 bottom corner of bag. Drain drippings into broiler pan, stopping before fat layer reaches opening; discard fat. Add broth mixture. Place broiler pan on stovetop over medium heat; scrape pan to loosen browned bits. Combine milk and cornstarch in a small bowl, stir well; add to pan. Bring to a boil; cook 1 minute, stirring constantly.

9. Strain gravy through a sieve into a bowl, and discard solids. Stir in ¼ teaspoon salt and ¼ teaspoon black pepper. Yield: 12 servings (serving size: 6 ounces turkey and about ¼ cup gravy).

CALORIES 375 (25% from fat); FAT 10.5g (sat 3.6g, mono 2.5g, poly 2.8g); PROTEIN 51.7g; CARB 15.7g; FIBER 0.2g; CHOL 140mg; IRON 3.6mg; SODIUM 809mg; CALC 91mg

Brined Maple Turkey
with Cream Gravy

Farmhouse Roast Turkey with Rosemary Gravy
(pictured on page 13)

Basting promotes browning, and hot drippings help seal the skin to hold in juices and keep the turkey moist. You'll have plenty of rosemary gravy to go over the stuffing and potatoes. And even better, you'll have leftover gravy to use on open-faced turkey sandwiches later. Of course, you may also substitute fat-free, less-sodium chicken broth for the Homemade Turkey Stock, if you prefer.

   1   (12-pound) fresh or frozen
       turkey, thawed
5 ⅓   cups Homemade Turkey Stock or
       5 ⅓ cups fat-free, less-sodium
       chicken broth, divided
   2   cups coarsely chopped onion
   1   cup coarsely chopped celery
   2   tablespoons chopped fresh
       rosemary, divided
1 ¾   teaspoons salt, divided
   ¾   teaspoon black pepper, divided
       Cooking spray
   2   tablespoons butter, melted
   ⅓   cup all-purpose flour
   ¼   cup water
   2   tablespoons cornstarch

1. Remove giblets and neck from turkey; reserve for Homemade Turkey Stock. Wrap turkey in plastic wrap and return to the refrigerator.
2. Prepare Homemade Turkey Stock.
3. Preheat oven to 325°.
4. Rinse turkey thoroughly with cold water, and pat dry. Trim excess fat. Combine onion, celery, 1 tablespoon rosemary, ½ teaspoon salt, and ¼ teaspoon pepper. Stuff body cavity with mixture. Tie ends of legs together with twine. Lift wing tips up and over back; tuck under turkey.
5. Place a roasting rack coated with cooking spray in a roasting pan. Place turkey, breast side up, on rack. Brush with butter; sprinkle evenly with 1 teaspoon salt and ¼ teaspoon pepper. Pour 1 cup Homemade Turkey Stock in bottom of pan. Insert a meat thermometer into meaty part of thigh, making sure not to touch bone. Cover turkey breast tightly with foil. Bake at 325° for 2 hours, basting with ⅓ cup Homemade Turkey Stock every 30 minutes (1 ⅓ cups total). Remove foil; bake an additional 1 ½ hours or until thermometer registers 180°, basting with ⅓ cup Homemade Turkey Stock every 30 minutes (1 cup total). Remove turkey from oven; let stand 30 minutes. Remove twine. Discard skin.
6. Place a zip-top plastic bag inside a 2-cup glass measure. Pour pan drippings into bag; let stand 10 minutes (fat will rise to the top). Seal bag; carefully snip off 1 bottom corner of bag. Drain drippings into a measuring cup, stopping before fat layer reaches opening. Reserve 2 tablespoons fat; discard remaining fat. Combine pan drippings with 2 cups Homemade Turkey Stock.
7. Heat 2 tablespoons reserved fat in bottom of roasting pan over medium heat. Add flour, stirring with a whisk. Cook 1 minute, stirring constantly. Stir in pan drippings mixture. Combine water and cornstarch, stirring with a whisk. Add cornstarch mixture to pan, stirring with a whisk. Bring to a boil, stirring frequently. Add 1 tablespoon rosemary. Reduce heat, and simmer 5 minutes or until sauce thickens. Stir in ¼ teaspoon salt and ¼ teaspoon pepper. Serve gravy with turkey. Yield: 12 servings (serving size: 6 ounces turkey and ⅓ cup gravy).

CALORIES 440 (26% from fat); FAT 12.6g (sat 3.8g, mono 3g, poly 3g); PROTEIN 71g; CARB 5.4g; FIBER 0.6g; CHOL 221mg; IRON 5.5mg; SODIUM 574mg; CALC 56mg

Homemade Turkey Stock

Turn turkey giblets and canned chicken broth into a rich stock to enhance Rosemary Gravy and Sausage and Mushroom Stuffing (recipe on page 26). Don't use livers in the stock—they make it bitter and cloudy. A cleaver works best to chop the neck.

   2   teaspoons vegetable oil
   1   turkey neck
   1   turkey heart
   1   turkey gizzard
   ½   cup chopped onion
   ½   cup chopped celery
   ½   cup chopped carrot
   8   cups cold water
   2   (14-ounce) cans fat-free,
       less-sodium chicken broth
   ½   teaspoon dried thyme
   ¼   teaspoon black peppercorns
   3   parsley sprigs
   1   bay leaf

1. Heat oil in a large stockpot or Dutch oven over medium-high heat. Chop neck, heart, and gizzard into 2-inch pieces; add to pan. Cook 5 minutes or until browned, stirring occasionally. Add onion, celery, and carrot; cook 4 minutes or until tender, stirring frequently. Stir in water and broth; bring to a boil. Add thyme, peppercorns, parsley, and bay leaf. Reduce heat; simmer 2 hours. Strain mixture through a sieve over a large bowl; discard solids. Cool to room temperature. Cover; chill overnight. Skim solidified fat from surface, and discard fat. Yield: 7 cups (serving size: 1 cup).
Note: Refrigerate leftover stock in an airtight container up to 1 week, or freeze up to 3 months.

CALORIES 27 (33% from fat); FAT 1g (sat 0.2g, mono 0.2g, poly 0.5g); PROTEIN 2.9g; CARB 0.9g; FIBER 0.1g; CHOL 8mg; IRON 0.3mg; SODIUM 217mg; CALC 3mg

(clockwise from left) Broccoli and Carrots
with Toasted Almonds; Mashed Honey-Roasted
Sweet Potatoes; Sausage and Mushroom
Stuffing; Gingered Cranberry Sauce;
Farmhouse Roast Turkey with Rosemary Gravy

Sausage and Mushroom Stuffing

    5   cups (1-inch) cubed white bread
        (about 7 [1-ounce] slices)
    5   cups (1-inch) cubed whole wheat
        bread (about 7 [1-ounce] slices)
    1   pound turkey Italian sausage
  Cooking spray
    1   teaspoon vegetable oil
    3   cups finely chopped onion
 1½   cups finely chopped celery
    1   (8-ounce) package presliced
        mushrooms (about 2 cups)
    1   teaspoon dried thyme
    1   teaspoon dried rubbed sage
    1   teaspoon dried rosemary
    ½   teaspoon dried marjoram
    ½   teaspoon black pepper
    ⅓   cup chopped fresh parsley
 1½   cups Homemade Turkey Stock
        (recipe on page 24) or 1½ cups
        fat-free, less-sodium chicken broth

1. Preheat oven to 250°.
2. Place bread in a single layer on 2 baking sheets. Bake at 250° for 1 hour or until dry. Set aside.
3. Remove casings from sausage. Cook sausage in a large nonstick skillet coated with cooking spray over medium heat until browned, stirring to crumble. Place sausage in a large bowl.
4. Heat oil in pan over medium heat. Add onion, celery, and mushrooms; cover and cook 10 minutes or until vegetables are tender, stirring occasionally. Remove from heat; stir in thyme and next 4 ingredients. Add onion mixture, bread, and parsley to sausage; toss gently to combine. Add Homemade Turkey Stock, and stir until moist.
5. Increase oven temperature to 350°.
6. Spoon bread mixture into a 13 x 9-inch baking dish coated with cooking spray. Cover and bake at 350° for 15 minutes. Uncover; bake an additional 20 minutes

or until top is crusty. Yield: 12 servings (serving size: about ¾ cup).

CALORIES 187 (28% from fat); FAT 5.9g (sat 1.6g, mono 2g, poly 1.5g); PROTEIN 12.4g; CARB 21.6g; FIBER 2.9g; CHOL 38mg; IRON 2.5mg; SODIUM 460mg; CALC 52mg

New England Sausage Stuffing with Chestnuts

    1   cup coarsely chopped bottled
        chestnuts
    1   (16-ounce) loaf French bread, cut
        into 1-inch cubes
    6   ounces mild pork sausage
    3   cups chopped onion
    2   cups chopped celery
 1½   cups fat-free, less-sodium chicken
        broth
    1   tablespoon dried rubbed sage
    1   teaspoon dried thyme
    ½   teaspoon salt
    ½   teaspoon black pepper
  Cooking spray

1. Preheat oven to 375°.
2. Arrange chopped chestnuts and bread cubes in a single layer on a jelly-roll pan. Bake at 375° for 10 minutes or until lightly browned.
3. Cook sausage in a large nonstick skillet over medium-high heat 4 minutes or until browned, stirring to crumble. Add onion and celery; sauté 6 minutes or until tender. Add broth, scraping pan to loosen browned bits.
4. Combine bread mixture, sausage mixture, sage, thyme, salt, and pepper, tossing to combine. Spoon into a 13 x 9-inch baking pan coated with cooking spray; cover with foil. Bake at 375° for 20 minutes. Uncover and bake an additional 10 minutes or until golden brown. Yield: 12 servings (serving size: about ⅔ cup).

CALORIES 214 (30% from fat); FAT 7.2g (sat 2.4g, mono 3.2g, poly 1.2g); PROTEIN 6.4g; CARB 30.6g; FIBER 3g; CHOL 10mg; IRON 1.5mg; SODIUM 498mg; CALC 55mg

Gingered Cranberry Sauce

Make up to a week ahead, and store, covered, in the refrigerator. The strong ginger flavor of this basic cranberry sauce goes well with the Farmhouse Roast Turkey with Rosemary Gravy (recipe on page 24).

 1½   cups sugar
    ½   cup water
    ⅓   cup chopped crystallized ginger
        (1 [2.7-ounce] bottle)
    1   (12-ounce) package fresh
        cranberries

1. Combine all ingredients in a medium saucepan. Bring to a boil; reduce heat, and simmer 9 minutes or until cranberries pop. Cool completely. Serve at room temperature. Yield: 12 servings (serving size: ¼ cup).

CALORIES 112 (0% from fat); FAT 0g; PROTEIN 0.2g; CARB 29g; FIBER 1.2g; CHOL 0mg; IRON 0.1mg; SODIUM 1.2mg; CALC 3mg

Cranberry-Fig Relish

    1   cup fresh orange juice (about
        4 oranges)
    ¾   cup chopped dried figs
    ½   cup dry red wine
    ½   cup granulated sugar
    ¼   cup packed brown sugar
    1   (12-ounce) package fresh cranberries
    ⅓   cup chopped pecans, toasted

1. Combine first 3 ingredients in a medium saucepan; bring to a boil. Cover, reduce heat, and simmer 10 minutes.
2. Add sugars and cranberries. Cook over medium heat 10 minutes or until mixture is slightly thick and cranberries pop; stirring occasionally. Cool slightly. Stir in pecans. Cover; chill. Yield: 12 servings (serving size: ¼ cup).

CALORIES 128 (18% from fat); FAT 2.6g (sat 0.2g, mono 1.4g, poly 0.8g); PROTEIN 1g; CARB 27.4g; FIBER 3g; CHOL 0mg; IRON 0.6mg; SODIUM 4mg; CALC 30mg

Old-Fashioned Mashed Potatoes

Nothing fancy here—just good, basic mashed potatoes that are great as is or topped with the gravy from the turkey (recipe on page 22). For extra flavor, sprinkle with chopped chives.

5 pounds cubed peeled baking potato
¾ cup warm 2% reduced-fat milk
2 tablespoons butter
1½ teaspoons salt
¾ teaspoon black pepper

1. Place potato in a medium saucepan; cover with water. Bring to a boil. Reduce heat, and simmer 15 minutes or until tender; drain.

2. Combine milk, butter, salt, and pepper in a large bowl. Add potato, and let stand 5 minutes or until butter melts.

3. Beat potato mixture with a mixer at medium speed until mixture is smooth. Yield: 12 servings (serving size: about ¾ cup).

CALORIES 169 (13% from fat); FAT 2.4g (sat 1.4g, mono 0.7g, poly 0.2g); PROTEIN 3.4g; CARB 34.2g; FIBER 3g; CHOL 6mg; IRON 0.6mg; SODIUM 329mg; CALC 33mg

Mashed Honey-Roasted Sweet Potatoes

Prepare this dish up to a day ahead, and store, covered, in the refrigerator.
To reheat, bake at 350°, covered, for 45 minutes. The temperature and time work well with
Sausage and Mushroom Stuffing (recipe on page 26), and the turkey can stand while this reheats.

6   pounds sweet potatoes, peeled and cut into
    (1-inch) cubes
Cooking spray
5   tablespoons honey, divided
4   tablespoons unsalted butter
¾   teaspoon salt

1. Preheat oven to 375°.
2. Place sweet potatoes in a single layer on 2 large baking
sheets coated with cooking spray. Lightly spray potatoes
with cooking spray. Bake at 375° for 1 hour or until
potatoes are tender, stirring occasionally. Place the
potatoes, ¼ cup honey, butter, and salt in a large bowl,
and beat with a mixer at medium speed until smooth.
Drizzle with 1 tablespoon honey. Yield: 12 servings
(serving size: ½ cup).

CALORIES 140 (25% from fat); FAT 3.9g (sat 2.4g, mono 1.1g, poly 0.2g); PROTEIN 1.4g;
CARB 26.2g; FIBER 2.4g; CHOL 10mg; IRON 0.4mg; SODIUM 154mg; CALC 24mg

Cider-Glazed Carrots

Cider vinegar gives these carrots the flavor of an apple cider reduction, but in a fraction of the time. To get a head start, boil the carrots a day ahead. Refrigerate them in a zip-top plastic bag, and sauté just before serving.

    9   cups (3-inch) julienne-cut carrot
        (about 2½ pounds)
    ¼   cup packed brown sugar
    2   tablespoons butter
    2   tablespoons cider vinegar
    ½   teaspoon dry mustard
    ½   teaspoon paprika
    ¼   teaspoon salt
    ¼   teaspoon celery seeds
    1   tablespoon chopped fresh parsley

1. Place carrot in a large saucepan; cover with water. Bring to a boil. Reduce heat; simmer 1 minute or until tender. Drain.
2. Combine sugar and next 6 ingredients in a large nonstick skillet over low heat; cook until butter melts, stirring frequently. Bring to a boil.
3. Reduce heat to medium; add carrots. Cook 3 minutes or until carrots are glazed and thoroughly heated, stirring constantly. Sprinkle with chopped parsley; toss to combine. Yield: 12 servings (serving size: about ⅔ cup).

CALORIES 75 (26% from fat); FAT 2.2g (sat 1.2g, mono 0.6g, poly 0.2g); PROTEIN 1g; CARB 14g; FIBER 2.8g; CHOL 5mg; IRON 0.6mg; SODIUM 103mg; CALC 31mg

Broccoli and Carrots with Toasted Almonds

Toast the almonds and blanch the vegetables a day ahead to ease preparation during the day's rush.

    ⅓   cup sliced almonds
    1   pound (1-inch) diagonally cut
        carrots (about 3 cups)
    1   (12-ounce) bag broccoli florets
        (about 6 cups)
    1   tablespoon butter
    ¼   cup finely chopped shallots
    ½   cup Homemade Turkey Stock
        (recipe on page 24) or ½ cup
        fat-free, less-sodium chicken
        broth
    ½   teaspoon salt
    ¼   teaspoon freshly ground black
        pepper

1. Preheat oven to 350°.
2. Spread almonds in a single layer in a shallow pan. Bake at 350° for 7 minutes or until lightly browned and fragrant, stirring occasionally. Cool completely, and set aside.
3. Place carrots in a large saucepan of boiling water; cook 3 minutes. Remove with a slotted spoon. Plunge into ice water, and drain. Place broccoli in boiling water; cook 2 minutes. Drain and plunge into ice water; drain.
4. Melt butter in a 12-inch nonstick skillet over medium-high heat. Add shallots; sauté 2 minutes or until tender. Reduce heat to medium. Add carrots, broccoli, Homemade Turkey Stock, salt, and pepper; cover and cook 6 minutes or until carrots and broccoli are crisp-tender. Sprinkle with almonds. Serve immediately. Yield: 12 servings (serving size: ½ cup).

CALORIES 54 (43% from fat); FAT 2.6g (sat 0.7g, mono 1.1g, poly 0.4g); PROTEIN 2.5g; CARB 6.3g; FIBER 2.3g; CHOL 5mg; IRON 0.6mg; SODIUM 130mg; CALC 36mg

Cider-Glazed Carrots

Roasted Brussels Sprouts with Ham and Garlic

Roasting brings out the best in Brussels sprouts. It lightly caramelizes their edges but keeps them tender inside. Don't trim too much from the stem ends of the sprouts, since they may fall apart. Country ham imparts saltiness to the dish; if it's unavailable in your market, substitute regular ham. Freeze leftover toasted breadcrumbs for up to 6 months; use them to top macaroni and cheese or casseroles.

1   (1-ounce) slice white bread
3   pounds Brussels sprouts, trimmed and halved
¼   cup finely chopped country ham (about 1 ounce)
2   tablespoons fresh lemon juice
1   teaspoon olive oil
½   teaspoon salt
3   garlic cloves, thinly sliced
Cooking spray
2   tablespoons grated fresh Parmesan cheese

1. Preheat oven to 425°.

2. Place bread in a food processor and pulse 2 times or until bread is crumbly. Sprinkle breadcrumbs on a baking sheet and bake at 425° for 5 minutes or until golden. Reduce oven temperature to 375°. Set aside 3 tablespoons toasted breadcrumbs, reserving remaining breadcrumbs for another use.

3. Combine sprouts and next 5 ingredients in a 3-quart baking dish coated with cooking spray, tossing to coat. Bake at 375° for 30 minutes or until sprouts are tender and lightly browned on edges, stirring twice.

4. Combine 3 tablespoons breadcrumbs and Parmesan cheese; sprinkle over sprouts. Serve immediately. Yield: 12 servings (serving size: ¾ cup).

CALORIES 58 (19% from fat); FAT 1.2g (sat 0.4g, mono 0.5g, poly 0.2g); PROTEIN 4.4g; CARB 9.6g; FIBER 3.6g; CHOL 2mg; IRON 1.4mg; SODIUM 211mg; CALC 57mg

Potato Rolls

Bake these rolls up to 1 month ahead. Cool completely, wrap in heavy-duty aluminum foil, and freeze. Thaw completely; reheat (wrapped in foil) at 375° for 12 minutes or until warm.

    2   cups cubed peeled baking potato
    4   teaspoons sugar, divided
    1   package dry yeast (about 2¼ teaspoons)
 4¼   cups bread flour, divided
    3   tablespoons butter, melted
 1½   teaspoons salt
    1   large egg
Cooking spray
    2   tablespoons bread flour

1. Place potato in a medium saucepan; cover with water. Bring to a boil. Reduce heat; simmer 15 minutes or until tender. Drain in a colander over a bowl; reserve 1 cup liquid. Mash potatoes with a fork.
2. Cool reserved cooking liquid to 105° to 115°. Stir in 1 teaspoon sugar and yeast. Let stand 5 minutes.
3. Lightly spoon 4¼ cups flour into dry measuring cups; level with a knife. Combine mashed potato, yeast mixture, 1 tablespoon sugar, 4 cups flour, butter, salt, and egg in a bowl; stir until well blended.
4. Turn dough out onto a floured surface. Knead until smooth and elastic (about 10 minutes); add up to ¼ cup flour, 1 tablespoon at a time, to prevent dough from sticking to hands (dough will feel sticky).
5. Place dough in a large bowl coated with cooking spray, turning to coat top. Cover and let rise in a warm place (85°), free from drafts, 45 minutes or until doubled in size. (Press 2 fingers into dough. If indentation remains, dough has risen enough.) Punch dough down; cover and let rest 10 minutes.
6. Divide dough in half; divide each half into 12 equal portions. Working with 1 portion at a time (cover remaining dough to keep from drying), shape into a 2-inch-long oval on a floured surface. Starting with a long edge, roll up tightly, pressing to eliminate air pockets; pinch seam and ends to seal. Place roll, seam side down, on a baking sheet coated with cooking spray.
7. Repeat procedure with remaining dough, placing 12 rolls on each of 2 baking sheets. Sift 2 tablespoons flour over rolls to lightly coat. Cover rolls and let rise 45 minutes or until doubled in size.
8. Preheat oven to 350°.
9. Bake at 350° for 10 minutes with 1 baking sheet on bottom rack and 1 baking sheet on second rack from top. Rotate baking sheets; bake 10 minutes or until rolls are browned on bottom, lightly browned on top, and sound hollow when tapped. Remove from pan; cool on wire racks. Yield: 24 servings (serving size: 1 roll).

CALORIES 121 (16% from fat); FAT 2.1g (sat 1g, mono 0.6g, poly 0.3g); PROTEIN 3.6g; CARB 21.6g; FIBER 0.9g; CHOL 13mg; IRON 1.2mg; SODIUM 165mg; CALC 7mg

Classic Pumpkin Pie

Bake the pie on a baking sheet in the lower third of the oven for a crisp crust.

Filling:
    ¾   cup packed brown sugar
 1¾   teaspoons pumpkin pie spice
    ¼   teaspoon salt
    1   (12-ounce) can evaporated low-fat milk
    2   large egg whites
    1   large egg
    1   (15-ounce) can unsweetened pumpkin
Crust:
    ½   (15-ounce) package refrigerated pie dough (such as Pillsbury)
Cooking spray
Topping:
    ¼   cup whipping cream
    1   tablespoon amaretto (almond-flavored liqueur)
    2   teaspoons powdered sugar

1. Position oven rack to lowest position.
2. Preheat oven to 425°.
3. To prepare filling, combine first 6 ingredients in a large bowl, stirring with a whisk until well combined. Add pumpkin; stir until smooth.
4. To prepare crust, roll dough into an 11-inch circle; fit into a 9-inch pie plate coated with cooking spray. Fold edges under and flute.
5. Pour pumpkin mixture into crust. Place pie on a baking sheet. Place baking sheet on lowest oven rack. Bake at 425° for 10 minutes. Reduce oven temperature to 350° (do not remove pie from oven); bake an additional 50 minutes or until almost set. Cool completely on a wire rack.
6. To prepare topping, beat whipping cream with a mixer at high speed until stiff peaks form. Add amaretto and powdered sugar, and beat until blended. Serve with pie. Yield: 12 servings (serving size: 1 wedge and about 1 tablespoon topping).

CALORIES 222 (30% from fat); FAT 7.4g (sat 3.7g, mono 0.7g, poly 0.1g); PROTEIN 4.1g; CARB 35.3g; FIBER 3g; CHOL 32mg; IRON 0.8mg; SODIUM 241mg; CALC 104mg

Classic Pumpkin Pie

Pumpkin Cake with
Cream Cheese Glaze

Pecan and
Date Ple

Pumpkin Cake with Cream Cheese Glaze

If you make the cake a day ahead, garnish with orange wedges shortly before serving. You can also bake the cake in a Bundt pan, but reduce the oven temperature to 325°.

Cake:
1½   cups granulated sugar
½   cup butter, softened
¾   cup egg substitute
1   teaspoon vanilla extract
1   (15-ounce) can pumpkin
3   cups sifted cake flour
1   teaspoon baking powder
1   teaspoon baking soda
1   teaspoon ground cinnamon
½   teaspoon salt
¼   teaspoon ground ginger
¼   teaspoon ground nutmeg
Cooking spray
Glaze:
½   cup powdered sugar
½   cup (4 ounces) ⅓-less-fat cream
    cheese, softened
½   teaspoon vanilla extract
3   tablespoons fresh orange juice
Garnish:
Fresh orange sections (optional)

1. Preheat oven to 350°.
2. To prepare cake, beat granulated sugar and butter with a mixer at medium speed until well blended (about 5 minutes). Add egg substitute, ¼ cup at a time, beating well after each addition. Beat in 1 teaspoon vanilla and pumpkin.
3. Combine flour and next 6 ingredients, stirring well with a whisk. Fold flour mixture into pumpkin mixture.
4. Spoon batter into a 10-inch tube pan coated with cooking spray. Bake at 350° for 55 minutes or until a wooden pick inserted in center comes out clean. Cool in pan 10 minutes on a wire rack. Remove from pan; place on wire rack.
5. To prepare glaze, place powdered sugar and cream cheese in a bowl, and beat with a mixer at medium speed until well blended. Beat in ½ teaspoon vanilla. Add orange juice, 1 tablespoon at a time, beating well after each addition. Drizzle warm cake with glaze. Cool cake completely on wire rack. Garnish cake with orange sections, if desired. Yield: 16 servings (serving size: 1 slice).

CALORIES 236 (29% from fat); FAT 7.5g (sat 4.6g, mono 1.7g, poly 0.3g); PROTEIN 3.9g; CARB 38.8g; FIBER 1.5g; CHOL 21mg; IRON 1.8mg; SODIUM 295mg; CALC 41mg

Pecan and Date Pie

Use moist and sticky whole dates in this pie instead of packaged dates, which are rolled in sugar. Coat your knife with cooking spray for easy chopping.

Crust:
1   cup all-purpose flour, divided
3   tablespoons ice water
1   teaspoon fresh lemon juice
2   tablespoons powdered sugar
¼   teaspoon salt
¼   cup vegetable shortening
Cooking spray
Filling:
½   cup whole pitted dates, chopped
⅓   cup chopped pecans
1   cup dark corn syrup
½   cup packed brown sugar
3   tablespoons all-purpose flour
1   teaspoon vanilla extract
¼   teaspoon salt
4   large eggs

1. Preheat oven to 325°.
2. To prepare crust, lightly spoon 1 cup flour into a dry measuring cup; level with a knife. Combine ¼ cup flour, water, and juice, stirring with a whisk until well blended to form a slurry.
3. Combine ¾ cup flour, powdered sugar, and ¼ teaspoon salt; cut in shortening with a pastry blender or 2 knives until mixture resembles coarse meal. Add slurry; toss with a fork until mixture is moist. Gently press mixture into a 4-inch circle on 2 sheets of heavy-duty plastic wrap that overlap; cover with 2 additional sheets of overlapping plastic wrap. Roll dough, still covered, into a 12-inch circle; freeze 10 minutes.
4. Remove top 2 sheets of plastic wrap; let dough stand 1 minute or until pliable. Fit dough, plastic-wrap side up, into a 9-inch pie plate coated with cooking spray. Remove remaining plastic wrap. Press dough into bottom and up sides of pan. Fold edges under; flute.
5. To prepare filling, sprinkle dates and pecans evenly over bottom of crust. Combine corn syrup and remaining ingredients in a large bowl; beat with a mixer at medium speed until well blended. Pour mixture into prepared crust. Bake at 325° for 55 minutes or until a knife inserted 1 inch from the edge comes out clean. Cool on a wire rack. Yield: 10 servings (serving size: 1 wedge).

CALORIES 321 (29% from fat); FAT 10.2g (sat 2.2g, mono 4.7g, poly 2.5g); PROTEIN 4.6g; CARB 55.8g; FIBER 1.5g; CHOL 85mg; IRON 1.5mg; SODIUM 198mg; CALC 33mg

Thanksgiving Table for Two

Enjoy the traditional flavors of the season without being overwhelmed with the leftovers.

Swiss Chard with Garlic and Oregano

After you rinse and drain the chard, there should be just enough water clinging to the leaves for it to wilt.

  10 cups coarsely chopped Swiss
      chard (about 10 ounces)
   1 teaspoon olive oil
   1 garlic clove, minced
  ¼ teaspoon dried oregano
  ⅛ teaspoon salt
  Dash of black pepper
   2 teaspoons red wine vinegar

1. Rinse Swiss chard with cold water; drain chard well.
2. Heat oil in a large nonstick skillet over medium-high heat. Add garlic, and sauté 1 minute or until slightly golden. Add chard. Cover and cook 1 minute or until chard begins to wilt. Stir in oregano, salt, and pepper. Cover and cook 5 minutes or until tender, stirring occasionally. Remove from heat; stir in vinegar. Yield: 2 servings (serving size: about ½ cup).

CALORIES 51 (46% from fat); FAT 2.6g (sat 0.4g, mono 1.7g, poly 0.3g); PROTEIN 2.7g; CARB 6.1g; FIBER 2.4g; CHOL 0mg IRON 2.8mg; SODIUM 454mg; CALC 80mg;

Maple-Glazed Winter Squash

Cook the squash in the same roasting pan as the Cornish hens and potatoes to save time. Just make sure to arrange the squash on the front of the pan so you can easily brush it with the syrup mixture when you open the oven door. Save the remaining squash to cube for soup or risotto.

   1 (1¾-pound) butternut squash
   Cooking spray
   4 teaspoons maple syrup, divided
   1 teaspoon butter, divided

1. Preheat oven to 375°.
2. Cut butternut squash 1 inch above bulb; save stem section for another use. Cut bulb in half lengthwise. Remove and discard seeds and membranes. Place squash halves, cut sides up, on a broiler pan coated with cooking spray; place 2 teaspoons maple syrup and ½ teaspoon butter in each squash half.
3. Bake at 375° for 1 hour or until squash halves are tender, brushing cut sides with syrup mixture every 20 minutes. Yield: 2 servings (serving size: 1 squash half).

CALORIES 86 (21% from fat); FAT 2g (sat 1.2g, mono 0.6g, poly 0.1g); PROTEIN 0.8g; CARB 17.9g; FIBER 2.4g; CHOL 5mg; IRON 0.7mg; SODIUM 24mg; CALC 45mg

(clockwise from back) Rosemary-Lemon
Cornish Hens with Roasted Potatoes;
Swiss Chard with Garlic and Oregano

Rosemary-Lemon Cornish Hens with Roasted Potatoes

You can easily vary this recipe by using thyme in place of rosemary or sprinkling ground red pepper and garlic powder over the potatoes.

 2 teaspoons crushed dried rosemary
 ½ teaspoon salt, divided
 ¼ teaspoon black pepper, divided
 2 (1¼-pound) Cornish hens
 ½ lemon, halved
 Cooking spray
 2 cups cubed Yukon gold or red potato
 2 teaspoons olive oil

1. Preheat oven to 375°.
2. Combine crushed dried rosemary, ¼ teaspoon salt, and ⅛ teaspoon pepper.
3. Remove and discard giblets from Cornish hens. Rinse hens with cold water and pat dry. Remove skin; trim excess fat. Working with 1 hen at a time, place 1 lemon piece in the cavity of hen, and then tie the ends of legs together with twine. Lift wing tips up and over back; tuck under hen. Repeat procedure with remaining hen and lemon piece. Rub hens with rosemary mixture. Place hens, breast sides up, on a broiler pan coated with cooking spray.

4. Toss potato with oil and sprinkle with ¼ teaspoon salt and ⅛ teaspoon pepper. Arrange potato around hens.
5. Insert a meat thermometer into meaty part of thigh, making sure not to touch bone. Bake at 375° for 1 hour or until thermometer registers 180°. Remove twine. Yield: 2 servings (serving size: 1 hen and about ¾ cup potatoes).

CALORIES 372 (28% from fat); FAT 11.4g (sat 2.4g, mono 5.5g, poly 2.1g); PROTEIN 41.8g; CARB 24.1g; FIBER 2.7g; CHOL 180mg; IRON 3mg; SODIUM 702mg; CALC 47mg

Pear-Cranberry Sauce

You can substitute an apple for one of the pears to vary this simple sauce.

 ⅓ cup fresh cranberries
 3 tablespoons water
 2 Bartlett pears, peeled and coarsely chopped
 1 tablespoon sugar
 ¼ teaspoon grated orange rind

1. Combine first 3 ingredients in a small saucepan. Cover and cook over medium-low heat 25 minutes or until cranberries pop, stirring occasionally.
2. Remove from heat; stir in sugar and rind. Cool to room temperature. Yield: 2 servings (serving size: about ⅓ cup).

CALORIES 118 (5% from fat); FAT 0.6g (sat 0.1g, mono 0.1g, poly 0.2g); PROTEIN 0.5g; CARB 30.4g; FIBER 2.9g; CHOL 0mg; IRON 0.3mg; SODIUM 0mg; CALC 13mg

Celery Salad

A cool, crisp salad adds crunch and contrast to the menu. You can substitute dried cranberries or raisins for the dried cherries and walnuts for the pecans.

 ¾ cup sliced celery
 ⅓ cup dried sweet cherries
 ⅓ cup frozen green peas, thawed
 3 tablespoons chopped fresh parsley
 1½ tablespoons fat-free mayonnaise
 1½ tablespoons plain low-fat yogurt
 1 tablespoon chopped pecans, toasted
 1½ teaspoons fresh lemon juice
 ⅛ teaspoon salt
 ⅛ teaspoon black pepper

1. Combine all ingredients; chill. Yield: 2 servings (serving size: about ⅔ cup).

CALORIES 160 (21% from fat); FAT 3.7g (sat 0.4g, mono 1.7g, poly 1.3g); PROTEIN 4.1g; CARB 27.5g; FIBER 4.5g; CHOL 0mg; IRON 1.3mg; SODIUM 332mg; CALC 71mg

Celery Salad

Apple Crumble with Golden Raisins

Baked apple—sweetened with raisins, orange juice, and cinnamon—is graced with a simple crumb topping.

2 tablespoons all-purpose flour
2 tablespoons granulated sugar, divided
1 tablespoon brown sugar
1 tablespoon chilled butter, cut into small pieces
1½ cups diced peeled Granny Smith apple
1 tablespoon golden raisins
2 tablespoons fresh orange juice
½ teaspoon fresh lemon juice
⅛ teaspoon ground cinnamon
Cooking spray

1. Preheat oven to 375°.

2. Combine flour, 1 tablespoon granulated sugar, and brown sugar in a medium bowl. Cut in butter with a pastry blender or 2 knives until mixture resembles coarse meal.

3. Combine 1 tablespoon granulated sugar, apple, and next 4 ingredients, tossing well. Divide apple mixture evenly between 2 (6-ounce) ramekins coated with cooking spray. Sprinkle evenly with flour mixture. Bake at 375° for 30 minutes or until golden brown. Yield: 2 servings.

CALORIES 223 (25% from fat); FAT 6.2g (sat 3.7g, mono 1.7g, poly 0.4g); PROTEIN 1.3g; CARB 43.1g; FIBER 2.4g; CHOL 16mg; IRON 0.7mg; SODIUM 61mg; CALC 17mg

(clockwise from front) Mashed Potato Latkes with Zucchini and Dill topped with Pear Applesauce; Eggplant and Green Pepper Kugel; Carrot-Wheat Berry Salad with Cumin and Raisins

Vegetarian Hanukkah

Join us in celebrating the Festival of Lights with this healthful, make-ahead vegetarian Hanukkah menu. This versatile menu makes a perfect vegetarian Thanksgiving or Christmas dinner, too.

Menu

serves 8

Mashed Potato Latkes with Zucchini and Dill

Pear Applesauce

Sweet-and-Sour Beet, Cabbage, and Tomato Soup

Eggplant and Green Pepper Kugel

Carrot-Wheat Berry Salad with Cumin and Raisins

Multigrain Honey Bread

Poached Figs in Wine

Mashed Potato Latkes with Zucchini and Dill

These potato cakes are made with mashed potatoes instead of traditional shredded potatoes. Combine and refrigerate the potato mixture up to a day ahead; dredge in matzo meal and sauté just before serving.

  4 cups cubed peeled Yukon gold potato (about 1¾ pounds)
  2 cups cubed zucchini
  1 cup diced leek
  ¼ cup cornstarch
  2 teaspoons minced fresh dill
  1½ teaspoons salt
  ½ teaspoon freshly ground black pepper
  1 large egg
  ½ cup matzo meal
  3 tablespoons vegetable oil, divided

1. Place potato in a saucepan, and cover with water. Bring to a boil. Reduce heat; simmer 15 minutes. Add zucchini and leek, and cook 6 minutes or until tender. Drain. Return mixture to pan; mash with a potato masher. Cool slightly. Stir in cornstarch and next 4 ingredients.
2. Divide potato mixture into 16 equal portions, shaping each into a ½-inch-thick patty. Dredge in matzo meal.
3. Heat 2¼ teaspoons oil in a large non-stick skillet over medium-high heat. Add 4 patties; cook 2 minutes on each side or until browned. Repeat procedure with remaining oil and patties. Yield: 8 servings (serving size: 2 patties).

CALORIES 185 (29% from fat); FAT 6g (sat 1g, mono 1.4g, poly 3.1g); PROTEIN 3.7g; CARB 30.4g; FIBER 2.6g; CHOL 27mg; IRON 1.1mg; SODIUM 456mg; CALC 24mg

Pear Applesauce

  ½ cup apple juice
  2 pounds Fuji apples, cored and cut into wedges
  2 pounds red Bartlett pears, cored and cut into wedges
  2 (3-inch) cinnamon sticks
  ½ lemon, cut into 2 pieces
  ¼ cup packed brown sugar

1. Combine first 5 ingredients in a large saucepan; bring to a boil. Cover, reduce heat, and simmer 45 minutes or until fruit is tender. Discard cinnamon sticks and lemon. Press fruit mixture through a sieve over a bowl using back of a spoon, and discard skins. Stir in brown sugar. Serve sauce at room temperature or chilled. Yield: 16 servings (serving size: ¼ cup).

CALORIES 80 (5% from fat); FAT 0.4g (sat 0.1g, mono 0.1g, poly 0.1g); PROTEIN 0.3g; CARB 20.7g; FIBER 1.6g; CHOL 0mg; IRON 0.2mg; SODIUM 2.1mg; CALC 12mg

Sweet-and-Sour Beet, Cabbage, and Tomato Soup

  4½ cups water
  6 cups shredded cabbage
  2 cups chopped onion
  2 cups diced peeled beets
  1½ cups canned petite diced tomatoes, undrained
  ½ cup tomato sauce
  ¼ cup chopped peeled celeriac (celery root)
  1 tablespoon brown sugar
  ¼ teaspoon salt
  ¼ teaspoon freshly ground black pepper
  2 tablespoons golden raisins
  1 tablespoon fresh lemon juice
  ½ cup sour cream
  4 teaspoons grated lemon rind

1. Bring water to a boil in a Dutch oven. Add cabbage and next 8 ingredients, and bring to a boil. Cover, reduce heat, and simmer 1 hour, stirring occasionally. Stir in raisins and juice. Simmer, partially covered, 15 minutes. Top each serving evenly with sour cream and rind. Yield: 8 servings (serving size: about 1 cup soup, 1 tablespoon sour cream, and ½ teaspoon rind).

CALORIES 114 (27% from fat); FAT 3.4g (sat 1.9g, mono 0.9g, poly 0.3g); PROTEIN 3.4g; CARB 20g; FIBER 4.8g; CHOL 6.3mg; IRON 1.3mg; SODIUM 295mg; CALC 75mg

Multigrain Honey Bread

The recipe makes two loaves, so freeze one to enjoy later. Wrap in plastic wrap, then aluminum foil, and store in the freezer for up to 2 months.

⅓ cup honey
2 packages dry yeast (about 4½ teaspoons)
4 cups warm water (100° to 110°)
8 cups all-purpose flour, divided
2 cups whole wheat flour
2 cups regular oats
1 cup wheat bran flakes cereal
1 cup toasted wheat germ
4 teaspoons salt
Cooking spray

1. Dissolve honey and yeast in warm water in a large bowl, and let stand 5 minutes. Lightly spoon flours into dry measuring cups; level with a knife. Add 7 cups all-purpose flour, whole wheat flour, and next 4 ingredients to yeast mixture; stir well to form a stiff dough. Turn dough out onto a floured surface. Knead until smooth and elastic (about 8 minutes); add enough remaining all-purpose flour, 1 tablespoon at a time, to prevent dough from sticking to hands (dough will feel sticky).
2. Place dough in a large bowl coated with cooking spray, turning to coat top. Cover and let rise in a warm place (85°), free from drafts, 45 minutes or until doubled in size. (Gently press 2 fingers into dough. If indentation remains, dough has risen enough.)
3. Punch dough down; cover and let rest 5 minutes. Divide in half. Working with 1 portion at a time (cover remaining dough to keep from drying), roll each portion into a 15 x 8-inch rectangle on a floured surface. Roll up each rectangle tightly, starting with a short edge, pressing firmly to eliminate air pockets; pinch seam and ends to seal. Place rolls, seam sides down, in 2 (9 x 5-inch) loaf pans coated with cooking spray. Cover;

let rise 45 minutes or until doubled in size.
4. Preheat oven to 350°.
5. Uncover dough; bake at 350° for 40 minutes or until loaves are browned on bottom and sound hollow when tapped. Remove from pans; cool on wire racks. Yield: 2 loaves, 18 slices per loaf (serving size: 1 slice).

CALORIES 166 (6% from fat); FAT 1.1g (sat 0.2g, mono 0.2g, poly 0.5g); PROTEIN 5.6g; CARB 34.2g; FIBER 2.7g; CHOL 0mg; IRON 2.4mg; SODIUM 270mg; CALC 12mg

Eggplant and Green Pepper Kugel

Kugel is traditionally a baked pudding that's made with potato or noodles. This version uses matzo meal and eggplant for a more savory flavor and a heartier texture.

1 large eggplant (about 2 pounds)
2 teaspoons vegetable oil
3 cups finely chopped onion
1½ cups finely chopped green bell pepper
3 tablespoons pine nuts
1½ teaspoons salt
½ teaspoon freshly ground black pepper
2 large eggs, lightly beaten
¾ cup matzo meal
Cooking spray
1 teaspoon paprika

1. Preheat oven to 450°.
2. Pierce eggplant several times with a fork; place on a foil-lined baking sheet. Bake at 450° for 20 minutes or until tender. Cool slightly; peel and chop. Place in a large bowl.
3. Heat oil in a large nonstick skillet over medium-high heat. Add onion, bell pepper, and nuts. Cook 6 minutes or until onion is tender. Add onion mixture, salt, black pepper, and eggs to eggplant; stir well to combine. Add matzo meal; toss gently to combine. Spoon mixture into an 11 x 7-inch

baking dish coated with cooking spray. Sprinkle with paprika. Bake at 450° for 35 minutes or until pudding is thoroughly heated and golden brown. Yield: 8 servings (serving size: about ¾ cup).

CALORIES 136 (30% from fat); FAT 4.5g (sat 0.9g, mono 2g, poly 1.1g); PROTEIN 5.4g; CARB 21g; FIBER 5g; CHOL 53mg; IRON 1.5mg; SODIUM 462mg; CALC 32mg

Carrot-Wheat Berry Salad with Cumin and Raisins

Make and chill up to 2 days ahead; sprinkle with fresh herbs just before serving.

½ cup uncooked wheat berries
1½ teaspoons salt, divided
2 pounds carrots, chopped
½ cup fresh lemon juice
2 teaspoons ground cumin
2 teaspoons paprika
¼ teaspoon ground red pepper
2 garlic cloves, minced
⅓ cup golden raisins
2 tablespoons extravirgin olive oil
3 tablespoons chopped fresh parsley
2 tablespoons chopped fresh cilantro

1. Place wheat berries and ½ teaspoon salt in a medium saucepan; cover with water to 2 inches above wheat berries. Bring to a boil. Reduce heat, and cook, uncovered, 50 minutes or until wheat berries are tender. Drain.
2. Cook half of carrots in a large pot of boiling water 2 minutes or until crisp-tender. Remove with a slotted spoon. Rinse with cold water; drain. Repeat with remaining carrots. Combine carrots and wheat berries in a large bowl; add 1 teaspoon salt, juice, cumin, paprika, pepper, and garlic. Stir in raisins and oil; toss well to combine. Cover; refrigerate 1 hour or until chilled. Sprinkle with parsley and cilantro. Yield: 8 servings (serving size: about ⅔ cup).

CALORIES 145 (25% from fat); FAT 4g (sat 0.5g, mono 2.5g, poly 0.4g); PROTEIN 3.2g; CARB 26.5g; FIBER 4.6g; CHOL 0mg; IRON 1.5mg; SODIUM 409mg; CALC 44mg

Poached Figs in Wine

Serve this simple dessert in wine stems or sherbet glasses. Prepare fig mixture up to 2 days ahead; cover and chill.
Whip cream at the last minute so it will remain fluffy. Sprinkle with grated orange rind for extra zip.

3 cups dried figs, halved (about 1 pound)
2 cups port or other sweet red wine
½ cup dry red wine
½ cup packed brown sugar
1 teaspoon grated orange rind
6 whole cloves
1 whole star anise
1 (3-inch) cinnamon stick
½ cup whipping cream
½ cup slivered almonds, toasted
Grated orange rind (optional)

1. Combine first 8 ingredients in a large saucepan; bring to a boil. Cover, reduce heat, and simmer over low heat 40 minutes. Cover; chill. Discard cloves, star anise, and cinnamon stick.

2. Place whipping cream in a medium bowl and beat with a mixer at high speed until soft peaks form. Top fig mixture with whipped cream and toasted almonds. Garnish with grated orange rind, if desired. Yield: 8 servings (serving size: ½ cup fig mixture, 2 tablespoons whipped cream, and 1 tablespoon almonds).

CALORIES 337 (26% from fat); FAT 9.6g (sat 3.8g, mono 3.9g, poly 1.4g); PROTEIN 3.6g; CARB 55.9g; FIBER 7.7g; CHOL 20mg; IRON 1.9mg; SODIUM 20mg; CALC 123mg

Leek-and-Bacon
Tart

Christmas Morning Breakfast

Once gifts have been opened, what's the first thing on everyone's mind? Breakfast! You'll need something substantial to hold you over until the big Christmas dinner later in the day. This hearty meal fits the bill.

Leek-and-Bacon Tart

This is a lighter version of the traditional quiche Lorraine. The leeks, which are milder than onions, can be chopped up to 2 days ahead and refrigerated in an airtight container.

Crust:
- 1 cup all-purpose flour
- ¼ teaspoon salt
- 2 tablespoons chilled butter, cut into small pieces
- 2 tablespoons vegetable shortening
- ¼ teaspoon cider vinegar
- 4 to 5 tablespoons ice water

Filling:
- 3 bacon slices, cut crosswise into thin strips
- 7 cups chopped leek (about 3 large)
- ½ teaspoon salt, divided
- ¼ teaspoon black pepper, divided
- 1¼ cups egg substitute
- ⅔ cup fat-free milk

1. To prepare crust, lightly spoon flour into a dry measuring cup; level with a knife. Combine flour and ¼ teaspoon salt in a bowl; cut in butter and shortening with a pastry blender or 2 knives until mixture resembles coarse meal. Add vinegar and ice water, 1 tablespoon at a time; toss with a fork until moist. Gently press mixture into a 4-inch circle on heavy-duty plastic wrap; cover dough with additional plastic wrap. Roll dough, still covered, into a 12-inch circle; chill 10 minutes.

2. Preheat oven to 425°.

3. Remove 1 sheet of plastic wrap; let dough stand 1 minute or until pliable. Fit dough, plastic-wrap side up, into a 10-inch round removable-bottom tart pan. Remove plastic wrap. Press dough against bottom and sides of pan. Fold edges under. Line dough with a piece of foil; arrange pie weights on foil. Bake at 425° for 10 minutes or until edge is lightly browned. Remove pie weights and foil; cool on a wire rack.

4. To prepare filling, heat a large nonstick skillet over medium heat until hot. Add bacon, and cook 4 minutes. Remove bacon from pan, reserving 2 teaspoons drippings in pan; set bacon aside. Add leek to drippings in pan; cover and cook 20 minutes, stirring occasionally. Sprinkle with ¼ teaspoon salt and ⅛ teaspoon pepper. Remove from heat. Arrange leek mixture and bacon in prepared crust.

5. Combine egg substitute, milk, ¼ teaspoon salt, and ⅛ teaspoon pepper; stir well with a whisk. Pour mixture into crust. Bake at 425° for 25 minutes or until a knife inserted in center comes out clean; let stand 10 minutes. Yield: 8 servings.

Note: You can use a commercial piecrust (such as Pillsbury) in place of the pastry crust. If you substitute a refrigerated piecrust, follow package instructions for prebaking. It will add 15 calories and 1.4 grams of fat to the nutrition figures for each serving.

CALORIES 213 (35% from fat); FAT 8.4g (sat 3.3g, mono 3.1g, poly 1.7g); PROTEIN 8.3g; CARB 26.5g; FIBER 1.5g; CHOL 12mg; IRON 3.3mg; SODIUM 379mg; CALC 95mg

Warm Ham with Shallots and Vinegar

- 1 tablespoon olive oil
- ⅓ cup minced shallots
- ⅓ cup red wine vinegar
- 2 tablespoons water
- 4 (4-ounce) slices smoked ham (about ¼ inch thick), cut into thin strips
- 2 tablespoons chopped fresh parsley

1. Heat oil in a 9-inch cast-iron or heavy skillet over medium heat. Add shallots, and sauté 2 minutes. Add vinegar and water; cook until reduced by half (about 1 minute). Add ham; cook 4 minutes or until thoroughly heated, stirring occasionally. Remove ham from pan; sprinkle with parsley. Yield: 8 servings (serving size: 2 ounces ham).

Note: You can purchase smoked ham in the deli section of the supermarket and have it cut into slices.

CALORIES 95 (43% from fat); FAT 4.5g (sat 1.2g, mono 2.6g, poly 0.4g); PROTEIN 11.2g; CARB 2.1g; FIBER 0.1g; CHOL 26mg; IRON 0.5mg; SODIUM 811mg; CALC 8mg

While some of these dishes require same-day preparation, you'll find that several can be made in advance.

(clockwise from left) Warm Ham with Shallots and Vinegar; Spiced Winter Fruit; Southwestern Breakfast Casserole

Southwestern Breakfast Casserole

You can assemble this entire casserole up to a week ahead. Bake the corn muffin mix ahead, and then store the muffins in an airtight container in the freezer for a couple of days. Assemble the casserole according to directions; cover and freeze. A day in advance, take it out of the freezer, and thaw in the refrigerator (about 24 hours). Uncover and let stand 30 minutes at room temperature before cooking; bake as directed.

1   (8½-ounce) package corn muffin mix
3   cups (½-inch) cubed white bread
8   ounces hot turkey Italian sausage
1   cup chopped onion
2½   cups fat-free milk
1   teaspoon ground cumin
⅛   teaspoon black pepper
1   (10-ounce) can diced tomatoes and green chiles, undrained
1   (8-ounce) carton egg substitute
Cooking spray
1   cup (4 ounces) shredded reduced-fat Monterey Jack or mild Cheddar cheese, divided

1. Prepare corn muffin mix according to package directions; cool. Crumble muffins into a large bowl; stir in bread. Set aside.
2. Remove casings from sausage. Cook sausage and onion in a large nonstick skillet over medium heat until browned, stirring to crumble. Drain.
3. Combine milk, cumin, pepper, tomatoes, and egg substitute; stir with a whisk until well blended. Add sausage mixture; stir well. Stir into bread mixture. Spoon half of bread mixture into an 11 x 7-inch baking dish coated with cooking spray. Top with ½ cup cheese. Spoon remaining bread mixture over cheese. Cover and refrigerate 8 hours or overnight.
4. Preheat oven to 350°.
5. Bake casserole at 350° for 20 minutes or until set. Top with ½ cup cheese, and bake an additional 20 minutes or until set. Let stand 10 minutes before serving. Yield: 8 servings.

CALORIES 271 (25% from fat); FAT 7.6g (sat 2.7g, mono 2.6g, poly 1.7g); PROTEIN 14.7g; CARB 33.9g; FIBER 1.6g; CHOL 22mg; IRON 2.1mg; SODIUM 700mg; CALC 290mg

Spiced Winter Fruit

This recipe also makes a simple and elegant holiday dessert when topped with low-fat vanilla ice cream. Quince, which is in season during the cool months, is a yellow-skinned fruit that looks and tastes like a cross between an apple and a pear but turns pink when cooked; cooking mellows its tartness. (If you can't find quince, just use 2 additional apples or pears cut into wedges.)

1   cup packed light brown sugar
1   teaspoon ground ginger
1   teaspoon ground cinnamon
½   teaspoon ground nutmeg
2   tablespoons butter
2   quinces, each cut into 8 wedges (about ¾ pound)
3   cups sliced peeled Bartlett or Anjou pear (about 1½ pounds)
2½   cups sliced peeled Granny Smith apple (about 1½ pounds)
¼   teaspoon freshly ground black pepper
Cinnamon sticks (optional)

1. Combine first 4 ingredients in a small bowl; set aside.
2. Melt butter in a large nonstick skillet over medium heat. Add quinces; cover and cook 6 minutes, stirring occasionally. Add sugar mixture, pear, and apple; cover and cook 12 minutes, stirring occasionally. Stir in pepper; garnish with cinnamon sticks, if desired. Yield: 8 servings (serving size: ¾ cup).

Note: This dish will keep up to 3 days if refrigerated in an airtight container. To serve, reheat over low heat.

CALORIES 219 (15% from fat); FAT 3.6g (sat 1.9g, mono 0.9g, poly 0.3g); PROTEIN 0.7g; CARB 50.1g; FIBER 4.5g; CHOL 8mg; IRON 1.1mg; SODIUM 38mg; CALC 38mg

extra touches

* Instead of a 10-foot tree this year, go small. Cover a table in red fabric, and put a small tree on top. It looks great surrounded by presents, and the cleanup is easier. Another idea is to place small branches in a pretty jar or glass and hang a single ornament on each branch.

* Set out bowls of unshelled nuts and fruits around your home. It's better to crack a few walnuts or eat some fruit than to munch on leftover desserts.

* Don't worry if you don't have a mantel on which to hang your stockings with care. Hang them on the doorknobs outside your kids' rooms for a great post-wake-up surprise filled with goodies, such as markers and toy cars.

Fresh Cranberry
Muffins

Fresh Cranberry Muffins

Feel free to use your imagination with this basic muffin recipe by substituting your other favorite fruits and flavors for the cranberries and orange rind. Some options we like: blueberries and lemon rind; chopped apple, pear, or pineapple and cinnamon; or mashed bananas and allspice.

> 2   cups all-purpose flour
> ⅔   cup sugar
> 2   teaspoons baking powder
> ¼   teaspoon salt
> 1   cup chopped fresh
>   cranberries
> ⅔   cup 2% reduced-fat milk
> ¼   cup butter, melted
> 1   teaspoon grated orange rind
> ½   teaspoon vanilla extract
> 1   large egg, lightly beaten
> Cooking spray

1. Preheat oven to 400°.
2. Lightly spoon flour into dry measuring cups; level with a knife. Combine flour, sugar, baking powder, and salt in a large bowl; stir well with a whisk. Stir in cranberries; make a well in center of mixture. Combine milk, butter, rind, vanilla, and egg; add to flour mixture, stirring just until moist. Spoon batter into 12 muffin cups coated with cooking spray. Bake at 400° for 18 minutes or until muffins spring back when touched lightly in center. Remove muffins from pan immediately; place on a wire rack. Yield: 12 servings (serving size: 1 muffin).

Note: These muffins, as well as the Almond Cake (recipe on page 47), freeze well. Bake them ahead, cool completely, and store in freezer bags. To serve, thaw at room temperature. Reheat in aluminum foil at 300° for 10 to 15 minutes or until thoroughly heated.

CALORIES 174 (26% from fat); FAT 5g (sat 2.7g, mono 1.4g, poly 0.4g); PROTEIN 3.2g; CARB 29.2g; FIBER 0.7g; CHOL 30mg; IRON 1.2mg; SODIUM 182mg; CALC 69mg

planning for a breakfast crowd

* Start a notebook several days in advance. Outline each task to be completed, and check it off as you go. You'll start the morning knowing all of the essential elements have been handled.

* Identify serving pieces for each dish ahead of time. Place a note card with the name of the recipe to be served on each piece. You'll save yourself from that last-minute frantic rush to find your favorite serving platter.

* Clean out the refrigerator and freezer to make room for storing dishes. Consider removing the refrigerator's storage drawers temporarily to free up space.

* Clean dishes as you go. If you start the day with an empty dishwasher, you'll find the cleanup less overwhelming. Knowing that a quick-to-clean kitchen awaits will free you to enjoy the company of friends and family.

* Designate an area for coffee and other beverages. Guests can serve themselves, and it creates an opportunity for them to feel at home.

Almond Cake

Since this cake is not too sweet or gooey, it's perfect for brunch. For a nonalcoholic version, omit the amaretto and substitute an equal amount of apple juice, or use $^1/_4$ cup water plus $^1/_2$ teaspoon almond extract.

1 $^1/_2$ cups all-purpose flour

$^3/_4$ cup sugar

$^1/_2$ cup chopped sliced almonds (about 2 ounces), toasted and divided

2 teaspoons baking powder

$^1/_2$ teaspoon salt

$^1/_4$ cup fat-free milk

$^1/_4$ cup butter, melted

$^1/_4$ cup amaretto (almond-flavored liqueur)

2 large eggs, lightly beaten

Cooking spray

1. Preheat oven to 350°.

2. Lightly spoon flour into dry measuring cups, and level with a knife. Combine flour, sugar, $^1/_4$ cup almonds, baking powder, and salt in a large bowl; stir well with a whisk. Combine milk, butter, amaretto, and eggs; add to flour mixture, stirring just until moist.

3. Spoon batter into a 9-inch round cake pan coated with cooking spray. Sprinkle batter with remaining almonds. Bake at 350° for 30 minutes or until a wooden pick inserted in center comes out clean. Cool cake in pan 10 minutes on a wire rack. Remove from pan. Cool completely on wire rack. Yield: 8 servings.

CALORIES 286 (35% from fat); FAT 11.1g (sat 4.4g, mono 4.6g, poly 1.3g); PROTEIN 5.8g; CARB 42g; FIBER 1.4g; CHOL 71mg; IRON 1.7mg; SODIUM 349mg; CALC 108mg

Fire and Spice Ham

Christmas Dinner

Though steeped in tradition, this Christmas Dinner menu is anything but ordinary. Simple, fresh, and delicious sides complement spicy ham for a truly memorable Yuletide meal.

Menu

serves 8

Fire and Spice Ham

Cinnamon Stewed Apples

Brussels Sprouts with Pecans

Arugula, Fennel, and
Parmesan Salad

Sweet Potato Cheesecake

Wine Note: *Ham accented with brown sugar and preserves needs a wine that will balance the sweetness. One option is a sparkling wine or Champagne. In this case, a creamy but crisp sparkler will provide just the right counterpoint.*

Fire and Spice Ham

1   (5½- to 6-pound) 33%-less-sodium
     smoked, fully cooked ham half
Cooking spray
½   cup red pepper jelly
½   cup pineapple preserves
¼   cup packed brown sugar
¼   teaspoon ground cloves

1. Preheat oven to 425°.
2. Trim fat and rind from ham half. Score outside of ham in a diamond pattern. Place ham on a broiler pan coated with cooking spray. Combine jelly and next 3 ingredients, stirring with a whisk until well blended. Brush about one-third of jelly mixture over ham.
3. Bake at 425° for 5 minutes. Reduce

oven temperature to 325° (do not remove ham from oven); bake an additional 45 minutes, basting ham with jelly mixture every 15 minutes. Transfer ham to a serving platter; let stand 15 minutes before slicing. Yield: 18 servings (serving size: about 3 ounces).

CALORIES 188 (23% from fat); FAT 4.9g (sat 1.6g, mono 2.3g, poly 0.5g); PROTEIN 18.4g; CARB 16.8g; FIBER 0g; CHOL 47mg; IRON 1.4mg; SODIUM 865mg; CALC 10mg

Cinnamon Stewed Apples

A terrific companion for ham or pork, this recipe can be doubled easily and will keep in the refrigerator for about a week. The sauce is somewhat thin just after cooking, but it will thicken upon standing.

6   cups chopped peeled Granny
     Smith apple (about 2 pounds)
½   cup packed brown sugar
¼   cup apple juice
1   teaspoon ground cinnamon
⅛   teaspoon ground nutmeg
⅛   teaspoon salt

1. Combine all ingredients in a large, heavy saucepan. Cover and cook over medium-low heat 45 minutes or until apple is tender, stirring occasionally. Let stand 5 minutes. Yield: 2 cups (serving size: ¼ cup).

CALORIES 121 (3% from fat); FAT 0.4g (sat 0.1g, mono 0g, poly 0.1g); PROTEIN 0.2g; CARB 31.3g; FIBER 2.3g; CHOL 0mg; IRON 0.4mg; SODIUM 42mg; CALC 19mg

Brussels Sprouts
with Pecans

Lure guests to their seats at your Christmas table with shimmering candlelight from glass hurricane lamps. Wrap the bases of the lamps with holiday greenery mixed with bright red berries.

Brussels Sprouts with Pecans

  2   teaspoons butter
  1   cup chopped onion
  4   garlic cloves, thinly sliced
  8   cups thinly sliced Brussels sprouts
        (about 1½ pounds)
  ½   cup fat-free, less-sodium chicken broth
1½   tablespoons sugar
  ½   teaspoon salt
  8   teaspoons coarsely chopped
        pecans, toasted

1. Melt butter in a large nonstick skillet over medium-high heat. Add onion and garlic; sauté 4 minutes or until lightly browned. Stir in Brussels sprouts; sauté 2 minutes. Add broth and sugar, and cook 5 minutes or until liquid almost evaporates, stirring frequently. Stir in salt. Sprinkle with pecans. Yield: 8 servings (serving size: about ⅔ cup).

CALORIES 82 (33% from fat); FAT 3g (sat 0.8g, mono 1.3g, poly 0.7g); PROTEIN 3.6g; CARB 12.6g; FIBER 3.9g; CHOL 3mg; IRON 1.3mg; SODIUM 207mg; CALC 45mg

Arugula, Fennel, and Parmesan Salad

  3   tablespoons fresh lemon juice
  2   teaspoons sugar
  1   teaspoon olive oil
  ½   teaspoon salt
  ¼   teaspoon black pepper
  4   cups thinly sliced fennel bulb
        (about 2 bulbs)
  1   cup thinly sliced red onion
  8   cups trimmed arugula
  ½   cup (2 ounces) shaved fresh
        Parmesan cheese

1. Combine first 5 ingredients in a small bowl; stir with a whisk. Combine fennel and onion in a large bowl; drizzle with dressing, tossing gently to coat.
2. Arrange 1 cup arugula on each of 8 plates. Top each serving with about ¾ cup fennel mixture and 1 tablespoon cheese. Yield: 8 servings.

CALORIES 62 (38% from fat); FAT 2.6g (sat 1.3g, mono 1g, poly 0.2g); PROTEIN 3.8g; CARB 7g; FIBER 2g; CHOL 5mg; IRON 0.7mg; SODIUM 289mg; CALC 141mg

Sweet Potato Cheesecake

Canned sweet potatoes and packaged graham cracker crumbs are great time-savers.

Crust:
  2   cups graham cracker crumbs
        (about 12 cookie sheets)
  3   tablespoons sugar
  2   tablespoons butter, melted
  1   tablespoon water
        Cooking spray
Filling:
  ½   cup vanilla fat-free yogurt
  2   (8-ounce) blocks ⅓-less-fat cream
        cheese, softened
  2   (8-ounce) blocks fat-free cream
        cheese, softened
  ⅓   cup all-purpose flour
1¼   cups sugar
  1   tablespoon vanilla extract
  1   tablespoon light molasses
  ¾   teaspoon ground cinnamon
  ½   teaspoon ground ginger
  ¼   teaspoon salt
  ¼   teaspoon ground nutmeg
  3   large eggs
  2   (15-ounce) cans sweet potatoes,
        drained

1. Preheat oven to 350°.
2. To prepare crust, combine first 4 ingredients, tossing with a fork until well blended. Press into bottom of a 9-inch springform pan coated with cooking spray. Bake at 350° for 10 minutes; cool on a wire rack. Reduce oven temperature to 325°.
3. To prepare filling, place yogurt and cheeses in a large bowl; beat with a mixer at high speed until smooth. Lightly spoon flour into a dry measuring cup; level with a knife. Add flour and next 7 ingredients to cheese mixture; beat well. Add eggs, 1 at a time, beating well after each addition.
4. Place sweet potatoes in a food processor; process until smooth. Add sweet potatoes to cheese mixture, stirring until well blended.
5. Pour cheese mixture into prepared pan. Bake at 325° for 1 hour and 20 minutes or until cheesecake center barely moves when pan is touched. Turn oven off. Cool cheesecake in closed oven 1 hour.
6. Remove cheesecake from oven, and run a knife around outside edge. Cool to room temperature. Cover and chill at least 8 hours. Yield: 16 servings (serving size: 1 wedge).

CALORIES 310 (29% from fat); FAT 10.1g (sat 5.5g, mono 3.2g, poly 1g); PROTEIN 10.3g; CARB 44g; FIBER 1.6g; CHOL 67mg; IRON 1.2mg; SODIUM 434mg; CALC 134mg

(clockwise from front) Herb, Garlic, and
Mustard-Crusted Fillet of Beef; Sautéed Leeks
and Broccolini with Balsamic Vinegar; Ciabatta;
Creamy Two-Cheese Polenta

Simple Christmas Supper

A creamy chocolate pie with a walnut crumb crust adds the finishing touch to this Italian-inspired Christmas menu. Prepare the bread and pie ahead, and you can have this meal ready to serve in less than 1 hour.

Herb, Garlic, and Mustard-Crusted Fillet of Beef

1 (2-pound) beef tenderloin, trimmed
Cooking spray
¾ teaspoon salt
¼ teaspoon freshly ground black pepper
3 tablespoons Dijon mustard
¼ cup chopped fresh basil
¼ cup chopped fresh parsley
1 tablespoon chopped fresh thyme
1 tablespoon chopped fresh oregano
3 garlic cloves, minced

1. Preheat oven to 400°.
2. Place beef on a broiler pan coated with cooking spray, and sprinkle with salt and pepper. Spread mustard evenly over beef. Combine basil and next 4 ingredients; pat evenly over beef.
3. Insert a meat thermometer into thickest portion of beef. Bake at 400° for 40 minutes or until thermometer registers 145° (medium-rare) or until desired degree of doneness.
4. Transfer beef to a cutting board. Cover loosely with foil, and let stand 10 minutes before slicing. Yield: 8 servings (serving size: 3 ounces).

CALORIES 154 (43% from fat); FAT 7.4g (sat 2.6g, mono 2.8g, poly 0.4g); PROTEIN 19.8g; CARB 1.4g; FIBER 0.3g; CHOL 57mg; IRON 2.8mg; SODIUM 404mg; CALC 23mg

Creamy Two-Cheese Polenta

If you're not serving this immediately, keep the polenta warm by covering it and placing it over very low heat. Stir occasionally.

4 cups 1% low-fat milk
1 cup water
1¼ teaspoons salt
¼ teaspoon freshly ground black pepper
1¼ cups instant dry polenta
⅓ cup (about 2½ ounces) mascarpone cheese
⅓ cup (about 1½ ounces) grated Parmigiano-Reggiano cheese

1. Combine first 4 ingredients in a medium saucepan over medium-high heat. Bring to a boil; gradually add polenta, stirring constantly with a whisk. Cook 2 minutes or until thick, stirring constantly. Remove from heat; stir in cheeses. Serve immediately. Yield: 8 servings (serving size: about ⅔ cup).

CALORIES 206 (28% from fat); FAT 6.4g (sat 3.7g, mono 0.7g, poly 0.1g); PROTEIN 8.5g; CARB 28.7g; FIBER 2.5g; CHOL 19mg; IRON 0.6mg; SODIUM 493mg; CALC 207mg

Sautéed Leeks and Broccolini with Balsamic Vinegar

4 center-cut bacon slices
1 pound broccolini, trimmed and cut in half crosswise
2 leeks, halved lengthwise and cut diagonally into 2-inch pieces
¼ teaspoon dried oregano
¼ teaspoon crushed red pepper
4 garlic cloves, thinly sliced
¼ cup fat-free, less-sodium chicken broth
1½ tablespoons balsamic vinegar
¾ teaspoon salt

1. Cook bacon in a large nonstick skillet over medium-high heat until crisp. Remove bacon from pan, reserving 2 teaspoons drippings in pan. Crumble bacon; set aside. Add broccolini and leeks to drippings in pan; sauté 4 minutes. Add oregano, pepper, and garlic; sauté 3 minutes. Stir in broth, vinegar, and salt; cook 30 seconds or until liquid almost evaporates. Sprinkle with crumbled bacon. Yield: 8 servings (serving size: about ¾ cup).

CALORIES 81 (32% from fat); FAT 2.9g (sat 1.1g, mono 1.2g, poly 0.4g); PROTEIN 3.8g; CARB 10.6g; FIBER 1.5g; CHOL 4mg; IRON 1.5mg; SODIUM 316mg; CALC 70mg;

Ciabatta

This bread gets its name from its shape; ciabatta is Italian for "slipper." Letting the sponge rest for 12 hours develops complex flavor. If you have any left over, try it with deli roast beef for quick, post-holiday sandwiches.

Sponge:

- 1 cup bread flour
- ½ cup warm fat-free milk (100° to 110°)
- ¼ cup warm water (100° to 110°)
- 1 tablespoon honey
- 1 package dry yeast (about 2¼ teaspoons)

Dough:

- 3½ cups bread flour, divided
- ½ cup semolina or pasta flour
- ¾ cup warm water (100° to 110°)
- ½ cup warm fat-free milk (100° to 110°)
- 1½ teaspoons salt
- 1 package dry yeast (about 2¼ teaspoons)
- 3 tablespoons semolina or pasta flour, divided

1. To prepare sponge, lightly spoon 1 cup bread flour into a dry measuring cup; level with a knife. Combine 1 cup bread flour and next 4 ingredients in a large bowl, stirring well with a whisk. Cover; chill 12 hours.

2. To prepare dough, let sponge stand at room temperature 30 minutes. Lightly spoon 3½ cups bread flour and ½ cup semolina flour into dry measuring cups; level with a knife. Add 3 cups bread flour, semolina flour, ¾ cup warm water, ½ cup warm milk, salt, and 1 package yeast to sponge; stir well to form a soft dough. Turn dough out onto a floured surface. Knead until smooth and elastic (about 8 minutes); add enough remaining bread flour, 1 tablespoon at a time, to prevent dough from sticking to hands. Divide dough in half.

3. Working with 1 portion at a time (cover remaining dough to keep from drying), roll each into a 13 x 5-inch oval. Place 3 inches apart on a large baking sheet sprinkled with 2 tablespoons semolina flour. Taper ends of dough to form a "slipper." Sprinkle 1 tablespoon semolina flour over dough. Cover and let rise in a warm place (85°), free from drafts, 45 minutes or until doubled in size.

4. Preheat oven to 425°.

5. Uncover dough. Bake at 425° for 18 minutes or until loaves are lightly browned and sound hollow when tapped. Remove from pan, and cool on a wire rack. Yield: 2 loaves, 16 servings (serving size: 1 slice).

CALORIES 150 (1% from fat); FAT 0.1g (sat 0g, mono 0.1g, poly 0g); PROTEIN 6.3g; CARB 32.1g; FIBER 1.3g; CHOL 0mg; IRON 2.1mg; SODIUM 227mg; CALC 21mg

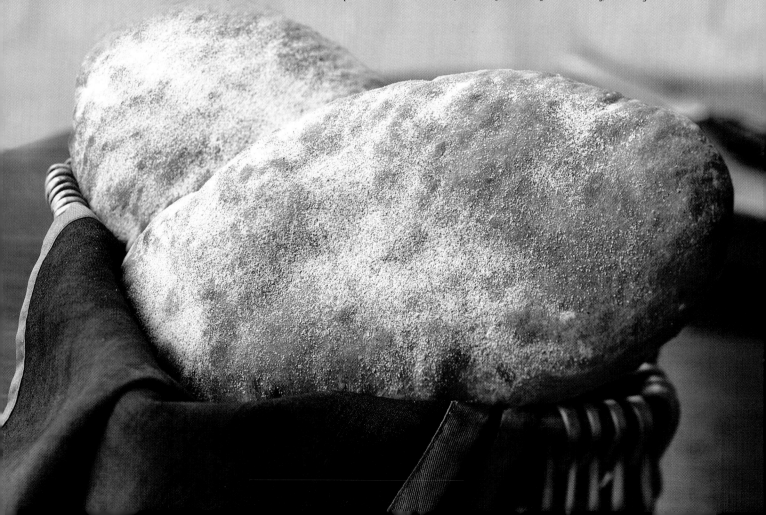

Orange, Arugula, and Kalamata Olive Salad

Blood oranges, available from December through March, add vibrant red color, so use them if you can find them. Pit the olives by crushing them with the blade of a chef's knife.

2	tablespoons fresh lemon juice
1½	teaspoons extravirgin olive oil
½	teaspoon salt
⅛	teaspoon freshly ground black pepper
8	cups trimmed arugula (about 8 ounces)
2	cups thinly sliced fennel bulb
¾	cup vertically sliced red onion
12	sliced pitted kalamata olives
2	cups coarsely chopped orange sections (about 2 pounds)

1. Combine first 4 ingredients. Combine arugula, fennel, onion, and olives in a large bowl. Drizzle lemon mixture over arugula mixture; toss gently to coat. Top with orange sections. Yield: 8 servings (serving size: about 1¼ cups).

CALORIES 62 (38% from fat); FAT 2.6g (sat 0.3g, mono 1.8g, poly 0.3g); PROTEIN 1.4g; CARB 9.4g; FIBER 2.3g; CHOL 0mg; IRON 0.6mg; SODIUM 254mg; CALC 65mg

Chocolate-Walnut Meringue Pie

Crust:

1½	cups low-fat graham cracker crumbs (about 10 cookie sheets)
½	cup finely ground walnuts
¼	cup butter, melted
	Cooking spray

Filling:

¾	cup sugar
3½	tablespoons cornstarch
	Dash of salt
2	cups evaporated fat-free milk
4	ounces semisweet chocolate, finely chopped
3	large egg yolks, lightly beaten
1	teaspoon vanilla extract

Meringue:

4	large egg whites
¼	teaspoon cream of tartar
¼	teaspoon salt
½	cup sugar
1	teaspoon vanilla extract

1. Preheat oven to 350°.
2. To prepare crust, combine first 3 ingredients, tossing well. Press into bottom and up sides of a 9-inch pie plate coated with cooking spray. Bake at 350° for 15 minutes or until lightly browned. Cool completely on a wire rack.
3. To prepare filling, combine ¾ cup sugar, cornstarch, and dash of salt in a medium saucepan; whisk in milk and chocolate. Bring to a boil over medium heat, stirring constantly. Cook 1 minute, stirring constantly. Remove from heat. Gradually add ½ cup chocolate mixture to egg yolks, stirring constantly with a whisk. Return egg mixture to pan. Cook over medium heat until thick (about 4 minutes), stirring constantly. Stir in 1 teaspoon vanilla. Spread mixture into prepared crust. Cover surface of chocolate mixture with plastic wrap.
4. Reduce oven temperature to 325°.
5. To prepare meringue, place the egg whites, cream of tartar, and ¼ teaspoon salt in a large bowl. Beat with a mixer at high speed until foamy. Add ½ cup sugar, 1 tablespoon at a time, beating until stiff peaks form. Add 1 teaspoon vanilla, beating just until blended. Remove plastic wrap from filling. Spread meringue evenly over filling, sealing to edge of crust.
6. Bake at 325° for 25 minutes. Cool 1 hour on a wire rack. Chill 3 hours or until pie is set. Yield: 12 servings (serving size: 1 wedge).

CALORIES 344 (30% from fat); FAT 11.4g (sat 5g, mono 2.9g, poly 2g); PROTEIN 8.5g; CARB 53.5g; FIBER 1.7g; CHOL 65mg; IRON 1.3mg; SODIUM 218mg; CALC 146mg

Chocolate-Walnut Meringue Pie

Kwanzaa Feast

Celebrate your cultural heritage, welcome the New Year, or gather family and friends for Sunday dinner with this traditional menu featuring many of the first fruits of the harvest.

Apple-Glazed Carrots with Bacon

2 bacon slices
1 cup chopped onion
2 (16-ounce) packages baby carrots
1½ cups apple cider
¼ cup packed brown sugar
¼ teaspoon ground red pepper
2 tablespoons chopped chives

1. Cook bacon slices in a small skillet over medium heat until crisp. Remove bacon from skillet, and crumble. Add onion to bacon drippings in skillet; sauté 3 minutes. Add carrots and next 3 ingredients; bring to a boil. Cook over medium heat 10 minutes or until carrots are tender. Do not drain.
2. Place carrot mixture in a large serving bowl. Sprinkle with crumbled bacon and chopped chives. Yield: 8 servings (serving size: ¾ cup).

CALORIES 115 (9% from fat); FAT 1.2g (sat 0.4g, mono 0.4g, poly 0.2g); PROTEIN 2.1g; CARB 26g; FIBER 4.2g; CHOL 2mg; IRON 0.9mg; SODIUM 86mg; CALC 45mg

Hoppin' John

1 tablespoon vegetable oil
⅔ cup chopped onion
½ cup chopped green bell pepper
⅓ cup chopped celery
2 garlic cloves, minced
1 teaspoon dried thyme
1 teaspoon crushed red pepper
½ teaspoon salt
¼ teaspoon ground black pepper
2 bay leaves
4 cups water
2 smoked ham hocks (about 1½ pounds)
1 (16-ounce) bag frozen black-eyed peas
1 cup uncooked jasmine or basmati rice
¾ cup chopped red bell pepper
⅓ cup chopped green onion tops

1. Heat oil in a Dutch oven over medium-high heat. Add onion, green bell pepper, celery, and garlic; sauté 5 minutes. Add thyme, red pepper, salt, black pepper, and bay leaves; cook 1 minute. Add water and ham hocks, and bring to a boil. Cover, reduce heat, and simmer 30 minutes. Add peas; cook an additional 30 minutes.
2. Remove ham hocks from pan; cool. Remove bones, skin, and fat from ham; finely chop ham. Discard bones, skin, and fat. Add rice and red bell pepper to pan; bring to a boil. Cover, reduce heat, and simmer 15 minutes. Remove from heat; stir in ham. Discard bay leaves. Spoon into a serving dish, and sprinkle with green onions. Yield: 8 servings (serving size: about 1 cup).

CALORIES 226 (12% from fat); FAT 2.7g (sat 0.7g, mono 1.2g, poly 0.6g); PROTEIN 13.6g; CARB 37g; FIBER 4.5g; CHOL 17mg; IRON 2.2mg; SODIUM 622mg; CALC 31mg

Quick Collard Greens

1 cup fat-free, less-sodium chicken broth, divided
4 garlic cloves, finely chopped
11 cups tightly packed chopped fresh collard greens (about 4½ pounds)
¼ teaspoon crushed red pepper
⅛ teaspoon salt

1. Heat ½ cup chicken broth in a large Dutch oven over medium heat until hot. Add garlic, and cook 2 minutes, stirring frequently.
2. Add collard greens and remaining ½ cup broth; stir well. Cover and cook 7 minutes, stirring occasionally. Remove from heat; stir in crushed red pepper and salt. Yield: 7 servings (serving size: 1 cup).

CALORIES 112 (14% from fat); FAT 1.7g (sat 0.3g, mono 0.2g, poly 0.7g); PROTEIN 7.4g; CARB 22.2g; FIBER 3.2g; CHOL 0mg; IRON 3.8mg; SODIUM 144mg; CALC 288mg

(clockwise from front) Braised Pork Roast
with Apple-Brandy Sauce; Triple-Corn
Spoon Bread; Apple-Glazed Carrots with
Bacon; whole-berry cranberry relish

Braised Pork Roast with Apple-Brandy Sauce

Cooked in the same pan with the roast, the chunky apple-brandy sauce picks up the herb rub's savory flavors.

  1 (2½-pound) rolled, boned pork loin roast
  1 tablespoon dried rubbed sage
1½ teaspoons dried thyme
  1 teaspoon salt, divided
  ½ teaspoon black pepper, divided
     Cooking spray
  1 teaspoon butter
  2 cups chopped onion
  ½ cup chopped celery
  ½ cup thawed apple juice concentrate, undiluted
  ½ cup applejack (apple brandy)
  1 (10½-ounce) can fat-free, less-sodium chicken broth
2⅔ cups peeled, chopped Granny Smith apple (about 1 pound)
  1 tablespoon water
  2 teaspoons cornstarch

1. Unroll roast; trim fat. Combine sage, thyme, ½ teaspoon salt, and ¼ teaspoon pepper; rub inside surface of roast with one-third of sage mixture. Reroll roast, securing at 1-inch intervals with twine. Rub outside surface of roast with remaining sage mixture.
2. Preheat oven to 425°.
3. Place a large Dutch oven coated with cooking spray over medium-high heat until hot. Add roast; brown on all sides. Remove roast from pan; set aside. Melt butter in pan. Add onion and celery; sauté 5 minutes. Return roast to pan. Combine ½ teaspoon salt, ¼ teaspoon pepper, apple juice, applejack, and broth; pour over roast.
4. Insert a meat thermometer into thickest portion of roast. Cover; bake at 425° for 20 minutes. Reduce oven temperature to 325° (do not remove roast from oven);

bake 30 minutes. Add apple; cover and bake 30 additional minutes or until meat thermometer registers 155° (slightly pink). Remove roast from pan, reserving apple mixture. Place roast on a platter; cover with aluminum foil. Let stand 10 minutes. Remove twine.
5. Combine water and cornstarch; stir into reserved apple mixture in pan. Bring mixture to a boil; cook 1 minute or until sauce is slightly thick. Serve sauce with pork. Yield: 8 servings (serving size: 3 ounces pork and ⅓ cup sauce).
Note: Use 1 cup apple juice concentrate and omit apple brandy, if desired.

CALORIES 301 (30% from fat); FAT 10.2g (sat 3.8g, mono 4.5g, poly 0.8g); PROTEIN 29.3g; CARB 17.4g; FIBER 1.7g; CHOL 81mg; IRON 1.7mg; SODIUM 426mg; CALC 45mg

Creamed-Spinach Gratin

Placing the creamed spinach in a casserole and topping it with sliced tomatoes gives the dish bright, festive touches of red and green.

  1 (10-ounce) package fresh spinach
     Cooking spray
  ⅔ cup chopped onion
  ¼ cup tub-style light cream cheese
  ½ teaspoon dried oregano
  ¼ teaspoon salt
  ¼ teaspoon black pepper
  1 cup (¼-inch-thick) sliced tomato
  ¼ cup dry breadcrumbs
  2 tablespoons finely grated fresh Parmesan cheese

1. Preheat oven to 375°.
2. Remove large stems from spinach. Tear spinach into 1-inch pieces; place in a colander. Rinse spinach under cold water; drain. Set aside.
3. Place a large Dutch oven coated with cooking spray over medium heat until hot. Add onion; sauté 3 minutes. Add spinach; cover and cook 2 minutes or until spinach wilts. Add cream cheese

and next 3 ingredients. Cook, uncovered, 1 additional minute or until cream cheese melts. Spoon spinach mixture into a 1-quart gratin dish or shallow casserole coated with cooking spray. Arrange tomato slices in a single layer over spinach; sprinkle with breadcrumbs and Parmesan cheese. Bake at 375° for 30 minutes or until golden. Yield: 6 servings (serving size: ½ cup).

CALORIES 72 (35% from fat); FAT 2.8g (sat 1.4g, mono 0.3g, poly 0.3g); PROTEIN 4.2g; CARB 8.5g; FIBER 2.8g; CHOL 7mg; IRON 1.8mg; SODIUM 265mg; CALC 105mg

Triple-Corn Spoon Bread

This moist, slightly sweet dish is a cross between corn bread dressing and creamed corn.

  1 cup fat-free sour cream
  3 tablespoons butter, melted
  1 large egg
  ½ cup chopped onion
  1 (15.25-ounce) can whole-kernel corn, undrained
  1 (14¾-ounce) can no-salt-added cream-style corn
  1 (8½-ounce) package corn muffin mix
     Cooking spray

1. Preheat oven to 350°.
2. Combine first 3 ingredients in a large bowl; stir well with a whisk. Stir in onion and next 3 ingredients, and pour into an 8-inch square baking dish coated with cooking spray. Bake at 350° for 1 hour or until spoon bread is set and lightly browned. Yield: 8 servings.

CALORIES 287 (28% from fat); FAT 9g (sat 3.9g, mono 2.1g, poly 0.5g); PROTEIN 6.2g; CARB 48.1g; FIBER 2.6g; CHOL 41mg; IRON 1.4mg; SODIUM 465mg; CALC 56mg

Classic
Pecan Pie

Classic Pecan Pie

From the first fall leaves to New Year's Day, this holiday classic can be served again and again.

Crust:
- 1 cup all-purpose flour
- 2 tablespoons granulated sugar
- ½ teaspoon baking powder
- ¼ teaspoon salt
- ¼ cup fat-free milk
- 1 tablespoon butter, melted
- Cooking spray

Filling:
- 1 large egg
- 4 large egg whites
- 1 cup light or dark-colored corn syrup
- ⅔ cup packed dark brown sugar
- ¼ teaspoon salt
- 1 cup pecan halves
- 1 teaspoon vanilla extract

1. To prepare crust, lightly spoon 1 cup flour into a dry measuring cup; level with a knife. Combine 1 cup flour, granulated sugar, baking powder, and ¼ teaspoon salt. Add milk and butter; toss with a fork until moist.

2. Press mixture gently into a 4-inch circle on heavy-duty plastic wrap, and cover dough with additional plastic wrap. Roll dough, still covered, into an 11-inch circle. Freeze 10 minutes or until plastic wrap can be easily removed.

3. Remove 1 sheet of plastic wrap; fit dough into a 9-inch pie plate coated with cooking spray. Remove top sheet of plastic wrap. Fold edges under; flute.

4. Preheat oven to 350°.

5. To prepare filling, beat egg and next 4 ingredients with a mixer at medium speed until well blended. Stir in pecan halves and vanilla. Pour mixture into prepared crust. Bake at 350° for 20 minutes; cover with foil. Bake an additional 20 minutes or until a knife inserted 1 inch from edge comes out clean. Do not overbake. Cool pie on a wire rack. Yield: 10 servings (serving size: 1 wedge).

CALORIES 288 (29% from fat); FAT 9.2g (sat 1.5g, mono 5.1g, poly 2g); PROTEIN 4.3g; CARB 48.1g; FIBER 1g; CHOL 25mg; IRON 1.1mg; SODIUM 253mg; CALC 52mg

New Year's Eve Menu for Two

Escape with the one you love to a quiet cabin in the woods for an intimate New Year's Eve celebration—or just pretend you're there. Cozy up to a warm glowing fireplace and a delicious, mouthwatering dinner for two.

Menu

serves 2

Tomato Crostini

Pepper-Crusted Filet Mignon
with Horseradish Cream

Spicy Roasted Potatoes
and Asparagus

Parmesan, Garlic, and Basil Twists

Sautéed Apple over Ice Cream

Wine Note: *For the filet mignon, a structured but soft and magnificently rich red wine is in order. And no New Year's Eve should be spent without some bubbly. Try a delicious California sparkler that's easy on the pocketbook.*

Pepper-Crusted Filet Mignon with Horseradish Cream

Horseradish and sour cream make a cooling yet spicy sauce for the peppery steaks.

    2   (4-ounce) beef tenderloin steaks,
        trimmed (about ¾ inch thick)
    ½   teaspoon sea salt
    ¼   teaspoon freshly ground black
        pepper
    1   teaspoon butter
Cooking spray
    1   garlic clove, minced
    ¼   cup fat-free sour cream
    ½   teaspoon prepared horseradish

1. Sprinkle both sides of steaks with salt and pepper.
2. Melt butter in a nonstick skillet coated with cooking spray over medium heat. Add steaks; cook 3 minutes on each side or until desired degree of doneness. Sprinkle steaks evenly with garlic, and cook 1 minute on each side over medium-low heat.
3. Combine sour cream and horseradish; serve with steaks. Yield: 2 servings (serving size: 1 steak and 2 tablespoons horseradish cream).

CALORIES 231 (44% from fat); FAT 11.3g (sat 4.8g, mono 4g, poly 0.5g); PROTEIN 25.2g; CARB 5.6g; FIBER 0.1g; CHOL 78mg; IRON 3.3mg; SODIUM 684mg; CALC 58mg

Spicy Roasted Potatoes and Asparagus

Move the potatoes to one side of the dish before you add the asparagus so the spears can cook in a single, even layer.

    2   teaspoons olive oil, divided
    ¼   teaspoon sea salt, divided
    ¼   teaspoon chopped fresh or
        ⅛ teaspoon dried thyme
    ⅛   teaspoon freshly ground black
        pepper
    ⅛   teaspoon crushed red pepper
    6   small red potatoes (about
        ¾ pound), quartered
Cooking spray
    2   tablespoons grated fresh Parmesan
        cheese
    1   teaspoon minced garlic, divided
    ½   pound asparagus spears

1. Preheat oven to 450°.
2. Combine 1 teaspoon oil, ⅛ teaspoon salt, thyme, peppers, and potatoes in an 11 x 7-inch baking dish coated with cooking spray. Bake at 450° for 20 minutes, stirring occasionally. Stir in cheese and ½ teaspoon garlic.
3. Snap off tough ends of asparagus. Combine 1 teaspoon oil, ⅛ teaspoon salt, ½ teaspoon garlic, and asparagus. Add asparagus mixture to baking dish. Bake 10 minutes or until asparagus is crisp-tender. Yield: 2 servings.

CALORIES 223 (27% from fat); FAT 6.8g (sat 1.9g, mono 3.9g, poly 0.6g); PROTEIN 9.1g; CARB 34.2g; FIBER 4.6g; CHOL 5mg; IRON 3.6mg; SODIUM 419mg; CALC 136mg

Pepper-Crusted Filet Mignon with Horseradish Cream; Spicy Roasted Potatoes and Asparagus

Tomato Crostini

If you can't get away for a weekend, create a rustic cabin ambience at home. Use table decorations focusing on natural items, such as pinecones, handmade candles, and neutral-colored linens. And don't forget a fire in the fireplace.

Tomato Crostini

Plum tomatoes usually have better flavor and are less watery than other tomatoes available during winter, so they are great for this recipe. If you're without a baking sheet, carefully arrange the bread slices directly on the oven rack.

- ½ cup chopped plum tomato
- 1 tablespoon chopped fresh basil
- 1 tablespoon chopped pitted green olives
- 1 teaspoon capers
- ½ teaspoon balsamic vinegar
- ½ teaspoon olive oil
- ⅛ teaspoon sea salt
- Dash of freshly ground black pepper
- 1 garlic clove, minced
- 4 (1-inch-thick) slices French bread baguette
- Cooking spray
- 1 garlic clove, halved

1. Preheat oven to 375°.
2. Combine first 9 ingredients.
3. Lightly coat both sides of bread slices with cooking spray, and arrange bread slices in a single layer on a baking sheet. Bake at 375° for 4 minutes on each side or until lightly toasted.
4. Rub 1 side of bread slices with halved garlic; top evenly with tomato mixture. Yield: 2 servings (serving size: 2 bread slices and about ⅓ cup tomato mixture).

CALORIES 109 (23% from fat); FAT 2.8g (sat 0.4g, mono 1.5g, poly 0.7g); PROTEIN 3.1g; CARB 18g; FIBER 1.4g; CHOL 0mg; IRON 1mg; SODIUM 373mg; CALC 30mg

Parmesan, Garlic, and Basil Twists

Because they begin with refrigerated breadstick dough, these twists are a snap to put together.

- 1 tablespoon olive oil
- 2 garlic cloves, minced
- 1 (11-ounce) can refrigerated soft breadstick dough
- ¼ cup chopped fresh basil
- ¼ cup (1 ounce) grated fresh Parmesan cheese
- ¼ teaspoon freshly ground black pepper
- Cooking spray

1. Preheat oven to 350°.
2. Heat oil in a small saucepan over medium heat. Add garlic; sauté 30 seconds. Remove from heat.
3. Unroll dough, separating into strips. Brush with garlic mixture. Sprinkle with basil, cheese, and pepper, gently pressing into dough. Twist breadsticks, and place on a baking sheet coated with cooking spray. Gently press ends of breadsticks onto baking sheet.
4. Bake at 350° for 15 minutes or until lightly browned. Yield: 1 dozen (serving size: 1 twist).

CALORIES 94 (30% from fat); FAT 3.1g (sat 0.8g, mono 1.4g, poly 0.6g); PROTEIN 2.9g; CARB 13g; FIBER 0.4g; CHOL 2mg; IRON 0.8mg; SODIUM 231mg; CALC 30mg

Sautéed Apple over Ice Cream

Use a bit of your favorite brandy in this dessert, and then enjoy sipping the rest alongside it.

- 1 tablespoon butter
- 1½ cups sliced peeled Fuji apple
- 1 tablespoon sugar
- 3 tablespoons brandy
- ¼ teaspoon fresh lemon juice
- ⅛ teaspoon ground ginger
- 1 cup vanilla reduced-fat ice cream

1. Melt butter in a small nonstick skillet over medium heat. Add apple; cook 5 minutes or until lightly browned, stirring frequently.
2. Add sugar, brandy, juice, and ginger; cook over medium-low heat 2 minutes or until apple is tender, stirring occasionally. Serve warm over ice cream. Yield: 2 servings (serving size: about ½ cup apple and ½ cup ice cream).

CALORIES 316 (23% from fat); FAT 8.2g (sat 4.7g, mono 1.7g, poly 0.4g); PROTEIN 3.3g; CARB 46.9g; FIBER 3.8g; CHOL 21mg; IRON 0.2mg; SODIUM 104mg; CALC 108mg

Festive New Year's Dinner

Ring in the New Year with a festive holiday dinner party featuring Champagne cocktails, soup sips, and a dazzling dessert. With the party secrets on page 68, you'll be able to savor time with your friends and welcome the New Year with style.

With the party secrets on page 68,

Menu

serves 6

Kir Champagne Cocktail

Pea-and-Pasta Soup Sips

Baked Fish with Roasted Potatoes, Tomatoes, and Salmoriglio Sauce

Three Kings Salad

Onion Biscuits

Easy Caramel-Banana Galette

Kir Champagne Cocktail

Serve plain Champagne (perhaps a more expensive brand) if you don't have time to make this recipe.

- 6   sugar cubes
- 6   tablespoons crème de cassis (black-currant-flavored liqueur)
- 3   cups Champagne, chilled

1. Place 1 sugar cube in the bottom of each of 6 Champagne glasses. Add 1 tablespoon crème de cassis and ½ cup Champagne to each of the glasses. Yield: 6 servings.

CALORIES 118 (0% from fat); FAT 0g; PROTEIN 0.4g; CARB 4.8g; FIBER 0g; CHOL 0mg; IRON 0.6mg; SODIUM 6mg; CALC 7mg

Baked Fish with Roasted Potatoes, Tomatoes, and Salmoriglio Sauce

Here's a main course that can be served directly from the dish in which it's baked.

- 6   cups peeled red potatoes, cut into ⅛-inch slices (about 2 pounds)
- 4   cups thinly sliced fennel bulb (about 2 small bulbs)
- 1   tablespoon olive oil, divided
- ¾   teaspoon kosher salt, divided
- ½   teaspoon black pepper, divided
- 1   teaspoon fennel seeds
- 3   garlic cloves, minced
- ¾   cup dry white wine
- 6   tablespoons chopped fresh flat-leaf parsley, divided
- 1   tablespoon grated orange rind
- 1½ teaspoons dried oregano
- 1   (28-ounce) can whole tomatoes, drained and chopped
- 6   (6-ounce) sea bass fillets or other firm white fish fillets
  Lemon rind strips (optional)
  Salmoriglio Sauce

1. Preheat oven to 450°.
2. Combine potatoes, sliced fennel, 2 teaspoons oil, ¼ teaspoon salt, and ¼ teaspoon pepper in a 13 x 9-inch baking dish; toss gently to coat. Bake at 450° for 30 minutes.
3. Heat 1 teaspoon oil in a medium nonstick skillet. Add fennel seeds and garlic; sauté 1 minute. Add ¼ teaspoon salt, ⅛ teaspoon pepper, wine, 4 tablespoons parsley, orange rind, oregano, and tomatoes; bring to a boil. Reduce heat; simmer 8 minutes.
4. Sprinkle fillets with ¼ teaspoon salt and ⅛ teaspoon pepper. Arrange fillets over potato mixture; spread tomato mixture over fillets. Bake at 450° for 20 minutes or until fish flakes easily when tested with a fork. Sprinkle with 2 tablespoons parsley; garnish with lemon rind strips, if desired. Serve with Salmoriglio Sauce. Yield: 6 servings (serving size: 1 fillet, about 1 cup potato mixture, and 2 teaspoons Salmoriglio Sauce).

(Totals include Salmoriglio Sauce) CALORIES 379 (26% from fat); FAT 10.9g (sat 1.9g, mono 5.8g, poly 2g); PROTEIN 37.2g; CARB 34.2g; FIBER 3.6g; CHOL 70mg; IRON 4.6mg; SODIUM 892mg; CALC 145mg

Salmoriglio Sauce

Salmoriglio (sahl-moh-REE-lyee-o) is a pungent Italian sauce of olive oil, lemon, garlic, and oregano. Freshness is key, so make it as close to serving time as possible.

- 2   tablespoons fresh lemon juice
- 2   tablespoons extravirgin olive oil
- 1½ teaspoons chopped fresh or ½ teaspoon dried oregano
- 1   teaspoon kosher salt
- 1   teaspoon grated lemon rind
- 2   garlic cloves, minced
  Dash of freshly ground black pepper

1. Combine all ingredients, stirring well with a whisk. Yield: ¼ cup (serving size: 2 teaspoons).

CALORIES 44 (92% from fat); FAT 4.5g (sat 0.6g, mono 3.3g, poly 0.4g); PROTEIN 0.1g; CARB 1.1g; FIBER 0.1g; CHOL 0mg; IRON 0.2mg; SODIUM 320mg; CALC 9mg

Baked Fish with Roasted Potatoes, Tomatoes, and Salmoriglio Sauce

Three Kings Salad

The colorful trio of beets, oranges, and red onion represents the three wise men from the nativity story. Section the oranges, cut the beets and onions, and make the vinaigrette ahead of time (store them in separate containers so the colors don't bleed). Assemble up to an hour before serving.

    4   navel oranges
    1   (15-ounce) can whole beets,
        drained
    3   tablespoons balsamic
        vinegar
    2   tablespoons walnut oil or
        olive oil
    ½   teaspoon salt
    ½   teaspoon black pepper
    ¾   cup thinly sliced red onion
    Pomegranate seeds (optional)

1. Peel and section oranges over a bowl; squeeze membranes to extract juice. Set sections aside; reserve 1½ tablespoons juice. Discard membranes.
2. Cut beets into wedges.
3. Combine reserved 1½ tablespoons juice, vinegar, oil, salt, and pepper in a medium bowl; stir well with a whisk.
4. Divide beet wedges and orange sections evenly among 6 salad plates. Top each serving with 2 tablespoons onion slivers. Drizzle with vinaigrette, and garnish with pomegranate seeds, if desired. Yield: 6 servings.

Note: To extract the pomegranate seeds, put on gloves, and cut the pomegranate into quarters. Coax seeds out from the base of the pomegranate with thumbs, being careful not to break seeds. Remove and discard white membrane. Reserve ⅓ cup seeds for garnish.

CALORIES 116 (37% from fat); FAT 4.8g (sat 0.4g, mono 3.2g, poly 0.9g); PROTEIN 1.7g; CARB 18.6g; FIBER 4.8g; CHOL 0mg; IRON 0.7mg; SODIUM 363mg; CALC 53mg

Pea-and-Pasta Soup Sips

    6   cups fat-free, less-sodium
          chicken broth
    1½   cups frozen green peas
    ¾   cup small uncooked pasta (such as
          pastina, orzo, or ditalini)
    2   tablespoons chopped fresh parsley
    3   tablespoons Riesling or other
          slightly sweet white wine
    2   tablespoons grated fresh Parmesan
          cheese

1. Bring broth to a boil in a large saucepan over medium-high heat. Add peas, pasta, and parsley. Reduce heat; simmer 5 minutes or until pasta is tender. Stir in wine. Spoon soup into each of 6 small cups; sprinkle with cheese. Yield: 6 servings (serving size: 1 cup soup and 1 teaspoon cheese).

CALORIES 118 (7% from fat); FAT 0.9g (sat 0.4g, mono 0.2g, poly 0.1g); PROTEIN 7.6g; CARB 16.7g; FIBER 1.7g; CHOL 2mg; IRON 1.2mg; SODIUM 562mg; CALC 40mg

Pea-and-Pasta
Soup Sips

*You don't necessarily have to serve soup in soup bowls. Try
mismatched coffee cups—you can find them for a couple of dollars
each on your next shopping trip to the flea market.*

dinner party secrets to success

- Have guests respond to invitations with regrets only so that you won't be overwhelmed by replies.

- Read each recipe, and highlight all of the ingredients you need to buy.

- Pick out serving utensils for each recipe. The fish entrée will be served straight from the oven, so you'll need a casserole carrier or trivet.

- Pick out the CDs you want to play, and set up the music equipment.

- Decide what you're going to wear ahead; the last thing you want is to discover something needs to be dry-cleaned or pressed as your guests are ringing the doorbell.

- Have the table set, flowers arranged, and anything non-food-related done the day before. You can then attend to the food on the day of the party.

- Clean the guest bathroom, and stock it with the necessary toiletries and towels.

- Plan tasks for the few who invariably ask, "What can I do to help?" Hand them an apron, and put them to work with the last-minute preparations, such as filling water glasses, lighting candles, opening wine, and plating salads. That way, you can visit with the helpers and enjoy a cocktail while you finish preparing the meal.

- Plan to serve the meal family-style so that each guest can serve himself rather than having the hostess prepare individual plates in the kitchen.

Onion Biscuits

You can prepare the biscuit dough a day in advance and refrigerate it. Remove dough from food processor, and cover in plastic wrap. Uncover the dough, shape it, and bake the biscuits the day of the party. If you're really pressed for time, serve some French bread instead of the biscuits.

Cooking spray
  1 cup minced fresh onion
 ½ teaspoon sugar
  2 cups all-purpose flour
  2 teaspoons baking powder
 ½ teaspoon baking soda
 ½ teaspoon salt
  3 tablespoons vegetable shortening
 ¾ cup low-fat buttermilk
  1 large egg, lightly beaten
  2 teaspoons water

1. Preheat oven to 450°.
2. Heat a small nonstick skillet coated with cooking spray over medium-high heat. Add onion and sugar; sauté 8 minutes or until golden brown. Cool.
3. Lightly spoon flour into dry measuring cups; level with a knife. Place flour, baking powder, baking soda, and salt in a food processor; pulse 2 times or until blended. Add shortening, and pulse 2 times or until combined. Sprinkle onion mixture over flour mixture. With processor on, slowly add buttermilk through food chute; process until dough forms a ball.
4. Turn dough out onto a floured surface; knead lightly 4 or 5 times. Pat dough into an 8 x 6-inch rectangle; cut into 12 squares. Place on a baking sheet. Combine egg and water; brush over biscuits. Bake at 450° for 11 minutes or until golden. Yield: 1 dozen (serving size: 1 biscuit).

CALORIES 114 (25% from fat); FAT 3.2g (sat 0.7g, mono 1.1g, poly 1.1g); PROTEIN 2.9g; CARB 18.3g; FIBER 0.8g; CHOL 0mg; IRON 1.1mg; SODIUM 252mg; CALC 70mg

Easy Caramel-Banana Galette

The only trick to making this simple dessert is leaving the caramel unstirred for 8 minutes; stirring can cause it to harden. To simplify the topping, substitute bottled fat-free caramel sauce for the sugar and water. Heat the sauce in the microwave for 1 minute, and then stir in the raisin mixture. The raisins should sit in the rum for at least 30 minutes—the longer, the better. Slice the bananas immediately before arranging them on the tart so they don't discolor. To dress the tart up even more, serve it warm with vanilla frozen yogurt.

 ¼ cup golden raisins
  2 tablespoons dark rum
 ½ (15-ounce) package refrigerated pie dough (such as Pillsbury)
Cooking spray
  3 cups (¼-inch-thick) diagonally sliced ripe banana (about 1½ pounds)
 ½ cup sugar
  2 tablespoons water

1. Combine raisins and rum in a small bowl; set aside.
2. Preheat oven to 425°.
3. Roll dough into a 10½-inch circle, and place on a foil-lined baking sheet coated with cooking spray. Arrange banana slices in concentric circles on dough, leaving a 1-inch border. Fold a 2-inch dough border over banana slices, pressing gently to seal (dough will partially cover slices). Bake at 425° for 30 minutes.
4. Combine sugar and water in a small saucepan; cook over medium heat until golden (about 8 minutes). Remove from heat; carefully stir in raisin mixture until combined. Cool slightly, and pour over banana slices. Cut into 6 wedges. Yield: 6 servings (serving size: 1 wedge).

CALORIES 318 (27% from fat); FAT 9.7g (sat 2.4g, mono 4g, poly 2.5g); PROTEIN 3.3g; CARB 57.3g; FIBER 2.5g; CHOL 0mg; IRON 0.9mg; SODIUM 160mg; CALC 35mg

Easy Caramel-
Banana Galette

holiday entertaining

Get a head start on festive party plans with our complete menus and entertaining ideas. You'll be confident, relaxed, and ready to enjoy the party along with your guests.

Sun-Dried Tomato Tapenade with Crostini (recipe on page 85)

Casual Weeknight Entertaining

With some make-ahead preparations, you can be ready to host a friendly holiday gathering any night of the week. This menu's great for anything, from a girls-only supper club to a gathering of couples minus the kids.

Menu

serves 10

Sherried Mushroom Soup

Herbed Turkey with Roasted Garlic Gravy

Cranberry, Apple, and Walnut Relish

Sourdough Stuffing with Apples and Ham

Streuseled Sweet Potato Casserole

Green Beans with Caramelized Onions

Vanilla Cheesecake with Cherry Topping

Sherried Mushroom Soup

The intense flavor of this soup dictates a small serving size of half a cup.

Broth:

- 2 tablespoons butter
- 1 tablespoon chopped fresh thyme
- 1 pound shallots, coarsely chopped
- 6 (14-ounce) cans fat-free, less-sodium chicken broth
- 2 ounces dried porcini mushrooms

Remaining Ingredients:

- 2 cups thinly sliced shiitake mushroom caps (about 4 ounces mushrooms)
- ¾ cup dry sherry
- 3 tablespoons chopped fresh chives

1. To prepare broth, melt butter in a Dutch oven over medium heat. Add thyme and shallots; cook 10 minutes or until shallots are golden brown. Stir in chicken broth and porcini mushrooms; bring to a boil. Reduce heat, and simmer, uncovered, 1 hour. Strain broth mixture through a sieve into a bowl, and discard solids.

2. Return broth mixture to pan. Stir in shiitake mushrooms and sherry; cook 10 minutes over low heat. Stir in chives. Serve immediately. Yield: 12 servings (serving size: about ½ cup).

CALORIES 52 (35% from fat); FAT 2g (sat 1.2g, mono 0.6g, poly 0.1g); PROTEIN 3g; CARB 2.5g; FIBER 0.2g; CHOL 5mg; IRON 0.4mg; SODIUM 401mg; CALC 4mg

Sherried Mushroom Soup

(clockwise from left) Green Beans with Caramelized Onions; Sourdough Stuffing with Apples and Ham; Cranberry, Apple, and Walnut Relish; Herbed Turkey with Roasted Garlic Gravy

countdown

- Make the cheesecake, and freeze it. Before freezing, chill the cooled cheesecake in the pan for 2 hours; then wrap the pan in heavy-duty plastic wrap.

UP TO 3 DAYS AHEAD
- Make the broth for the Sherried Mushroom Soup; refrigerate.
- Make the relish, and store it in the refrigerator.
- Prepare the onion mixture for the stuffing; cover and store in the refrigerator. You can also toast the bread for the stuffing and store it in an airtight container.

UP TO 2 DAYS AHEAD
- Prepare the onions for the green beans; refrigerate.

THE DAY BEFORE
- Make the garlic-herb rub; rub under the skin of the turkey. Chill.
- Assemble the potato mixture, and sprinkle with streusel.
- Move cheesecake from freezer to refrigerator to begin thawing.

THE DAY OF THE PARTY
- Cook the turkey.
- Bake Streuseled Sweet Potato Casserole.
- Just before serving the Sherried Mushroom Soup, add the shiitakes, sherry, and chives, and then heat.
- Combine the onion mixture, bread, and broth for the stuffing; bake.
- Add the onions to the beans in a last-minute sauté just before serving.

Herbed Turkey with Roasted Garlic Gravy

Garlic-Herb Rub:
- 1 cup fresh flat-leaf parsley leaves
- ¼ cup fresh sage leaves
- ¼ cup fresh rosemary leaves
- ¼ cup fresh thyme leaves
- 12 garlic cloves

Turkey:
- 1 whole garlic head
- 1 (15-pound) fresh or frozen turkey, thawed
- Cooking spray

Roasted Garlic Gravy:
- 2½ cups fat-free, less-sodium chicken broth
- ¼ cup all-purpose flour

1. Preheat oven to 325°.
2. To prepare garlic-herb rub, place first 5 ingredients in a food processor; process until finely minced.
3. To prepare turkey, remove the white papery skin from garlic head (do not peel or separate cloves). Wrap garlic head in foil. Set aside.
4. Remove and discard giblets and neck from turkey. Rinse turkey with cold water; pat dry. Trim excess fat. Starting at neck cavity, loosen skin from breast and drumsticks by inserting fingers, gently pushing between skin and meat. Spread garlic-herb rub under loosened skin and rub over breast and drumsticks. Gently press skin to secure. Lift wing tips up and over back; tuck under turkey.
5. Place turkey on a broiler pan coated with cooking spray. Insert a meat thermometer into meaty part of thigh, making sure not to touch bone. Bake at 325° for 1 hour. Add garlic head to pan; bake an additional 2 hours or until thermometer registers 180°. Place turkey on a platter, reserving pan drippings; let stand 20 minutes. Discard skin.
6. To prepare gravy, place a zip-top plastic bag inside a 4-cup glass measure. Pour pan drippings into bag; let stand 10 minutes (fat will rise to the top). Seal bag; snip off 1 bottom corner of bag. Drain drippings into glass measure, stopping before fat layer reaches opening (you should have about ⅔ cup). Reserve 1 tablespoon fat; discard remaining fat. Add enough broth to drippings to measure 3 cups.
7. Separate roasted garlic cloves; squeeze to extract garlic pulp. Discard skins. Heat reserved fat in a medium saucepan over medium heat. Add garlic pulp and flour; cook 30 seconds or until lightly browned, whisking constantly. Gradually add broth mixture, stirring with a whisk until blended. Bring to a boil over high heat, stirring constantly. Remove from heat. Yield: 15 servings (serving size: 6 ounces turkey and about 3 tablespoons gravy).

CALORIES 299 (23% from fat); FAT 7.5g (sat 2.4g, mono 1.8g, poly 2.1g); PROTEIN 50.6g; CARB 3.9g; FIBER 0.4g; CHOL 148mg; IRON 3.8mg; SODIUM 232mg; CALC 58mg

Cranberry, Apple, and Walnut Relish

- 1 cup sugar
- ½ cup cranberry-apple juice
- 1 pound fresh cranberries
- 4 cups diced peeled Granny Smith apple (about 1 pound)
- ⅔ cup coarsely chopped walnuts

1. Combine sugar, juice, and cranberries in a large saucepan; bring to a boil over medium-high heat. Reduce heat; simmer 15 minutes or until cranberries pop and mixture thickens.
2. Remove from heat; stir in apple and walnuts. Spoon into a bowl; cool. Cover and chill at least 4 hours. Yield: 4 cups (serving size: ⅓ cup).

CALORIES 121 (25% from fat); FAT 3.3g (sat 0.2g, mono 0.7g, poly 2.1g); PROTEIN 1.5g; CARB 23.2g; FIBER 2.1g; CHOL 0mg; IRON 0.3mg; SODIUM 2mg; CALC 7mg

Sourdough Stuffing with Apples and Ham

Before serving, combine the onion mixture and bread; then add the broth and bake.

  1 (1-pound) loaf sourdough bread, cut into ½-inch cubes (about 12 cups)
  2 tablespoons butter
  2 cups vertically sliced red onion
  2 cups thinly sliced celery
  2 cups chopped 33%-less-sodium ham (about 10 ounces)
  2 cups diced peeled Braeburn apple
  ½ teaspoon dried thyme
  ½ teaspoon poultry seasoning
  ½ teaspoon freshly ground black pepper
  ¼ teaspoon salt
  1 (14-ounce) can fat-free, less-sodium chicken broth
Cooking spray

1. Preheat oven to 350°.
2. Arrange the bread cubes in single layers on 2 baking sheets. Bake at 350° for 18 minutes or until toasted. Remove from oven.
3. Increase oven temperature to 375°.
4. Melt butter in a large nonstick skillet over medium-high heat. Add onion and celery; sauté 4 minutes or until tender. Add ham and next 5 ingredients; sauté 2 minutes.
5. Combine onion mixture and bread, tossing gently to combine. Add broth, and toss gently to coat. Spoon mixture into a 13 x 9-inch baking dish coated with cooking spray.
6. Cover and bake at 375° for 10 minutes. Uncover and bake an additional 35 minutes or until golden brown. Yield: 12 servings (serving size: about 1 cup).

CALORIES 179 (25% from fat); FAT 4.5g (sat 1.9g, mono 1.7g, poly 0.5g); PROTEIN 9.1g; CARB 25.4g; FIBER 2.2g; CHOL 18mg; IRON 1.5mg; SODIUM 609mg; CALC 45mg

Streuseled Sweet Potato Casserole

Add ⅛ teaspoon ground red pepper if you want to add a bit of heat to this sweet dish.

 14 cups (1-inch) cubed peeled sweet potato (about 5 pounds)
  ½ cup half-and-half
  ½ cup maple syrup
  1 teaspoon vanilla extract
  ¾ teaspoon salt
  1 large egg, lightly beaten
Cooking spray
  ½ cup all-purpose flour
  ½ cup packed brown sugar
  ¼ cup chilled butter, cut into small pieces
  ½ cup chopped pecans

1. Preheat oven to 375°.
2. Place potato in a Dutch oven; cover with water. Bring to a boil. Reduce heat; simmer 12 minutes or until tender. Drain.
3. Combine half-and-half and next 4 ingredients in a large bowl; stir with a whisk. Add potato to egg mixture; beat with a mixer at medium speed until smooth. Spoon potato mixture into a 13 x 9-inch baking dish coated with cooking spray.
4. Combine flour and sugar in a food processor; pulse to combine. Add chilled butter; pulse until mixture resembles coarse meal. Stir in pecans; sprinkle over potato mixture.
5. Cover and bake at 375° for 15 minutes. Uncover; bake an additional 25 minutes or until topping is browned and potatoes are thoroughly heated. Yield: 18 servings (serving size: about ½ cup).

CALORIES 250 (23% from fat); FAT 6.3g (sat 2.4g, mono 2.5g, poly 1g); PROTEIN 3.3g; CARB 46.1g; FIBER 2.7g; CHOL 22mg; IRON 1.2mg; SODIUM 149mg; CALC 49mg

Streuseled Sweet Potato Casserole

Green Beans with Caramelized Onions

- 2 tablespoons olive oil, divided
- 2 (16-ounce) packages frozen pearl onions, thawed
- 1 tablespoon sugar
- 1 teaspoon salt, divided
- 2 pounds green beans, trimmed
- ½ teaspoon black pepper

1. Heat 1 tablespoon oil in a large nonstick skillet over medium heat. Pat onions dry with paper towels; add to pan. Increase heat to medium-high; sauté onions 5 minutes. Add sugar and ½ teaspoon salt; sauté 15 minutes or until onions are tender and golden brown. Spoon into a bowl.

2. Heat 1 tablespoon oil in pan over medium-high heat. Add beans; sauté 8 minutes or until crisp-tender. Add onions, ½ teaspoon salt, and pepper; cook 2 minutes or until mixture is thoroughly heated. Yield: 10 servings (serving size: 1 cup).

CALORIES 89 (29% from fat); FAT 2.9g (sat 0.4g, mono 2g, poly 0.3g); PROTEIN 2.5g; CARB 15.4g; FIBER 4.6g; CHOL 0mg; IRON 1.4mg; SODIUM 249mg; CALC 67mg

Vanilla Cheesecake with Cherry Topping

Crust:
- ¾ cup graham cracker crumbs
- ¼ cup sugar
- 2 tablespoons butter, melted
- 2 teaspoons water
- Cooking spray

Filling:
- 3 (8-ounce) blocks fat-free cream cheese, softened
- 2 (8-ounce) blocks ⅓-less-fat cream cheese, softened
- 1 cup sugar
- 3 tablespoons all-purpose flour
- ¼ teaspoon salt
- 1 (8-ounce) carton fat-free sour cream
- 4 large eggs
- 2 teaspoons vanilla extract
- 1 vanilla bean, split lengthwise

Topping:
- ⅔ cup tawny port or other sweet red wine
- ½ cup sugar
- 2 (10-ounce) bags frozen pitted dark sweet cherries
- 2 tablespoons fresh lemon juice
- 4 teaspoons cornstarch
- 4 teaspoons water

1. Preheat oven to 400°.

2. To prepare crust, combine first 3 ingredients, tossing with a fork. Add 2 teaspoons water; toss with a fork until moist and crumbly. Gently press mixture into bottom and 1½ inches up sides of a 9-inch springform pan coated with cooking spray. Bake at 400° for 5 minutes; cool on a wire rack.

3. Reduce oven temperature to 325°.

4. To prepare filling, beat cheeses with a mixer at high speed until smooth. Combine 1 cup sugar, flour, and salt, stirring with a whisk. Add to cheese mixture; beat well. Add sour cream; beat well. Add eggs, 1 at a time, beating well after each addition. Stir in vanilla extract. Scrape seeds from vanilla bean; stir seeds into cheese mixture, reserving bean halves.

5. Pour cheese mixture into prepared pan; bake at 325° for 1 hour and 15 minutes or until cheesecake center barely moves when pan is touched. Remove cheesecake from oven; run a knife around outside edge. Cool to room temperature. Cover and chill at least 8 hours.

6. To prepare topping, combine port, ½ cup sugar, cherries, and reserved vanilla bean halves in a large saucepan; bring to a boil. Cook 5 minutes or until cherries are thawed and mixture is syrupy. Remove vanilla bean halves; discard.

7. Combine lemon juice, cornstarch, and 4 teaspoons water, stirring with a whisk until well blended. Stir cornstarch mixture into cherry mixture; bring to a boil. Reduce heat; simmer 3 minutes or until mixture is slightly thickened and shiny. Remove from heat; cool to room temperature. Cover and chill. Serve over cheesecake. Yield: 16 servings (serving size: 1 slice cheesecake and about 2 tablespoons topping).

CALORIES 324 (30% from fat); FAT 10.7g (sat 6.1g, mono 3.2g, poly 0.7g); PROTEIN 12.2g; CARB 42.8g; FIBER 1g; CHOL 83mg; IRON 0.8mg; SODIUM 458mg; CALC 134mg

Fill small vases with a single flower or herb to adorn each place setting. See Simply Decorating (page 85) and 6 Steps to Seasonal Style (page 96) for more holiday decorating ideas.

Vanilla Cheesecake
with Cherry Topping

Wine and Cheese Party

Lean on the ease and simplicity of a wine and cheese party for holiday entertaining. With good planning, most of the menu can be assembled 1 or 2 hours ahead. See Selecting and Serving Wine (page 346) for more information.

Menu

serves 16

Smoky Red Pepper Dip with fresh vegetable tray

Endive Stuffed with Goat Cheese and Walnuts

Spice-Crusted Shrimp with Rémoulade Sauce

Pork-Filled Dijon-Pepper Biscuits

Spiced Fig and Walnut Bread

Mini Mocha-Toffee Crunch Cheesecakes

Marinated olives

Fresh fruit and nuts

Assorted cheeses

Commercial breadsticks, toasted baguette slices, and crispy crackers

Red and white wine

Smoky Red Pepper Dip

Serve this flavorful spread with toasted pita triangles or as the centerpiece of a fresh vegetable tray full of colorful selections like broccoli, carrots, celery, and snow peas. Stir in a few tablespoons of chopped fresh flat-leaf parsley or cilantro to add color and interest to the dip.

2 medium red bell peppers
2 cups sliced red onion
2 garlic cloves
¼ cup dry breadcrumbs
¼ cup plain fat-free yogurt
1 tablespoon red wine vinegar
2 teaspoons olive oil
⅛ teaspoon salt
⅛ teaspoon hot sauce

1. Preheat broiler.
2. Cut bell peppers in half lengthwise; discard seeds and membranes. Place pepper halves, skin sides up, on a foil-lined baking sheet; flatten with hand. Arrange onion and garlic around peppers on baking sheet. Broil 10 minutes or until blackened. Place peppers in a zip-top plastic bag; seal. Let stand 15 minutes; peel.
3. Place peppers, onion, and garlic in a food processor; process until finely chopped. Add remaining ingredients; process until smooth. Serve with fresh vegetables. Yield: 1¾ cups (serving size: 1 tablespoon).

CALORIES 13 (28% from fat); FAT 0.4g (sat 0.1g, mono 0.3g, poly 0.1g); PROTEIN 0.4g; CARB 1.9g; FIBER 0.3g; CHOL 0mg; IRON 0.1mg; SODIUM 21mg; CALC 9mg

Spice-Crusted Shrimp with Rémoulade Sauce

Sauce:
¼ cup low-fat mayonnaise
¼ cup plain fat-free yogurt
1½ tablespoons fresh lime juice
1 teaspoon grated lime rind
1 teaspoon capers, chopped
Dash of ground red pepper

Shrimp:
2 teaspoons ground cumin
2 teaspoons paprika
1 teaspoon ground coriander
½ teaspoon garlic powder
¼ teaspoon salt
⅛ teaspoon black pepper
48 large shrimp, peeled and deveined (about 1½ pounds)
1 tablespoon olive oil, divided
Cilantro sprigs (optional)

1. To prepare sauce, combine first 6 ingredients in a bowl; stir with a whisk.
2. To prepare shrimp, combine cumin and next 5 ingredients. Add shrimp; toss well. Heat 1½ teaspoons oil in a large nonstick skillet over medium-high heat; add half of shrimp. Cook 3 minutes on each side or until done. Remove shrimp; keep warm. Repeat procedure with remaining oil and shrimp. Serve shrimp with sauce. Garnish with cilantro, if desired. Yield: 16 servings (serving size: 3 shrimp and about 1½ teaspoons sauce).

CALORIES 50 (29% from fat); FAT 1.6g (sat 0.2g, mono 0.7g, poly 0.3g); PROTEIN 6.9g; CARB 1.9g; FIBER 0.3g; CHOL 61mg; IRON 1.2mg; SODIUM 150mg; CALC 24mg

Spice-Crusted Shrimp with
Rémoulade Sauce; Pork-Filled
Dijon-Pepper Biscuits

Pork-Filled Dijon-Pepper Biscuits

For easy cleanup, line the broiler pan with foil before roasting.

    1   (1-pound) pork tenderloin
    4   cups water
    2   tablespoons sugar
    1   tablespoon salt
 1½   teaspoons dried thyme
    1   teaspoon whole allspice
    1   bay leaf
    1   teaspoon dried rosemary,
        crushed
    4   teaspoons olive oil, divided
        Cooking spray
        Dijon-Pepper Biscuits
   ¾   cup purchased cranberry-orange
        relish

1. Trim fat from pork. Combine pork and next 6 ingredients in a large heavy-duty zip-top plastic bag. Seal; marinate in refrigerator 2½ hours.
2. Preheat oven to 350°.
3. Remove pork from bag; discard marinade. Pat pork dry with a paper towel. Combine rosemary and 1 teaspoon oil; rub over pork.
4. Heat remaining 1 tablespoon oil in a nonstick skillet over medium-high heat. Add pork; cook 5 minutes, browning on all sides. Place pork on a broiler pan coated with cooking spray. Bake at 350° for 35 minutes or until a thermometer registers 160° (slightly pink). Wrap in foil; chill 3 hours or overnight.
5. Cut pork diagonally across grain into 24 slices. Place 1 slice pork on each bottom half of split Dijon-Pepper Biscuits. Top each slice with 1½ teaspoons relish; cover with top halves. Yield: 24 appetizers (serving size: 1 appetizer).

(Totals include Dijon-Pepper Biscuits) CALORIES 102 (29% from fat); FAT 3.3g (sat 1.2g, mono 1.6g, poly 0.3g); PROTEIN 5.2g; CARB 12.9g; FIBER 0.4g; CHOL 15mg; IRON 0.8mg; SODIUM 243mg; CALC 36mg

Dijon-Pepper Biscuits

    2   cups all-purpose flour
    2   teaspoons baking powder
   ¾   teaspoon coarsely ground pepper
   ½   teaspoon salt
   ⅛   teaspoon garlic powder
    3   tablespoons butter, cut into small
        pieces and chilled
   ½   cup 1% low-fat milk
    2   tablespoons Dijon mustard
        Cooking spray

1. Preheat oven to 425°.
2. Lightly spoon flour into dry measuring cups; level with a knife. Combine flour and next 4 ingredients in a bowl; cut in butter with a pastry blender or 2 knives until mixture resembles coarse meal. Combine milk and mustard; add to flour mixture. Stir until flour mixture is moist.
3. Turn dough out onto a lightly floured surface. Knead 5 or 6 times. Roll dough to about ½-inch thickness; cut with a 1¾-inch biscuit cutter. Place on a baking sheet coated with cooking spray. Bake at 425° for 12 to 15 minutes or until lightly browned. Yield: 2 dozen (serving size: 1 biscuit).

CALORIES 55 (28% from fat); FAT 1.7g (sat 0.8g, mono 0.7g, poly 0.1g); PROTEIN 1.3g; CARB 8.5g; FIBER 0.3g; CHOL 4mg; IRON 0.6mg; SODIUM 134mg; CALC 33mg

planning the party

Visit the wine store. Ask for assistance in selecting wines and cheeses to complement menu items; if possible, sample your choices.

Select four to five wines. A mixture of reds and whites is recommended.
* Merlot or Cabernet Sauvignon
* Riesling
* Sauvignon Blanc
* Sparkling wine or Champagne
* Zinfandel

Be sure to have plenty of wine glasses. It's often easier to rent glasses. Balloon-shaped glasses can be used to serve both red and white wine. The exception is Champagne or sparkling wine, which should be served in tall, narrow flute or tulip-shaped glasses.

Choose fresh fruit and vegetables. Fresh fruits and vegetables do double duty as accompaniments to the food and as simple yet beautiful table decorations.

Purchase specialty breads and desserts. Shop your neighborhood bakery for specialty breads or desserts, or bake your own.

Select an assortment of cheeses. Generally, mild cheeses pair well with both red and white wine. We suggest:
* Brie, Camembert, or other rich and creamy cheeses
* Chèvre (goat cheese)
* Gorgonzola or other blue cheese
* Parmigiano-Reggiano
* Cheddar, colby, or Monterey Jack

Endive Stuffed with Goat Cheese and Walnuts

350° for 1 hour or until a wooden pick inserted in center comes out clean. Cool in pan 10 minutes on a wire rack; remove from pan. Cool completely on wire rack. Yield: 1 loaf, 12 servings (serving size: 1 slice).

CALORIES 246 (25% from fat); FAT 6.8g (sat 1.2g, mono 1.8g, poly 3.4g); PROTEIN 5.5g; CARB 42.2g; FIBER 2g; CHOL 37mg; IRON 2.1mg; SODIUM 238mg; CALC 104mg

Endive Stuffed with Goat Cheese and Walnuts

This appetizer is perfect for a wine and cheese party. Every bite packs a contrast of flavors and textures—salty, sweet, tangy, bitter, creamy, and crunchy.

⅓ cup coarsely chopped walnuts
2 tablespoons honey, divided
Cooking spray
¼ cup balsamic vinegar
3 tablespoons orange juice
16 Belgian endive leaves (about 2 heads)
16 small orange sections (about 2 navel oranges)
⅓ cup (1½ ounces) crumbled goat cheese or blue cheese
1 tablespoon minced fresh chives
¼ teaspoon cracked black pepper

1. Preheat oven to 350°.
2. Combine walnuts and 1 tablespoon honey; spread on a baking sheet coated with cooking spray. Bake at 350° for 10 minutes, stirring after 5 minutes.
3. Combine 1 tablespoon honey, vinegar, and orange juice in a small saucepan. Bring mixture to a boil over high heat, and cook until reduced to 3 tablespoons (about 5 minutes).
4. Fill each endive leaf with 1 orange section. Top each section with 1 teaspoon cheese and 1 teaspoon walnuts; arrange on a plate. Drizzle vinegar mixture evenly over leaves, and sprinkle evenly

with chives and pepper. Yield: 16 servings (serving size: 1 stuffed leaf).

CALORIES 46 (45% from fat); FAT 2.3g (sat 0.6g, mono 0.4g, poly 1.2g); PROTEIN 1.3g; CARB 5.9g; FIBER 1g; CHOL 2mg; IRON 0.3mg; SODIUM 15mg; CALC 22mg

Spiced Fig and Walnut Bread

2 cups all-purpose flour
¾ cup sugar
1½ teaspoons baking powder
1½ teaspoons ground cinnamon
1 teaspoon ground ginger
½ teaspoon baking soda
½ teaspoon salt
½ teaspoon ground allspice
¼ teaspoon ground nutmeg
½ cup chopped walnuts
8 dried Black Mission figs, chopped
1 cup low-fat buttermilk
⅓ cup molasses
2 tablespoons vegetable oil
2 large eggs
Cooking spray

1. Preheat oven to 350°.
2. Lightly spoon flour into dry measuring cups; level with a knife. Combine flour and next 8 ingredients in a large bowl; make a well in center of mixture. Stir in walnuts and figs. Combine buttermilk, molasses, oil, and eggs in a bowl; add to flour mixture. Stir just until moist.
3. Spoon batter into an 8 x 4-inch loaf pan coated with cooking spray. Bake at

Mini Mocha-Toffee Crunch Cheesecakes

36 commercial prebaked miniature phyllo dough shells
1½ teaspoons instant coffee granules
1 teaspoon hot water
1 teaspoon Kahlúa (coffee-flavored liqueur)
½ cup sugar
½ cup (4 ounces) ⅓-less-fat cream cheese
½ cup (4 ounces) block-style fat-free cream cheese
1 tablespoon all-purpose flour
¼ teaspoon vanilla extract
1 large egg
3 tablespoons toffee bits (such as Heath)

1. Preheat oven to 350°.
2. Place 1 phyllo shell into each of 36 miniature muffin cups.
3. Combine coffee granules, hot water, and Kahlúa in a small bowl. Place coffee mixture, sugar, and next 5 ingredients in a food processor; process until smooth. Spoon about 1 tablespoon cheese mixture into each shell; discard remaining filling. Sprinkle cheesecakes evenly with toffee bits.
4. Bake at 350° for 15 minutes or until set. Remove from pans; cool on a wire rack. Yield: 3 dozen (serving size: 1 cheesecake).

CALORIES 55 (38% from fat); FAT 2.3g (sat 0.8g, mono 0.9g, poly 0.6g); PROTEIN 1.5g; CARB 6.5g; FIBER 0g; CHOL 10mg; IRON 0.1mg; SODIUM 47mg; CALC 10mg

Holiday Open House

There's no better way to bring friends and family together in one spot during the holidays than with an open house. Dazzle your guests with our eclectic holiday buffet and dramatic decorating ideas.

Menu

serves 16

West Indies Shrimp

Chipotle-Chicken Stew

Antipasto Bowl

Sun-Dried Tomato Tapenade
with Crostini

Baked Potato-and-Bacon Soup

Cornmeal Cheese Twists

Hot Spiced Cheer

Coconut-Macadamia Nut Cookies

West Indies Shrimp

You can cook and peel the shrimp early in the day and then cover and chill. You can make the marinade in the morning, but don't combine the two components until about 45 minutes to 1 hour before you expect your guests to arrive.

 12 cups water
  2 pounds unpeeled medium shrimp
  2 teaspoons Old Bay seasoning
  1 cup chopped onion
  1 cup chopped green bell pepper
 ⅔ cup cider vinegar
1½ tablespoons vegetable oil
  1 teaspoon salt
 ¼ teaspoon black pepper

1. Bring water to a boil in a large saucepan. Add shrimp and seasoning; cook 3 minutes or until done. Drain and cool completely. Place shrimp in a large zip-top plastic bag. Add onion and remaining ingredients to bag; seal and marinate in refrigerator 30 minutes, turning bag occasionally. Remove shrimp from bag, reserving marinade. Peel shrimp; place in a large bowl. Add reserved marinade; toss gently to coat. Yield: 18 servings (serving size: about 2 shrimp).

CALORIES 57 (28% from fat); FAT 1.8g (sat 0.3g, mono 0.4g, poly 0.8); PROTEIN 7.9g; CARB 2.1g; FIBER 0.3g; CHOL 57mg; IRON 1.1mg; SODIUM 260mg; CALC 23mg

Chipotle-Chicken Stew

Chipotles give this stew a Southwestern flair that's guaranteed to take the chill off winter. Make and store the stew in the refrigerator the day before the party. Reheat over medium-low heat; stir in the cilantro before serving.

   Cooking spray
  3 pounds skinless, boneless chicken breast, cut into bite-sized pieces
  1 tablespoon olive oil
  3 cups chopped onion
  6 garlic cloves, minced
  2 cups (1-inch) cubed peeled red potato (about 1 pound)
1½ cups (1-inch-thick) slices carrot
 ¼ cup tomato paste
1½ teaspoons ground cumin
  6 cups fat-free, less-sodium chicken broth
  3 (14.5-ounce) cans no-salt-added diced tomatoes, undrained
  3 drained canned chipotle chiles in adobo sauce, finely chopped
 ½ teaspoon salt
  2 tablespoons chopped fresh cilantro

1. Place a large Dutch oven coated with cooking spray over medium-high heat. Add chicken; sauté 7 minutes or until browned. Remove chicken from pan; keep warm.
2. Add oil to pan. Add onion; sauté 7 minutes or until lightly browned. Add garlic; sauté 1 minute. Add potato and next 6 ingredients; bring to a boil. Reduce heat, and simmer 25 minutes or until vegetables are tender. Add chicken and salt; cover and cook 10 minutes. Stir in chopped cilantro. Yield: 16 servings (serving size: 1 cup).

CALORIES 173 (12% from fat); FAT 2.3g (sat 0.5g, mono 1g, poly 0.5g); PROTEIN 22.7g; CARB 14.6g; FIBER 1.6g; CHOL 49mg; IRON 1.6mg; SODIUM 361mg; CALC 54mg

Chipotle-Chicken Stew

West Indies Shrimp

Antipasto Bowl

This assortment of vegetables and cheese takes less than 30 minutes to prepare, but if you want to get as much as possible done in advance, make the vinaigrette a few days early. You can store this appetizer in the refrigerator for up to 8 hours, but don't go longer than that, or it will affect the texture and flavor of the ingredients.

3 cups (2-inch) sliced asparagus (about ¾ pound)
3 cups quartered mushrooms (about ¾ pound)
1 cup red bell pepper strips
½ cup pitted ripe olives
3 ounces part-skim mozzarella cheese, cubed (about ⅔ cup)
1 (14-ounce) can quartered artichoke hearts, drained
1 (11.5-ounce) jar pickled pepperoncini peppers, drained
⅓ cup cider vinegar
¼ cup finely chopped fresh parsley
2 tablespoons extravirgin olive oil
2 teaspoons dried oregano
1 teaspoon sugar
¼ teaspoon salt
¼ teaspoon black pepper
3 garlic cloves, minced

1. Steam asparagus, covered, 2 minutes. Drain and plunge into ice water; drain well. Combine asparagus, mushrooms, and next 5 ingredients in a large bowl.
2. Combine vinegar and next 7 ingredients in a small bowl; stir well with a whisk. Pour vinaigrette over vegetable mixture, tossing gently to coat. Cover and marinate in refrigerator 2 hours, stirring occasionally. Yield: 20 servings (serving size: ½ cup).
Note: This dish can either be served chilled or at room temperature.

CALORIES 49 (50% from fat); FAT 2.7g (sat 0.7g, mono 1.5g, poly 0.3g); PROTEIN 2.5g; CARB 5g; FIBER 1.2g; CHOL 2mg; IRON 1.2mg; SODIUM 263mg; CALC 50mg

Sun-Dried Tomato Tapenade with Crostini
(pictured on page 71)

This recipe takes about 30 minutes to prepare and can be made up to 2 days in advance. Store the tapenade, covered, in the refrigerator, and garnish with parsley immediately before serving.

- 2 cups boiling water
- 1 cup sun-dried tomatoes, packed without oil (about 3 ounces)
- ½ cup pitted kalamata olives
- 2 tablespoons dried basil
- 2 tablespoons fresh lemon juice
- 1 garlic clove, minced
- 2 teaspoons olive oil
- 72 (½-inch-thick) slices diagonally cut French bread baguette (about 2 loaves)
- Cooking spray
- Chopped fresh parsley (optional)

1. Combine boiling water and sun-dried tomatoes; cover and let stand 15 minutes or until soft. Drain tomatoes in a colander over a bowl, reserving ¾ cup liquid. Combine tomatoes, reserved liquid, olives, basil, lemon juice, and garlic in a blender or food processor; process until smooth. Place tomato mixture in a small bowl; stir in oil. Cover and chill.
2. Preheat oven to 350°.
3. Place half of bread slices on a baking sheet coated with cooking spray. Lightly coat bread slices with cooking spray. Bake at 350° for 4 minutes. Turn bread slices over; lightly coat with cooking spray. Bake an additional 4 minutes. Repeat with remaining bread slices. Cool completely.
4. Garnish tapenade with parsley, if desired, and serve with crostini. Yield: 24 servings (serving size: 3 crostini and 1 tablespoon tapenade).

CALORIES 77 (19% from fat); FAT 1.6g (sat 0.3g, mono 0.9g, poly 0.4g); PROTEIN 2.5g; CARB 13.6g; FIBER 1.3g; CHOL 0mg; IRON 1.1mg; SODIUM 239mg; CALC 29mg

simply decorating

Cooking Light photo stylists offer season-simplifying ideas for jazzing up the holidays at your house.

Fill a goldfish bowl with ornaments. This makes an easy, low-maintenance holiday centerpiece.

There's a reason clove-spiked oranges are an enduring tradition—they smell like holiday cheer. Set a row of them on a windowsill, tuck one in an overnight guest's linen drawer, or simply place several in a bright bowl in your kitchen.

To dress up your mantel, arrange branches of fresh pine across the top, line up several tall white or frosted glasses (or whatever kind strikes your fancy), and fill them with fat candy canes.

Make your own invitations. Use pom-pom balls from a craft store, spices, or pine cones and twigs from the yard. No rules—just be creative.

If you're serving aperitifs or wine with dinner, invite your friends to pour their own. Tie a piece of pine or rosemary to the bottle. The subtle scent will stay on their fingertips throughout the evening.

Baked Potato-and-Bacon Soup

Bake the potatoes and shred the cheese the day before making the soup. If the soup needs to simmer for a while on the stove, you may need to add more chicken broth.

5¼ pounds baking potatoes
7 bacon slices
4½ cups chopped onion
1 teaspoon salt
5 garlic cloves, minced
1 bay leaf
7½ cups 1% low-fat milk
¾ teaspoon black pepper
3 cups fat-free, less-sodium chicken broth
⅓ cup chopped fresh parsley (optional)
1¼ cups sliced green onions
1¼ cups (5 ounces) finely shredded reduced-fat sharp Cheddar cheese

1. Preheat oven to 400°.
2. Pierce potatoes with a fork; bake at 400° for 1 hour or until tender. Cool slightly. Partially mash potatoes, including skins, with a potato masher; set aside.
3. Cook bacon in a Dutch oven over medium heat until crisp. Remove bacon from pan; crumble. Add onion to bacon drippings in pan; sauté 5 minutes. Add salt, garlic, and bay leaf; sauté 2 minutes. Add potato, milk, pepper, and broth; bring to a boil. Reduce heat, and simmer 10 minutes. Stir in parsley, if desired. Top individual servings with bacon, green onions, and cheese. Yield: 18 servings (serving size: 1 cup soup, about 1 teaspoon bacon, about 1 tablespoon green onions, and about 1 tablespoon cheese).

CALORIES 237 (30% from fat); FAT 7.8g (sat 3.5g, mono 3.1g, poly 0.8g); PROTEIN 10.5g; CARB 31.8g; FIBER 3.1g; CHOL 15mg; IRON 2mg; SODIUM 394mg; CALC 228mg

Cornmeal Cheese Twists

Measure the cornmeal and grate the cheese ahead.

¼ cup water
4 large egg whites
1 cup yellow cornmeal
1 cup (4 ounces) grated Asiago cheese
1 cup (4 ounces) grated fresh Parmesan cheese
1 teaspoon paprika
Cooking spray
4 (11-ounce) cans refrigerated soft breadsticks (such as Pillsbury)

1. Preheat oven to 375°.
2. Combine water and egg whites in a shallow bowl. Combine cornmeal, cheeses, and paprika in a shallow bowl. Coat 2 baking sheets with cooking spray.

Baked Potato-and-Bacon Soup; Cornmeal Cheese Twists

3. Unroll breadstick dough, separating into strips. Roll each piece into a 7-inch-long strip. Dip 2 strips in egg white mixture, and dredge in cornmeal mixture. Twist strips together, pinching ends to seal; place on baking sheet. Repeat procedure with remaining dough strips, egg white mixture, and cornmeal mixture. Bake at 375° for 15 minutes or until golden brown. Yield: 2 dozen twists (serving size: 1 twist).

CALORIES 202 (24% from fat); FAT 5.3g (sat 2.2g, mono 1.6g, poly 1.2g); PROTEIN 8.3g; CARB 29.9g; FIBER 0.3g; CHOL 8mg; IRON 1.7mg; SODIUM 521mg; CALC 107mg

Coconut-Macadamia Nut Cookies

Hot Spiced Cheer

If you don't have cheesecloth, remove the tea leaves from an ordinary tea bag, fill the empty bag with the cloves and ginger, and tie it securely with the tea bag string; let the cinnamon sticks float separately while simmering. Serve in a decorative punch bowl alongside a small pitcher of rum marked with a label or card. You may want to have an extra tea bag and more of the cider mixture handy in case you have thirsty guests.

    10   whole cloves
     4   (3-inch) cinnamon sticks
     4   pieces crystallized ginger,
         chopped
     1   gallon apple cider
     4   cups pineapple juice
     2   cups orange juice
    ¼   cup fresh lemon juice
    ⅓   cup sugar
    ¼   teaspoon salt
         White rum (optional)

1. Place first 3 ingredients on a double layer of cheesecloth. Gather edges of cheesecloth together; tie securely.
2. Combine cheesecloth bag, cider, and next 5 ingredients in a large stockpot; bring to a boil. Reduce heat, and simmer 20 minutes. Discard cheesecloth bag.

Serve with rum, if desired. Yield: 22 cups (serving size: 1 cup).

CALORIES 133 (1% from fat); FAT 0.2g (sat 0g, mono 0g, poly 0.1g); PROTEIN 0.4g; CARB 33g; FIBER 0.5g; CHOL 0mg; IRON 0.8mg; SODIUM 33mg; CALC 23mg

Coconut-Macadamia Nut Cookies

You can make these cookies a day or two ahead; store them in an airtight container.

     1   cup all-purpose flour
     1   cup regular oats
     1   cup packed brown sugar
    ⅓   cup golden raisins
    ⅓   cup flaked sweetened coconut
    ¼   cup chopped macadamia nuts
    ½   teaspoon baking soda
    ¼   cup butter, melted
     3   tablespoons water
     2   tablespoons honey
         Cooking spray

1. Preheat oven to 325°.
2. Lightly spoon flour into a dry measuring cup; level with a knife. Combine flour and next 6 ingredients. Combine butter, water, and honey, stirring well to combine. Add butter mixture to flour mixture, stirring until well blended. Drop by level tablespoons 2 inches apart onto baking sheets coated with cooking spray. Bake at 325° for 10 minutes or until almost set. Cool on pans 2 to 3 minutes or until firm. Remove cookies from pans, and cool on wire racks. Yield: 2½ dozen (serving size: 1 cookie).

CALORIES 90 (30% from fat); FAT 3g (sat 1.5g, mono 1.2g, poly 0.2g); PROTEIN 1.1g; CARB 15.4g; FIBER 0.5g; CHOL 4mg; IRON 0.5mg; SODIUM 43mg; CALC 10mg

Elegant Entertaining

All that glitters is definitely gold when you're hosting a classy dinner party Cooking Light-style. All your guests' dreams will come true when they sit down to this elegant dinner.

Menu

serves 12

Cream of Mushroom Soup with Sherry

Roast Beef with
Horseradish-Mustard Sauce

Mashed potatoes

Steamed zucchini

Challah

Grand Marnier Soufflé with
Vanilla Sauce

Wine Note: *Roast beef calls for a big, soft wine of substance. Such wines often cost a fortune, but a stellar Syrah is a steal.*

Cream of Mushroom Soup with Sherry

This soup is an elegant first course. Half-and-half and sherry enrich the soup and infuse it with flavor. Using a blender rather than a food processor gives the soup a silky texture.

  2 teaspoons olive oil
  2 cups chopped onion
  1 cup thinly sliced carrot
 ⅔ cup chopped celery
  8 cups sliced button mushrooms
     (about 1½ pounds)
  4 cups sliced shiitake mushroom
     caps (about 7 ounces)
  2 garlic cloves, minced
  1 cup water
  1 teaspoon dried rubbed sage
 ¼ teaspoon salt
 ¼ teaspoon black pepper
  4 (14-ounce) cans fat-free,
     less-sodium chicken broth
  6 tablespoons half-and-half
 ¼ cup dry sherry
 ¼ cup chopped fresh parsley

1. Heat oil in a Dutch oven over medium-high heat. Add onion, carrot, and celery; sauté 6 minutes or until tender. Reduce heat to medium; add mushrooms and garlic. Cook 7 minutes or until mushrooms are tender, stirring frequently. Add water, sage, salt, pepper, and broth; bring to a simmer. Cover and simmer 25 minutes. Remove from heat, and cool 5 minutes.

2. Place half of mushroom mixture in a blender; process until smooth. Pour pureed soup into a large bowl. Repeat procedure with remaining mushroom mixture. Return soup to pan. Stir in half-and-half and sherry; cook over low heat 5 minutes or until thoroughly heated, stirring frequently. Sprinkle each serving with 1 teaspoon parsley. Yield: 12 servings (serving size: 1 cup).

CALORIES 71 (24% from fat); FAT 1.9g (sat 0.7g, mono 0.8g, poly 0.2g); PROTEIN 4.7g; CARB 8.4g; FIBER 1.9g; CHOL 3mg; IRON 1.2mg; SODIUM 321mg; CALC 26mg

Roast Beef with Horseradish-
Mustard Sauce with mashed
potatoes and steamed zucchini

Challah

This traditional Jewish bread has a moist, rich texture and is often braided.

½ teaspoon sugar
1 package dry yeast (about 2¼ teaspoons)
¾ cup warm water (100° to 110°)
¼ cup vegetable oil
1 large egg, lightly beaten
3⅓ cups all-purpose flour
1¼ teaspoons salt
Cooking spray
2 teaspoons water
1 large egg yolk, lightly beaten

1. Dissolve sugar and yeast in warm water in a large bowl; let mixture stand 5 minutes. Add oil and egg, stirring with a whisk until combined. Lightly spoon flour into dry measuring cups; level with a knife. Add flour and salt to yeast mixture; beat with a mixer at medium speed until smooth.

2. Turn dough out onto a lightly floured surface. Knead until smooth and elastic (about 10 minutes). Place dough in a large bowl coated with cooking spray, turning to coat top. Cover and let rise in a warm place (85°), free from drafts, 1 hour or until doubled in size. (Press 2 fingers into dough. If indentation remains, dough has risen enough.)

3. Punch dough down; shape into a ball. Return dough to bowl; cover and let rise 1 hour or until doubled in size.

4. Punch dough down; turn dough out onto a lightly floured surface. Cover and let rest 15 minutes.

5. Divide dough into 3 equal portions. Working with 1 portion at a time (cover remaining dough to keep from drying), shape each portion into a 15-inch rope.

Place ropes lengthwise on a baking sheet coated with cooking spray (do not stretch); pinch ends together at 1 end to seal. Braid ropes, and pinch loose ends together to seal. Cover and let rise 1 hour or until doubled in size.

6. Preheat oven to 375°.

7. Uncover dough. Combine 2 teaspoons water and egg yolk; brush over braid. Bake at 375° for 35 minutes or until loaf is browned on bottom and sounds hollow when tapped. Remove from pan; cool on a wire rack. Yield: 1 loaf, 16 servings (serving size: 1 slice).

CALORIES 124 (30% from fat); FAT 4.1g (sat 0.7g, mono 1g, poly 2.1g); PROTEIN 3.2g; CARB 19.5g; FIBER 0.7g; CHOL 27mg; IRON 1.4mg; SODIUM 188mg; CALC 3mg

Challah

When hosting an elegant dinner party, it's fine to mix your sterling, silver plate, or pewter platters with pitchers, candleholders, and other serving pieces.

Roast Beef with Horseradish-Mustard Sauce

A dry rub of coriander, pepper, salt, and garlic encrusts the roast. Use leftover roast and sauce along with Swiss cheese to make great sandwiches on toasted sourdough or Crusty Rye Loaf (recipe on page 180).

Roast Beef:
- 2 tablespoons ground coriander seeds
- 1 tablespoon cracked black pepper
- 2 teaspoons kosher salt
- 5 garlic cloves, crushed
- 1 (3-pound) sirloin tip roast, trimmed
- Cooking spray

Sauce:
- ¾ cup prepared horseradish
- ½ cup stone-ground mustard
- ¼ cup white vinegar

1. Preheat oven to 450°.
2. To prepare roast beef, combine first 4 ingredients; rub over roast. Place roast on a broiler pan coated with cooking spray. Insert a meat thermometer into thickest portion of roast. Bake at 450° for 20 minutes.
3. Reduce oven temperature to 300° (do not remove roast from oven); bake an additional 40 minutes or until thermometer registers 145° (medium-rare) or until desired degree of doneness. Place roast on a cutting board; cover loosely with foil. Let stand 15 minutes (temperature of roast will increase 5° upon standing). Cut roast against grain into thin slices.
4. To prepare sauce, combine horseradish, mustard, and vinegar. Serve with roast

beef. Yield: 12 servings (serving size: 3 ounces beef and 2 tablespoons sauce).

CALORIES 203 (36% from fat); FAT 8.1g (sat 2.8g, mono 3.1g, poly 0.4g); PROTEIN 24.9g; CARB 5.3g; FIBER 2.4g; CHOL 70mg; IRON 2.9mg; SODIUM 575mg; CALC 37mg

Grand Marnier Soufflé with Vanilla Sauce

In order to serve 12 guests, you'll need to make 2 soufflés.

Sauce:
- 2 large egg yolks, lightly beaten
- 1 cup whole milk
- 2½ tablespoons sugar
- 1 teaspoon vanilla extract
- Dash of salt

Soufflé:
- Cooking spray
- 1 tablespoon sugar
- 3 large egg yolks, lightly beaten
- 3 tablespoons all-purpose flour
- ⅔ cup 2% reduced-fat milk
- ¼ cup sugar
- 1 tablespoon butter
- 3 tablespoons Grand Marnier (orange-flavored liqueur)
- 2 teaspoons vanilla extract
- 5 large egg whites
- ½ teaspoon cream of tartar
- ⅛ teaspoon salt
- 2 tablespoons sugar

1. To prepare sauce, place 2 egg yolks in a medium bowl. Combine whole milk and 2½ tablespoons sugar in a small, heavy saucepan over medium heat; heat to 180° or until tiny bubbles form around edge (do not boil).
2. Gradually add hot milk mixture to 2 egg

yolks, stirring constantly with a whisk. Return mixture to pan; cook over medium heat until thick and bubbly (about 3 minutes), stirring constantly. Remove from heat. Stir in 1 teaspoon vanilla and dash of salt. Pour into a glass bowl; cover and chill.
3. Preheat oven to 375°.
4. To prepare soufflé, coat a 1½-quart soufflé dish with cooking spray; sprinkle with 1 tablespoon sugar.
5. Place 3 egg yolks in a medium bowl; set aside. Place flour in a small, heavy saucepan; gradually add 2% milk, stirring with a whisk. Stir in ¼ cup sugar; add butter. Cook over medium heat until thick (about 5 minutes), stirring constantly. Gradually add hot milk mixture to 3 egg yolks, stirring constantly with a whisk. Return mixture to pan; cook over medium heat until thick and bubbly (about 3 minutes), stirring constantly. Stir in liqueur and 2 teaspoons vanilla; cook 1 minute, stirring constantly. Remove from heat.
6. Place egg whites, cream of tartar, and ⅛ teaspoon salt in a large bowl; beat with a mixer at high speed until soft peaks form. Gradually add 2 tablespoons sugar, 1 tablespoon at a time, beating until stiff peaks form. Gently stir one-fourth egg white mixture into milk mixture; gently fold in remaining egg white mixture.
7. Spoon into prepared soufflé dish. Place soufflé dish in a 9-inch square baking pan; add hot water to pan to a depth of 1 inch. Bake at 375° for 30 minutes or until puffy and set. Spoon about 3 tablespoons sauce over each serving. Serve immediately. Yield: 6 servings.

CALORIES 242 (30% from fat); FAT 8.1g (sat 3.7g, mono 2.7g, poly 0.8g); PROTEIN 7.9g; CARB 30g; FIBER 0.1g; CHOL 190mg; IRON 0.7mg; SODIUM 179mg; CALC 104mg

Mix-and-Match Dinner Party

We all love options! Let your entertaining prowess garner you all of the accolades you deserve when you offer your entire menu on your buffet or table and let everyone pick and choose.

Roast Lamb with Rosemary and Garlic

This roast cooks with just a simple rub of rosemary and garlic; coarse salt goes on the lamb the second it emerges from the oven.

1 (3-pound) rolled boneless leg of lamb, trimmed
1 tablespoon chopped fresh rosemary
3 garlic cloves, minced
1 teaspoon kosher or sea salt

1. Preheat oven to 450°.
2. Secure roast at 1-inch intervals with twine. Rub surface of roast with rosemary and garlic. Place roast on rack of a broiler pan or roasting pan; insert a meat thermometer into thickest portion of roast. Bake at 450° for 1 hour and 15 minutes or until thermometer registers 145°

(medium-rare) to 160° (medium).
3. Sprinkle roast with salt. Place roast on a cutting board; cover loosely with foil. Let stand 10 minutes (temperature of roast will increase 5° upon standing). Remove twine before slicing. Yield: 8 servings (serving size: 3 ounces).

CALORIES 165 (36% from fat); FAT 6.6g (sat 2.4g, mono 2.9g, poly 0.4g); PROTEIN 24.2g; CARB 0.5g; FIBER 0g; CHOL 76mg; IRON 1.9mg; SODIUM 293mg; CALC 12mg

Orange-Sage Roasted Turkey

Fresh sage leaves are a must for the best flavor. We also recommend fresh orange juice, but you can use frozen for convenience.

1 (15-pound) fresh or frozen turkey, thawed
Cooking spray
½ cup chopped fresh sage
2 tablespoons grated orange rind
1⅛ teaspoons salt, divided
1¼ cups fresh orange juice (about 3 oranges), divided
2 tablespoons honey, divided
1 orange, quartered
1 tablespoon cornstarch

1. Preheat oven to 325°.
2. Remove and discard giblets and neck from turkey. Rinse turkey with cold water; pat dry. Trim excess fat. Starting at neck cavity, loosen skin from breast and drumsticks by inserting fingers, gently pushing between skin and meat. Lift wing tips up and over back; tuck under turkey.

3. Place turkey on the rack of a broiler pan or roasting pan coated with cooking spray. Combine the sage, rind, and 1 teaspoon salt. Rub sage mixture under loosened skin and inside the body cavity. Combine ¼ cup juice and 1 tablespoon honey; pour over turkey. Place orange quarters inside body cavity.
4. Insert a meat thermometer into meaty part of thigh, making sure not to touch bone. Bake at 325° for 3 hours or until thermometer registers 180°. Cover turkey loosely with foil, and let stand for 10 minutes. Discard skin and orange quarters. Remove turkey from pan, reserving pan drippings for sauce. Place turkey on a platter; keep warm.
5. To make the sauce, pour reserved pan drippings into a zip-top plastic bag. Seal bag; snip off 1 corner of bag. Drain drippings into a medium saucepan, stopping before fat layer reaches the opening; discard fat. (You should have about ⅔ cup drippings; add enough water or fat-free, low-sodium chicken broth to make up the difference, if necessary.)
6. Add ⅛ teaspoon salt, ½ cup juice, and 1 tablespoon honey to drippings in pan; bring to a boil. Reduce heat; simmer 1 minute. Combine ½ cup juice and cornstarch in a small bowl; add to drippings mixture. Bring to a boil; cook 1 minute, stirring constantly. Serve sauce with turkey. Yield: 16 servings (serving size: 5 ounces turkey and 2 tablespoons sauce).

CALORIES 261 (24% from fat); FAT 7.1g (sat 2.3g, mono 1.5g, poly 2g); PROTEIN 41.7g; CARB 5.1g; FIBER 0.1g; CHOL 108mg; IRON 2.6mg; SODIUM 264mg; CALC 44mg

Roast Lamb with
Rosemary and Garlic

Corn Bread, Cherry, and Bacon Stuffing

Make the corn bread croutons a day ahead (place them in an airtight container)
or up to a week in advance (keep them in the freezer).

⅔ cup fat-free milk

2 large eggs

2 (8½-ounce) packages corn muffin mix

Cooking spray

6 bacon slices

2 cups chopped onion

2 cups diced carrot

2 cups diced celery

½ cup dried tart cherries

2 cups fat-free, less-sodium chicken broth

1 cup chopped fresh parsley

1 teaspoon dried thyme

½ teaspoon salt

¼ teaspoon black pepper

1. Preheat oven to 400°.

2. Combine milk and eggs in a bowl; stir well with a whisk. Stir in muffin mix; let stand 2 minutes. Pour corn bread mixture into a 13 x 9-inch baking dish coated with cooking spray. Bake at 400° for 20 minutes or until a wooden pick inserted in center comes out clean. Cool; cut into ½-inch cubes. Place on a baking sheet; bake at 400° for 10 minutes or until golden brown.

3. Cook bacon in a large nonstick skillet over medium heat until crisp. Remove bacon from pan, reserving 1 teaspoon drippings in pan. Crumble bacon; set aside. Add onion, carrot, and celery to pan; sauté 5 minutes over medium-high heat. Stir in cherries and broth, and cook 5 minutes.

4. Combine corn bread cubes, bacon, onion mixture, parsley, thyme, salt, and pepper in a large bowl; stir until well blended. Spoon corn bread mixture into a 13 x 9-inch baking dish coated with cooking spray. Bake at 400° for 20 minutes or until thoroughly heated, stirring after 10 minutes. Yield: 12 servings (serving size: ¾ cup).

CALORIES 248 (28% from fat); FAT 7.6g (sat 2g, mono 3g, poly 2.1g); PROTEIN 5.7g; CARB 39g; FIBER 2.9g; CHOL 41mg; IRON 2.1mg; SODIUM 524mg; CALC 113mg

Corn Bread, Cherry, and Bacon Stuffing

Potato and Sun-Dried Tomato au Gratin

This can be assembled and refrigerated up to 24 hours ahead. Let stand 30 minutes at room temperature, and then bake as directed. You can substitute any sharp Italian cheese (such as Romano, provolone, or Asiago) for the Parmesan.

Potato and Sun-Dried
Tomato au Gratin

    1   cup boiling water
    ¾   cup sun-dried tomatoes, packed
        without oil (about 2 ounces)
    3   pounds peeled baking potato, cut
        into ¼-inch-thick slices
Cooking spray
    1   tablespoon butter
    1   cup chopped onion
    ½   teaspoon dried oregano
    ¼   teaspoon salt
    ¼   teaspoon black pepper
    ¼   cup all-purpose flour
    2¼ cups fat-free milk
    2   cups (8 ounces) grated fresh
        Parmesan cheese

1. Combine water and sun-dried tomatoes in a bowl; cover and let stand 30 minutes or until soft. Drain and coarsely chop; set aside.
2. Preheat oven to 350°.
3. Place potato in a large saucepan, and cover with water; bring to a boil. Reduce heat; simmer 15 minutes or until tender. Drain well. Arrange potato in a 13 x 9-inch baking dish coated with cooking spray.
4. Melt butter in pan over medium heat. Add onion; cook 3 minutes or until tender. Add sun-dried tomatoes, oregano, salt, and pepper; cook 2 minutes. Lightly spoon flour into a dry measuring cup; level with a knife. Sprinkle tomato mixture with flour; cook 1 minute, stirring constantly. Gradually add milk, stirring with a whisk until blended. Remove from heat; add cheese, stirring until cheese melts. Pour sauce over potatoes, tossing gently to coat. Bake at 350° for 20 minutes or until bubbly and golden. Yield: 10 servings (serving size: about ¾ cup).

CALORIES 279 (25% from fat); FAT 7.6g (sat 4.6g, mono 2.1g, poly 0.4g); PROTEIN 13.7g; CARB 38g; FIBER 2.9g; CHOL 19mg; IRON 1.2mg; SODIUM 558mg; CALC 353mg

Brussels Sprouts with Browned Garlic

To trim Brussels sprouts, discard the tough outer leaves, and trim off about 1/4 inch from the stems. Don't trim too much from the stems, or the sprouts will fall apart. If you're not fond of Brussels sprouts, try substituting green beans. Be sure to brown the garlic over low heat because it can burn in a flash.

    6   cups trimmed Brussels sprouts,
        halved (about 2 pounds)
    1   tablespoon olive oil,
        divided
    ½   teaspoon salt
    ⅛   teaspoon black pepper
Cooking spray
    3   garlic cloves, thinly sliced
    1   tablespoon fresh lemon juice

1. Preheat oven to 425°.
2. Combine the Brussels sprouts, 1½ teaspoons oil, salt, and pepper. Place sprouts mixture in a 13 x 9-inch baking dish coated with cooking spray. Bake at 425° for 25 minutes or until sprouts are crisp-tender. Keep warm.
3. Heat 1½ teaspoons olive oil in a small skillet over medium-low heat. Add garlic, and cook 3 minutes or until golden brown, stirring occasionally. Remove from heat; stir in juice. Add to sprouts mixture; toss well. Yield: 8 servings (serving size: ¾ cup).

CALORIES 68 (30% from fat); FAT 2.3g (sat 0.3g, mono 1.3g, poly 0.3g); PROTEIN 3.9g; CARB 10.7g; FIBER 4.9g; CHOL 0mg; IRON 1.7mg; SODIUM 175mg; CALC 50mg

Roasted Red Onions

    4   medium red onions, peeled and
        halved (about 4 pounds)
Cooking spray
    2   teaspoons olive oil
    1   teaspoon balsamic vinegar
    ¾   teaspoon salt
    ¼   teaspoon black pepper

1. Preheat oven to 400°.
2. Arrange onions, cut sides down, in a 13 x 9-inch baking pan or on a broiler pan coated with cooking spray. Combine oil and next 3 ingredients in a small bowl; stir with a whisk. Drizzle onions with oil mixture. Bake at 400° for 1½ hours or until very tender. Yield: 8 servings (serving size: 1 onion half).

CALORIES 99 (15% from fat); FAT 1.7g (sat 0.3g, mono 0.9g, poly 0.4g); PROTEIN 2.6g; CARB 19.6g; FIBER 4.2g; CHOL 0mg; IRON 0.5mg; SODIUM 227mg; CALC 46mg

Buttermilk-Dill Rolls

You can make the dough for these simple rolls up to 2 weeks ahead and freeze it in a heavy-duty zip-top plastic bag. Thaw in the refrigerator, shape, and bake as directed. These rolls are also good without the dill if you prefer to omit it.

1½ cups warm low-fat buttermilk
    (100° to 110°)
2 tablespoons vegetable oil
2 teaspoons sugar
1 package dry yeast (about 2¼
    teaspoons)
3¼ cups all-purpose flour,
    divided
2 teaspoons dried dill
1 teaspoon kosher salt,
    divided
  Cooking spray
1½ teaspoons cornmeal
1 large egg white, lightly beaten

1. Combine first 4 ingredients in a large bowl; let stand 5 minutes. Lightly spoon flour into dry measuring cups; level with a knife. Add 3 cups flour, dill, and ½ teaspoon salt to buttermilk mixture. Turn dough out onto a floured surface. Knead until smooth and elastic (about 10 minutes); add enough of remaining flour, 1 tablespoon at a time, to prevent dough from sticking to hands (dough will feel sticky).
2. Place dough in a large bowl coated with cooking spray, turning to coat top. Cover and let rise in a warm place (85°), free from drafts, 45 minutes or until doubled in size. (Press 2 fingers into dough. If indentation remains, dough has risen enough.) Punch dough down. Cover; let rest 5 minutes. Divide in half. Working with 1 portion at a time (cover remaining dough to keep from drying), shape portion into 6 (2-inch-long) ovals on a floured surface. Roll up each portion tightly, starting with a long edge and

pressing firmly to eliminate air pockets; pinch seam and ends to seal. Place rolls, seam sides down, on a large baking sheet sprinkled with cornmeal. Repeat with remaining dough portion.
3. Preheat oven to 375°.
4. Brush egg white over rolls, and sprinkle with ½ teaspoon salt. Bake at 375° for 25 minutes or until the rolls are browned on bottom and sound hollow when tapped. Remove rolls from pan; cool on wire racks. Yield: 12 servings (serving size: 1 roll).

CALORIES 158 (19% from fat); FAT 3.3g (sat 0.8g, mono 0.9g, poly 1.3g); PROTEIN 4.9g; CARB 26.6g; FIBER 1g; CHOL 0mg; IRON 1.6mg; SODIUM 181mg; CALC 46mg

6 steps to seasonal style

Make your home look great for the holidays in ways that aren't laborious or expensive, courtesy of the *Cooking Light* photo stylists.

1. Fruit of elegance: This year, instead of making a pricey style statement with new holiday china, try putting a neatly folded napkin on each guest's dinner plate and topping it with an ornamental fruit, such as a lime, lemon, or orange, along with a leafy herb sprig. ▶

2. Talking points: Collectibles can double as tabletop helpers as well as conversation pieces. Toy soldiers? Use them to hold name cards for your dinner guests. Small vases? Fill them with a single flower to adorn each place setting. The personal connection makes the dinner special.

3. Fresh entry: Help guests feel festive right away by putting a bowl of bright green apples on a table outside your front door.

4. Sweet spotlight: Showcase dessert by inverting a wide vase in the center

of the dinner table, topping it with the plate holding your cake or pie, and arranging greenery or fruit around it. (Melt some candle wax on the inverted bottom of the vase to keep the plate steady.)

5. Lose the visual stress: A little pre-season housecleaning will get you in the mood and make the coming festivities feel more fresh.

◀ **6. Aroma, with love:** Put some star anise, cloves, nutmeg, marjoram, allspice, orange zest, and mint (or any nicely scented spices you have on hand) into a mortar. Lightly grind them once or twice with a pestle, and then sprinkle in a little rose- or orange-flower water. Your mixture is now ready to go wherever there are noses to please—in the middle of the table, by your front door, etc.

Pumpkin Cheesecake

Cheesecakes are best when they're made ahead. You can prepare this one
up to 3 days before the party; just cover and chill it until time to serve.

Crust:

56 reduced-fat vanilla wafers (about 8 ounces)

1 tablespoon butter, melted

Cooking spray

Filling:

3 (8-ounce) blocks fat-free cream cheese, softened

2 (8-ounce) blocks ⅓-less-fat cream cheese, softened

½ cup granulated sugar

½ cup packed brown sugar

3 tablespoons all-purpose flour

1 teaspoon ground cinnamon

½ teaspoon ground nutmeg

½ teaspoon ground ginger

¼ teaspoon salt

Dash of allspice

2 teaspoons vanilla extract

4 large eggs

1 (15-ounce) can pumpkin

1. Preheat oven to 400°.

2. To prepare crust, place wafers in a food processor; pulse 2 to 3 times or until finely ground. Add butter; pulse 10 times or until mixture resembles coarse meal. Firmly press mixture into bottom of a 9-inch springform pan coated with cooking spray. Bake at 400° for 10 minutes; cool on a wire rack.

3. Reduce oven temperature to 325°.

4. To prepare filling, beat cheeses with a mixer at high speed until smooth. Add granulated sugar and next 8 ingredients, beating well. Add eggs, 1 at a time, beating well after each addition. Add pumpkin; beat well.

5. Pour cheese mixture into prepared crust; bake at 325° for 1½ hours or until cheesecake center barely moves when pan is touched. Remove cheesecake from oven; run a knife around outside edge. Cool to room temperature; cover and chill at least 8 hours. Yield: 16 servings (serving size: 1 slice).

CALORIES 256 (34% from fat); FAT 9.8g (sat 5.3g, mono 2.9g, poly 0.5g); PROTEIN 11.4g; CARB 29.3g; FIBER 1.4g; CHOL 86mg; IRON 1.2mg; SODIUM 479mg; CALC 172mg

Croquant (recipe
on page 104)

holiday gifts

Surprise your friends with homemade specialties. Whether your holiday gift list includes a gourmet, a busy family, or a sweet tooth, you can be sure they'll all be pleased.

Spicy Oatmeal Crisps (recipe on page 108)

Sauces, Jams, and Candies

From rich, gooey caramel sauce to the sweet-tart pop of vibrant sugary cranberries, we've got sauces, jams, and candies that will be well received.

Caramel Sauce

Pour sauce into a syrup pitcher, an interesting cruet, or a French jelly jar; cover with wax paper, and secure with gold or silver elastic ribbon.

 2 cups sugar
 ½ cup water
 2 tablespoons butter
1½ cups evaporated fat-free milk
 1 teaspoon vanilla extract
Dash of salt

1. Combine sugar and water in a heavy saucepan; place over medium-low heat. Cook 13 minutes or until sugar dissolves (do not stir). Cover; increase heat to medium. Boil 1 minute (this will dissolve any sugar crystals clinging to sides of pan). Uncover; boil 10 additional minutes or until amber or golden (do not stir).
2. Remove from heat; let stand 1 minute. Add butter, stirring until it melts. Add milk, stirring constantly (caramel will harden and stick to spoon). Place pan over medium heat; cook, stirring constantly, 3 minutes or until caramel melts and mixture is smooth. Remove from heat; stir in vanilla and salt. Pour sauce into a bowl; serve warm or chilled. Store in an airtight container in the refrigerator. Yield: 2½ cups (serving size: 1 tablespoon).

CALORIES 52 (10% from fat); FAT 0.6g (sat 0.4g, mono 0.2g, poly 0g); PROTEIN 0.7g; CARB 11.1g; FIBER 0g; CHOL 2mg; IRON 0mg; SODIUM 19mg; CALC 28mg

Caramel Sauce

Golden Vanilla Syrup

For a gift, attach your favorite pancake recipe—perhaps Buttermilk Pancakes (recipe on page 165). This syrup is also good drizzled over ice cream or pound cake.

 1 vanilla bean, split lengthwise
 2 cups granulated sugar
1½ cups water
 ⅓ cup fresh lemon juice, strained
 1 tablespoon light brown sugar

1. Scrape seeds from vanilla bean; place seeds and bean in a small bowl.
2. Combine granulated sugar and next 3 ingredients in a medium saucepan. Bring to a boil over medium-high heat, stirring until sugar dissolves. Reduce heat; simmer 5 minutes. Remove from heat. Add vanilla bean and seeds, stirring gently. Cool syrup to room temperature.
3. Pour syrup and vanilla bean into a glass container. Cover and chill. Yield: 2¼ cups (serving size: 2 tablespoons).
Note: Store in the refrigerator for up to 1 month.

CALORIES 89 (0% from fat); FAT 0g; PROTEIN 0g; CARB 23.1g; FIBER 0g; CHOL 0mg; IRON 0mg; SODIUM 1mg; CALC 1mg

Maple-Blueberry Syrup

Give in a tall decorative bottle or empty syrup bottle nestled in a basket.

 2 cups maple syrup
 1 (12-ounce) bag frozen blueberries
 1 tablespoon fresh lemon juice

1. Combine syrup and blueberries in a medium saucepan. Bring to a boil over medium-high heat, stirring occasionally. Remove from heat; stir in juice. Pour into a bowl; cover and chill. Serve warm. Yield: 3 cups (serving size: about 3 tablespoons).
Note: Store in the refrigerator for up to 2 weeks.

CALORIES 116 (2% from fat); FAT 0.2g (sat 0g, mono 0g, poly 0.1g); PROTEIN 0.1g; CARB 29.6g; FIBER 0.6g; CHOL 0mg; IRON 0.5mg; SODIUM 4mg; CALC 29mg

Sugared Cranberries,
page 103

Apple Butter

This treat needs to be stored in an airtight container in the refrigerator; a clear glass jar with a secure lid will work best. To decorate, tie a cinnamon stick and star anise to the jar with ribbon or raffia.

  4 pounds Granny Smith apples, peeled, cored, and quartered
  1 cup apple cider
  ¼ cup packed dark brown sugar
  1 tablespoon fresh lemon juice
  ¼ teaspoon salt
Dash of ground cloves
  2 (3-inch) cinnamon sticks
  1 star anise

1. Combine apples and cider in a large stockpot; bring to a boil. Reduce heat; simmer, partially covered, 30 minutes or until apples are tender.
2. Place mixture in a food processor; pulse 6 times or until chunky. Return to pan.
3. Stir in sugar and remaining ingredients. Cook over low heat 1 hour or until thick, stirring occasionally. Discard cinnamon and star anise. Cover and chill. Yield: 4 cups (serving size: ¼ cup).
Note: Store in an airtight container in refrigerator up to 1 month.

CALORIES 76 (4% from fat); FAT 0.3g (sat 0.1g, mono 0g, poly 0.1g); PROTEIN 0.2g; CARB 19.6g; FIBER 1.8g; CHOL 0mg; IRON 0.1mg; SODIUM 40mg; CALC 7mg

Red Onion Marmalade

Spoon marmalade into airtight glass jars with screw-on lids. Store in the refrigerator. On a gift tag, suggest spreading the marmalade on rosemary focaccia or using it as a sauce for grilled tenderloin; note to keep refrigerated.

  2 tablespoons olive oil
  8 cups thinly sliced red onion (about 2 pounds)
  1 teaspoon fresh thyme leaves
  1 bay leaf
  ¾ teaspoon fine sea salt
  3 garlic cloves, minced
  1 cup Cabernet Sauvignon or other dry red wine
  ¼ cup packed brown sugar
  2 tablespoons balsamic vinegar
  ¼ teaspoon freshly ground black pepper

1. Heat oil in a large nonstick skillet over medium heat. Add onion, thyme, and bay leaf. Cover; cook 25 minutes, stirring occasionally.

2. Stir in salt and garlic; cook, uncovered, 2 minutes, stirring frequently. Stir in wine, brown sugar, and vinegar; bring to a boil. Reduce heat; simmer 12 minutes or until liquid almost evaporates and becomes syrupy.
3. Remove from heat; stir in pepper. Cool to room temperature. Discard bay leaf. Yield: 3 cups (serving size: ¼ cup).
Note: Store in the refrigerator for up to 1 week.

CALORIES 77 (28% from fat); FAT 2.4g (sat 0.3g, mono 1.7g, poly 0.2g); PROTEIN 1g; CARB 10.5g; FIBER 1.4g; CHOL 0mg; IRON 0.4mg; SODIUM 149mg; CALC 22mg

Spicy Thyme and Garlic Oil

For a gift, pour the oil into small (about 4-ounce) decorative glass bottles, and then package each with a fresh baguette, a small dipping bowl for the oil, and some colorful napkins in a beautiful basket. Include a note or gift card stating to keep the oil refrigerated.

  1 cup extravirgin olive oil
  ½ teaspoon crushed red pepper
  4 garlic cloves, halved
  2 bay leaves, crumbled
  1 (4-inch) thyme sprig

1. Combine all ingredients in a small, heavy saucepan. Cook over medium-low heat until thermometer registers 200°. Reduce heat to low; cook 20 minutes (do not allow temperature to rise above 220°). Cool to room temperature.
2. Strain oil mixture through a sieve into a bowl; discard solids. Store in refrigerator. Yield: 1 cup (serving size: 1 tablespoon).
Note: Store in the refrigerator in a glass container for 1 week.

CALORIES 119 (100% from fat); FAT 13.5g (sat 1.8g, mono 10g, poly 1.1g); PROTEIN 0g; CARB 0g; FIBER 0g; CHOL 0mg; IRON 0.1mg; SODIUM 0mg; CALC 0mg

Preserved Lemons

This classic Moroccan condiment brings lemony zing to lamb and poultry dishes. We've added saffron for earthy flavor and beautiful golden orange color. Pack in a widemouthed glass pint container. Attach this recipe suggestion to the gift: For subtle lemon-saffron flavor, stir 2 chopped preserved lemon slices into 2 cups cooked basmati rice or couscous.

  1 tablespoon kosher salt
  ½ teaspoon saffron threads, crushed
  2 cups thinly sliced lemon
     (about 3 lemons)
  ¼ cup fresh lemon juice
  1 tablespoon olive oil

Preserved Lemons

2. Add cheese to melted chips, and beat at medium speed of a mixer until smooth. Add 1 package powdered sugar to cheese mixture; beat until well blended.

3. Press mixture into a 6-inch square on heavy-duty plastic wrap, and cover with additional plastic wrap. Chill at least 1 hour.

4. Remove top sheet of plastic wrap; cut mixture into 48 squares. Roll each square into a ball; place on wax paper. Roll half of balls in cocoa; roll remaining balls in ¼ cup powdered sugar.

5. Place 2 tablespoons chips in a heavy-duty zip-top plastic bag, and microwave at HIGH 1 minute or until chips are softened. Knead bag until smooth. Snip a tiny hole in corner of bag; drizzle chocolate over balls rolled in cocoa. Serve at room temperature. Yield: 4 dozen (serving size: 1 piece).

Note: Store truffles in a single layer in an airtight container in the freezer for up to 1 month. Let stand at room temperature 1 hour before serving.

CALORIES 54 (18% from fat); FAT 1.1g (sat 0.7g, mono 0.4g, poly 0g); PROTEIN 0.4g; CARB 11.4g; FIBER 0.3g; CHOL 2mg; IRON 0.1mg; SODIUM 10mg; CALC 3mg

1. Combine salt and saffron. Place one lemon slice in bottom of a widemouthed 2-cup glass container. Sprinkle with a dash of salt mixture. Repeat layers with remaining lemon slices and salt mixture. Cover and let stand at room temperature 3 days.

2. After 3 days, press lemon slices down with a spoon. Pour juice and oil over lemon slices. Place a ramekin, custard cup, or clean decorative stone on top of lemon slices (to weigh them down). Cover and let stand at room temperature 5 days. Yield: 1 cup (serving size: 1 tablespoon).

Note: Preserved lemons can be stored at room temperature up to 1 month, or refrigerated up to 6 months.

CALORIES 11 (74% from fat); FAT 0.9g (sat 0.1g, mono 0.6g, poly 0.1g); PROTEIN 0.1g; CARB 1g; FIBER 0.2g; CHOL 0mg; IRON 0.1mg; SODIUM 353mg; CALC 2mg

Mint-Chocolate Truffles

After placing truffles in miniature baking cups, nestle them in a small box lined with parchment paper and tied with a bit of French wire ribbon.

⅓ cup semisweet mint-chocolate chips
½ cup (4 ounces) ⅓-less-fat cream cheese, softened
1 (16-ounce) package powdered sugar, sifted
¼ cup unsweetened cocoa
¼ cup sifted powdered sugar
2 tablespoons semisweet mint-chocolate chips

1. Place ⅓ cup chips in a medium glass bowl, and microwave at HIGH 1 minute or until chips are almost melted, stirring until smooth. Cool.

Sugared Cranberries
(pictured on page 101)

Because of the contrast between the tart cranberries and sugary coating, the flavor of this snack pops in your mouth. The berries are steeped in hot sugar syrup to tame their tangy bite. For gift-giving, package in parchment-lined tins. If you can't find superfine sugar, make your own by processing granulated sugar in a food processor for 1 minute.

2 cups granulated sugar
2 cups water
2 cups fresh cranberries
¾ cup superfine sugar

1. Combine granulated sugar and water in a small saucepan over low heat, stirring until sugar dissolves. Bring to a simmer; remove from heat (do not boil or cranberries may pop when added). Stir in cranberries; pour mixture into a bowl. Cover and refrigerate 8 hours or overnight.

2. Drain cranberries in a colander over a bowl, reserving liquid, if desired. Place superfine sugar in a shallow dish. Add cranberries, rolling to coat. Spread cranberries in a single layer on a baking sheet; let stand at room temperature 1 hour or until dry. Yield: 9 servings (serving size: about ⅓ cup).

Note: Store in an airtight container in a cool place up to 1 week.

CALORIES 118 (0% from fat); FAT 0g; PROTEIN 0.1g; CARB 30.4g; FIBER 0.9g; CHOL 0mg; IRON 0.1mg; SODIUM 0mg; CALC 2mg

Buttermilk Pralines

1½ cups sugar
½ cup whole buttermilk
1½ tablespoons light-colored corn syrup
½ teaspoon baking soda
Dash of salt
⅔ cup chopped pecans, toasted
1½ teaspoons butter
1 tablespoon vanilla extract

1. Combine first 5 ingredients in a large saucepan. Cook over low heat until sugar dissolves, stirring constantly. Continue cooking over low heat until a candy thermometer registers 234° (about 10 minutes); stir occasionally. Remove from heat; let stand 5 minutes.
2. Stir in nuts, butter, and vanilla; beat with a wooden spoon until mixture begins to lose its shine (about 6 minutes). Drop by teaspoonfuls onto wax paper. Let stand 20 minutes or until set. Yield: 30 servings (serving size: 1 praline).
Note: Store pralines in an airtight container for up to 2 weeks.

CALORIES 65 (30% from fat); FAT 2.2g (sat 0.4g, mono 1.2g, poly 0.6g); PROTEIN 0.4g; CARB 11.4g; FIBER 0.3g; CHOL 1mg; IRON 0.1mg; SODIUM 36mg; CALC 7mg

Buttermilk Pralines

Peppered Peanut Brittle

To wrap, place pieces of brittle in clear food-safe cellophane bags, and tie with ribbon.

Cooking spray
1½ cups sugar
⅓ cup light-colored corn syrup
3 tablespoons water
1½ teaspoons vanilla extract
1 teaspoon fresh lemon juice
½ teaspoon salt
1½ cups roasted peanuts
1 teaspoon baking soda
1 teaspoon butter
½ teaspoon crushed red pepper
¼ teaspoon cracked black pepper
⅛ teaspoon ground red pepper

1. Coat a large jelly-roll pan with cooking spray.
2. Combine sugar and next 5 ingredients in a large saucepan; bring to a boil over medium-high heat. Cook 10 minutes or until sugar dissolves and candy thermometer registers 325°, stirring occasionally. Remove mixture from heat; stir in peanuts and remaining ingredients. (Baking soda will cause mixture to bubble and become opaque.)
3. Quickly pour mixture into prepared pan, spreading to edges. Let stand 1 hour; break into pieces. Yield: about 1¼ pounds (serving size: about 1 ounce).
Note: Store in an airtight container for up to 2 weeks.

CALORIES 105 (32% from fat); FAT 3.7g (sat 0.6g, mono 1.8g, poly 1.1g); PROTEIN 1.7g; CARB 17.6g; FIBER 0.6g; CHOL 0mg; IRON 0.2mg; SODIUM 166mg; CALC 4mg

Croquant
(pictured on page 98)

Instead of high-fat pralines, toffee, or brittle, give *croquant* (French for "crisp")—a cream- and butter-free combination of caramelized sugar and almonds. Package in a paper-lined confection box or pretty bowl with a note to crumble over ice cream, layer into parfaits, or simply eat like brittle.

3 cups sugar
¾ cup water
1½ cups sliced almonds, toasted
Cooking spray

1. Combine sugar and water in a medium, heavy saucepan,

being careful not to splash sides of pan. Stir gently over high heat just until sugar dissolves (do not stir beyond this point). Using a clean pastry brush dipped in water, brush inside walls of pan to loosen any sugar particles.

2. Cook sugar mixture over high heat until light golden brown (about 10 to 15 minutes; do not leave unattended). Remove pan from heat; gently stir in almonds. Immediately pour almond mixture onto a jelly-roll pan coated with cooking spray. Cool completely; break into pieces. Store in an airtight container up to 5 days. Yield: 20 servings (serving size: about 1½ ounces).

CALORIES 159 (20% from fat); FAT 3.6g (sat 0.3g, mono 2.3g, poly 0.9g); PROTEIN 1.5g; CARB 31.3g; FIBER 0.7g; CHOL 0mg; IRON 0mg; SODIUM 0mg; CALC 19mg

Toasted Pecan Divinity
(pictured on cover)

Here's a traditional holiday candy that contrasts the sweetness of a confection with the flavor of buttery toasted pecans. Wrap in little cellophane bags, and tie with a sprig of pine and red ribbon.

    4   dozen pecan halves (about 4 ounces)
    1   tablespoon butter, melted
    ¼   teaspoon salt
    2½ cups sugar
    ⅔   cup water
    ½   cup light-colored corn syrup
    2   large egg whites
    1   teaspoon vanilla extract

1. Preheat oven to 350°.
2. Combine pecans and butter, and toss well. Spread mixture evenly onto a jelly-roll pan. Bake at 350° for 12 minutes, stirring once. Remove from oven; sprinkle with salt.
3. Combine sugar, water, and corn syrup in a medium saucepan. Bring to a boil over medium heat; cover and cook 3 minutes. Uncover and cook, without stirring, until a candy thermometer registers 250° (about 8 minutes). Remove from heat.
4. Beat egg whites in a large bowl with a heavy-duty stand mixer at high speed until stiff peaks form; beat in vanilla. Pour hot syrup in a thin stream over beaten egg whites while continuing to beat at high speed. Beat until mixture is stiff (about 3 minutes). Working quickly, drop by rounded teaspoonfuls onto wax paper. Gently press a pecan half on top of each piece of candy. Store divinity in an airtight container. Yield: 4 dozen (serving size: 1 piece).

CALORIES 70 (24% from fat); FAT 1.9g (sat 0.3g, mono 1g, poly 0.5g); PROTEIN 0.4g; CARB 13.5g; FIBER 0.2g; CHOL 1mg; IRON 0.1mg; SODIUM 20mg; CALC 2mg

Caramel Popcorn

Let the popcorn cool completely before dividing it into holiday tins for giving.

      Cooking spray
    1   cup packed dark brown sugar
    ½   cup light-colored corn syrup
    ⅓   cup butter
    1   tablespoon light molasses
    1½ teaspoons vanilla extract
    ½   teaspoon baking soda
    ½   teaspoon salt
    12 cups popcorn (popped without salt or fat)

1. Preheat oven to 250°.
2. Coat a large jelly-roll pan with cooking spray.
3. Combine sugar, corn syrup, butter, and molasses in a medium saucepan; bring to a boil over medium heat. Cook 5 minutes; stir once. Remove from heat; stir in vanilla, baking soda, and salt. Place popcorn in a large bowl. Pour sugar mixture over popcorn in a steady stream; stir to coat.
4. Spread popcorn mixture onto prepared pan. Bake at 250° for 1 hour, stirring every 15 minutes.
5. Remove from oven; stir to break up any large clumps. Cool 15 minutes. Serve warm or at room temperature. Yield: 18 servings (serving size: ⅔ cup).
Note: Store in an airtight container for up to 1 week.

CALORIES 126 (26% from fat); FAT 3.6g (sat 2.2g, mono 1.1g, poly 0.2g); PROTEIN 0.7g; CARB 23.9g; FIBER 0.8g; CHOL 9mg; IRON 0.4mg; SODIUM 151mg; CALC 15mg

Peppered Cheese Chips

    12 (6-inch) flour tortillas
        Cooking spray
    ¼   cup grated Parmesan cheese
    ½   teaspoon ground red pepper
    ½   teaspoon black pepper

1. Preheat oven to 350°.
2. Lightly coat each tortilla with cooking spray; cut each into 4 wedges. Combine cheese and peppers in a small bowl; sprinkle over tortilla wedges. Arrange wedges in a single layer on a baking sheet. Bake at 350° for 10 minutes or until lightly browned. Yield: 4 dozen chips (serving size: 4 chips).

CALORIES 112 (27% from fat); FAT 3.4g (sat 1g, mono 1.4g, poly 0.5g); PROTEIN 3g; CARB 16.7g; FIBER 1.1g; CHOL 1mg; IRON 1.1mg; SODIUM 229mg; CALC 60mg

Cookies and Coffee Cakes

Here are our favorite cookie and coffee cake recipes that make great holiday gifts. Check out more cookie recipes in the desserts chapter (beginning on page 336).

Black-and-White Cake Cookies
(pictured at right)

Package these cakelike cookies in an antique cookie jar or holiday tin.

Cookies:

1½	cups all-purpose flour
1½	teaspoons baking powder
½	teaspoon salt
⅔	cup applesauce
1	cup granulated sugar
¼	cup butter, softened
1½	teaspoons vanilla extract
2	large egg whites

Frosting:

1½	cups powdered sugar, divided
3	tablespoons 2% reduced-fat milk, divided
¼	teaspoon almond extract
2	tablespoons unsweetened cocoa

1. Preheat oven to 375°.
2. To prepare cookies, lightly spoon flour into dry measuring cups; level with a knife. Combine flour, baking powder, and salt, stirring with a whisk.
3. Place applesauce in a fine sieve; let stand 15 minutes.
4. Combine drained applesauce, granulated sugar, and butter in a large bowl; beat with a mixer at medium speed 2 minutes or until well blended. Beat in vanilla and egg whites. Add flour mixture; beat at low speed until blended.
5. Drop dough by level tablespoons 2 inches apart onto parchment-lined baking sheets. Bake at 375° for 10 minutes or until set (not browned). Cool on pans 2 minutes or until firm. Remove from pans; cool completely on wire racks.
6. To prepare frosting, combine ¾ cup powdered sugar, 1 tablespoon milk, and almond extract in a bowl, stirring well with a whisk until smooth. Working with 1 cookie at a time, hold cookie over bowl, and spread about 1 teaspoon white frosting over half of cookie (scrape excess frosting from edges). Let stand 10 minutes or until frosting is set.
7. Combine ¾ cup powdered sugar and cocoa in a bowl.

Gradually add 2 tablespoons milk; stir with a whisk until smooth. Hold 1 cookie over bowl; spread about 1 teaspoon chocolate frosting over other half of cookie (scrape excess frosting from edges). Repeat procedure. Let stand 10 minutes or until frosting is set. Yield: 2 dozen (serving size: 1 cookie).

CALORIES 106 (17% from fat); FAT 2g (sat 1.2g, mono 0.6g, poly 0.1g); PROTEIN 1.3g; CARB 21.4g; FIBER 0.4g; CHOL 5mg; IRON 0.4mg; SODIUM 100mg; CALC 14mg

Oatmeal-Raisin Cookies

¾	cup packed brown sugar
6	tablespoons butter, softened
¼	cup granulated sugar
1	large egg
6	tablespoons fat-free milk
1	teaspoon vanilla extract
1½	cups all-purpose flour
¾	teaspoon baking soda
½	teaspoon ground cinnamon
¼	teaspoon salt
¼	teaspoon ground nutmeg
1½	cups quick-cooking oats
¾	cup raisins
	Cooking spray

1. Preheat oven to 375°.
2. Place first 3 ingredients in a bowl; beat with a mixer at medium speed until light and fluffy. Add egg, and beat well. Add milk and vanilla extract; beat well.
3. Lightly spoon flour into dry measuring cups; level with a knife. Combine flour and next 4 ingredients; gradually add to creamed mixture, beating well. Stir in oats and raisins.
4. Drop dough by rounded tablespoonfuls onto baking sheets coated with cooking spray. Bake at 375° for 9 minutes or until lightly browned. Cool on wire racks. Yield: 4 dozen (serving size: 1 cookie).

CALORIES 63 (26% from fat); FAT 1.8g (sat 1g, mono 0.5g, poly 0.1g); PROTEIN 1g; CARB 11g; FIBER 0.5g; CHOL 8mg; IRON 0.5mg; SODIUM 46mg; CALC 9mg

Alaska Molasses
Cookies, page 108

Black-and-White
Cake Cookies

Double Chocolate
Cookies, page 109

Chocolate Chip
Meringues, page 112

Alaska Molasses Cookies
(pictured on page 107)

For gift-giving, package cookies in a colorful bag accented with a beautiful bow.

½ cup applesauce
1¼ cups sugar, divided
6 tablespoons butter, softened
¼ cup dark molasses
1 large egg
1 cup all-purpose flour
1 cup whole wheat pastry flour
2 teaspoons baking soda
1 teaspoon ground cinnamon
½ teaspoon salt
½ teaspoon ground ginger
½ teaspoon ground cloves
Cooking spray

1. Spoon applesauce onto several layers of heavy-duty paper towels; spread to ½-inch thickness. Cover with additional paper towels; let stand 5 minutes. Scrape into a bowl using a rubber spatula.
2. Combine applesauce, 1 cup sugar, and butter; beat with a mixer at medium speed until well blended (about 3 minutes). Add molasses and egg; beat well.
3. Lightly spoon flours into dry measuring cups; level with a knife. Combine flours and next 5 ingredients, stirring well with a whisk. Gradually add flour mixture to sugar mixture, beating

until blended. Cover and freeze dough 30 minutes or until firm.
4. Preheat oven to 375°.
5. With moist hands, shape dough into 32 (1-inch) balls. Roll balls in ¼ cup sugar. Place 3 inches apart on baking sheets coated with cooking spray. Bake at 375° for 8 to 10 minutes. Cool on pans 5 minutes. Remove from pans; cool completely on wire racks. Yield: 32 cookies (serving size: 1 cookie).

CALORIES 88 (25% from fat); FAT 2.4g (sat 1.4g, mono 0.7g, poly 0.1g); PROTEIN 1.2g; CARB 16g; FIBER 0.7g; CHOL 12mg; IRON 0.7mg; SODIUM 141mg; CALC 16mg

Spicy Oatmeal Crisps
(pictured on page 99)

Pepper may sound like an odd ingredient for a cookie, but it complements the other spices well. Wrap the cookies in a gift box. For an easy way to package an assortment of cookies in the same gift box, divide the cookies into stacks that are the appropriate height for your gift box. Tie stacks with colorful string before placing in box.

¾ cup all-purpose flour
1 teaspoon ground cinnamon
½ teaspoon baking soda
½ teaspoon ground allspice
½ teaspoon grated whole nutmeg
¼ teaspoon salt
¼ teaspoon ground cloves
¼ teaspoon freshly ground black pepper (optional)
1 cup packed brown sugar
5 tablespoons butter, softened
1 teaspoon vanilla extract
1 large egg
½ cup regular oats
Cooking spray

1. Preheat oven to 350°.
2. Lightly spoon flour into dry measuring cups; level with a knife. Combine flour, next 6 ingredients, and pepper, if desired, in a medium bowl. Beat sugar, butter, and vanilla in a large bowl with a mixer at medium speed until light and fluffy. Add egg; beat well. Stir in flour mixture and oats.
3. Drop by level tablespoons 2 inches apart onto baking sheets coated with cooking spray. Bake at 350° for 12 minutes or until crisp. Cool on pan 2 to 3 minutes or until firm. Remove cookies from pan, and cool on wire racks. Yield: 2 dozen (serving size: 1 cookie).

CALORIES 81 (34% from fat); FAT 3.1g (sat 1.7g, mono 0.9g, poly 0.3g); PROTEIN 1.5g; CARB 12.2g; FIBER 0.7g; CHOL 15mg; IRON 0.6mg; SODIUM 71mg; CALC 12mg

Ginger Shortbread
(pictured on cover)

Though it's lightened, this traditional-style wedge-shaped shortbread has all of the buttery flavor and tender flaky texture of the original. For more pronounced ginger flavor, increase the ground ginger by $1/2$ teaspoon. For a plain version, leave out both the ground and the crystallized ginger. Place in a cookie tin with other assorted cookies for a perfect gift idea.

- $3/4$ cup plus 3 tablespoons sifted cake flour
- $1/4$ cup granulated sugar
- 1 teaspoon ground ginger
- Dash of salt
- 5 tablespoons unsalted butter, softened
- 1 tablespoon ice water
- Cooking spray
- 1 tablespoon turbinado or other coarse sugar
- $1/4$ ounce crystallized ginger, cut into 16 thin slices

1. Combine flour, $1/4$ cup sugar, ground ginger, and salt, stirring with a whisk.
2. Place butter in a medium bowl; beat with a mixer at medium speed until smooth (about 1 minute). Add flour mixture; beat at low speed just until combined. Add ice water, and stir just until combined. Press mixture gently into a 4-inch circle on plastic wrap, and cover with additional plastic wrap. Chill for 20 minutes.
3. Preheat oven to 350°.
4. Slightly overlap 2 sheets of plastic wrap on a slightly damp surface. Unwrap chilled dough and place on plastic wrap. Cover dough with 2 additional sheets of overlapping plastic wrap. Roll dough, still covered, into an 8-inch circle (edges of circle will crack slightly). Remove top sheets of plastic wrap, and fit dough, plastic wrap side up, onto a baking sheet coated with cooking spray. Remove remaining plastic wrap.
5. Sprinkle the dough with 1 tablespoon coarse sugar, and press gently to help sugar adhere to dough. Lightly score the dough into 16 wedges, cutting into, but not through, dough. Place 1 piece of the crystallized ginger in each wedge, and press gently to help adhere.
6. Bake at 350° for 25 minutes or until light gold in color.

Remove from oven; cool 5 minutes. Cut through score lines to make 16 wedges. Place on a wire rack; cool completely. Yield: 16 cookies (serving size: 1 cookie).

CALORIES 77 (42% from fat); FAT 3.6g (sat 2.3g, mono 0.9g, poly 0.2g); PROTEIN 0.7g; CARB 10.7g; FIBER 0.2g; CHOL 9mg; IRON 0.6mg; SODIUM 10mg; CALC 3mg

Double Chocolate Cookies
(pictured on page 107)

White chocolate chips and dried cherries add a special holiday touch to these yummy treats. You can use dried cranberries if you prefer. A small enamel or galvanized bucket makes a terrific gift container. Line with a colorful napkin or tissue paper. Tie a bow on the handle.

- $1 1/4$ cups all-purpose flour
- $1/2$ teaspoon baking powder
- $1/4$ teaspoon salt
- 5 tablespoons butter, softened
- $1/2$ cup granulated sugar
- $1/2$ cup packed brown sugar
- $1 1/2$ teaspoons vanilla extract
- 1 large egg white
- $1/3$ cup dried tart cherries
- $1/4$ cup semisweet chocolate chunks
- $2 1/2$ tablespoons premium white chocolate chips
- Cooking spray

1. Preheat oven to 350°.
2. Lightly spoon flour into dry measuring cups; level with a knife. Combine flour, baking powder, and salt, stirring with a whisk.
3. Combine butter and sugars in a large bowl; beat with a mixer at medium speed until well blended. Add vanilla and egg white; beat 1 minute. Stir in flour mixture, cherries, chocolate chunks, and chocolate chips.
4. Drop by level tablespoons 2 inches apart onto baking sheets coated with cooking spray. Place pans in freezer 5 minutes. Bake at 350° for 10 minutes or until lightly browned. Cool on pans 2 minutes. Remove from pans; cool completely on wire racks. Yield: 2 dozen (serving size: 1 cookie).

CALORIES 98 (30% from fat); FAT 3.3g (sat 2g, mono 1g, poly 0.1g); PROTEIN 1g; CARB 16.6g; FIBER 0.4g; CHOL 7mg; IRON 0.5mg; SODIUM 63mg; CALC 12mg

For a chocolaty gift anyone would love, package Double Chocolate Cookies in a tin with other chocolate favorites such as Black-and-White Cake Cookies (recipe on page 106) and Chocolate Chip Meringues (recipe on page 112).

Macadamia Butter Cookies with Dried Cranberries

The dough is somewhat sticky; chilling it briefly makes handling easier. Wrap stacks of cookies in cellophane bags, and tie with colorful ribbon. Give the stacks individually, or place a few in a small basket.

⅔ cup macadamia nuts
½ cup granulated sugar
½ cup packed light brown sugar
1 teaspoon vanilla extract
1 large egg
1¼ cups all-purpose flour
½ teaspoon baking soda
¼ teaspoon salt
⅛ teaspoon ground nutmeg
½ cup sweetened dried cranberries, chopped
1 tablespoon granulated sugar

1. Preheat oven to 375°.
2. Place nuts in a food processor; process until smooth (about 2 minutes), scraping sides of bowl once. Combine macadamia butter, ½ cup granulated sugar, and brown sugar in a large bowl; beat with a mixer at medium speed. Add vanilla and egg, and beat well.
3. Lightly spoon flour into dry measuring cups; level with a knife. Combine flour, baking soda, salt, and nutmeg, stirring with a whisk. Add flour mixture to sugar mixture; beat at low speed just until combined (mixture will be very thick). Stir in cranberries. Chill 10 minutes.
4. Divide chilled dough into 30 equal portions; roll each portion into a ball. Place 1 tablespoon granulated sugar in a small bowl. Lightly press each ball into sugar. Place 15 balls, sugar side up, on each of 2 baking sheets covered with parchment paper.
5. Gently press top of each cookie with a fork. Dip fork in water; gently press top of each cookie again to form a criss-cross pattern.
6. Bake cookies, 1 baking sheet at a time, at 375° for 9 minutes or until golden. Remove cookies from pans; cool on wire racks. Yield: 30 cookies (serving size: 1 cookie).

CALORIES 76 (30% from fat); FAT 2.5g (sat 0.4g, mono 1.8g, poly 0.1g); PROTEIN 1g; CARB 13.2g; FIBER 0.6g; CHOL 7mg; IRON 0.5mg; SODIUM 44mg; CALC 7mg

Macadamia Butter Cookies with Dried Cranberries

Raspberry Strippers

Think of these as a variation of thumbprint cookies. Vanilla butter cookies are filled with fruit preserves and drizzled with a powdered sugar glaze. You may substitute other preserves, such as apricot, if desired. Arrange the colorful treats in a single layer on a festive platter, and take to a friend.

⅓ cup granulated sugar
5 tablespoons butter, softened
1½ teaspoons vanilla extract
1 large egg white
1 cup all-purpose flour
2 tablespoons cornstarch
¼ teaspoon baking powder
¼ teaspoon salt
Cooking spray
⅓ cup raspberry or apricot preserves
½ cup powdered sugar
2 teaspoons fresh lemon juice
¼ teaspoon almond or vanilla extract

1. Preheat oven to 375°.
2. Beat granulated sugar and butter with a mixer at medium speed until well blended (about 5 minutes). Add 1½ teaspoons vanilla and egg white; beat well. Lightly spoon flour into a dry measuring cup; level with a knife. Combine flour, cornstarch, baking powder, and salt, stirring well with a whisk. Add flour mixture to sugar mixture, stirring until well blended (dough will be stiff).

3. Turn dough out onto a lightly floured surface; divide in half. Roll each portion into a 12-inch log. Place logs 3 inches apart on a baking sheet coated with cooking spray. Form a ½-inch-deep indentation down length of each log using an index finger or end of a wooden spoon. Spoon preserves into indentation. Bake at 375° for 20 minutes or until lightly browned. Remove to a cutting board.

4. Combine powdered sugar, lemon juice, and almond extract; stir well with a whisk. Drizzle mixture over warm logs. Immediately cut each log diagonally into 12 slices. (Do not separate slices.) Cool 10 minutes; separate slices. Transfer slices to wire racks. Cool completely. Yield: 2 dozen (serving size: 1 cookie).

Note: Storing these cookies in a single layer ensures that their icing stays intact.

CALORIES 75 (30% from fat); FAT 2.5g (sat 1.5g, mono 0.7g, poly 0.2g); PROTEIN 0.7g; CARB 12.4g; FIBER 0.2g; CHOL 6mg; IRON 0.3mg; SODIUM 56mg; CALC 4mg

Christmas Sugar Wafers with Vanilla Icing
(pictured on cover)

Place in a holiday tin with other assorted cookies for gift-giving. Be sure the vanilla icing is dry before stacking.

Cookies:

  6 tablespoons granulated sugar
  ¼ cup butter
  2 tablespoons dark brown sugar
1½ teaspoons vanilla extract
  2 large egg whites
1½ cups all-purpose flour
  3 tablespoons cornstarch
  ½ teaspoon baking powder
  ¼ teaspoon baking soda
  ¼ teaspoon salt
    Cooking spray

Vanilla Icing:

  1 cup powdered sugar
  2 teaspoons warm water
  1 teaspoon light-colored corn syrup
  ¼ teaspoon vanilla extract
    Dash of salt

1. Preheat oven to 375°.

2. To prepare cookies, place first 3 ingredients in a large bowl; beat with a mixer at medium speed until well blended (about 5 minutes). Beat in 1½ teaspoons vanilla. Add egg whites, 1 at a time, beating well after each addition.

3. Lightly spoon flour into dry measuring cups; level with a knife. Combine flour and next 4 ingredients, stirring well with a whisk. Add to butter mixture; beat well. Turn dough out onto a lightly floured surface (dough will be soft). Divide dough into 4 equal portions. Roll each portion into an 8-inch circle between 2 sheets of plastic wrap. Freeze dough 20 minutes or until plastic wrap can be easily removed.

4. Working with 1 portion of dough at a time (keep remaining dough in freezer), remove top sheet of plastic wrap. Cut dough with a 3-inch cookie cutter, dipping cutter in flour before each use; place cookies on baking sheets coated with cooking spray. Discard bottom sheet of plastic wrap; reserve remaining dough scraps. Repeat procedure with remaining frozen dough.

5. Gently gather reserved dough into a ball; repeat rolling, freezing, and cutting procedure.

6. Bake at 375° for 8 minutes or until cookies are lightly browned. Remove from baking sheet; cool on a wire rack.

7. To prepare icing, combine powdered sugar and remaining 4 ingredients in a small bowl; stir with a fork until combined. Drizzle icing over cookies, or spoon icing into a small heavy-duty zip-top plastic bag; cut a tiny hole in 1 corner of bag, and pipe designs onto cookies. Yield: 2 dozen (serving size: 1 cookie).

CALORIES 94 (22% from fat); FAT 2.3g (sat 1.4g, mono 0.6g, poly 0.3g); PROTEIN 0.1g; CARB 17.9g; FIBER 0.3g; CHOL 5mg; IRON 0.4mg; SODIUM 75mg; CALC 5mg

Christmas Sugar Wafers
with Vanilla Icing

Chocolate Chip Meringues
(pictured on page 107)

These cookies will keep for a week in an airtight container. Just trim the container with some raffia or ribbon, and you've got a nice holiday gift.

   3   large egg whites
  ¼   teaspoon cream of tartar
  ⅛   teaspoon salt
  ¾   cup sugar
  ¼   cup unsweetened cocoa, divided
  ½   cup semisweet chocolate minichips
  ¼   teaspoon vanilla extract

1. Preheat oven to 250°.
2. Cover a baking sheet with parchment paper; secure with masking tape.
3. Place egg whites, cream of tartar, and salt in a large bowl; beat with a mixer at high speed until foamy. Combine sugar and 3 tablespoons cocoa, stirring with a whisk. Gradually add sugar mixture to egg white mixture, 1 tablespoon at a time, beating at medium speed until stiff peaks form. Gently fold in minichips and vanilla.
4. Spoon mixture into a pastry bag fitted with a ½-inch round tip, or a large zip-top plastic bag with 1 corner snipped to form a ½-inch opening. Pipe 30 (2-inch-round) mounds ¼ inch apart onto prepared baking sheet. Bake at 250° for 1½ hours.
5. Turn oven off; cool meringues in closed oven 1 hour. Carefully remove meringues from paper. Using a fine sieve, dust meringues with 1 tablespoon cocoa. Yield: 30 cookies (serving size: 1 cookie).

CALORIES 26 (42% from fat); FAT 1.2g (sat 0.7g, mono 0.1g, poly 0.1g); PROTEIN 0.7g; CARB 3.1g; FIBER 0.2g; CHOL 0mg; IRON 0.2mg; SODIUM 15mg; CALC 3mg

Chocolate-Toffee Puffs

Package this candy in tissue paper–lined gift bags with holiday trim.

   4   large egg whites
  ⅓   cup granulated sugar
  1   cup sifted powdered sugar
  ½   cup unsweetened cocoa
  2   (1.4-ounce) chocolate-covered toffee bars (such as Heath), crushed
Cooking spray

1. Preheat oven to 350°.
2. Beat egg whites in a large bowl with a mixer at high speed until soft peaks form. Gradually add granulated sugar, beating egg whites until stiff peaks form.
3. Combine powdered sugar, cocoa, and crushed candy in a small bowl, and mix well. Fold half of cocoa mixture into egg whites (egg whites will deflate quickly). Fold in remaining cocoa mixture until smooth. Drop egg mixture by rounded tablespoonfuls onto a baking sheet coated with cooking spray. Bake at 350° for 15 minutes (puffs will be soft in center). Yield: 2 dozen (serving size: 1 cookie).

CALORIES 52 (24% from fat); FAT 1.4g (sat 0.9g, mono 0.5g, poly 0.1g); PROTEIN 1.1g; CARB 9.9g; FIBER 0.7g; CHOL 1.7mg; IRON 0.3mg; SODIUM 19mg; CALC 7mg

Gingerbread Squares

Place these moist gingerbread squares in a parchment paper–lined gift box.

1¼   cups all-purpose flour
  1   teaspoon ground ginger
  1   teaspoon ground cinnamon
  ½   teaspoon baking soda
  ½   cup granulated sugar
  ½   cup low-fat buttermilk
  ½   cup molasses
  ⅓   cup butter, melted
  1   large egg, lightly beaten
Cooking spray
  1   tablespoon powdered sugar

1. Preheat oven to 350°.
2. Lightly spoon flour into dry measuring cups; level with a knife. Combine flour, ginger, cinnamon, and baking soda, stirring with a whisk.
3. Combine granulated sugar and the next 4 ingredients in a large bowl, stirring mixture with a whisk. Stir in flour mixture. Pour the batter into a 9-inch square baking pan coated with cooking spray.
4. Bake at 350° for 25 minutes or until a wooden pick inserted in center comes out clean. Cool in pan on a wire rack. Sprinkle gingerbread with powdered sugar. Yield: 25 servings (serving size: 1 [1¾-inch] square).

CALORIES 84 (30% from fat); FAT 2.8g (sat 1.6g, mono 0.8g, poly 0.2g); PROTEIN 1.1g; CARB 14g; FIBER 0.2g; CHOL 15mg; IRON 0.7mg; SODIUM 61mg; CALC 22mg

Caramel Cloud Bars

These bar cookies are nothing short of heavenly. Find fun-shaped boxes at any craft store to package the bars in style.

Cooking spray
1 tablespoon all-purpose flour
1½ cups sugar
¼ cup light butter, melted
¼ cup evaporated fat-free milk
4 large egg whites
2 cups all-purpose flour
¼ teaspoon salt
¼ teaspoon baking soda
⅔ cup premium white chocolate chips
½ cup chopped macadamia nuts
½ cup caramel sundae syrup

1. Preheat oven to 350°.
2. Coat a 13 x 9-inch baking pan with cooking spray; dust with 1 tablespoon flour.
3. Place sugar, butter, evaporated milk, and egg whites in a large bowl, and beat with a mixer at medium speed 1 minute. Lightly spoon 2 cups flour into dry measuring cups, and level with a knife. Combine 2 cups flour, salt, and baking soda in a small bowl, stirring well with a whisk. Gradually add flour mixture to sugar mixture, and beat with a mixer at low speed just until blended. Stir in chips and macadamia nuts.
4. Spoon batter into prepared pan. Microwave syrup at HIGH 45 seconds or until warm; stir. Drizzle caramel syrup diagonally across batter. Bake at 350° for 30 minutes or until a wooden pick inserted in center comes out clean. Cool. Yield: 2 dozen (serving size: 1 bar).

CALORIES 171 (30% from fat); FAT 5.7g (sat 2.5g, mono 2.6g, poly 0.2g); PROTEIN 2.6g; CARB 28.4g; FIBER 0.5g; CHOL 5mg; IRON 0.6mg; SODIUM 91mg; CALC 22mg

Lemon-Ginger Biscotti

Lemon-Ginger Biscotti

2½ cups all-purpose flour
1 cup sugar
1 teaspoon baking soda
½ teaspoon ground ginger
¼ teaspoon salt
¼ cup finely chopped crystallized ginger
2 tablespoons grated lemon rind
1 tablespoon fresh lemon juice
3 large eggs, lightly beaten
Cooking spray
1 tablespoon water
1 large egg white, lightly beaten
1 tablespoon sugar

1. Preheat oven to 350°.
2. Lightly spoon flour into dry measuring cups; level with a knife. Combine flour and next 4 ingredients in a large bowl, stirring with a whisk. Stir in crystallized ginger. Combine rind, juice, and 3 eggs; add to flour mixture, stirring until well blended (dough will be crumbly). Turn dough out onto a lightly floured surface; knead lightly 7 or 8 times. Divide dough in half. Shape each portion into a 9-inch-long roll. Place rolls 6 inches apart on a baking sheet coated with cooking spray; flatten each roll to a 1-inch thickness. Combine water and egg white; brush over rolls. Sprinkle rolls evenly with 1 tablespoon sugar.
3. Bake at 350° for 20 minutes. Remove rolls from baking sheet; cool 10 minutes on a wire rack. Cut each roll diagonally into 15 (¾-inch) slices. Carefully stand slices upright on baking sheet. Reduce oven temperature to 325°; bake 20 minutes (cookies will be slightly soft in center but will harden as they cool). Remove from baking sheet; cool completely on a wire rack. Yield: 30 biscotti (serving size: 1 biscotto).

CALORIES 77 (7% from fat); FAT 0.6g (sat 0.2g, mono 0.2g, poly 0.1g); PROTEIN 1.8g; CARB 16.1g; FIBER 0.3g; CHOL 21mg; IRON 0.6mg; SODIUM 70mg; CALC 6mg

Caramel Cloud Bars

White Chocolate-Cashew Coffee Biscotti
(pictured on cover)

To present as a gift, wrap biscotti in cellophane tied with ribbon, and place in a cheery holiday mug.

- ½ cup granulated sugar
- ½ cup packed brown sugar
- 2 tablespoons butter, softened
- 1 teaspoon vanilla extract
- 2 large eggs
- 1 large egg white
- 2½ cups all-purpose flour
- ¼ cup instant coffee granules
- 3 tablespoons unsweetened cocoa
- 1 teaspoon baking soda
- ½ teaspoon ground cinnamon
- ¼ teaspoon salt
- ⅛ teaspoon ground nutmeg
- ¾ cup dry-roasted cashews, coarsely chopped
- Cooking spray
- 1 tablespoon granulated sugar
- 3 ounces premium white chocolate, chopped

1. Preheat oven to 350°.
2. Place first 6 ingredients in a large bowl, and beat with a mixer at medium speed until well blended.
3. Lightly spoon flour into dry measuring cups; level with a knife. Combine flour and next 6 ingredients; gradually add to sugar mixture, beating until well blended. Stir in cashews. Turn dough out onto a lightly floured surface; knead lightly 7 times. Divide dough in half. Shape each portion into a 12-inch-long roll. Place rolls on a baking sheet coated with cooking spray; pat to ¾-inch thickness. Sprinkle rolls evenly with 1 tablespoon granulated sugar.
4. Bake at 350° for 22 minutes. Remove rolls from baking sheet; cool 10 minutes on a wire rack. Cut each roll diagonally into 21 (½-inch) slices. Carefully stand slices upright on baking sheet. Reduce oven temperature to 325°; bake 20 minutes (cookies will be slightly soft in center but will harden as they cool). Remove from baking sheet, and cool completely on wire rack.
5. Place chocolate in a small heavy-duty zip-top plastic bag; microwave at HIGH 1 minute or until chocolate is soft. Knead bag until smooth. Snip a tiny hole in 1 corner of bag; drizzle chocolate over biscotti. Yield: 30 biscotti (serving size: 1 biscotto).

CALORIES 83 (30% from fat); FAT 2.8g (sat 1.1g, mono 0.9g, poly 0.3g); PROTEIN 1.8g; CARB 13g; FIBER 0.4g; CHOL 12mg; IRON 0.7mg; SODIUM 56mg; CALC 13mg

Orange-Pistachio Baklava

Our variation of this Lebanese classic has half the fat of the original. To create a holiday gift, place each slice of baklava in a foil-covered paper muffin cup liner, and arrange in a sturdy white gift box with a cellophane window that hints of the sweets inside.

- Butter-flavored cooking spray
- 1¼ cups chopped pistachios
- ¾ cup wheat saltine cracker crumbs (about 20 crackers)
- ⅓ cup sugar
- ½ teaspoon ground cinnamon
- 12 sheets frozen phyllo pastry, thawed
- 2 tablespoons butter, melted
- ¾ cup honey
- ½ cup thawed orange juice concentrate, undiluted
- ⅓ cup water
- 1 teaspoon ground cinnamon
- ⅛ teaspoon ground cloves

1. Coat a 13 x 9-inch baking pan with cooking spray; set aside. Combine pistachios, cracker crumbs, sugar, and ½ teaspoon cinnamon in a bowl; set aside.
2. Working with 1 phyllo sheet at a time, lightly coat each sheet with cooking spray. Fold phyllo sheet in half crosswise to form a 13 x 8½-inch rectangle; lightly coat both sides of rectangle with cooking spray. Place in bottom of prepared pan, and sprinkle 3 tablespoons pistachio mixture over phyllo. Repeat procedure with 9 sheets of phyllo, cooking spray, and remaining pistachio mixture, ending with pistachio mixture.
3. Lightly coat remaining 2 sheets of phyllo with cooking spray. Fold each sheet in half crosswise to form a 13 x 8½-inch rectangle; lightly coat both sides of each rectangle with cooking spray. Layer each into baking pan.
4. Preheat oven to 350°. With a very sharp knife, score diamond shapes, ¾ inch deep, into layers of phyllo. Drizzle butter over phyllo. Bake at 350° for 25 minutes or until golden.
5. Combine honey and next 4 ingredients in a small saucepan; bring to a boil. Reduce heat; simmer, uncovered, 5 minutes, stirring frequently. Remove from heat; drizzle honey mixture over phyllo. Cool completely in pan. With a sharp knife, cut completely through layers of phyllo (following the original score lines) to form diamond shapes. Yield: 16 servings (serving size: 1 [3¼ x 2¼-inch] piece).

CALORIES 210 (33% from fat); FAT 7.8g (sat 1.9g, mono 3.4g, poly 1.6g); PROTEIN 3.7g; CARB 33.4g; FIBER 1.7g; CHOL 4mg; IRON 1.2mg; SODIUM 113mg; CALC 20mg

Banana Coffee Cake
with Macadamia
Nuts and Coconut

Banana Coffee Cake with Macadamia Nuts and Coconut

Substitute pecans if you don't have macadamia nuts. This gift is best delivered warm from the oven with nothing more than a simple cake stand.

Cooking spray
1⅓ cups all-purpose flour
½ teaspoon salt
½ teaspoon baking powder
¼ teaspoon baking soda
1 cup mashed ripe banana (about 2 large bananas)
¾ cup granulated sugar
3 tablespoons vegetable oil
1 teaspoon vanilla extract
¼ teaspoon ground nutmeg
1 large egg
¼ cup packed dark brown sugar
1 tablespoon water
2 teaspoons butter
2 tablespoons chopped macadamia nuts, toasted
2 tablespoons flaked sweetened coconut

1. Preheat oven to 350°.
2. Coat a 9-inch round cake pan with cooking spray; line bottom of pan with wax paper. Coat wax paper with cooking spray.
3. Lightly spoon flour into dry measuring cups, and level with a knife. Combine flour, salt, baking powder, and baking soda in a bowl, stirring with a whisk. Combine banana and next 5 ingredients in a bowl; beat with a mixer at medium speed 1 minute or until well blended. Add flour mixture to banana mixture, and beat until blended. Pour batter into prepared cake pan.
4. Bake at 350° for 30 minutes or until a wooden pick inserted in center comes out clean. Cool in pan 10 minutes on a wire rack; remove from pan. Carefully peel off wax paper.
5. Combine brown sugar, water, and butter in a small saucepan; bring to a boil. Cook 1 minute, stirring constantly. Remove from heat; stir in nuts and coconut. Spread over cake. Serve cake warm. Yield: 12 servings (serving size: 1 wedge).

CALORIES 189 (28% from fat); FAT 5.8g (sat 1.4g, mono 1.9g, poly 2.1g); PROTEIN 2.3g; CARB 32.6g; FIBER 1g; CHOL 19mg; IRON 0.9mg; SODIUM 159mg; CALC 22mg

Apple Cake with Almonds

We tested this dish with Braeburn apples, but Granny Smith will also work. Present the gift on a plate. An ornament makes a great gift tag.

    5 tablespoons butter, divided
    2 cups chopped peeled cooking apple
 1½ cups all-purpose flour
 1½ teaspoons baking powder
  ⅛ teaspoon salt
    1 cup granulated sugar
  ½ cup (4 ounces) block-style fat-free cream cheese
 1¼ teaspoons vanilla extract, divided
  ½ teaspoon almond extract
  ½ cup 1% low-fat milk
    1 large egg, lightly beaten
    1 large egg white, lightly beaten
  Cooking spray
    2 tablespoons sliced almonds, toasted
  ⅓ cup sifted powdered sugar
    2 teaspoons water

1. Preheat oven to 350°.

2. Melt 1 tablespoon butter in a large nonstick skillet over medium-high heat. Add apple, and cook 5 minutes or until apple is tender.

3. Lightly spoon flour into dry measuring cups; level with a knife. Combine flour, baking powder, and salt in a bowl, stirring with a whisk. Combine ¼ cup butter, granulated sugar, cream cheese, 1 teaspoon vanilla, and almond extract in a large bowl; beat with a mixer at medium speed until blended.

4. Combine milk, egg, and egg white. Add flour mixture and milk mixture alternately to cream cheese mixture, beginning and ending with flour mixture. Stir in apple. Pour batter into a 9-inch round cake pan coated with cooking spray. Sprinkle with almonds.

5. Bake at 350° for 55 minutes or until a wooden pick inserted in center comes out clean. Cool in pan 10 minutes on a wire rack; remove from pan.

6. Combine ¼ teaspoon vanilla, powdered sugar, and water in a small bowl. Drizzle over cake. Serve cake warm or at room temperature. Yield: 12 servings (serving size: 1 wedge).

CALORIES 225 (25% from fat); FAT 6.2g (sat 3.4g, mono 2g, poly 0.5g); PROTEIN 4.4g; CARB 38.5g; FIBER 1.3g; CHOL 32mg; IRON 1mg; SODIUM 201mg; CALC 74mg

Blueberry Buckle with Walnuts and Ginger

In a buckle, fruit is baked into a streusel-topped cake. The subtle bite of fresh ginger adds a tangy freshness and light spiciness to the batter.

Crumbs:
    2 tablespoons all-purpose flour
    2 tablespoons brown sugar
  ⅛ teaspoon ground cinnamon
    1 tablespoon butter
    2 tablespoons chopped walnuts, toasted
Cake:
 1¼ cups all-purpose flour
 1¼ teaspoons baking powder
  ⅛ teaspoon salt
  ½ cup granulated sugar
  ⅓ cup packed brown sugar
 3½ tablespoons butter, softened
 1½ teaspoons grated peeled fresh ginger
    1 teaspoon vanilla extract
    1 large egg
  ½ cup 1% low-fat milk
  Cooking spray
    2 cups frozen blueberries
 1½ teaspoons powdered sugar

1. Preheat oven to 350°.

2. To prepare crumbs, combine first 3 ingredients in a small bowl; cut in 1 tablespoon butter with a pastry blender or 2 knives until mixture resembles coarse meal. Stir in walnuts.

3. To prepare cake, lightly spoon 1¼ cups flour into dry measuring cups; level with a knife. Combine 1¼ cups flour, baking powder, and salt in a bowl, stirring with a whisk. Combine granulated sugar and next 5 ingredients in a large bowl; beat with a mixer at medium speed until well blended. Add flour mixture and milk alternately to butter mixture, beginning and ending with flour mixture.

4. Pour batter into a 9-inch round cake pan coated with cooking spray. Sprinkle with blueberries and crumbs. Bake at 350° for 1 hour or until a wooden pick inserted in center comes out clean. Cool in pan 10 minutes on a wire rack; remove from pan. Sift powdered sugar over cake. Serve cake warm or at room temperature. Yield: 12 servings (serving size: 1 wedge).

CALORIES 189 (29% from fat); FAT 6g (sat 3g, mono 1.6g, poly 0.9g); PROTEIN 2.7g; CARB 31.8g; FIBER 1.2g; CHOL 30mg; IRON 1mg; SODIUM 134mg; CALC 57mg

Coffee cakes make the perfect home-baked gift to share with friends and neighbors at any time of the year.

Cranberry-Hazelnut Coffee Cake

Streusel:
- ¼ cup sifted cake flour
- ¼ cup packed brown sugar
- ¼ cup chopped hazelnuts
- ½ teaspoon ground cinnamon
- 1 tablespoon butter, melted

Cake:
- 1⅔ cups sifted cake flour
- 1 cup granulated sugar
- 1½ teaspoons baking powder
- ¼ teaspoon baking soda
- ¼ teaspoon salt
- 1 teaspoon vanilla extract
- 1 (8-ounce) carton fat-free sour cream, divided
- 1 large egg
- 1 large egg white
- 5 tablespoons butter, softened

Remaining Ingredients:
- Cooking spray
- 2 cups fresh cranberries, chopped

1. Preheat oven to 350°.

2. To prepare streusel, combine first 5 ingredients in a bowl, and toss well. Set aside.

3. To prepare cake, combine 1⅔ cups flour and next 4 ingredients, stirring well with a whisk. Combine vanilla, ¼ cup sour cream, egg, and egg white in a small bowl; stir with a whisk. Place remaining sour cream and 5 tablespoons butter in a large bowl; beat at medium speed of a mixer until well blended (about 2 minutes). Add flour mixture to butter mixture alternately with egg mixture, beginning and ending with flour mixture.

4. Spread half of batter into a 9-inch springform pan coated

with cooking spray. Sprinkle cranberries over batter. Spread remaining batter over cranberries. Sprinkle streusel mixture over batter. Bake at 350° for 45 minutes or until a wooden pick inserted in center comes out clean. Cool on a wire rack. Yield: 10 servings (serving size: 1 wedge).

CALORIES 293 (30% from fat); FAT 9.8g (sat 4.7g, mono 3.9g, poly 0.6g); PROTEIN 4.9g; CARB 46.6g; FIBER 0.4g; CHOL 41mg; IRON 2mg; SODIUM 265mg; CALC 63mg

Cherry-Almond Cake

To give away, place the cake on a clear glass plate. Encircle the sides of the cake with holiday ribbon approximately 1½ inches wide.

- 1 cup all-purpose flour
- 1 teaspoon baking powder
- ⅛ teaspoon salt
- ⅛ teaspoon ground cloves
- ⅔ cup granulated sugar
- 3½ tablespoons butter, softened
- 3 tablespoons fat-free cream cheese
- 2 tablespoons almond paste
- ¼ teaspoon almond extract
- 1 large egg
- ⅓ cup 1% low-fat milk
- Cooking spray
- 2 tablespoons chopped almonds, toasted
- 2 tablespoons granulated sugar
- 1 (14.5-ounce) can pitted tart red cherries in water, drained
- 1 teaspoon powdered sugar

1. Preheat oven to 350°.

2. Lightly spoon flour into a dry measuring cup; level with a knife. Combine flour, baking powder, salt, and cloves in a bowl, stirring with a whisk. Combine ⅔ cup granulated sugar and next 5 ingredients in a large bowl; beat with a mixer at medium speed until blended.

3. Add flour mixture and milk alternately to sugar mixture, beginning and ending with flour mixture. Pour batter into a 9-inch round cake pan coated with cooking spray.

4. Combine almonds and 2 tablespoons granulated sugar; sprinkle over batter. Arrange cherries on top. Bake at 350° for 50 minutes or until a wooden pick inserted in center comes out clean. Cool in pan 10 minutes on a wire rack; remove from pan. Sift powdered sugar over top of cake. Yield: 12 servings (serving size: 1 wedge).

CALORIES 191 (24% from fat); FAT 5.1g (sat 2.4g, mono 1.6g, poly 0.4g); PROTEIN 3.7g; CARB 26.8g; FIBER 1.8g; CHOL 27mg; IRON 2.3mg; SODIUM 137mg; CALC 61mg

Cranberry-Hazelnut Coffee Cake

Loaf Breads and Sweet Rolls

Breads warm the heart and soul throughout the holiday season. Whether for breakfast, lunch, or dinner, they comfort everyone and complete any meal.

Apricot-Amaretto Bread

When giving this bread as a holiday gift, include homemade or store-bought apricot fruit spread.

2¼ cups all-purpose flour
2½ teaspoons baking powder
½ teaspoon baking soda
½ teaspoon salt
½ teaspoon ground allspice
½ cup chopped dried apricots
¼ cup sliced almonds, toasted and divided
¾ cup sugar
¾ cup fat-free milk
¼ cup amaretto (almond-flavored liqueur)
3 tablespoons vegetable oil
½ teaspoon almond extract
1 large egg white
1 large egg
Cooking spray
1 tablespoon sugar

1. Preheat oven to 350°.
2. Lightly spoon flour into dry measuring cups; level with a knife. Combine flour and next 4 ingredients in a large bowl. Stir in apricots and 3 tablespoons almonds; make a well in center of mixture. Combine ¾ cup sugar and next 6 ingredients in a bowl; add to flour mixture, stirring just until moist. Spoon batter into an 8 x 4-inch loaf pan coated with cooking spray. Sprinkle with 1 tablespoon almonds and 1 tablespoon sugar.
3. Bake at 350° for 45 minutes or until a wooden pick inserted in center comes out clean. Cool in pan 10 minutes on a wire rack; remove from pan. Cool completely on wire rack. Yield: 1 loaf, 14 servings (serving size: 1 slice).
Note: For a nonalcoholic version, omit amaretto and increase fat-free milk to 1 cup; add ½ teaspoon almond extract.

CALORIES 188 (22% from fat); FAT 4.5g (sat 0.8g, mono 1.6g, poly 1.7g); PROTEIN 3.8g; CARB 33.7g; FIBER 0.9g; CHOL 16mg; IRON 1.4mg; SODIUM 149mg; CALC 77mg

Pear-and-Poppy Seed Loaf

Wrap up this loaf in a plain piece of wax paper tied with a silver wire ribbon. This bread makes a nice gift for the hostess of a wine and cheese party. Be sure to include a recipe card with these directions for a quick cheese spread: Soften Gorgonzola or blue cheese in the microwave, stir in fat-free plain yogurt, and cool.

2¼ cups all-purpose flour
3 tablespoons poppy seeds
1½ teaspoons baking powder
1 teaspoon baking soda
½ teaspoon salt
⅛ teaspoon ground cardamom
1 cup chopped peeled ripe pear
1 cup low-fat buttermilk
⅔ cup sugar
¼ cup honey
2 tablespoons butter, melted
1 teaspoon vanilla extract
1 large egg
Cooking spray

1. Preheat oven to 350°.
2. Lightly spoon flour into dry measuring cups; level with a knife. Combine flour and next 5 ingredients in a bowl. Stir in pear; make a well in center of mixture. Combine buttermilk and next 5 ingredients in a bowl; stir well with a whisk. Add to flour mixture; stir just until moist. Spoon into an 8 x 4-inch loaf pan coated with cooking spray.
3. Bake at 350° for 1 hour and 5 minutes or until a wooden pick inserted in center comes out clean. Cool in pan 10 minutes on a wire rack; remove from pan. Cool completely on wire rack. Yield: 1 loaf, 14 servings (serving size: 1 slice).

CALORIES 173 (17% from fat); FAT 3.2g (sat 1.4g, mono 0.7g, poly 0.8g); PROTEIN 3.5g; CARB 33.3g; FIBER 1g; CHOL 20mg; IRON 1.3mg; SODIUM 261mg; CALC 83mg

Pear-and-Poppy
Seed Loaf

Bake and transport homemade breads in lightweight recyclable aluminum pans available at most supermarkets. Wrap pans of bread with a large linen napkin. Or place bread in gift bags, and tie with ribbon.

Pumpkin-Orange Spice Loaf

Wrap loaf in plastic wrap, cinch top with festive ribbon, and place decorative stickers around the top and sides. The bread can also be baked in miniature loaf pans for 45 minutes and wrapped as smaller individual gifts.

1½ cups all-purpose flour
½ cup whole wheat flour
2 teaspoons baking powder
½ teaspoon baking soda
1½ teaspoons ground cinnamon
½ teaspoon salt
¼ teaspoon ground ginger
¼ teaspoon ground cloves
1 cup sugar
1 cup canned pumpkin
½ cup fat-free milk
¼ cup butter, softened
1 tablespoon grated orange rind
¼ cup fresh orange juice
1 large egg
Cooking spray

1. Preheat oven to 350°.
2. Lightly spoon flours into dry measuring cups; level with a knife. Combine flours and next 6 ingredients in a large bowl; make a well in center of mixture. Combine sugar and next 6 ingredients in a bowl; stir with a whisk. Add to flour mixture; stir just until moist. Pour batter into an 8 x 4-inch loaf pan coated with cooking spray. Bake at 350° for 1 hour and 10 minutes or until a wooden pick inserted in center comes out clean. Cool in pan 10 minutes on a wire rack; remove from pan. Cool completely on wire rack. Yield: 1 loaf, 12 servings (serving size: 1 slice).

CALORIES 193 (22% from fat); FAT 4.7g (sat 2.6g, mono 1.3g, poly 0.3g); PROTEIN 3.5g; CARB 35.4g; FIBER 2g; CHOL 29mg; IRON 1.5mg; SODIUM 283mg; CALC 76mg

Spicy Pumpkin Bread

If you're tempted to fiddle with the spices (such as substituting pumpkin-pie spice for the allspice, cinnamon, nutmeg, and cloves), think again. We tried it that way in our Test Kitchens, but it wasn't as good. There's just something special about this four-spice combination. Simply wrap loaves with colorful fall-colored ribbon for a beautiful presentation.

3½ cups all-purpose flour
2 teaspoons baking powder
1 teaspoon ground allspice
1 teaspoon ground cinnamon
1 teaspoon ground nutmeg
¾ teaspoon salt
½ teaspoon baking soda
½ teaspoon ground cloves
1⅓ cups packed brown sugar
¾ cup fat-free milk
⅓ cup vegetable oil
2 teaspoons vanilla extract
2 large eggs
1 (15-ounce) can pumpkin
Cooking spray
⅓ cup chopped walnuts

1. Preheat oven to 350°.
2. Lightly spoon flour into dry measuring cups; level with a knife. Combine flour and next 7 ingredients in a large bowl; make a well in center of mixture. Combine sugar and next 5 ingredients in a bowl; stir well with a whisk until smooth. Add to flour mixture, stirring just until moist.
3. Spoon batter into 2 (8 x 4-inch) loaf pans coated with cooking spray, and sprinkle with walnuts. Bake at 350° for 1 hour or until a wooden pick inserted in center comes out clean. Cool loaves in pans 10 minutes on a wire rack; remove from pans. Cool loaves completely; cut each loaf into 12 slices. Yield: 2 loaves, 24 slices (serving size: 1 slice).

CALORIES 161 (26% from fat); FAT 4.7g (sat 0.8g, mono 1.3g, poly 2.3g); PROTEIN 3.1g; CARB 26.9g; FIBER 1.3g; CHOL 18mg; IRON 1.4mg; SODIUM 138mg; CALC 46mg

Sour Cream Raspberry Swirl Loaf

This cake freezes well for up to 2 months. Place loaf on a wooden tray draped with a linen napkin for gift-giving.

⅓ cup seedless raspberry jam

3 tablespoons chopped walnuts, toasted

1½ cups all-purpose flour

1 teaspoon baking powder

¼ teaspoon baking soda

⅛ teaspoon salt

¾ cup granulated sugar

¼ cup butter, softened

2 teaspoons grated lemon rind

1⅛ teaspoons vanilla extract, divided

1 large egg

1 large egg white

¾ cup fat-free sour cream

Cooking spray

¼ cup sifted powdered sugar

1½ teaspoons 2% reduced-fat milk

1. Preheat oven to 350°.

2. Combine raspberry jam and walnuts in a small bowl.

3. Lightly spoon flour into dry measuring cups; level with a knife. Combine flour, baking powder, baking soda, and salt in a bowl, stirring with a whisk. Combine granulated sugar, butter, lemon rind, 1 teaspoon vanilla, egg, and egg white in a large bowl; beat with a mixer at medium speed until well blended. Add flour mixture and sour cream alternately to sugar mixture, beginning and ending with flour mixture.

4. Spread half of batter into an 8 x 4-inch loaf pan coated with cooking spray. Spoon raspberry mixture over top, leaving a ¼-inch border. Spread remaining batter over raspberry mixture.

5. Bake at 350° for 55 minutes or until a wooden pick inserted in center comes out clean. Cool in pan 10 minutes on a wire rack; remove from pan. Cool completely on wire rack. Combine ⅛ teaspoon vanilla, powdered sugar, and milk in a small bowl, stirring well with a whisk. Drizzle over loaf. Yield: 1 loaf, 12 servings (serving size: 1 slice).

CALORIES 184 (26% from fat); FAT 5.4g (sat 2.6g, mono 1.6g, poly 0.9g); PROTEIN 3.2g; CARB 31.2g; FIBER 0.7g; CHOL 28mg; IRON 1.2mg; SODIUM 155mg; CALC 53mg

Sour Cream Raspberry Swirl Loaf

Apricot-Cream Cheese Braid

The finished braids can be covered and refrigerated for several days or frozen for up to 1 month. The extra loaves are great gifts; wrap in plastic, and cinch with a bow. Feel free to substitute any kind of fruit preserves.

Dough:
- ½ cup granulated sugar
- ⅓ cup butter
- ½ teaspoon salt
- 1 (8-ounce) carton light sour cream
- 2 packages dry yeast (about 4½ teaspoons)
- ½ cup warm water (100° to 110°)
- 2 large eggs, lightly beaten
- 4 cups all-purpose flour

Filling:
- ⅔ cup apricot preserves
- ¼ cup granulated sugar
- 1 teaspoon vanilla extract
- 2 (8-ounce) blocks ⅓-less-fat cream cheese, softened
- 1 large egg, lightly beaten
- Cooking spray

Glaze:
- 1½ cups sifted powdered sugar
- 2 tablespoons fat-free milk
- 1 teaspoon vanilla extract

1. To prepare dough, combine first 4 ingredients in a saucepan over medium heat, stirring until sugar dissolves. Remove from heat; cool. Dissolve yeast in warm water in a large bowl and let stand 5 minutes. Stir in sour cream mixture and 2 eggs. Lightly spoon flour into dry measuring cups, and level with a knife. Gradually stir flour into sour cream mixture (dough will be soft and sticky). Cover dough and chill 8 hours or overnight.

2. To prepare filling, combine preserves and next 4 ingredients in a medium bowl; beat with a mixer at medium speed until well blended.

3. Divide dough into 4 equal portions. Turn each portion out onto a lightly floured surface; knead lightly 4 or 5 times. Roll each portion into a 12 x 8-inch rectangle. Spread one-fourth of filling over each portion, leaving a ½-inch border. Starting at a long side, carefully roll up each portion jelly-roll fashion; pinch seam and ends to seal.

4. Place 2 loaves on each of 2 baking sheets coated with cooking spray. Cut 4 (¼-inch-deep) "X"s in top of each loaf with scissors. Cover and let rise in a warm place (85°), free

from drafts, 25 minutes or until doubled in size.

5. Preheat oven to 375°.

6. Place 1 baking sheet in oven (cover remaining loaves to keep from drying). Bake at 375° for 15 minutes or until lightly browned. Repeat procedure with remaining loaves. Cool loaves slightly.

7. To prepare glaze, combine powdered sugar, milk, and 1 teaspoon vanilla, stirring with a whisk. Drizzle warm loaves with glaze. Yield: 4 loaves, 10 slices per loaf (serving size: 1 slice).

CALORIES 145 (31% from fat); FAT 5g (sat 3g, mono 1.5g, poly 0.3g); PROTEIN 3.3g; CARB 21.6g; FIBER 0.5g; CHOL 30mg; IRON 0.8mg; SODIUM 102mg; CALC 26mg

Freezer Cinnamon-Fruit Rolls

These frozen rolls are good for busy mornings—let them stand at room temperature 30 minutes, and then bake 20 minutes. Make them in disposable foil pans for easy gift-giving; present the glaze in a small jar or zip-top plastic bag with these instructions: Microwave at HIGH 15 to 30 seconds, stir until smooth, and drizzle over warm rolls.

Dough:
- 1 package dry yeast (about 2¼ teaspoons)
- ¼ cup warm water (100° to 110°)
- ½ cup fat-free milk
- ⅓ cup granulated sugar
- ¼ cup butter, melted
- 1 teaspoon vanilla extract
- ½ teaspoon salt
- 1 large egg, lightly beaten
- 3¾ cups all-purpose flour, divided
- Cooking spray

Filling:
- ⅔ cup packed brown sugar
- ½ cup golden raisins
- ½ cup chopped dried apricots
- ½ cup chopped pecans
- 1 tablespoon ground cinnamon
- 2 tablespoons butter, melted

Glaze:
- 1 cup powdered sugar
- 2 tablespoons fat-free milk

1. Dissolve yeast in warm water in a large bowl; let stand 5 minutes. Stir in ½ cup milk and next 5 ingredients. Lightly spoon flour into dry measuring cups; level with a knife. Add 3½ cups flour to yeast mixture, stirring until blended. Turn dough out onto a floured surface. Knead until smooth and elastic (about 10

Freezer Cinnamon-
Fruit Rolls

minutes); add enough of remaining flour, 1 tablespoon at a time, to prevent dough from sticking to hands (dough will feel sticky).

2. Place dough in a large bowl coated with cooking spray, turning to coat top. Cover and let rise in a warm place (85°), free from drafts, 1 hour or until doubled in size. (Gently press 2 fingers into dough. If indentation remains, dough has risen enough.) Punch dough down; cover and let rest 5 minutes.

3. To prepare filling, combine brown sugar and next 4 ingredients.

4. Roll dough into an 18 x 10-inch rectangle on a floured surface. Brush 2 tablespoons melted butter over dough. Sprinkle 1½ cups filling over dough, leaving a ½-inch border. Beginning with a long side, roll up dough jelly-roll fashion; pinch seam to seal (do not seal ends of roll).

5. Place a long piece of dental floss or thread under dough ¾ inch from end of roll. Cross ends of floss over top of dough roll; slowly pull ends to cut through dough. Repeat procedure to make 24 rolls. Coat 2 (9-inch) square foil baking pans with

cooking spray. Sprinkle remaining filling evenly into bottom of pans. Place 12 rolls, cut sides up, in each prepared pan. Cover and let rise 1½ hours or until doubled in size.

6. Preheat oven to 350°.

7. Uncover rolls. Bake at 350° for 20 minutes or until browned. Invert onto a serving platter.

8. To prepare glaze, combine powdered sugar and 2 tablespoons milk, stirring until smooth. Drizzle over warm rolls. Yield: 24 servings (serving size: 1 roll).

To Freeze Unbaked Rolls: Prepare through Step 5. Cover with plastic wrap. Wrap tightly with heavy-duty foil. Store in freezer for up to 2 months.

To Prepare Frozen Unbaked Rolls: Remove rolls from freezer; let stand at room temperature 30 minutes. Uncover and bake at 350° for 20 minutes or until browned.

CALORIES 193 (24% from fat); FAT 5.1g (sat 2g, mono 1.9g, poly 0.8g); PROTEIN 3.1g; CARB 34.4g; FIBER 1.4g; CHOL 17mg; IRON 1.5mg; SODIUM 87mg; CALC 28mg

holiday recipes

From "A+" appetizers to deliciously decadent desserts, every recipe you need for any holiday occasion is here—be it a quick post-shopping lunch, Christmas Eve dinner, or impromptu family brunch.

Double-Coconut Cake with Fluffy Coconut Frosting
(recipe on page 313)

Cranberry
Cosmopolitans
(recipe on page 154)

appetizers and beverages

Warm up your holiday guests with tasty bites and mugs of good cheer. From familiar flavors to exotic inspirations, these starters and sippers will satisfy everyone's party appetite.

Spiced Parmesan Cheese Crisps

About 15 minutes after you start this recipe, you can start munching on this crunchy snack—perhaps while watching holiday movies. You can also make these up to a day ahead and store them in an airtight container. They're great with Wild Mushroom and Artichoke Dip (recipe on page 131).

 10 egg roll wrappers
Cooking spray
  2 large egg whites, lightly beaten
  1 cup (4 ounces) grated fresh Parmesan cheese
  1 teaspoon dried oregano
  1 teaspoon dried basil
 ½ teaspoon ground red pepper

1. Preheat oven to 425°.
2. Place egg roll wrappers in a single layer on baking sheets coated with cooking spray. Lightly brush with egg whites; cut each wrapper into 8 wedges. Combine cheese and next 3 ingredients, and sprinkle evenly over wedges. Bake at 425° for 5 minutes or until lightly browned. Yield: 80 crisps (serving size: 4 crisps).

CALORIES 75 (24% from fat); FAT 2g (sat 1.1g, mono 0.5g, poly 0.1g); PROTEIN 4.3g; CARB 9.6g; FIBER 0.4g; CHOL 6mg; IRON 0.7mg; SODIUM 203mg; CALC 88mg

---

5 secrets to cocktail party success

1. For a two- to four-hour event (with no dinner afterward), serve up to eight hors d'oeuvres.

2. Set out low-maintenance cheeses, crudités with dip, and spiced nuts on a buffet table. Good cheese selections include aged Cheddar, Camembert, aged Swiss, and goat and blue cheeses.

3. Serve four "light bites" per guest for the first two hours. Great examples include:

- Sugary Spice Pecans (recipe on page 128)
- Baked Feta with Marinara (recipe on page 132)
- Mini Frittatas with Ham and Cheese (recipe on page 140).

4. For the last two hours of the party, allow two "substantial" appetizers per person, such as:

- Swiss Chard Spanakopita Casserole (recipe on page 144)
- Vietnamese Rolls with Peanut Dipping Sauce (recipe on page 145)
- Shrimp Ceviche Cocktail (recipe on page 137).

5. As a finale, serve something sweet, such as fruit or chocolate, which signals the party's nearing an end.

Asian Party Mix

Sesame rice crackers and wasabi peas add crunch and fire to this old favorite. Dried green peas coated with wasabi are available by the pound in some supermarkets, often in the bulk foods department. Don't worry if you can't find them; the mix is fine without them. Rice crackers are crunchy and airy, with the mild taste of rice. Look for them in the snack or Asian section of your grocery store. For a unique Asian touch, serve the mix in a bright red straw basket with chop sticks emerging as an unexpected decorative "garnish."

  2 cups crispy corn cereal squares (such as Corn Chex)
  2 cups crispy rice cereal squares (such as Rice Chex)
  2 cups sesame rice crackers, broken
  1 cup tiny fat-free pretzel twists
 ¾ cup wasabi peas
 ¼ cup lightly salted dry-roasted peanuts
  3 tablespoons unsalted butter
  1 tablespoon sugar
  1 tablespoon curry powder
  1 tablespoon low-sodium soy sauce
  1 teaspoon Worcestershire sauce
 ½ teaspoon garlic powder
 ½ teaspoon ground cumin
 ¼ teaspoon salt
 ¼ teaspoon ground red pepper
Cooking spray

1. Preheat oven to 200°.
2. Combine first 6 ingredients in a large bowl; set aside. Melt butter in a small saucepan over medium heat. Add sugar and next 7 ingredients, stirring with a whisk. Pour butter mixture over cereal mixture, tossing gently to coat. Spread mixture on a jelly-roll pan coated with cooking spray. Bake at 200° for 45 minutes. Cool completely before serving. Yield: 8 cups (serving size: ½ cup).

CALORIES 116 (29% from fat); FAT 3.7g (sat 1.6g, mono 1.3g, poly 0.6g); PROTEIN 2.9g; CARB 18.6g; FIBER 1.2g; CHOL 6mg; IRON 2.8mg; SODIUM 269mg; CALC 38mg

Asian-Spiced Pecans

2 tablespoons low-sodium soy sauce
1 tablespoon tomato paste
2 teaspoons Thai seasoning (such as Spice Islands)
1 teaspoon butter, melted
Dash of black pepper
Dash of ground red pepper
4 cups pecan halves
Cooking spray
⅛ teaspoon salt

1. Preheat oven to 350°.
2. Combine first 6 ingredients in a large bowl, and stir well with a whisk. Add pecan halves; toss well. Spread mixture evenly onto a jelly-roll pan coated with cooking spray.
3. Bake at 350° for 12 minutes, stirring once. Remove from oven, and sprinkle with salt. Cool completely. Yield: 4 cups (serving size: 2 tablespoons).
Note: Store in an airtight container in a cool, dark place up to 1 month; in refrigerator up to 3 months; or in freezer up to 8 months.

CALORIES 93 (90% from fat); FAT 9.3g (sat 0.8g, mono 5.7g, poly 2.3g); PROTEIN 1.1g; CARB 2.6g; FIBER 0.9g; CHOL 0mg; IRON 0.3mg; SODIUM 61mg; CALC 5mg

Sugary Spice Pecans

1 cup sugar
½ cup water
1 teaspoon ground cinnamon
Dash of ground cloves
2 cups pecan halves
1 teaspoon vanilla extract
Cooking spray

1. Combine first 4 ingredients in a medium saucepan. Cook over medium heat until sugar dissolves, stirring constantly (about 8 minutes). Add pecans and vanilla; cook until all syrup is absorbed and pecans are coated, stirring constantly (about 12 minutes). Spread pecan mixture on a baking sheet coated with cooking spray (pecans will have a sugar coating). Separate pecans halves. Cool completely. Yield: 3½ cups (serving size: 2 tablespoons).
Note: Store in an airtight container in a cool, dark place up to 1 month; in refrigerator up to 3 months; or in freezer up to 8 months.

CALORIES 80 (60% from fat); FAT 5.3g (sat 0.4g, mono 3.3g, poly 1.3g); PROTEIN 0.6g; CARB 8.6g; FIBER 0.5g; CHOL 0mg; IRON 0.2mg; SODIUM 0mg; CALC 4mg

Graham Cracker-and-Pecan Praline Popcorn

The brown sugar mixture heats up quickly and burns easily, so don't leave it unattended while cooking.

10 cups popcorn (popped without salt or fat)
2 cups honey-flavored bear-shaped graham crackers (such as Teddy Grahams)
½ cup coarsely chopped pecans
Cooking spray
1 cup packed dark brown sugar
¼ cup light-colored corn syrup
1½ tablespoons butter

1. Preheat oven to 325°.
2. Combine the first 3 ingredients in a large bowl. Spread popcorn mixture onto a foil-lined jelly-roll pan coated with cooking spray.
3. Combine brown sugar, corn syrup, and butter in a medium saucepan. Bring to a boil over medium heat, stirring constantly. Cover; cook 1 minute. Uncover; cook, without stirring, until candy thermometer registers 290° (about 5 minutes).
4. Drizzle brown sugar mixture over popcorn mixture; toss to coat. Bake at 325° for 30 minutes, stirring once. Cool completely in pan on a wire rack, and break into large pieces. Yield: 12 cups (serving size: ½ cup).
Note: Store in an airtight container up to 2 weeks.

CALORIES 97 (32% from fat); FAT 3.5g (sat 0.7g, mono 1.6g, poly 0.9g); PROTEIN 1g; CARB 16.4g; FIBER 0.7g; CHOL 2mg; IRON 0.5mg; SODIUM 47mg; CALC 7mg

healthy holiday choice

Most nuts are naturally high in fat, but it's monounsaturated, one of the "good" fats and an important part of a healthy diet. And since they're so healthy, nuts make a great addition to any holiday party buffet spread. Simply fill silver bowls or goblets with walnuts, almonds, hazelnuts, Brazil nuts, cashews, or pecans. Place one bowl on the buffet and one or two others in other guest-gathering locales.

But nuts aren't just for the buffet alone. They make the perfect gift idea as well. For a quick gift, simply pour a cup or two into a cellophane bag, and tie it up with a pine sprig and raffia for a natural look. Or add one or two sweet or savory nut recipes to your holiday baking, and package the nuts in a small holiday tin or other container. The recipient will be glad to know that the gift that's good for his or her heart is given from the bottom of yours!

Roasted-Poblano Guacamole with Garlic and Parsley

Roasted Tomato and Green Chile Salsa

Roasted-Poblano Guacamole with Garlic and Parsley

Cooking Light Test Kitchens Staffer Kathryn Conrad likes to serve this dip whenever she's entertaining. "It's always such a welcome change from the traditional holiday fare," she says.

2   poblano chiles (about 6 ounces)
2   plum tomatoes (about 6 ounces)
2   garlic cloves, unpeeled
1⅓ cups ripe peeled avocado, seeded and coarsely mashed (about 3)
3   tablespoons chopped fresh flat-leaf parsley
2   tablespoons fresh lime juice
¼   teaspoon salt
2   tablespoons grated queso añejo or Parmesan cheese
2   tablespoons sliced radishes
7   ounces baked tortilla chips (about 7 cups)

1. Preheat broiler.
2. Cut poblanos in half lengthwise; discard seeds and membranes. Place poblano halves (skin sides up), tomatoes, and garlic on a foil-lined baking sheet. Broil 12 minutes or until poblanos are blackened, turning tomatoes once. Place poblanos in a zip-top plastic bag; seal. Let stand 10 minutes. Peel poblanos, tomatoes, and garlic.
3. Place poblanos, tomatoes, and garlic in a food processor, and pulse until coarsely chopped. Combine poblano mixture, avocado, parsley, juice, and salt in a bowl. Sprinkle with cheese and radishes. Serve with tortilla chips. Yield: 8 servings (serving size: ¼ cup guacamole and about ¾ cup chips).

CALORIES 179 (38% from fat); FAT 7.5g (sat 1.3g, mono 4.1g, poly 1.5g); PROTEIN 3.6g; CARB 27g; FIBER 4.8g; CHOL 2mg; IRON 1mg; SODIUM 280mg; CALC 57mg

Roasted Tomato and Green Chile Salsa

6   plum tomatoes (about 1 pound)
3   garlic cloves, unpeeled
2   jalapeño peppers
⅓   cup chopped fresh cilantro
¼   cup finely chopped onion
1   teaspoon fresh lime juice
¼   teaspoon salt

1. Preheat broiler.
2. Place tomatoes, garlic, and jalapeños on a foil-lined baking sheet. Broil 16 minutes, turning after 8 minutes. Cool; peel tomatoes and garlic. Combine garlic and peppers in a molcajete, mortar, or bowl; pound with a pestle or back of a spoon to form a paste. Add tomatoes; crush using pestle or spoon. Combine tomato mixture, cilantro, and remaining ingredients. Yield: 6 servings (serving size: ¼ cup).

CALORIES 23 (12% from fat); FAT 0.3g (sat 0g, mono 0.1g, poly 0.1g); PROTEIN 0.9g; CARB 5g; FIBER 1.2g; CHOL 0mg; IRON 0.5mg; SODIUM 106mg; CALC 10mg

Artichokes with Roasted-Pepper Dip

Serve this dip with raw vegetables, pita chips, or plain crackers at your next cocktail party. It's a great stress-buster because it can be made a day ahead. Just before your party begins, bring the artichokes to room temperature, place half the dip in a small serving bowl, and top with cheese and capers.

2   red bell peppers
2   artichokes
12 cups water
3   lemon slices
1   bay leaf
2   teaspoons olive oil
2   teaspoons Dijon mustard
1   teaspoon red wine vinegar
¼   teaspoon dried fines herbes
⅛   teaspoon black pepper
1   tablespoon finely crumbled feta cheese
½   teaspoon capers

1. Preheat broiler.
2. Cut bell peppers in half lengthwise, discarding seeds and membranes. Place bell pepper halves, skin sides up, on a foil-lined baking sheet; flatten bell peppers with your hand. Broil 10 minutes or until blackened. Place bell pepper halves in a zip-top plastic bag and seal. Let stand 20 minutes. Peel and set aside.
3. Cut off artichoke stems; remove bottom leaves. Trim 1 inch from tops of artichokes. Bring water, lemon slices, and bay leaf to a boil in a large Dutch oven. Add artichokes; cover, reduce heat, and simmer 25 minutes or until a leaf near center of each artichoke pulls out easily. Drain well; discard lemon and bay leaf. Set aside.
4. Combine bell peppers, oil, mustard, and vinegar in a blender; process until smooth. Combine bell pepper mixture, fines herbes, and black pepper. Spoon ⅔ cup into a serving bowl; sprinkle with feta and capers. Serve with artichokes. Cover and chill remaining dip. Yield: 2 servings (serving size: 1 artichoke and ⅓ cup dip).

CALORIES 105 (30% from fat); FAT 3.5g (sat 0.9g, mono 1.9g, poly 0.4g); PROTEIN 4.2g; CARB 17.3g; FIBER 7.1g; CHOL 3mg; IRON 2.6mg; SODIUM 234mg; CALC 80mg

Artichokes with
Roasted-Pepper Dip

Deviled Dip

This spicy onion dipping sauce is ideal as a light appetizer for an open house or holiday meal. Serve with crudités, such as carrots, celery, radishes, cucumber, bell peppers, or cherry tomatoes.

Cooking spray
  1 cup minced red onion
  1 tablespoon sugar
  2 tablespoons water
  1 tablespoon white wine vinegar
1½ cups 1% low-fat cottage cheese
  ¼ cup fat-free mayonnaise
  1 teaspoon hot sauce
  ¼ teaspoon salt
  ¼ teaspoon chili powder
  ⅛ teaspoon garlic powder

1. Place a skillet coated with cooking spray over medium-high heat until hot. Add onion, and sauté 4 minutes or until tender. Stir in sugar, water, and vinegar; cover and cook 1 minute. Remove from heat; cool.
2. Place cottage cheese in a food processor, and process until smooth. Spoon into a bowl, and stir in onion mixture, mayonnaise, and remaining ingredients. Cover and chill. Yield: 2 cups (serving size: 1 tablespoon).

CALORIES 14 (19% from fat); FAT 0.3g (sat 0.1g, mono 0.1g, poly 0.1g); PROTEIN 1.4g; CARB 1.5g; FIBER 0.1g; CHOL 1mg; IRON 0mg; SODIUM 78mg; CALC 8mg

Tex-Mex Black Bean Dip

Load up fat-free corn or flour tortilla chips with a helping of this favorite authentic Southwestern dip served warm or at room temperature. Red corn tortilla chips add the perfect seasonal touch.

  1 (15-ounce) can black beans, drained
  1 teaspoon vegetable oil
  ½ cup chopped onion
  2 garlic cloves, minced
  ½ cup diced tomato
  ⅓ cup bottled picante sauce
  ½ teaspoon chili powder
  ½ teaspoon ground cumin
  ¼ cup (1 ounce) shredded reduced-fat Monterey Jack cheese
  ¼ cup chopped fresh cilantro
  1 tablespoon fresh lime juice

1. Place beans in a bowl; partially mash until chunky. Set aside.
2. Heat oil in a medium nonstick skillet over medium heat. Add onion and garlic, and sauté 4 minutes or until tender. Add beans, tomato, and next 3 ingredients; cook 5 minutes or until thick, stirring constantly. Remove from heat; add cheese, cilantro, and lime juice, stirring until cheese melts. Yield: 1⅔ cups (serving size: 1 tablespoon).

CALORIES 14 (26% from fat); FAT 0.5g (sat 0.2g, mono 0.1g, poly 0.1g); PROTEIN 0.7g; CARB 2.4g; FIBER 0.7g; CHOL 1mg; IRON 0.2mg; SODIUM 75mg; CALC 12mg

Wild Mushroom and Artichoke Dip

Try this mushroom and artichoke dip with Spiced Parmesan Cheese Crisps (recipe on page 127). They're a great combo to munch on while watching your favorite Christmas flicks—from *It's a Wonderful Life* to *National Lampoon's Christmas Vacation.*

  1 teaspoon olive oil
  2 cups sliced shiitake mushroom caps (about 4 ounces)
  1 (6-ounce) package portobello mushrooms, chopped
  ½ cup low-fat mayonnaise
  ¼ cup (1 ounce) grated fresh Parmesan cheese
  ¼ cup finely chopped celery
  ¼ cup finely chopped onion
  ¼ cup thinly sliced green onions
  2 tablespoons chopped fresh parsley
  1 teaspoon garlic powder
  1 teaspoon black pepper
  ¾ teaspoon salt
  ¼ teaspoon ground red pepper
  1 (14-ounce) can artichoke hearts, drained and coarsely chopped
  1 (8-ounce) block ⅓-less-fat cream cheese
  1 (8-ounce) block fat-free cream cheese
Cooking spray

1. Preheat oven to 350°.
2. Heat oil in a large nonstick skillet over medium-high heat. Add mushrooms; sauté 5 minutes or until tender. Combine mushrooms, mayonnaise, and remaining ingredients except cooking spray in a large bowl, stirring until well blended.
3. Spoon mixture into a 2-quart casserole coated with cooking spray. Bake at 350° for 30 minutes or until thoroughly heated. Yield: 5 cups (serving size: ¼ cup).

CALORIES 66 (30% from fat); FAT 2.2g (sat 1g, mono 0.3g, poly 0.1g); PROTEIN 4.5g; CARB 7.6g; FIBER 1.2g; CHOL 6mg; IRON 0.2mg; SODIUM 377mg; CALC 50mg

Presentation is everything when it comes to party dips and spreads. Rather than serving dip in a typical bowl, use antique cups, parfait glasses, gourds, or bread rounds as serving containers.

Creamy Oysters Rockefeller Dip

36 (¼-inch-thick) slices diagonally cut French bread baguette (about 9 ounces)
½ (1-ounce) slice white bread
1 (12-ounce) container standard oysters, undrained
1 cup coarsely chopped green onions
1 cup coarsely chopped celery
½ cup chopped fresh parsley
½ teaspoon butter
1 (10-ounce) package frozen chopped spinach, thawed and drained
¼ cup (1 ounce) grated fresh Parmesan cheese
¼ cup (2 ounces) ⅓-less-fat cream cheese
¼ cup evaporated fat-free milk
1 tablespoon fresh lemon juice
1 tablespoon Worcestershire sauce
1½ teaspoons anchovy paste
¼ teaspoon black pepper

1. Preheat oven to 375°.
2. Arrange baguette slices on 2 baking sheets; bake baguette slices at 375° for 8 minutes or until crisp.
3. Preheat broiler.
4. Place ½ (1-ounce) bread slice in a food processor; pulse 10 times or until coarse crumbs form to measure ¼ cup.
5. Drain oysters in a colander over a bowl, reserving 2 tablespoons oyster liquid. Place oysters on a broiler pan, and broil 7 minutes or until edges of oysters curl. Cool and chop.
6. Place onions, celery, and parsley in a blender or food processor, and process until finely chopped.
7. Melt butter in a Dutch oven over medium-high heat. Add onion mixture; sauté 5 minutes or until tender. Add spinach; cook 2 minutes or until thoroughly heated. Stir in oysters, ¼ cup breadcrumbs, 2 tablespoons oyster liquid, cheeses, and remaining ingredients; cook 2 minutes or until well blended, stirring constantly. Yield: 18 servings (serving size: 2 tablespoons dip and 2 bread slices).

CALORIES 83 (26% from fat); FAT 2.4g (sat 1.1g, mono 0.6g, poly 0.3g); PROTEIN 4.6g; CARB 11.1g; FIBER 1.3g; CHOL 16mg; IRON 2.3mg; SODIUM 213mg; CALC 80mg

Baked Feta with Marinara

1 teaspoon fresh lemon juice
¼ teaspoon crushed red pepper
2 garlic cloves, minced
1 (14.5-ounce) can diced tomatoes with basil, garlic, and oregano, drained
1 (4-ounce) package crumbled feta cheese
Cooking spray
32 (½-inch-thick) slices diagonally cut French bread baguette, toasted

1. Preheat oven to 350°.
2. Combine first 4 ingredients in a bowl. Sprinkle feta evenly into a 6-inch gratin dish or small shallow baking dish coated with cooking spray. Top with tomato mixture. Bake at 350° for 20 minutes. Serve as a spread with bread slices. Yield: 16 servings (serving size: 2 tablespoons spread and 2 bread slices).

CALORIES 107 (20% from fat); FAT 2.4g (sat 1.3g, mono 0.3g, poly 0.2g); PROTEIN 4.1g; CARB 16.9g; FIBER 1g; CHOL 6mg; IRON 1mg; SODIUM 352mg; CALC 72mg

Warm Pumpkin-Cheese Dip

1¼ cups plain low-fat yogurt
½ teaspoon butter
1 cup thinly sliced leek
2 teaspoons chopped fresh or ½ teaspoon dried thyme
1 teaspoon salt
¾ cup (3 ounces) goat cheese
⅓ cup evaporated fat-free milk
1 (15-ounce) can pumpkin
3 large egg whites

1. Preheat oven to 375°.
2. Spoon yogurt onto several layers of heavy-duty paper towels; spread to ½-inch thickness. Cover with additional paper towels; let stand 5 minutes. Scrape into a large bowl using a rubber spatula.
3. Melt butter in a skillet over medium-high heat. Add leek; sauté 5 minutes or until tender. Remove from heat; stir in thyme and

salt. Place yogurt, cheese, and next 3 ingredients in a large bowl; beat with a mixer at medium speed just until smooth. Stir in leek mixture. Spoon pumpkin mixture into a 1-quart baking dish. Bake at 375° for 25 minutes or until dip is bubbly and lightly browned. Serve warm. Yield: 3½ cups (serving size: ¼ cup).

CALORIES 57 (36% from fat); FAT 2.3g (sat 1.6g, mono 0.5g, poly 0.1g); PROTEIN 3.9g; CARB 5.5g; FIBER 1g; CHOL 7mg; IRON 0.7mg; SODIUM 306mg; CALC 81mg

Spiced Red Lentil Dip with Pita Crisps

Dip:
- 1 cup dried small red lentils
- 1 bay leaf
- 1 tablespoon olive oil
- 1 cup finely chopped onion
- 2 tablespoons pine nuts
- 1 tablespoon tomato paste
- 1 teaspoon fine sea salt
- 1 teaspoon ground coriander seeds
- ½ teaspoon ground cumin
- ½ teaspoon ground caraway seeds
- ⅛ teaspoon ground red pepper
- 3 garlic cloves, minced
- 3 tablespoons fresh lemon juice

Pita Crisps:
- 4 (6-inch) pitas, each cut into 5 wedges
- Cooking spray
- ⅛ teaspoon fine sea salt
- ⅛ teaspoon freshly ground black pepper

1. Preheat oven to 350°.
2. Place lentils and bay leaf in a saucepan; cover with water to 2 inches above lentils. Bring to a boil. Cover, reduce heat, and simmer 8 minutes or until tender. Drain well. Discard bay leaf.
3. Heat oil in a small nonstick skillet over medium-high heat. Add onion and nuts, and sauté 5 minutes or until nuts are lightly browned. Stir in tomato paste and next 6 ingredients; cook 5 minutes, stirring occasionally. Stir in juice. Combine lentils and onion mixture in a food processor; process until smooth.
4. Coat 1 side of each pita wedge with cooking spray; sprinkle wedges evenly with ⅛ teaspoon salt and black pepper. Arrange pita wedges in a single layer on a baking sheet. Bake at 350° for 20 minutes or until golden. Yield: 10 servings (serving size: about ¼ cup dip and 2 pita crisps).

CALORIES 159 (15% from fat); FAT 2.6g (sat 0.4g, mono 1.4g, poly 0.6g); PROTEIN 7.4g; CARB 27g; FIBER 3.9g; CHOL 0mg; IRON 2mg; SODIUM 395mg; CALC 46mg

Spiced Red Lentil Dip with Pita Crisps

Creamy Hummus

- ¾ cup water
- ½ cup tahini (sesame-seed paste)
- 6 garlic cloves, peeled
- 6 tablespoons fresh lemon juice
- 1 tablespoon extravirgin olive oil
- 1 teaspoon ground cumin
- ½ teaspoon salt
- ¼ teaspoon black pepper
- 2 (19-ounce) cans chickpeas (garbanzo beans), rinsed and drained

1. Place the first 3 ingredients in a food processor, and process until the mixture is smooth. Add lemon juice and remaining ingredients, and process until the mixture is smooth, scraping sides of bowl occasionally. Yield: 4 cups (serving size: 1 tablespoon).

CALORIES 34 (40% from fat); FAT 1.5g (sat 0.2g, mono 0.6g, poly 0.6g); PROTEIN 1.2g; CARB 4.3g; FIBER 0.9g; CHOL 0mg; IRON 0.3mg; SODIUM 69mg; CALC 8mg

Spinach-and-Artichoke Dip

People are always looking for that quintessential open-house dip. Well, this is it! Hands down, this is our best party spinach dip ever.

- 2 cups (8 ounces) shredded part-skim mozzarella cheese, divided
- ½ cup fat-free sour cream
- ¼ cup (1 ounce) grated fresh Parmesan cheese, divided
- ¼ teaspoon black pepper
- 3 garlic cloves, crushed
- 1 (14-ounce) can artichoke hearts, drained and chopped
- 1 (8-ounce) block ⅓-less-fat cream cheese, softened
- 1 (8-ounce) block fat-free cream cheese, softened
- ½ (10-ounce) package frozen chopped spinach, thawed, drained, and squeezed dry
- 1 (13.5-ounce) package baked tortilla chips (about 16 cups)

1. Preheat oven to 350°.
2. Combine 1½ cups mozzarella, sour cream, 2 tablespoons Parmesan, pepper, and next 5 ingredients in a large bowl, and stir until well blended. Spoon mixture into a 1½-quart baking dish. Sprinkle with ½ cup mozzarella and 2 tablespoons Parmesan. Bake at 350° for 30 minutes or until bubbly and golden brown. Serve with tortilla chips. Yield: 5½ cups (serving size: ¼ cup dip and about 6 chips).

CALORIES 148 (30% from fat); FAT 5g (sat 2.9g, mono 1.5g, poly 0.5g); PROTEIN 7.7g; CARB 18.3g; FIBER 1.5g; CHOL 17mg; IRON 0.6mg; SODIUM 318mg; CALC 164mg

Fluffy Fruit Dip with Almond Brickle Chips

Serve this make-ahead dip with an assortment of fresh fruits, such as red and green grapes, apple slices, and strawberries.

- ¼ cup low-fat sour cream
- ¼ cup peach preserves
- 1 (7-ounce) jar marshmallow creme
- ¼ cup almond brickle chips (such as Heath)

1. Combine first 3 ingredients in a bowl, stirring with a whisk until blended. Cover mixture; chill at least 2 hours or up to 2 days. Stir in brickle chips just before serving. Yield: 1½ cups (serving size: 1 tablespoon dip).

CALORIES 52 (17% from fat); FAT 1g (sat 0.3g, mono 0g, poly 0g); PROTEIN 0.2g; CARB 10.8g; FIBER 0g; CHOL 2mg; IRON 0mg; SODIUM 23mg; CALC 23mg

Spinach-and-Artichoke Dip

Holiday Buffet Menu

serves 12

Many of these dishes can be prepared ahead and assembled the morning of the party. They hold up beautifully on the buffet, giving you time to spend with your guests.

Pomegranate Cocktail (recipe on page 155)

Curried Crab Spread (recipe on page 136)

Butternut, Goat Cheese, and Walnut Spread (recipe below)

Chicken and Lemon Pot Stickers with Soy-Scallion Dipping Sauce (recipe on page 146)

Swiss Chard Spanakopita Casserole (recipe on page 144)

Poached Shrimp with Bay Leaves and Lemon (recipe on page 138)

Apple Cider-Glazed Pork Tenderloin (recipe on page 248)

Buttermilk-Chive Biscuits (recipe on page 159)

Lemon-Ginger Biscotti (recipe on page 113)

Butternut, Goat Cheese, and Walnut Spread

Toast baguette slices 1 day ahead; store at room temperature in a zip-top plastic bag. Prepare and chill the spread up to 1 day ahead; serve at room temperature.

  1 medium butternut squash (about 1½ pounds)
Cooking spray
  1 whole garlic head
  2 tablespoons fresh lemon juice
½ teaspoon salt
  1 (3-ounce) package goat cheese
¼ cup chopped walnuts, toasted
36 (½-inch-thick) slices French bread baguette, toasted (about 18 ounces)

1. Preheat oven to 400°.
2. Cut squash in half lengthwise; remove and discard seeds and membrane. Place squash halves, cut sides down, on a foil-lined

jelly-roll pan coated with cooking spray. Remove white papery skin from garlic head (do not peel or separate cloves). Wrap garlic head in foil. Place garlic on pan with squash. Bake at 400° for 30 minutes or until squash is tender. Cool slightly. Scoop out pulp from squash, and discard skins. Separate garlic cloves, and squeeze to extract garlic pulp. Discard skins.
3. Place squash, garlic, juice, salt, and cheese in a food processor; process until smooth. Spoon mixture into a bowl, and sprinkle evenly with nuts. Serve with baguette slices. Yield: 12 servings (serving size: about 2½ tablespoons spread and 3 baguette slices).

CALORIES 183 (22% from fat); FAT 4.4g (sat 1.4g, mono 1.2g, poly 1.4g); PROTEIN 6.5g; CARB 30g; FIBER 2.9g; CHOL 3mg; IRON 1.7mg; SODIUM 407mg; CALC 68mg

Pineapple-Apricot Cheese Spread

  1 (8-ounce) can crushed pineapple in juice, undrained
½ cup finely chopped dried apricots
¼ cup mango chutney, chopped
¼ cup brandy
½ teaspoon ground ginger
  2 cups (8 ounces) shredded reduced-fat Cheddar cheese
  2 (8-ounce) blocks fat-free cream cheese, softened
¼ cup butter, softened
128 gingersnaps
Edible flowers (optional)

1. Drain pineapple in a sieve over a bowl, reserving 3 tablespoons juice. Combine pineapple, reserved juice, apricots, chutney, brandy, and ginger in a small saucepan; bring to a boil. Reduce heat; simmer 5 to 7 minutes or until thick, stirring frequently. Place in a bowl; chill thoroughly.
2. Place cheeses and butter in a food processor, and process mixture until smooth, scraping sides of processor bowl occasionally.
3. Combine cheese mixture and chilled pineapple mixture; spoon into a serving bowl. Cover and chill. Serve with gingersnaps. Garnish with edible flowers, if desired. Yield: 64 appetizers (serving size: 1 tablespoon cheese spread and 2 gingersnaps).

CALORIES 89 (28% from fat); FAT 2.8g (sat 1.2g, mono 1.0g, poly 0.2g); PROTEIN 2.9g; CARB 13.4g; FIBER 0.4g; CHOL 4mg; IRON 1mg; SODIUM 163mg; CALC 50mg

At each end of your holiday buffet table, stock more than enough napkins and flatware for all guests. Designate one or more locations where guests may leave their dirty dishes and glassware during the party.

Warm Mushroom Spread

With this make-ahead appetizer, you'll be ready to go with minimal prep time on the day of the event. Prepare and refrigerate the dip up to 1 day in advance and then reheat in the microwave for a couple of minutes. Toast the crostini up to 3 days prior to the party, and store at room temperature in a zip-top plastic bag. Use truffle oil on the bread, if desired.

32 (½-inch-thick) slices diagonally cut French bread baguette (about 1 pound)
 2 tablespoons olive oil, divided
 ½ cup finely chopped shallots
 1 garlic clove, minced
 4 cups chopped portobello mushrooms (about 1 pound)
 4 cups chopped shiitake mushrooms (about 1 pound)
 1 cup Madeira wine
 ⅓ cup chopped fresh parsley
 1 teaspoon dried thyme
 1 teaspoon salt
 ¼ teaspoon freshly ground black pepper
 ⅓ cup reduced-fat sour cream
 1½ teaspoons balsamic vinegar
 1 tablespoon chopped fresh parsley

1. Preheat broiler.
2. Place bread slices in a single layer on a large baking sheet. Brush 1 side of bread slices evenly with 1 tablespoon oil. Broil 1 minute or until lightly browned.
3. Heat 1 tablespoon oil in a large nonstick skillet over medium-high heat. Add shallots and garlic; sauté 1 minute. Add mushrooms; sauté 5 minutes or until tender. Add wine, ⅓ cup parsley, thyme, salt, and pepper; bring to a boil. Cook 15 minutes or until liquid almost evaporates. Remove from heat; stir in sour cream and vinegar. Spoon into a serving bowl, and sprinkle with 1 tablespoon parsley. Yield: 16 servings (serving size: 2 tablespoons spread and 2 bread slices).

CALORIES 190 (24% from fat); FAT 5g (sat 1g, mono 2.1g, poly 1.5g); PROTEIN 3.9g; CARB 27.3g; FIBER 2.5g; CHOL 2mg; IRON 1.3mg; SODIUM 331mg; CALC 18mg

how to: REMOVE MUSHROOM GILLS

Carefully remove the dark gills on the underside of the portobellos with a spoon or a butter knife. Removing the gills will keep the Warm Mushroom Spread from turning a dark gray color.

White Bean Spread with Fennel

 2 tablespoons light mayonnaise
 1 tablespoon fresh lemon juice
 ¼ teaspoon salt
 ⅛ teaspoon black pepper
 1 (16-ounce) can cannellini beans or other white beans, rinsed and drained
 ¼ cup finely chopped fennel bulb
 2 tablespoons finely chopped fennel fronds
 1 tablespoon finely chopped red onion

1. Combine first 5 ingredients in a food processor, and pulse 5 times or until beans are coarsely chopped. Combine bean mixture, fennel bulb, fennel fronds, and onion in a small bowl. Yield: 5 servings (serving size: ¼ cup).

CALORIES 130 (16% from fat); FAT 2.3g (sat 0.4g, mono 0g, poly 0.1g); PROTEIN 6.8g; CARB 21.3g; FIBER 4.6g; CHOL 2mg; IRON 2.9mg; SODIUM 172mg; CALC 72mg

Curried Crab Spread

 ½ cup minced celery
 ½ cup minced green bell pepper
 ½ cup minced red bell pepper
 ½ cup ⅓-less-fat cream cheese
 ⅓ cup light mayonnaise
 1 teaspoon curry powder
 1 teaspoon hot sauce
 ½ teaspoon salt
 ½ teaspoon grated lemon rind
 ¼ teaspoon dry mustard
 ¼ teaspoon black pepper
 1 pound lump crabmeat, shell pieces removed
36 (½-inch-thick) slices diagonally cut French bread baguette (about 18 ounces)
 1 tablespoon olive oil

1. Combine first 11 ingredients in a large bowl, stirring until well combined. Gently fold in crabmeat.
2. Preheat broiler.
3. Place bread slices in a single layer on a baking sheet. Brush 1 side of bread slices evenly with olive oil. Broil 1 minute or until lightly browned. Serve with spread. Yield: 18 servings (serving size: about 2 tablespoons spread and 2 bread slices).

CALORIES 156 (27% from fat); FAT 4.6g (sat 1g, mono 1.4g, poly 0.8g); PROTEIN 7.6g; CARB 21g; FIBER 1.8g; CHOL 22mg; IRON 0.8mg; SODIUM 359mg; CALC 33mg

Shrimp Ceviche
Cocktail

Shrimp Ceviche Cocktail

These ceviche "cocktails" feature seafood that's been cooked and combined with fresh vegetables, hot sauce, lime juice, and just a little ketchup. It's an easy, refreshing crowd-pleaser, and you don't have to track down the just-off-the-boat fresh fish necessary for classic marinate-only ceviche. *Cooking Light* Food Stylist Kellie Kelley praises this appetizer for its freshness and flavor. She suggests serving it at your next holiday cocktail party with tostadas, tortilla chips, or saltines. And don't forget the lime garnish for a fresh, festive look.

½   cup chopped onion
6   cups water
¾   cup fresh lime juice, divided
1   pound medium shrimp
1   cup chopped peeled cucumber
½   cup ketchup
⅓   cup chopped fresh cilantro
2   tablespoons Mexican hot sauce (such as Tamazula)
1   tablespoon olive oil
¼   teaspoon salt

1. Place chopped onion in a colander; rinse with cold water. Drain.
2. Bring 6 cups water and ¼ cup lime juice to a boil in a Dutch oven. Add shrimp; cook 3 minutes or until done. Drain and rinse with cold water; peel shrimp and devein, if desired. Combine shrimp and ½ cup juice in a large bowl; cover and chill 1 hour. Stir in onion, cucumber, and remaining ingredients. Serve immediately or chill until ready to serve. Yield: 6 servings (serving size: ½ cup).

CALORIES 138 (25% from fat); FAT 3.8g (sat 0.6g, mono 1.9g, poly 0.8g); PROTEIN 16.2g; CARB 10.8g; FIBER 0.8g; CHOL 115mg; IRON 2.1mg; SODIUM 483mg; CALC 53mg

Poached Shrimp with Bay Leaves and Lemon

If you love shrimp, this party-pleaser is for you. Prepare and chill several hours in advance.

3 quarts water

1½ tablespoons salt

1 tablespoon mustard seeds

6 whole black peppercorns

6 bay leaves

1 celery stalk, halved

1 carrot, halved

2 pounds medium shrimp, peeled and deveined

2 teaspoons grated lemon rind

½ cup fresh lemon juice

1 tablespoon extravirgin olive oil

½ teaspoon salt

¼ teaspoon freshly ground black pepper

1. Combine first 7 ingredients in a Dutch oven; bring to a boil. Reduce heat; simmer 15 minutes. Add shrimp; cook 3 minutes. Drain shrimp. Place shrimp in a shallow dish.

2. Combine lemon rind and next 4 ingredients. Add to shrimp and toss well. Cover and chill until ready to serve. Yield: 12 servings (serving size: 3 ounces).

CALORIES 94 (24% from fat); FAT 2.5g (sat 0.4g, mono 1.1g, poly 0.6g); PROTEIN 15.4g; CARB 1.7g; FIBER 0.1g; CHOL 115mg; IRON 1.9mg; SODIUM 313mg; CALC 46mg

Hiziki Caviar with Lemon Tofu Cream and Chives

Look for *hiziki*, a black ribbonlike seaweed, in Asian markets; substitute dried nori seaweed sheets if hiziki isn't available. This recipe isn't quick, but if you have the time and inclination, it's quite impressive. Use the leftover tofu cream as a dip for crudités.

Caviar:

1 ounce dried hiziki seaweed
1 teaspoon dark sesame oil
½ teaspoon vegetable oil
⅔ cup water
1½ tablespoons low-sodium soy sauce
1 garlic clove, minced

Remaining Ingredients:

1 lemon
48 sesame-flavored rice crackers
½ cup Lemon Tofu Cream
48 (1-inch) pieces sliced fresh chives
48 pieces matchstick-cut carrot

1. To prepare caviar, place seaweed in a large bowl; cover with hot water to 2 inches above seaweed. Cover and let stand 30 minutes or until soft. Drain. Rinse with cold water, and drain. Place seaweed in a food processor; process until minced.
2. Heat oils in a large nonstick skillet over medium heat. Add seaweed; cook 3 minutes, stirring occasionally. Add ⅔ cup water, soy sauce, and garlic; bring to a boil. Reduce heat; simmer 6 minutes or until liquid evaporates.
3. To prepare remaining ingredients, peel lemon; cut lengthwise into 6 wedges. Cut each wedge crosswise into 8 pieces.
4. Place 1 teaspoon seaweed caviar on each cracker. Place Lemon Tofu Cream in a small zip-top plastic bag; seal. Snip a small hole in 1 corner of bag; pipe about ½ teaspoon tofu cream onto each

Hiziki Caviar with Lemon Tofu Cream and Chives

cracker. Place 1 lemon triangle, 1 chive piece, and 1 carrot piece on each cracker. Yield: 16 servings (serving size: 3 crackers).

(Totals include Lemon Tofu Cream) CALORIES 40 (20% from fat); FAT 0.9g (sat 0.1g, mono 0.3g, poly 0.5g); PROTEIN 1.1g; CARB 7g; FIBER 0.5g; CHOL 0mg; IRON 0.6mg; SODIUM 127mg; CALC 16mg

Lemon Tofu Cream

1 (2-inch) piece peeled fresh ginger
2 tablespoons fresh lemon juice
1 tablespoon vegetable oil
½ teaspoon fine sea salt
8 ounces firm tofu, drained

1. Finely grate ginger; place ginger on several layers of damp cheesecloth. Gather edges of cheesecloth together; squeeze over a small bowl to extract 1 teaspoon ginger juice.
2. Combine ginger juice, lemon juice, oil, salt, and tofu in a food processor; process until smooth. Yield: 1 cup (serving size: 2 tablespoons).

CALORIES 34 (66% from fat); FAT 2.5g (sat 0.3g, mono 0.6g, poly 1.4g); PROTEIN 2g; CARB 1.1g; FIBER 0.1g; CHOL 0mg; IRON 0.3mg; SODIUM 154mg; CALC 10mg

Roasted Bell Pepper-and-Olive Crostini

2 large red bell peppers, roasted and peeled (about 1 pound)
2 large yellow bell peppers, roasted and peeled (about 1 pound)
⅔ cup sliced pitted kalamata olives
2 tablespoons thinly sliced fresh basil
1 tablespoon capers
1 tablespoon red wine vinegar
⅛ teaspoon black pepper
2 garlic cloves, minced
32 (½-inch-thick) slices diagonally cut French bread baguette, toasted

1. Cut bell peppers into 1 x ¼-inch julienne strips. Combine bell pepper strips and next 6 ingredients in a bowl. Cover bell pepper mixture, and let stand at room temperature 2 hours.
2. Spoon about 1 tablespoon bell pepper mixture onto each bread slice. Yield: 32 appetizers (serving size: 2 appetizers).
Note: You may substitute ⅓ cup sliced green olives and ⅓ cup sliced black olives for kalamata olives, if desired.

CALORIES 114 (21% from fat); FAT 2.7g (sat 0.4g, mono 1.6g, poly 0.5g); PROTEIN 3.3g; CARB 19.6g; FIBER 1.2g; CHOL 0mg; IRON 1mg; SODIUM 305mg; CALC 31mg

Mini Frittatas with Ham and Cheese

Mini Frittatas with Ham and Cheese

These bite-sized ham-and-cheese frittatas, baked in miniature muffin pans, are one of our favorite recipes. They're a great treat to grace your annual Christmas buffet table. And the best feature of all is that they can be made ahead and served at room temperature.

Cooking spray
½ cup finely chopped onion
⅔ cup chopped reduced-fat ham (about 2 ounces)
⅓ cup (about 1½ ounces) shredded reduced-fat extrasharp Cheddar cheese
2 tablespoons chopped fresh chives
⅛ teaspoon dried thyme
⅛ teaspoon black pepper
4 large egg whites
1 large egg

1. Preheat oven to 350°.

2. Heat a large nonstick skillet coated with cooking spray over medium-high heat. Add onion, and sauté 2 minutes or until crisp-tender. Add ham, and sauté 3 minutes. Remove from heat, and cool 5 minutes. Combine cheese and next 5 ingredients in a large bowl, and stir gently with a whisk. Add ham mixture, stirring with a whisk. Spoon ham mixture into 24 miniature muffin cups coated with cooking spray. Bake at 350° for 20 minutes or until set. Yield: 8 servings (serving size: 3 frittatas).

CALORIES 39 (30% from fat); FAT 1.3g (sat 0.5g, mono 0.2g, poly 0.1g); PROTEIN 4.4g; CARB 2.3g; FIBER 0.4g; CHOL 32mg; IRON 0.2mg; SODIUM 121mg; CALC 80mg

Pissaladière Tartlets

"I like that this recipe has so much make-ahead potential," *Cooking Light* Test Kitchens Staffer Tiffany Vickers says. "And what's even better is that it looks more difficult to make than it really is!"

    1 tablespoon olive oil
   10 cups thinly vertically sliced onion (about 4 medium)
   ¼ teaspoon salt
    3 canned anchovy fillets, chopped
   ¼ cup balsamic vinegar
    1 teaspoon chopped fresh thyme
   ¼ cup niçoise olives, pitted and chopped
   24 (½-ounce) slices very thin white bread
Cooking spray
   ¼ teaspoon fresh thyme leaves

1. Heat olive oil in a large nonstick skillet over medium-high heat. Add onion, and sauté 10 minutes. Stir in salt and anchovies; sauté 10 minutes. Stir in vinegar and chopped thyme. Reduce heat to medium-low; cook 3 minutes or until liquid is absorbed, stirring frequently. Stir in olives. Cool to room temperature.
2. Preheat oven to 375°.
3. Trim crusts from bread; reserve crusts for another use. Lightly coat both sides of bread with cooking spray. Place 1 slice into each of 24 miniature muffin cups, pressing bread into pan to form cups (bread tips will stick up). Bake at 375° for 10 minutes or until dry and golden. Carefully remove bread cups from pan; cool on a wire rack. Spoon 1 heaping tablespoon onion mixture into each bread cup. Sprinkle evenly with whole thyme leaves. Yield: 12 servings (serving size: 2 tartlets).

CALORIES 122 (30% from fat); FAT 4g (sat 0.4g, mono 2.5g, poly 0.4g); PROTEIN 2.9g; CARB 18.3g; FIBER 1.8g; CHOL 1mg; IRON 0.8mg; SODIUM 281mg; CALC 39mg

Mini Black Bean Cakes with Green Onion Cream and Avocado Salsa

Cooking Light Test Kitchens Director Vanessa Johnson likes to serve these mini black bean cakes whenever she's hosting an open house or holiday party. "It's a great appetizer if you're looking for something unique," she says. "It's out-of-the-ordinary, which makes for a great addition to any holiday spread. Seasoned black beans kick up the Southwestern flavor, while the sour cream topping tempers the heat."

Cakes:
   ½ cup bottled salsa
    2 teaspoons ground cumin
    2 (19-ounce) cans seasoned black beans (such as La Costeña), rinsed and drained
    1 cup dry breadcrumbs, divided
   ¼ cup thinly sliced green onions
   ½ teaspoon salt
Cooking spray
Toppings:
   ½ cup reduced-fat sour cream
   ¼ cup thinly sliced green onions
   ¼ cup diced peeled avocado
   ¼ cup chopped plum tomato
    1 teaspoon fresh lime juice

1. Preheat oven to 375°.
2. To prepare cakes, combine first 3 ingredients in a food processor; process until smooth. Stir in ½ cup breadcrumbs, ¼ cup green onions, and salt.
3. Divide mixture into 24 equal portions, shaping each into a ½-inch-thick patty. Place ½ cup breadcrumbs in a shallow dish. Dredge patties in breadcrumbs. Place patties on a baking sheet coated with cooking spray. Bake at 375° for 14 minutes, turning after 7 minutes.
4. To prepare toppings, combine sour cream and ¼ cup green onions in a small bowl. Combine avocado, tomato, and juice in a small bowl. Top each patty with 1 teaspoon green onion cream and 1 teaspoon avocado salsa. Yield: 12 servings (serving size: 2 cakes).

CALORIES 99 (25% from fat); FAT 2.8g (sat 1g, mono 0.5g, poly 0.2g); PROTEIN 3.8g; CARB 16.3g; FIBER 0.7g; CHOL 5mg; IRON 1.6mg; SODIUM 421mg; CALC 61mg

quick-fix appetizers

If you're short on time during the holidays—like the majority of us—here's a list of items you can pick up at the market and have on hand for unexpected guests. No recipes needed!

* Jar of olives (black, green, or Greek kalamata)
* Grissini (skinny breadsticks)
* Herb-flavored cheese
* 8-ounce package cream cheese; top with your favorite preserves or jelly (we recommend fig preserves, jalapeño jelly, or mint jelly)
* Tub of fruited cream cheese; serve with gingersnaps and fresh fruit, such as strawberries, apple slices, and grapes
* Jar of lemon curd; serve with pound cake or angel food cake
* An assortment of flavored tea bags, flavored coffee, and hot cocoa

Curried Chickpea Canapés with Ginger-Carrot Butter

These canapés are made with chickpea flour, but you can also make them with polenta or grits. Get a jump start on things by making them up to 2 days ahead and refrigerating. Cut and heat just before serving.

Canapés:
    1   cup chickpea flour
    2⅔ cups cold water
    ¾   teaspoon fine sea salt
    Cooking spray
    1   tablespoon curry powder

Butter:
    2⅓ cups thinly sliced carrot
    2   cups water
    1   tablespoon butter
    1   tablespoon honey
    2   teaspoons minced peeled fresh ginger
    1   tablespoon fresh lemon juice
    ¼   teaspoon fine sea salt
    ⅛   teaspoon white pepper

Remaining Ingredients:
    2   tablespoons sliced almonds, toasted
    2   tablespoons finely chopped fresh cilantro

1. To prepare canapés, lightly spoon flour into a dry measuring cup; level with a knife. Combine flour, 2⅔ cups water, and ¾ teaspoon salt in a medium saucepan, stirring with a whisk. Bring to a boil, stirring constantly. Cover, reduce heat, and simmer 20 minutes. Uncover; stir with a whisk until smooth. Pour into an 11 x 7-inch baking dish coated with cooking spray; sprinkle evenly with curry powder. Chill 1 hour or until firm.

2. Preheat oven to 375°.

3. Cut chickpea mixture into 40 (1-inch) squares; place on a jelly-roll pan coated with cooking spray. Bake at 375° for 20 minutes or until golden. Cool.

4. To prepare butter, combine carrot and next 4 ingredients in a saucepan; bring to a boil. Cover, reduce heat, and simmer 7 minutes or until tender. Increase heat to medium-high; uncover and cook 12 minutes or until liquid evaporates.

5. Combine carrot mixture, lemon juice, ¼ teaspoon salt, and pepper in a food processor; process until smooth. Pour in a zip-top bag; seal. Snip a small hole in 1 corner of bag; pipe 1 teaspoon mixture onto each canapé. Sprinkle canapés with almonds and cilantro. Yield: 20 servings (serving size: 2 canapés).

CALORIES 36 (30% from fat); FAT 1.2g (sat 0.4g, mono 0.4g, poly 0.1g); PROTEIN 1.2g; CARB 5.5g; FIBER 0.8g; CHOL 2mg; IRON 0.5mg; SODIUM 127mg; CALC 13mg

Curried Chickpea Canapés with Ginger-Carrot Butter

Roasted Cauliflower Skewers with Sweet Peppers and Cumin

Roasting cauliflower amplifies its flavor. Add flair to these skewers by dressing them up with colorful ribbon or decorative paper.

    3   tablespoons fresh lemon juice
    1   tablespoon extravirgin olive oil
    1   teaspoon fine sea salt
    1   teaspoon ground cumin
    1   teaspoon ground coriander seeds
    ½   teaspoon cumin seeds
    ½   teaspoon crushed red pepper
    30 cauliflower florets (about 1 medium head)
    1   large yellow bell pepper, cut into 15 (1-inch) squares
    1   large red bell pepper, cut into 15 (1-inch) squares
    ½   cup chopped fresh cilantro

1. Preheat oven to 450°.

2. Combine first 7 ingredients in a large bowl; stir with a whisk. Add cauliflower and bell pepper squares; toss gently to coat.

3. Spoon vegetables into a single layer on a jelly-roll pan. Bake at 450° for 25 minutes or until lightly browned and crisp-tender, stirring after 15 minutes. Cool completely; stir in cilantro.

4. Thread 1 cauliflower floret and 1 bell pepper square onto each of 30 (6-inch) skewers. Yield: 15 servings (serving size: 2 skewers).

CALORIES 25 (40% from fat); FAT 1.1g (sat 0.1g, mono 0.7g, poly 0.1g); PROTEIN 1g; CARB 3.6g; FIBER 1.5g; CHOL 0mg; IRON 0.4mg; SODIUM 167mg; CALC 15mg

Baby Vegetable Antipasto

Place the prepared vegetables in the marinade immediately so they won't discolor. Be sure to use fresh mozzarella, which comes packed in water and is usually found with the specialty cheeses. While this is perfect for a holiday hors d'oeuvre party, it's also wonderful just about anytime of the year.

Marinade:

  3 tablespoons white wine vinegar

  1 tablespoon chopped fresh flat-leaf parsley

  1 tablespoon chopped fresh basil

  2 teaspoons extravirgin olive oil

  ½ teaspoon salt

Dash of sugar

Dash of freshly ground black pepper

  1 garlic clove, crushed

Vegetables:

  8 baby artichokes (about 1½ pounds)

20 small red potatoes (about 12 ounces)

  3 bunches baby carrots with tops (about 1½ pounds), peeled

  2 bunches small radishes with tops (about 1½ pounds)

  1 cup torn radicchio

  1 head Belgian endive, separated into leaves (about 4 ounces)

Remaining Ingredients:

20 pitted ripe olives

  3 ounces fresh mozzarella cheese, cubed

1. To prepare marinade, combine first 8 ingredients in a small bowl, and stir well with a whisk.

2. To prepare vegetables, working with 1 artichoke at a time, cut off stem to the base. Remove bottom leaves and tough outer leaves, leaving tender heart and bottom; trim about 1 inch from top of artichoke. Steam artichokes, covered, 20 minutes or until tender; cool to room temperature. Cut artichokes in half lengthwise. Remove fuzzy thistle from bottom with a spoon.

3. Steam potatoes, covered, 6 minutes or until tender. Cool to room temperature.

4. Trim carrot stems to 2 inches. Steam carrots, covered, 20 seconds. Plunge into ice water; drain well.

5. Trim radish tops to 1 inch.

6. Place artichokes, potatoes, carrots, radishes, radicchio, and endive in a large bowl. Drizzle with marinade; toss gently to coat. Cover and marinate in refrigerator 2 hours.

7. Arrange vegetables on a platter; top with olives and cheese. Yield: 10 servings (serving size: about 1¼ cups).

CALORIES 127 (30% from fat); FAT 4.2g (sat 1.5g, mono 1.9g, poly 0.4g); PROTEIN 6.4g; CARB 19.5g; FIBER 6g; CHOL 7mg; IRON 2.1mg; SODIUM 386mg; CALC 127mg

Swiss Chard Spanakopita Casserole

This casserole recipe is much quicker and easier to assemble than the traditional classic individual pastries, offering you just what you need before hosting a dinner—time.

Cooking spray

2¼ cups minced white onion

¾ cup minced green onions

3 garlic cloves, minced

9 cups chopped trimmed Swiss chard (about 1½ pounds)

6 tablespoons chopped fresh parsley

3 tablespoons minced fresh mint

1 cup (4 ounces) crumbled feta cheese

½ cup (2 ounces) freshly grated Parmesan cheese

½ teaspoon salt

¼ teaspoon black pepper

3 large egg whites, lightly beaten

10 (18 x 14-inch) sheets frozen phyllo dough, thawed

1. Preheat oven to 350°.

2. Heat a large nonstick skillet coated with cooking spray over medium-high heat. Add white onion; sauté 7 minutes or until golden. Add green onions and garlic, and sauté 1 minute. Stir in chard; cook 2 minutes or until chard wilts. Stir in parsley and mint, and cook 1 minute. Place in a large bowl; cool slightly. Stir in cheeses, salt, pepper, and egg whites.

3. Place 1 phyllo sheet on a large cutting board (cover remaining phyllo to keep from drying), and coat with cooking spray. Top with 1 phyllo sheet, and coat with cooking spray. Repeat procedure with 3 additional sheets.

4. Cut stack into a 14-inch square. Place square in center of a 13 x 9-inch baking dish coated with cooking spray, allowing phyllo to extend up long sides of dish. Cut 14 x 4-inch piece into 2 (7 x 4-inch) rectangles. Fold each rectangle in half lengthwise. Place each rectangle against an empty side at short ends of dish. Spread chard mixture evenly over phyllo. Repeat Step 3 with remaining phyllo sheets. Place 18 x 14-inch phyllo stack over chard mixture. Fold overhanging phyllo edges to center. Coat with cooking spray. Score phyllo by making 2 lengthwise cuts and 3 crosswise cuts to form 12 rectangles. Bake at 350° for 40 minutes or until golden. Yield: 12 servings.

CALORIES 121 (35% from fat); FAT 4.7g (sat 2.8g, mono 1.4g, poly 0.3g); PROTEIN 6.1g; CARB 13.6g; FIBER 1.6g; CHOL 14mg; IRON 1.3mg; SODIUM 449mg; CALC 134mg

Swiss Chard Spanakopita Casserole

Vietnamese Rolls
with Peanut Dipping
Sauce

Vietnamese Rolls with Peanut Dipping Sauce

Crunchy vegetables pair with chicken in this refreshing appetizer. You can make the sauce and chicken mixture
a few hours before your guests arrive, but assemble the rolls just before serving so they don't dry out.

Sauce:

½ cup seasoned rice vinegar
¼ cup honey
¼ teaspoon salt
⅓ cup finely chopped roasted peanuts

Rolls:

1 tablespoon peanut oil
4 teaspoons minced peeled fresh ginger
4 garlic cloves, minced
1 pound skinless, boneless chicken breasts, cut into
   ¼-inch-wide strips
⅓ cup hoisin sauce
1 teaspoon hot chili sauce (such as Sriracha)
12 (8-inch) round sheets rice paper
3 cups thinly sliced romaine lettuce
36 (2-inch) julienne-cut seeded peeled cucumber strips
36 (2-inch) julienne-cut red bell pepper strips
36 mint leaves

1. To prepare sauce, combine first 3 ingredients in a small bowl,
stirring until honey dissolves. Stir in peanuts.

2. To prepare rolls, heat oil in a large nonstick skillet over
medium-high heat. Add ginger, garlic, and chicken; sauté
5 minutes. Combine chicken mixture, hoisin sauce, and chili
sauce; chill.

3. Add hot water to a large, shallow dish to a depth of 1 inch.
Place 1 rice paper sheet in the dish. Let stand for 30 seconds or
just until rice sheet is soft. Place rice sheet on a flat surface.
Arrange ¼ cup romaine lettuce over half of sheet, leaving a
1-inch border. Top the lettuce with ¼ cup chicken mixture,
3 cucumber strips, 3 bell pepper strips, and 3 mint leaves. Fold
sides of rice sheet over filling and, starting with filled side, roll
up jelly-roll fashion. Gently press seam to seal roll. Place the
roll, seam side down, on a serving platter (cover roll to keep
from drying).

4. Repeat procedure with remaining sheets of rice paper,
lettuce, chicken mixture, cucumber strips, bell pepper strips,
and mint leaves. Cut each roll in half diagonally. Serve rolls
with sauce. Yield: 12 servings (serving size: 2 roll halves and
about 1½ tablespoons sauce).

CALORIES 176 (23% from fat); FAT 4.5g (sat 0.7g, mono 1.8g, poly 1.3g); PROTEIN 11.9g;
CARB 22.9g; FIBER 2g; CHOL 22mg; IRON 1.4mg; SODIUM 422mg; CALC 39mg

Chicken and Lemon Pot Stickers with Soy-Scallion Dipping Sauce

Pot Stickers:

- ½ cup dry sherry
- ½ cup water
- ½ ounce dried shiitake mushrooms
- ¾ cup finely chopped bok choy (about ½ pound)
- ⅓ cup chopped green onions
- ¼ cup finely chopped water chestnuts
- 1 tablespoon low-sodium soy sauce
- 2 teaspoons minced peeled fresh ginger
- 2 teaspoons grated lemon rind
- 1 teaspoon salt
- 1 teaspoon dark sesame oil

Dash of hot sauce

- ½ pound ground chicken or turkey
- 24 won ton wrappers
- 2 tablespoons cornstarch
- ¼ cup vegetable oil, divided
- 1 cup water, divided

Sauce:

- 5 tablespoons mirin (sweet rice wine)
- ¼ cup low-sodium soy sauce
- ¼ cup seasoned rice vinegar
- 3 tablespoons chopped green onions
- 1 teaspoon chile paste with garlic

1. To prepare pot stickers, bring sherry and ½ cup water to a boil in a small saucepan. Remove from heat; add mushrooms. Cover and let stand 30 minutes or until mushrooms are tender. Drain and discard liquid. Finely chop mushrooms. Combine mushrooms, bok choy, and next 9 ingredients, stirring well.

2. Working with 1 won ton wrapper at a time (cover remaining wrappers with a damp towel to keep from drying), spoon about 1½ teaspoons chicken mixture into center of each wrapper. Moisten edges of dough with water; bring 2 opposite corners to center, pinching points to seal. Bring remaining 2 corners to center, pinching points to seal. Pinch 4 edges together to seal. Place pot stickers on a large baking sheet sprinkled with cornstarch.

3. Heat 2 tablespoons oil in a large nonstick skillet over medium-high heat. Add half of pot stickers; cook 2 minutes or until bottoms are golden brown. Carefully add ½ cup water to pan; cover and cook 4 minutes. Uncover and cook 3 minutes or until liquid evaporates. Repeat procedure with 2 tablespoons oil, remaining pot stickers, and ½ cup water.

4. To prepare sauce, combine mirin and next 4 ingredients.

Serve with pot stickers. Yield: 12 servings (serving size: 2 pot stickers and about 2 teaspoons sauce).

CALORIES 196 (19% from fat); FAT 4.2g (sat 0.8g, mono 1.7g, poly 0.9g); PROTEIN 4.4g; CARB 32g; FIBER 2.6g; CHOL 2mg; IRON 1.4mg; SODIUM 567mg; CALC 49mg

Herbed Ricotta Won Tons with Spicy Tomato Sauce

Won Tons:

- 1 cup part-skim ricotta cheese
- ¼ cup blanched almonds, toasted
- ½ teaspoon all-purpose flour
- ½ cup chopped fresh mint
- 2 tablespoons grated fresh Parmesan cheese
- 2 tablespoons fresh flat-leaf parsley leaves
- 2 tablespoons finely chopped fresh chives
- 1 tablespoon grated lemon rind
- ½ teaspoon fine sea salt
- ¼ teaspoon freshly ground black pepper
- 1 large egg white
- 1 garlic clove, chopped
- 30 won ton wrappers

Cooking spray

- 1 large egg white, lightly beaten

Sauce:

- 1 (28-ounce) can whole tomatoes, drained
- 1 teaspoon olive oil
- ⅔ cup chopped onion
- 2 teaspoons finely grated orange rind
- 1 teaspoon sugar
- 1 habanero pepper, finely chopped
- 2 tablespoons chopped fresh basil

1. To prepare won tons, place colander in a 2-quart glass measure or medium bowl. Line colander with 2 layers of cheesecloth, allowing cheesecloth to extend over edges of bowl. Spoon ricotta into colander. Gather edges of cheesecloth together; tie securely. Refrigerate 1 hour. Gently squeeze cheesecloth bag to remove excess liquid; discard liquid. Spoon ricotta into a food processor.

2. Preheat oven to 350°.

3. Place almonds and flour in a spice or coffee grinder, and process until finely ground. Set aside 3 tablespoons almond mixture; add remaining almond mixture, mint, and next 8 ingredients to food processor. Process until smooth.

4. Working with 1 won ton wrapper at a time (cover remaining wrappers with a damp towel to keep from drying), spoon about

Herbed Ricotta Won
Tons with Spicy
Tomato Sauce

2 teaspoons ricotta mixture into center of each wrapper. Moisten edges of dough with water; bring 2 opposite corners together. Press edges together to seal, forming a triangle.

5. Place won tons on 2 baking sheets lined with parchment paper and coated with cooking spray. Brush won tons with lightly beaten egg white; sprinkle with reserved almond mixture.

6. Bake at 350° for 15 minutes or until lightly browned. Cool won tons 5 minutes on a wire rack.

7. To prepare sauce, place tomatoes in food processor; process until finely chopped. Heat oil in a large nonstick skillet over medium-high heat. Add onion, and sauté 3 minutes. Stir in orange rind, sugar, and habanero pepper; sauté 2 minutes. Reduce heat to medium. Stir in tomatoes and basil; cook 10 minutes, stirring mixture occasionally. Serve sauce with won tons. Yield: 15 servings (serving size: 2 won tons and about 1 tablespoon sauce).

CALORIES 120 (29% from fat); FAT 3.9g (sat 2.2g, mono 1g, poly 0.4g); PROTEIN 5.8g; CARB 15.5g; FIBER 1.9g; CHOL 10mg; IRON 1.3mg; SODIUM 456mg; CALC 111mg

new year's celebration

Whether you're ushering in the Chinese New Year or celebrating to the tune of "Auld Lang Syne," Chicken and Lemon Pot Stickers with Soy-Scallion Dipping Sauce and Herbed Ricotta Won Tons with Spicy Tomato Sauce will help you start the year off with a bang.

Baked Italian Oysters

This hot appetizer is served on the half shell for an elegant presentation. The ground red pepper lends
a subtle heat to the breadcrumb topping. Slide the pan of oysters into the oven as you ask your guests to be seated.
By the time everyone is settled, the oysters will be ready to serve.

1½ (1-ounce) slices white bread
    Cooking spray
 ⅓ cup sliced green onions
 ¼ cup chopped fresh parsley
 2 garlic cloves, minced
 ¼ cup Italian-seasoned breadcrumbs
 ¼ cup (1 ounce) grated fresh Parmesan cheese
 1 teaspoon fresh lemon juice
 ⅛ teaspoon ground red pepper
 ⅛ teaspoon black pepper
24 oysters on the half shell
 8 lemon wedges

1. Preheat oven to 450°.

2. Place bread in a food processor, and pulse 10 times or until coarse crumbs form to measure ¾ cup.

3. Heat a medium nonstick skillet coated with cooking spray over medium heat. Add onions, parsley, and garlic; cook 5 minutes, stirring constantly. Remove from heat; stir in fresh breadcrumbs, Italian-seasoned breadcrumbs, and next 4 ingredients. Place oysters on a jelly-roll pan. Sprinkle breadcrumb mixture evenly over oysters.

4. Bake at 450° for 7 minutes or until edges of oysters curl. Serve with lemon wedges. Yield: 8 servings (serving size: 3 oysters).

CALORIES 76 (30% from fat); FAT 2.5g (sat 1g, mono 0.5g, poly 0.5g); PROTEIN 5.4g; CARB 7.7g; FIBER 0.4g; CHOL 26mg; IRON 3.3mg; SODIUM 234mg; CALC 77mg

Toasted Shrimp Appetizers

1 garlic clove, peeled
2 green onions, cut into 1-inch pieces
1½ teaspoons cornstarch
1½ teaspoons dry sherry
1 large egg white
½ pound medium shrimp, peeled and deveined
½ cup canned water chestnuts
24 slices party-style rye bread
¼ cup sweet-and-sour simmer sauce

1. Preheat oven to 375°. Drop garlic through food chute with food processor on; process until minced. Add green onions; process until chopped. Add cornstarch, sherry, and egg white; process until well blended. Add shrimp and water chestnuts; pulse mixture until finely chopped.

2. Spread about 1 tablespoon shrimp mixture over each bread slice. Place bread slices on a baking sheet. Bake at 375° for 10 minutes or until shrimp mixture is done. Serve warm with sweet-and-sour sauce. Yield: 2 dozen appetizers (serving size: 1 appetizer and ½ teaspoon sauce.)

CALORIES 49 (7% from fat); FAT 0.4g (sat 0.1g, mono 0.1g, poly 0.1g); PROTEIN 2.9g; CARB 8.6g; FIBER 1.2g; CHOL 14mg; IRON 0.7mg; SODIUM 87mg; CALC 12mg

Buffalo Shrimp with Blue Cheese Dip

48 large shrimp (about 2 pounds)
2 tablespoons dark brown sugar
2 tablespoons chopped onion
3 tablespoons cider vinegar
2 tablespoons water
2 tablespoons ketchup
1 tablespoon Worcestershire sauce
2 to 4 teaspoons hot sauce
¼ teaspoon black pepper
1 garlic clove, chopped
¾ cup fat-free cottage cheese
3 tablespoons skim milk
2 tablespoons (½ ounce) crumbled blue cheese
⅛ teaspoon black pepper
Cooking spray
Celery sticks and leaves (optional)

1. Peel and devein shrimp, leaving tails intact. Place shrimp in a shallow dish; cover and chill.

2. Combine sugar and next 8 ingredients in a blender; cover and process until smooth. Pour sugar mixture into a small saucepan. Place over medium-low heat; cook 10 minutes, stirring occasionally. Cool and pour over shrimp. Cover and marinate in refrigerator 30 minutes, turning shrimp occasionally.

3. Combine cottage cheese, milk, blue cheese, and ⅛ teaspoon pepper in a blender; cover and process until mixture is smooth. Spoon into a bowl; cover and chill.

4. Preheat broiler. Remove shrimp from marinade, reserving marinade. Arrange shrimp in a single layer on a broiler pan coated with cooking spray; broil 3 minutes. Turn shrimp over; baste with marinade. Broil 3 minutes or until shrimp are done. Serve with cheese dip; garnish with celery sticks and leaves, if desired. Yield: 16 appetizers (serving size: 3 shrimp and 1 tablespoon dip).

CALORIES 54 (12% from fat); FAT 0.7g (sat 0.2g, mono 0.1g, poly 0g); PROTEIN 9g; CARB 3.1g; FIBER 0.1g; CHOL 64mg; IRON 1.2mg; SODIUM 125mg; CALC 23mg

Cheese Fondue with Apples

¼ cup all-purpose flour
¾ cup (3 ounces) shredded Emmenthaler or Swiss cheese
⅛ teaspoon ground nutmeg
1 garlic clove, halved
¾ cup fat-free, less-sodium chicken broth
¼ cup dry white wine
1 teaspoon kirsch (cherry brandy)
3 Pink Lady apples, each cored and cut into 9 wedges

1. Lightly spoon flour into a dry measuring cup; level with a knife. Combine flour, cheese, and nutmeg, tossing well.

2. Rub cut sides of garlic on inside of a medium, heavy saucepan. Add broth and wine to pan; bring to a simmer over medium heat.

3. Add one-third cheese mixture to pan; stir with a whisk until combined. Repeat twice with remaining cheese mixture. Reduce heat to medium-low. Cook 5 minutes or until smooth, stirring frequently.

4. Remove cheese mixture from heat; stir in kirsch. Pour mixture into a fondue pot. Keep warm over low flame. Serve with apple wedges. Yield: 9 servings (serving size: 3 apple wedges and about 2 tablespoons fondue).

CALORIES 84 (32% from fat); FAT 3g (sat 1.8g, mono 0.7g, poly 0.2g); PROTEIN 3.4g; CARB 9.9g; FIBER 1.3g; CHOL 9mg; IRON 0.3mg; SODIUM 80mg; CALC 101mg

Tempeh Satay with Curried Cashew Sauce

Tempeh:

¼ cup rice vinegar

¼ cup low-sodium soy sauce

¼ cup mirin (sweet rice wine)

2 teaspoons minced peeled fresh ginger

2 teaspoons vegetable oil

1 garlic clove, crushed

1 pound tempeh, cut into 40 cubes

Sauce:

Cooking spray

1 cup chopped onion

2 teaspoons minced peeled fresh ginger

¼ teaspoon fine sea salt

2 garlic cloves, chopped

2 teaspoons curry powder

½ teaspoon ground turmeric

1 cup water

2 tablespoons chopped cashews

1 tablespoon fresh lemon juice

1. To prepare tempeh, combine first 6 ingredients in a large nonstick skillet; add tempeh, tossing lightly to coat. Bring to a boil. Cover, reduce heat to low, and simmer 15 minutes.
2. Uncover tempeh mixture, and increase heat to medium-high. Cook 4 minutes or until golden brown, turning frequently. Cool.
3. To prepare sauce, heat a small saucepan coated with cooking spray over medium-high heat. Add onion, ginger, salt, and garlic; sauté 5 minutes. Stir in curry powder and turmeric; sauté 1 minute. Add water. Bring to a boil; cook 1 minute. Cool 5 minutes.
4. Pour onion mixture into a blender, and add cashews and lemon juice. Process until smooth. Place a toothpick in each tempeh cube. Serve with warm cashew sauce. Yield: 20 servings (serving size: 2 tempeh cubes and about 2 teaspoons sauce).

CALORIES 50 (32% from fat); FAT 1.8g (sat 0.4g, mono 0.3g, poly 0.7g); PROTEIN 4g; CARB 4.1g; FIBER 1.7g; CHOL 0mg; IRON 0.7mg; SODIUM 241mg; CALC 32mg

Spicy Chicken Bites with Cucumber Dip

1 pound skinless, boneless chicken breasts, cut into 1-inch pieces

¼ cup minced onion

1 large garlic clove, minced

1 egg, lightly beaten

⅓ cup dry breadcrumbs

1 teaspoon ground ginger

½ teaspoon ground cumin

½ teaspoon curry powder

½ teaspoon salt

½ teaspoon ground red pepper

¼ teaspoon black pepper

3 tablespoons all-purpose flour

2 teaspoons vegetable oil, divided

¼ teaspoon paprika, divided

Cucumber Dip

1. Place half of chicken in a food processor, and pulse 6 times or until chicken is coarsely chopped. Spoon into a large bowl; repeat procedure with remaining chicken. Add onion, garlic, and egg. Combine breadcrumbs and next 6 ingredients; add to chicken mixture, stirring well. Shape mixture into 40 (1-inch) balls.
2. Place flour in a medium bowl. Roll each chicken ball in flour; place in an 11 x 7-inch baking dish. Microwave at MEDIUM-HIGH (70% power) 6 minutes, stirring every 2 minutes.
3. Combine oil and paprika in a skillet; place over medium heat until hot. Add chicken balls; cook 10 minutes, stirring occasionally. Serve warm with Cucumber Dip. Yield: 40 appetizer servings (serving size: 1 chicken ball and 1½ teaspoons dip).

(Totals include Cucumber Dip) CALORIES 27 (23% from fat); FAT 0.7g (sat 0.2g, mono 0.2g, poly 0.2g); PROTEIN 3.3g; CARB 1.8g; FIBER 0.1g; CHOL 12mg; IRON 0.2mg; SODIUM 49mg; CALC 16mg

Cucumber Dip

1 cup grated seeded peeled cucumber

1 cup plain low-fat yogurt

1 teaspoon dried dill

½ teaspoon lemon juice

1. Place cucumber on several layers of paper towels; cover with additional paper towels. Let stand 15 minutes, pressing down occasionally. Combine cucumber and remaining ingredients in a bowl; cover and chill. Yield: 1⅓ cups (serving size: 1 tablespoon).

CALORIES 8 (22% from fat); FAT 0.2g (sat 0.1g, mono 0.1g, poly 0g); PROTEIN 0.9g; CARB 1g; FIBER 0.1g; CHOL 0.6mg; IRON 0.1mg; SODIUM 8mg; CALC 23mg

Spicy Rum Punch

You can steep the juice in advance and then add the ginger beer and rum just before serving so that the punch will be fizzy. Ginger beer, which actually contains no alcohol, tastes like a spicy ginger ale.

¼ cup chopped crystallized ginger
2 tablespoons black peppercorns
6 star anise
4 (3-inch) cinnamon sticks
2 (64-ounce) bottles cranberry juice cocktail
2 cups dark rum
4 (12-ounce) bottles ginger beer (such as Stewart's)

1. Combine first 5 ingredients in a large Dutch oven; bring to a boil. Remove from heat; let stand 30 minutes.
2. Strain cranberry mixture through a fine sieve into a bowl; discard solids. Chill thoroughly. Stir in rum and ginger beer just before serving. Yield: 20 servings (serving size: about ¾ cup).

CALORIES 205 (0% from fat); FAT 0g; PROTEIN 0.2g; CARB 38.2g; FIBER 0.2g; CHOL 0mg; IRON 0.1mg; SODIUM 4mg; CALC 13mg

Wasabi Bloody
Marys

For a two-hour holiday cocktail party, estimate three drinks,
three glasses, and three napkins for each guest.

Wasabi Bloody Marys

½   cup fresh lime juice
1½ tablespoons wasabi paste
6   cups low-sodium vegetable juice
3   tablespoons Worcestershire sauce
1¼ teaspoons hot pepper sauce
¾   teaspoon salt
1½ cups vodka

1. Combine lime juice and wasabi; stir with a whisk until wasabi dissolves.
2. Combine wasabi and lime mixture, vegetable juice, Worcestershire sauce, pepper sauce, and salt in a pitcher. Chill thoroughly.
3. Stir in vodka. Serve over ice. Yield: 8 servings (serving size: about 1 cup).

CALORIES 166 (0% from fat); FAT 0g; PROTEIN 1.6g; CARB 11.3g; FIBER 1.8g; CHOL 0mg; IRON 1.2mg; SODIUM 395mg; CALC 43mg

Citrus Wassail

12 whole cloves
3   (3-inch) cinnamon sticks
1   (750-milliliter) bottle Cabernet Sauvignon or other dry red wine
1   (64-ounce) bottle cranberry-tangerine juice drink
2   (12-ounce) cans frozen citrus beverage concentrate (such as Five Alive), thawed and undiluted
½   cup water

1. Place cloves and cinnamon sticks on a 6-inch square of cheesecloth; tie ends of cheesecloth securely.
2. Place spice bag, wine, and remaining ingredients in a 4- to 6-quart electric slow cooker; stir well. Cover with lid; cook on low-heat setting 7 hours. Discard spice bag. Serve warm or chilled. Yield: 3¼ quarts (serving size: 1 cup).
Note: For a nonalcoholic beverage, replace the wine with 3¼ cups purple grape juice and increase the cloves to 40.

CALORIES 175 (0% from fat); FAT 0g; PROTEIN 0.1g; CARB 46.2g; FIBER 0g; CHOL 0mg; IRON 0.2mg; SODIUM 25mg; CALC 4mg

Holiday Glögg

This lightened version of a traditional Swedish holiday punch takes the chill off those deep-freeze winter nights.

3½ cups water
1   tablespoon whole cloves
¼   teaspoon ground cardamom
2   (3-inch) cinnamon sticks
2   (750-milliliter) bottles dry red wine
1   cup raisins
1   cup sugar

1. Combine first 4 ingredients in a large saucepan; bring to a boil. Reduce heat; simmer 20 minutes.
2. Strain liquid through a sieve into a bowl, discarding cloves and cinnamon sticks. Return liquid to saucepan. Stir in wine, raisins, and sugar, and cook mixture over medium heat just until sugar is dissolved and mixture is thoroughly heated. Serve warm. Yield: 18 servings (serving size: ½ cup).
Note: Nonalcoholic dry red wine may be substituted for regular wine, if desired.

CALORIES 86 (1% from fat); FAT 0.1g; PROTEIN 0.3g; CARB 17.8g; FIBER 0.6g; CHOL 0mg; IRON 0.3mg; SODIUM 5mg; CALC 6mg

Warm Spiced Cranberry Cocktail

5½ cups cranberry juice cocktail
2½ cups orange juice
11 whole cloves
3   (¼-inch-thick) slices orange, each cut into 3 wedges (optional)
Freshly grated nutmeg (optional)

1. Combine first 3 ingredients in a medium saucepan, and bring juice mixture to a boil. Reduce heat, and simmer juice mixture 7 minutes. Discard cloves.
2. Pour juice mixture into mugs, and garnish with orange wedges and grated nutmeg, if desired. Yield: 2 quarts (serving size: 1 cup).

CALORIES 133 (3% from fat); FAT 0.4g (sat 0g, mono 0.1g, poly 0.1g); PROTEIN 0.6g; CARB 32.9g; FIBER 0.3g; CHOL 0mg; IRON 0.4mg; SODIUM 4mg; CALC 13mg

Cranberry Liqueur

2 cups sugar
1 cup water
1 (12-ounce) package fresh cranberries
3 cups vodka

1. Combine sugar and water in a medium saucepan; cook over medium heat 5 minutes or until sugar dissolves, stirring constantly. Remove from heat, and cool completely.
2. Place cranberries in a food processor; process 2 minutes or until finely chopped. Combine sugar mixture and cranberries in a large bowl; stir in vodka.
3. Pour cranberry mixture into clean jars; secure with lids. Let stand 3 weeks in a cool, dark place, shaking every other day.
4. Strain cranberry mixture through a cheesecloth-lined sieve into a bowl, and discard solids. Carefully pour liqueur into clean bottles or jars. Yield: 4½ cups (serving size: ¼ cup).
Note: Store refrigerated or at room temperature up to 1 year.

CALORIES 200 (0% from fat); FAT 0g; PROTEIN 0g; CARB 23.4g; FIBER 0.4g; CHOL 0mg; IRON 0mg; SODIUM 0.8mg; CALC 1.2mg

Cranberry Cosmopolitans
(pictured on page 126)

½ cup Cranberry Liqueur (recipe above)
¼ cup Cointreau (orange-flavored liqueur)
2 tablespoons lime juice

1. Place crushed ice in a martini shaker. Add liqueur, Cointreau, and lime juice; strain into martini glasses. Yield: 2 cocktails.

CALORIES 283 (0% from fat); FAT 0.1g; PROTEIN 0.1g; CARB 34.6g; FIBER 0.5g; CHOL 0mg; IRON 0.1mg; SODIUM 3mg; CALC 4mg

not just for sipping
Cranberry Liqueur strikes the ideal balance of a pure, simple syrup infused with intensely tart cranberries and the spirit of vodka. But instead of simply sipping this evocative recipe in liqueur glasses, you've got several other options as well.

- Pour it over homemade fruitcake, drenching the holiday staple.
- Drizzle it over ice cream or fruit for a glamorous dessert.
- Give it away as party favors in small decanters or glass bottles embellished with beaded toppers. Or substitute it for a bottle of wine at the next dinner party you attend as a little "thank you" to the hostess for a wonderful evening.

Cranberry-Raspberry Spritzer

To garnish this drink, thread fresh cranberries and fresh lemon slices onto wooden skewers.

3 cups unsweetened raspberry-flavored sparkling water, chilled
3 cups cranberry-raspberry juice drink, chilled
¼ cup plus 2 tablespoons crème de cassis (black currant-flavored liqueur), divided

1. Combine sparkling water and cranberry-raspberry juice drink in a pitcher; stir well.
2. Spoon 1 tablespoon crème de cassis into each of 6 glasses, and add 1 cup juice mixture to each. Yield: 6 servings.
Note: For a nonalcoholic version, omit the crème de cassis; the recipe works fine without it.

CALORIES 82 (0% from fat); FAT 0g; PROTEIN 0.4g; CARB 16.5g; FIBER 0g; CHOL 0mg; IRON 0.2mg; SODIUM 3mg; CALC 3mg

Cranberry-
Raspberry
Spritzer

Open House Brunch

serves 8

Mini Frittatas with Ham and Cheese (recipe on page 140)

Asian Party Mix (recipe on page 127)

Mulled Cranberry-Orange Cider (recipe below)

Mulled Cranberry-Orange Cider

  4 whole cloves

  4 whole allspice

  2 star anise

  1 (3-inch) cinnamon stick, broken in half

  5 cups apple cider

  3 cups cranberry juice cocktail

 ¼ cup packed brown sugar

  4 orange slices

  8 star anise (optional)

  8 small orange slices (optional)

1. Place first 4 ingredients on a cheesecloth square. Gather edges of cheesecloth together; tie securely. Combine spice bag, cider, cranberry juice, sugar, and 4 orange slices in a Dutch oven. Bring to a boil. Reduce heat; simmer, partially covered, 10 minutes. Remove from heat; let stand 30 minutes. Discard spice bag and orange slices. Serve with additional anise and orange slices, if desired. Yield: 8 servings (serving size: 1 cup).

CALORIES 155 (1% from fat); FAT 0.1g (sat 0g, mono 0g, poly 0.1g); PROTEIN 0.6g; CARB 38.5g; FIBER 0.1g; CHOL 0mg; IRON 0.3mg; SODIUM 20mg; CALC 21mg

Pomegranate Cocktail

You may substitute fresh orange juice for the blood orange.

  2 cups pomegranate juice

1½ cups vodka

  1 cup grenadine

  1 cup fresh blood orange juice (about 2 oranges)

 ½ cup fresh lime juice (about 2 limes)

1. Combine all ingredients in a pitcher. Serve over ice. Yield: 12 servings (serving size: ½ cup).

CALORIES 171 (1% from fat); FAT 0.1g (sat 0g, mono 0g, poly 0.1g); PROTEIN 0.2g; CARB 28.3g; FIBER 0.1g; CHOL 0mg; IRON 0.2mg; SODIUM 14mg; CALC 6mg

Holiday Eggnog

2⅓ cups 2% reduced-fat milk

  1 (8-ounce) carton frozen egg substitute, partially thawed

 ¼ cup nonfat dry milk

 ¼ cup sugar

  1 teaspoon vanilla extract

 ½ teaspoon rum flavoring

 ⅛ teaspoon ground nutmeg

  6 ice cubes

Additional ground nutmeg (optional)

1. Combine first 8 ingredients in a blender; process until smooth. Pour into small glasses; sprinkle with nutmeg, if desired. Serve immediately. Yield: 10 servings (serving size: ½ cup).

CALORIES 72 (14% from fat); FAT 1.1g (sat 0.7g, mono 0.3g, poly 0g); PROTEIN 5.2g; CARB 9.8g; FIBER 0g; CHOL 5mg; IRON 0.5mg; SODIUM 78mg; CALC 114mg

Coffee Royale

This holiday season, invite everyone over for coffee. They'll all agree that this cup of java is far from ordinary. Full of flavor, this beverage will have you savoring every sip.

1¼ cups 1% low-fat milk

  1 tablespoon sugar

 ¼ teaspoon ground cinnamon

2¾ cups hot strong brewed coffee

 ½ cup amaretto (almond-flavored liqueur)

  6 (3-inch) cinnamon sticks (optional)

1. Combine milk, sugar, and cinnamon in a medium saucepan. Place over medium heat; cook 2 minutes or until sugar dissolves, stirring constantly. Remove from heat; stir in coffee and amaretto. Pour into mugs; garnish with cinnamon sticks, if desired. Yield: 6 servings (serving size: ¾ cup).

Note: You may omit the amaretto; just increase the coffee to 3¼ cups.

CALORIES 96 (6% from fat); FAT 0.6g (sat 0.4g, mono 0.2g, poly 0g); PROTEIN 1.8g; CARB 10.9g; FIBER 0g; CHOL 2mg; IRON 0.5mg; SODIUM 28mg; CALC 66mg

After a long day of sledding and building snowmen, chase away the cold with Hot Chocolate or Hot White Chocolate with Ginger. Serve these sweet mugs with festive holiday cookies (recipes beginning on page 106 and 336).

holiday perks

For an informal holiday get-together with the girls, serve coffee and dessert straight from your coffee table. Use a variety of new and antique containers for serving an array of innovative coffee condiments. Here are some suggestions:

- Scatter peppermint disks on the coffee table.
- Stand cinnamon sticks or peppermint sticks in a silver-rimmed punch cup or crystal toothpick holder.
- Place colored and flavored sugar sprinkles in a glass or crystal salt shaker.
- Serve grated chocolate, miniature chocolate chips, or shaved chocolate curls from a decorative salt cellar.
- Pour coffee-flavored drops, liqueurs, and syrups into cruets.
- Drizzle honey into a syrup pitcher.
- Nestle chocolate-covered coffee beans in a silver cup, interesting mug, or beautiful small bowl.
- Spoon turbinado (large-crystal) sugar into an antique jelly container, pickle canister, or sugar container.
- Place vanilla sugar in a tall salt cellar.
- Stand rock-sugar swizzlers in a demitasse cup or mug.

Tahitian Coffee

Melted vanilla low-fat ice cream forms a sweet, foamy top layer for this drink.

2¾ cups hot strong brewed coffee
¼ cup dark rum
1 tablespoon sugar
½ cup vanilla low-fat ice cream
4 (3-inch) cinnamon sticks (optional)

1. Combine first 3 ingredients in a pitcher, stirring until sugar dissolves. Pour into mugs, and top with ice cream. Garnish with cinnamon sticks, if desired. Yield: 4 servings (serving size: ¾ cup coffee and 2 tablespoons ice cream).

CALORIES 75 (6% from fat); FAT 0.5g (sat 0.3g, mono 0g, poly 0g); PROTEIN 0.9g; CARB 8.5g; FIBER 0.3g; CHOL 1.3mg; IRON 0.1mg; SODIUM 15mg; CALC 28mg

Hot Chocolate

⅓ cup unsweetened cocoa
5½ cups fat-free milk, divided
1 tablespoon vanilla extract
1 (14-ounce) can fat-free sweetened condensed milk
1 (3-inch) cinnamon stick (optional)
30 miniature marshmallows

1. Place cocoa in a 3-quart electric slow cooker. Gradually add 1 cup fat-free milk, stirring with a whisk until well blended. Add 4½ cups fat-free milk, vanilla, and condensed milk, stirring with a whisk until well blended. Add cinnamon stick, if desired. Cover with lid; cook on low-heat setting 4 to 8 hours. Discard cinnamon stick. Stir well with a whisk before serving. Ladle hot chocolate into mugs; top with marshmallows. Yield: 10 servings (serving size: ¾ cup hot chocolate and 3 marshmallows).

CALORIES 173 (3% from fat); FAT 0.6g (sat 0.3g, mono 0.2g, poly 0g); PROTEIN 8.7g; CARB 34.1g; FIBER 1g; CHOL 5mg; IRON 0.5mg; SODIUM 101mg; CALC 284mg

Hot White Chocolate with Ginger

⅔ cup chopped peeled fresh ginger
½ cup sugar
¼ cup water
8 cups fat-free milk
1 cup chopped premium white baking chocolate (about 4 ounces; such as Ghirardelli)

1. Combine ginger, sugar, and water in a large saucepan; cook over medium-high heat until sugar dissolves and mixture is golden (about 5 minutes); stir frequently. Remove from heat; cool slightly.
2. Add milk and chocolate; stir with a whisk. Heat over medium-low heat to 180° or until bubbles form around edge of pan, stirring frequently (do not boil). Strain mixture into a bowl; discard solids. Yield: 8 servings (serving size: 1 cup).

CALORIES 210 (21% from fat); FAT 5g (sat 3g, mono 1.4g, poly 0.2g); PROTEIN 9.2g; CARB 32.8g; FIBER 0g; CHOL 7mg; IRON 0.1mg; SODIUM 139mg; CALC 331mg

Hot
Chocolate

breads

The aroma of fresh-baked bread warms hearts and kitchens alike throughout the holidays. Be it breakfast, lunch, or a very special dinner, our savory and sweet loaves and rolls rise to the occasion.

Citrus-Cream Cheese
Pull-Apart Rolls
(recipe on page185)

Buttermilk-Chive Biscuits

Not only are these biscuits perfect for our Holiday Buffet Menu (page 135), but they also make great gifts. When giving as a gift, include a handwritten gift card with these instructions: To reheat, place in a 300° oven for 10 minutes.

  2 cups all-purpose flour
  1 tablespoon baking powder
 ½ teaspoon baking soda
 ½ teaspoon salt
 ¼ cup chilled butter, cut into small pieces
 ¾ cup low-fat buttermilk
  1 large egg, lightly beaten
 ¼ cup chopped fresh chives

1. Preheat oven to 400°.
2. Lightly spoon flour into dry measuring cups; level with a knife. Combine flour, baking powder, baking soda, and salt in a large bowl; cut in butter with a pastry blender or 2 knives until mixture resembles coarse meal. Combine buttermilk and egg, and stir in chives. Add buttermilk mixture to flour mixture, and stir just until moist.
3. Turn dough out onto a heavily floured surface; knead lightly 5 times. Roll dough to a ½-inch thickness; cut with a 2-inch biscuit cutter. Place dough rounds, 1 inch apart, on a baking sheet. Bake at 400° for 12 minutes or until golden. Serve warm or at room temperature. Yield: 20 biscuits (serving size: 1 biscuit).

CALORIES 74 (33% from fat); FAT 2.7g (sat 1.6g, mono 0.8g, poly 0.2g); PROTEIN 2g; CARB 10.2g; FIBER 0.4g; CHOL 17mg; IRON 0.7mg; SODIUM 199mg; CALC 56mg

Sweet Potato Biscuits

To prepare as a gift, place biscuit squares in stacks of four, wrap each stack with colorful plastic wrap, and tie with ribbon.

  2 cups all-purpose flour
 ⅓ cup yellow cornmeal
2½ teaspoons baking powder
 ½ teaspoon salt
 ⅓ cup chilled butter, cut into small pieces
  1 cup mashed cooked sweet potato
 ½ cup fat-free milk
  2 tablespoons honey

1. Preheat oven to 400°.
2. Lightly spoon flour into dry measuring cups; level with a knife. Combine flour, cornmeal, baking powder, and salt in a bowl; cut in butter with a pastry blender or 2 knives until mixture resembles coarse meal. Add sweet potato, milk, and honey; stir just until moist.
3. Turn dough out onto a heavily floured surface; knead lightly 5 times. Pat dough into a 9-inch square; cut into 16 squares. Place biscuits on a baking sheet. Bake at 400° for 20 minutes or until golden. Yield: 16 biscuits (serving size: 1 biscuit).

CALORIES 134 (28% from fat); FAT 4.1g (sat 2.4g, mono 1.1g, poly 0.3g); PROTEIN 2.5g; CARB 21.9g; FIBER 1.2g; CHOL 11mg; IRON 1.1mg; SODIUM 196mg; CALC 60mg

Sun-Dried Tomato Semolina Biscuits

Semolina is durum wheat that's more coarsely ground than all-purpose flour. It's similar to fine cornmeal, which will work as a substitute. The dough will be sticky, but don't add more flour; it would make the biscuits dry.

  2 cups boiling water
 10 sun-dried tomatoes, packed without oil
  2 cups all-purpose flour
 ¼ cup semolina flour or yellow cornmeal
  1 tablespoon sugar
1½ teaspoons baking powder
 ¾ teaspoon salt
 ½ teaspoon baking soda
  1 teaspoon dried basil
 ¼ teaspoon ground red pepper
 ¼ cup chilled butter, cut into small pieces
  1 cup low-fat buttermilk
    Cooking spray

1. Combine boiling water and sun-dried tomatoes in a bowl; let stand 15 minutes. Drain and chop.
2. Preheat oven to 425°.
3. Lightly spoon flours into dry measuring cups, and level with a knife. Combine flours and next 6 ingredients in a bowl, and cut in butter with a pastry blender or 2 knives until mixture resembles coarse meal. (Flour mixture and butter can also be combined in a food processor; pulse until mixture resembles coarse meal.) Add chopped tomatoes and buttermilk, and stir just until moist.
4. Turn dough out onto a heavily floured surface; knead lightly 5 times. Roll to a ½-inch thickness; cut with a 2½-inch biscuit cutter. Place on a baking sheet coated with cooking spray. Bake at 425° for 15 minutes or until golden. Yield: 1 dozen (serving size: 1 biscuit).

CALORIES 140 (29% from fat); FAT 4.5g (sat 2.6g, mono 1.3g, poly 0.3g); PROTEIN 3.4g; CARB 21.3g; FIBER 0.9g; CHOL 10mg; IRON 1.4mg; SODIUM 345mg; CALC 67mg

Pumpkin Biscuits with
Orange-Honey Butter

Pumpkin Biscuits with Orange-Honey Butter

Try these with your Thanksgiving feast. They're likely to become a new tradition. Or if you'd prefer,
serve them as part of a country-style breakfast with bacon or baked ham.

2   cups all-purpose flour
3   tablespoons sugar
2   teaspoons baking powder
1   teaspoon ground cinnamon
½   teaspoon baking soda
½   teaspoon salt
¼   teaspoon ground nutmeg
¼   cup chilled butter, cut into small pieces
¾   cup fat-free buttermilk
½   cup canned pumpkin
Cooking spray
¼   cup Orange-Honey Butter

1. Preheat oven to 450°.
2. Lightly spoon flour into dry measuring cups, and level with
a knife. Combine flour and next 6 ingredients; cut in chilled
butter with a pastry blender or 2 knives until mixture resembles
coarse meal.
3. Combine buttermilk and pumpkin; add to flour mixture,
stirring just until moist. Turn dough out onto a lightly floured

surface; knead lightly 5 times. Roll dough to a ½-inch thickness. Cut into 12 biscuits with a 2½-inch biscuit cutter. Place
biscuits on a baking sheet coated with cooking spray. Bake
at 450° for 11 minutes or until golden. Serve warm with
Orange-Honey Butter. Yield: 12 servings (serving size: 1
biscuit and 1 teaspoon butter).

(Totals include Orange-Honey Butter) CALORIES 153 (33% from fat); FAT 5.6g
(sat 3.4g, mono 1.6g, poly 0.3g); PROTEIN 2.9g; CARB 23.1g; FIBER 1g; CHOL 15mg;
IRON 1.2mg; SODIUM 311mg; CALC 68mg

Orange-Honey Butter

½   cup butter, softened
½   cup honey
½   teaspoon grated orange rind

1. Combine all ingredients in a medium bowl; beat with a
mixer at medium speed until well blended. Store in refrigerator.
Yield: 1¼ cups (serving size: 1 teaspoon).

CALORIES 22 (61% from fat); FAT 1.5g (sat 0.9g, mono 0.5g, poly 0.1g); PROTEIN 0g;
CARB 2.3g; FIBER 0g; CHOL 4mg; IRON 0mg; SODIUM 16mg; CALC 1mg

Cranberry Scones

1¾ cups all-purpose flour
½ cup granulated sugar
¼ cup yellow cornmeal
2 teaspoons baking powder
¼ teaspoon baking soda
¼ teaspoon salt
2 tablespoons chilled butter, cut into small pieces
½ cup halved fresh cranberries
½ cup low-fat buttermilk
½ teaspoon grated orange rind
1 large egg, lightly beaten
Cooking spray
1 teaspoon powdered sugar

1. Preheat oven to 375°.
2. Lightly spoon flour into dry measuring cups; level with a knife. Combine flour and next 5 ingredients in a bowl; cut in butter with a pastry blender or 2 knives until mixture resembles coarse meal. Add cranberries, tossing to coat.
3. Combine buttermilk, rind, and egg; add to flour mixture, stirring just until moist (dough will be sticky).
4. Turn dough out onto a lightly floured surface, and knead lightly 5 times with floured hands. Pat dough into a 7-inch circle on a baking sheet coated with cooking spray. Cut dough into 10 wedges, cutting into but not through dough. Bake at 375° for 30 minutes or until golden. Sift powdered sugar over scones; serve warm. Yield: 10 scones (serving size: 1 scone).

CALORIES 168 (17% from fat); FAT 3.2g (sat 1.7g, mono 0.9g, poly 0.3g); PROTEIN 3.7g; CARB 31.2g; FIBER 1.1g; CHOL 28mg; IRON 1.4mg; SODIUM 231mg; CALC 75mg

Coffee-Nut Scones

⅔ cup 1% low-fat milk
2½ tablespoons instant coffee granules
1 teaspoon vanilla extract
1 large egg, lightly beaten
2¼ cups all-purpose flour
⅓ cup sugar
2½ teaspoons baking powder
¾ teaspoon salt
¼ teaspoon ground cinnamon
¼ cup chilled butter, cut into small pieces
3 tablespoons finely chopped walnuts
Cooking spray
2 teaspoons 1% low-fat milk
2 teaspoons sugar

1. Combine ⅔ cup milk and coffee granules in a microwave-safe bowl. Microwave at HIGH 1 minute; stir until coffee dissolves. Cover and chill completely. Stir in vanilla and egg.
2. Preheat oven to 425°.
3. Lightly spoon flour into dry measuring cups; level with a knife. Combine flour and next 4 ingredients in a bowl; cut in butter with a pastry blender or 2 knives until mixture resembles coarse meal. (Flour mixture and butter can also be combined in a food processor; pulse until mixture resembles coarse meal.) Stir in walnuts. Add milk mixture, stirring just until moist (dough will be sticky).
4. Turn dough out onto a lightly floured surface; knead lightly 4 times with floured hands. Pat dough into an 8-inch circle on a baking sheet coated with cooking spray. Cut dough into 10 wedges, cutting into but not completely through dough. Brush dough with 2 teaspoons milk; sprinkle with 2 teaspoons sugar. Bake at 425° for 20 minutes or until browned. Serve warm. Yield: 10 scones (serving size: 1 scone).

CALORIES 207 (30% from fat); FAT 7g (sat 3.3g, mono 1.9g, poly 1.3g); PROTEIN 4.9g; CARB 31g; FIBER 1g; CHOL 35mg; IRON 1.7mg; SODIUM 361mg; CALC 101mg

santa's scone surprise

Don a velvety red Santa hat and surprise your coworkers with a midmorning snack of scones, such as Coffee-Nut Scones (recipe at right), and a fresh, hot pot of flavored roasted coffee. It'll be a perfect break from a busy workday and will spread some much-needed office holiday cheer. Remember: When cutting your scones, cut through the circle of dough, but don't separate the wedges. This allows them to bake as one large scone, and they will be much moister than scones baked separately.

Ham and Cheese Scones

Scones make wonderful seasonal "dunkers" for coffee, cocoa, and soups. Ham and Cheese Scones are a great accompaniment to a steaming bowl of chili. Serve as a warm-up to a tree-trimming get-together or as a savory breakfast sensation.

Ham and Cheese Scones

  2 cups all-purpose flour
  1 tablespoon baking powder
  2 teaspoons sugar
  ¼ teaspoon salt
  ¼ teaspoon ground red pepper
  3 tablespoons chilled butter, cut into small pieces
  ¾ cup (3 ounces) shredded reduced-fat extrasharp
     Cheddar cheese
  ¾ cup chopped 33%-less-sodium ham (about 3 ounces)
  ¾ cup fat-free buttermilk
  2 large egg whites
Cooking spray

1. Preheat oven to 400°.
2. Lightly spoon flour into dry measuring cups; level with a knife. Combine flour, baking powder, sugar, salt, and pepper in a large bowl; cut in butter with a pastry blender or 2 knives until mixture resembles coarse meal. Stir in cheese and ham. Combine buttermilk and egg whites, stirring with a whisk. Add to flour mixture, stirring just until moist.
3. Turn dough out onto a lightly floured surface; knead lightly 4 or 5 times with floured hands. Pat dough into an 8-inch circle on a baking sheet coated with cooking spray. Cut into 8 wedges, cutting into but not through dough. Bake at 400° for 20 minutes or until lightly browned. Yield: 8 servings (serving size: 1 scone).

CALORIES 217 (30% from fat); FAT 7.2g (sat 4.1g, mono 1.6g, poly 0.4g); PROTEIN 10.4g; CARB 27.1g; FIBER 0.9g; CHOL 26mg; IRON 1.8mg; SODIUM 519mg; CALC 235mg

Strawberry Yogurt Scones

  1½ cups all-purpose flour
  ⅔   cup whole wheat flour
  ½   cup sugar
  2   teaspoons baking powder
  ½   teaspoon baking soda
  ¼   teaspoon salt
  ¾   cup chopped strawberries
  ⅔   cup strawberry fat-free yogurt
  3   tablespoons butter, melted
  ½   teaspoon grated orange rind
  1   large egg white, lightly beaten
Cooking spray
  2   teaspoons sugar

1. Preheat oven to 400°.
2. Lightly spoon flours into dry measuring cups; level with a knife. Combine flours, ½ cup sugar, baking powder, baking soda, and salt in a large bowl. Combine strawberries, yogurt, butter, rind, and egg white; add to flour mixture, stirring just until moist.
3. Turn dough out onto a lightly floured surface; knead lightly 4 times with floured hands. Pat into an 8-inch circle on a baking sheet coated with cooking spray. Cut into 12 wedges, cutting into but not through dough; sprinkle with 2 teaspoons sugar. Bake at 400° for 20 minutes or until lightly browned. Yield: 12 servings (serving size: 1 scone).

CALORIES 152 (20% from fat); FAT 3.3g (sat 1.9g, mono 0.9g, poly 0.3g); PROTEIN 3.6g; CARB 27.7g; FIBER 1.5g; CHOL 8mg; IRON 1.1mg; SODIUM 227mg; CALC 78mg

Cranberry-Orange Muffins

These easy-to-make, freezable, cake-style muffins feature two traditional holiday flavors—orange and cranberry. Keep extras in the freezer to serve to drop-in guests or for breakfast on-the-go. Microwave at HIGH 20 to 30 seconds to reheat.

1½   cups all-purpose flour
3   tablespoons yellow cornmeal
1½   teaspoons baking powder
½   teaspoon baking soda
¼   teaspoon salt
¾   cup sugar
¼   cup butter, softened
2   teaspoons grated orange rind
1   large egg
1   large egg white
⅓   cup fat-free buttermilk
¼   cup part-skim ricotta cheese
⅔   cup dried cranberries, coarsely chopped
Cooking spray

1. Preheat oven to 375°.

2. Lightly spoon flour into dry measuring cups; level with a knife. Combine flour and next 4 ingredients.

3. Place sugar and butter in a large bowl; beat with a mixer at medium speed until well blended (about 2 minutes). Add rind, and beat to combine. Add egg and egg white, 1 at a time, beating well after each addition.

4. Combine buttermilk and ricotta, stirring well with a whisk. Add flour mixture and buttermilk mixture alternately to sugar mixture, beginning and ending with flour mixture. Fold in cranberries. Spoon batter into 12 muffin cups coated with cooking spray. Bake at 375° for 20 minutes or until a wooden pick inserted in center comes out clean. Cool in pan 10 minutes on a wire rack; remove from pan. Cool completely on wire rack. Yield: 12 servings (serving size: 1 muffin).

CALORIES 184 (24% from fat); FAT 4.9g (sat 2.8g, mono 1.4g, poly 0.3g); PROTEIN 3.5g; CARB 31.6g; FIBER 1g; CHOL 30mg; IRON 1mg; SODIUM 225mg; CALC 63mg

White Chocolate-Apricot Muffins

Combining the chocolate with the dry ingredients disperses it and creates chocolate pockets throughout the muffins. To mince crystallized ginger, coat your knife with cooking spray to keep it from sticking.

1¾ cups all-purpose flour
½ cup sugar
1 tablespoon minced crystallized ginger
1½ teaspoons baking powder
½ teaspoon salt
2 ounces premium white baking chocolate, finely chopped
¾ cup 1% low-fat milk
3 tablespoons butter, melted
1 large egg, lightly beaten
Cooking spray
½ cup apricot preserves
1 tablespoon sugar

1. Preheat oven to 400°.
2. Lightly spoon flour into dry measuring cups; level with a knife. Combine flour and next 5 ingredients in a medium bowl; stir well with a whisk. Make a well in center of mixture. Combine milk, butter, and egg; stir well with a whisk. Add to flour mixture, stirring just until moist.
3. Spoon about 1 tablespoon batter into each of 12 muffin cups coated with cooking spray. Spoon 2 teaspoons preserves into center of each muffin cup (do not spread over batter); top with remaining batter. Sprinkle evenly with 1 tablespoon sugar.
4. Bake at 400° for 22 minutes or until muffins spring back when touched lightly in center. Remove from pan. Cool completely on a wire rack. Yield: 1 dozen (serving size: 1 muffin).

CALORIES 199 (24% from fat); FAT 5.3g (sat 2.9g, mono 1.6g, poly 0.4g); PROTEIN 3.3g; CARB 35.3g; FIBER 0.7g; CHOL 27mg; IRON 1.2mg; SODIUM 212mg; CALC 72mg

muffin merriment

Muffins are a quick and easy way to get breakfast on the table in a flash. Not only are they a time-saver for you, but they're also always well received when presented as a gift. Here are some fun and creative ideas for gift-giving:

- Slip muffins into a new muffin pan after they've cooled, and package them with a copy of the recipe attached.
- Invite a friend over for coffee and muffins. Then send her off with a take-home batch of her very own.
- Place muffins in a wire basket lined with a colorful, seasonal cloth napkin, and tie on a gift tag.

Whole Wheat Orange Juice Muffins

Whole Wheat Orange Juice Muffins

Before you rush out the door for holiday grocery shopping, be sure to grab a muffin. These muffins can be baked and frozen up to a month in advance. Just pop them in the toaster oven or microwave for a quick warm-up.

1½ cups all-purpose flour
½ cup whole wheat flour
½ cup sugar
2 teaspoons baking powder
¾ teaspoon salt
½ teaspoon ground cinnamon
1 cup orange juice
¼ cup vegetable oil
1½ teaspoons grated lemon rind
1 large egg, lightly beaten
½ cup golden raisins
Cooking spray
1 tablespoon sugar

1. Preheat oven to 400°.
2. Lightly spoon flours into dry measuring cups; level with a knife. Combine flours and next 4 ingredients in a medium bowl; stir well with a whisk. Make a well in center of mixture. Combine juice, oil, rind, and egg; add to flour mixture, stirring just until moist. Stir in raisins. Spoon batter into 12 muffin cups coated with cooking spray. Sprinkle evenly with 1 tablespoon sugar. Bake at 400° for 20 minutes or until muffins spring back when touched lightly in center. Remove from pan. Cool completely on a wire rack. Yield: 1 dozen (serving size: 1 muffin).

CALORIES 189 (26% from fat); FAT 5.5g (sat 1g, mono 1.6g, poly 2.5g); PROTEIN 3.2g; CARB 33g; FIBER 1.4g; CHOL 18mg; IRON 1.3mg; SODIUM 235mg; CALC 58mg

Buttermilk
Pancakes

Buttermilk Pancakes

These light and fluffy hotcakes are easy to make and easy to eat, and they may be the ultimate
comfort food. They're a great beginning to a day filled with shopping. Try topping with maple syrup,
fresh fruit, or jams and jellies for a breakfast that's perfect for the whole family.

1   cup all-purpose flour
2   tablespoons sugar
1   teaspoon baking powder
½   teaspoon baking soda
¼   teaspoon salt
1   cup low-fat buttermilk
1   tablespoon vegetable oil
1   large egg, lightly beaten
Cooking spray

1. Lightly spoon flour into a dry measuring cup; level with a
knife. Combine flour and next 4 ingredients in a large bowl;
make a well in center of mixture. Combine buttermilk, oil,
and egg. Add to flour mixture; stir until smooth.

2. Spoon about ¼ cup batter for each pancake onto a hot
nonstick griddle or nonstick skillet coated with cooking
spray. Turn pancakes when tops are covered with bubbles
and edges look cooked. Yield: 9 (4-inch) pancakes (serving
size: 1 pancake).

CALORIES 99 (26% from fat); FAT 2.9g (sat 0.8g, mono 0.9g, poly 1g); PROTEIN 3.2g;
CARB 14.9g; FIBER 0.4g; CHOL 25mg; IRON 0.8mg; SODIUM 211mg; CALC 69mg

Stuffed French Toast

You'll love this bread pudding–like dish, not only for its layers of smooth cream cheese stuffing and cinnamon raisin bread, but also because of its efficiency. You can throw it together the night before and pop it in the oven shortly before brunch—perfect for the hectic holiday season.

24 (1-ounce) slices cinnamon-raisin bread
Cooking spray
3 cups 1% low-fat milk
2 cups egg substitute, divided
1 cup half-and-half
1 cup sugar, divided
1 tablespoon vanilla extract
⅛ teaspoon ground nutmeg
1 (8-ounce) block fat-free cream cheese, softened
1 (8-ounce) block ⅓-less-fat cream cheese, softened
Bottled cinnamon-sugar (optional)

1. Trim crusts from bread, and arrange half of bread in a 13 x 9-inch baking dish coated with cooking spray.

2. Combine milk, 1½ cups egg substitute, half-and-half, and ½ cup sugar in a large bowl, stirring with a whisk. Pour half of milk mixture over bread in dish.

3. Combine ½ cup egg substitute, ½ cup sugar, vanilla, ground nutmeg, and cream cheeses in a food processor or blender, and process until smooth. Pour cream cheese mixture over moist bread in dish. Top with remaining bread, and pour remaining milk mixture over bread. Cover and refrigerate 8 hours or overnight.

4. Preheat oven to 350°.

5. Uncover and bake at 350° for 55 minutes. Let stand 10 minutes before serving. Sprinkle with cinnamon-sugar, if desired. Yield: 12 servings (serving size: 1 piece).

CALORIES 340 (30% from fat); FAT 11.3g (sat 5.1g, mono 3.3g, poly 0.9g); PROTEIN 16.7g; CARB 43.2g; FIBER 1.5g; CHOL 26mg; IRON 3.7mg; SODIUM 447mg; CALC 197mg

Stuffed French
Toast

Classic Banana Bread

Classic Banana Bread

We love this bread's moist texture and simple flavor. Banana bread should form a crack down the center as it bakes—a sign that the baking soda is doing its job.

 2 cups all-purpose flour
 ¾ teaspoon baking soda
 ½ teaspoon salt
 1 cup sugar
 ¼ cup butter, softened
 2 large eggs
 1½ cups mashed ripe banana (about 3 bananas)
 ⅓ cup plain low-fat yogurt
 1 teaspoon vanilla extract
 Cooking spray

1. Preheat oven to 350°.
2. Lightly spoon flour into dry measuring cups, and level with a knife. Combine flour, baking soda, and salt, stirring mixture with a whisk.
3. Place sugar and butter in a large bowl, and beat with a mixer at medium speed until well blended (about 1 minute). Add eggs, 1 at a time, beating well after each addition. Add banana, yogurt, and vanilla; beat until blended. Add flour mixture; beat at low speed just until moist. Spoon batter into an 8 x 4-inch loaf pan coated with cooking spray. Bake at 350° for 1 hour or until a wooden pick inserted in center comes out clean. Cool in pan 10 minutes on a wire rack; remove from pan. Cool completely on wire rack. Yield: 1 loaf, 14 servings (serving size: 1 slice).

CALORIES 187 (21% from fat); FAT 4.3g (sat 2.4g, mono 1.2g, poly 0.3g); PROTEIN 3.3g; CARB 34.4g; FIBER 1.1g; CHOL 40mg; IRON 1mg; SODIUM 198mg; CALC 20mg

Hazelnut-Pear Bread

 ⅓ cup hazelnuts (about 1¾ ounces)
 1 cup coarsely shredded peeled pear
 ¾ cup sugar
 3 tablespoons vegetable oil
 ½ teaspoon grated lemon rind
 ½ teaspoon vanilla extract
 1 large egg, lightly beaten
 1 large egg white, lightly beaten
 1½ cups all-purpose flour
 ½ cup whole wheat flour
 1¼ teaspoons baking powder
 ¾ teaspoon ground cinnamon
 ½ teaspoon salt
 ½ teaspoon baking soda
 Baking spray with flour

1. Preheat oven to 350°. Place hazelnuts on a baking sheet. Bake at 350° for 15 minutes, stirring once. Turn nuts out onto a towel. Roll up towel, and rub off skins. Chop nuts; set aside.
2. Combine pear and next 6 ingredients in a large bowl. Lightly spoon flours into dry measuring cups; level with a knife. Combine hazelnuts, flours, and next 4 ingredients, and add to pear mixture, stirring just until flour mixture is moist. Spoon batter into an 8 x 4-inch loaf pan coated with baking spray. Bake at 350° for 1 hour and 5 minutes or until a wooden pick inserted in center comes out clean. Cool in pan 10 minutes on a wire rack; remove from pan. Cool completely on wire rack. Yield: 1 loaf, 12 servings (serving size: 1 slice).

CALORIES 198 (32% from fat); FAT 7.1g (sat 0.7g, mono 3.7g, poly 2.1g); PROTEIN 3.8g; CARB 31.4g; FIBER 2g; CHOL 15mg; IRON 1.3mg; SODIUM 264mg; CALC 43mg

"Absolutely irresistible! This bread is a winner with both kids and adults alike. And it's great as a gift or a snack. When giving as a gift, wrap in a holiday tea towel, and tie with a bow and fresh greenery."
—Kathryn Conrad, Test Kitchens Staffer

Marbled-Chocolate
Banana Bread

Marbled-Chocolate Banana Bread

Marbled-Chocolate Banana Bread is a *Cooking Light* all-time favorite recipe. It has become a staple in our staff's own homes.

  2 cups all-purpose flour
 ¾ teaspoon baking soda
 ½ teaspoon salt
  1 cup sugar
 ¼ cup butter, softened
1½ cups mashed ripe banana (about 3 bananas)
 ½ cup egg substitute
 ⅓ cup plain low-fat yogurt
 ½ cup semisweet chocolate chips
Cooking spray

1. Preheat oven to 350°.

2. Lightly spoon flour into dry measuring cups; level with a knife. Combine flour, baking soda, and salt, stirring with a whisk.

3. Place sugar and butter in a large bowl; beat with a mixer at medium speed until well blended (about 1 minute). Add banana, egg substitute, and yogurt; beat until blended. Add flour mixture; beat at low speed just until moist.

4. Place chocolate chips in a medium microwave-safe bowl, and microwave at HIGH 1 minute or until almost melted; stir until smooth. Cool slightly. Add 1 cup batter to chocolate, stirring until well combined. Spoon chocolate batter alternately with plain batter into an 8 x 4-inch loaf pan coated with cooking spray. Swirl batters together using a knife. Bake at 350° for 1 hour and 15 minutes or until a wooden pick inserted in center comes out clean. Cool in pan 10 minutes on a wire rack; remove from pan. Cool completely on wire rack. Yield: 1 loaf, 16 slices (serving size: 1 slice).

CALORIES 183 (23% from fat); FAT 4.7g (sat 2.8g, mono 1.4g, poly 0.2g); PROTEIN 3.1g; CARB 33.4g; FIBER 1.3g; CHOL 8mg; IRON 1.1mg; SODIUM 180mg; CALC 18mg

our staff raves

"Banana bread is always such a crowd-pleaser at any time of year, but it's especially popular during the holidays. Marbled-Chocolate Banana Bread is like a great standard recipe, but with a twist." —Tiffany Vickers, Test Kitchens Staffer

Cranberry Quick Bread with Raisins and Hazelnuts

The batter is a pale tan color, but the finished bread is a rich golden brown. The fruit in this easy quick bread helps it stay moist. You can use chopped walnuts in place of the hazelnuts.

1⅓ cups all-purpose flour
 ⅔ cup whole wheat flour
  1 cup sugar
  1 teaspoon baking powder
 ½ teaspoon baking soda
 ¼ teaspoon salt
 ¾ cup apple juice
  3 tablespoons vegetable oil
  1 teaspoon grated orange rind
  1 large egg, lightly beaten
1⅓ cups chopped fresh cranberries
 ⅓ cup golden raisins
 ¼ cup chopped hazelnuts
Cooking spray

1. Preheat oven to 350°.

2. Lightly spoon flours into dry measuring cups; level with a knife. Combine flours and next 4 ingredients in a large bowl; make a well in center of mixture. Combine juice, oil, rind, and egg; add to flour mixture, stirring just until moist. Fold in cranberries, raisins, and hazelnuts.

3. Spoon batter into a 9 x 5-inch loaf pan coated with cooking spray. Bake at 350° for 50 minutes or until a wooden pick inserted in center comes out clean. Cool in pan 10 minutes on a wire rack; remove from pan. Cool completely on wire rack. Yield: 1 loaf, 16 servings (serving size: 1 slice).

CALORIES 162 (23% from fat); FAT 4.2g (sat 0.6g, mono 1.6g, poly 1.8g); PROTEIN 2.6g; CARB 29.6g; FIBER 1.6g; CHOL 13mg; IRON 1mg; SODIUM 112mg; CALC 27mg

Dried Fruit-and-Walnut Loaf

Cardamom is an aromatic spice in the ginger family. If you prefer, you can substitute an equal amount of ground ginger, nutmeg, or cinnamon. Whichever spice you choose, you can be sure your kitchen will smell like the season.

2¼ cups all-purpose flour
½ cup sugar
1½ teaspoons baking powder
¾ teaspoon salt
½ teaspoon baking soda
¼ teaspoon ground cardamom
1 cup sweetened applesauce
⅓ cup low-fat sour cream
¼ cup honey
3 tablespoons vegetable oil
1 teaspoon vanilla extract
1 large egg, lightly beaten
¾ cup finely chopped dried mixed fruit or fruit bits
    (about 5 ounces)
¼ cup finely chopped walnuts
   Cooking spray

1. Preheat oven to 350°.
2. Lightly spoon flour into dry measuring cups; level with a knife. Combine flour and next 5 ingredients in a large bowl; make a well in center of mixture. Combine applesauce and next 5 ingredients; add to flour mixture, stirring just until moist. Fold in fruit and nuts.
3. Spoon batter into a 9 x 5-inch loaf pan coated with cooking spray. Bake at 350° for 1 hour or until a wooden pick inserted in center comes out clean. Cool in pan 10 minutes on a wire rack; remove from pan. Cool completely on wire rack. Yield: 1 loaf, 14 servings (serving size: 1 slice).

CALORIES 209 (24% from fat); FAT 5.4g (sat 1.1g, mono 1.5g, poly 2.4g); PROTEIN 3.4g; CARB 37.9g; FIBER 1.7g; CHOL 17mg; IRON 1.4mg; SODIUM 205mg; CALC 38mg

Dried Plum-and-Port Bread

This quick bread won our Test Kitchens' highest rating. It's great for dessert, as a snack, or for breakfast. Prunes are actually dried plums; we use the latter name in our title because more people find it appealing.

2 cups chopped pitted prunes
1¾ cups port or other sweet red wine
1½ cups all-purpose flour
½ cup whole wheat or all-purpose flour
¾ cup packed brown sugar
2½ teaspoons baking powder
½ teaspoon salt
½ teaspoon ground cinnamon
¼ cup vegetable oil
¼ cup plain low-fat yogurt
2 teaspoons grated lemon rind
1 teaspoon vanilla extract
2 large eggs, lightly beaten
   Cooking spray
1 tablespoon turbinado sugar or granulated sugar

1. Combine prunes and port in a small saucepan; bring to a boil. Cover and remove from heat; let stand 30 minutes.
2. Preheat oven to 350°.
3. Lightly spoon flours into dry measuring cups; level with a knife. Combine flours and next 4 ingredients in a medium bowl; stir well with a whisk. Make a well in center of mixture. Drain prunes in a colander over a bowl, reserving liquid. Combine reserved liquid, oil, and next 4 ingredients; stir well with a whisk. Stir in prunes. Add to flour mixture, stirring just until moist.
4. Spoon batter into a 9 x 5-inch loaf pan coated with cooking spray; sprinkle with turbinado sugar. Bake at 350° for 1 hour and 15 minutes or until a wooden pick inserted in center comes out clean. Cool in pan 10 minutes on a wire rack; remove from pan. Cool completely on wire rack. Yield: 1 loaf, 12 servings (serving size: 1 slice).
Note: If using a glass baking dish, decrease oven temperature by 25° and bake about 10 minutes less than the recipe states.

CALORIES 254 (21% from fat); FAT 5.9g (sat 1.2g, mono 1.8g, poly 2.5g); PROTEIN 4.5g; CARB 48g; FIBER 3.1g; CHOL 37mg; IRON 2.1mg; SODIUM 222mg; CALC 100mg

---

bread storage and freezing

Bread will stay fresh up to 5 days if stored at room temperature rather than in the refrigerator. However, if your bread contains anything perishable, such as a cream cheese filling, store it in the refrigerator rather than at room temperature.

If you need to store bread longer—perhaps to make ahead for Christmas gift-giving—store it in the freezer. Wrap a whole loaf tightly in plastic wrap, then in heavy-duty aluminum foil; freeze up to a month. To thaw, let stand at room temperature. To freeze individual slices, place in small heavy-duty zip-top plastic bags. Remove excess air from bags; seal and freeze for up to a month. Or wrap slices in plastic wrap and aluminum foil as noted above. Thaw at room temperature, or microwave at HIGH for 15 to 30 seconds.

Dried Plum-and-Port
Bread

Sweet Potato-Streusel Quick Bread

To make this quick bread even quicker, we used the microwave to cook the potato and to soften the butter for the streusel topping. Use an electric knife to get clean slices.

 1 large sweet potato (about 12 ounces)
 2 teaspoons butter
 ⅓ cup chopped pecans
 2 tablespoons dark brown sugar
1½ cups all-purpose flour
 ½ cup whole wheat flour
 ¾ cup packed dark brown sugar
 2 teaspoons baking powder
 1 teaspoon ground cinnamon
 ¾ teaspoon salt
 ¼ teaspoon ground nutmeg
 ⅔ cup fresh orange juice
 3 tablespoons vegetable oil
 1 large egg, lightly beaten
Cooking spray

1. Preheat oven to 350°.
2. Pierce potato with a fork; place on a paper towel in microwave oven. Microwave at HIGH 7 minutes, turning after 4 minutes. Wrap potato in paper towel; let stand 5 minutes. Peel potato; mash to measure 1 cup.
3. Place butter in a small microwave-safe bowl. Microwave at MEDIUM 20 seconds or until soft. Stir in pecans and 2 tablespoons sugar.
4. Lightly spoon flours into dry measuring cups and level with a knife. Combine flours, ¾ cup sugar, and next 4 ingredients in a large bowl, stirring with a whisk. Add mashed sweet potato, juice, oil, and egg, stirring until well blended.
5. Spoon batter into an 8 x 4-inch loaf pan coated with cooking spray. Drop pecan mixture by spoonfuls over top of loaf; gently press into batter.
6. Bake at 350° for 1 hour or until a wooden pick inserted in center comes out clean. Cool 5 minutes in pan on a wire rack; remove from pan. Cool completely on wire rack. Yield: 1 loaf, 16 servings (serving size: 1 slice).

CALORIES 174 (28% from fat); FAT 5.4g (sat 1g, mono 1.9g, poly 2.2g); PROTEIN 2.8g; CARB 29.5g; FIBER 1.5g; CHOL 15mg; IRON 1.2mg; SODIUM 187mg; CALC 57mg

Pumpkin-Date Loaf with Cream Cheese Swirl

 ½ cup (4 ounces) block-style ⅓-less-fat cream cheese
 2 tablespoons granulated sugar
 1 teaspoon vanilla extract
 1 large egg white, lightly beaten
 2 cups all-purpose flour
1½ teaspoons pumpkin-pie spice
 1 teaspoon baking powder
 ½ teaspoon salt
 ¼ teaspoon baking soda
 1 large egg, lightly beaten
 1 large egg yolk, lightly beaten
1¼ cups packed dark brown sugar
 ¾ cup canned pumpkin
 3 tablespoons vegetable oil
 ¾ cup whole pitted dates, chopped (about 5 ounces)
Cooking spray

1. Preheat oven to 350°.
2. Combine first 4 ingredients in a small bowl; beat with a mixer at medium speed until blended.
3. Lightly spoon flour into dry measuring cups, and level with a knife. Combine flour and next 4 ingredients in a medium bowl, stirring well with a whisk. Combine egg, egg yolk, and brown sugar in a medium bowl; stir with a whisk until well blended. Add pumpkin and oil; stir well with a whisk. Stir in dates. Add to flour mixture, stirring just until moist.
4. Spoon batter into a 9 x 5-inch loaf pan coated with cooking spray. Spoon cream cheese mixture over batter; swirl batters together using tip of a knife. Bake at 350° for 1 hour or until a wooden pick inserted in center comes out clean. Cool in pan 10 minutes on a wire rack; remove from pan. Cool completely on wire rack. Yield: 1 loaf, 16 servings (serving size: 1 slice).

CALORIES 208 (22% from fat); FAT 5.1g (sat 1.7g, mono 1.3g, poly 1.7g); PROTEIN 3.5g; CARB 38.1g; FIBER 1.6g; CHOL 32mg; IRON 1.4mg; SODIUM 167mg; CALC 50mg

Pumpkin-Date Loaf with
Cream Cheese Swirl

Whole Wheat
Rolls

Whole Wheat Rolls

  2 tablespoons sugar, divided
  1 package dry yeast (about 2¼ teaspoons)
  ¼ cup warm water (100° to 110°)
1½ cups all-purpose flour, divided
  1 cup whole wheat flour
  ½ teaspoon salt
  ¼ cup warm 1% low-fat milk
  1 tablespoon vegetable oil
  1 large egg
Cooking spray
  1 tablespoon butter, melted

1. Dissolve 1 teaspoon sugar and yeast in warm water; let stand 5 minutes. Lightly spoon flours into dry measuring cups; level with a knife. Place 1¼ cups all-purpose flour, whole wheat flour, 5 teaspoons sugar, and salt in a food processor; pulse 2 times or until blended. With processor on, add yeast mixture, milk, oil, and egg through food chute; process until dough forms a ball. Process 1 additional minute.

2. Turn dough out onto a lightly floured surface. Knead until smooth and elastic (about 5 minutes); add enough of remaining flour, 1 tablespoon at a time, to prevent dough from sticking to hands. Place in a large bowl coated with cooking spray, turning to coat top. Cover; let rise in a warm place (85°), free from drafts, 1 hour or until doubled in size. (Press 2 fingers into dough. If indentation remains, dough has risen enough.) Punch dough down; cover and let rest 5 minutes.

3. Coat 12 muffin cups with cooking spray. Divide dough into 12 equal portions. Divide each portion into 3 pieces; shape each piece into a ball. Dip balls in melted butter; place 3 balls in each muffin cup. Cover and let rise 45 minutes or until doubled in bulk. Preheat oven to 400°. Uncover dough; bake at 400° for 15 minutes. Remove from pans; serve warm. Yield: 1 dozen (serving size: 1 roll).

CALORIES 132 (22% from fat); FAT 3.2g (sat 1g, mono 1g, poly 0.7g); PROTEIN 4.0g; CARB 22.3g; FIBER 1.8g; CHOL 20mg; IRON 1.3mg; SODIUM 113mg; CALC 15mg

take a dip

To accompany your bread, you usually have two choices: butter or olive oil. If you choose olive oil, here are some serving suggestions:
- Pour the oil into small, wide bowls to facilitate dipping.
- Add freshly ground black pepper to the oil in one bowl.
- Combine the olive oil with a small amount of flavored oil such as Spicy Thyme and Garlic Oil (recipe on page 102). Add a garlic clove or sprig of thyme to help guests identify the flavor.

Poppy Seed and Onion Crescent Rolls

  1 package dry yeast (about 2¼ teaspoons)
  1 cup warm water (100° to 110°)
  1 cup warm 2% reduced-fat milk (100° to 110°)
  2 tablespoons butter
1½ tablespoons sugar
  1 large egg
5½ to 6 cups all-purpose flour, divided
  ½ cup whole wheat flour
  2 teaspoons salt
Cooking spray
1½ tablespoons olive oil
  2 cups chopped onion
  1 large egg
  1 tablespoon 2% reduced-fat milk
  1 teaspoon poppy seeds

1. Dissolve yeast in warm water in a large mixing bowl; let stand 5 minutes. Add 1 cup milk, butter, sugar, and 1 egg, and beat with a mixer at medium speed until well blended. Lightly spoon flours into dry measuring cups; level with a knife. Add 3 cups all-purpose flour and whole wheat flour to yeast mixture; beat until blended. Let stand 15 minutes. Add salt, and beat well. Stir in 2 cups all-purpose flour to form a soft dough.

2. Turn dough out onto a floured surface. Knead until smooth and elastic (about 10 minutes); add enough of remaining flour, ¼ cup at a time, to prevent dough from sticking to hands. Place dough in a large bowl coated with cooking spray, turning to coat top. Cover; let rise in a warm place (85°), free from drafts, 1 hour or until doubled in size. (Press 2 fingers into dough. If indentation remains, dough has risen enough.)

3. Heat oil in a large nonstick skillet over medium-high heat. Add onion; cook 10 minutes or until golden.

4. Punch dough down. Cover; let rest 5 minutes. Divide in half. Working with 1 portion at a time, roll each portion into a 14-inch circle. Spread half of onion mixture over each portion; cut each portion into 12 wedges. Roll up each wedge tightly, beginning at wide end. Place, point sides down, on baking sheets coated with cooking spray. Combine 1 egg and 1 tablespoon milk, stirring with a whisk; brush over rolls. Sprinkle evenly with poppy seeds. Let rise, uncovered, 30 minutes or until doubled in size.

5. Preheat oven to 375°.

6. Bake at 375° for 23 minutes or until golden. Serve warm. Yield: 2 dozen (serving size: 1 roll).

CALORIES 159 (16% from fat); FAT 2.9g (sat 1g, mono 1.2g, poly 0.4g); PROTEIN 4.8g; CARB 28.3g; FIBER 1.5g; CHOL 21mg; IRON 1.7mg; SODIUM 217mg; CALC 26mg

Dinner rolls are delicious at any time of the year, but tuck in a slice of turkey or ham, and you've got an extraspecial holiday indulgence.

Herb Cloverleaf Rolls

  1 package dry yeast (about 2¼ teaspoons)
  2 teaspoons sugar
 ¼ cup warm water (100° to 110°)
 ¾ cup 1% low-fat milk
 ½ cup evaporated skim milk
  4 cups bread or all-purpose flour, divided
1½ tablespoons butter, melted
  1 teaspoon salt
 ½ teaspoon dried rosemary
 ½ teaspoon dried thyme
 ½ teaspoon dried oregano
 ¼ teaspoon black pepper
Cooking spray
  1 tablespoon water
  1 large egg white, lightly beaten

1. Dissolve yeast and sugar in warm water in a large bowl; let stand 5 minutes. Stir in milks. Lightly spoon flour into dry measuring cups; level with a knife. Add 3 cups flour, butter, and next 5 ingredients to yeast mixture; stir until blended. Turn dough out onto a lightly floured surface. Knead until smooth and elastic (about 10 minutes), adding enough of remaining flour, 1 tablespoon at a time, to prevent dough from sticking to hands.
2. Place dough in a large bowl coated with cooking spray, turning to coat top. Cover and let rise in a warm place (85°), free from drafts, 1 hour or until doubled in size. (Press 2 fingers into dough. If indentation remains, dough has risen enough.) Punch dough down; turn dough out onto a lightly floured surface. Cover and let rest 10 minutes. Divide into 18 equal portions. Working with 1 portion at a time (cover remaining dough to keep from drying), divide each portion into 3 pieces; shape each piece into a ball. Coat muffin pans with cooking spray; place 3 balls in each muffin cup. Cover; let rise 30 minutes or until doubled in size.
3. Preheat oven to 350°.
4. Uncover dough. Combine water and egg white, and brush over dough. Bake at 350° for 20 minutes. Serve warm. Yield: 1½ dozen (serving size: 1 roll).

CALORIES 111 (10% from fat); FAT 1.1g (sat 0.7g, mono 0.3g, poly 0g); PROTEIN 4.8g; CARB 21.6g; FIBER 0.1g; CHOL 3mg; IRON 1.4mg; SODIUM 152mg; CALC 35mg

Anadama Rolls with Sage

  1 package dry yeast (about 2¼ teaspoons)
Dash of sugar
 ¼ cup warm water (100° to 110°)
 ¾ cup 1% low-fat milk
 ¼ cup molasses
3¼ cups bread or all-purpose flour, divided
 ½ cup yellow cornmeal
  2 tablespoons butter, melted
  1 teaspoon dried rubbed sage
 ¾ teaspoon salt
Cooking spray
  2 teaspoons water
  1 large egg white, lightly beaten

1. Dissolve yeast and sugar in warm water in a large bowl; let stand 5 minutes. Stir in milk and molasses. Lightly spoon flour into dry measuring cups; level with a knife. Add 3 cups flour, cornmeal, and next 3 ingredients to yeast mixture; stir until blended. Turn dough out onto a lightly floured surface. Knead until smooth and elastic (about 10 minutes), adding enough of remaining flour, 1 tablespoon at a time, to prevent dough from sticking to hands.
2. Place dough in a large bowl coated with cooking spray, turning to coat top. Cover and let rise in a warm place (85°), free from drafts, 1 hour or until doubled in size. (Press 2 fingers into dough. If indentation remains, dough has risen enough.) Punch dough down; turn dough out onto a lightly floured surface. Cover and let rest 5 minutes. Divide into 18 equal portions. Working with 1 portion at a time (cover remaining dough to keep from drying), shape each into a ball. Place balls of dough 2 inches apart on baking sheets coated with cooking spray. Cover and let rise 30 minutes or until doubled in size.
3. Preheat oven to 350°.
4. Uncover dough. Cut a ¼-inch-deep "X" in top of each roll. Combine 2 teaspoons water and egg white; brush over dough. Bake at 350° for 13 minutes or until golden brown. Serve warm. Yield: 1½ dozen (serving size: 1 roll).

CALORIES 122 (11% from fat); FAT 1.5g (sat 0.9g, mono 0.4g, poly 0.1g); PROTEIN 4.1g; CARB 24.0g; FIBER 1.0g; CHOL 4mg; IRON 1.6mg; SODIUM 117mg; CALC 23mg

Buttermilk-Oat Rolls

¾ cup regular oats
½ cup boiling water
1 tablespoon sugar
1 package dry yeast (about 2¼ teaspoons)
1½ teaspoons sugar
¼ cup warm water (100° to 110°)
2¼ cups bread or all-purpose flour, divided
¼ cup low-fat buttermilk
1 tablespoon butter, melted
¾ teaspoon salt
Cooking spray
1 tablespoon water
1 large egg white, lightly beaten
1 tablespoon regular oats

1. Combine first 3 ingredients; stir until well blended. Let stand 5 minutes.

2. Dissolve yeast and 1½ teaspoons sugar in warm water; let stand 5 minutes. Lightly spoon flour into dry measuring cups; level with a knife. Add oat mixture, 1¾ cups flour, buttermilk, butter, and salt to yeast mixture, stirring to form a soft dough. Turn out onto a lightly floured surface. Knead until smooth and elastic (about 8 minutes), adding enough of remaining flour, 1 tablespoon at a time, to prevent dough from sticking to hands (dough will be slightly sticky).

3. Place dough in a large bowl coated with cooking spray, turning to coat top. Cover and let rise in a warm place (85°), free from drafts, 45 minutes or until doubled in size. (Press 2 fingers into dough. If indentation remains, dough has risen enough.) Punch dough down; cover and let rest 5 minutes. Divide into 12 equal portions. Working with 1 portion at a time (cover remaining dough to keep from drying), shape each into a ball. Place balls in a 9-inch square baking pan coated with cooking spray. Cover; let rise 30 minutes or until doubled in size.

4. Preheat oven to 375°. Uncover dough. Combine 1 tablespoon water and egg white; brush over dough. Sprinkle with oats. Bake at 375° for 25 minutes or until lightly browned. Serve warm. Yield: 1 dozen (serving size: 1 roll).

CALORIES 138 (16% from fat); FAT 2.5g (sat 0.8g, mono 0.7g, poly 0.6g); PROTEIN 4.7g; CARB 24.3g; FIBER 1.3g; CHOL 3mg; IRON 1.5mg; SODIUM 163mg; CALC 14mg

Buttermilk-Oat Rolls

Olive and Asiago Rolls

You can substitute Parmesan for Asiago and use green olives, if you prefer.

1 tablespoon sugar

1 package dry yeast (about 2¼ teaspoons)

¾ cup warm water (100° to 110°)

3⅔ cups bread flour

½ cup whole wheat flour

¾ cup 1% low-fat milk

2 tablespoons chopped fresh oregano

1 teaspoon salt

1 teaspoon olive oil

Cooking spray

3 tablespoons chopped pitted kalamata olives

1 tablespoon water

1 large egg white, lightly beaten

½ cup (2 ounces) grated Asiago cheese

1. Dissolve sugar and yeast in warm water in a large bowl; let stand 5 minutes. Lightly spoon flours into dry measuring cups; level with a knife. Add flours, milk, and next 3 ingredients to yeast mixture; beat with a mixer at medium speed until smooth.
2. Turn dough out onto a lightly floured surface. Knead until smooth and elastic (about 10 minutes).

3. Place dough in a large bowl coated with cooking spray, turning to coat top. Cover; let rise in a warm place (85°), free from drafts, 45 minutes or until doubled in size. (Press 2 fingers into dough. If indentation remains, dough has risen enough.)
4. Punch dough down. Cover and let rest 5 minutes. Turn dough out onto a lightly floured surface. Arrange olives over dough; knead gently 4 or 5 times or until olives are incorporated into dough. Cover and let rest 10 minutes.
5. Punch dough down. Divide into 16 equal portions. Working with 1 portion at a time (cover remaining dough to keep from drying), roll into 2-inch balls. Place on baking sheets coated with cooking spray. Cover; let rise 30 minutes or until doubled in size. Cut a ¼-inch-deep "X" in top of each roll.
6. Preheat oven to 375°.
7. Combine 1 tablespoon water and egg white; brush over rolls. Bake at 375° for 18 minutes or until golden brown. Remove from oven; immediately sprinkle with cheese. Serve warm. Yield: 16 rolls (serving size: 1 roll).

CALORIES 161 (15% from fat); FAT 2.7g (sat 0.9g, mono 1.1g, poly 0.4g); PROTEIN 6.1g; CARB 27.5g; FIBER 1.3g; CHOL 4mg; IRON 1.6mg; SODIUM 212mg; CALC 58mg

Sour Cream-Green Onion Fan Tans

1   package dry yeast (about 2¼ teaspoons)
1   teaspoon sugar
¼   cup warm water (100° to 110°)
4¼ cups bread or all-purpose flour, divided
¾   cup 1% low-fat milk
½   cup low-fat sour cream
1   teaspoon salt
¾   teaspoon ground cumin
Cooking spray
3   tablespoons butter, melted and divided
½   cup minced green onions, divided

1. Dissolve yeast and sugar in warm water in a large bowl; let stand 5 minutes. Lightly spoon flour into dry measuring cups; level with knife. Add 4 cups flour, milk, and next 3 ingredients to yeast mixture; stir until blended. Turn dough out onto a lightly floured surface. Knead until smooth and elastic (about 10 minutes), adding enough of remaining flour, 1 tablespoon at a time, to prevent dough from sticking to hands.
2. Place dough in a large bowl coated with cooking spray, turning to coat top. Cover; let rise in a warm place (85°), free from drafts, 1 hour or until doubled in size. (Press 2 fingers into dough. If indentation remains, dough has risen enough.) Punch dough down; cover and let rest 5 minutes. Divide dough into 3 equal portions. Working with 1 portion at a time (cover remaining dough to keep from drying), roll each portion into a 12 x 9-inch rectangle on a lightly floured surface. Brush each rectangle with 1½ teaspoons butter; sprinkle with about 2½ tablespoons onions. Cut each rectangle lengthwise into 6 (1½-inch) strips. Stack 6 strips, coated sides up, one on top of another. Cut each stack into 8 (1½-inch) sections. Place each stacked section, cut side down, in a muffin cup coated with cooking spray. Brush remaining butter over dough. Cover; let rise 30 minutes or until doubled in size.
3. Preheat oven to 400°.
4. Bake at 400° for 17 minutes or until golden brown. Serve warm. Yield: 2 dozen (serving size: 1 roll).
Food Processor Variation: Dissolve yeast and sugar in warm water in a small bowl; let stand 5 minutes. Lightly spoon flour into dry measuring cups; level with a knife. Place 4 cups flour, sour cream, salt, and cumin in a food processor; pulse 2 times or until blended. With processor on, slowly add yeast mixture and milk through food chute; process until dough forms a ball. Process 1 additional minute. Turn dough out onto a lightly floured surface. Knead until smooth and elastic (about 10

minutes); add enough of remaining flour, 1 tablespoon at a time, to prevent dough from sticking to hands. Place dough in a large bowl coated with cooking spray, turning to coat top. Let rise, and shape. Proceed with recipe as directed.

CALORIES 97 (18% from fat); FAT 1.9g (sat 1.3g, mono 0.4g, poly 0.1g); PROTEIN 3.5g; CARB 18.7g; FIBER 0.1g; CHOL 6mg; IRON 1.1mg; SODIUM 114mg; CALC 22mg

Cornmeal Cloverleaf Rolls

1   package dry yeast (about 2¼ teaspoons)
1   tablespoon sugar
¼   cup warm water (100° to 110°)
1½ cups 2% reduced-fat milk
4⅓ cups all-purpose flour, divided
⅓   cup cornmeal
3   tablespoons butter, melted
1¼ teaspoons salt
Cooking spray
1   large egg white, lightly beaten
1   tablespoon water
1   teaspoon cornmeal

1. Dissolve yeast and sugar in warm water in a large bowl; let stand 5 minutes. Stir in milk. Lightly spoon flour into dry measuring cups; level with a knife. Add 4 cups flour, ⅓ cup cornmeal, butter, and salt to yeast mixture; beat with a mixer at medium speed until smooth. Turn dough out onto a floured surface. Knead until smooth and elastic (about 10 minutes); add enough of remaining flour, 1 tablespoon at a time, to prevent dough from sticking to hands (dough will feel sticky).
2. Place dough in a large bowl coated with cooking spray, turning to coat top. Cover; let rise in a warm place (85°), free from drafts, 1 hour or until doubled in size. (Press 2 fingers into dough. If indentation remains, dough has risen enough.) Punch dough down; cover and let rest 10 minutes. Divide into 18 equal portions. Working with 1 portion at a time (cover remaining dough to keep from drying), divide each portion into 3 pieces; shape each piece into a ball. Coat muffin pans with cooking spray; place 3 dough balls in each muffin cup. Cover; let rise 10 minutes or until doubled in size.
3. Preheat oven to 350°.
4. Uncover rolls. Combine egg white and 1 tablespoon water; brush over rolls. Sprinkle with 1 teaspoon cornmeal. Bake at 350° for 25 minutes. Serve warm. Yield: 1½ dozen (serving size: 1 roll).

CALORIES 152 (16% from fat); FAT 2.7g (sat 1.5g, mono 0.7g, poly 0.2g); PROTEIN 4.4g; CARB 26.9g; FIBER 1.1g; CHOL 7mg; IRON 1.6mg; SODIUM 196mg; CALC 30mg

Crusty Rye Loaf

This bread is a great choice for corned beef, roast beef, or pastrami sandwiches. We especially like it with leftover Roast Beef with Horseradish-Mustard Sauce (recipe on page 91) topped with Swiss cheese. The sponge can be made ahead and refrigerated for up to 24 hours, but bring it back to room temperature before making the bread.

Sponge:
- 1 package dry yeast (about 2 1/4 teaspoons)
- 2/3 cup warm water (100° to 110°)
- 1/2 cup rye flour—medium
- 1/4 cup bread flour

Bread:
- 2 cups bread flour
- 1/2 cup rye flour—medium
- 1/2 cup water
- 2 teaspoons caraway seeds
- 1 1/4 teaspoons salt
- 2 tablespoons bread flour
- Cooking spray

1. To prepare sponge, dissolve yeast in warm water in a large bowl; let stand 5 minutes. Lightly spoon 1/2 cup rye flour and 1/4 cup bread flour into dry measuring cups; level with a knife. Add 1/2 cup rye flour and 1/4 cup bread flour to yeast mixture, stirring with a whisk. Cover and let stand in a warm place (85°), free from drafts, 2 hours.

2. To prepare bread, lightly spoon 2 cups bread flour and 1/2 cup rye flour into dry measuring cups; level with a knife. Add 2 cups bread flour, 1/2 cup rye flour, 1/2 cup water, caraway seeds, and salt to sponge; beat with a mixer at medium speed until smooth.

3. Turn dough out onto a lightly floured surface. Knead until smooth and elastic (about 10 minutes); add 2 tablespoons bread flour, 1 tablespoon at a time, to prevent dough from sticking to hands.

4. Shape dough into a round loaf; place loaf on a baking sheet coated with cooking spray. Cover and let rise 1 1/2 hours or until doubled in size. (Press 2 fingers into dough. If indentation remains, dough has risen enough.)

5. Preheat oven to 425°.

6. Uncover and pierce loaf 1 inch deep in several places with a wooden pick. Bake at 425° for 30 minutes or until loaf is browned on bottom and sounds hollow when tapped. Let stand 20 minutes before slicing. Yield: 1 loaf, 12 servings (serving size: 1 slice).

CALORIES 131 (5% from fat); FAT 0.7g (sat 0.1g, mono 0.1g, poly 0.3g); PROTEIN 4.3g; CARB 26.7g; FIBER 2.2g; CHOL 0mg; IRON 1.5mg; SODIUM 246mg; CALC 9mg

Spinach-Feta Bread

- 1 (1-pound) loaf frozen white bread dough
- 1 cup (4 ounces) crumbled feta cheese
- 1/3 cup (3 ounces) 1/3-less-fat cream cheese
- 1/2 teaspoon dried oregano
- 1/4 teaspoon salt
- 1 (14-ounce) can artichoke hearts, drained and chopped
- 1 (10-ounce) package frozen chopped spinach, thawed, drained, and squeezed dry
- 3 garlic cloves, minced
- 1 large egg white
- Cooking spray
- 2 tablespoons (1/2 ounce) grated fresh Parmesan cheese

1. Thaw dough in refrigerator 12 hours.

2. Combine feta and next 7 ingredients in a bowl.

3. Roll dough into a 16 x 10-inch rectangle on a lightly floured surface. Spread spinach mixture over dough, leaving a 1/2-inch border. Beginning with a long side, roll up dough, jelly-roll fashion; pinch seam and ends to seal. Place roll, seam side down, on a baking sheet coated with cooking spray. Cut diagonal slits into top of roll using a sharp knife. Cover; let rise in a warm place (85°), free from drafts, 1 hour or until doubled in size.

4. Preheat oven to 350°.

5. Sprinkle Parmesan cheese on top of roll. Bake at 350° for 45 minutes or until golden. Yield: 16 servings (serving size: 1 slice).

CALORIES 143 (23% from fat); FAT 3.7g (sat 2.2g, mono 1g, poly 0.3g); PROTEIN 6.4g; CARB 21.7g; FIBER 1.2g; CHOL 14mg; IRON 1.7mg; SODIUM 461mg; CALC 99mg

Spinach-Feta Bread

Walnut and
Rosemary Loaves

Walnut and Rosemary Loaves

Inside the dark crust is a creamy white bread flecked with rosemary and bits of walnuts.

Not only is this bread great with soups, it's also excellent for sandwiches.

2   cups warm 1% low-fat milk (100° to 110°)
¼   cup warm water (100° to 110°)
3   tablespoons sugar
2   tablespoons butter, melted
2   teaspoons salt
2   packages dry yeast (about 4½ teaspoons)
5½ cups all-purpose flour, divided
1   cup chopped walnuts
3   tablespoons coarsely chopped fresh rosemary
1   large egg, lightly beaten
Cooking spray
1   tablespoon yellow cornmeal
1   tablespoon 1% low-fat milk
1   large egg, lightly beaten

1. Combine first 5 ingredients in a large bowl, stirring with a whisk. Add yeast, stirring with a whisk; let stand 5 minutes. Lightly spoon flour into dry measuring cups; level with a knife. Add 2 cups flour to yeast mixture, stirring with a whisk. Cover and let rise in a warm place (85°), free from drafts, 15 minutes.

2. Add 2½ cups flour, walnuts, rosemary, and 1 egg to yeast mixture, stirring with a whisk. Turn dough out onto a lightly floured surface. Knead until smooth and elastic (about 10 minutes), adding enough of remaining flour, ¼ cup at a time, to prevent dough from sticking to hands.

3. Place dough in a large bowl coated with cooking spray, turning dough to coat top. Cover and let rise 1 hour or until doubled in size. (Press 2 fingers into dough. If indentation remains, dough has risen enough.)

4. Preheat oven to 400°.

5. Punch dough down; turn dough out onto a lightly floured surface. Divide dough in half, shaping each portion into a round. Place loaves on a baking sheet dusted with cornmeal. Cover and let rise 30 minutes or until doubled in size.

6. Combine 1 tablespoon milk and 1 egg, stirring with a whisk; brush over loaves. Make 3 diagonal cuts ¼-inch-deep across top of each loaf using a sharp knife.

7. Place loaves in oven. Reduce oven temperature to 375°; bake 40 minutes or until bottom of each loaf sounds hollow when tapped. Let stand 20 minutes before slicing. Yield: 2 loaves, 12 servings per loaf (serving size: 1 slice).

CALORIES 170 (28% from fat); FAT 5.2g (sat 1.2g, mono 1g, poly 2.6g); PROTEIN 5.2g; CARB 25.7g; FIBER 1.3g; CHOL 21mg; IRON 1.7mg; SODIUM 222mg; CALC 39mg

Apple "Fritters"

After a long day making holiday preparations, enjoy an Apple "Fritter" with a hot cup of tea or coffee.

Filling:

  1 tablespoon butter
  3 cups chopped peeled Granny Smith apple (about 1 pound)
  ½ cup apple juice
  2 tablespoons granulated sugar
  1 teaspoon ground cinnamon

Dough:

  2 packages dry yeast (about 4½ teaspoons)
  1 cup warm 1% low-fat milk (100° to 110°)
  5 cups all-purpose flour, divided
  ⅔ cup granulated sugar
  3 tablespoons butter, melted
  1 teaspoon salt
  2 large eggs, lightly beaten
    Cooking spray

Glaze:

1½ cups powdered sugar
  4 teaspoons butter, melted
  1 tablespoon apple juice
  ⅛ teaspoon ground cinnamon

1. To prepare filling, melt 1 tablespoon butter in a large nonstick skillet over medium-high heat. Add apple; sauté 3 minutes. Add ½ cup apple juice, 2 tablespoons granulated sugar, and 1 teaspoon cinnamon. Reduce heat to medium-low; simmer 3 minutes or until liquid is almost absorbed. Remove from heat; cool.

2. To prepare dough, dissolve yeast in warm milk in a large bowl. Let stand 5 minutes or until foamy. Lightly spoon flour into dry measuring cups; level with a knife. Add 3½ cups flour, ⅔ cup granulated sugar, 3 tablespoons melted butter, salt, and eggs to yeast mixture, stirring until smooth. Add 1 cup flour; stir until a soft dough forms.

3. Turn dough out onto a lightly floured surface. Knead until smooth and elastic (about 10 minutes); add enough of remaining flour, 1 tablespoon at a time, to prevent dough from sticking to hands (dough will feel sticky).

4. Place dough in a large bowl coated with cooking spray, turning to coat top. Cover and let rise in a warm place (85°), free from drafts, 1½ hours or until doubled in size. (Press 2 fingers into dough. If indentation remains, dough has risen enough.)

5. Punch dough down. Cover; let rest 5 minutes. Divide dough into 24 equal portions. Working with 1 portion at a time (cover remaining dough to keep from drying), roll into a 3-inch circle

on a lightly floured surface. Spoon 2 teaspoons filling into center of dough; gather dough over filling to form a ball, pinching seam to seal. Place balls, seam side down, in muffin cups coated with cooking spray. Cover; let rise 40 minutes or until doubled in size.

6. Preheat oven to 400°.

7. Uncover dough; bake at 400° for 20 minutes or until lightly browned. Remove from pan; cool on a wire rack.

8. To prepare glaze, combine powdered sugar and remaining 3 ingredients; drizzle over rolls. Yield: 2 dozen (serving size: 1 roll).

CALORIES 191 (16% from fat); FAT 3.4g (sat 1.8g, mono 1g, poly 0.3g); PROTEIN 3.9g; CARB 36.4g; FIBER 1.3g; CHOL 25mg; IRON 1.4mg; SODIUM 136mg; CALC 21mg

Spanish Buns

When you want the flavor and texture of homemade yeast rolls but don't have the time or energy for the kneading, double-rising, and shaping of traditional yeast rolls, this recipe solves your problem. Pour the batter into the pan, let it rise, and then bake and serve.

  3 cups all-purpose flour, divided
  ¾ cup granulated sugar
  1 teaspoon salt
  1 teaspoon freshly grated whole or ground nutmeg
  1 package quick-rise yeast (about 2¼ teaspoons)
  1 cup warm 1% low-fat milk (100° to 110°)
  ½ cup butter, melted
  4 large eggs
  2 teaspoons vanilla extract
    Cooking spray
  1 tablespoon powdered sugar

1. Lightly spoon flour into dry measuring cups; level with a knife. Combine 2 cups flour, ¾ cup sugar, salt, nutmeg, and yeast in a large bowl. Add milk and butter; stir with a wooden spoon until smooth. Add eggs, 1 at a time, beating well after each addition. Stir in vanilla. Add 1 cup flour; stir until smooth.

2. Scrape batter into a 13 x 9-inch baking pan coated with cooking spray. Coat dough with cooking spray. Cover and let rise in a warm place (85°), free from drafts, 1 hour or until doubled in size (batter should become bubbly on surface).

3. Preheat oven to 350°.

4. Bake at 350° for 30 minutes or until golden brown and a toothpick inserted in center comes out clean. Cool in pan on a wire rack. Sprinkle with powdered sugar. Cut into squares. Yield: 16 servings (serving size: 1 square).

CALORIES 203 (33% from fat); FAT 7.5g (sat 4.2g, mono 2.3g, poly 0.5g); PROTEIN 4.8g; CARB 29g; FIBER 0.8g; CHOL 70mg; IRON 1.4mg; SODIUM 229mg; CALC 29mg

Pennsylvania Dutch Tea Rolls

These rolls are one of Projects Editor Mary Creel's favorite holiday recipes. "The name throws you off because they're not dainty little breads to serve with tea. However, they're light and fluffy, and they have a wonderful yeasty flavor. They also rise high in the pan. Neither you nor your dinner guests will be able to stop at just one!"

5¼ cups all-purpose flour, divided
1⅓ cups warm 1% low-fat milk (100° to 110°)
1 package quick-rise yeast (about 2¼ teaspoons)
½ cup sugar
¼ cup butter, melted and cooled to room temperature
1 teaspoon salt
1 large egg, lightly beaten
Cooking spray
3 tablespoons 1% low-fat milk
1½ teaspoons poppy seeds

1. Lightly spoon flour into dry measuring cups, and level with a knife. Combine 2 cups flour, warm milk, and yeast in a large bowl. Cover mixture with plastic wrap, and let stand 1½ hours (batter should become very bubbly and almost triple in size).
2. Add 3 cups flour, sugar, butter, salt, and egg to batter; stir with a wooden spoon 3 minutes or until well combined. Turn dough out onto a lightly floured surface. Knead until smooth and elastic (about 8 minutes); add enough of remaining flour, 1 tablespoon at a time, to prevent dough from sticking to hands (dough will feel sticky).

3. Place dough in a large bowl coated with cooking spray, turning to coat top. Cover and let rise in a warm place (85°), free from drafts, 1½ hours or until doubled in size. (Press 2 fingers into dough. If indentation remains, dough has risen enough.)
4. Turn dough out onto a lightly floured surface; lightly dust dough with flour, and pat into a 10 x 8-inch rectangle. Divide dough by making 3 lengthwise cuts and 4 crosswise cuts to form 20 equal pieces; shape each piece into a ball. Place balls in a 13 x 9-inch baking pan coated with cooking spray.
5. Lightly coat dough with cooking spray. Cover with plastic wrap, and let rise 1 hour or until doubled in size.
6. Preheat oven to 375°.
7. Brush 3 tablespoons milk lightly over dough; sprinkle with poppy seeds. Bake at 375° for 20 minutes or until browned. Cool rolls in pan 5 minutes. Serve rolls warm, or cool completely on a wire rack. Yield: 20 servings (serving size: 1 roll).

CALORIES 173 (17% from fat); FAT 3.2g (sat 1.7g, mono 0.9g, poly 0.3g); PROTEIN 4.6g; CARB 31.3g; FIBER 1g; CHOL 18mg; IRON 1.7mg; SODIUM 154mg; CALC 31mg

Saffron and Raisin Breakfast Bread

Saffron breads are a tradition in southwestern England and throughout many Nordic countries, especially Sweden and Finland. Serve toasted or plain with honey for a special holiday breakfast or brunch.

1⅓ cups warm fat-free milk (100° to 110°)
¼ teaspoon saffron threads, crushed
1 package dry yeast (about 2¼ teaspoons)
1 teaspoon sugar
½ cup warm water (100° to 110°)
5¼ cups bread flour, divided
1½ cups raisins
¼ cup sugar
3 tablespoons butter, melted and cooled
1 teaspoon salt
Cooking spray

1. Combine milk and saffron; let stand 10 minutes.
2. Dissolve yeast and 1 teaspoon sugar in warm water in a large bowl, and let stand 5 minutes or until foamy. Stir in milk mixture. Lightly spoon flour into dry measuring cups, and level with a knife. Add 5 cups flour, raisins, ¼ cup sugar, butter, and salt to milk mixture, stirring to form a soft dough. Turn dough out onto a floured surface. Knead until smooth and elastic (about 8 minutes), and add enough of remaining flour, 1 tablespoon at a time, to prevent dough from sticking to hands (dough will feel sticky).
3. Place dough in a large bowl coated with cooking spray, turning to coat top. Cover; let rise in a warm place (85°), free from drafts, 1½ hours or until doubled in size. (Press 2 fingers into dough. If indentation remains, dough has risen enough.) Punch dough down; cover and let rest 5 minutes. Divide in half, and shape each portion into a 5-inch round loaf. Place loaves 3 inches apart on a large baking sheet coated with cooking spray. Make 2 diagonal cuts ¼-inch-deep across top of each loaf using a sharp knife. Cover and let rise 30 minutes or until doubled in size.
4. Preheat oven to 375°.
5. Uncover dough. Bake at 375° for 30 minutes or until loaves are browned on bottom and sound hollow when tapped. Remove from pan; cool on wire racks. Yield: 2 loaves, 20 servings (serving size: 1 slice).

CALORIES 199 (11% from fat); FAT 2.4g (sat 1.2g, mono 0.6g, poly 0.3g); PROTEIN 5.4g; CARB 39.5g; FIBER 1.4g; CHOL 5mg; IRON 1.9mg; SODIUM 145mg; CALC 33mg

christmas around the world

In Germany, he's *'Der Weihnachtsmann'* or Father Christmas. In France, he's *'Père Noël.'* In Belgium, he's *'Sinterklaas'* or Saint Nicholas. And in America, he's best known as Santa Claus. And just as there are differences in our names for that jolly old elf, there are differences in the ways the world celebrates the holidays. But one thing that is consistent is our affinity for Christmas breads. We love to eat them—and give them. In parts of England and in the Nordic countries, it's tradition to serve saffron bread for breakfast or brunch. In Greece, you'll find *Christopsomo*. In Italy, *panettone*. And in Denmark, *julekage*. Branch out this year and try one of our international Christmas delights. Bring a little Christmas, and perhaps a little of Italy or Sweden, to your holiday table today.

Saffron and Raisin Breakfast Bread

Citrus-Cream Cheese Pull-Apart Rolls
(pictured on page 158)

If you're looking for a great make-ahead American tradition for Christmas morning, this is it! Place on a holiday plate on your coffee table and enjoy while opening your gifts. Note: The cream cheese mixture sinks to the bottom of the rolls. Place a piece of foil under the pan in case the sugar mixture runs over.

    1   (25-ounce) package frozen roll dough
        Cooking spray
    ¼   cup butter, melted
    ½   cup sweetened dried cranberries or chopped
        dried apricots
    1   cup granulated sugar, divided
    ⅔   cup (6 ounces) ⅓-less-fat cream cheese,
        softened
    2   tablespoons fresh orange juice
    1   large egg
    1   tablespoon grated lemon rind
    1   tablespoon grated orange rind
    1   cup powdered sugar
    5   teaspoons fresh lemon juice

1. Thaw roll dough at room temperature 30 minutes.
2. Cut rolls in half. Place 24 halves, cut sides down, in bottom of each of 2 (9-inch) round cake pans coated with cooking spray. Brush butter evenly over rolls. Cover and let rise in a warm place (85°), free from drafts, 30 minutes. Sprinkle with dried cranberries. Combine ¼ cup granulated sugar, cream cheese, orange juice, and egg in a bowl; beat with a mixer at medium speed until well blended. Pour cream cheese mixture evenly over rolls. Combine ¾ cup granulated sugar and rinds. Sprinkle evenly over rolls. Cover and let rise 1 hour or until doubled in size.
3. Preheat oven to 350°.
4. Bake at 350° for 20 minutes. Cover with foil. Bake an additional 5 minutes or until rolls in center of cake pans are done. Remove from oven; cool 15 minutes. Combine powdered sugar and lemon juice. Drizzle over rolls. Yield: 4 dozen (serving size: 2 rolls).

Overnight Variation: After pouring cream cheese mixture over rolls, cover with plastic wrap and refrigerate 12 hours. Gently remove plastic wrap from rolls; sprinkle with rind mixture. Let stand at room temperature 30 minutes or until dough has doubled in size. Proceed with recipe as directed.

CALORIES 174 (29% from fat); FAT 5.6g (sat 2.8g, mono 1.9g, poly 0.6g); PROTEIN 3.6g; CARB 27.7g; FIBER 0.6g; CHOL 20mg; IRON 0.3mg; SODIUM 203mg; CALC 10mg

Christopsomo
(Greek Christmas Bread)

Mahleb, a spice made from ground black cherry pits, is often used for flavoring, but we've used the easier-to-find aniseed.

    1   package dry yeast (about 2¼ teaspoons)
    1   tablespoon sugar
    ½   cup warm water (100° to 110°)
    6   tablespoons butter, softened
    2   large eggs
  3½   cups all-purpose flour, divided
    ⅓   cup sugar
    2   tablespoons nonfat dry milk
    2   teaspoons aniseed, crushed
    ½   teaspoon salt
        Cooking spray
    1   large egg white, lightly beaten
    8   candied cherries

1. Dissolve yeast and 1 tablespoon sugar in warm water in a large bowl; let stand 5 minutes. Add butter and eggs; beat with a mixer at medium speed until smooth. Lightly spoon flour into dry measuring cups; level with a knife. Combine 3 cups flour, ⅓ cup sugar, dry milk, aniseed, and salt; add to yeast mixture, beating well. Turn dough out onto a lightly floured surface. Knead until smooth and elastic (about 10 minutes); add enough of remaining flour, 1 tablespoon at a time, to prevent dough from sticking to hands.
2. Place dough in a large bowl coated with cooking spray, turning to coat top. Cover; let rise in a warm place (85°), free from drafts, about 1½ hours. Dough will not double in size. (Press 2 fingers into dough. If indentation remains, dough has risen enough.)
3. Punch dough down; let rest 5 minutes. Pinch 2 (1½-inch) balls off dough; cover and set aside. Shape remaining dough into an 8-inch round; place on a baking sheet coated with cooking spray. Brush with egg white. Shape each dough ball into an 8-inch-long rope; cut a 2-inch slash into each end of ropes. Place 1 rope across middle of dough; brush middle of rope with egg white. Place other rope across middle of rope, forming a cross. Curl slashed ends together to form a circle at end of each rope; place a cherry in middle of each circle. Arrange 4 cherries around center of cross. Cover and let rise 1 hour.
4. Preheat oven to 350°.
5. Uncover dough. Bake at 350° for 35 minutes or until loaf sounds hollow when tapped. Remove loaf from pan, and cool on a wire rack. Yield: 16 servings (serving size: 1 wedge).

CALORIES 185 (26% from fat); FAT 5.3g (sat 1.1g, mono 2.2g, poly 1.6g); PROTEIN 4.5g; CARB 29.8g; FIBER 1g; CHOL 28mg; IRON 1.6mg; SODIUM 140mg; CALC 24mg

Julekage

Julekage
(Danish Christmas Fruit Loaf)

Dough:

4 1/4   cups all-purpose flour, divided
3   tablespoons granulated sugar, divided
1/3   cup chopped almonds
1/3   cup raisins
1/4   cup nonfat dry milk
2   tablespoons chopped candied citron
2   tablespoons chopped candied lemon peel
2   tablespoons chopped candied orange peel
1   teaspoon salt
1   teaspoon grated lemon rind
1/2   teaspoon ground cardamom
1   package dry yeast (about 2 1/4 teaspoons)
1/2   cup warm water (100° to 110°)
6   tablespoons butter, softened
1   teaspoon vanilla extract
2   large eggs, lightly beaten
Cooking spray
1   tablespoon fat-free milk
1/8   teaspoon salt
1   large egg
1   tablespoon turbinado or granulated sugar

Glaze:

1/2   cup sifted powdered sugar
2   teaspoons water
1/4   teaspoon almond extract

1. To prepare dough, lightly spoon flour into dry measuring cups; level with a knife. Combine 4 cups flour, 2 tablespoons granulated sugar, and next 9 ingredients in a large bowl.

2. Dissolve 1 tablespoon granulated sugar and yeast in warm water in a large bowl; let stand 5 minutes. Stir in butter, vanilla, and 2 eggs until well blended. Gradually add flour mixture, stirring to combine. Turn dough out onto a lightly floured surface. Knead until smooth and elastic (about 8 minutes); add enough of remaining flour, 1 tablespoon at a time, to prevent dough from sticking to hands.

3. Place dough in a large bowl coated with cooking spray, turning to coat top. Cover and let rise in a warm place (85°), free from drafts, 1 hour and 45 minutes. Dough will not double in size. (Press 2 fingers into dough. If indentation remains, dough has risen enough.)

4. Punch dough down, and let rest 5 minutes. Roll into an 11 x 9-inch rectangle on a lightly floured surface. Roll up rectangle tightly, starting with a short edge, pressing firmly to eliminate air pockets; pinch seam and ends to seal. Place, seam side down, in a 9 x 5-inch loaf pan coated with cooking spray. Cover and let rise 1 1/2 hours.

5. Preheat oven to 375°.

6. Uncover dough. Combine fat-free milk, 1/8 teaspoon salt, and 1 egg; brush lightly over loaf. Sprinkle with turbinado sugar. Bake at 375° for 45 minutes or until loaf sounds hollow when tapped. Remove from pan; cool on a wire rack.

7. To prepare glaze, combine powdered sugar, 2 teaspoons water, and almond extract in a small bowl. Drizzle over loaf. Yield: 1 loaf, 16 servings (serving size: 1 slice).

CALORIES 234 (26% from fat); FAT 6.7g (sat 1.3g, mono 3g, poly 1.8g); PROTEIN 5.9g; CARB 37.6g; FIBER 1.4g; CHOL 42mg; IRON 1.9mg; SODIUM 249mg; CALC 47mg

Panettone
(Italian Christmas Bread)

This Italian fruitcake-style yeast bread is typically baked into a tall, cylindrical shape (empty coffee cans work great as baking pans). While its origins are sketchy, one legend holds that in the late 1400s, a young Milanese nobleman fell in love with the daughter of a baker named Toni and created "Pan de Toni" to impress his love's father.

Marinated Fruit:

⅓ cup golden raisins
⅓ cup chopped dried apricots
⅓ cup dried tart cherries
¼ cup Triple Sec (orange-flavored liqueur) or orange juice

Dough:

1 package dry yeast (about 2¼ teaspoons)
¼ teaspoon granulated sugar
¼ cup warm water (100° to 110°)
3¾ cups all-purpose flour, divided
6 tablespoons butter, melted
¼ cup fat-free milk
¼ cup granulated sugar
½ teaspoon salt
1 large egg
1 large egg yolk
2 tablespoons pine nuts
Cooking spray
1 teaspoon butter, melted
2 teaspoons turbinado or granulated sugar

1. To prepare marinated fruit, combine first 4 ingredients in a small bowl; let stand 1 hour. Drain fruit in a sieve over a bowl, reserving fruit and 2 teaspoons liqueur separately.

2. To prepare dough, dissolve yeast and ¼ teaspoon granulated sugar in warm water in a small bowl; let stand 5 minutes. Lightly spoon flour into dry measuring cups; level with a knife. Combine ½ cup flour, 6 tablespoons butter, and next 5 ingredients in a large bowl; beat with a mixer at medium speed 1 minute or until smooth. Add yeast mixture and ½ cup flour; beat 1 minute. Stir in marinated fruit, 2½ cups flour, and pine nuts. Turn dough out onto a lightly floured surface. Knead until smooth and elastic (about 8 minutes); add enough of remaining flour, 1 tablespoon at a time, to prevent dough from sticking to hands.

3. Place dough in a large bowl coated with cooking spray, turning to coat top. Cover and let rise in a warm place (85°), free from drafts, about 1½ hours. Dough will not double in size. (Press 2 fingers into dough. If indentation remains, dough has risen enough.)

4. Punch dough down; let rest 5 minutes. Divide in half, shaping each portion into a ball. Place balls into 2 (13-ounce) coffee cans coated with cooking spray. Cover and let rise 1 hour.

5. Preheat oven to 375°.

6. Uncover dough. Place coffee cans on bottom rack in oven, and bake at 375° for 30 minutes or until browned and loaf sounds hollow when tapped. Remove bread from cans, and cool on a wire rack. Combine reserved 2 teaspoons liqueur and 1 teaspoon butter; brush over loaves. Sprinkle evenly with turbinado sugar. Yield: 2 loaves, 8 servings per loaf (serving size: 1 slice).

CALORIES 211 (28% from fat); FAT 6.6g (sat 1.3g, mono 2.7g, poly 2.1g); PROTEIN 4.5g; CARB 33.8g; FIBER 1.4g; CHOL 27mg; IRON 1.9mg; SODIUM 137mg; CALC 19mg

Panettone

salads and soups

Add color, texture, and flavor to your holiday meals with the welcoming additions of seasonal soups and salads.

White Turkey Chili
(recipe on page 208)

Mushroom Salad with Maple Dressing

2   tablespoons lime juice
2   tablespoons maple syrup
¼   teaspoon low-sodium soy sauce
¼   teaspoon sesame oil
⅛   teaspoon black pepper
1½ teaspoons vegetable oil
    Cooking spray
1   (8-ounce) package button mushrooms, quartered
6   cups gourmet salad greens
⅓   cup chopped green onions
1   tablespoon finely chopped fresh cilantro

1. Combine first 5 ingredients in a small bowl, and stir well with a whisk.
2. Heat vegetable oil in a large nonstick skillet coated with cooking spray over medium-high heat. Add mushrooms; sauté 6 minutes or until tender. Remove from heat; add maple mixture, tossing to coat. Combine greens, onions, and cilantro in a large bowl. Add mushroom mixture, tossing to coat. Serve salad immediately. Yield: 4 servings (serving size: 1½ cups).

CALORIES 78 (28% from fat); FAT 2.4g (sat 0.4g, mono 0.5g, poly 1.3g); PROTEIN 3g; CARB 12.9g; FIBER 2.9g; CHOL 0mg; IRON 1.8mg; SODIUM 37mg; CALC 56mg

Winter Salad

2   tablespoons raspberry vinegar
1   tablespoon fresh orange juice
1   tablespoon balsamic vinegar
2   teaspoons extravirgin olive oil
½   teaspoon sugar
½   teaspoon low-sodium soy sauce
¼   teaspoon black pepper
¼   teaspoon Dijon mustard
⅛   teaspoon salt
8   cups mixed salad greens
1   cup grapefruit sections
1   cup thinly sliced red onion
¼   cup coarsely chopped walnuts

1. Combine first 9 ingredients. Combine salad greens, grapefruit, onion, and walnuts in a large bowl. Drizzle with vinegar mixture; toss. Yield: 6 servings (serving size: 1½ cups).

CALORIES 80 (53% from fat); FAT 4.7g (sat 0.4g, mono 1.8g, poly 2.2g); PROTEIN 3g; CARB 8.1g; FIBER 2.4g; CHOL 0mg; IRON 1.1mg; SODIUM 75mg; CALC 39mg

---

Shopper's Lunch
serves 4
This hearty menu will give you the energy to wrap all those presents.

Winter Vegetable Soup (recipe on page 206)

Warm Spinach Salad with Mushroom Vinaigrette (recipe below)

Olive and Asiago Rolls (recipe on page 178)

Warm Spinach Salad with Mushroom Vinaigrette

Radicchio, a slightly bitter red lettuce, pairs nicely with sweet balsamic and sherry vinegars.

6   cups fresh spinach
1½ cups torn radicchio
2   tablespoons (½-inch) sliced green onions
½   pound shiitake mushrooms
½   teaspoon olive oil
1   tablespoon finely chopped fresh or 1 teaspoon dried rubbed sage
1½ teaspoons finely chopped fresh or ½ teaspoon dried thyme
2   garlic cloves, minced
3½ tablespoons sherry vinegar
⅛   teaspoon salt
⅛   teaspoon black pepper
1½ teaspoons balsamic vinegar
2   hard-cooked large eggs, quartered lengthwise

1. Combine first 3 ingredients in a large bowl.
2. Remove and discard stems from mushrooms, reserving caps. Heat oil in a large nonstick skillet over medium-high heat. Add mushroom caps; sauté 5 minutes. Reduce heat to medium. Add sage, thyme, and garlic; sauté 3 minutes. Stir in sherry vinegar, salt, and pepper; bring to a boil. Remove from heat.
3. Pour mushroom mixture over spinach mixture, tossing well to coat. Drizzle with balsamic vinegar. Place about 1 cup salad on each of 4 plates; top each serving with 2 egg quarters. Yield: 4 servings.

CALORIES 105 (30% from fat); FAT 3.5g (sat 0.9g, mono 1.4g, poly 0.5g); PROTEIN 6g; CARB 11.9g; FIBER 2.2g; CHOL 106mg; IRON 2.6mg; SODIUM 160mg; CALC 71mg

Caesar Salad with Roasted Peppers

Dressing:

2 large whole garlic heads

¼ cup fat-free mayonnaise

1½ teaspoons Dijon mustard

1 teaspoon anchovy paste

Dash of black pepper

3 tablespoons red wine vinegar

1 tablespoon olive oil

Salad:

2 yellow bell peppers

2 red bell peppers

14 cups torn romaine lettuce

¼ cup (1 ounce) finely grated fresh Parmesan cheese, divided

4 (1-ounce) slices rye bread, cubed and toasted

1. Preheat oven to 400°.

2. To prepare dressing, remove white papery skin from garlic heads (do not peel or separate cloves). Wrap each head separately in foil. Bake garlic heads at 400° for 1 hour; cool. Cut crosswise; squeeze to extract garlic pulp to measure 3 tablespoons. Discard skins. Place garlic, mayonnaise, mustard, anchovy paste, and black pepper in a food processor; process until smooth. With food processor on, slowly pour vinegar and olive oil through food chute; process until well blended.

3. Preheat broiler.

4. To prepare salad, cut bell peppers in half lengthwise; discard seeds and membranes. Place bell pepper halves, skin sides up, on a foil-lined baking sheet; flatten with hand. Broil 15 minutes or until blackened. Place in a zip-top plastic bag; seal. Let stand 15 minutes. Peel and cut into 1-inch strips. Combine dressing, lettuce, 2 tablespoons cheese, and bread cubes in a large bowl; toss gently to coat. Divide salad evenly among 8 salad plates. Arrange yellow and red bell pepper strips on top of salads. Sprinkle evenly with 2 tablespoons cheese. Yield: 8 servings (serving size: 2 cups).

CALORIES 111 (30% from fat); FAT 3.7g (sat 1g, mono 1.7g, poly 0.5g); PROTEIN 5g; CARB 15.3g; FIBER 3.4g; CHOL 2mg; IRON 2.2mg; SODIUM 378mg; CALC 98mg

Caesar Salad with Roasted Peppers

Endive, Sweet Lettuce,
and Cashew Salad

Endive, Sweet Lettuce, and Cashew Salad

Walnut oil adds subtle and delicate flavor. If you can't find it, use light olive oil.
Cashews lend a crunchy texture and slightly sweet flavor, but you can use walnuts in their place.

2 tablespoons minced shallots
2 tablespoons honey
1 tablespoon sherry vinegar
2 teaspoons walnut oil
½ teaspoon salt
8 cups torn green leaf lettuce
4 cups sliced Belgian endive (about 3 heads)
2 tablespoons roasted unsalted cashews, coarsely chopped

1. Combine first 5 ingredients; stir with a whisk. Add lettuce,
endive, and cashews; toss to coat. Serve immediately. Yield:
8 servings (serving size: about 1¼ cups).

CALORIES 55 (35% from fat); FAT 2.1g (sat 0.3g, mono 0.8g, poly 0.9g); PROTEIN 1.3g;
CARB 9.2g; FIBER 2g; CHOL 0mg; IRON 0.4mg; SODIUM 173mg; CALC 40mg

New Year's Day
Brunch Menu

serves 8

Wasabi Bloody Marys (recipe on page 153)

Endive, Sweet Lettuce, and Cashew Salad
(recipe at left)

Mixed citrus fruits

Mediterranean Spinach Strata
(recipe on page 215)

Blood Orange Layer Cake (recipe on page 316)

Belgian Endive-
and-Apple Salad

Belgian Endive-and-Apple Salad

You can make the dressing early in the day and toss the apples with it to keep them from browning.

2 tablespoons minced shallots
2 tablespoons white wine vinegar
2 tablespoons red wine vinegar
½ teaspoon salt
½ teaspoon black pepper
1 tablespoon olive oil
1 tablespoon walnut oil or olive oil
4 cups julienne-cut Golden Delicious apple (about 2 large)
3 heads Belgian endive, halved and thinly sliced lengthwise (about 4 cups)
2 tablespoons chopped fresh parsley

1. Combine first 5 ingredients; add oils, stirring well with a whisk. Add apple, tossing well; cover and chill.

2. Combine apple mixture, endive, and parsley in a large bowl; toss well to coat. Serve immediately. Yield: 6 servings (serving size: 1⅓ cups).

CALORIES 92 (47% from fat); FAT 4.8g (sat 0.5g, mono 3.3g, poly 0.7g); PROTEIN 0.5g; CARB 13g; FIBER 2.1g; CHOL 0mg; IRON 0.4mg; SODIUM 199mg; CALC 9mg

holiday chargers

Chargers, or service plates, are a good way to add texture and color to your holiday table. Chargers are oversized plates that are slightly larger than dinner plates. They are made from a variety of materials—china, pewter, brass, or acrylic. Food is never served directly on chargers, which are purely decorative, but first-course salad plates or soup bowls can be set on top of chargers. Chargers are removed from the table before dinner plates are served.

- Mix and match china and charger patterns to form interesting combinations.
- Use gold- or silver-colored chargers with

all kinds of china. Often, these can be purchased inexpensively from the housewares section of discount stores.

Fill a pedestal bowl with clementines for a quick centerpiece,
or use single fruits as rests for place cards at each table setting.

Clementine Salad with Spiced Walnuts and Pickled Onions

Winter offers a small window of opportunity to use pomegranates and clementines. For instructions on seeding a pomegranate, see page 197.

Onions:

  ½   cup water
  ½   cup red wine vinegar
  ¼   cup sugar
  1   cup vertically sliced red onion

Dressing:

  1   tablespoon orange juice
  2   teaspoons olive oil
  1   teaspoon Dijon mustard

Remaining Ingredients:

  8   cups gourmet salad greens
  2   cups clementine sections (about 6 clementines)
  ¾   cup Spiced Walnuts (recipe at right)
  6   tablespoons pomegranate seeds

1. To prepare onions, combine first 3 ingredients in a small saucepan. Bring to a boil; remove from heat. Reserve 2 tablespoons vinegar mixture. Combine remaining vinegar mixture and onion in a small bowl; cool to room temperature.
2. To prepare dressing, combine reserved 2 tablespoons vinegar mixture, orange juice, oil, and mustard; stir well with a whisk.
3. Combine dressing and salad greens in a large bowl; toss well. Divide evenly among 6 salad plates. Top each with ⅓ cup

clementines, about 2 tablespoons onions, 2 tablespoons Spiced Walnuts, and 1 tablespoon pomegranate seeds. Yield: 6 servings.

(Totals include Spiced Walnuts) CALORIES 175 (27% from fat); FAT 5.3g (sat 0.6g, mono 2g, poly 2.5g); PROTEIN 2.9g; CARB 31.7g; FIBER 3.9g; CHOL 0mg; IRON 1.2mg; SODIUM 58mg; CALC 49mg

Spiced Walnuts

Keep these sweet, spicy nuts on hand to add to salads, serve as snacks, or give as gifts.

  1   cup walnut halves
  ½   cup sugar
  ¼   cup water
  ½   teaspoon ground cinnamon
  ¼   teaspoon salt
  Dash of ground red pepper
  Cooking spray

1. Preheat oven to 350°.
2. Arrange walnuts in a single layer on a baking sheet. Bake at 350° for 10 minutes or until lightly browned.
3. Combine sugar and next 4 ingredients in a small saucepan. Cook, without stirring, until a candy thermometer registers 238° (about 8 minutes). Remove from heat; stir in walnuts. Pour onto baking sheet coated with cooking spray. Cool completely; break into small pieces. Yield: 2 cups (serving size: 2 tablespoons).
Note: Store remaining walnuts in an airtight container.

CALORIES 60 (51% from fat); FAT 3.4g (sat 0.3g, mono 0.8g, poly 2.2g); PROTEIN 0.8g; CARB 7.3g; FIBER 0.3g; CHOL 0mg; IRON 0.2mg; SODIUM 37mg; CALC 6mg

Clementine Salad with Spiced Walnuts and Pickled Onions

Pear, Walnut, and
Blue Cheese Salad
with Cranberry
Vinaigrette

Pear, Walnut, and Blue Cheese Salad with Cranberry Vinaigrette

Vinaigrette:

- ½ cup canned whole-berry cranberry sauce
- ¼ cup fresh orange juice (about 1 orange)
- 2 tablespoons balsamic vinegar
- 1 tablespoon olive oil
- 1 teaspoon sugar
- 1 teaspoon minced peeled fresh ginger
- ¼ teaspoon salt

Salad:

- 18 Bibb lettuce leaves (about 2 heads)
- 2 cups sliced peeled pear (about 2 pears)
- 2 tablespoons fresh orange juice
- 1 cup (⅛-inch-thick) slices red onion, separated into rings
- ⅓ cup (1.3 ounces) crumbled blue cheese
- 2 tablespoons coarsely chopped walnuts, toasted

1. To prepare vinaigrette, place first 7 ingredients in a medium bowl; stir well with a whisk.
2. To prepare salad, divide lettuce leaves evenly among 6 salad plates. Toss pear with 2 tablespoons orange juice. Divide pear and onion evenly among leaves. Top each serving with about 1 tablespoon cheese and 1 teaspoon walnuts. Drizzle each serving with about 2½ tablespoons vinaigrette. Yield: 6 servings.

CALORIES 151 (35% from fat); FAT 5.8g (sat 1.5g, mono 2.2g, poly 1.3g); PROTEIN 3.1g; CARB 23.8g; FIBER 3g; CHOL 5mg; IRON 0.8mg; SODIUM 192mg; CALC 63mg

Orange, Date, and Endive Salad with Lemon-Cardamom Dressing

Dressing:

- ½ teaspoon cardamom seeds, toasted
- ¼ cup low-fat buttermilk
- 1 tablespoon extravirgin olive oil
- 2 teaspoons chopped fresh mint
- 1 teaspoon grated lemon rind
- ¼ teaspoon salt
- ¼ teaspoon freshly ground black pepper

Salad:

- 12 Belgian endive leaves
- 3 cups blood orange sections
- 1 cup thinly sliced radish
- 1 cup thinly vertically sliced red onion
- ½ cup thinly sliced pitted dates (about 5 whole)
- 4 teaspoons chopped fresh mint

1. To prepare dressing, place cardamom in a spice or coffee grinder; process until finely ground. Combine cardamom, buttermilk, and next 5 ingredients.
2. To prepare salad, arrange 3 endive leaves on each of 4 salad plates. Top each with ¾ cup orange sections, ¼ cup radish, ¼ cup onion, 2 tablespoons dates, and 1 teaspoon mint. Drizzle each serving with 1 tablespoon dressing. Yield: 4 servings.

CALORIES 187 (20% from fat); FAT 4.1g (sat 0.7g, mono 2.8g, poly 0.4g); PROTEIN 3.2g; CARB 38.2g; FIBER 7g; CHOL 1mg; IRON 1mg; SODIUM 179mg; CALC 112mg

Red Cabbage, Cranberry, and Apple Slaw

The slaw marinates in the refrigerator for a couple of hours, allowing the vinaigrette to permeate the cabbage and plump the cranberries. Stir in the apples just before serving to keep them bright.

5   cups thinly sliced red cabbage (about
    1½ pounds)
½   cup dried cranberries
⅓   cup rice vinegar
⅓   cup sugar
2   tablespoons white wine vinegar
2   teaspoons olive oil
¾   teaspoon salt
½   teaspoon freshly ground black pepper
2¼ cups thinly sliced Granny Smith apple
¼   cup chopped pecans, toasted

1. Combine cabbage and cranberries in a large bowl. Combine vinegar and next 5 ingredients, stirring with a whisk; drizzle over cabbage mixture, tossing gently to coat. Cover and chill 2 hours. Add apple, and toss well to combine. Sprinkle with pecans. Yield: 8 servings (serving size: 1 cup).

CALORIES 131 (29% from fat); FAT 4.2g (sat 0.4g, mono 2.4g, poly 1g); PROTEIN 1.7g; CARB 23.6g; FIBER 3.8g; CHOL 0mg; IRON 0.7mg; SODIUM 236mg; CALC 46mg

Persimmon and
Fennel Salad

Rye Berry Salad with
Orange Vinaigrette

Persimmon and Fennel Salad

The easiest way to peel persimmons is to cut the fruit into wedges and remove the peel from each wedge with a paring knife. We prefer nonastringent Fuyu persimmons in this salad. Serve with a holiday meal of roasted pork or chicken.

    2   tablespoons finely chopped shallots
    2   tablespoons red wine vinegar
    2   teaspoons sugar
 1½   teaspoons olive oil
    ½   teaspoon salt
    ¼   teaspoon freshly ground black pepper
    3   cups thinly sliced fennel bulb (about 1 large bulb)
    ¼   cup chopped fresh chives
    4   persimmons, each cut into 6 wedges and peeled
    ¼   cup (1 ounce) crumbled goat cheese

1. Combine the first 6 ingredients in a large bowl, stirring well with a whisk. Add fennel, chives, and persimmons, and toss gently to coat. Divide fennel mixture evenly among 4 plates. Top each serving with 1 tablespoon crumbled goat cheese. Yield: 4 servings.

CALORIES 103 (30% from fat); FAT 3.4g (sat 1.3g, mono 1.6g, poly 0.2g); PROTEIN 2.6g; CARB 17.5g; FIBER 2.1g; CHOL 3mg; IRON 1.4mg; SODIUM 355mg; CALC 55mg

staff holiday favorite

Test Kitchens Staffer Mike Wilson is a big fan of this holiday-inspired salad. "This is a great way to use persimmons without cooking them to death," Mike says. "The fresh, sweet, and creamy texture of the persimmons goes well with crisp fennel. This is a great salad for Thanksgiving, Christmas Eve dinner, or whenever persimmons are in season."

Rye Berry Salad with Orange Vinaigrette

Any of the whole grains—wheat berries, whole grain rye, buckwheat groats, or a mix of them—will work in this salad. Substitute raisins if you don't have currants.

    3   cups water
    1   cup uncooked rye berries or wheat berries
    1   cup hot water
    3   tablespoons dried currants
 1½   cups finely chopped celery
    ¼   cup chopped fresh parsley
    ¾   teaspoon salt, divided
    ¼   teaspoon freshly ground black pepper
    ¼   cup finely chopped shallots
    1   tablespoon grated orange rind
    1   tablespoon fresh orange juice
    2   teaspoons Champagne vinegar or white wine
        vinegar
    2   tablespoons olive oil

1. Combine 3 cups water and rye berries in a saucepan; bring to a boil. Cover, reduce heat, and simmer 1 hour. Drain.
2. Combine 1 cup hot water and currants in a small bowl; let stand 30 minutes. Drain well.
3. Combine rye berries, currants, celery, parsley, ½ teaspoon salt, and pepper.
4. Combine ¼ teaspoon salt, shallots, rind, juice, and vinegar in a small bowl, stirring well. Let stand 5 minutes. Stir in oil with a whisk. Pour shallot mixture over rye mixture; toss well to coat. Yield: 6 servings (serving size: about ⅔ cup).

CALORIES 174 (27% from fat); FAT 5.3g (sat 0.6g, mono 3.3g, poly 0.4g); PROTEIN 4.8g; CARB 29.3g; FIBER 5.2g; CHOL 0mg; IRON 1.8mg; SODIUM 329mg; CALC 41mg

Orange-Basmati Salad with Pine Nuts and Pomegranate Seeds

Although best served immediately, this dish can be covered and chilled for a couple of hours. Try it with roasted chicken.

2   cups water
1   cup uncooked basmati rice
1   teaspoon salt, divided
¼   cup white wine vinegar
2   teaspoons grated orange rind
¼   cup fresh orange juice
1½ tablespoons extravirgin olive oil
¼   teaspoon freshly ground black pepper
2   cups orange sections (about 3 oranges)
½   cup pomegranate seeds
¼   cup pine nuts, toasted
3   tablespoons chopped fresh flat-leaf parsley

1. Bring water to a boil in a medium saucepan over medium-high heat. Add rice and ¾ teaspoon salt; cover, reduce heat, and simmer 15 minutes or until liquid is absorbed. Remove from heat; fluff rice with a fork. Cool completely.
2. Combine ¼ teaspoon salt, vinegar, and next 4 ingredients, stirring with a whisk. Combine rice, vinegar mixture, orange sections, and remaining ingredients; toss gently. Yield: 6 servings (serving size: about ⅔ cup).

CALORIES 225 (27% from fat); FAT 6.8g (sat 1.1g, mono 3.7g, poly 1.7g); PROTEIN 4.8g; CARB 38g; FIBER 2.1g; CHOL 0mg; IRON 1.1mg; SODIUM 393mg; CALC 35mg

how to: SEED A POMEGRANATE

Pomegranate juice stains, so be careful when extracting the seeds. Carefully cut the fruit in half, submerge in a large bowl of water, and slowly turn the shell inside out to dislodge the seeds. Removing the seeds underwater prevents juice from squirting out and staining.

Orange-Basmati Salad with Pine Nuts and Pomegranate Seeds

Beet and Black-Eyed Pea Salad

Add black-eyed peas to your Christmas table with this colorful salad that combines them with beets, feta cheese, and toasted pecans. To save time, substitute 3 cups of canned black-eyed peas, rinsed and drained, for the dried peas. You may also use canned beets instead of fresh.

    1   cup dried black-eyed peas
   1/3 cup rice vinegar
    2   tablespoons olive oil
    2   tablespoons spicy brown mustard
    2   teaspoons sugar
    1   teaspoon grated orange rind
   1/2 teaspoon salt
    7   cups coarsely chopped peeled beets (about 2 1/2 pounds)
   1/4 cup (1 ounce) crumbled feta cheese
    2   tablespoons chopped pecans, toasted
    2   tablespoons chopped fresh parsley

1. Sort and wash black-eyed peas; place in a small saucepan. Cover with water to 2 inches above peas; bring to a boil. Cook 2 minutes. Remove from heat; cover and let stand 1 hour. Drain peas, and return to pan. Cover with water to 2 inches above peas. Bring to a boil; cover, reduce heat, and simmer 30 minutes or until tender. Drain.
2. Combine vinegar and next 5 ingredients in a small bowl; stir well with a whisk.
3. Steam beets, covered, 25 minutes or until done. Arrange beets on a platter, and top with peas. Sprinkle with cheese, pecans, and parsley. Drizzle vinaigrette over salad. Yield: 8 servings (serving size: 1 cup).

CALORIES 184 (29% from fat); FAT 6g (sat 1.2g, mono 3.5g, poly 0.9g); PROTEIN 5.2g; CARB 28.6g; FIBER 7.8g; CHOL 3mg; IRON 2.1mg; SODIUM 359mg; CALC 127mg

Beet and Black-Eyed Pea Salad

Warm Lentil-Ham Salad with Dijon Cream

You can serve this main-dish salad at room temperature or chilled. Dried lentils are ideal for weeknight dinners because they require no soaking and cook in about 20 minutes.

    1   cup dried lentils
   1/2 cup reduced-fat sour cream
    2   tablespoons Dijon mustard
    2   tablespoons fat-free milk
    1   tablespoon white wine vinegar
    1   teaspoon chopped fresh or 1/4 teaspoon dried thyme
   1/4 teaspoon black pepper
 1 1/3 cups chopped cooked ham
   3/4 cup chopped celery
   3/4 cup chopped red onion

1. Place lentils in a large saucepan, and cover with water to 2 inches above lentils. Bring lentils to a boil; cover, reduce heat, and simmer 20 minutes or until tender. Drain well.
2. Combine sour cream and next 5 ingredients in a large bowl. Add lentils, ham, celery, and onion; toss well. Yield: 4 servings (serving size: about 1 1/3 cups).

CALORIES 291 (20% from fat); FAT 6.6g (sat 3.1g, mono 1.2g, poly 0.6g); PROTEIN 24.4g; CARB 35.6g; FIBER 15.8g; CHOL 37mg; IRON 5.5mg; SODIUM 649mg; CALC 114mg

Warm Lentil-Ham Salad
with Dijon Cream

This year, consider creating a holiday centerpiece with fruits and vegetables that are also featured in the dishes you're serving. See page 348 for a listing of fresh winter fruits and vegetables.

Chicken-Apple Crunch Salad

Inspired by the classic Waldorf salad, this version features chunks of white-meat chicken and sweet-tangy Granny Smith apples.

  2   cups cubed cooked chicken breast
  1   cup chopped Granny Smith apple
  ½   cup chopped celery
  ¼   cup raisins
  2   tablespoons chopped green onions
  ⅓   cup low-fat mayonnaise
  1   tablespoon reduced-fat sour cream
  1   teaspoon fresh lemon juice
  ¼   teaspoon salt
  ¼   teaspoon freshly ground black pepper
  ⅛   teaspoon ground cinnamon

1. Combine first 5 ingredients in a large bowl. Combine mayonnaise and next 5 ingredients, stirring well with a whisk. Add mayonnaise mixture to chicken mixture, tossing well to coat. Yield: 4 servings (serving size: 1 cup).

CALORIES 207 (19% from fat); FAT 4.4g (sat 1.2g, mono 1.2g, poly 1.4g); PROTEIN 22.4g; CARB 18.4g; FIBER 1.1g; CHOL 61mg; IRON 1.2mg; SODIUM 402mg; CALC 32mg

Wild Rice-and-Apricot Salad

  1   cup uncooked wild rice
  3   cups water
  ½   cup dried apricots, cut into ¼-inch strips
  5   shallots, halved (about ¼ pound)
  2   teaspoons olive oil, divided
  ½   cup thinly sliced green onions
  2   tablespoons chopped fresh parsley
  2   tablespoons water
  2   tablespoons balsamic vinegar
  ¼   teaspoon grated orange rind
  ¼   teaspoon salt
  ⅛   teaspoon black pepper

1. Combine rice and 3 cups water in a saucepan; bring to a boil.

Cover, reduce heat, and simmer 30 minutes. Add apricots; simmer an additional 15 minutes. Drain and set aside.
2. Preheat oven to 400°. Combine shallots and 1 teaspoon oil in a shallow baking dish. Bake at 400° for 20 minutes or until shallots are soft and edges are dark brown.
3. Combine rice mixture, shallots, green onions, and parsley in a bowl; toss gently, and set aside.
4. Combine 1 teaspoon oil, 2 tablespoons water, and next 4 ingredients in a bowl; stir with a whisk. Pour over rice mixture; toss gently. Yield: 4 servings (serving size: 1 cup).

CALORIES 250 (10% from fat); FAT 2.7g (sat 0.4g, mono 1.7g, poly 0.5g); PROTEIN 7.4g; CARB 50.4g; FIBER 4g; CHOL 0mg; IRON 2.2mg; SODIUM 159mg; CALC 26mg

Apple and Smoked Salmon Salad

This recipe is adapted from one of our favorite Thai cookbooks, *Cracking the Coconut* by Su-Mei Yu.

Dressing:
  ¼   cup granulated sugar
  ¼   cup Thai fish sauce
  2   tablespoons light brown sugar
  ¼   teaspoon kosher or sea salt
  ½   cup fresh lime juice
Salad:
  3   cups thinly sliced Granny Smith apple (about ¾ pound)
  ½   cup thinly sliced shallots
  ½   cup thinly sliced kumquats or 1 cup pomegranate seeds
  1   teaspoon minced serrano chile
  4   ounces thinly sliced smoked salmon, cut into ¼-inch-wide strips

1. To prepare dressing, combine first 4 ingredients in a small saucepan. Bring to a boil; cook 1 minute or until sugars dissolve. Cool; stir in lime juice.
2. To prepare salad, combine apple and next 4 ingredients in a medium bowl. Drizzle dressing over salad, and toss gently to coat. Yield: 8 servings (serving size: ½ cup).

CALORIES 100 (7% from fat); FAT 0.8g (sat 0.2g, mono 0.3g, poly 0.2g); PROTEIN 3.6g; CARB 21.2g; FIBER 1.4g; CHOL 3mg; IRON 0.4mg; SODIUM 868mg; CALC 18mg

Golden Oyster Bisque

Saffron colors this holiday favorite a rich yellow-gold. You won't miss it if
you omit it, though; the bisque will simply look paler, like oyster stew or chowder.

2 (8-ounce) containers standard oysters,
    undrained
1 (8-ounce) bottle clam juice
1 tablespoon hot water
¼ teaspoon saffron threads, crushed
1 teaspoon butter
1 cup coarsely chopped red onion
1 cup coarsely chopped celery
¼ cup all-purpose flour
¾ teaspoon ground coriander seeds
3 cups 2% reduced-fat milk
¼ cup chopped fresh flat-leaf parsley
¼ teaspoon salt
⅛ teaspoon ground red pepper

1. Drain oysters in a colander over a bowl, reserving
liquid. Add enough clam juice to oyster liquid to
equal 1 cup, and set aside. Reserve remaining
clam juice for another use. Coarsely chop oysters.

2. Combine water and saffron in a small bowl;
set aside.

3. Melt butter in a large saucepan over medium
heat. Add chopped onion and celery, and cook for
5 minutes, stirring frequently. Lightly spoon flour
into a dry measuring cup, and level with a knife.
Stir flour and coriander into onion mixture, and
cook 1 minute. Add oyster liquid, saffron water,
and milk, stirring with a whisk. Cook until thick
(about 12 minutes), stirring frequently. Add oysters, parsley, salt, and pepper. Cook 3 minutes or
until edges of oysters curl. Yield: 6 servings (serving size: 1 cup).

CALORIES 153 (30% from fat); FAT 5.1g (sat 2.4g, mono 1.1g, poly 0.7g);
PROTEIN 10.6g; CARB 16.2g; FIBER 1.2g; CHOL 53mg; IRON 5.7mg;
SODIUM 313mg; CALC 205mg

Oyster-Crab Bisque

3 (12-ounce) containers standard oysters, undrained
Cooking spray
1 cup chopped onion
½ cup chopped celery
½ cup chopped green bell pepper
2 garlic cloves, minced
½ cup all-purpose flour
1 (14-ounce) can fat-free, less-sodium chicken broth
½ teaspoon dried thyme
1 bay leaf
½ cup sliced green onions
1 (12-ounce) can evaporated fat-free milk
1 pound lump crabmeat, shell pieces removed
¼ teaspoon salt
¼ teaspoon black pepper

1. Drain oysters in a colander over a bowl, reserving 1 cup oyster liquid.

2. Heat a large Dutch oven coated with cooking spray over medium-high heat. Add chopped onion, celery, bell pepper, and garlic; sauté 5 minutes. Lightly spoon flour into a dry measuring cup, and level with a knife. Add flour to onion mixture, and cook 1 minute, stirring constantly. Gradually add reserved oyster liquid and broth, stirring with a whisk until blended. Stir in thyme and bay leaf, and bring to a boil. Add oysters, green onions, and milk, and cook 3 minutes or until edges of oysters curl. Gently stir in crabmeat, salt, and black pepper, and cook 1 minute or until thoroughly heated. Discard bay leaf. Yield: 7 servings (serving size: about 1½ cups).

CALORIES 263 (18% from fat); FAT 5.3g (sat 1.2g, mono 0.7g, poly 1.8g); PROTEIN 29.5g; CARB 22.2g; FIBER 1.2g; CHOL 147mg; IRON 11.4mg; SODIUM 631mg; CALC 293mg

Oyster-Crab Bisque

Homemade breads make great accompaniments to these hearty soups.
Check out our seasonal bread offerings beginning on page 158.

Thai Shrimp Bisque

Marinade:

1½ pounds medium shrimp

1½ tablespoons grated lime rind

⅓ cup fresh lime juice

1½ tablespoons ground coriander

1 tablespoon minced fresh cilantro

1 tablespoon minced peeled fresh ginger

1½ teaspoons sugar

¼ teaspoon ground red pepper

2 garlic cloves, crushed

Shrimp Stock:

2 cups water

¼ cup dry white wine

1 tablespoon tomato paste

Soup:

1 teaspoon olive oil

½ cup chopped onion

⅓ cup chopped celery

1 (14-ounce) can light coconut milk

1 tablespoon tomato paste

¼ cup all-purpose flour

1 cup 2% reduced-fat milk

1 tablespoon grated lime rind

1 tablespoon minced fresh cilantro

½ teaspoon salt

1. To prepare marinade, peel shrimp, reserving shells. Combine shrimp and next 8 ingredients in a large zip-top plastic bag; seal and marinate in refrigerator 30 minutes.

2. To prepare shrimp stock, combine reserved shrimp shells, water, wine, and 1 tablespoon tomato paste in a large Dutch oven. Bring mixture to a boil. Reduce heat; simmer until liquid is reduced to 1 cup (about 10 minutes). Strain mixture through a sieve over a bowl, and discard solids.

3. To prepare soup, heat olive oil in a large Dutch oven over medium heat. Add onion and celery, and sauté 8 minutes or until browned. Add 1 cup shrimp stock, coconut milk, and 1 tablespoon tomato paste, scraping pan to loosen browned bits. Bring to a boil. Lightly spoon flour into a dry measuring cup, and level with a knife. Combine flour and reduced-fat milk in a small bowl, stirring with a whisk. Add to pan; reduce heat, and simmer until thick (about 5 minutes). Add shrimp and marinade, and cook 5 minutes. Stir in 1 tablespoon lime rind, 1 tablespoon cilantro, and salt. Yield: 4 servings (serving size: 1½ cups).

CALORIES 201 (30% from fat); FAT 6.7g (sat 3.2g, mono 1.7g, poly 1.2g); PROTEIN 19.9g; CARB 15.2g; FIBER 0.9g; CHOL 133mg; IRON 3.3mg; SODIUM 380mg; CALC 117mg

Pumpkin Soup

1 tablespoon butter

1 cup chopped onion

3 tablespoons all-purpose flour

½ teaspoon curry powder

¼ teaspoon ground cumin

¼ teaspoon ground nutmeg

2 garlic cloves, crushed

1 cup (½-inch) cubed peeled sweet potato

¼ teaspoon salt

2 (14-ounce) cans fat-free, less-sodium chicken broth

1 (15-ounce) can pumpkin

1 cup 1% low-fat milk

1 tablespoon fresh lime juice

2 tablespoons chopped fresh chives (optional)

1. Melt butter in a Dutch oven over medium-high heat. Add onion; sauté 3 minutes. Stir in flour and next 4 ingredients; sauté 1 minute. Add sweet potato, salt, broth, and pumpkin; bring to a boil. Reduce heat; simmer, partially covered, 20 minutes or until potato is tender, stirring occasionally. Remove from heat; cool 10 minutes.

2. Place half of pumpkin mixture in a blender or food processor; process until smooth. Pour pureed soup into a large bowl. Repeat procedure with remaining pumpkin mixture. Return soup to pan; stir in milk. Cook over medium heat 6 minutes or until thoroughly heated, stirring frequently (do not boil). Remove from heat; stir in juice. Garnish with chives, if desired. Yield: 6 servings (serving size: 1 cup).

CALORIES 121 (21% from fat); FAT 2.8g (sat 1.6g, mono 0.7g, poly 0.2g); PROTEIN 5.1g; CARB 19.7g; FIBER 3.5g; CHOL 7mg; IRON 1.5mg; SODIUM 565mg; CALC 85mg

Triple-Ginger Butternut Squash Soup

2 butternut squash (about 1¾ pounds)
1 teaspoon olive oil
1 cup chopped onion
3 tablespoons chopped crystallized ginger
1 teaspoon ground ginger
1 (1-inch) piece peeled fresh ginger
2 (14-ounce) cans vegetable broth
¼ cup thinly sliced green onions
4 teaspoons chopped dry-roasted peanuts
4 teaspoons low-fat sour cream

1. Pierce each squash with a fork. Microwave at HIGH 20 minutes or until tender, and cool. Cut each squash in half lengthwise, discarding seeds and membrane. Remove pulp.
2. Heat oil in a Dutch oven over medium heat. Add chopped onion, and cook 5 minutes or until golden. Place onion, squash, and gingers in a blender, and process until smooth. Return squash mixture to pan. Stir in vegetable broth, and cook 5 minutes or until thoroughly heated. Spoon 1½ cups soup into each of 4 individual soup bowls. Top each serving with 1 tablespoon green onions, 1 teaspoon chopped peanuts, and 1 teaspoon sour cream. Yield: 4 servings.

CALORIES 164 (21% from fat); FAT 3.9g (sat 0.7g, mono 1.4g, poly 0.5g); PROTEIN 5g; CARB 33.1g; FIBER 8g; CHOL 3mg; IRON 1.7mg; SODIUM 905mg; CALC 117mg

Rustic Potato Chowder

To warm up after a sleigh ride or a day of window shopping, cozy up with a bowl of this easy-to-make soup.

Parsley Butter:
1 cup fresh parsley leaves (about 1 bunch)
1 tablespoon butter
Soup:
6 cups water
3½ cups fresh parsley sprigs (about 1½ bunches)
4½ cups cubed peeled Yukon gold or red potato (about 2 pounds)
¾ cup cubed carrot
1 teaspoon salt

1. To prepare parsley butter, process parsley leaves and butter in a food processor until well blended.
2. To prepare soup, combine water and parsley sprigs in a large saucepan; bring to a boil. Reduce heat, and simmer 15 minutes.

Strain mixture through a sieve over a large bowl, reserving broth, and discard solids. Return broth to pan; add potato, carrot, and salt. Bring to a boil. Reduce heat; simmer 15 minutes or until vegetables are tender. Remove 1½ cups vegetables from soup with a slotted spoon. Place remaining soup and vegetables in a food processor, and process until smooth; pour into pan. Return 1½ cups vegetables to soup. Bring to a boil, and stir in parsley butter. Yield: 6 servings (serving size: 1 cup).

CALORIES 115 (16% from fat); FAT 2.1g (sat 1.2g, mono 0.6g, poly 0.1g); PROTEIN 2.7g; CARB 22.2g; FIBER 2.7g; CHOL 5mg; IRON 1.5mg; SODIUM 427mg; CALC 26mg

Cheddar Chicken Chowder

This chowder is one of Food Stylist Kellie Kelley's family favorites. "It's rich and filling," she says. "And it's great for those cold winter nights."

2 bacon slices
1 pound skinless, boneless chicken breast, cut into bite-sized pieces
1 cup chopped onion
1 cup diced red bell pepper
2 garlic cloves, minced
4½ cups fat-free, less-sodium chicken broth
1¾ cups chopped peeled red potato
2¼ cups frozen whole-kernel corn
½ cup all-purpose flour
2 cups 2% reduced-fat milk
¾ cup (3 ounces) shredded Cheddar cheese
½ teaspoon salt
¼ teaspoon black pepper

1. Cook bacon in a Dutch oven over medium-high heat until crisp. Remove bacon from pan; crumble. Set aside. Add chicken, onion, bell pepper, and garlic to drippings in pan; sauté 5 minutes. Add broth and potato, and bring to a boil. Cover, reduce heat, and simmer 20 minutes or until potato is tender. Add corn; stir well.
2. Lightly spoon flour into a dry measuring cup; level with a knife. Place flour in a bowl. Gradually add milk, stirring with a whisk until blended; add to soup. Bring to a boil over medium-high heat. Reduce heat to medium, and simmer 15 minutes or until thick, stirring frequently. Stir in Cheddar cheese, salt, and black pepper. Top with crumbled bacon. Yield: 7 servings (serving size: 1½ cups).

CALORIES 306 (22% from fat); FAT 7.5g (sat 4g, mono 2.2g, poly 0.6g); PROTEIN 25g; CARB 33.7g; FIBER 2.9g; CHOL 58mg; IRON 1.6mg; SODIUM 376mg; CALC 193mg

Quick Chicken-Corn Chowder

You can have this soup on the table in less than 30 minutes, which is ideal anytime of year
but is especially good during the hustle and bustle of the holiday season.

2 tablespoons butter

¼ cup chopped onion

¼ cup chopped celery

1 jalapeño pepper, seeded and minced

2 tablespoons all-purpose flour

3 cups 2% reduced-fat milk

2 cups chopped roasted skinless, boneless chicken breasts (about 2 breast halves)

1½ cups fresh or frozen corn kernels (about 3 ears)

1 teaspoon chopped fresh or ¼ teaspoon dried thyme

¼ teaspoon ground red pepper

⅛ teaspoon salt

1 (14¾-ounce) can cream-style corn

1. Melt butter in a large Dutch oven over medium heat. Add onion, celery, and jalapeño, and cook 3 minutes or until tender, stirring frequently. Add flour, and cook 1 minute, stirring constantly. Stir in milk and remaining ingredients. Bring to a boil, and cook until thick (about 5 minutes), stirring frequently. Yield: 6 servings (serving size: about 1 cup).

CALORIES 257 (28% from fat); FAT 8.1g (sat 4.4g, mono 2.4g, poly 0.8g); PROTEIN 19.1g; CARB 28.6g; FIBER 1.9g; CHOL 52mg; IRON 0.4mg; SODIUM 668mg; CALC 165mg

Winter Vegetable Soup

Potatoes, squash, and white beans combine for a substantial main-dish soup.

- 1 teaspoon olive oil
- 2 ounces pancetta, chopped
- 1 cup chopped onion
- 3 garlic cloves, minced
- 2 cups cubed peeled acorn squash
- 2 cups chopped peeled red potato
- ½ cup chopped celery
- ½ cup chopped carrot
- 1 teaspoon dried basil
- ¼ teaspoon ground cinnamon
- ¼ teaspoon dried thyme
- 1 (28-ounce) can whole tomatoes, drained and chopped
- 2 (14-ounce) cans fat-free, less-sodium chicken broth
- 4 cups chopped kale
- 1 (15.5-ounce) can navy beans or other small white beans, rinsed and drained

1. Heat oil in a Dutch oven over medium-high heat. Add pancetta; sauté 3 minutes. Add chopped onion and garlic; sauté 3 minutes. Add squash and next 6 ingredients, stirring to combine; cook 4 minutes, stirring occasionally. Add tomatoes; cook 2 minutes.

2. Stir in broth; bring to a boil. Reduce heat; simmer 8 minutes. Add kale; simmer 5 minutes. Add beans, and simmer 4 minutes or until potato and kale are tender. Yield: 4 servings (serving size: about 2 cups).

CALORIES 349 (27% from fat); FAT 10.4g (sat 3.3g, mono 4.6g, poly 1.4g); PROTEIN 14.4g; CARB 55g; FIBER 10.5g; CHOL 10mg; IRON 4.2mg; SODIUM 1,076mg; CALC 213mg

Escarole, Endive, and Pasta Soup

- 1 tablespoon olive oil
- 1 cup chopped carrot
- 2 garlic cloves, minced
- 6 cups Rich Turkey Stock (recipe at right)
- 3 cups coarsely chopped escarole
- 3 cups coarsely chopped curly endive
- 1½ cups uncooked small seashell pasta
- ½ teaspoon salt
- 1 (3-inch) piece Parmigiano-Reggiano cheese rind

1. Heat oil in a large saucepan over medium-low heat. Add

carrot; cook 5 minutes, stirring occasionally. Add garlic; sauté 30 seconds. Stir in stock and remaining ingredients; bring to a boil. Cover, reduce heat, and simmer 7 minutes or until shells are tender. Discard rind. Yield: 4 servings (serving size: about 1½ cups).

CALORIES 258 (25% from fat); FAT 7.1g (sat 1.4g, mono 3.5g, poly 1.4g); PROTEIN 16.4g; CARB 31.2g; FIBER 4.4g; CHOL 25mg; IRON 2.6mg; SODIUM 707mg; CALC 64mg

holiday soup basic

The secret to a great soup is the stock. Rich Turkey Stock (recipe below) is an outstanding stock to use and is included in the following recipes:

- Broccoli Rabe, Butternut Squash, and White Bean Soup (recipe on page 207)
- Curried Couscous, Spinach, and Roasted Tomato Soup (recipe on page 207)
- Escarole, Endive, and Pasta Soup (recipe at left)
- Leek and Potato Stew (recipe on page 210)

Rich Turkey Stock

Carcass and skin from a cooked 12-pound turkey
- 2 carrots, each cut in half crosswise
- 1 celery stalk, cut in half crosswise
- 1 large onion, quartered
- 1 whole garlic head, halved
- 5 cups water
- 3 (14-ounce) cans fat-free, less-sodium chicken broth
- ¼ teaspoon black peppercorns

1. Preheat oven to 425°.
2. Cut turkey carcass into quarters. Place carcass, skin, carrot, celery, onion, and garlic on a jelly-roll pan or shallow roasting pan. Bake at 425° for 45 minutes, stirring once.
3. Place bones and vegetable mixture, water, broth, and peppercorns in a large stockpot. Bring to a boil; cover, reduce heat, and simmer 2 hours. Strain mixture through a sieve into a bowl, reserving stock. Discard solids. Cover and chill stock 8 hours or overnight. Skim solidified fat from surface; discard fat. Yield: 9 cups (serving size: 1 cup).
Note: Store the turkey stock in an airtight container in the refrigerator for up to 1 week, or freeze for up to 3 months.

CALORIES 53 (34% from fat); FAT 2g (sat 0.6g, mono 0.6g, poly 0.5g); PROTEIN 7.3g; CARB 0.5g; FIBER 0g; CHOL 17mg; IRON 0.4mg; SODIUM 257mg; CALC 5mg

Broccoli Rabe, Butternut Squash, and White Bean Soup

Curried Couscous, Spinach, and Roasted Tomato Soup

Broccoli Rabe, Butternut Squash, and White Bean Soup

To make this simple-to-prepare soup even easier, look for chopped peeled squash in the produce section of your supermarket.

  2 cups (¾-inch) cubed peeled butternut squash
Cooking spray
  1 tablespoon olive oil, divided
  8 ounces broccoli rabe (rapini), trimmed
  ½ cup finely chopped onion
  1 garlic clove, minced
4½ cups Rich Turkey Stock (recipe on page 206)
  1 (16-ounce) can cannellini beans or other white beans, rinsed and drained
  ¼ teaspoon salt

1. Preheat oven to 450°.
2. Arrange squash in a single layer on a jelly-roll pan coated with cooking spray. Drizzle with 1½ teaspoons oil, and toss well to coat. Bake at 450° for 25 minutes or until lightly browned. Set aside.
3. Cut broccoli rabe crosswise into thirds. Cook broccoli rabe in boiling water 5 minutes; drain. Set aside.
4. Heat 1½ teaspoons oil in a large saucepan over medium heat. Add onion and garlic; cook 5 minutes, stirring frequently. Add squash, stock, and beans; cook 10 minutes. Place 1½ cups vegetable mixture in a blender or food processor; process until smooth. Return pureed mixture to pan; stir in broccoli rabe and salt. Cook 5 minutes or until thoroughly heated. Yield: 4 servings (serving size: 1¾ cups).

CALORIES 195 (28% from fat); FAT 6g (sat 1.1g, mono 3.2g, poly 0.9g); PROTEIN 15.4g; CARB 26g; FIBER 6.9g; CHOL 19mg; IRON 2.2mg; SODIUM 756mg; CALC 100mg

Curried Couscous, Spinach, and Roasted Tomato Soup

Israeli couscous is toasted semolina pasta; each grain is about half the size of a green pea. Even in hot soup, this kind of couscous retains al dente firmness for a long time.

  4 plum tomatoes, each cut into 8 wedges (about ¾ pound)
  1 teaspoon olive oil
  1 teaspoon butter
  1 cup finely chopped onion
  ½ cup uncooked toasted Israeli couscous
1½ teaspoons curry powder
  ¼ teaspoon salt
  1 garlic clove, minced
4½ cups Rich Turkey Stock (recipe on page 206)
  1 (6-ounce) package fresh baby spinach

1. Preheat oven to 450°.
2. Combine tomato wedges and olive oil on a baking sheet lined with foil, tossing the tomato wedges well to coat. Bake at 450° for 15 minutes or until tomato wedges are tender and lightly browned.
3. Melt butter in a large saucepan over medium-high heat. Add onion, and sauté 3 minutes. Add couscous, curry powder, salt, and garlic, and sauté 3 minutes. Add tomato wedges and turkey stock, and bring to a boil. Reduce heat, and simmer 7 minutes or until couscous is almost tender. Stir in spinach, and cook 2 minutes or just until spinach wilts. Yield: 4 servings (serving size: 1½ cups).

CALORIES 339 (15% from fat); FAT 5.8g (sat 1.5g, mono 1.9g, poly 1.3g); PROTEIN 18.6g; CARB 55.1g; FIBER 4.8g; CHOL 21mg; IRON 3.3mg; SODIUM 486mg; CALC 64mg

Chicken, Sausage, and Rice Soup

4 ounces hot turkey Italian sausage
2 (2½-ounce) skinless, boneless chicken thighs, cut into ½-inch pieces
Cooking spray
1½ cups frozen chopped onion
2 thyme sprigs
⅓ cup chopped celery
⅓ cup chopped carrot
2 (14-ounce) cans fat-free, less-sodium chicken broth
1 (3½-ounce) bag boil-in-bag brown rice
1 tablespoon chopped fresh parsley
¼ teaspoon salt
⅛ teaspoon black pepper

1. Remove casings from sausage. Combine sausage and chicken in a large saucepan coated with cooking spray over high heat; cook 2 minutes, stirring to crumble sausage. Add onion and thyme sprigs; cook 2 minutes, stirring occasionally. Add celery, carrot, and broth; bring to a boil.
2. Remove rice from bag; stir into broth mixture. Cover, reduce heat to medium, and cook 7 minutes or until rice is tender. Discard thyme sprigs. Stir in parsley, salt, and pepper. Yield: 4 servings (serving size: 1½ cups).

CALORIES 245 (19% from fat); FAT 5.2g (sat 1.5g, mono 1.8g, poly 1.5g); PROTEIN 18.4g; CARB 30g; FIBER 3.4g; CHOL 56mg; IRON 1.6mg; SODIUM 754mg; CALC 35mg

Turkey Mole Soup

1 teaspoon olive oil
1¼ pounds ground turkey
1 cup chopped onion
1 cup chopped green bell pepper
2 tablespoons chili powder
4 garlic cloves, minced
¼ cup bottled mole (such as La Costeña)
2 (14-ounce) cans fat-free, less-sodium chicken broth
½ cup raisins
½ teaspoon salt
½ teaspoon black pepper
1 (19-ounce) can black beans, drained
1 (14.5-ounce) can diced tomatoes, undrained
1 (4.5-ounce) can chopped green chiles, undrained
3 (6-inch) corn tortillas, cut into ¼-inch strips
½ cup chopped fresh cilantro

1. Heat oil in a Dutch oven over medium heat. Add turkey; cook 5 minutes or until browned, stirring to crumble. Add onion and next 3 ingredients; cook 5 minutes, stirring frequently. Combine mole and broth, stirring with a whisk. Add broth mixture, raisins, and next 5 ingredients to turkey mixture, stirring to combine; bring to a boil. Cover; reduce heat. Simmer 20 minutes.
2. Preheat oven to 425°.
3. Place tortilla strips on a baking sheet. Bake at 425° for 5 minutes or until golden brown.
4. Spoon 1¼ cups soup into each of 8 bowls. Divide tortilla strips evenly among servings. Top each serving with 1 tablespoon cilantro. Yield: 8 servings.

CALORIES 281 (28% from fat); FAT 8.8g (sat 1.7g, mono 2.7g, poly 2g); PROTEIN 19.5g; CARB 30.6g; FIBER 7.1g; CHOL 56mg; IRON 3.4mg; SODIUM 926mg; CALC 89mg

White Turkey Chili
(pictured on page 188)

1 tablespoon butter
1½ cups chopped onion
½ cup chopped celery
½ cup chopped red bell pepper
1 tablespoon minced seeded jalapeño pepper
1 garlic clove, minced
3 cups chopped cooked turkey (about 15 ounces)
2 (19-ounce) cans cannellini beans or other white beans, drained and divided
4 cups fat-free, less-sodium chicken broth
1 (4.5-ounce) can chopped green chiles, undrained
1 cup frozen whole-kernel corn
1½ teaspoons ground cumin
1 teaspoon chili powder
½ teaspoon salt
¼ teaspoon black pepper
1 cup 1% low-fat milk
½ cup chopped fresh cilantro

1. Melt butter in a large Dutch oven over medium-high heat. Add onion and next 4 ingredients; sauté 5 minutes. Add turkey, 1½ cups beans, broth, and next 6 ingredients; bring to a boil. Cover, reduce heat, and simmer 15 minutes.
2. Mash remaining beans; add beans and milk to turkey mixture. Simmer, uncovered, 20 minutes or until mixture is thick, stirring frequently. Stir in cilantro. Yield: 11 servings (serving size: 1 cup).

CALORIES 172 (20% from fat); FAT 3.9g (sat 1.5g, mono 0.8g, poly 1g); PROTEIN 16.4g; CARB 17.6g; FIBER 4.2g; CHOL 33mg; IRON 2.3mg; SODIUM 485mg; CALC 79mg

Chicken Chili
with Pesto

Chicken Chili with Pesto

Swirl in a generous dollop of pesto before serving to liven up this classic white chili.

2   teaspoons vegetable oil
¾   cup finely chopped onion
¾   pound skinless, boneless chicken breast, cut into
    bite-sized pieces
1½ cups finely chopped carrot
¾   cup finely chopped red bell pepper
¾   cup thinly sliced celery
¼   cup canned chopped green chiles
¾   teaspoon dried oregano
½   teaspoon ground cumin
¼   teaspoon salt
⅛   teaspoon black pepper
1   (16-ounce) can cannellini beans or other white beans,
    rinsed and drained
1   (14-ounce) can fat-free, less-sodium chicken broth
3   tablespoons Classic Pesto

1. Heat oil in a Dutch oven over medium-high heat. Add onion and chicken; sauté 5 minutes. Add carrot, bell pepper, and celery; sauté 4 minutes. Add chiles and next 6 ingredients, and bring to a boil.
2. Cover, reduce heat, and simmer 25 minutes. Stir in Classic Pesto. Yield: 4 servings (serving size: 1¼ cups).
Note: The chili and pesto can be made ahead and frozen for up to 3 months. Prepare and freeze 3 tablespoons Classic Pesto. Prepare the chili without Classic Pesto, and spoon into a freezer-safe container. Cool completely in refrigerator; cover and freeze. Thaw chili and pesto in refrigerator. Place chili in a large skillet; cook over medium-low heat until thoroughly heated, stirring occasionally. Stir in Classic Pesto.

CALORIES 327 (23% from fat); FAT 8.5g (sat 1.8g, mono 3.4g, poly 2.5g); PROTEIN 30.3g; CARB 30.7g; FIBER 5.9g; CHOL 52mg; IRON 4.1mg; SODIUM 769mg; CALC 134mg

Classic Pesto

2   tablespoons coarsely chopped walnuts or pine nuts
2   garlic cloves, peeled
3   tablespoons extravirgin olive oil
4   cups basil leaves (about 4 ounces)
½   cup (2 ounces) grated fresh Parmesan cheese
¼   teaspoon salt

1. Drop nuts and garlic through food chute with food processor on; process until minced. Add oil; pulse 3 times. Add basil, cheese, and salt; process until finely minced, scraping sides of bowl once. Yield: ¾ cup (serving size: 1 tablespoon).

CALORIES 58 (82% from fat); FAT 5.3g (sat 1.3g, mono 3g, poly 0.8g); PROTEIN 2.1g; CARB 0.9g; FIBER 0.6g; CHOL 3mg; IRON 0.5mg; SODIUM 125mg; CALC 72mg

After Christmas tree hunting, warm up with a bowl of Nonstop, No-Chop Chili (recipe below) or Slow-Cooker Chicken Stew (recipe on page 212).

Nonstop, No-Chop Chili

¾ pound ground round

Cooking spray

2 cups water

1½ cups frozen whole-kernel corn

1 cup bottled salsa

2 tablespoons chili powder

1 tablespoon sugar

2½ teaspoons ground cumin

1½ teaspoons dried oregano

¼ teaspoon salt

1 (16-ounce) can chili beans, undrained

1 (14.5-ounce) can no-salt-added diced tomatoes, undrained

1. Cook ground round in a large Dutch oven coated with cooking spray over medium-high heat 4 minutes or until beef is browned, stirring occasionally. Stir in water and remaining ingredients; bring to a boil. Reduce heat; simmer 25 minutes, stirring occasionally. Yield: 6 servings (serving size: about 1 cup).

CALORIES 254 (28% from fat); FAT 8g (sat 2.8g, mono 2.4g, poly 0.6g); PROTEIN 18g; CARB 30.5g; FIBER 7.2g; CHOL 24mg; IRON 3.9mg; SODIUM 649mg; CALC 96mg

Leek and Potato Stew

2 bacon slices

3 cups chopped leek

4½ cups Rich Turkey Stock (recipe on page 206)

4 cups cubed peeled Yukon gold potato

½ teaspoon salt

½ teaspoon chopped fresh or ¼ teaspoon dried thyme

2 tablespoons chopped fresh flat-leaf parsley

1. Cook bacon in a saucepan over medium-high heat until crisp. Add leek. Cover; reduce heat to medium-low. Cook 3 minutes. Add stock, potato, salt, and thyme; bring to a boil. Reduce heat; simmer 15 minutes or until potato is tender. Remove 1 cup potato with a slotted spoon; place in a blender. Add ½ cup cooking liquid; process until smooth. Return mixture to pan. Sprinkle with parsley. Yield: 4 servings (serving size: 2 cups).

CALORIES 312 (26% from fat); FAT 9.1g (sat 3.1g, mono 3.7g, poly 1.5g); PROTEIN 13.4g; CARB 44.5g; FIBER 4.3g; CHOL 26mg; IRON 2.5mg; SODIUM 686mg; CALC 59mg

Chinese Beef-and-Mushroom Stew with Whole Spices

2 cups boiling water

1 cup dried black mushrooms

Cooking spray

1 (1½-pound) beef brisket, trimmed and cubed

1½ cups chopped green onions, divided

1 teaspoon grated peeled fresh ginger

4 garlic cloves, minced

1¼ cups water

3 tablespoons low-sodium soy sauce

2 tablespoons sake (rice wine)

2 tablespoons brown sugar

½ teaspoon mixed peppercorns

3 star anise

3 whole cloves

2 dried red chiles

1 (14-ounce) can less-sodium beef broth

1 (3-inch) cinnamon stick

1 teaspoon dark sesame oil

2½ cups hot cooked basmati rice

1. Combine boiling water and dried mushrooms. Cover and let stand 30 minutes. Remove mushrooms with a slotted spoon. Chop mushrooms; set aside. Strain soaking liquid through a cheesecloth- or paper towel-lined sieve into a bowl. Discard solids; reserve 1 cup soaking liquid.

2. Heat a large Dutch oven coated with cooking spray over medium-high heat. Add beef, and cook 8 minutes on all sides or until browned. Add ¾ cup onion, ginger, and garlic, and cook 1 minute, stirring frequently. Stir in reserved soaking liquid, 1¼ cups water, and next 9 ingredients, and bring to a boil. Cover, reduce heat, and simmer 1 hour. Stir in mushrooms. Cover and simmer 40 minutes or until beef is tender. Remove beef mixture with a slotted spoon. Discard star anise, cloves, dried chiles, and cinnamon stick. Bring liquid to a boil, and cook 3 minutes or until reduced to 1 cup. Stir in ¾ cup onion and oil. Serve beef mixture over rice with sauce. Yield: 5 servings (serving size: ⅔ cup beef mixture, about 3 tablespoons sauce, and ½ cup rice).

CALORIES 379 (24% from fat); FAT 10.1g (sat 3.1g, mono 4.4g, poly 0.9g); PROTEIN 34.1g; CARB 33g; FIBER 1.9g; CHOL 80mg; IRON 4.2mg; SODIUM 460mg; CALC 33mg

Beef, Beer, and Barley Stew

Beef, Beer, and Barley Stew

Serve this stew as part of a hearty autumn menu with Roasted Cipollini Onions (recipe on page 282) and Sweet Potato Tart with Pecan Crust (recipe on page 331).

2 tablespoons olive oil
1 pound beef stew meat
1 teaspoon salt, divided
¼ teaspoon black pepper
3 cups coarsely chopped onion
2 bay leaves
2 thyme sprigs
2 tablespoons tomato paste
2 cups (1½-inch-thick) slices carrot
2 cups chopped peeled turnips (about 1 pound)
¾ cup uncooked pearl barley
5 garlic cloves, minced and divided
2 (8-ounce) packages mushrooms, quartered
3 cups water
3 cups low-salt beef broth
2 tablespoons Worcestershire sauce
1 (12-ounce) bottle dark beer (such as Guinness Stout)
3 small beets
3 tablespoons chopped fresh parsley
1 teaspoon thyme leaves
2 tablespoons prepared horseradish

1. Heat oil in a stockpot over medium-high heat. Sprinkle beef with ½ teaspoon salt and pepper. Add beef to pan; sauté 10 minutes or until browned. Remove from pan. Add onion, bay leaves, and thyme sprigs to pan. Cover, reduce heat, and cook 10 minutes, stirring occasionally.

2. Uncover; stir in tomato paste. Increase heat to medium-high. Add carrot, turnip, barley, 4 garlic cloves, and mushrooms; sauté 3 minutes. Add beef, ½ teaspoon salt, water, broth, Worcestershire sauce, and beer; bring to a boil. Reduce heat; simmer, covered, 1½ hours. Discard bay leaves and thyme sprigs.

3. While stew is simmering, trim beets, leaving root and 1 inch of stem on each; scrub with a brush. Place in a medium saucepan, and cover with water; bring to a boil. Cover, reduce heat, and simmer 35 minutes or until tender. Drain; rinse with cold water. Drain; cool. Leave root and stem on beets; rub off skins. Cut each beet into 6 wedges.

4. Combine parsley, thyme leaves, and 1 garlic clove. Ladle about 2 cups stew into each of 6 bowls. Top each serving with 3 beet wedges, about 1½ teaspoons parsley mixture, and 1 teaspoon horseradish. Yield: 6 servings.

CALORIES 379 (27% from fat); FAT 11.4g (sat 2.9g, mono 6g, poly 1.1g); PROTEIN 24.5g; CARB 45.2g; FIBER 10.2g; CHOL 47mg; IRON 4.8mg; SODIUM 654mg; CALC 85mg

Slow-Cooker Chicken Stew

1 pound skinless, boneless chicken breast, chopped
1 pound skinless, boneless chicken thighs, chopped
2 cups mushrooms, halved
2 cups water
1 cup frozen small whole onions
1 cup (½-inch) sliced celery
1 cup thinly sliced carrot
1 teaspoon paprika
½ teaspoon salt
½ teaspoon dried rubbed sage
½ teaspoon dried thyme
½ teaspoon black pepper
1 (14-ounce) can fat-free, less-sodium chicken broth
1 (6-ounce) can tomato paste
¼ cup water
3 tablespoons cornstarch
2 cups frozen green peas

1. Combine first 14 ingredients in an electric slow cooker. Cover with lid; cook on high-heat setting 4 hours or until carrot is tender. Combine water and cornstarch in a small bowl, stirring with a whisk until blended. Add cornstarch mixture and peas to slow cooker; stir well. Cover and cook on high-heat setting 30 additional minutes. Yield: 8 servings (serving size: 1½ cups).

CALORIES 212 (14% from fat); FAT 3.4g (sat 0.9g, mono 0.9g, poly 0.9g); PROTEIN 28.1g; CARB 16.7g; FIBER 4.1g; CHOL 80mg; IRON 2.7mg; SODIUM 551mg; CALC 51mg

Jamaican Chicken Stew

1 cup uncooked long-grain rice
2 teaspoons olive oil
1 cup chopped onion
1½ teaspoons bottled minced garlic
1 pound skinless, boneless chicken breast, cut into bite-sized pieces
1 teaspoon curry powder
1 teaspoon dried thyme
½ teaspoon ground allspice
½ teaspoon crushed red pepper
½ teaspoon cracked black pepper
¼ cup dry red wine
2 tablespoons capers
1 (15-ounce) can black beans, rinsed and drained
1 (14.5-ounce) can diced tomatoes, undrained

1. Cook the rice according to package directions, omitting salt and fat.
2. While rice cooks, heat oil in a large nonstick skillet over medium-high heat. Add onion and garlic; sauté 3 minutes or until tender. Combine chicken and next 5 ingredients in a bowl. Add chicken mixture to pan; sauté 4 minutes. Stir in wine, capers, beans, and tomatoes. Cover, reduce heat, and simmer 10 minutes or until tender. Serve over rice. Yield: 4 servings (serving size: 1½ cups stew and ¾ cup rice).

CALORIES 465 (10% from fat); FAT 5g (sat 1g, mono 2.2g, poly 1g); PROTEIN 38.5g; CARB 66g; FIBER 5.9g; CHOL 66mg; IRON 6mg; SODIUM 799mg; CALC 101mg

Spicy Turkey and Sweet Potato Gumbo

1 (6-ounce) box long-grain and wild rice mix
2 (4-ounce) links hot turkey Italian sausage
1 cup chopped onion
1 cup chopped celery
1 cup chopped green bell pepper
4 garlic cloves, minced
½ cup all-purpose flour
2 cups (¼-inch) cubed peeled sweet potato
1 teaspoon dried thyme
1 teaspoon dried oregano
2 (14-ounce) cans fat-free, less-sodium chicken broth
1 (14½-ounce) can diced tomatoes with green pepper and onion, undrained
1 bay leaf
2 cups chopped cooked dark-meat turkey
½ teaspoon hot sauce

1. Cook rice according to package directions, omitting seasoning packet.
2. Remove casings from sausage. Cook sausage in a Dutch oven over medium heat until browned, stirring to crumble. Add onion, celery, and bell pepper, and cook 4 minutes, stirring frequently. Add garlic, and cook 1 minute. Lightly spoon flour into a dry measuring cup, and level with a knife. Stir in flour, and cook 6 minutes or until lightly browned, stirring constantly. Add sweet potato and next 5 ingredients, and bring to a boil. Cover, reduce heat, and simmer 15 minutes. Add turkey and hot sauce; cook, uncovered, 3 minutes. Discard bay leaf. Serve over rice. Yield: 6 servings (serving size: 1⅓ cups gumbo and ½ cup rice).

CALORIES 379 (18% from fat); FAT 7.5g (sat 2.3g, mono 2.2g, poly 2.3g); PROTEIN 27.3g; CARB 48.9g; FIBER 4.8g; CHOL 72mg; IRON 3.8mg; SODIUM 804mg; CALC 68mg

Post-Turkey
Day Posole

Post-Turkey Day Posole

For some, the best part of Thanksgiving dinner is the leftovers. Post-Turkey Day Posole capitalizes on this truth.
This Mexican stew is traditionally topped with shredded cabbage, sliced radishes, cilantro, and lime wedges.

1   tablespoon olive oil
1   canned chipotle chile in adobo sauce
¾   cup finely chopped onion
¾   cup finely chopped celery
¾   cup finely chopped carrot
2   tablespoons minced fresh garlic
2   teaspoons chili powder
2   cups shredded leftover cooked turkey (light
     and dark meat)
3   cups fat-free, less-sodium chicken broth
½   cup tomato puree
½   teaspoon salt
¼   teaspoon freshly ground black pepper
1   (15.5-ounce) can white hominy, drained

1. Heat oil in a large heavy saucepan over medium-high heat. Finely chop chile. Add chile and next 5 ingredients to pan, and sauté 5 minutes or until tender. Add remaining ingredients, and bring to a simmer.

2. Cover and cook 45 minutes or until slightly thick, stirring occasionally. Yield: 4 servings (serving size: 1¼ cups).

CALORIES 286 (29% from fat); FAT 9g (sat 1.8g, mono 4.2g, poly 1.9g); PROTEIN 22g; CARB 29g; FIBER 5.5g; CHOL 41mg; IRON 2.5mg; SODIUM 1,121mg; CALC 66mg

meatless main dishes

For genuine crowd-pleasers, it's hard to beat casseroles, pizzas, and pastas. These dishes, along with our other meatless favorites, are perfect for weeknight meals during the holidays.

Quick Pizza Margherita
(recipe on page 233)

Mediterranean Spinach Strata

Fresh tomatoes and spinach pair well with nutty Asiago and tangy feta cheese in this make-ahead dish that's great for a holiday brunch, lunch, or dinner. Substitute Parmesan, Romano, or sharp provolone cheese for the Asiago, if you prefer. Presliced mushrooms and packaged spinach provide a head start.

2 (8-ounce) loaves French bread baguette, cut into
   1-inch-thick slices
Cooking spray
1 cup chopped onion
4 garlic cloves, minced
1 (8-ounce) package presliced mushrooms
1 tablespoon all-purpose flour
2 (6-ounce) packages fresh baby spinach
½ teaspoon salt, divided
½ teaspoon black pepper, divided
3 cups thinly sliced plum tomato (about 1 pound)
1 (4-ounce) package crumbled feta cheese
¾ cup (3 ounces) grated Asiago cheese, divided
3 cups fat-free milk
2 tablespoons Dijon mustard
1½ teaspoons dried oregano
5 large eggs, lightly beaten
4 large egg whites, lightly beaten

1. Preheat oven to 350°.
2. Place bread slices in a single layer on a baking sheet. Bake at 350° for 12 minutes or until lightly browned.
3. Heat a large nonstick skillet coated with cooking spray over medium-high heat. Add onion, garlic, and mushrooms; sauté 5 minutes or until tender. Sprinkle flour over mushroom mixture; cook 1 minute, stirring constantly. Add 1 package of spinach, and cook 3 minutes or until spinach wilts. Add remaining spinach, and cook 3 minutes or until spinach wilts. Stir in ¼ teaspoon salt and ¼ teaspoon pepper.
4. Place half of bread slices in bottom of a 13 x 9-inch baking dish coated with cooking spray. Spread spinach mixture over bread. Top with tomato slices; sprinkle evenly with feta and half of Asiago cheese. Arrange remaining bread slices over cheese. Combine ¼ teaspoon salt, ¼ teaspoon pepper, milk, and next 4 ingredients, stirring well with a whisk. Pour over bread; sprinkle with remaining Asiago cheese. Cover and chill 8 hours or overnight.

5. Preheat oven to 350°.
6. Uncover strata; bake at 350° for 40 minutes or until lightly browned and set. Serve warm. Yield: 10 servings.

CALORIES 297 (29% from fat); FAT 9.5g (sat 4.4g, mono 2.8g, poly 1g); PROTEIN 17.9g; CARB 36g; FIBER 3.1g; CHOL 125mg; IRON 3.5mg; SODIUM 720mg; CALC 332mg

Tomato Goat Cheese Strata

Similar to a frittata, this savory bread pudding starts on the stovetop and finishes in the oven. Using a large cast-iron skillet will help you get a crisp, brown crust.

1 cup 2% reduced-fat milk
3 tablespoons chopped fresh parsley
5 large egg whites, lightly beaten
3 large eggs, lightly beaten
2 teaspoons olive oil
2 cups thinly sliced onion
1 tablespoon chopped fresh sage
2 garlic cloves, sliced
½ teaspoon crushed red pepper
1 (28-ounce) can diced tomatoes with basil, garlic, and
   oregano, undrained
8 cups (1-inch) cubed sourdough bread (about 8 ounces)
¾ cup (3 ounces) crumbled goat cheese

1. Preheat oven to 450°.
2. Combine first 4 ingredients in a bowl, stirring mixture well with a whisk.
3. Heat oil in a large cast-iron or ovenproof skillet over high heat. Add onion; sauté 2 minutes. Add chopped sage and sliced garlic; sauté 1 minute. Add pepper and tomatoes, stirring well. Bring to a boil, and cook 1 minute. Stir bread into tomato mixture, and top with goat cheese. Pour egg mixture over tomato mixture (pan will be very full).
4. Carefully place pan in oven, and bake at 450° for 25 minutes or until egg is set. Let stand 5 minutes. Cut strata into 4 wedges. Yield: 4 servings (serving size: 1 wedge).

CALORIES 415 (30% from fat); FAT 13.9g (sat 5.7g, mono 5.2g, poly 1.4g); PROTEIN 23g; CARB 50.3g; FIBER 5.4g; CHOL 174mg; IRON 3.9mg; SODIUM 880mg; CALC 246mg

During the holidays, you always need to have reinforcements—in other words, food that can be made ahead and served at all kinds of gatherings. Now when friends unexpectedly drop by your house one evening, send in the Savory Cheesecake!

Savory
Cheesecake

Savory Cheesecake

You can serve this versatile dish as an appetizer or entrée for brunch, or as a side dish with roast turkey. Make cheesecake up to 2 days ahead, if desired. Cover with foil; place in a zip-top plastic bag, and refrigerate. Serve at room temperature.

Cooking spray
¼ cup finely crushed onion melba toasts (about 9 pieces), divided
3 tablespoons minced shallots
2½ cups trimmed watercress
¼ teaspoon freshly ground black pepper
2 cups 1% low-fat cottage cheese
¾ cup (3 ounces) shredded provolone or Gruyère cheese
¼ cup all-purpose flour
¼ teaspoon salt
1 (11-ounce) can no-salt-added whole-kernel corn, drained
2 large eggs
2 large egg whites
Watercress sprigs (optional)

1. Coat bottom of an 8-inch springform pan with cooking spray, and sprinkle with 2 tablespoons melba toast crumbs. Set aside.
2. Preheat oven to 325°.
3. Place a medium nonstick skillet coated with cooking spray over medium-high heat until hot. Add shallots; sauté 1 minute. Add trimmed watercress and pepper; sauté 2 minutes.
4. Place 2 tablespoons onion melba toast crumbs, cottage cheese, and next 6 ingredients in a food processor, and process until smooth. Add watercress mixture, and process until chopped.
5. Pour mixture into prepared springform pan. Bake at 325° for 1 hour and 15 minutes or until almost set. Remove from oven; cool 15 minutes. Cover and chill 2 hours. Serve at room temperature. Garnish with watercress sprigs, if desired. Yield: 6 servings (serving size: 1 wedge).
Note: One (10-ounce) package frozen chopped spinach, thawed and well-drained, may be substituted for trimmed watercress, if desired.

CALORIES 218 (28% from fat); FAT 6.9g (sat 3.3g, mono 1.0g, poly 0.5g); PROTEIN 18.9g; CARB 21.4g; FIBER 1.6g; CHOL 84mg; IRON 1.2mg; SODIUM 610mg; CALC 182mg

Southwestern Broccoli Quiche

You can substitute an 11-ounce can of refrigerated breadstick dough for the corn bread twists.

1 (11.5-ounce) can refrigerated corn bread twist dough (such as Pillsbury)
Cooking spray
1 teaspoon vegetable oil
½ cup chopped onion
2 garlic cloves, minced
1 jalapeño pepper, seeded and chopped
½ cup frozen whole-kernel corn
½ cup chopped red bell pepper
½ teaspoon dried oregano
½ teaspoon ground cumin
⅛ teaspoon ground red pepper
1 (10-ounce) package frozen chopped broccoli, thawed, drained, and squeezed dry
1 cup evaporated fat-free milk
3 large egg whites
1 large egg
½ teaspoon salt
¾ cup (3 ounces) reduced-fat sharp Cheddar cheese

1. Preheat oven to 350°.
2. Unroll dough; unfold layers (do not separate into strips). Place layers lengthwise, end to end, in an 11 x 7-inch baking dish coated with cooking spray. Pinch ends in middle to seal; press dough up sides of dish. Set aside.
3. Heat oil in a large nonstick skillet over medium-high heat. Add onion, garlic, and jalapeño; sauté 3 minutes or until soft. Add corn and next 5 ingredients, and sauté 5 minutes or until vegetables are soft and liquid evaporates. Remove from heat; cool 5 minutes.
4. Combine milk, egg whites, egg, and salt; stir well. Sprinkle cheese over dough. Spoon broccoli mixture into pan. Pour milk mixture over broccoli mixture. Place dish on a baking sheet. Bake at 350° for 45 minutes; cover and bake an additional 10 minutes or until set. Let stand 10 minutes. Yield 6 servings.

CALORIES 307 (32% from fat); FAT 11g (sat 3.1g, mono 3g, poly 4.2g); PROTEIN 15.6g; CARB 36.9g; FIBER 2.4g; CHOL 40mg; IRON 2.4mg; SODIUM 820mg; CALC 224mg

Barley-Mushroom Pilaf

    3   cups vegetable broth
  ⅓   cup dried porcini mushrooms, chopped (about
        ⅓ ounce)
1 ½   cups uncooked quick-cooking barley
    2   tablespoons olive oil
    3   cups quartered shiitake mushroom caps (about
        8 ounces)
    2   cups chopped onion
  ¾   teaspoon salt
  ½   teaspoon dried rosemary
    1   (8-ounce) package presliced mushrooms
  ¼   cup dry Marsala wine
    2   teaspoons sherry vinegar

1. Combine broth and porcini mushrooms in a large saucepan. Bring to a boil; stir in barley. Cover, reduce heat, and simmer 12 minutes or until tender.
2. While barley cooks, heat oil in a Dutch oven over medium-high heat. Add shiitake mushrooms, onion, salt, rosemary, and presliced mushrooms; sauté 5 minutes. Stir in Marsala; cook 1 minute. Stir in barley mixture and vinegar; cook 2 minutes or until thoroughly heated, stirring frequently. Yield: 4 servings (serving size: 1 ½ cups).

CALORIES 415 (19% from fat); FAT 8.7g (sat 1.3g, mono 5.2g, poly 1.5g); PROTEIN 15.3g; CARB 66.6g; FIBER 15g; CHOL 0mg; IRON 4.6mg; SODIUM 805mg; CALC 46mg

Beet Risotto with Greens, Goat Cheese, and Walnuts

    2   teaspoons olive oil
    1   cup chopped onion
    1   cup Arborio rice
    1   tablespoon minced peeled fresh ginger
    2   teaspoons finely chopped fresh rosemary
  ½   cup dry white wine
    3   cups finely chopped peeled beets
  ½   cup water
  ¼   teaspoon fine sea salt
    1   (14-ounce) can vegetable broth
    6   cups finely sliced Swiss chard
  ½   cup (2 ounces) crumbled goat cheese
  ¼   cup chopped walnuts, toasted

1. Heat oil in a Dutch oven over medium-high heat. Add onion, and sauté 3 minutes. Add rice, ginger, and rosemary, and sauté 1 minute. Add wine. Cook 3 minutes or until liquid is nearly absorbed, stirring constantly. Add beets, water, salt, and broth; bring to a boil. Cover, reduce heat, and simmer 20 minutes or until beets are tender, stirring occasionally.
2. Stir in chard; cook 5 minutes. Add cheese, stirring until blended. Sprinkle each serving with 1 tablespoon walnuts. Yield: 4 servings (serving size: 1 ½ cups).

CALORIES 412 (30% from fat); FAT 13.7g (sat 4.9g, mono 4g, poly 3.6g); PROTEIN 14.1g; CARB 57.5g; FIBER 4.1g; CHOL 14mg; IRON 2.1mg; SODIUM 611mg; CALC 92mg

Cheesy Spinach Polenta

Even though you have a house full of guests and presents to unwrap, don't panic! With very little effort you can still serve a joyous, welcoming brunch that includes this spinach polenta. You can even assemble the polenta the day before. Simply prepare, cover, and chill. You'll be ready to bake it the day of your brunch.

    2   (10-ounce) packages frozen chopped spinach,
        thawed and drained
    2   tablespoons all-purpose flour
    1   cup evaporated skim milk
  ½   cup low-salt vegetable broth
    2   teaspoons dry sherry
  ¼   teaspoon salt
  ¼   teaspoon black pepper
  ⅛   teaspoon ground red pepper
  ½   cup grated Parmesan cheese, divided
Basic Polenta
Cooking spray
    4   large hard-cooked eggs, peeled and sliced
Oregano sprigs (optional)

1. Press spinach between paper towels until spinach is barely moist, and set aside.
2. Combine flour and milk in a small saucepan, stirring with a whisk until blended; cook 1 minute, stirring constantly. Gradually add broth and next 4 ingredients, stirring with a whisk. Cook milk mixture over medium heat 4 minutes or until thick and bubbly, stirring constantly. Remove from heat, and stir in ¼ cup Parmesan cheese. Set aside.

Cheesy Spinach
Polenta

3. Preheat oven to 350°. Prepare Basic Polenta; spread in bottoms of 8 individual gratin dishes coated with cooking spray. Spread spinach evenly over polenta in each dish. Divide egg slices evenly over spinach in each dish. Pour 3 tablespoons cheese sauce over egg slices; sprinkle each gratin with 1½ teaspoons Parmesan cheese. Bake at 350° for 30 minutes or until lightly browned. Let stand 15 minutes before serving. Garnish with oregano, if desired. Yield: 8 servings.

(Totals include Basic Polenta) CALORIES 190 (24% from fat); FAT 5g (sat 1.8g, mono 1.6g, poly 0.6g); PROTEIN 11.7g; CARB 25.3g; FIBER 3.1g; CHOL 112mg; IRON 2.9mg; SODIUM 461mg; CALC 241mg

Basic Polenta

1¼   cups cornmeal
½   teaspoon salt
4   cups water

1. Place cornmeal and salt in a large saucepan. Gradually add water, stirring constantly with a whisk. Bring to a boil; reduce heat to medium. Cook, uncovered, 10 minutes, stirring frequently. Yield: 4 servings (serving size: 1 cup).

CALORIES 158 (4% from fat); FAT 0.7g (sat 0.1g, mono 0.2g, poly 0.3g); PROTEIN 3.7g; CARB 33.5g; FIBER 3.2g; CHOL 0mg; IRON 1.8mg; SODIUM 297mg; CALC 7.1mg

Polenta Gratin with Mushrooms and Fontina

Keep convenience products, such as packaged salad greens, on hand for quick meals during the holidays.
With the addition of a green salad, this comforting meatless main dish can be on the table in about 15 minutes.

1 (16-ounce) tube of polenta, cut into
¼-inch-thick slices

Cooking spray

1 (8-ounce) package presliced
mushrooms

1 teaspoon bottled minced garlic

¼ teaspoon salt

⅓ cup sun-dried tomato Alfredo sauce
(such as Classico)

¼ cup chopped fresh basil

¼ cup (1 ounce) shredded fontina
cheese

1. Preheat oven to 500°.

2. Arrange polenta slices in an 11 x 7-inch baking dish coated with cooking spray, allowing slices to overlap.

3. Heat a medium nonstick skillet coated with cooking spray over medium-high heat. Add mushrooms; cook 2 minutes, stirring frequently. Stir in garlic and salt. Cover, reduce heat, and cook 2 minutes. Stir in Alfredo sauce and basil.

4. Spoon mushroom mixture evenly over polenta. Top with cheese. Bake at 500° for 7 minutes or until thoroughly heated. Yield: 3 servings.

CALORIES 221 (30% from fat); FAT 7.4g (sat 3.9g, mono 1.7g, poly 1.2g); PROTEIN 8.3g; CARB 28.7g; FIBER 4.2g; CHOL 29mg; IRON 2.4mg; SODIUM 739mg; CALC 82mg

Polenta Gratin with
Mushrooms and Fontina

Ragù Finto with Cheese Polenta

Ragù—or meat sauce—is the perfect antidote to cold weather. But here's a *finto* (fake) ragù that stands in just as well. It'll have you saying *"Bellisimo!"*

Ragù:

- 2 cups boiling water, divided
- ½ cup dried porcini mushrooms (about ½ ounce)
- 1 cup sun-dried tomatoes, packed without oil (about 2 ounces)
- 1 tablespoon olive oil
- 1½ cups finely chopped red onion
- 1 tablespoon minced garlic cloves
- 5 cups finely chopped cremini mushrooms (about 1 pound)
- 2 teaspoons minced fresh or ½ teaspoon dried rosemary
- ½ teaspoon salt
- ¼ teaspoon crushed red pepper
- 1 cup dry red wine
- 2 tablespoons minced fresh flat-leaf parsley

Polenta:

- ¾ cup yellow cornmeal
- ¼ teaspoon salt
- 1½ cups water
- 1½ cups fat-free milk
- ½ cup (2 ounces) shredded Gruyère cheese
- 2 tablespoons grated fresh Parmesan cheese

1. To prepare ragù, combine 1 cup boiling water and porcini mushrooms in a bowl; cover and let stand 15 minutes. Drain mushrooms through a sieve over a bowl, reserving soaking liquid. Discard porcini stems; finely chop caps.

2. Combine 1 cup boiling water and sun-dried tomatoes in a bowl. Cover and let stand 15 minutes. Drain and finely chop tomatoes.

3. Heat oil in a Dutch oven over medium heat. Add onion and garlic; cover and cook 10 minutes, stirring occasionally. Add cremini mushrooms, rosemary, salt, and red pepper. Cover and cook 5 minutes. Uncover and cook 5 minutes or until liquid almost evaporates.

4. Add chopped porcini caps, reserved soaking liquid, chopped tomatoes, wine, and parsley; bring to a boil. Reduce heat; simmer 12 minutes.

5. To prepare polenta, place cornmeal and salt in a large saucepan. Gradually add 1½ cups water and milk, stirring constantly with a whisk; bring to a boil. Reduce heat to medium; cook 5 minutes, stirring frequently.

6. Remove from heat; stir in Gruyère. Serve with ragù; sprinkle with Parmesan. Yield: 4 servings (serving size: about 1 cup ragù, 1 cup polenta, and 1½ teaspoons Parmesan).

CALORIES 334 (28% from fat); FAT 10.3g (sat 4g, mono 4.5g, poly 1.1g); PROTEIN 17.8g; CARB 46g; FIBER 6.2g; CHOL 20mg; IRON 3.4mg; SODIUM 905mg; CALC 361mg

Vegetarian Burritos

- 1 (3½-ounce) bag boil-in-bag long-grain rice
- 1 tablespoon salt-free garlic-and-herb spice blend
- ¼ teaspoon ground cumin
- 1 (15-ounce) can black beans
- 6 (8-inch) flour tortillas
- ¾ cup (3 ounces) shredded reduced-fat sharp Cheddar cheese
- 6 tablespoons sliced green onions
- 6 tablespoons salsa
- 6 tablespoons plain low-fat yogurt

1. Cook rice according to package directions, omitting salt and fat.

2. Combine spice blend, cumin, and beans in a medium saucepan; bring to a boil. Reduce heat; simmer 5 minutes, stirring occasionally. Remove from heat; stir in rice.

3. Spoon about ⅓ cup of bean mixture down center of each tortilla. Top each with 2 tablespoons cheese, 1 tablespoon green onions, 1 tablespoon salsa, and 1 tablespoon yogurt; roll up. Yield: 6 servings (serving size: 1 burrito).

CALORIES 326 (18% from fat); FAT 6.7g (sat 2.5g, mono 1.5g, poly 0.5g); PROTEIN 14.1g; CARB 53.2g; FIBER 4.6g; CHOL 11mg; IRON 2.8mg; SODIUM 730mg; CALC 255mg

holiday breakaway

If at some point during the holidays you get a craving for food that isn't tied to the season, don't be alarmed. It's normal and happens to everyone. So when that irrepressible feeling comes your way, try informal, fuss-free recipes (such as Vegetarian Burritos [recipe above] and Polenta Gratin with Mushrooms and Fontina [recipe on page 220]) that will leave you time to shop, wrap presents, or plan more holiday meals.

Baked Burritos

If you're looking to add color and spice to your mealtimes leading up to *Navidad,* try these burritos. They're packed with south-of-the-border flavor.

  1 cup packaged cabbage-and-carrot coleslaw
  1 cup (4 ounces) preshredded reduced-fat Mexican blend
      or Cheddar cheese, divided
  1 cup bottled salsa
  ½ cup chopped red onion
  ½ cup chopped green bell pepper
  ½ cup minced fresh cilantro
  2 tablespoons fresh lime juice
  1 (16-ounce) can pinto beans, rinsed and drained
  1 (2.25-ounce) can sliced ripe olives, drained
  6 (8-inch) fat-free flour tortillas
Cooking spray
  ½ cup chopped green onions

1. Preheat oven to 425°.
2. Combine coleslaw, ½ cup cheese, salsa, and next 6 ingredients in a large bowl; stir until blended. Spread ⅔ cup coleslaw mixture down center of each tortilla; roll up. Place burritos on a baking sheet coated with cooking spray. Sprinkle burritos with ½ cup cheese and green onions.
3. Bake at 425° for 13 minutes or until cheese melts. Yield: 6 servings (serving size: 1 burrito).

CALORIES 250 (10% from fat); FAT 2.7g (sat 0.9g, mono 1.2g, poly 0.6g); PROTEIN 13.4g; CARB 44g; FIBER 5g; CHOL 3mg; IRON 3.6mg; SODIUM 858mg; CALC 200mg

Layered Tamale Casserole

  ¼ cup water
  2 (15-ounce) cans black beans, drained
Cooking spray
  3 cups sliced onion (about 2 large)
2½ cups thinly sliced zucchini (about 2 medium)
1¾ cups (¼-inch) julienne-cut red bell pepper (about
      2 medium)
  2 garlic cloves, minced
  1 cup frozen whole-kernel corn, thawed
  1 teaspoon ground cumin
  ¼ teaspoon ground red pepper
  5 (8-inch) flour tortillas
1¼ cups green taco sauce
1½ cups (6 ounces) shredded Monterey Jack cheese

1. Place water and beans in a food processor; process until smooth. Set aside. Place a large nonstick skillet coated with cooking spray over medium-high heat until hot.
2. Add onion, zucchini, bell pepper, and garlic; sauté 10 minutes. Add corn, cumin, and ground red pepper; cook 2 minutes. Set aside.
3. Preheat oven to 350°. Coat a 3-quart round soufflé dish with cooking spray. Place 1 tortilla in bottom. Spread ½ cup bean mixture over tortilla. Spoon 1 cup onion mixture over top. Top with ¼ cup sauce. Sprinkle with ¼ cup cheese. Repeat with remaining ingredients, ending with ½ cup cheese. Bake at 350° for 45 minutes or until thoroughly heated. Yield: 8 servings (serving size: 1½ cups).

CALORIES 272 (31% from fat); FAT 9.5g (sat 4.3g, mono 2.8g, poly 0.6g); PROTEIN 12.9g; CARB 41.1g; FIBER 6.3g; CHOL 19mg; IRON 2.1mg; SODIUM 877mg; CALC 266mg

Black-Bean Enchilada Casserole

  1 cup (4 ounces) shredded reduced-fat Monterey Jack
      cheese, divided
  1 cup cooked brown basmati rice or long-grain rice
  1 cup fat-free sour cream
  ½ cup chopped fresh cilantro
  ⅓ cup chopped green onions
  1 teaspoon ground cumin
  1 teaspoon chili powder
  1 (15-ounce) can black beans, rinsed and drained
  1 jalapeño pepper, seeded and chopped
  1 (19-ounce) can red enchilada sauce
Cooking spray
 12 (6-inch) corn tortillas

1. Preheat oven to 350°.
2. Combine ½ cup cheese, rice, and next 7 ingredients in a large bowl. Spread ¼ cup enchilada sauce in an 11 x 7-inch baking dish coated with cooking spray. Heat remaining enchilada sauce in a skillet 2 minutes or until warm; remove from heat. Dredge both sides of 6 tortillas in warm sauce; arrange tortillas, overlapping, over sauce in baking dish. Top with 1¾ cups bean mixture. Dredge both sides of remaining tortillas in warm sauce; arrange tortillas, overlapping, over bean mixture. Top with remaining bean mixture, remaining sauce, and ½ cup cheese. Bake at 350° for 40 minutes or until bubbly. Yield: 6 servings (serving size: 1 [3½-inch] square).

CALORIES 323 (20% from fat); FAT 7.2g (sat 2.4g, mono 2.6g, poly 1.7g); PROTEIN 16.1g; CARB 49.5g; FIBER 5.5g; CHOL 12mg; IRON 2.5mg; SODIUM 683mg; CALC 269mg

White Bean
Enchiladas

White Bean Enchiladas

This easy enchilada casserole can be prepared up to 1 day ahead. Since the enchiladas
are baked in a baking dish, the casserole reheats well in the microwave, too.

2   tablespoons fat-free sour cream
1   (16-ounce) can cannellini beans or other white beans,
    rinsed and drained
½   cup (2 ounces) preshredded reduced-fat Mexican
    blend or Cheddar cheese, divided
2   tablespoons canned chopped green chiles
1   tablespoon sliced green onions
1   tablespoon chopped fresh cilantro
1   teaspoon ground cumin
1   (10-ounce) can enchilada sauce (such as Old El Paso),
    divided
¼   cup water
6   (6-inch) corn tortillas
Cooking spray
1   tablespoon minced fresh cilantro (optional)

1. Preheat oven to 350°.

2. Combine sour cream and beans in a food processor; process
until almost smooth. Stir in ¼ cup cheese, chiles, onions,
chopped cilantro, and cumin.

3. Combine ⅓ cup enchilada sauce and ¼ cup water in a
small nonstick skillet over medium-low heat. Dip 1 tortilla in
sauce mixture to soften, and transfer to a plate. Spread ¼ cup
bean mixture down center of tortilla; roll up. Place roll, seam
side down, in an 11 x 7-inch baking dish coated with cooking
spray. Repeat procedure with remaining tortillas and bean mixture. Add remaining sauce to pan; cook 1 minute. Spoon over
enchiladas; sprinkle with ¼ cup cheese.

4. Bake at 350° for 30 minutes or until bubbly. Sprinkle with
minced cilantro, if desired. Yield: 3 servings (serving size:
2 enchiladas).

CALORIES 372 (19% from fat); FAT 8g (sat 1.6g, mono 2.1g, poly 3.6g); PROTEIN 17.5g;
CARB 60.5g; FIBER 6.2g; CHOL 3mg; IRON 3.9mg; SODIUM 1,076mg; CALC 291mg

Creamy Indian Lentils and Rice

Celebrate Hanukkah with this meatless main dish. Serve with *naan* (an Indian flat bread) or pita bread.

- 1 tablespoon vegetable oil
- 2 cups thinly sliced onion
- 1 cup uncooked long-grain brown rice
- 1 tablespoon curry powder
- 2 teaspoons mustard seeds
- 1 teaspoon salt
- ½ teaspoon black pepper
- 4 cups water
- 1 cup dried lentils
- 1 cup chopped fresh cilantro
- ½ cup low-fat sour cream

1. Heat oil in a large Dutch oven over medium-high heat. Add onion; sauté 8 minutes or until golden brown, stirring occasionally. Add rice and next 4 ingredients; sauté 1 minute. Add water and lentils; bring to a boil. Cover, reduce heat, and simmer 1 hour. Remove from heat; stir in cilantro and sour cream. Yield: 6 servings (serving size: 1 cup).

CALORIES 297 (20% from fat); FAT 6.5g (sat 2.1g, mono 2g, poly 1.7g); PROTEIN 13.2g; CARB 48g; FIBER 6.3g; CHOL 8mg; IRON 4.5mg; SODIUM 411mg; CALC 78mg

Creamy Indian Lentils and Rice

the holidays, unplugged

Put those fancy appliances away and get back to basics this holiday season. With the chaos that frequently accompanies the holidays, you need to keep recipes on hand that emphasize simplicity and comfort. You don't need recipes that require plugging in several appliances to get the job done. White Bean Enchiladas (recipe on page 223) and Quick Pizza Margherita (recipe on page 233) are just two great examples of stress-free fare.

Lentil Dal with Garlic-and-Cumin-Infused Oil

Dal is served with traditional Indian meals. It's either spooned over rice or pureed and used as a sauce for dipping *naan* and *chapati*—traditional Indian flat breads.

- 1¼ cups dried pink or yellow lentils
- ½ teaspoon ground turmeric
- 4 cups water
- 1 cup chopped plum tomato
- 1 teaspoon salt
- 1 tablespoon vegetable oil
- 1½ teaspoons cumin seeds
- 4 garlic cloves, sliced
- ¼ teaspoon ground red pepper
- ⅓ cup minced fresh cilantro, divided
- 1 tablespoon fresh lemon juice

1. Place lentils and turmeric in a large saucepan; cover with 4 cups water. Bring to a boil; cover, reduce heat, and simmer 15 minutes, stirring occasionally. Add tomato; cook 5 minutes or until lentils are tender. Stir in salt; keep warm.
2. Heat oil in a small skillet over medium-high heat. Add cumin seeds and garlic; cook 2 minutes or until garlic is golden, stirring constantly. Stir in red pepper, and remove from heat. Pour oil mixture over lentils, and stir in 2 tablespoons cilantro. Spoon dal into each of 5 bowls, and sprinkle with remaining cilantro and lemon juice. Yield: 5 servings (serving size: 1 cup).

CALORIES 202 (16% from fat); FAT 3.5g (sat 0.5g, mono 0.8g, poly 1.9g); PROTEIN 14.1g; CARB 30.6g; FIBER 15.3g; CHOL 0mg; IRON 5.1mg; SODIUM 479mg; CALC 39mg

Asian Noodle, Tofu, and Vegetable Stir-Fry

The dish gets a boost of rich flavor from a stock made with soaked dried mushrooms,
which makes the stir-fry extraspecial for those out-of-towners who might be visiting.

2 ounces uncooked bean threads (cellophane
   noodles)

½ ounce dried wood ear mushrooms (about 6)

1 cup boiling water

2 teaspoons peanut oil or vegetable oil

1 cup coarsely chopped onion

1 tablespoon minced seeded jalapeño pepper

2 teaspoons minced peeled fresh ginger

2 garlic cloves, minced

3 cups (¼-inch) diagonally sliced carrot (about
   1 pound)

¼ teaspoon salt

7 cups (1-inch) sliced bok choy

2 tablespoons low-sodium soy sauce

1 (12.3-ounce) package reduced-fat firm tofu, cubed

3 tablespoons water

2 teaspoons cornstarch

1 teaspoon dark sesame oil or chili oil

1. Place noodles in a large bowl; cover with warm water. Let stand 20 minutes. Drain; set aside.

2. Combine mushrooms and boiling water in a bowl; let stand 20 minutes. Strain through a sieve into a bowl, reserving mushroom liquid. Cut mushrooms into strips.

3. Heat peanut oil in a wok or nonstick Dutch oven over medium-high heat. Add onion, jalapeño, ginger, and garlic; stir-fry 1 minute. Add mushrooms, carrot, and salt; stir-fry 2 minutes. Stir in ¼ cup reserved mushroom liquid; cover and cook 3 minutes or until carrot is crisp-tender and liquid evaporates.

4. Add bok choy; stir-fry 1 minute. Stir in noodles, remaining mushroom liquid, soy sauce, and tofu; cook 2 minutes.

5. Combine 3 tablespoons water and cornstarch; add to pan. Bring to a boil; cook 2 minutes or until slightly thick. Drizzle with sesame oil. Yield: 4 servings (serving size: 2 cups).

CALORIES 195 (29% from fat); FAT 6.4g (sat 1g, mono 1.9g, poly 2.8g); PROTEIN 10.3g; CARB 27.4g; FIBER 6.1g; CHOL 0mg; IRON 2.6mg; SODIUM 539mg; CALC 206mg

Asian Noodle,
Tofu, and
Vegetable Stir-Fry

Broccoli-Tofu Stir-Fry

This simple meatless stir-fry has a subtle yet addictive sauce. To cut preparation time, use precut broccoli florets. They're near the salad greens in the supermarket.

    1   (3½-ounce) bag boil-in-bag brown rice
    2   tablespoons low-sodium soy sauce
    2   tablespoons oyster sauce
 2½   teaspoons cornstarch
    2   teaspoons rice vinegar
    2   teaspoons dark sesame oil
    2   teaspoons vegetable oil
    1   pound firm tofu, drained and cut into ½-inch cubes
  ¼   teaspoon salt
    2   cups broccoli florets
  ¾   cup water
 1½   tablespoons bottled minced garlic

1. Cook rice according to package directions.
2. While rice cooks, combine soy sauce and next 4 ingredients in a small bowl, stirring with a whisk; set aside.
3. Heat vegetable oil in a large nonstick skillet over medium-high heat. Add tofu; sprinkle with salt. Cook 8 minutes or until golden brown, tossing frequently. Remove tofu from pan; keep warm. Add broccoli, water, and garlic to pan. Cover; cook 4 minutes or until crisp-tender, stirring occasionally. Uncover; add soy sauce mixture and tofu, stirring gently to coat. Cook 2 minutes or until sauce thickens, stirring occasionally. Serve over rice. Yield: 4 servings (serving size: 1 cup stir-fry and ½ cup rice).

CALORIES 451 (17% from fat); FAT 8.3g (sat 1.4g, mono 2.6g, poly 3.8g); PROTEIN 16.2g; CARB 78g; FIBER 4.4g; CHOL 0mg; IRON 2.8mg; SODIUM 581mg; CALC 87mg

Broccoli-Tofu
Stir-Fry

Spinach Gnocchi

We kept the gnocchi simple—kneading in a little spinach and then dressing the "dumplings" with only butter and Parmesan.

    4   large peeled baking potatoes (about 2¼ pounds)
    2   cups all-purpose flour, divided
    1   teaspoon salt
  ¼   teaspoon black pepper
  ¼   teaspoon ground nutmeg
    1   large egg, lightly beaten
    1   large egg white, lightly beaten
    1   (10-ounce) package frozen chopped spinach, thawed, drained, and squeezed dry
  Cooking spray
  14   cups water
    6   tablespoons butter, melted
  ¾   cup (3 ounces) finely grated fresh Parmesan cheese

1. Place potatoes in a saucepan, and add water to cover. Bring to a boil; partially cover. Cook 35 minutes or until tender. Drain; cool. Place potatoes in a bowl; mash. Lightly spoon flour into dry measuring cups; level with a knife. Combine potatoes, 1½ cups flour, salt, and next 4 ingredients, stirring to form a soft dough.
2. Turn dough out onto a well-floured surface; knead in spinach. Add enough of remaining flour, 1 tablespoon at a time, to prevent dough from sticking to hands. Divide dough into 6 portions, and shape each portion into an 18-inch-long rope. Cut each rope into 18 (1-inch) pieces; roll each piece into a ball. Drag tines of a fork through half of each ball, forming a concave shape. Place on a baking sheet coated with cooking spray.
3. Bring 14 cups water to a boil in a large Dutch oven. Add one-third of gnocchi; cook 1½ minutes (do not overcook, or gnocchi will fall apart). Remove gnocchi with a slotted spoon; place in a colander to drain. Repeat procedure with remaining gnocchi. Toss with butter and cheese; serve immediately. Yield: 9 servings (serving size: 12 gnocchi).

CALORIES 333 (30% from fat); FAT 11.2g (sat 6.6g, mono 3.2g, poly 0.6g); PROTEIN 10.6g; CARB 47.4g; FIBER 3.4g; CHOL 52mg; IRON 2.5mg; SODIUM 533mg; CALC 163mg

These vegetarian dishes offer a great change of pace any night of the week.

Tempeh and Wild Mushroom Fricassee

Fricassee often refers to a thick and chunky meat-based stew. Tempeh, which is made from soybeans, replaces the meat in this recipe. It's found alongside tofu in the refrigerated section of many supermarkets as well as health food stores.

Cooking spray
12 ounces tempeh, cut into ½-inch cubes
¼ cup dry white wine
2 tablespoons low-sodium soy sauce
4 cups thinly sliced leek (about 4 large)
2 cups sliced button mushrooms
2 cups sliced cremini mushrooms
2 cups chopped shiitake mushroom caps (about 4 ounces)
2 (4-inch) portobello mushroom caps, gills removed, chopped
1 tablespoon all-purpose flour
⅓ cup celery leaves
2 thyme sprigs
1 parsley sprig
½ cup thinly sliced garlic (about 20 cloves)
1 (14-ounce) can vegetable broth
1 tablespoon fresh lemon juice
¼ teaspoon fine sea salt
¼ teaspoon freshly ground black pepper
2 tablespoons chopped fresh parsley
1 tablespoon grated lemon rind (optional)

1. Heat a Dutch oven coated with cooking spray over medium-high heat. Add tempeh; sauté 8 minutes or until golden brown. Add wine and soy sauce; cook 15 seconds or until liquid almost evaporates. Remove tempeh from pan.

2. Add leek and mushrooms to pan; sauté 5 minutes. Stir in flour; cook 1 minute, stirring frequently. Tie celery leaves, thyme sprigs, and parsley sprig together securely with string. Add herbs, garlic, and broth to pan; bring to a boil. Add tempeh, stirring well. Cover, reduce heat, and simmer 15 minutes.

3. Uncover and cook 3 minutes or until thick. Discard herbs. Stir in lemon juice, salt, and pepper; sprinkle with parsley. Garnish each serving with ½ teaspoon lemon rind, if desired. Yield: 6 servings (serving size: 1 cup).

CALORIES 317 (30% from fat); FAT 10.4g (sat 2g, mono 2.6g, poly 3.6g); PROTEIN 23.7g; CARB 37.8g; FIBER 8.6g; CHOL 0mg; IRON 6.2mg; SODIUM 898mg; CALC 206mg

Braised Shallots and Fall Vegetables with Red Wine Sauce

Serve this chunky and saucy vegetable dish with a mound of creamy mashed potatoes.

2 tablespoons butter

1 tablespoon olive oil

20 large shallots, peeled and separated (about 2 pounds)

6 carrots, quartered lengthwise and cut into 2-inch-thick pieces (about ¾ pound)

2½ cups quartered mushrooms (about ⅓ pound)

4 large parsnips, cut into 1-inch pieces

Red Wine Sauce, divided

1½ teaspoons minced fresh rosemary

¼ teaspoon salt

⅛ teaspoon black pepper

2 bay leaves

2 thyme sprigs

3 tablespoons chopped fresh parsley

1 garlic clove, minced

1. Heat butter and oil in a large Dutch oven over medium-high heat. Add shallots and carrots; sauté 10 minutes, stirring frequently. Add mushrooms and parsnips; sauté 10 minutes. Add 1 cup Red Wine Sauce, rosemary, and next 4 ingredients; bring to a boil. Reduce heat, and simmer 20 minutes. Discard bay leaves and thyme sprigs.

2. Drizzle vegetables with remaining Red Wine Sauce. Combine parsley and garlic; sprinkle over each serving. Yield: 6 servings

(serving size: 1½ cups braised vegetables and ¼ cup wine sauce).

(Totals include Red Wine Sauce) CALORIES 317 (32% from fat); FAT 11.1g (sat 4.4g, mono 5.1g, poly 0.9g); PROTEIN 7.1g; CARB 52.3g; FIBER 6.1g; CHOL 16mg; IRON 4.2mg; SODIUM 386mg; CALC 126mg

Red Wine Sauce

4 cups boiling water

⅓ cup dried porcini mushrooms (about ½ ounce)

1 tablespoon olive oil

2 cups diced carrot

1½ cups quartered button mushrooms

1 cup diced onion

1 cup diced celery

1 cup chopped red bell pepper

4 garlic cloves, minced

2 thyme sprigs

1 bay leaf

1 (2-inch) rosemary sprig

3 tablespoons tomato paste

2 tablespoons all-purpose flour

¼ teaspoon salt

⅛ teaspoon black pepper

2 cups Merlot or other dry red wine

1 tablespoon low-sodium soy sauce

1 tablespoon butter

1. Combine boiling water and porcini mushrooms; set aside.
2. Heat oil in a large Dutch oven over medium heat; add carrot and next 8 ingredients. Cook 30 minutes or until browned, stirring frequently. Stir in tomato paste, flour, salt, and black pepper; cook 1 minute. Stir in porcini mixture and wine, scraping pan to loosen browned bits. Bring to a boil; reduce heat, and simmer 30 minutes. Strain through a colander into a large bowl, pressing vegetable mixture with the back of a spoon to remove as much sauce as possible. Return sauce to pan, discarding solids. Bring to a boil; cook until reduced to 2½ cups (about 5 minutes). Stir in soy sauce and butter. Yield: 2½ cups (serving size: ¼ cup).

CALORIES 42 (56% from fat); FAT 2.6g (sat 0.9g, mono 1.3g, poly 0.2g); PROTEIN 0.7g; CARB 4.4g; FIBER 0.7g; CHOL 3mg; IRON 0.6mg; SODIUM 121mg; CALC 11mg

New-Tradition Lasagna with Spinach Noodles

Try a new tradition in your home this Christmas with a novel spin on lasagna. Substitute prepackaged spinach lasagna noodles and a good jarred low-fat marinara sauce. The noodle recipe makes plenty, in case some fall apart. You can make the sauce in advance and store it in airtight containers; freeze up to 2 months or refrigerate up to 3 days.

½   cup (2 ounces) grated fresh Parmesan cheese
 1   tablespoon butter, softened
¼   teaspoon salt
¼   teaspoon black pepper
⅛   teaspoon grated whole nutmeg
 1   (15-ounce) carton fat-free ricotta cheese
 6   cups Marinara Sauce
Cooking spray
 9   cooked Homemade Spinach Lasagna Noodles
¼   cup thinly sliced fresh basil, divided
 2   cups (8 ounces) shredded part-skim mozzarella cheese, divided

1. Preheat oven to 350°.
2. Combine first 6 ingredients in a bowl. Spoon 1 cup marinara sauce into a 13 x 9-inch baking dish coated with cooking spray. Arrange 3 noodles over sauce; top with 1 cup ricotta mixture, 2 cups marinara sauce, 2 tablespoons basil, and ⅔ cup mozzarella cheese. Repeat layers, ending with noodles. Spread 1 cup marinara sauce over noodles; top with ⅔ cup mozzarella. Cover and bake at 350° for 1 hour. Let stand 15 minutes. Yield: 9 servings.

(Totals include Marinara Sauce and Homemade Spinach Lasagna Noodles)
CALORIES 267 (36% from fat); FAT 10.7g (sat 5g, mono 4g, poly 0.7g); PROTEIN 19.8g; CARB 25.3g; FIBER 1.6g; CHOL 64mg; IRON 2.1mg; SODIUM 827mg; CALC 385mg

Marinara Sauce

 1   tablespoon olive oil
¼   cup chopped onion
 4   garlic cloves, thinly sliced
½   teaspoon salt
½   teaspoon sugar
½   teaspoon black pepper
 2   (14.5-ounce) cans diced tomatoes, undrained
 1   (28-ounce) can crushed tomatoes, undrained

1. Heat oil in a saucepan over medium-high heat. Add onion and garlic. Cook 3 minutes or until tender; stir constantly. Stir in salt and remaining ingredients; bring to a boil. Reduce heat; simmer 30 minutes. Yield: 6 cups (serving size: ⅔ cup).

CALORIES 55 (31% from fat); FAT 1.9g (sat 0.2g, mono 1.2g, poly 0.2g); PROTEIN 1.9g; CARB 8.8g; FIBER 1.1g; CHOL 0mg; IRON 1.1mg; SODIUM 394mg; CALC 56mg

Homemade Spinach Lasagna Noodles

1½ cups all-purpose flour
 3   tablespoons frozen chopped spinach, thawed, drained, and squeezed dry
½   teaspoon salt
 2   teaspoons olive oil
 2   large eggs, lightly beaten

1. Lightly spoon flour into dry measuring cups, and level with a knife. Place flour, spinach, and salt in a food processor; pulse 3 times or until blended. With processor on, slowly pour oil and eggs through food chute; process until dough forms a ball. Turn dough out onto a lightly floured surface, and knead until smooth and elastic (about 10 minutes). Dust dough lightly with flour; let stand 10 minutes.
2. Divide dough into 4 equal portions. Working with 1 portion at a time, pass dough through smooth rollers of pasta machine on widest setting. Continue moving width gauge to narrower settings; pass dough through rollers once at each setting, dusting with flour, if needed. Repeat procedure with remaining dough. Cut each pasta sheet into 3 (11 x 2-inch) strips. Hang pasta on a wooden drying rack 10 minutes. Cook pasta in boiling water 2 minutes or until al dente; drain. Yield: 12 noodles (serving size: 1 noodle).

CALORIES 77 (21% from fat); FAT 1.8g (sat 0.4g, mono 0.9g, poly 0.3g); PROTEIN 2.8g; CARB 12.1g; FIBER 0.5g; CHOL 37mg; IRON 0.9mg; SODIUM 111mg; CALC 9mg

Baked Eggplant with Mushroom-and-Tomato Sauce

This is a great winter recipe that's very hearty and satisfying. Serve with a green salad
and a loaf of crusty Italian bread for a casual Christmas Eve dinner.

1 peeled eggplant, cut into ¼-inch-thick slices
Cooking spray
1 cup chopped onion
½ teaspoon dried Italian seasoning
¼ teaspoon salt
2 garlic cloves, chopped
1 (8-ounce) package presliced mushrooms
¼ teaspoon black pepper, divided
1 (8-ounce) can no-salt-added tomato sauce, divided
⅔ cup (about 3 ounces) shredded part-skim mozzarella cheese, divided
¼ cup (1 ounce) grated fresh Parmesan cheese

1. Preheat broiler.

2. Arrange eggplant slices on a baking sheet coated with cooking spray; broil 3 minutes on each side or until lightly browned.

3. Preheat oven to 375°.

4. Heat a large nonstick skillet coated with cooking spray over medium heat; add onion and next 4 ingredients. Cover and cook 7 minutes or until tender, stirring occasionally. Increase heat to medium-high; uncover and cook 2 minutes or until liquid evaporates.

5. Spread half of mushroom mixture in bottom of a 1½-quart round baking dish coated with cooking spray. Arrange half of eggplant slices over mushroom mixture; sprinkle with ⅛ teaspoon pepper. Top with ½ cup tomato sauce and ⅓ cup mozzarella. Spread remaining mushroom mixture over mozzarella; top with remaining eggplant slices. Sprinkle with ⅛ teaspoon pepper; top with remaining tomato sauce. Cover and bake at 375° for 1 hour. Sprinkle with ⅓ cup mozzarella and Parmesan. Bake, uncovered, 5 minutes or until cheese melts. Let stand 10 minutes. Yield: 4 servings.

CALORIES 168 (30% from fat); FAT 5.6g (sat 3.2g, mono 1.5g, poly 0.5g); PROTEIN 10.9g; CARB 21g; FIBER 6.1g; CHOL 16mg; IRON 2.1mg; SODIUM 369mg; CALC 236mg

Baked Eggplant with
Mushroom-and-
Tomato Sauce

2-Minute, 24-Hour Casserole

This is the ultimate make-ahead recipe for the holidays. It takes 2 minutes to assemble, but it needs to sit in the refrigerator overnight before you cook it so the dry pasta can soak up most of the sauce's liquid.

7½ cups fat-free Italian herb pasta sauce (such as Muir Glen)
  1 pound uncooked penne (tube-shaped pasta)
  1 (8-ounce) package presliced mushrooms
  1 (8-ounce) block ⅓-less-fat cream cheese, softened
  ½ cup low-fat sour cream
Cooking spray
  1 cup (4 ounces) preshredded part-skim mozzarella cheese

1. Combine first 3 ingredients in a large bowl; stir until blended.
2. Beat cream cheese and sour cream with a mixer at low speed until smooth (about 2 minutes).
3. Spread half of pasta mixture in bottom of a 3-quart casserole coated with cooking spray; spread cream cheese mixture evenly over pasta mixture. Top with remaining pasta mixture; sprinkle with mozzarella cheese.
4. Cover and refrigerate 24 hours.
5. Preheat oven to 350°.
6. Bake, covered, at 350° for 50 minutes. Uncover; bake an additional 10 minutes or until cheese is browned. Yield: 10 servings.

CALORIES 370 (23% from fat); FAT 9.6g (sat 5.5g, mono 2.6g, poly 0.7g); PROTEIN 14.6g; CARB 55.9g; FIBER 4.4g; CHOL 28mg; IRON 3.8mg; SODIUM 602mg; CALC 142mg

Linguine and Spinach with Gorgonzola Sauce

Cloaked in a creamy Gorgonzola sauce, this rich-tasting pasta dish comes together in a flash—perfect for a low-key New Year's Eve.

  1 (9-ounce) package fresh linguine
  1 tablespoon butter
  1 tablespoon all-purpose flour
  1 (12-ounce) can evaporated low-fat milk
¾ cup (3 ounces) crumbled Gorgonzola cheese
¾ teaspoon salt
¼ teaspoon black pepper
  1 (6-ounce) package fresh baby spinach (about 6 cups)

1. Cook linguine according to package directions, omitting salt and fat.
2. While pasta cooks, melt butter in a medium saucepan over medium heat. Add flour; cook 1 minute, stirring constantly with a whisk. Gradually add milk, stirring constantly with a whisk. Increase heat to medium-high; bring to a boil, stirring constantly. Reduce heat, and simmer 3 minutes or until sauce thickens slightly, stirring frequently. Remove from heat; stir in cheese, salt, and pepper. Combine sauce, pasta, and spinach, tossing gently to coat. Yield: 4 servings (serving size: 1¼ cups).

CALORIES 379 (29% from fat); FAT 12.2g (sat 7.5g, mono 1.5g, poly 0.8g); PROTEIN 19.6g; CARB 48.3g; FIBER 4.6g; CHOL 80mg; IRON 3.7mg; SODIUM 898mg; CALC 411mg

Pasta with Chickpeas and Vegetables

Using some of the pasta cooking liquid restores body and flavor to the dish. We liked chickpeas here, but you can use any kind of canned beans. The vegetables make this pasta toss slightly sweet, so increase the crushed red pepper if you want to make it hotter.

 12 cups water
  3 cups peeled, halved, and thinly sliced butternut squash
  2 cups small cauliflower florets
  1 cup (1-inch-thick) diagonally cut carrot
  2 red onions, cut into 1-inch-thick wedges
  8 ounces uncooked penne (tube-shaped pasta)
2½ cups cherry tomatoes, halved
  2 tablespoons olive oil
  1 tablespoon ground cumin
  ½ teaspoon crushed red pepper
  4 garlic cloves, sliced
  3 thyme sprigs
  1 (15½-ounce) can chickpeas (garbanzo beans), drained
  ½ cup dry white wine
  ½ teaspoon fine sea salt
  ¼ teaspoon black pepper
  ½ cup chopped fresh parsley

1. Bring water to a boil in a large stockpot or Dutch oven. Add squash, cauliflower, carrot, and onion, and cook 2 minutes. Remove vegetables with a slotted spoon; drain well.
2. Return water to a boil. Add pasta; cook 10 minutes or until done. Drain in a colander over a bowl; reserve ½ cup liquid.
3. Return vegetables to pan; add tomatoes and next 6 ingredients. Cook 2 minutes over medium-high heat, stirring occasionally. Add reserved cooking liquid and wine; cook 15 minutes or until squash is tender, stirring occasionally. Discard thyme sprigs.
4. Add pasta, salt, and black pepper to pan, and stir to combine. Sprinkle with parsley. Yield: 5 servings (serving size: about 2½ cups).

CALORIES 398 (18% from fat); FAT 8g (sat 1.1g, mono 4.4g, poly 1.6g); PROTEIN 12.5g; CARB 69.6g; FIBER 10.4g; CHOL 0mg; IRON 4.3mg; SODIUM 450mg; CALC 123mg

Pasta with Mushrooms
and Pumpkin-
Gorgonzola Sauce

Pasta with Mushrooms and Pumpkin-Gorgonzola Sauce

This is a good recipe to use up the Gorgonzola cheese left over from your wine and cheese party. Any short pasta will work in this dish. We recommend our favorite brand of cheese: Saladena Gorgonzola; it gives the sauce a luscious consistency.

  1   pound uncooked pennette (small penne)
  1   tablespoon olive oil
  5   cups thinly sliced shiitake mushroom caps
  4   cups vertically sliced onion
  4   garlic cloves, minced
  1   teaspoon chopped fresh sage
  1   (12-ounce) can evaporated milk
1½ tablespoons cornstarch
1½ tablespoons cold water
 ½ cup (2 ounces) crumbled Gorgonzola cheese
 ½ cup canned pumpkin
  1   teaspoon salt
 ½ teaspoon freshly ground black pepper
 ⅛ teaspoon grated whole nutmeg
    Sage sprigs (optional)

1. Cook pasta according to package directions, omitting salt and fat. Keep pasta warm.
2. Heat oil in a Dutch oven over medium-high heat. Add mushrooms, onion, and garlic; cover and cook 3 minutes. Uncover; cook 5 minutes or until tender, stirring occasionally.
3. Combine chopped sage and milk in a saucepan over medium heat; bring to a simmer. Combine cornstarch and water, stirring with a whisk. Add cornstarch mixture and cheese to milk mixture, stirring with a whisk. Cook 2 minutes or until thick and smooth, stirring constantly. Remove from heat; stir in pumpkin, salt, pepper, and nutmeg.
4. Add pasta and pumpkin mixture to mushroom mixture; toss well to combine. Garnish with sage sprigs, if desired. Yield: 6 servings (serving size: 1½ cups).

CALORIES 462 (13% from fat); FAT 6.5g (sat 2.8g, mono 1.7g, poly 0.4g); PROTEIN 19.9g; CARB 83.1g; FIBER 7.3g; CHOL 11mg; IRON 3.7mg; SODIUM 636mg; CALC 265mg

Quick Pizza Margherita
(pictured on page 214)

Baking the dough before topping it with tomato keeps the crust crisp. Be sure to use fresh mozzarella, which comes packed in water and can be found with other gourmet cheeses.

  1   (13.8-ounce) can refrigerated pizza crust dough
    Cooking spray
  1   teaspoon extravirgin olive oil, divided
  1   garlic clove, halved
  5   plum tomatoes, thinly sliced (about ¾ pound)
  1   cup (4 ounces) shredded fresh mozzarella cheese
  1   teaspoon balsamic vinegar
 ½ cup thinly sliced fresh basil
 ⅛ teaspoon salt
 ⅛ teaspoon black pepper

1. Preheat oven to 400°.
2. Unroll dough onto a baking sheet coated with cooking spray; pat into a 13 x 11-inch rectangle. Bake at 400° for 8 minutes. Remove crust from oven, and brush with ½ teaspoon oil. Rub crust with cut sides of garlic.
3. Arrange tomato slices on crust, leaving a ½-inch border; sprinkle evenly with cheese. Bake at 400° for 12 minutes or until cheese melts and crust is golden.
4. Combine ½ teaspoon oil and vinegar, stirring with a whisk.
5. Sprinkle pizza evenly with sliced basil, salt, and pepper. Drizzle vinegar mixture evenly over pizza. Cut pizza into 8 pieces. Yield: 4 servings (serving size: 2 pieces).

CALORIES 371 (27% from fat); FAT 11.1g (sat 3.9g, mono 2.7g, poly 0.4g); PROTEIN 15.7g; CARB 51g; FIBER 2.5g; CHOL 22mg; IRON 3mg; SODIUM 907mg; CALC 161mg

staff favorite

Let's face it, pizza is obviously not going to be your stand-in for turkey and dressing, but it makes a great weeknight or weekend meal just about anytime during the holidays. And we think that Quick Pizza Margherita (recipe above) is just the thing when you're craving something quick and easy. "In the time it takes to have a pizza delivered, you can have Quick Pizza Margherita already on the table," Assistant Food Stylist Kathleen Kanen says. "One can of pizza dough and a few simple ingredients create this quick, delicious pizza. It's also a good idea for a 'trim-the-tree party.'"

Pizza with Caramelized Fennel, Onion, and Olives

Dough:

1½ teaspoons dry yeast

⅔ cup warm water (100° to 110°)

2 cups all-purpose flour, divided

½ teaspoon salt

Cooking spray

2 teaspoons yellow cornmeal

Topping:

1 tablespoon olive oil

4 cups thinly sliced fennel bulb (about 4 small bulbs)

2 cups thinly sliced onion

½ teaspoon salt

¼ teaspoon dried oregano

¼ teaspoon dried thyme

¼ teaspoon black pepper

Remaining Ingredients:

1 cup bottled tomato-basil pasta sauce (such as Classico)

1 cup (4 ounces) shredded part-skim mozzarella cheese

¼ cup coarsely chopped pitted kalamata olives

1. To prepare dough, dissolve yeast in warm water in a large bowl, and let stand 5 minutes. Lightly spoon flour into dry measuring cups; level with a knife. Add 1¾ cups flour and ½ teaspoon salt to yeast mixture, and beat with a mixer at medium speed until smooth. Turn dough out onto a floured surface. Knead until smooth and elastic (about 10 minutes); add enough of remaining flour, 1 tablespoon at a time, to prevent dough from sticking to hands (dough will feel sticky).

2. Place dough in a large bowl coated with cooking spray, turning to coat top. Cover and let rise in a warm place (85°), free from drafts, 45 minutes or until doubled in size. (Press 2 fingers into dough. If indentation remains, dough has risen enough.) Punch dough down; knead 5 times, and let rest 15 minutes. Roll dough into a 12-inch circle on a floured surface. Place dough on a 12-inch pizza pan or baking sheet coated with cooking spray and sprinkled with cornmeal. Crimp edges of dough with fingers to form a rim.

3. To prepare topping, heat oil in a large nonstick skillet coated with cooking spray over medium-high heat. Add fennel and next 5 ingredients, and cook 20 minutes or until golden, stirring frequently.

4. Preheat oven to 450°.

5. Spread sauce over dough, leaving a ½-inch border; sprinkle with fennel mixture, cheese, and olives. Bake at 450° for 18 minutes or until browned. Yield: 6 servings (serving size: 1 wedge).

CALORIES 296 (23% from fat); FAT 7.5g (sat 2.6g, mono 3.7g, poly 0.6g); PROTEIN 11.9g; CARB 45.4g; FIBER 4.5g; CHOL 10mg; IRON 3.1mg; SODIUM 653mg; CALC 220mg

Spinach Pizza Purses

Here's a great substitute for the traditional pizza—these pizza purses aren't as cheesy. If you're short on time, you can substitute preseasoned tomato sauce from a jar or can.

Crust:

¼ teaspoon sugar

1 package dry yeast (about 2¼ teaspoons)

¼ cup warm water (100° to 110°)

1 cup all-purpose flour

1 cup whole wheat flour

½ cup water

1 teaspoon olive oil

¼ teaspoon salt

Cooking spray

Filling:

2 cups (2-inch) red bell pepper strips

¾ cup (3 ounces) grated fresh Parmesan cheese

2 (10-ounce) packages frozen chopped spinach, thawed, drained, and squeezed dry

1 tablespoon cornmeal

Sauce:

1 cup chopped tomato

1 teaspoon dried basil

1 teaspoon dried oregano

¼ teaspoon onion powder

1 garlic clove, minced

1 (15-ounce) can tomato sauce

Olive Pizza

1. To prepare crust, dissolve sugar and yeast in ¼ cup warm water in a large bowl; let stand 5 minutes. Lightly spoon flours into dry measuring cups; level with a knife. Stir flours, ½ cup water, oil, and salt into yeast mixture to form a soft dough. Turn dough out onto a lightly floured surface, and knead until smooth and elastic (about 5 minutes). Place dough in a large bowl coated with cooking spray, turning to coat top. Cover and let rise in a warm place (85°), free from drafts, 40 minutes or until doubled in size. (Press 2 fingers into dough. If indentation remains, dough has risen enough.)
2. Punch dough down. Divide dough into 8 equal portions, and roll each dough portion into a 5-inch circle on a lightly floured surface.
3. Preheat oven to 350°.
4. To prepare filling, combine bell pepper, Parmesan cheese, and spinach in a medium bowl; stir until combined. Spoon ½ cup filling into center of each dough circle. Gather edges of each dough circle together, and press firmly to seal, forming a purse. Place on a baking sheet coated with cooking spray and sprinkled with cornmeal.
5. Bake at 350° for 25 minutes or until lightly browned.
6. To prepare sauce, combine chopped tomato and next 5 ingredients in a medium saucepan; bring to a boil. Reduce heat, and simmer 5 minutes. Serve pizza purses with sauce. Yield: 8 servings (serving size: 1 purse and ¼ cup sauce).

CALORIES 208 (19% from fat); FAT 4.4g (sat 2g, mono 1.4g, poly 0.6g); PROTEIN 11.1g; CARB 33.8g; FIBER 6.2g; CHOL 7mg; IRON 4mg; SODIUM 622mg; CALC 230mg

Olive Pizza

Store-bought pizza dough tastes just as good as a homemade crust and saves you time in the kitchen—especially if you're behind on your holiday shopping.

  2 (13.8-ounce) cans refrigerated pizza crust dough
Cooking spray
  1 tablespoon cornmeal
  3 tomatoes, cut into ¼-inch-thick slices (about 1¼ pounds)
1½ cups (6 ounces) shredded part-skim mozzarella cheese
  1 cup (4 ounces) crumbled feta cheese
  ½ cup sliced pitted kalamata olives
Freshly ground black pepper (optional)

1. Preheat oven to 450°.
2. Unroll dough portions crosswise onto a large baking sheet coated with cooking spray and sprinkled with cornmeal. Slightly overlap edges of dough, pinching edges together to seal. Pat dough into a 15 x 12-inch rectangle. Bake at 450° for 2 minutes. Top with tomato and next 3 ingredients. Bake an additional 12 minutes or until cheese melts. Garnish with pepper, if desired. Yield: 8 servings.

CALORIES 389 (29% from fat); FAT 12.5g (sat 4.6g, mono 3.6g, poly 0.5g); PROTEIN 16.4g; CARB 51.4g; FIBER 2.0g; CHOL 26mg; IRON 2.9mg; SODIUM 1102mg; CALC 242mg

main dishes

Whether you're planning a come-as-you-are brunch or a showstopping supper, your holiday entertaining just got easier. Though steeped in tradition, these entrées are anything but ordinary.

Tunisian-Spiced Turkey with Garlic
Couscous and Harissa Gravy
(recipe on page 266)

Lemon and Dill Fish with Red Cabbage and Caraway over Mashed Potatoes

Fish:
- 1 tablespoon chopped fresh dill
- 1 teaspoon grated lemon rind
- ¼ teaspoon salt
- ¼ teaspoon freshly ground black pepper
- 4 (6-ounce) skinless halibut or other firm white fish fillets

Potatoes:
- 5 cups cubed red potato (about 1¾ pounds)
- ½ cup 2% reduced-fat milk
- ¼ cup chopped fresh chives
- 2 teaspoons prepared horseradish
- ¾ teaspoon salt
- ½ teaspoon freshly ground black pepper

Cabbage:
- 1 teaspoon vegetable oil
- ½ cup finely chopped onion
- ½ teaspoon caraway seeds
- 1 cup shredded peeled Granny Smith apple (about ¾ pound)
- 6 cups very thinly sliced red cabbage
- ¼ teaspoon salt
- ¼ teaspoon freshly ground black pepper

Remaining Ingredients:
- Cooking spray
- 1½ tablespoons fresh lemon juice

1. To prepare fish, combine first 4 ingredients, and rub over fish. Cover and chill 1 hour.
2. To prepare potatoes, place potatoes in a large saucepan; cover with water. Bring to a boil; cook 12 minutes or until very tender. Drain. Return potato to pan. Add milk and next 4 ingredients; mash with a potato masher to desired consistency. Keep warm.
3. To prepare cabbage, heat oil in a large nonstick skillet over medium-high heat. Add onion and caraway; sauté 3 minutes. Add apple; sauté 2 minutes. Add cabbage, ¼ teaspoon salt, and ¼ teaspoon pepper. Cover; cook 5 minutes or until tender. Keep warm.
4. Preheat broiler.
5. Place fish on a broiler pan coated with cooking spray; broil 10 to 12 minutes or until fish flakes easily when tested with a fork. Drizzle lemon juice over fish. Serve with potatoes and cabbage. Yield: 4 servings (serving size: 1 fillet, 1 cup potato, and 1 cup cabbage).

CALORIES 423 (14% from fat); FAT 6.5g (sat 1.5g, mono 2g, poly 1.8g); PROTEIN 42.6g; CARB 49g; FIBER 7.6g; CHOL 58mg; IRON 3.9mg; SODIUM 875mg; CALC 223mg

Rosemary-Scented Salmon

- 2 cups alder wood chips
- ¾ cup fresh lime juice
- 3 tablespoons minced fresh rosemary
- 2 tablespoons olive oil
- 1½ teaspoons prepared horseradish
- 1 (3-pound) salmon fillet, halved crosswise
- 1½ teaspoons cracked black pepper
- ¾ teaspoon salt
- Cooking spray
- Lemon slices (optional)
- Lime slices (optional)
- Rosemary sprigs (optional)

1. Soak alder wood chips in water 1 to 24 hours. Drain well.
2. Combine lime juice and next 3 ingredients in a large zip-top plastic bag. Add salmon; seal. Marinate in refrigerator 3 hours, turning bag occasionally. Remove salmon from bag; reserve marinade. Sprinkle pepper and salt over salmon; set aside.
3. Prepare charcoal fire in meat smoker; let burn 15 to 20 minutes. Place alder wood chips on top of coals. Place water pan in smoker; add reserved marinade. Add hot tap water to fill pan.
4. Coat grill rack with cooking spray; place rack in smoker. Arrange salmon on grill rack, skin side down, allowing enough room between salmon pieces for air to circulate. Cover with smoker lid, and cook 50 minutes or until salmon flakes easily when tested with a fork.
5. Place salmon on a platter; garnish with lemon slices, lime slices, and rosemary sprigs, if desired. Yield: 12 servings (serving size: 3 ounces).

CALORIES 169 (45% from fat); FAT 8.5g (sat 1.9g, mono 4.2g, poly 1.8g); PROTEIN 20.8g; CARB 1.2g; FIBER 0.2g; CHOL 54mg; IRON 0.5mg; SODIUM 191mg; CALC 14mg

Shake up the holidays. There's no rule stating that turkey or ham must grace the menu. Fish and shellfish recipes are just as appropriate for Thanksgiving or Christmas as for Fourth of July or Labor Day celebrations.

Bourbon-Brown Sugar Salmon with Onion Sauce

Cereal nuggets create a crunchy topping for meaty salmon. Serve with roasted potatoes and asparagus for a Christmas Eve dinner or New Year's Eve meal.

    1   (2¼-pound) salmon fillet
    3   cups thinly sliced onion
    ½   cup packed brown sugar
    ½   cup water
    ½   cup bourbon
    1   tablespoon low-sodium soy sauce
    1   teaspoon freshly ground black pepper
    ¾   teaspoon salt
    6   tarragon sprigs
    4   thyme sprigs
    ⅓   cup nutlike cereal nuggets (such as Grape-Nuts)
    ¼   cup chopped pecans
        Cooking spray
    ¾   teaspoon salt
    2   tablespoons packed brown sugar
    2   tablespoons honey
  1½   teaspoons water

1. Place salmon in a 13 x 9-inch baking dish. Combine onion and next 8 ingredients; pour over salmon. Cover and marinate in refrigerator 2 hours, turning occasionally.
2. Preheat oven to 350°.
3. Place cereal and pecans in a baking pan. Bake at 350° for 7 minutes or until toasted. Place mixture in a food processor; pulse 4 times or until finely chopped.
4. Remove salmon from dish, and reserve marinade. Arrange salmon fillet diagonally on a broiler pan coated with cooking spray. Sprinkle with ¾ teaspoon salt. Combine 2 tablespoons sugar, honey, and 1½ teaspoons water, stirring with a whisk. Spread honey mixture over salmon, and sprinkle with cereal mixture, gently pressing into salmon. Bake salmon fillet at 350° for 20 minutes or until fish flakes easily when tested with a fork.
5. While salmon bakes, place reserved marinade in a small saucepan. Discard tarragon and thyme sprigs. Bring marinade to a boil over medium-high heat, and cook until reduced to ¾ cup (about 10 minutes). Serve sauce with salmon. Yield: 6 servings (serving size: about 4½ ounces salmon and 2 tablespoons sauce).

CALORIES 437 (30% from fat); FAT 14.7g (sat 2.9g, mono 6.8g, poly 3.8g); PROTEIN 32.2g; CARB 39.5g; FIBER 2.2g; CHOL 72mg; IRON 3.2mg; SODIUM 793mg; CALC 57mg

Seared Scallops with Pomegranate Sauce

Seared Scallops with Pomegranate Sauce

This vibrant dish is perfect for Christmas just because of its color alone. You can buy pomegranate juice at markets specializing in Middle Eastern foods, or make fresh juice by squeezing the fruit as you would an orange. Protect your hands from stains with gloves.

    2   large pomegranates, halved crosswise
    ¼   cup balsamic vinegar
    2   tablespoons low-sodium soy sauce
    ⅛   teaspoon freshly ground black pepper
        Dash of ground red pepper
  1½   pounds sea scallops
    2   teaspoons vegetable oil
    ¼   teaspoon salt
    ¼   teaspoon sugar
    ⅛   teaspoon freshly ground black pepper
    3   cups trimmed watercress (about 1 bunch)
    ¾   cup pomegranate seeds (about 1 pomegranate)

1. Squeeze juice from pomegranate halves using a citrus reamer or juicer to measure 1 cup. Combine juice, vinegar, soy sauce, ⅛ teaspoon black pepper, and red pepper in a small saucepan; bring to a boil. Reduce heat; simmer until reduced by half (about 15 minutes), stirring frequently. Keep warm.
2. Rinse scallops; pat dry. Heat oil in a cast-iron skillet over medium-high heat. Sprinkle scallops with salt, sugar, and ⅛ teaspoon black pepper. Add scallops to pan; cook 2 minutes on each side or until done.
3. Arrange ½ cup watercress on each of 6 plates; divide scallops evenly among plates. Drizzle each serving with 1 tablespoon sauce; sprinkle with 2 tablespoons seeds. Yield: 6 servings.

CALORIES 175 (14% from fat); FAT 2.7g (sat 0.2g, mono 1g, poly 0.8g); PROTEIN 20.2g; CARB 17.9g; FIBER 0.7g; CHOL 37mg; IRON 0.7mg; SODIUM 592mg; CALC 53mg

Linguine with Mussels and Red Sauce

This recipe is really easy to prepare and is best served in wide-rimmed soup bowls. If you have small bread plates, include them at each place setting. The plates can be used for chunks of crusty bread or for the shells after the mussels are eaten.

42 mussels (about 1½ pounds), scrubbed and debearded
2 tablespoons cornmeal
1 tablespoon olive oil
½ cup finely chopped onion
1 garlic clove, minced
1 cup dry white wine
1 tablespoon dried basil
½ teaspoon crushed red pepper
1 (28-ounce) can plum tomatoes with basil, undrained and chopped
2 (8-ounce) cans no-salt-added tomato sauce
9 cups hot cooked linguine (about 1 pound uncooked pasta)
¼ cup chopped fresh parsley

1. Discard any open mussels. Place remaining mussels in a large bowl, and cover with cold water. Sprinkle with cornmeal, and let stand 30 minutes. Drain and rinse mussels; set aside. Discard cornmeal.

2. Heat olive oil in a large Dutch oven over medium-low heat until hot. Add chopped onion and minced garlic, and cook 5 minutes, stirring frequently. Add wine; bring to a boil over medium heat, and cook 5 minutes. Add basil, pepper, tomatoes, and tomato sauce; reduce heat, and simmer, uncovered, 10 minutes.

3. Spread mussels, hinged side down, over tomato mixture. Cover and cook over high heat 3 minutes or until mussels open; discard any unopened shells.

4. Spoon linguine into large soup bowls, and top with red sauce, mussels, and chopped parsley. Yield: 12 servings (serving size: ¾ cup cooked linguine, ½ cup red sauce, 3 mussels, and 1 teaspoon chopped parsley).

CALORIES 229 (12% from fat); FAT 3.0g (sat 0.6g, mono 1.1g, poly 0.5g); PROTEIN 13.1g; CARB 36.5g; FIBER 2.6g; CHOL 16mg; IRON 4.4mg; SODIUM 289mg; CALC 48mg

Linguine with Mussels and Red Sauce

Spiced Shrimp
Skewers with
Clementine Salsa

Spiced Shrimp Skewers with Clementine Salsa

Don't be intimidated by the long list of ingredients—more than half are spices.
Crisp jícama adds texture, and you can leave the seeds in the chiles for an especially hot salsa. Serve this dish
with cooked rice to balance the earthy-flavored shrimp and fiery-sweet salsa.

Shrimp:

½ teaspoon ground cinnamon
½ teaspoon paprika
¼ teaspoon salt
¼ teaspoon ground ginger
¼ teaspoon ground coriander seeds
¼ teaspoon ground cumin
⅛ teaspoon ground red pepper
⅛ teaspoon freshly ground black pepper
Dash of ground nutmeg
36 jumbo shrimp (about 2½ pounds), peeled and
   deveined
Cooking spray

Salsa:

6 cups clementine sections (about 6 clementines)
1½ cups chopped peeled jícama
1 cup finely chopped red onion
1 tablespoon minced peeled fresh ginger
1 tablespoon fresh lime juice
1 tablespoon extravirgin olive oil
2 teaspoons chopped fresh thyme
½ teaspoon salt
¼ teaspoon freshly ground black pepper
2 serrano chiles, seeded and finely chopped

1. To prepare shrimp, combine first 9 ingredients in a large bowl; stir well. Add shrimp, tossing well to coat. Cover and marinate in refrigerator 4 hours.

2. Soak 12 (6-inch) wood skewers in water 30 minutes.

3. Preheat grill or grill pan.

4. Thread 3 shrimp onto each skewer. Place skewers on grill rack or grill pan coated with cooking spray; cook 3 minutes on each side or until shrimp are done.

5. To prepare salsa, combine clementine and next 9 ingredients, stirring well. Serve salsa with shrimp. Yield: 6 servings (serving size: 2 skewers and about ⅔ cup salsa).

CALORIES 135 (22% from fat); FAT 3.3g (sat 0.5g, mono 1.8g, poly 0.6g); PROTEIN 9.7g; CARB 15.9g; FIBER 3.3g; CHOL 64mg; IRON 1.5mg; SODIUM 360mg; CALC 49mg

Buy a few extra clementines to brighten a fresh fruit basket during the holidays. They peel effortlessly and don't have seeds. Both children and adults will love the slightly sweet, tart flavor.

Seafood Lasagna Florentine

Sitting down to a nice meal during the holidays can be the highlight of a family's day, and it's even more special when the cook doesn't have to do all the work. That's why this dish makes a wonderful gift for a deserving seafood-loving family. Enclose in a disposable container, and add a prepackaged salad kit to round out the meal.

2   (10-ounce) packages frozen chopped spinach, thawed and drained
½   cup all-purpose flour
2   cups 2% reduced-fat milk
¼   teaspoon salt
¼   teaspoon ground nutmeg
⅛   teaspoon ground red pepper
⅛   teaspoon ground black pepper
1   large garlic clove, crushed
¼   cup dry white wine
⅔   cup grated Parmesan cheese, divided
1   pound bay scallops
½   cup chopped fresh basil
1   tablespoon lemon juice
½   pound lump crabmeat, drained and shell pieces removed
1   large egg, lightly beaten
9   cooked lasagna noodles
½   teaspoon paprika

1. Preheat oven to 350°. Press spinach between paper towels until barely moist; set aside.
2. Place flour in a shallow baking pan. Bake at 350° for 30 minutes or until lightly browned, stirring after 15 minutes. Spoon flour into a large saucepan; gradually add milk, stirring with a whisk. Stir in salt and next 4 ingredients; cook over medium heat 5 minutes or until thick, stirring constantly. Add wine; cook 1 additional minute, stirring constantly. Remove from heat; stir in ½ cup cheese and scallops. Cool slightly; stir in basil, lemon juice, crabmeat, and egg.
3. Increase oven temperature to 400°. Spoon ¼ cup seafood sauce into a 13 x 9-inch baking dish. Arrange 3 lasagna noodles in a single layer over seafood sauce; top with one-third spinach. Spoon one-third of remaining seafood sauce over spinach. Repeat layers twice, ending with seafood sauce. Combine remaining cheese and paprika; sprinkle cheese mixture over lasagna. Cover and bake at 400° for 30 minutes. Bake, uncovered, 10 additional minutes. Let stand 10 minutes before serving. Yield: 9 servings.

CALORIES 275 (15% from fat); FAT 4.7g (sat 2.1g, mono 1g, poly 0.4g); PROTEIN 25.2g; CARB 33.3g; FIBER 2.5g; CHOL 67mg; IRON 3.1mg; SODIUM 419mg; CALC 240mg

Apple Orchard Pot Roast

This autumnal roast is the ideal one-dish meal for welcoming family home for the holidays. Add bread and a salad, if you choose.

1   (3-pound) boneless beef bottom round roast
2   teaspoons vegetable oil
1½ cups apple juice
1   cup dry white wine
½   cup orange juice
½   teaspoon salt
6   garlic cloves, peeled
6   whole cloves
2   (1 x 3-inch) orange rind strips
1   (3-inch) cinnamon stick
8   turnips (about 1 pound), peeled
6   carrots (about ¾ pound), peeled and cut into thirds
4   parsnips (about ¾ pound), peeled and cut into thirds
2   peeled baking potatoes (about 1 pound), halved and quartered
1   peeled sweet potato (about 1 pound), halved and quartered

1. Preheat oven to 300°.
2. Trim fat from roast. Heat oil in a Dutch oven over medium-high heat until hot. Add roast; cook 5 minutes, browning on all sides. Add apple juice, wine, and orange juice; scrape pan to loosen browned bits. Add salt and next 4 ingredients. Bring to a boil; remove from heat. Cover; bake at 300° for 1 hour.
3. Turn roast over. Add vegetables; cover and bake 2 additional hours. Increase oven temperature to 400° (do not remove roast from oven). Bake, uncovered, 20 minutes or until very tender. Remove roast and vegetables from pan. Cover roast with foil; let stand 10 minutes before slicing. Strain cooking liquid through a sieve; discard solids. Serve with roast and vegetables. Yield: 8 servings (serving size: 3 ounces beef, about 1 cup vegetable mixture, and ¼ cup gravy).

CALORIES 335 (18% from fat); FAT 6.7g (sat 2.1g, mono 2.5g, poly 0.9g); PROTEIN 32.2g; CARB 36g; FIBER 4.9g; CHOL 73mg; IRON 5.1mg; SODIUM 274mg; CALC 70mg

Standing Rib Roast with
Madeira Sauce and Herbed
Yorkshire Puddings

Standing Rib Roast with Madeira Sauce and Herbed Yorkshire Puddings

Yorkshire pudding, a holiday classic for generations, derives its name from the Yorkshire region of northern England. Let the roast rest while you finish the sauce and make the puddings; this will make the roast easier to carve.

Roast:
- 1 (5-pound) French-cut rib-eye roast, trimmed
- 1 garlic clove, halved
- ½ teaspoon salt
- ½ teaspoon freshly ground black pepper
- Cooking spray

Sauce:
- 1 cup water
- 2 tablespoons all-purpose flour
- ½ cup Madeira
- ½ cup beef broth
- ½ teaspoon black pepper

Puddings:
- 1½ cups all-purpose flour
- 1 teaspoon salt
- ¾ teaspoon freshly ground black pepper
- 1½ cups 1% low-fat milk
- 1 tablespoon chopped fresh or 1 teaspoon dried thyme
- 1 tablespoon chopped fresh parsley
- 1 teaspoon grated lemon rind
- 5 large egg whites
- 2 large eggs

1. Preheat oven to 450°.

2. To prepare roast, rub roast on all sides with garlic. Sprinkle with ½ teaspoon salt and ½ teaspoon pepper. Place roast, fat side up, on a broiler pan coated with cooking spray. Insert a meat thermometer into thickest portion of roast, making sure not to touch bone. Bake at 450° for 25 minutes. Reduce oven temperature to 300° (do not remove roast from oven), and bake an additional 1½ hours or until thermometer registers 160° (medium) or until desired degree of doneness. Place roast on a platter, and let stand while finishing sauce and Yorkshire puddings. Reserve 1½ tablespoons drippings from pan for puddings, and set aside.

3. To prepare sauce, wipe remaining drippings from pan with paper towels, leaving browned bits on bottom of pan. Combine water and 2 tablespoons flour in a small bowl. Add Madeira to pan, and bring to a boil over medium-high heat, scraping bottom of pan with a wooden spoon to loosen browned bits. Add flour mixture; cook 1 minute or until slightly thick. Stir in broth and ½ teaspoon pepper; cook 2 minutes. Keep warm.

4. Increase oven temperature to 450°.

5. To prepare puddings, coat 12 muffin cups with reserved pan drippings. Lightly spoon 1½ cups flour into dry measuring cups; level with a knife. Combine 1½ cups flour, 1 teaspoon salt, and ¾ teaspoon pepper in a medium bowl. Gradually add milk, stirring with a whisk until smooth. Add thyme and next 4 ingredients, stirring with a whisk until smooth. Spoon batter into prepared cups. Bake at 450° for 15 minutes. Reduce oven temperature to 375° (do not remove puddings from oven); bake an additional 15 minutes or until golden. Yield: 12 servings (serving size: 3 ounces beef, 2 tablespoons sauce, and 1 pudding).

CALORIES 304 (38% from fat); FAT 12.8g (sat 5g, mono 5.2g, poly 0.6g); PROTEIN 29g; CARB 16.1g; FIBER 0.6g; CHOL 106mg; IRON 3.5mg; SODIUM 410mg; CALC 58mg

wine suggestion

For centuries, the British have enjoyed red Bordeaux wines (also called "claret") with hearty, warming fare, such as this classic roast. You can find a wide range of Bordeaux wines to suit any budget.

how to: DEGLAZE THE PAN

To use browned bits in the bottom of a pan to flavor gravy, deglaze the pan by pouring wine, broth, or other liquid into it and scraping flavorful bits into the liquid. We scraped up bits after adding Madeira to this recipe. Reducing the liquid intensifies the flavor.

Beef Tenderloin with Parsnip-Mushroom Ragoût

Ragoût:

1½ cups boiling water

2 cups dried porcini mushrooms (about 2 ounces)

2 teaspoons butter

½ cup chopped shallots

3 tablespoons minced garlic (about 9 cloves)

1 teaspoon minced fresh or ¼ teaspoon dried thyme

3 cups coarsely chopped parsnips (about 1 pound)

12 cups quartered button mushrooms (about 1½ pounds)

½ cup port wine

2 tablespoons chopped fresh parsley

½ teaspoon salt

½ teaspoon freshly ground black pepper

Beef:

½ teaspoon salt

½ teaspoon freshly ground black pepper

1 (3-pound) beef tenderloin, trimmed and cut in half crosswise

Cooking spray

Sauce:

1 teaspoon butter

⅓ cup (2-inch) julienne-cut carrot

⅓ cup vertically sliced shallots

¼ cup port wine

1 (14-ounce) can less-sodium beef broth

¼ teaspoon salt

¼ teaspoon freshly ground black pepper

1. To prepare ragoût, pour boiling water over porcini mushrooms; let stand 20 minutes. Strain through a sieve into a bowl; reserve liquid. Finely chop porcini mushrooms; divide in half.
2. Melt 2 teaspoons butter in a large nonstick skillet over medium heat. Add ½ cup shallots, garlic, and thyme; cook 1 minute, stirring frequently. Add parsnips; cook 2 minutes, stirring occasionally. Add button mushrooms; cook 10 minutes, stirring occasionally. Add half of porcini mushrooms and ½ cup wine; bring to a boil. Cover, reduce heat, and cook 15 minutes or until parsnips are tender. Stir in parsley, ½ teaspoon salt, and ½ teaspoon pepper. Set aside; keep warm.
3. Preheat oven to 450°.
4. To prepare beef, rub ½ teaspoon salt and ½ teaspoon pepper over tenderloin. Heat a large ovenproof skillet coated with cooking spray over medium-high heat. Add tenderloin; cook 5 minutes, browning on all sides. Bake at 450° for

20 minutes or until a thermometer registers 160° (medium) or until desired degree of doneness. Place tenderloin on a cutting board; cover loosely with foil. Let stand 10 minutes (temperature of tenderloin will increase 5° upon standing).
5. To prepare sauce, melt 1 teaspoon butter in pan over medium-high heat. Add carrot and ⅓ cup shallots; sauté 3 minutes. Add reserved porcini mushroom liquid, remaining porcini mushrooms, ¼ cup wine, and broth; bring to a boil. Cook until reduced to 1½ cups (about 10 minutes). Stir in ¼ teaspoon salt and ¼ teaspoon pepper. Cut beef into thin slices; serve with ragoût and sauce. Yield: 12 servings (serving size: 3 ounces tenderloin, ⅔ cup ragoût, and 2 tablespoons sauce).

CALORIES 265 (35% from fat); FAT 10.3g (sat 3.9g, mono 3.8g, poly 0.6g); PROTEIN 28.8g; CARB 14.1g; FIBER 3.4g; CHOL 74mg; IRON 5.2mg; SODIUM 330mg; CALC 36mg

Pepper-Crusted Beef Tenderloin with Kumquat Marmalade

1½ cups vertically sliced onion

½ cup halved, seeded, and vertically sliced kumquats

½ cup carrot juice or orange juice

1 tablespoon Dijon mustard

¼ teaspoon salt

2 thyme sprigs

1 bay leaf

2 teaspoons rice vinegar

2 teaspoons olive oil

1½ to 2 tablespoons freshly ground mixed peppercorns or black peppercorns

4 (4-ounce) beef tenderloin steaks, trimmed (about ¾ inch thick)

½ teaspoon salt

1. Combine first 7 ingredients in a small saucepan, and bring mixture to a boil. Reduce heat, and simmer 15 minutes or until liquid almost evaporates, stirring occasionally. Remove mixture from heat. Discard thyme sprigs and bay leaf. Stir in rice vinegar, and cool.
2. Heat oil in a large nonstick skillet over medium-high heat. Place pepper in a shallow dish. Dredge steaks in pepper; sprinkle evenly with ½ teaspoon salt. Add beef to pan; cook 3 minutes on each side or until desired degree of doneness. Serve with marmalade. Yield: 4 servings (serving size: 1 steak and about ¼ cup marmalade).

CALORIES 211 (29% from fat); FAT 6.9g (sat 1.9g, mono 3.3g, poly 0.4g); PROTEIN 23.8g; CARB 17.1g; FIBER 3.4g; CHOL 60mg; IRON 4.1mg; SODIUM 611mg; CALC 62mg

The secret to holiday entertaining is in the planning. Have the table set, the flowers arranged, and anything not related to food done the day before so you can devote your time to enjoying the food, family, and guests during the celebration.

Beef Tenderloin with
Parsnip-Mushroom Ragoût

Individual Beef Wellingtons

¾ pound mushrooms, quartered
Butter-flavored cooking spray
¼ cup chopped shallots
2 garlic cloves, minced
2 teaspoons all-purpose flour
½ teaspoon dried marjoram
⅛ teaspoon black pepper
1 (10½-ounce) can beef consommé, divided
2 tablespoons minced fresh parsley
6 (4-ounce) beef tenderloin steaks (1 inch thick)
1½ teaspoons Worcestershire sauce
6 sheets frozen phyllo dough, thawed
½ cup sweet Marsala
1 tablespoon plus 1½ teaspoons cornstarch

1. Place mushrooms in a food processor, and process until finely chopped.
2. Place a large skillet coated with cooking spray over medium-high heat until hot. Add mushrooms, shallots, and garlic, and sauté 2 minutes or until tender. Stir in flour, dried marjoram, and pepper. Gradually add ¼ cup beef consommé, and stir well. Cook 5 minutes or until liquid evaporates; stir constantly (mixture will be thick). Remove mixture from heat, and stir in parsley; set aside.
3. Preheat oven to 425°.
4. Trim fat from steaks. Place a large skillet coated with cooking spray over medium-high heat until hot. Add steaks; cook 1½ minutes on each side or until browned. Drain on paper towels. Place steaks on a broiler pan coated with cooking spray. Drizzle ¼ teaspoon Worcestershire sauce over each steak; top each with 3 tablespoons mushroom mixture.
5. Layer 6 sheets phyllo, spraying each lightly with cooking spray. Cut 6 (6½ x 4½-inch) rectangles. Thinly slice excess phyllo for topping. Drape a phyllo rectangle over each steak, tucking edges of phyllo under steak. Crumple phyllo strips into 6 balls; place one on top of each phyllo-wrapped steak. Lightly coat with cooking spray. Bake at 425° for 15 minutes or until desired degree of doneness.
6. Combine remaining consommé, wine, and cornstarch in a small saucepan, and stir well. Bring to a boil; cook 1 minute, stirring constantly. Serve with steaks. Yield: 6 servings (serving size: 1 steak and ¼ cup sauce).

CALORIES 234 (25% from fat); FAT 6.8g (sat 2.0g, mono 2.1g, poly 0.3g); PROTEIN 27.7g; CARB 17.2g; FIBER 1.2g; CHOL 60mg; IRON 4.3mg; SODIUM 424mg; CALC 18mg

Veal Medallions with Apple-Thyme Sauce

To prevent the apple from turning brown, chop it while the sauce is reducing. After that step, this recipe comes together rather quickly.

Sauce:
1 cup dry sherry
1¾ cups fat-free, less-sodium chicken broth
¼ cup thawed apple juice concentrate, undiluted
1 tablespoon water
1½ teaspoons cornstarch
½ cup chopped Granny Smith apple
½ teaspoon chopped fresh or ⅛ teaspoon dried thyme
Veal:
4 (2-ounce) veal medallions
⅛ teaspoon salt
⅛ teaspoon black pepper
2 teaspoons vegetable oil

1. To prepare sauce, bring sherry to a boil in a medium saucepan over medium-high heat; cook until reduced to 2 tablespoons (about 8 minutes). Add broth and apple juice concentrate; cook until reduced to 1 cup (about 12 minutes). Combine water and cornstarch in a small bowl. Add to broth mixture; bring to a boil. Cook 1 minute, stirring constantly. Remove from heat; stir in apple and thyme. Cover and keep warm.
2. To prepare veal, sprinkle veal with salt and pepper. Heat oil in a medium nonstick skillet over medium-high heat. Add veal; cook 3 minutes on each side or until lightly browned. Serve veal with sauce. Yield: 2 servings (serving size: 2 medallions and ½ cup sauce).

CALORIES 331 (28% from fat); FAT 10.4g (sat 2.4g, mono 3.4g, poly 2.8g); PROTEIN 30.2g; CARB 26.3g; FIBER 0.8g; CHOL 101mg; IRON 1.7mg; SODIUM 662mg; CALC 40mg

successful holiday dinner tips

* At this time of year, refrigerator storage space is at a premium, so start a new holiday ritual: a weekly refrigerator cleaning. Designate a day (the day before trash pickup is a good one) to reclaim refrigerator space from old leftovers and expired items and make room for seasonal dishes.

* Identify serving pieces and utensils for each dish ahead. Place a slip of paper with the name of the recipe to be served on each piece. You'll save yourself from that last-minute rush to find your favorite serving platter.

* Clean up as you go. Start the dinner party with an empty trash can and an empty dishwasher, and wash pots and pans as you use them.

Pistachio-Encrusted Rack of Lamb

This striking yet simple entrée will win you applause. You can prepare the mustard
mixture earlier in the day. The breadcrumb mixture (minus the lemon juice) can also be prepared ahead;
just remember to add the juice before patting the pistachio crust onto the lamb.

3 (1-ounce) slices day-old white bread
⅓ cup finely chopped pistachios
1¼ teaspoons grated lemon rind
2½ tablespoons finely chopped fresh parsley
¼ cup lemon juice
¾ teaspoon salt, divided
¼ cup finely chopped fresh chives
¼ cup finely chopped fresh mint
2½ tablespoons Dijon mustard
2 garlic cloves, minced
2 (1½-pound) French-cut racks of lamb (8 ribs each),
   trimmed
Cooking spray
Mint sprigs (optional)

1. Preheat oven to 425°.
2. Place bread in a food processor; pulse 10 times or until
coarse crumbs form to measure about 1¼ cups.

3. Combine breadcrumbs, nuts, rind, parsley, lemon juice,
and ½ teaspoon salt in a small bowl.
4. Combine chives, mint, mustard, and garlic in a small bowl.
5. Sprinkle lamb with ¼ teaspoon salt. Heat a large nonstick
skillet coated with cooking spray over medium-high heat.
Add lamb racks, and cook 2 minutes on each side or until
browned. Spread mustard mixture evenly over meaty portion
of lamb racks. Carefully pat breadcrumb mixture into mustard mixture.
6. Place lamb on a broiler pan coated with cooking spray.
Bake at 425° for 35 minutes or until a thermometer registers
145° (medium-rare) to 160° (medium). Place lamb on a
platter; cover with foil. Let stand 10 minutes before serving
(temperature will increase 5° upon standing). Cut each rack
into 4 pieces (2 ribs per piece). Garnish with mint sprigs, if
desired. Yield: 8 servings (serving size: 1 piece, 2 ribs).

CALORIES 206 (47% from fat); FAT 10.8g (sat 3.1g, mono 4.6g, poly 1.5g); PROTEIN 18.5g;
CARB 8.5g; FIBER 0.9g; CHOL 52mg; IRON 2.1mg; SODIUM 472mg; CALC 37mg

Pork Medallions with
Cranberries and Apples

4. Add 1 teaspoon oil to pan. Add onion; cover, reduce heat, and cook 5 minutes or until golden brown, stirring frequently. Return pork to pan; add juice mixture, apple, and cranberries. Bring to a simmer; cover and cook 3 minutes or until cranberries pop and pork is done, stirring occasionally. Garnish with sage sprigs, if desired. Yield: 4 servings (serving size: 2 pork medallions and ⅓ cup fruit mixture).

CALORIES 262 (30% from fat); FAT 8.7g (sat 2g, mono 5.1g, poly 0.9g); PROTEIN 24.8g; CARB 20.9g; FIBER 2.2g; CHOL 74mg; IRON 1.8mg; SODIUM 409mg; CALC 20mg

Apple Cider-Glazed Pork Tenderloin

This pork tenderloin is a good choice for a small holiday dinner or for buffet biscuit sandwiches. Reduce the apple cider and chicken broth to a flavorful syrup to brush over the cooked pork. Serve apple chutney and stone-ground mustard alongside the pork and Buttermilk-Chive Biscuits (recipe on page 159).

  2 tablespoons dried rosemary, crushed
  1 tablespoon minced peeled fresh ginger
  1 tablespoon grated orange rind
  1 tablespoon olive oil
  ½ teaspoon salt
  ¼ teaspoon freshly ground black pepper
  6 garlic cloves, minced
  3 (1-pound) pork tenderloins, trimmed
  3 cups apple cider
  3 whole cloves
  2 bay leaves
  1 cup fat-free, less-sodium chicken
     broth

1. Combine first 7 ingredients, and rub evenly over pork. Place pork in a dish; cover and chill 1 hour.
2. Combine cider, cloves, and bay leaves in a large skillet; bring to a boil over medium-high heat. Cook until reduced to 1½ cups (about 10 minutes). Add broth; bring to a boil. Add pork; cover and simmer 20 minutes or until a thermometer registers 155° (slightly pink). Remove pork from pan and let stand 10 minutes for internal temperature to rise to 160°. Bring cooking liquid to a boil. Cook until reduced to ¾ cup (about 8 minutes). Strain cooking liquid through a fine sieve into a bowl; discard solids. Spoon sauce over pork. Cut pork into thin slices. Yield: 12 servings (serving size: 3 ounces).

CALORIES 183 (25% from fat); FAT 5.1g (sat 1.5g, mono 2.6g, poly 0.5g); PROTEIN 24.2g; CARB 8.7g; FIBER 0.4g; CHOL 74mg; IRON 1.6mg; SODIUM 198mg; CALC 17mg

Pork Medallions with Cranberries and Apples

Cranberries are traditionally associated with Thanksgiving and Christmas. And rightfully so—they are only in season from October to December. So now's the time to use them! Serve this pork dish with nutty wild rice or a blend of white and wild rice.

  ½ cup apple juice
  ½ cup fat-free, less-sodium chicken broth
  1 tablespoon brown sugar
1½ teaspoons cornstarch
  ½ teaspoon salt
  ¼ teaspoon dried rubbed sage
  ⅛ teaspoon coarsely ground black pepper
  1 (1-pound) pork tenderloin, trimmed
  1 tablespoon all-purpose flour
  4 teaspoons olive oil, divided
     Cooking spray
  ½ cup finely chopped onion
  1 cup thinly sliced peeled Rome apple
  ¾ cup fresh cranberries
     Fresh sage sprigs (optional)

1. Combine first 7 ingredients in a small bowl, stirring well with a whisk.
2. Cut pork crosswise into 8 pieces. Place each piece between 2 sheets of heavy-duty plastic wrap; flatten each piece to ¾-inch thickness using a meat mallet or rolling pin. Dredge each pork piece in flour.
3. Heat 3 teaspoons oil in a large nonstick skillet coated with cooking spray over medium-high heat. Add pork; cook 2½ minutes on each side or until browned. Remove pork from pan.

Pork Loin with Olivada, Spinach, and Rice Stuffing

This roast can be assembled and refrigerated up to 2 days ahead. To cook, let stand at room temperature 30 minutes, and then proceed with baking instructions. Overnight brining tenderizes the pork and keeps it juicy.

Brine:

- 8 cups water
- ¾ cup sugar
- ¾ cup kosher salt
- 2 tablespoons grated lemon rind
- 2 tablespoons chopped fresh oregano
- 2 garlic cloves, crushed
- 1 (3½-pound) center-cut boneless pork loin roast, trimmed

Stuffing:

- ¾ cup uncooked jasmine rice
- 1 (6-ounce) package fresh baby spinach
- ½ teaspoon salt
- ½ cup pitted kalamata olives, finely chopped
- 1 teaspoon crushed red pepper
- 1 teaspoon grated lemon rind
- 2 teaspoons fresh lemon juice

Remaining Ingredient:

- 1 tablespoon freshly ground black pepper

1. To brine pork, combine first 6 ingredients in a large non-aluminum bowl or pan; stir until sugar and salt dissolve. Add pork. Cover; refrigerate 8 hours or overnight. Remove pork from bowl; discard brine.

2. Preheat oven to 325°.

3. Starting off-center, slice pork lengthwise, cutting to, but not through, other side. Open uneven portions, laying pork flat. Turning knife blade parallel to surface of cutting board, slice larger portion of pork in half horizontally, cutting to, but not through, other side; open flat. Place heavy-duty plastic wrap over pork; pound to an even thickness using a meat mallet or rolling pin. Refrigerate until ready to use.

4. To prepare stuffing, cook rice according to package directions, omitting salt and fat. Add spinach and ½ teaspoon salt to hot rice, stirring until spinach wilts. Stir in olives, red pepper, 1 teaspoon rind, and juice.

5. Spread rice mixture over pork, leaving a ½-inch border. Roll up pork, jelly-roll fashion, starting with a long side. Secure both ends with twine; secure middle at 2-inch intervals with twine. Rub black pepper over pork. Place pork on a broiler pan. Bake at 325° for 1 hour and 20 minutes or until a thermometer registers 155° (slightly pink). Let pork stand 10 minutes for juice to reabsorb and for temperature to rise to 160° before slicing. Yield: 12 servings (serving size: 1 [6-ounce] slice stuffed pork).

CALORIES 232 (33% from fat); FAT 8.5g (sat 3g, mono 3.9g, poly 0.7g); PROTEIN 25.2g; CARB 12.2g; FIBER 0.8g; CHOL 68mg; IRON 1.7mg; SODIUM 780mg; CALC 44mg

This fall-colored dish won the highest marks from just about everyone who tasted it. Since it elicited rave reviews in our Test Kitchens, we've no doubt it will do the same in your home.

Pecan-Crusted Pork with
Red Onion Marmalade and
Roasted Sweet Potatoes

Pecan-Crusted Pork with Red Onion Marmalade and Roasted Sweet Potatoes

    2   pounds peeled sweet potatoes, cut into ½-inch-thick slices
Cooking spray
    ¼   cup packed brown sugar, divided
    1   bacon slice, cut into 1-inch pieces
    1   teaspoon vegetable oil
    1   medium red onion, sliced and separated into rings
        (about 1½ cups)
    ¼   cup water
    ¼   cup balsamic vinegar
    1   tablespoon grated peeled fresh ginger
    1   pound pork tenderloin
    ½   cup all-purpose flour, divided
    ⅓   cup ground pecans
    ½   teaspoon cracked black pepper
    2   large egg whites, lightly beaten
    1   tablespoon butter
    4   teaspoons finely chopped pecans, toasted

1. Preheat oven to 400°.
2. Arrange potato slices in a 13 x 9-inch baking dish coated with cooking spray. Sprinkle with 2 tablespoons sugar; arrange bacon on top. Bake at 400° for 30 minutes. Turn potatoes over; bake an additional 30 minutes or until tender. Keep warm.
3. Heat oil in a large nonstick skillet over medium-high heat. Add onion and 2 tablespoons sugar; cook 6 minutes or until onion is tender and lightly browned, stirring frequently. Stir in water, vinegar, and ginger; bring to a boil. Cook 3 minutes, and remove from heat. Remove onions from skillet; set aside.
4. Trim fat from pork, and cut crosswise into 8 pieces. Place each piece between 2 sheets of heavy-duty plastic wrap, and flatten to ½-inch thickness, using a meat mallet or rolling pin.
5. Lightly spoon flour into a dry measuring cup; level with a knife. Place ¼ cup flour in a shallow dish. Combine ¼ cup flour, ground pecans, and pepper in a separate shallow dish. Dredge pork in flour, shaking off excess. Dip pork in egg whites; dredge in pecan mixture, coating both sides.
6. Melt butter in a large nonstick skillet coated with cooking spray over medium-high heat. Arrange pork in pan in a single layer. Cook 3 minutes on each side or until browned. Top pork with onion mixture; sprinkle with chopped pecans. Serve with sweet potatoes. Yield: 4 servings (serving size: 2 cutlets, ¼ cup onion marmalade, and ¾ cup sweet potatoes).

CALORIES 685 (30% from fat); FAT 23.2g (sat 5.4g, mono 11.4g, poly 4.9g); PROTEIN 33.2g; CARB 87.3g; FIBER 9.1g; CHOL 86mg; IRON 4.5mg; SODIUM 190mg; CALC 89mg

Roasted Spiced-Pork Tenderloin with Beet, Apple, and Caraway Salsa

Pork:
    ½   cup water
    ⅓   cup fresh orange juice
    ¼   cup fresh lime juice
  2½   tablespoons chopped peeled fresh lemongrass
    1   tablespoon minced fresh cilantro
    1   tablespoon Thai fish sauce
    1   tablespoon low-sodium soy sauce
    1   teaspoon brown sugar
    1   teaspoon grated peeled fresh ginger
    2   garlic cloves, minced
    1   (1-pound) pork tenderloin, trimmed
  Cooking spray
Salsa:
    2   cups diced Granny Smith apple
    1   cup diced, cooked beets
    ¼   cup sliced green onions
    ¼   cup diced seeded Anaheim chile
    1   tablespoon chopped fresh mint
    2   teaspoons rice vinegar
    ½   teaspoon caraway seeds, crushed
    ½   teaspoon brown sugar
    ¼   teaspoon salt
    ¼   teaspoon freshly ground black pepper

1. To prepare pork, combine first 11 ingredients in a large zip-top plastic bag; seal. Marinate in refrigerator 4 to 12 hours, turning bag occasionally.
2. Preheat oven to 450°.
3. Heat a large nonstick skillet coated with cooking spray over medium-high heat. Remove pork from bag, reserving marinade. Pat pork dry with paper towels. Add pork to pan, and cook 6 minutes, browning on all sides. Remove pork from pan, and place on a broiler pan coated with cooking spray. Place reserved marinade in a small saucepan, and bring to a boil. Remove from heat. Bake pork at 450° for 25 minutes or until a thermometer registers 155° (slightly pink), basting occasionally with reserved marinade. Let stand 10 minutes for internal temperature to rise to 160°, and cut into thin slices.
4. To prepare salsa, combine apple and next 9 ingredients. Serve with pork. Yield: 4 servings (serving size: 3 ounces pork and about ½ cup salsa).

CALORIES 225 (17% from fat); FAT 4.3g (sat 1.4g, mono 1.8g, poly 0.5g); PROTEIN 25.7g; CARB 21.5g; FIBER 3.1g; CHOL 74mg; IRON 2.5mg; SODIUM 721mg; CALC 35mg

Holiday Ham Menu

serves 8

Cranberry-Glazed Ham (recipe below)

Potato-Gorgonzola Gratin (recipe on page 287)

Green beans

Green salad

Buttermilk-Chive Biscuits (recipe on page 159)

Old-Fashioned Caramel Layer Cake (recipe on page 311)

Cranberry-Glazed Ham

1 (7-pound) 33%-less-sodium smoked, fully cooked
    ham half
½ cup whole-berry cranberry sauce
3 tablespoons brown sugar
1 tablespoon spicy brown mustard

1. Preheat oven to 325°. Trim fat and rind from ham. Score outside of ham in a diamond pattern. Place ham on a broiler pan lined with foil. Bake at 325° for 1 hour.
2. Combine cranberry sauce, sugar, and mustard; brush over ham. Bake an additional 35 minutes. Transfer ham to a platter; let stand 10 minutes before slicing. Yield: 25 servings (serving size: 3 ounces).

CALORIES 173 (57% from fat); FAT 11g (sat 4g, mono 5.2g, poly 1.7g); PROTEIN 13g; CARB 5.2g; FIBER 0g; CHOL 46mg; IRON 0.8mg; SODIUM 96mg; CALC 2mg

Guinness Baked Ham

1 (6½- to 7-pound) 33%-less-sodium smoked, fully
    cooked ham half
Cooking spray
¼ cup country-style Dijon mustard
¼ cup flat Guinness Stout
2 tablespoons minced fresh parsley
1 tablespoon dark brown sugar
½ teaspoon ground cinnamon
Parsley sprigs (optional)

1. Preheat oven to 425°. Trim fat and rind from ham. Score outside of ham in a diamond pattern. Place ham on a broiler pan coated with cooking spray.

2. Combine mustard and next 4 ingredients, and brush over ham. Bake at 425° for 5 minutes. Reduce heat to 325°; continue baking 1 hour. Baste ham with mustard mixture every 15 minutes. Transfer ham to a platter; let stand 15 minutes before slicing. Garnish with parsley, if desired. Yield: 23 servings (serving size: 3 ounces).

CALORIES 127 (43% from fat); FAT 6.1g (sat 2.0g, mono 2.9g, poly 0.7g); PROTEIN 24.2g; CARB 3.3g; FIBER 0g; CHOL 51mg; IRON 0mg; SODIUM 935mg; CALC 2mg

Gingersnap-Crusted Ham with Apricot-Mustard Sauce

Whole hams usually weigh at least 15 pounds; ham halves, which are labeled either "shank" or "butt end," are more manageable. A bone-in shank is easier to carve than the butt end, which contains part of the hip bone.

Ham:
1 (8-pound) 33%-less-sodium smoked, fully cooked
    ham half
2 tablespoons apricot preserves
2 tablespoons Dijon mustard
½ cup brown sugar
½ cup gingersnap crumbs (about 9 cookies, finely
    crushed)
Sauce:
1½ cups apricot preserves
½ cup dry Marsala
3 tablespoons Dijon mustard
½ teaspoon ground allspice

1. Preheat oven to 325°.
2. To prepare ham, trim fat and rind from ham. Score outside of ham in a diamond pattern. Place ham on a boiler pan lined with foil. Bake at 325° for 1 hour. Remove ham from oven, and cool slightly. Increase oven temperature to 375°.
3. Combine 2 tablespoons preserves and 2 tablespoons mustard, stirring with a whisk. Combine sugar and crumbs. Brush preserves mixture over ham. Carefully press crumb mixture onto preserves mixture (some crumb mixture will fall onto pan). Bake at 375° for 45 minutes. Place ham on a platter; let stand 15 minutes before slicing.
4. To prepare sauce, combine 1½ cups preserves and next 3 ingredients in a small saucepan. Bring to a boil; cook 5 minutes. Serve sauce with ham. Yield: 24 servings (serving size: about 3½ ounces ham and 2 teaspoons sauce).

CALORIES 233 (24% from fat); FAT 6.3g (sat 1.9g, mono 2.9g, poly 0.7g); PROTEIN 21.2g; CARB 22.4g; FIBER 0.4g; CHOL 53mg; IRON 1.9mg; SODIUM 1,076mg; CALC 23mg

As important as they are, it's not the candles, the silverware, the centerpiece, or even the side dishes that your guests are going to focus on. It's undoubtedly the holiday ham or turkey that will receive the most attention. For an easy, quick, and impressive presentation, garnish the serving platter with a variety of fresh herbs.

Gingersnap-Crusted
Ham with Apricot-
Mustard Sauce

Asparagus, Ham, and Fontina Bread Puddings

These savory bread puddings are baked and served in individual custard cups. "While individually proportioned and simple, they're a very rich-tasting holiday dish," Test Kitchens Director Vanessa Johnson says.

1 pound asparagus
1 teaspoon olive oil
1 cup chopped onion
Cooking spray
5 (1.4-ounce) slices firm white sandwich bread
 (such as Pepperidge Farm Farmhouse), cut into
 ½-inch cubes
½ cup chopped reduced-fat ham
¾ cup (3 ounces) shredded fontina cheese
1⅔ cups fat-free milk
¾ cup egg substitute
2 teaspoons Dijon mustard
½ teaspoon dried basil
¼ teaspoon salt
¼ teaspoon black pepper

1. Cut a 3-inch tip from each asparagus spear, reserving stalks for another use. Cut asparagus tips into ½-inch pieces.

2. Heat olive oil in a nonstick skillet over medium-high heat. Add chopped onion, and sauté 5 minutes or until onion is tender, stirring frequently. Add asparagus; cover and cook 4 minutes, stirring once. Remove from heat, and set aside.

3. Coat 6 (10-ounce) custard cups or ramekins with cooking spray; place in a large baking pan. Place bread cubes evenly into custard cups. Top evenly with asparagus mixture, ham, and cheese. Combine milk and remaining 5 ingredients, stirring with a whisk. Pour evenly into custard cups, and let stand 20 minutes.

4. Preheat oven to 375°.

5. Add hot water to pan to a depth of 1 inch. Cover and bake at 375° for 30 minutes. Uncover and bake for an additional 15 minutes. Let stand 10 minutes before serving. Yield: 6 servings.

CALORIES 237 (30% from fat); FAT 7.9g (sat 3.3g, mono 2.4g, poly 0.9g); PROTEIN 16.4g; CARB 26.2g; FIBER 3.9g; CHOL 23mg; IRON 2mg; SODIUM 624mg; CALC 223mg

Asparagus, Ham,
and Fontina Bread
Puddings

Venison Medallions with Cherry-Wine Sauce

Talk about a quick holiday dish—this entrée is cooked on the stovetop and can be ready in less than 45 minutes! You can substitute 4-ounce beef tenderloin fillets for the venison steaks.

½   cup port or other sweet red wine
½   cup dried tart cherries
½   teaspoon dried thyme
1   (14¼-ounce) can fat-free beef broth
16   whole allspice
16   juniper berries (optional)
½   teaspoon salt, divided
⅛   teaspoon black pepper
6   (4-ounce) venison tenderloin steaks (about 1½ inches thick)
   Cooking spray
2   teaspoons butter
½   cup minced shallots
2   garlic cloves, minced
2   teaspoons water
1   teaspoon cornstarch

1. Combine first 4 ingredients in a small saucepan. Bring to a boil. Remove from heat. Cover; set aside.
2. Place allspice and, if desired, juniper berries in a spice or coffee grinder; process until finely ground. Sprinkle ½ teaspoon allspice mixture, ¼ teaspoon salt, and pepper over venison. Coat a large nonstick skillet with cooking spray. Melt butter in skillet over medium-high heat. Add venison; cook 5 minutes on each side or until browned. Reduce heat to medium; cook 3 minutes on each side or until desired degree of doneness. Remove venison from skillet; keep warm.
3. Add shallots and garlic to skillet; sauté 2 minutes. Add cherry mixture, 1 teaspoon allspice mixture, and ¼ teaspoon salt; bring to a boil. Reduce heat; simmer, uncovered, until reduced to 1 cup (about 3 minutes). Combine water and cornstarch; add to cherry mixture. Bring to a boil; cook, stirring constantly, 1 minute. Serve sauce with venison. Yield: 6 servings (serving size: 3 ounces venison and 2 tablespoons sauce).
Note: You may substitute ½ cup cranberry juice for the port, if desired.

CALORIES 208 (18% from fat); FAT 4.1g (sat 1.9g, mono 1.1g, poly 0.6g); PROTEIN 27.3g; CARB 11.9g; FIBER 0.9g; CHOL 99mg; IRON 4.4mg; SODIUM 368mg; CALC 19mg

Loin of Venison with Wild-Mushroom Sauce

¾   teaspoon salt, divided
¼   teaspoon black pepper, divided
1   (2-pound) boneless venison loin
1   tablespoon butter
3   cups sliced shiitake mushroom caps (about ½ pound)
¼   cup minced shallots
¾   cup port or other sweet red wine
1   cup beef broth
2¼   teaspoons cornstarch

1. Preheat oven to 500°. Sprinkle ½ teaspoon salt and ⅛ teaspoon pepper over venison loin. Place venison on a broiler pan. Insert meat thermometer into thickest portion of loin. Bake at 500° for 20 minutes or until thermometer registers 160° (medium). Remove from oven. Cover venison loosely with foil; let stand 10 minutes.
2. Melt butter in a large nonstick skillet over medium-high heat. Add sliced mushrooms and shallots, and sauté 4 minutes or until tender. Add ¼ teaspoon salt, ⅛ teaspoon pepper, and wine, and cook 2 minutes. Combine broth and cornstarch, stirring well; add to mushroom mixture in skillet. Bring to a boil, and cook 1 minute, stirring constantly. Remove from heat. Cut venison into ¼-inch-thick slices, and serve with sauce. Yield: 8 servings (serving size: 3 ounces venison and ¼ cup sauce).

CALORIES 162 (40% from fat); FAT 4.3g (sat 2.0g, mono 1.1g, poly 0.6g); PROTEIN 26.9g; CARB 2.9g; FIBER 0.3g; CHOL 99mg; IRON 4.7mg; SODIUM 389mg; CALC 13mg

Venison Menu

serves 6

Venison Medallions with Cherry-Wine Sauce
(recipe at left)

Rice pilaf

Rutabaga gratin

Steamed asparagus

Classic Pumpkin Pie (recipe on page 31)

Roasted Chicken with Clementine-and-Cranberry Sauce

If you're looking for a quick dinner solution, you can make the sauce and serve it over sautéed chicken breasts.

1	(4-pound) chicken
½	teaspoon kosher salt
¼	teaspoon black pepper
1	clementine, quartered
½	cup fresh orange juice (about 2 oranges)
½	cup fresh cranberries
2	tablespoons sugar
½	cup fat-free, less-sodium chicken broth
1½	teaspoons cornstarch
2	tablespoons Madeira wine or water
2	cups clementine sections (about 6 clementines)

1. Preheat oven to 450°.

2. Remove and discard giblets and neck from chicken. Rinse chicken with cold water; pat dry. Trim excess fat. Starting at neck cavity, loosen skin from breast and drumsticks by inserting fingers, gently pushing between skin and meat. Rub salt and pepper under loosened skin, and sprinkle in body cavity. Place clementine quarters in cavity. Place chicken, breast side down, on a broiler pan. Insert a meat thermometer into meaty part of thigh, making sure not to touch bone. Bake at 450° for 25 minutes. Reduce oven temperature to 350°. Turn chicken breast side up; bake at 350° for 1 hour or until thermometer registers 180°. Cover chicken loosely with foil; let stand 10 minutes. Discard skin.

3. Place orange juice, cranberries, and sugar in a medium saucepan. Cook over medium-high heat 5 minutes or until cranberries pop; add broth. Combine cornstarch and wine in a small dish; stir into cranberry mixture. Bring to a boil; cook 1 minute, stirring constantly. Remove from heat; stir in clementine sections. Yield: 4 servings (serving size: 3 ounces chicken and ½ cup sauce).

CALORIES 285 (21% from fat); FAT 6.6g (sat 1.8g, mono 2.3g, poly 1.5g); PROTEIN 26.2g; CARB 28.8g; FIBER 3.6g; CHOL 76mg; IRON 1.3mg; SODIUM 275mg; CALC 38mg

Roast Chicken Provençale

Thinking of roasting a chicken? Think big. Large roasters have a greater proportion of meat to bone, and leftovers are a time-saver. Look for herbes de Provence, a combination of dried herbs (basil, lavender, marjoram, rosemary, sage, savory, and thyme), in the spice section of supermarkets. Rubbing the paste under the skin means that even though the skin is discarded, the meat keeps the flavor.

2	tablespoons dried herbes de Provence
2	tablespoons fresh lemon juice
2	teaspoons kosher salt
½	teaspoon black pepper
3	garlic cloves, minced
1	(7-pound) roasting chicken
1	small onion, quartered
	Cooking spray
⅓	cup Sauvignon Blanc or other dry white wine
⅔	cup fat-free, less-sodium chicken broth
1	tablespoon chilled butter, cut into small pieces

1. Preheat oven to 400°.

2. Combine first 5 ingredients in a small bowl; mash to a paste consistency.

3. Remove and discard giblets and neck from chicken. Rinse chicken with cold water; pat dry. Trim excess fat. Starting at neck cavity, loosen skin from breast and drumsticks by inserting fingers, gently pushing between skin and meat.

4. Rub seasoning mixture under loosened skin. Place onion in body cavity. Lift wing tips up and over back; tuck under chicken. Tie legs together with string.

5. Place chicken, breast side up, on a broiler pan coated with cooking spray. Insert a meat thermometer into breast, making sure not to touch bone. Bake at 400° for 1 hour and 20 minutes or until thermometer registers 180°. Remove chicken from pan. Cover with foil, and let stand 10 minutes. Discard skin.

6. Place a zip-top plastic bag inside a 2-cup glass measure. Pour pan drippings into bag; let stand 10 minutes (fat will rise to top). Seal bag; carefully snip off 1 bottom corner. Drain drippings into pan, stopping before fat layer reaches opening; discard fat.

7. Place pan over medium-high heat. Stir in wine, scraping pan to loosen browned bits. Add broth; bring to a boil. Cook until reduced to ⅔ cup (about 3 minutes). Remove from heat; add butter, stirring with a whisk until well blended. Serve sauce with chicken. Yield: 12 servings (serving size: about 4 ounces chicken and about 1 tablespoon sauce).

CALORIES 204 (37% from fat); FAT 8.4g (sat 2.6g, mono 3.1g, poly 1.7g); PROTEIN 28.2g; CARB 1g; FIBER 0.3g; CHOL 86mg; IRON 1.7mg; SODIUM 433mg; CALC 25mg

Spicy Apple-Glazed
Chick 'n' Grits Gorgonzola

Spicy Apple-Glazed Chick 'n' Grits Gorgonzola

"Sweet apple butter paired with zesty, pungent Gorgonzola makes this a great recipe idea for a holiday brunch," Assistant Food Stylist
Kathleen Kanen says. "It can easily be prepared in less than an hour and kept warm by covering until company arrives."

4   (4-ounce) skinless, boneless chicken breast halves
Cooking spray
¼   cup apple butter
¼   cup spicy brown mustard
¼   teaspoon salt
¼   teaspoon ground red pepper
⅛   teaspoon black pepper
Gorgonzola Cheese Grits
2   tablespoons chopped green onions

1. Preheat oven to 350°.
2. Place each chicken breast half between 2 sheets of heavy-duty plastic wrap; flatten to ½-inch thickness using a meat mallet or rolling pin. Place chicken in a baking pan coated with cooking spray.
3. Combine apple butter, mustard, salt, red pepper, and black pepper; brush over chicken. Bake at 350° for 20 minutes. Cut chicken into ½-inch-thick slices.
4. Spoon Gorgonzola Cheese Grits into each of 4 shallow serving bowls. Top with chicken, and sprinkle with green

onions. Yield: 4 servings (serving size: 1 cup grits, 3 ounces chicken, and 1½ teaspoons green onions).

(Totals include Gorgonzola Cheese Grits) CALORIES 371 (30% from fat); FAT 12.4g (sat 6.2g, mono 3.3g, poly 0.9g); PROTEIN 41.8g; CARB 21.5g; FIBER 1g; CHOL 94mg; IRON 6.8mg; SODIUM 1,209mg; CALC 190mg

Gorgonzola Cheese Grits

2   (14-ounce) cans fat-free, less-sodium chicken broth
¾   cup uncooked quick-cooking grits
1   cup (4 ounces) crumbled Gorgonzola cheese
⅓   cup fat-free sour cream
¼   teaspoon ground nutmeg
¼   teaspoon freshly ground black pepper

1. Bring broth to a boil in a medium saucepan; add grits, stirring constantly. Reduce heat to low; simmer, covered, 5 minutes or until thick, stirring occasionally. Remove from heat; stir in cheese and remaining ingredients. Yield: 4 cups (serving size: 1 cup).

CALORIES 182 (41% from fat); FAT 8.3g (sat 5.3g, mono 2.2g, poly 0.2g); PROTEIN 14.4g; CARB 11.9g; FIBER 0.7g; CHOL 21mg; IRON 5.6mg; SODIUM 795mg; CALC 154mg

Pan-Grilled Chicken with Cranberry Salsa

Just because the flavors in this dish are complex doesn't mean the preparation is. You can have this seasonal Tex-Mex dish on the table in less than 25 minutes, making it the perfect casual weeknight meal.

4   (4-ounce) skinless, boneless chicken breast halves
¼   teaspoon salt
⅛   teaspoon black pepper
⅓   cup minced green onions
1   tablespoon minced pickled jalapeño peppers
2   teaspoons balsamic vinegar
1   (12-ounce) container cranberry-orange sauce (such as Ocean Spray)
2   tablespoons minced fresh cilantro, divided
1½ tablespoons lime juice, divided
2   tablespoons ⅓-less-fat cream cheese

1. Place each chicken breast half between 2 sheets of heavy-duty plastic wrap. Flatten to ½-inch thickness using a meat mallet or rolling pin. Sprinkle with salt and black pepper. Heat grill pan over medium-high heat; cook chicken 5 minutes on each side or until done. Keep warm.
2. Combine onions, jalapeño, vinegar, and cranberry sauce in a medium bowl. Stir in 1 tablespoon cilantro and 1 tablespoon lime juice.
3. Combine 1 tablespoon cilantro, 1½ teaspoons lime juice, and cream cheese in a small bowl; stir well to combine. Spoon cranberry salsa evenly onto each of 4 individual plates. Place chicken on top of salsa; top with a dollop of cilantro cream. Serve immediately. Yield: 4 servings (serving size: 1 chicken breast half, ⅓ cup salsa, and 2 teaspoons cilantro cream).

CALORIES 292 (8% from fat); FAT 2.5g (sat 0.9g, mono 0.6g, poly 0.4g); PROTEIN 26.9g; CARB 38g; FIBER 0.3g; CHOL 69mg; IRON 1.2mg; SODIUM 397mg; CALC 26mg

Pan-Grilled Chicken with Cranberry Salsa

Herbed Chicken Parmesan

Herbed Chicken Parmesan

If you're needing a change from traditional holiday fare, try this Italian-inspired poultry dish.

⅓   cup (1½ ounces) grated fresh Parmesan cheese, divided
¼   cup dry breadcrumbs
1   tablespoon minced fresh parsley
½   teaspoon dried basil
¼   teaspoon salt, divided
1   large egg white, lightly beaten
1   pound chicken breast tenders
1   tablespoon butter
1½ cups bottled fat-free tomato-basil pasta sauce
2   teaspoons balsamic vinegar
¼   teaspoon black pepper
⅓   cup (1½ ounces) shredded provolone cheese

1. Preheat broiler.
2. Combine 2 tablespoons Parmesan, breadcrumbs, parsley, basil, and ⅛ teaspoon salt in a shallow dish. Place egg white in a shallow dish. Dip each chicken tender in egg white; dredge in breadcrumb mixture. Melt butter in a large nonstick skillet over medium-high heat. Add chicken; cook 3 minutes on each side or until done. Set aside.
3. Combine ⅛ teaspoon salt, pasta sauce, vinegar, and pepper in a microwave-safe bowl. Cover with plastic wrap; vent. Microwave mixture at HIGH 2 minutes or until thoroughly heated. Pour over chicken in pan. Sprinkle evenly with remaining Parmesan and provolone cheese. Wrap handle of pan with foil; broil 2 minutes or until cheese melts. Yield: 4 servings.

CALORIES 308 (30% from fat); FAT 10.4g (sat 5.7g, mono 3g, poly 0.6g); PROTEIN 35.9g; CARB 16.2g; FIBER 1.8g; CHOL 88mg; IRON 2.3mg; SODIUM 808mg; CALC 249mg

Chicken and Basmati Rice Pilau with Saffron, Spinach, and Cardamom

The cardamom in the pilaf is left whole, so the pods need to be bruised or crushed slightly to allow the flavor to escape.
Serve this dish with both yogurt and cilantro relish flavored with a little crushed garlic and ground, toasted cumin.
If you don't have a nonstick skillet large enough to hold 10 cups, use a Dutch oven.

1½ cups uncooked basmati rice

¾ cup dried lentils

Cooking spray

10 skinless, boneless chicken thighs (about 1¼ pounds)

2 cups vertically sliced onion

2 teaspoons chopped peeled fresh ginger

1 cup shredded carrot

4 cardamom pods, lightly crushed

½ teaspoon grated orange rind

½ cup fresh orange juice (about 2 oranges)

1 teaspoon salt

¼ teaspoon black pepper

2½ cups warm fat-free, less-sodium chicken broth

⅛ teaspoon saffron threads, crushed

1 (6-ounce) package fresh baby spinach, coarsely chopped

1 teaspoon butter

½ cup blanched almonds

1. Cover rice with cold water. Let stand 20 minutes. Drain and rinse with cold water. Drain.

2. Sort and rinse lentils. Place lentils in a small saucepan; cover with water 2 inches above lentils. Bring to a boil. Reduce heat; simmer 20 minutes or until almost tender. Drain.

3. Heat a large nonstick skillet coated with cooking spray over medium-high heat. Add chicken; cook 4 minutes on each side or until lightly browned. Remove chicken from pan. Add onion and ginger to pan, and sauté 7 minutes or until tender. Add carrot and cardamom; sauté 2 minutes. Return chicken to pan. Add rice, lentils, rind, juice, salt, and pepper. Combine broth and saffron; stir until saffron is dissolved. Add saffron mixture to pan; bring to a simmer. Cover and cook 15 minutes or until rice is almost tender and liquid is absorbed. Stir in spinach. Remove from heat. Cover with a towel; place lid over towel. Let stand 10 minutes.

4. Melt butter in a small skillet over medium heat. Add almonds; cook 5 minutes or until lightly browned, stirring frequently. Sprinkle almonds over chicken mixture. Yield: 5 servings (serving size: 2 cups).

CALORIES 601 (19% from fat); FAT 12.7g (sat 2.2g, mono 6.1g, poly 2.8g); PROTEIN 40.1g; CARB 85.8g; FIBER 14.5g; CHOL 96mg; IRON 7.4mg; SODIUM 837mg; CALC 119mg

Chicken and Basmati Rice
Pilau with Saffron,
Spinach, and Cardamom

Chicken Braised with Figs on Wilted Escarole

Chicken:

  1   cup port or other sweet red wine
  1   cup dried figs, halved
  ¼   cup all-purpose flour
  ¾   teaspoon salt, divided
  ½   teaspoon freshly ground black pepper, divided
  4   chicken thighs (about 1 pound), skinned
  4   chicken drumsticks (about 1 pound), skinned
  2   chicken breast halves (about 1 pound), skinned
  2   tablespoons olive oil, divided
  ¾   pound small shallots, peeled
  1   tablespoon minced fresh thyme
  ½   teaspoon ground fennel seeds
  2   garlic cloves, crushed
  1   (14-ounce) can fat-free, less-sodium chicken broth
  ¼   cup honey
  ¼   cup cider vinegar

Escarole:

  1   tablespoon olive oil
1½   pounds escarole, coarsely chopped
  ½   cup fat-free, less-sodium chicken broth
  ¼   teaspoon salt
  ¼   teaspoon freshly ground black pepper

1. Preheat oven to 350°.

2. To prepare chicken, bring port to a boil in a medium saucepan. Add figs; remove from heat. Let stand, covered, 30 minutes or until soft.

3. Combine flour, ½ teaspoon salt, and ¼ teaspoon pepper in a large zip-top plastic bag; add chicken. Seal; shake to coat. Heat 1 tablespoon oil in a large Dutch oven over medium-high heat. Add half of chicken to pan; cook 5 minutes on each side or until lightly browned. Remove chicken from pan. Repeat procedure with 1 tablespoon oil and remaining chicken. Return chicken to pan. Add fig mixture, ¼ teaspoon salt, ¼ teaspoon pepper, shallots, and next 4 ingredients. Cover; bake at 350° for 25 minutes. Stir in honey. Bake, uncovered, at 350° for 25 minutes. Stir in vinegar; place mixture in a large bowl. Cover; keep warm.

4. To prepare escarole, heat 1 tablespoon oil in pan over medium heat. Add escarole; cook 5 minutes or until escarole begins to wilt. Add ½ cup broth; cover and cook 5 minutes or until tender. Stir in ¼ teaspoon salt and ¼ teaspoon pepper. Serve chicken mixture over escarole. Yield: 6 servings (serving size: 1 breast half or 1 thigh and 1 drumstick, about ¾ cup sauce, and about ½ cup escarole).

CALORIES 423 (24% from fat); FAT 11.4g (sat 2g, mono 6.2g, poly 1.8g); PROTEIN 33.9g; CARB 48.7g; FIBER 8.6g; CHOL 97mg; IRON 4mg; SODIUM 694mg; CALC 151mg

Green Chile-Chicken Casserole

1⅓   cups fat-free, less-sodium chicken broth
  1   cup canned chopped green chiles, drained
  1   cup chopped onion
  1   cup fat-free sour cream
  ¾   teaspoon salt
  ½   teaspoon ground cumin
  ½   teaspoon freshly ground black pepper
  2   (10½-ounce) cans condensed 98%-fat-free cream of chicken soup, undiluted (such as Campbell's)
  1   garlic clove, minced
Cooking spray
24   (6-inch) corn tortillas
  4   cups shredded cooked chicken breast (about 1 pound)
  2   cups (8 ounces) finely shredded sharp Cheddar cheese

1. Preheat oven to 350°.

2. Combine first 9 ingredients in a large saucepan, stirring with a whisk. Bring to a boil, stirring constantly. Remove from heat.

3. Spread 1 cup soup mixture in a 13 x 9-inch baking dish coated with cooking spray. Arrange 6 tortillas over soup mixture, and top with 1 cup chicken and ½ cup cheese. Repeat layers 3 times, ending with cheese. Spread remaining soup mixture over cheese. Bake at 350° for 30 minutes or until bubbly. Yield: 12 servings (serving size: about ¾ cup).

CALORIES 335 (29% from fat); FAT 10.8g (sat 5.9g, mono 2.7g, poly 1.2g); PROTEIN 23.9g; CARB 34.3g; FIBER 3.2g; CHOL 66mg; IRON 1.5mg; SODIUM 693mg; CALC 270mg

the gift of dinner

Green Chile-Chicken Casserole (recipe above) is perfect to give as a gift to a neighbor or friend. You can always give the casserole in a glass dish, making the dish a part of the gift, too. But if you're looking for a less expensive route, purchase a set of disposable plastic or aluminum baking containers from your supermarket. You'll find that they're inexpensive, convenient, and made for baking in the oven.

Game Hens with Pesto Rub
and Roasted Potatoes

Game Hens with Pesto Rub and Roasted Potatoes

Golden roasted potatoes are a great match for the hens, which are
flavored with basil and Parmesan. Use kitchen shears or a sharp knife to split the hens.

4   cups loosely packed fresh basil leaves
⅓   cup (about 1½ ounces) grated fresh Parmesan cheese
1   tablespoon water
1   tablespoon olive oil
¼   teaspoon salt
⅛   teaspoon black pepper
2   garlic cloves, chopped
4   (22-ounce) Cornish hens
Cooking spray
7   cups small red potatoes, quartered (about 2 pounds)
1   tablespoon olive oil
½   teaspoon salt
¼   teaspoon black pepper
1   cup fat-free, less-sodium chicken broth
1   tablespoon water
1   teaspoon cornstarch
Basil sprigs (optional)

1. Preheat oven to 375°.

2. Combine first 7 ingredients in a food processor, and process until smooth.

3. Remove and discard giblets and necks from hens. Rinse hens with cold water; pat dry. Starting at neck cavity, loosen skin from breast and drumsticks by inserting fingers, gently pushing between skin and meat. Rub pesto under loosened skin. Gently press skin to secure. Lift wing tips up and over back; tuck under hens.

4. Place hens on a broiler pan coated with cooking spray. Insert a meat thermometer into meaty part of thigh, making sure not to touch bone.

5. Combine potatoes and next 3 ingredients, tossing well to coat. Arrange potatoes around hens; bake at 375° for 45 minutes or until thermometer registers 180° and potatoes are tender.

6. Remove hens and potatoes from pan, and cover loosely with foil. Let stand 10 minutes. Discard skin. Cut hens in half, and cover loosely with foil.

7. Place a zip-top plastic bag inside a 2-cup glass measure. Pour pan drippings into bag; let stand 10 minutes (fat will rise to top). Seal bag; carefully snip off 1 bottom corner of bag. Drain drippings into pan, stopping before fat layer reaches opening; discard fat.

8. Place pan over medium-high heat. Stir in broth, scraping pan to loosen browned bits. Combine 1 tablespoon water and cornstarch, stirring well with a whisk. Add to pan. Bring to a boil; cook until reduced to ½ cup (about 3 minutes). Serve sauce with hens and potatoes. Garnish with basil sprigs, if desired. Yield: 8 servings (serving size: ½ hen, about ¾ cup potatoes, and 1 tablespoon sauce).

CALORIES 299 (27% from fat); FAT 9g (sat 2.4g, mono 4.2g, poly 1.4g); PROTEIN 28.9g; CARB 25g; FIBER 3.1g; CHOL 113mg; IRON 2.8mg; SODIUM 434mg; CALC 120mg

Orange-Ginger Glazed Cornish Hens

Line your pan with foil for easy cleanup. Don't worry if the sweet glaze burns on the foil; it won't burn on the hens.
Cooking the hens and green beans in the oven together saves time and ensures that everything will be ready at once.

¾ cup fresh orange juice (about 3 oranges)
2 tablespoons minced peeled fresh ginger
2 tablespoons honey
1 tablespoon low-sodium soy sauce
1 tablespoon water
2 teaspoons cornstarch
2 (1½-pound) Cornish hens, skinned and halved
Cooking spray
½ teaspoon salt
½ teaspoon ground ginger

1. Preheat oven to 475°.

2. Combine first 4 ingredients in a small saucepan; bring to a boil. Combine water and cornstarch in a small bowl, stirring with a whisk. Add to juice mixture in pan, stirring with a whisk. Cook 2 minutes or until thick and glossy, stirring constantly.

3. Place hen halves, meaty sides up, on a foil-lined jelly-roll pan coated with cooking spray; sprinkle hen halves with salt and ground ginger. Spoon juice mixture evenly over hen halves.

4. Insert a meat thermometer into meaty part of thigh, making sure not to touch bone. Bake at 475° for 25 minutes or until thermometer registers 180°. Yield: 4 servings (serving size: 1 hen half).

CALORIES 188 (18% from fat); FAT 3.8g (sat 1g, mono 1.2g, poly 0.9g); PROTEIN 22.5g; CARB 15.6g; FIBER 0.3g; CHOL 99mg; IRON 1mg; SODIUM 487mg; CALC 19mg

Cornish Hens Menu

serves 4

Orange-Ginger Glazed Cornish Hens
(recipe at left)

Oven-roasted green beans*

Long-grain and wild rice blend

* Combine 1 pound green beans (trimmed), 2 teaspoons olive oil, ½ teaspoon salt, and ⅛ teaspoon black pepper. Arrange in a single layer on a baking sheet coated with cooking spray; place in oven on rack below hens. Bake at 475° for 10 minutes or until tender, turning once. Remove from oven; toss with 2 teaspoons fresh lemon juice.

Orange-Ginger Glazed
Cornish Hens

Herb-Roasted Turkey
with Cheese Grits

Herb-Roasted Turkey with Cheese Grits

12   thyme sprigs

1   rosemary sprig

1   sage sprig

2   tablespoons bottled minced garlic

2   tablespoons minced shallots

1   teaspoon freshly ground black pepper

1   (12-pound) fresh or frozen turkey, thawed

3   tablespoons fresh lemon juice

2   lemons, each cut in half

Cooking spray

Cheese Grits

1. Preheat oven to 350°.

2. Remove leaves from thyme sprigs to measure 2 tablespoons chopped; reserve stems. Remove leaves from rosemary sprig to measure 2 tablespoons chopped; reserve stem. Remove leaves from sage sprig to measure 2 tablespoons chopped; reserve stem. Combine chopped thyme, chopped rosemary, chopped sage, garlic, shallots, and pepper in a small bowl.

3. Remove and discard giblets and neck from turkey. Rinse turkey with cold water, and pat dry. Trim excess fat. Starting at neck cavity, loosen skin from breast and drumsticks by inserting fingers, gently pushing between skin and meat. Rub herb mixture under skin and sprinkle in body cavity. Drizzle lemon juice over skin. Place reserved stems and lemon halves in body cavity. Tie ends of legs with cord. Lift wing tips up and over back, and tuck under turkey.

4. Place turkey on a broiler pan coated with cooking spray or on a rack set in a shallow roasting pan. Insert a meat thermometer into meaty part of thigh, making sure not to touch bone. Bake at 350° for 3 hours or until thermometer registers 180° (cover turkey loosely with foil if it gets too brown). Remove turkey from oven. Cover loosely with foil; let stand 10 minutes before carving. Discard skin. Serve with Cheese Grits. Yield: 12 servings (serving size: 6 ounces turkey and about ½ cup Cheese Grits).

(Totals include Cheese Grits) CALORIES 354 (29% from fat); FAT 11.3g (sat 4.5g, mono 2.5g, poly 2.5g); PROTEIN 53.5g; CARB 6.6g; FIBER 0.6g; CHOL 138mg; IRON 5.8mg; SODIUM 406mg; CALC 140mg

Cheese Grits

4   cups water

1   cup uncooked quick-cooking grits

1   cup (4 ounces) shredded reduced-fat sharp Cheddar cheese

1   tablespoon butter

1½   teaspoons garlic powder

½   teaspoon dried thyme

½   teaspoon salt

1. Bring water to a boil in a medium saucepan, and gradually add grits, stirring constantly. Cover, reduce heat to low, and simmer 5 minutes or until thick, stirring occasionally. Remove grits from heat, and stir in shredded cheese and remaining ingredients. Yield: 12 servings (serving size: about ½ cup).

CALORIES 58 (43% from fat); FAT 2.8g (sat 1.7g, mono 0.8g, poly 0.1g); PROTEIN 3.4g; CARB 5.1g; FIBER 0.3g; CHOL 9mg; IRON 2.5mg; SODIUM 286mg; CALC 87mg

Cooking Light's
Ultimate Roasted Turkey

This nearly perfect recipe won the highest rating in our Test Kitchens.

¾   cup apple cider
 5   tablespoons dark corn syrup, divided
 1   (12-pound) fresh or frozen turkey, thawed
 1   tablespoon poultry seasoning
 1   tablespoon dried rubbed sage
 1   teaspoon salt
¼   teaspoon black pepper
 4   garlic cloves, sliced
 2   onions, quartered
 2   Golden Delicious apples, cored and quartered
Cooking spray
 1   teaspoon butter
 1   (14-ounce) can fat-free, less-sodium chicken broth
 1   tablespoon cornstarch

1. Preheat oven to 375°.
2. Combine cider and 4 tablespoons corn syrup in a small saucepan; bring to a boil. Remove from heat; set aside.
3. Remove and reserve giblets and neck from turkey. Rinse turkey with cold water; pat dry. Trim excess fat. Lift wing tips up and over back; tuck under turkey. Combine poultry seasoning, sage, salt, and pepper. Rub seasoning mixture into skin and body cavity. Place half each of garlic, onion quarters, and apple quarters into body cavity. Place turkey, breast side up, in a shallow roasting pan coated with cooking spray. Arrange remaining garlic, onion, and apple around turkey in pan. Insert a meat thermometer into meaty part of thigh, making sure not to touch bone. Bake at 375° for 45 minutes. Baste turkey with cider syrup; cover with foil. Bake at 375° an additional 2 hours and 15 minutes or until thermometer registers 180°, basting with cider syrup 4 times at regular intervals. Let stand 10 minutes. Discard skin. Remove turkey from pan, reserving drippings for sauce. Place turkey on a platter; keep warm.
4. Strain drippings through a colander into a bowl; discard solids. Place a zip-top plastic bag inside a 2-cup glass measure. Pour drippings into bag; let stand 10 minutes (fat will rise to top). Seal bag; carefully snip off 1 bottom corner. Drain drippings into a bowl, stopping before fat layer reaches opening; discard fat.
5. While turkey bakes, melt butter in a medium saucepan over medium-high heat. Add reserved giblets and neck; sauté 2 minutes on each side or until browned. Add broth, and bring to a boil. Cover, reduce heat, and simmer 45 minutes. Strain mixture through a colander into a bowl, discarding solids.

Reserve ¼ cup broth mixture. Combine remaining broth mixture with drippings in roasting pan on stovetop over medium heat, scraping pan to loosen browned bits. Combine ¼ cup reserved broth mixture and cornstarch; add to roasting pan. Add 1 tablespoon corn syrup, stirring with a whisk. Bring to a boil; cook 1 minute. Serve gravy with turkey (gravy will be dark and thin). Yield: 12 servings (serving size: 6 ounces turkey and about 3 tablespoons gravy).

CALORIES 331 (24% from fat); FAT 8.8g (sat 3g, mono 1.9g, poly 2.5g); PROTEIN 50.4g; CARB 9.4g; FIBER 0.1g; CHOL 130mg; IRON 3.2mg; SODIUM 396mg; CALC 52mg

Spice-Rubbed Smoked Turkey with Roasted-Pear Stuffing and Cranberry Syrup

While the turkey is smoking, closely monitor the grill to make sure the coals burn with continuous smoke. Never stuff a turkey before smoking it because the temperature inside the grill is less stable than in an oven.

 1   (12-pound) fresh or frozen turkey, thawed
 3   tablespoons brown sugar
 1   tablespoon kosher salt
 2   teaspoons ground cumin
 2   teaspoons dried oregano
 2   teaspoons dried rubbed sage
 2   teaspoons dry mustard
 1   teaspoon dried thyme
 1   teaspoon ground coriander
 6   hickory wood chunks
Cooking spray
Roasted-Pear Stuffing
Cranberry Syrup

1. To prepare turkey, remove and discard giblets and neck. Rinse turkey with cold water, and pat dry. Trim excess fat. Starting at neck cavity, loosen skin from breast and drumsticks by inserting fingers, gently pushing between skin and meat. Lift wing tips up and over back, and tuck under turkey. Place turkey on a jelly-roll pan. Combine brown sugar and next 7 ingredients. Rub seasoning mixture over and under skin. Cover turkey with plastic wrap; refrigerate 8 hours.
2. Soak wood chunks in water 1 hour, and drain well. Place a large disposable aluminum foil pan in center of bottom grill rack. Place 25 charcoal briquettes on each side of pan; ignite briquettes. Place wood chunks over hot coals. Coat top grill rack with cooking spray; place over foil pan and hot coals. Uncover turkey; remove from jelly-roll pan. Place on top rack over foil pan. Insert a meat thermometer into meaty part of

thigh, making sure not to touch bone. Cover and smoke turkey 2½ hours or until thermometer registers 180°, adding 8 additional briquettes to each side of drip pan every hour. (Cover turkey loosely with foil if it becomes too brown. Turkey will be a deep mahogany brown when done.) Discard skin. Serve with Roasted-Pear Stuffing and Cranberry Syrup. Yield: 12 servings (serving size: 6 ounces turkey, ⅔ cup stuffing, and 2½ tablespoons syrup).

Note: Try to resist checking the turkey too often. Lifting the grill lid decreases the temperature significantly.

(Totals include Roasted-Pear Stuffing and Cranberry Syrup) CALORIES 593 (21% from fat); FAT 14.1g (sat 3.5g, mono 5.4g, poly 3.1g); PROTEIN 54.3g; CARB 61.3g; FIBER 2.6g; CHOL 166mg; IRON 4.6mg; SODIUM 511mg; CALC 104mg

Spice-Rubbed Smoked Turkey with Roasted-Pear Stuffing and Cranberry Syrup

Roasted-Pear Stuffing

You may substitute apples for the pears. If you have pear brandy, by all means, use it in place of the sherry and brandy.

    2 teaspoons olive oil
    4 cups sliced peeled Bosc pear (about 3½ pounds)
    1 cup diced onion
    1 cup diced peeled celeriac (celery root)
    3 garlic cloves, minced
    ½ cup dry sherry
    ½ cup brandy
    5 cups (½-inch) cubed dense white bread (about 8 ounces)
    1 cup fat-free, less-sodium chicken broth
    ½ cup chopped hazelnuts, toasted
    2 teaspoons chopped fresh or ½ teaspoon dried thyme
    ½ teaspoon salt
    ¼ teaspoon freshly ground black pepper
    2 large eggs, lightly beaten

1. Preheat oven to 350°.

2. Heat oil in a large nonstick skillet over medium-high heat. Add pear slices, and cook, without stirring, 2 minutes or until golden brown. Carefully turn pear slices; cook 2 minutes or until golden brown. Add onion, celeriac, and garlic; sauté 3 minutes or until lightly browned. Add sherry and brandy, and cook until liquid almost evaporates. Remove from heat; cool.

3. Combine pear mixture, bread, and remaining ingredients in a large bowl, tossing gently. Spoon bread mixture into a 2-quart casserole. Cover with lid, and bake at 350° for 45 minutes or until thoroughly heated. Yield: 12 servings (serving size: ⅔ cup).

CALORIES 167 (30% from fat); FAT 5.6g (sat 0.8g, mono 3.6g, poly 0.7g); PROTEIN 4.2g; CARB 26.4g; FIBER 2.4g; CHOL 37mg; IRON 1.2mg; SODIUM 265mg; CALC 51mg

Cranberry Syrup

    1½ cups sugar
     1 (750-milliliter) bottle ruby port or other sweet red wine
     2 cups fresh or frozen cranberries
     1 tablespoon thawed orange juice concentrate
     1 teaspoon chopped peeled fresh ginger
     3 garlic cloves, chopped

1. Combine sugar and port in a Dutch oven. Bring to a boil, and cook 4 minutes or until sugar dissolves. Add cranberries, orange juice, ginger, and garlic, and cook over medium heat until reduced to 3 cups (about 20 minutes). Press cranberry mixture through a fine sieve over a bowl, discarding solids. Yield: 2 cups (serving size: 2½ tablespoons).

Note: Cranberry Syrup can be stored, covered, in the refrigerator for up to 1 week.

CALORIES 134 (0% from fat); FAT 0g; PROTEIN 0.2g; CARB 34.3g; FIBER 0.1g; CHOL 0mg; IRON 0.2mg; SODIUM 6mg; CALC 7mg

Tunisian-Spiced Turkey with Garlic Couscous and Harissa Gravy
(pictured on page 236)

This spicy entrée is cooked breast side down for 45 minutes and then flipped to finish cooking; this unusual procedure helps keep the breast meat moist. Prepare the spice paste and the yogurt mixture for the gravy up to 1 day ahead; store separately in the refrigerator. Use 1 teaspoon crushed red pepper in the gravy if you prefer milder heat.

Turkey:

1½ tablespoons black peppercorns
1 tablespoon whole cloves
1 tablespoon cardamom pods
1 tablespoon olive oil
1½ teaspoons ground cinnamon
1 teaspoon salt
½ teaspoon ground nutmeg
1 (12-pound) fresh or frozen turkey, thawed
Cooking spray
2 (14-ounce) cans fat-free, less-sodium chicken broth

Gravy:

⅓ cup water
2 tablespoons cornstarch
2 teaspoons coriander seeds
1 teaspoon caraway seeds
1 teaspoon cumin seeds
2 teaspoons crushed red pepper
2 red jalapeño or Fresno peppers, seeded and chopped
2 garlic cloves, minced
¾ cup plain low-fat yogurt
½ teaspoon salt
¼ teaspoon freshly ground black pepper

Couscous:

1 tablespoon olive oil
8 garlic cloves, crushed
1 cup water
2 (14-ounce) cans fat-free, less-sodium chicken broth
2½ cups uncooked couscous
½ cup dried currants
¼ cup chopped fresh flat-leaf parsley
¼ cup chopped fresh cilantro
½ teaspoon salt
¼ teaspoon freshly ground black pepper

1. Preheat oven to 400°.
2. To prepare turkey, place first 3 ingredients in a small skillet, and cook over medium-low heat 2 minutes or until toasted and fragrant, shaking pan frequently. Place peppercorn mixture in a spice or coffee grinder; process until finely ground. Place mixture in a small bowl. Stir in 1 tablespoon oil, cinnamon, 1 teaspoon salt, and nutmeg to form a paste.
3. Remove and discard giblets and neck from turkey. Rinse turkey with cold water; pat dry. Trim excess fat. Starting at neck cavity, loosen skin from breast and drumsticks by inserting fingers, gently pushing between skin and meat. Rub spice paste under loosened skin, and rub over breast and drumsticks. Lift wing tips up and over back; tuck under turkey.
4. Place turkey, breast side down, on rack of a broiler pan or roasting pan coated with cooking spray. Pour 2 cans broth into shallow roasting pan, and place rack in pan. Bake at 400° for 45 minutes. Carefully turn over (breast side up). Insert a meat thermometer into thigh, making sure not to touch bone. Bake 1 hour and 15 minutes or until thermometer registers 180°. Let stand 10 minutes.
5. To prepare gravy, place a zip-top plastic bag inside a 2-cup glass measure. Pour pan drippings into bag; let stand 10 minutes (fat will rise to the top). Seal bag; carefully snip off 1 bottom corner of bag. Drain drippings into a medium saucepan, stopping before fat layer reaches opening; discard fat. Bring to a boil. Reduce heat; simmer 5 minutes. Combine ⅓ cup water and cornstarch, stirring with a whisk. Stir cornstarch mixture into drippings; bring to a boil. Reduce heat; simmer 3 minutes or until slightly thick.
6. Place coriander, caraway, and cumin in a small skillet; cook over medium-low heat 2 minutes or until toasted and fragrant, shaking pan frequently. Place mixture in a spice or coffee grinder; process until finely ground. Add crushed red pepper, jalapeño, and 2 garlic cloves; process until a paste forms. Remove spice paste from grinder; combine spice paste and yogurt. Add yogurt mixture to drippings mixture; simmer 3 minutes. Stir in ½ teaspoon salt and ¼ teaspoon black pepper.
7. To prepare couscous, heat 1 tablespoon oil in a large nonstick saucepan over medium-high heat. Add 8 garlic cloves; sauté 1 minute. Add 1 cup water and 2 cans broth to pan; bring to a boil. Stir in couscous and currants. Cover and remove from heat; let stand 8 minutes. Fluff with a fork. Stir in parsley, cilantro, ½ teaspoon salt, and ¼ teaspoon black pepper. Serve turkey with couscous and gravy. Discard skin before serving. Yield: 12 servings (serving size: 6 ounces turkey, about ¾ cup couscous, and about 2 tablespoons gravy).

CALORIES 521 (24% from fat); FAT 13.7g (sat 4g, mono 4.6g, poly 3.2g); PROTEIN 57.8g; CARB 38.1g; FIBER 3.2g; CHOL 132mg; IRON 4.4mg; SODIUM 771mg; CALC 105mg

Mahogany Turkey Breast with Vegetable Gravy

The glaze gives a dark sheen to the turkey and lends a rich, caramelized flavor to the chunky gravy.
Roasting the turkey on vegetables instead of a rack keeps it moist and adds fragrance to the pan drippings,
which are the base of the gravy. For a pretty presentation, garnish the platter with a variety of herbs.

2 cups thinly sliced onion
1 cup sliced carrot
½ cup thinly sliced celery
Cooking spray
3 tablespoons low-sodium soy sauce, divided
1 (14-ounce) can fat-free, less-sodium chicken broth, divided
1 (5- to 6-pound) bone-in turkey breast
½ teaspoon black pepper
¼ teaspoon salt
2 tablespoons dry sherry or Madeira
2 tablespoons molasses
1 tablespoon all-purpose flour

1. Preheat oven to 350°.

2. Combine onion, carrot, and celery in a roasting pan coated with cooking spray. Add 1 tablespoon soy sauce and ⅔ cup broth; stir to coat. Place turkey breast, skin side up, on vegetables. Sprinkle with pepper and salt. Insert meat thermometer into turkey breast, making sure not to touch bone. Bake at 350° for 1 hour; baste turkey with 2 tablespoons pan drippings every 30 minutes. Combine 2 tablespoons soy sauce, sherry, and molasses. Bake turkey an additional 45 minutes or until thermometer registers 180°, brushing with sherry mixture every 15 minutes. Place turkey on a platter. Cover turkey loosely with foil; let stand 15 minutes. Do not discard drippings.

3. Combine remaining chicken broth and flour, stirring with a whisk until well blended to form a slurry. Strain onion mixture and drippings through a colander over a bowl, reserving both. Place a zip-top plastic bag inside a 2-cup glass measure. Pour drippings into bag; let stand 10 minutes (fat will rise to the top). Seal bag; carefully snip off 1 bottom corner of bag. Drain drippings into a medium saucepan, stopping before fat layer reaches opening; discard fat. Add reserved onion mixture to pan; stir in slurry. Bring to a boil; reduce heat and simmer 5 minutes. Serve turkey with gravy. Yield: 8 servings (serving size: 6 ounces turkey and 3 tablespoons gravy).

CALORIES 336 (23% from fat); FAT 8.6g (sat 2.8g, mono 1.8g, poly 2.5g); PROTEIN 51.8g; CARB 9.6g; FIBER 1.2g; CHOL 129mg; IRON 3.6mg; SODIUM 543mg; CALC 70mg

Mahogany Turkey Breast
with Vegetable Gravy

Make-Ahead Turkey Breast with Herb Stuffing, Vanilla Sweet Potatoes, and steamed broccoli

Make-Ahead Turkey Breast with Herb Stuffing and Vanilla Sweet Potatoes

This turkey dinner from George Bernas, chef at Brandywine Inn in Dayton, Ohio, is the ultimate make-ahead meal. The turkey is poached the day before, and then it's seasoned and reheated in an oven the day it's served.

Stock:

- 4 quarts water
- 1 cup (2-inch-thick) slices carrot
- ½ cup (1-inch-thick) slices celery
- 1 teaspoon dried thyme
- ¼ teaspoon black pepper
- 3 garlic cloves
- 3 bay leaves
- 2 tomatoes, quartered
- 1 onion, quartered
- ½ lemon
- 1 (6-pound) whole turkey breast, skinned

Turkey:

- 1 teaspoon olive oil
- ½ teaspoon dried thyme
- ¼ teaspoon salt
- ¼ teaspoon garlic powder
- ¼ teaspoon black pepper

Stuffing:

- ¼ cup butter
- 1 cup diced onion
- 1 cup diced celery
- 16 cups (1-inch) cubed stale bread (about 1½ pounds)
- 2 teaspoons poultry seasoning
- 1 teaspoon dried thyme
- ½ teaspoon salt
- ½ teaspoon garlic powder
- ½ teaspoon dried tarragon
- ½ teaspoon dried rubbed sage
- ¼ teaspoon black pepper

Gravy:

- ¼ cup butter
- ⅓ cup all-purpose flour

Remaining Ingredient:

Vanilla Sweet Potatoes

1. To prepare stock, combine first 10 ingredients in a large stockpot. Bring to a boil; add turkey. Return to a boil; reduce heat, and simmer 1½ hours or until turkey reaches 180° (use an instant-read thermometer). Carefully remove turkey from stock. Cover turkey; refrigerate. Strain stock through a colander into a large bowl; discard solids, and return stock to pot. Reduce heat; continue to simmer stock until reduced to 2 quarts (about 1½ hours). Cover and chill stock 8 hours. Skim fat from surface of stock, if necessary.

2. Preheat oven to 250°.

3. To prepare turkey, rub turkey with oil. Sprinkle with ½ teaspoon thyme, ¼ teaspoon salt, ¼ teaspoon garlic powder, and ¼ teaspoon pepper. Wrap turkey in heavy-duty plastic wrap and foil (double-wrapping helps retain moisture when reheating). Bake at 250° for 2 hours or until thoroughly heated.

4. To prepare stuffing, melt ¼ cup butter in a large Dutch oven over medium-high heat. Add diced onion and diced celery; sauté 3 minutes. Stir in bread cubes and next 7 ingredients. Stir in 2½ cups turkey stock. Place in a 13 x 9-inch baking dish. Bake at 250° for 1 hour and 55 minutes along with turkey as it is reheating.

5. While turkey and stuffing cook, prepare gravy. Melt ¼ cup butter in a large saucepan over medium heat. Stir in flour; reduce heat, and cook 15 minutes or until lightly browned. Gradually add reserved 5½ cups turkey stock, stirring with a whisk until blended. Bring to a boil; reduce heat, and simmer until reduced to 3 cups (about 2 hours).

6. Uncover turkey; remove turkey breast halves from bone. Slice turkey, and serve with stuffing, gravy, and Vanilla Sweet Potatoes. Yield: 6 servings (serving size: 5 ounces turkey, about 1⅓ cups stuffing, ½ cup gravy, and ⅔ cup Vanilla Sweet Potatoes).

(Totals include Vanilla Sweet Potatoes) CALORIES 945 (24% from fat); FAT 25.7g (sat 13.8g, mono 7.8g, poly 2.3g); PROTEIN 64.9g; CARB 110.5g; FIBER 8g; CHOL 197mg; IRON 7.9mg; SODIUM 1,262mg; CALC 254mg

Vanilla Sweet Potatoes

- 2 pounds sweet potatoes
- ¾ cup 1% low-fat milk
- ¼ cup packed brown sugar
- 2 tablespoons vanilla extract
- 2 tablespoons butter, softened

1. Pierce potatoes with a fork, and arrange in a circle on paper towels in microwave oven. Microwave at HIGH 10 minutes or until tender, rearranging potatoes after 5 minutes. Wrap in a towel; let stand 5 minutes. Peel and mash potatoes. Combine potato, milk, and remaining ingredients. Place in a 1-quart casserole; cover and microwave at MEDIUM (50% power) 7 minutes or until thoroughly heated. Yield: 6 servings (serving size: ⅔ cup).

CALORIES 241 (17% from fat); FAT 4.6g (sat 2.7g, mono 1.2g, poly 0.4g); PROTEIN 3.5g; CARB 44.6g; FIBER 4.5g; CHOL 12mg; IRON 1mg; SODIUM 77mg; CALC 78mg

Sautéed Duck Breast with Cherry-Pistachio Salsa

Duck is the only poultry we recommend serving medium-rare. If you cook it past that, it will lack flavor and be slightly tough.

1½ cups dried sweet or tart cherries (about 8 ounces)
1½ cups boiling water
 1 dried chipotle chile
 ½ cup shelled dry-roasted pistachios, coarsely chopped
 ⅓ cup finely chopped red onion
 ¼ cup chopped fresh cilantro
 2 tablespoons fresh lime juice
 1 teaspoon chili powder
 1 teaspoon honey
 1 jalapeño pepper, seeded and finely chopped
1¼ teaspoons salt, divided
 1 teaspoon black pepper
 8 (6-ounce) boneless duck breast halves, skinned
 1 teaspoon vegetable oil
Cooking spray

1. Combine first 3 ingredients in a large bowl; let stand 30 minutes. Drain well; discard chile. Combine cherries, pistachios, and next 6 ingredients. Stir in ¼ teaspoon salt.
2. Sprinkle 1 teaspoon salt and pepper over duck. Heat oil in a large nonstick skillet coated with cooking spray over medium-high heat. Add duck; sauté 6 minutes on each side or until desired degree of doneness. Serve with salsa. Yield: 8 servings (serving size: 1 duck breast half and about ⅓ cup salsa).

CALORIES 354 (29% from fat); FAT 11.4g (sat 2.7g, mono 4g, poly 2.4g); PROTEIN 37.1g; CARB 23.1g; FIBER 3.3g; CHOL 131mg; IRON 8.4mg; SODIUM 469mg; CALC 32mg

---

Thanksgiving with a Twist Menu

serves 8

Sautéed Duck Breast with Cherry-Pistachio Salsa
(recipe above)

Blue Corn Bread Dressing (recipe on page 293)

Roasted Asparagus with Balsamic Browned Butter
(recipe on page 276)

Molasses Cake with Lemon Cream Cheese Frosting
(recipe on page 306)

Wine Note: *Pinot Noir is just the ticket alongside duck. And with dessert, try tawny port, with flavors of vanilla, brown sugar, and roasted nuts.*

Honey-Basted Duck with Balsamic Lentils

Fall-off-the-bone tenderness and a Provençal sweetness are the hallmarks of this dish. Because duck has a thick layer of fat that melts as it cooks, drain the roasting pan a couple of times during cooking. Allow the herbs to penetrate the meat overnight for the best flavor—but the dish will still be good if you don't have time to do so.

Duck:
 1 tablespoon chopped fresh or 1 teaspoon dried thyme
 1 tablespoon dried herbes de Provence
 2 teaspoons freshly ground black pepper
 1 teaspoon salt
 3 garlic cloves, minced
 2 (5-pound) whole ducks
 ½ cup honey
 2 tablespoons balsamic vinegar
 1 tablespoon dried herbes de Provence

Lentils:
 1 shallot, peeled and cut in half
 2 whole cloves
 4 cups water
 2 cups petite green lentils
 2 garlic cloves, peeled
 1 cup balsamic vinegar
 1 tablespoon Dijon mustard
 ¼ teaspoon salt
 1 teaspoon olive oil
 1 cup finely chopped shallots
 ½ cup finely chopped carrot
 2 teaspoons chopped fresh thyme
 ¼ teaspoon freshly ground black pepper
Thyme sprig (optional)

1. To prepare duck, combine first 5 ingredients. Remove and discard giblets and necks from ducks. Cut off wing tips. Rinse ducks with cold water; pat dry. Trim excess fat. Starting at neck cavity, loosen skin from breast and drumsticks by inserting fingers, gently pushing between skin and meat. Rub herb mixture under loosened skin; rub over breast and drumsticks. Cover and refrigerate 8 hours or overnight.
2. Preheat oven to 325°.
3. Combine honey, 2 tablespoons vinegar, and 1 tablespoon herbes de Provence; set aside.
4. Score duck skin several times with a paring knife (do not cut into meat). Place ducks in a roasting pan, breast side up. Cover pan tightly with foil. Bake at 325° for 1½ hours. Carefully remove ducks from pan. Drain and discard drippings from pan.

Carefully place ducks in pan, breast side down. Cover and bake at 325° for 1½ hours.

5. Carefully remove ducks from pan, and discard drippings. Cool ducks slightly. Remove and discard skin. Carefully place ducks in pan, breast side up. Baste with honey mixture. Bake, uncovered, at 325° for 30 minutes, basting every 10 minutes. Let stand 10 minutes. Reserve drumsticks. Remove remaining meat from bones; discard bones.

6. To prepare lentils, stud shallot halves with cloves. Combine shallot halves, water, lentils, and 2 garlic cloves in a large saucepan; bring to a boil. Cover, reduce heat, and simmer 20 minutes or until lentils are tender. Remove from heat; let stand 10 minutes. Drain and discard shallot halves.

7. Bring 1 cup vinegar to a boil in a small saucepan. Cook until reduced to ¼ cup (about 10 minutes). Stir in mustard and ¼ teaspoon salt; set aside.

8. Heat olive oil in a large nonstick skillet over medium-high heat. Add chopped shallots, carrot, 2 teaspoons thyme, and ¼ teaspoon pepper, and sauté for 3 minutes. Add shallot mixture and mustard mixture to lentils, and toss well. Place lentils on a platter. Arrange drumsticks around lentils, and top lentils with pulled meat. Garnish with a thyme sprig, if desired. Yield: 8 servings (serving size: about 4 ounces duck and ⅔ cup lentils).

CALORIES 498 (25% from fat); FAT 13.7g (sat 4.9g, mono 4.7g, poly 1.8g); PROTEIN 38.8g; CARB 55.8g; FIBER 8g; CHOL 101mg; IRON 6.9mg; SODIUM 518mg; CALC 101mg

Honey-Basted Duck with
Balsamic Lentils

Cranberry Sauce with
Apple Cider
(recipe on page 273)

side dishes

Complement your entrées and create

an impressive array of festive meals

with accompaniments that sparkle

with flavor.

Rustic Applesauce

A combination of sweet Braeburns and tart Granny Smiths gives this applesauce a pleasant balance—ideal for a fall harvest dinner. Mashing the apples creates a chunky sauce; for a smoother version, process part or all of the apple mixture in a food processor or blender. Substitute full-fat sour cream if your market doesn't carry crème fraîche.

   4   cups cubed peeled Braeburn or Pink Lady apple
   4   cups cubed peeled Granny Smith apple
   ½   cup packed brown sugar
   2   teaspoons grated lemon rind
   3   tablespoons fresh lemon juice
   1   teaspoon ground cinnamon
   1   teaspoon vanilla extract
Dash of salt
   2   tablespoons crème fraîche

1. Combine first 8 ingredients in a Dutch oven over medium heat. Cook 25 minutes or until apples are tender, stirring occasionally.
2. Remove from heat; mash to desired consistency with a fork or potato masher. Stir in crème fraîche. Serve warm or chilled. Yield: 7 servings (serving size: about ½ cup).

CALORIES 140 (12% from fat); FAT 1.8g (sat 1g, mono 0.5g, poly 0.2g); PROTEIN 0.3g; CARB 32.5g; FIBER 2.3g; CHOL 3mg; IRON 0.5mg; SODIUM 30mg; CALC 31mg

Baked Apples and Pears with Raisins

   2   medium peeled Golden Delicious apples, cored and each cut into 8 wedges
   2   medium peeled ripe pears, cored and each cut into 8 wedges
   ¼   cup raisins
   ½   cup water
   2   tablespoons honey
   2   teaspoons grated orange rind
Orange rind strips (optional)

1. Preheat oven to 350°. Combine apple wedges, pear wedges, and raisins in a 1½-quart baking dish; toss well. Combine water, honey, and grated orange rind in a bowl, and stir well. Pour over apple mixture. Cover and bake at 350° for 45 minutes or until tender. Serve warm or chilled. Garnish with orange rind strips, if desired. Yield: 8 servings (serving size: ½ cup).

CALORIES 71 (4% from fat); FAT 0.3g; PROTEIN 0.5g; CARB 18.4g; FIBER 1.7g; CHOL 0mg; IRON 0.1mg; SODIUM 1mg; CALC 30mg

Cranberry Sauce with Apple Cider
(pictured at left)

Apple cider stands in for water to add dimension to this cranberry sauce, which is great with roasted ham, pork, or turkey. Try some as a relish on a sandwich made with holiday leftovers.

   1   cup sugar
   1   cup apple cider or apple juice
   1   (12-ounce) package fresh cranberries

1. Combine all ingredients in a medium saucepan; bring to a boil over medium-high heat. Reduce heat; simmer 10 minutes or until cranberries pop, stirring occasionally. Chill. Yield: 8 servings (serving size: ¼ cup).

CALORIES 135 (0% from fat); FAT 0g; PROTEIN 0.3g; CARB 35g; FIBER 1.8g; CHOL 0mg; IRON 0.1mg; SODIUM 1mg; CALC 3mg

Cran-Apple Relish

If you're looking for a holiday condiment with versatility, this is it. Dollop onto Leek, Potato, and Caraway Latkes (recipe on page 288), enjoy as a condiment with turkey or ham, or package in a jar tied with ribbon as a holiday gift for a friend.

   5   cups chopped peeled cooking apple (such as McIntosh or Braeburn; 2 pounds)
   2   cups fresh cranberries
   2   cups water
   ¾   cup packed dark brown sugar
   ½   cup white wine vinegar
   ¼   teaspoon ground cloves
   1   (3-inch) cinnamon stick

1. Combine all ingredients in a large, heavy saucepan. Bring to a boil. Reduce heat; simmer 1 hour, stirring occasionally. Continue to cook until thick (about 30 minutes), stirring frequently. Discard cinnamon. Mash with a potato masher. Cover and chill. Yield: 18 servings (serving size: ¼ cup).

CALORIES 69 (3% from fat); FAT 0.2g (sat 0g, mono 0g, poly 0.1g); PROTEIN 0.1g; CARB 17.8g; FIBER 1.4g; CHOL 0mg; IRON 0.3mg; SODIUM 5mg; CALC 12mg

Cranberries aren't just for eating—they're for decorating, too. Any clear container becomes a holiday creation when filled with the bright red berries. Add candles or a few flower stems, and it's worthy of a dining room centerpiece.

Cranberry-Kumquat-Date Relish

Make this relish ahead, and keep it refrigerated. Serve with turkey as an alternative to the usual cranberry sauce.

    1   (12-ounce) package fresh cranberries
    1   cup kumquats, quartered
    ¾   cup sugar
    ½   cup chopped pitted dates

1. Combine first 3 ingredients in a food processor, and pulse 10 times or until fruit is coarsely chopped. Add dates, and pulse 5 times or until blended. Cover and chill. Yield: 10 servings (serving size: ¼ cup).

CALORIES 111 (1% from fat); FAT 0.1g (sat 0g, mono 0g, poly 0.1g); PROTEIN 0.5g; CARB 29g; FIBER 3.4g; CHOL 0mg; IRON 0.3mg; SODIUM 2mg; CALC 14mg

Cranberry Chutney

Cranberry Salsa

The sweet-tart flavor of this fresh salsa sparks up simple chicken, turkey, or pork. You can make it up to 2 days before serving.

    2   cups fresh cranberries
    1½ cups coarsely chopped orange sections (about 3 oranges)
    ⅓   cup chopped red onion
    ⅓   cup fresh orange juice
    3   tablespoons sugar
    2   tablespoons chopped fresh cilantro
    ¼   teaspoon salt
    1   jalapeño pepper, seeded and finely chopped

1. Place cranberries in a food processor, and pulse 2 or 3 times or until coarsely chopped. Combine cranberries, chopped orange sections, and remaining ingredients in a large bowl, tossing gently to combine. Cover and chill. Yield: 3 cups (serving size: ¼ cup).

CALORIES 36 (3% from fat); FAT 0.1g (sat 0g, mono 0g, poly 0.1g); PROTEIN 0.4g; CARB 9.2g; FIBER 1.3g; CHOL 0mg; IRON 0.1mg; SODIUM 50mg; CALC 13mg

Cranberry Chutney

Slivered almonds add crunch to this chutney. Its flavor works well with shrimp or chicken.

    4   cups fresh cranberries
    2   cups packed brown sugar
    1   cup raisins
    1   cup water
    ½   cup slivered almonds, toasted
    ¼   cup fresh lemon juice
    1   teaspoon salt
    1   teaspoon grated onion
    ⅛   teaspoon ground cloves

1. Combine all ingredients in a large saucepan, and bring to a boil. Reduce heat, and simmer 35 minutes or until thickened. Yield: 3½ cups (serving size: ¼ cup).

CALORIES 199 (11% from fat); FAT 2.5g (sat 0.2g, mono 1.6g, poly 0.6g); PROTEIN 1.4g; CARB 44.2g; FIBER 2.2g; CHOL 0mg; IRON 1.2mg; SODIUM 184mg; CALC 47mg

Herbed Fruit Compote

Instead of cranberry sauce at the traditional holiday feast, try this tangy relish with roasted turkey or beef. This sweet-savory compote goes particularly well with ham.

  1   teaspoon olive oil
1½   cups chopped onion
  2   cups water
  ½   cup chopped dried pears
  ½   cup chopped dried apricots
  ½   cup dried tart cherries
  ½   cup raisins
  ¼   cup sweet Marsala
  2   tablespoons honey
  ¼   teaspoon dried thyme
  ¼   teaspoon dried rubbed sage

1. Heat oil in a large saucepan over medium heat. Add onion; cover and cook 10 minutes, stirring occasionally. Add water and remaining ingredients; bring to a boil. Reduce heat; simmer until thick (about 20 minutes). Pour into a bowl; cool. Yield: 3½ cups (serving size: ¼ cup).
Note: You may substitute apple juice for Marsala, if desired.

CALORIES 80 (6% from fat); FAT 0.5g (sat 0.1g, mono 0.5g, poly 0.1g); PROTEIN 0.9g; CARB 20g; FIBER 1.4g; CHOL 0mg; IRON 0.7mg; SODIUM 7mg; CALC 15mg

Golden Spiced Fruit

  ½   cup golden raisins
  ½   cup Riesling or other slightly sweet
         white wine
  ⅓   cup sugar
1½   teaspoons grated peeled fresh ginger
  1   (1-inch) julienne-cut lemon rind strip
  1   (3-inch) cinnamon stick
1½   cups (1-inch) cubed fresh pineapple
1½   cups chopped peeled Golden Delicious apple (about
         2 apples)
  2   teaspoons cornstarch
  2   teaspoons water

1. Combine first 6 ingredients in a large saucepan over medium-high heat, and add pineapple and apple. Bring to a boil; reduce heat, and simmer 10 minutes or until apple is soft. Remove from heat. Cover and let stand 15 minutes. Remove lemon rind and cinnamon stick. Return fruit mixture to a simmer. Combine cornstarch and water; stir into fruit mixture. Cook until slightly thick (about 4 minutes). Yield: 2 cups (serving size: ¼ cup).

CALORIES 93 (2% from fat); FAT 0.2g (sat 0g, mono 0g, poly 0.1g); PROTEIN 0.5g; CARB 24g; FIBER 1.2g; CHOL 1mg; IRON 0.4mg; SODIUM 3mg; CALC 10mg

Brown Sugar-Balsamic Glazed Oranges

The oranges can be prepared up to 2 hours ahead of dinnertime; cover and chill. Serve with your Thanksgiving or Christmas turkey dinner.

  2   medium navel oranges (about 1 pound)
  2   tablespoons brown sugar
  1   tablespoon balsamic vinegar

1. Peel oranges, and cut each crosswise into ¼-inch-thick slices. Divide oranges evenly between 2 plates. Combine brown sugar and vinegar; drizzle vinegar mixture over oranges. Cover and marinate in refrigerator 2 hours. Yield: 2 servings.

CALORIES 111 (1% from fat); FAT 0.1g (sat 0g, mono 0g, poly 0g); PROTEIN 1.7g; CARB 28.3g; FIBER 7.3g; CHOL 0mg; IRON 0.4mg; SODIUM 5mg; CALC 74mg

Orange Beets

  2   large beets (about 1½ pounds)
  1   tablespoon butter
  1   tablespoon grated orange rind
  ¾   cup fresh orange juice (about 2 oranges)
  1   teaspoon lemon juice
  ⅛   teaspoon salt
  ⅛   teaspoon black pepper
1½   tablespoons chopped almonds, toasted

1. Leave root and 1 inch of stem on beets, and scrub with a brush. Place in a large saucepan; cover with water. Bring to a boil; cover, reduce heat, and simmer 1 hour or until tender. Drain; rinse with cold water. Drain; cool. Trim off beet roots; rub off skins. Cut beets into cubes to measure 3½ cups.
2. Melt butter in a large nonstick skillet over medium heat. Add beets, rind, and next 4 ingredients. Bring to a boil; cook until liquid is the consistency of a thin syrup (about 12 minutes), stirring occasionally. Sprinkle with almonds. Yield: 6 servings (serving size: ½ cup).

CALORIES 89 (29% from fat); FAT 2.9g (sat 1.3g, mono 1.1g, poly 0.3g); PROTEIN 2.4g; CARB 14.8g; FIBER 1.2g; CHOL 5mg; IRON 1mg; SODIUM 157mg; CALC 27mg

Roasted Asparagus with Balsamic Browned Butter

This side makes a great addition to a Christmas Eve spread. You can trim the asparagus ahead, but for the best flavor, roast it just before serving. Cooking the butter until it's slightly brown gives the dish a nutty flavor; watch carefully, though, since the butter can burn easily.

40 asparagus spears, trimmed (about 2 pounds)
Cooking spray
¼ teaspoon kosher salt
⅛ teaspoon black pepper
2 tablespoons butter
2 teaspoons low-sodium soy sauce
1 teaspoon balsamic vinegar

1. Preheat oven to 400°.
2. Arrange asparagus in a single layer on a baking sheet; coat with cooking spray. Sprinkle with salt and pepper. Bake at 400° for 12 minutes or until tender.
3. Melt butter in a small skillet over medium heat, and cook 3 minutes or until lightly browned, shaking pan occasionally. Remove from heat, and stir in soy sauce and vinegar. Drizzle over asparagus, tossing well to coat. Serve immediately. Yield: 8 servings (serving size: 5 spears).

CALORIES 45 (60% from fat); FAT 3g (sat 1.8g, mono 0.9g, poly 0.2g); PROTEIN 1.9g; CARB 3.9g; FIBER 1.7g; CHOL 8mg; IRON 0.7mg; SODIUM 134mg; CALC 18mg

5 smart holiday produce picks

With all the hustle and bustle of the holidays, it's easy to get run down and catch a cold. To keep you feeling your best, choosing produce that helps your immune system is important. Here are a few good food choices that are incorporated in our side dish recipes. Not only will servings of these foods help you fight colds and the flu, but they'll also be a welcome addition to your holiday table because they taste so good.

1. **Broccoli:** One cup meets your daily need for vitamin C and has 33 percent more vitamin A than the same amount of green beans.

2. **Brussels Sprouts:** This cousin of cabbage gives you more than 3 grams of fiber per cup.

3. **Cranberries:** Summer berries don't provide the infection-fighting components of cranberries.

4. **Persimmons:** You'll get two-thirds more vitamin C from a persimmon than a peach.

5. **Sweet Potatoes:** Their orange flesh is an excellent source of beta-carotene.

Broccoli with Almond-Breadcrumb Topping

Cooking the broccoli first on the stove speeds up the baking time of this vegetable casserole.

6 cups chopped broccoli
⅓ cup dry breadcrumbs
2 tablespoons grated Parmesan cheese
2 tablespoons finely chopped almonds
1 teaspoon dried basil
1 teaspoon dried oregano
¼ teaspoon salt
¼ teaspoon black pepper

1. Preheat oven to 450°.
2. Cook broccoli in boiling water 2 minutes, and drain. Rinse with cold water; drain well. Place broccoli in an 11 x 7-inch baking dish. Combine breadcrumbs and next 6 ingredients; sprinkle breadcrumb mixture over broccoli. Bake at 450° for 15 minutes or until breadcrumbs are golden brown. Yield: 8 servings (serving size: ¾ cup).

CALORIES 52 (29% from fat); FAT 1.7g (sat 0.4g, mono 0.7g, poly 0.4g); PROTEIN 3.4g; CARB 7.3g; FIBER 2.5g; CHOL 1mg; IRON 1.1mg; SODIUM 153mg; CALC 69mg

Broccoli, Cheese, and Rice Casserole

This casserole is quickly assembled, so it's easy to make ahead and pop in the oven before dinner. It's also kid-friendly.

1 cup uncooked instant rice
½ cup chopped onion
¼ cup fat-free milk
4 ounces light processed cheese, cubed (such as Velveeta Light)
2 tablespoons butter, softened
2 (10-ounce) packages frozen chopped broccoli, thawed and drained
1 (10¾-ounce) can condensed reduced-fat, reduced-sodium cream of mushroom soup, undiluted

1. Preheat oven to 350°.
2. Combine all ingredients in a large bowl, and spoon into a 2-quart casserole. Bake at 350° for 45 minutes. Yield: 8 servings (serving size: ½ cup).

CALORIES 137 (29% from fat); FAT 4.4g (sat 1.7g, mono 1.4g, poly 0.9g); PROTEIN 6.6g; CARB 19.2g; FIBER 2.2g; CHOL 8mg; IRON 1.1mg; SODIUM 410mg; CALC 160mg

Broccoli, Cheese, and
Rice Casserole

One of the advantages of vegetable side dishes is their ability to add bright and vivid color to your holiday table. In some ways, they're decorations all on their own.

Broccolini with Pepper Dressing

Broccolini is a cross between broccoli and Chinese kale. It has long, thin, edible stalks topped with tiny buds that resemble broccoli florets. The flavor is reminiscent of broccoli, but with a peppery bite. Substitute broccoli or asparagus if you can't find broccolini.

- ⅓ cup finely chopped red bell pepper
- 2 tablespoons finely chopped shallots
- 2 tablespoons rice vinegar
- 1 tablespoon fresh lime juice
- 1 tablespoon sugar
- 2 teaspoons minced peeled fresh ginger
- 1 teaspoon vegetable oil
- ½ teaspoon salt
- ¼ teaspoon crushed red pepper
- 1 pound broccolini, trimmed

1. Combine first 9 ingredients in a bowl; toss well.
2. Steam broccolini, covered, 5 minutes or until crisp-tender; drain. Spoon pepper dressing over broccolini. Yield: 4 servings (serving size: 1 cup broccolini and 2 tablespoons pepper dressing).

CALORIES 60 (24% from fat); FAT 1.6g (sat 0.2g, mono 0.3g, poly 0.9g); PROTEIN 3.5g; CARB 10.5g; FIBER 3g; CHOL 0mg; IRON 1.1mg; SODIUM 325mg; CALC 57mg

Lemon-Scented Broccoli Soufflé

Serve this soufflé straight out of the oven. Plunge the serving spoon into the middle of the dish—the soufflé will fall, but its airy texture will remain.

- ¾ pound finely chopped broccoli
- ⅓ cup all-purpose flour
- 1½ cups 1% low-fat milk
- ⅓ cup fat-free sour cream
- 1 tablespoon grated lemon rind
- ¾ teaspoon salt
- 3 large egg yolks
- 1 garlic clove, minced
- 6 large egg whites
- Cooking spray

1. Preheat oven to 325°.

2. Cook broccoli in boiling water 4 minutes or until tender. Drain. Cool to room temperature on paper towels.
3. Lightly spoon flour into a dry measuring cup; level with a knife. Combine flour and milk in a saucepan; stir well. Bring to a boil over medium heat; cook 1 minute, stirring constantly. Reduce heat to medium-low. Stir in sour cream, rind, salt, yolks, and garlic; cook 1 minute or until thick, stirring constantly. Pour mixture into a large bowl, and stir in broccoli.
4. Beat egg whites with a mixer at high speed until stiff peaks form. Gently stir one-third of egg whites into broccoli mixture; fold in remaining egg whites. Spoon into a 2-quart soufflé dish coated with cooking spray. Place on middle rack of oven. Bake at 325° for 40 minutes. Serve immediately. Yield: 6 servings (serving size: ¾ cup).

CALORIES 117 (27% from fat); FAT 3.5g (sat 1.3g, mono 1.2g, poly 0.4g); PROTEIN 8.9g; CARB 12.2g; FIBER 0.9g; CHOL 110mg; IRON 0.8mg; SODIUM 398mg; CALC 121mg

Wilted Cabbage with Toasted Cumin

Savoy cabbage has crinkled pale green leaves and a mellow flavor; you can also use napa (Chinese) cabbage, which has a similarly mild taste. If you can't find sherry vinegar, substitute cider vinegar.

- 2 teaspoons olive oil
- 12 cups coarsely chopped Savoy cabbage (about 2 pounds)
- ½ cup water
- ½ teaspoon salt
- ¼ teaspoon freshly ground black pepper
- 1 teaspoon cumin seeds
- 1 tablespoon sherry vinegar

1. Heat olive oil in a Dutch oven over medium heat. Add cabbage and water. Cook 6 minutes or until cabbage wilts, stirring occasionally. Stir in salt and black pepper.
2. Place cumin seeds in a small nonstick skillet; cook over medium heat 1 minute or until seeds are toasted and fragrant, shaking pan frequently. Add toasted cumin seeds and vinegar to cabbage; cook 6 minutes or until tender, stirring mixture occasionally. Yield: 6 servings (serving size: 1 cup).

CALORIES 58 (28% from fat); FAT 1.8g (sat 0.2g, mono 1.2g, poly 0.2g); PROTEIN 3.1g; CARB 9.9g; FIBER 4.8g; CHOL 0mg; IRON 1mg; SODIUM 239mg; CALC 59mg

Brussels Sprouts with Crisp Prosciutto

    3 cups trimmed halved Brussels sprouts (about 1½ pounds)
    ¼ cup chopped prosciutto (about 1½ ounces)
 Cooking spray
    1 tablespoon butter
    ½ teaspoon salt
    ¼ teaspoon freshly ground black pepper
    1 tablespoon fresh lemon juice

1. Cook Brussels sprouts in boiling water 3 minutes or until crisp-tender; drain.
2. Heat a large nonstick skillet over medium heat; add prosciutto. Cook 6 minutes or until crisp, stirring occasionally. Remove from pan; set aside.
3. Heat pan coated with cooking spray over medium-high heat. Add Brussels sprouts; sauté 3 minutes or until lightly browned. Add butter, salt, and pepper, stirring until butter melts. Remove from heat; drizzle with juice. Add prosciutto; toss to combine. Yield: 6 servings (serving size: about ¾ cup).

CALORIES 79 (33% from fat); FAT 2.9g (sat 1.5g, mono 0.9g, poly 0.3g); PROTEIN 5.5g; CARB 10.4g; FIBER 4.3g; CHOL 9mg; IRON 1.7mg; SODIUM 350mg; CALC 50mg

Lemon-Dill Carrots

When the oven is already packed with other holiday dishes, this stovetop vegetable side saves time and space.

    1 teaspoon olive oil
    3 cups diagonally sliced carrot
    ¼ cup fat-free, less-sodium chicken broth
    1 teaspoon grated lemon rind
    1 tablespoon fresh lemon juice
    ½ teaspoon celery salt
    ¼ teaspoon black pepper
    1 tablespoon minced fresh or 1 teaspoon
       dried dill

1. Heat oil in a large nonstick skillet over medium-high heat. Add carrot; sauté 2 minutes. Stir in broth and next 4 ingredients. Cover; reduce heat to medium-low, and cook 10 minutes or until carrots are tender, stirring occasionally. Remove from heat; stir in dill. Yield: 6 servings (serving size: ½ cup).

CALORIES 33 (25% from fat); FAT 0.9g (sat 0.1g, mono 0.6g, poly 0.1g); PROTEIN 0.7g; CARB 6.1g; FIBER 1.8g; CHOL 0mg; IRON 0.4mg; SODIUM 214mg; CALC 20mg

Brussels Sprouts with
Crisp Prosciutto

Orange-Glazed Carrots

2 tablespoons butter

⅓ cup honey

2 tablespoons minced fresh parsley

½ teaspoon salt

¼ teaspoon black pepper

¼ teaspoon orange extract

Dash of dried thyme

1½ pounds baby carrots

1. Preheat oven to 375°.

2. Place butter in a small microwave-safe bowl; microwave at HIGH 20 seconds or until melted. Stir in honey and next 5 ingredients.

3. Place carrots in a 1-quart casserole, and pour honey mixture over carrots. Cover and bake at 375° for 1 hour or until tender. Yield: 5 servings (serving size: ½ cup).

CALORIES 169 (26% from fat); FAT 4.9g (sat 2.9g, mono 1.4g, poly 0.3g); PROTEIN 1.5g; CARB 32.6g; FIBER 4.4g; CHOL 12mg; IRON 0.9mg; SODIUM 331mg; CALC 42mg

Carrot Soufflé

Because this dish contains no beaten egg whites, it's not a true soufflé. Instead, the name is derived from its light, airy texture. Similar in color and flavor to sweet potato casserole, it pairs well with ham or turkey.

7 cups chopped carrot (about 2 pounds)

⅔ cup granulated sugar

¼ cup fat-free sour cream

3 tablespoons all-purpose flour

2 tablespoons butter, melted

1 teaspoon baking powder

1 teaspoon vanilla extract

¼ teaspoon salt

3 large eggs, lightly beaten

Cooking spray

1 teaspoon powdered sugar

1. Preheat oven to 350°.

2. Cook carrot in boiling water 15 minutes or until very tender; drain. Place carrot in a food processor; process until smooth. Add granulated sugar and next 7 ingredients; pulse to combine.

3. Spoon mixture into a 2-quart baking dish coated with cooking spray. Bake at 350° for 40 minutes or until puffed and set. Sprinkle with powdered sugar. Yield: 8 servings (serving size: ½ cup).

CALORIES 187 (25% from fat); FAT 5.1g (sat 2.5g, mono 1.6g, poly 0.5g); PROTEIN 4.2g; CARB 32.3g; FIBER 3.5g; CHOL 88mg; IRON 1.1mg; SODIUM 233mg; CALC 86mg

Braised Fennel with Orange

Serve this side with ham, pork chops, or roasted pork tenderloin.

2 quarts water

4 large fennel bulbs, each cut into 8 wedges (about 1½ pounds)

1 tablespoon olive oil

2 teaspoons sugar

1 cup fat-free, less-sodium chicken broth

1 tablespoon grated orange rind

⅓ cup fresh orange juice (about 1 orange)

2 teaspoons sherry vinegar

½ teaspoon salt

⅛ teaspoon freshly ground black pepper

2 tablespoons chopped fennel fronds

1. Bring 2 quarts of water to a boil in a large saucepan. Add fennel wedges. Cook 5 minutes or until crisp-tender, and drain.

2. Heat oil in a large nonstick skillet over medium-high heat. Add fennel wedges and sugar, and sauté 3 minutes. Add chicken broth and next 5 ingredients. Reduce heat, and simmer 25 minutes or until liquid almost evaporates. Sprinkle with fennel fronds. Yield: 6 servings (serving size: 1 cup).

CALORIES 85 (28% from fat); FAT 2.6g (sat 0.3g, mono 1.7g, poly 0.2g); PROTEIN 2.6g; CARB 14.8g; FIBER 5g; CHOL 0mg; IRON 1.2mg; SODIUM 353mg; CALC 81mg

Braised Fennel with Orange

Green Beans with
Roasted-Onion
Vinaigrette

Green Beans with Roasted-Onion Vinaigrette

To simplify things on Thanksgiving day, make and refrigerate the vinaigrette and steam and chill the green beans a day ahead.

  2   red onions, peeled (about 1 pound)
  4   teaspoons olive oil, divided
 ¼   teaspoon salt
 ¼   teaspoon black pepper
  2   fresh thyme sprigs
  1   tablespoon chopped fresh dill
  3   tablespoons Champagne vinegar or white wine vinegar
  1   tablespoon stone-ground mustard
  2   pounds green beans, trimmed, steamed, and chilled

1. Preheat oven to 400°.
2. Cut onions in half vertically. Drizzle cut side of each onion half with ¼ teaspoon oil. Sprinkle halves evenly with salt and pepper. Place 1 thyme sprig on 1 onion half; top with other half. Wrap in foil. Repeat procedure with remaining thyme and onion halves. Bake wrapped onions at 400° for 1 hour or until tender. Cool to room temperature. Discard thyme, and chop onions. Combine 1 tablespoon olive oil, onion, dill, vinegar, and mustard in a small bowl.

3. Toss beans with vinaigrette. Yield: 8 servings (serving size: about 4 ounces green beans and ¼ cup vinaigrette).

CALORIES 83 (29% from fat); FAT 2.7g (sat 0.4g, mono 1.7g, poly 0.4g); PROTEIN 2.9g; CARB 14g; FIBER 4.8g; CHOL 0mg; IRON 1.6mg; SODIUM 109mg; CALC 65mg

Green Beans with Crushed Walnuts

This simple dish relies on freshly ground nutmeg. Look for whole nutmeg in the spice aisle, and store in the freezer for up to a year.

 1¼   pounds green beans, trimmed
  2   teaspoons butter
  2   tablespoons finely crushed walnuts
 ½   teaspoon salt
 ¼   teaspoon freshly ground whole nutmeg

1. Place beans in a large saucepan of boiling water; cook 5 minutes. Drain.
2. Heat butter in a large nonstick skillet over medium-high heat. Add walnuts; sauté 1 minute, stirring constantly. Add beans, salt, and nutmeg; cook 1 minute. Yield: 6 servings (serving size: ⅔ cup).

CALORIES 52 (52% from fat); FAT 3g (sat 1g, mono 0.6g, poly 1.3g); PROTEIN 1.8g; CARB 5.8g; FIBER 2.8g; CHOL 3mg; IRON 0.9mg; SODIUM 213mg; CALC 31mg

When it comes to holiday preparations, saving time is essential. Chop green peppers or onions ahead if you know you'll be using them, and freeze them in zip-top freezer bags up to 3 months. It's also a good idea to freeze any leftover veggies as well. They're great for combining to make soups and stews.

Green Beans Provençale

These simply prepared green beans are perfect for any holiday meal, supper club, or just a casual weeknight side.

   4   cups (2-inch) cut green beans (about ¾ pound)
   1   teaspoon olive oil
   ½   cup sliced green onions
   4   garlic cloves, crushed
   2   cups plum tomato, seeded and thinly sliced (about ¾ pound)
   2   tablespoons chopped fresh basil or 2 teaspoons dried basil
   ¼   teaspoon salt
   ⅛   teaspoon black pepper

1. Arrange green beans in a steamer basket over boiling water; cover and steam 5 minutes or until tender. Drain.
2. Heat oil in a large nonstick skillet over medium-high heat. Add onions and garlic; sauté 1 minute. Add beans; sauté 3 minutes. Add tomato and remaining ingredients; sauté 2 minutes. Yield: 4 servings (serving size: 1 cup).

CALORIES 72 (20% from fat); FAT 1.6g (sat 0.2g, mono 0.9g, poly 0.3g); PROTEIN 3.2g; CARB 14g; FIBER 3.8g; CHOL 0mg; IRON 1.8mg; SODIUM 164mg; CALC 62mg

Caramelized Pearl Onions

This side will be a tasty and beautiful addition to your Christmas buffet table. We found in testing that the frozen pearl onions worked fine, making this recipe quick and easy.

   1   tablespoon butter
   1   tablespoon sugar
   1   (16-ounce) package frozen pearl onions, thawed
   1⅔ cups coarsely chopped red bell pepper
   1   teaspoon chopped fresh or ¼ teaspoon dried rosemary
   ½   teaspoon salt
   ¼   teaspoon black pepper

1. Melt butter in a nonstick skillet over medium-high heat. Add sugar and onions; sauté 8 minutes or until golden brown. Stir in bell pepper and remaining ingredients; sauté 2 minutes. Yield: 6 servings (serving size: ½ cup).

CALORIES 69 (29% from fat); FAT 2.2g (sat 1.3g, mono 0.5g, poly 0.2g); PROTEIN 1.5g; CARB 12.3g; FIBER 1.2g; CHOL 5mg; IRON 0.4mg; SODIUM 210mg; CALC 21mg

Roasted Cipollini Onions

Cipollini (chip-oh-LEE-nee) are sometimes called wild onions. If you can't find them in the supermarket or an Italian market, substitute pearl onions. Briefly blanching the onions makes them easy to peel. This side goes well with beef.

   2   quarts water
   4   pounds cipollini onions
   4   rosemary sprigs
   1   cup dry red wine
   ½   cup low-sodium soy sauce
   ⅓   cup balsamic vinegar
   2   tablespoons olive oil
   2   tablespoons honey
Rosemary sprigs (optional)

1. Preheat oven to 475°.
2. Bring water to a boil in a stockpot. Add onions; cook 30 seconds. Drain; cool. Peel onions; arrange in a single layer on a jelly-roll pan. Top with 4 rosemary sprigs.
3. Combine wine and next 4 ingredients, stirring with a whisk. Pour wine mixture over onions. Bake at 475° for 30 minutes, turning twice.
4. Remove onions from pan with a slotted spoon. Carefully pour cooking liquid into a small saucepan; bring to a boil. Reduce heat; simmer 3 minutes or until mixture is consistency of a thin syrup. Pour over onions; toss well to coat. Garnish with rosemary sprigs, if desired. Yield: 10 servings (serving size: about ⅓ cup).

CALORIES 187 (15% from fat); FAT 3.1g (sat 0.4g, mono 2g, poly 0.2g); PROTEIN 3.3g; CARB 32.5g; FIBER 1.2g; CHOL 0mg; IRON 1mg; SODIUM 522mg; CALC 54mg

Roasted Parsnips

Roasted Parsnips

The natural sweetness of parsnips comes alive when they're roasted and caramelized. This is a great side dish to serve with ham or pork tenderloin.

  3 tablespoons balsamic vinegar
  1 tablespoon brown sugar
  2 teaspoons chopped fresh rosemary
  2 pounds (2-inch-thick) slices peeled parsnip
  1 large red onion, peeled and quartered
Cooking spray
  1 tablespoon olive oil
  ½ teaspoon salt
  ¼ teaspoon freshly ground black pepper

1. Combine first 5 ingredients in a large zip-top plastic bag; seal and marinate in refrigerator 1 hour, turning twice. Remove parsnip and onion; discard marinade.
2. Preheat oven to 500°.
3. Place parsnip and onion in a shallow roasting pan coated with cooking spray. Drizzle with olive oil, and toss to coat. Sprinkle with salt and pepper. Bake at 500° for 30 minutes or until parsnip is tender, stirring often. Yield: 4 servings (serving size: about 1 cup).

CALORIES 235 (16% from fat); FAT 4.2g (sat 0.6g, mono 2.8g, poly 0.4g); PROTEIN 3.2g; CARB 49.3g; FIBER 11.9g; CHOL 0mg; IRON 1.7mg; SODIUM 319mg; CALC 97mg

Basic Mashed Potatoes

No holiday spread is complete without mashed potatoes, since they complement just about any main dish—whether it be turkey, ham, or beef. In this basic recipe, chicken broth and milk make the potatoes rich, and sour cream gives them tang. And if you're cooking a turkey or roast, don't forget the gravy!

  3 pounds cubed peeled baking potato
  ½ cup 2% reduced-fat milk
  ½ cup fat-free, less-sodium chicken broth
  3 tablespoons reduced-fat sour cream
  1 teaspoon salt
  ½ teaspoon black pepper
  ¼ cup butter, softened

1. Place potato in a saucepan, and cover with water. Bring to a boil. Reduce heat; simmer 15 minutes or until tender.
2. Drain and return potato to pan. Add milk and broth; mash to desired consistency. Cook 2 minutes or until thoroughly heated, stirring constantly. Stir in sour cream, salt, and pepper. Top with butter. Yield: 8 servings (serving size: ¾ cup).

CALORIES 162 (30% from fat); FAT 5.4g (sat 3.4g, mono 1.4g, poly 0.2g); PROTEIN 3.7g; CARB 25.4g; FIBER 2.2g; CHOL 15mg; IRON 1mg; SODIUM 306mg; CALC 32mg

Creamy Herbed
Mashed Potatoes

Creamy Herbed Mashed Potatoes

Yukon golds make brilliant mashed potatoes, thanks to their balance
of waxiness and starch. Because yellow potatoes are more flavorful
than others, they don't need a lot of fat to taste rich. Mash the
potatoes by hand just until creamy—overworking the potatoes will
make them gummy.

    4 cups cubed peeled Yukon gold potato
       (about 2 pounds)
   ½ cup 2% reduced-fat milk
   ¼ cup low-fat sour cream
    3 tablespoons butter
    3 tablespoons chopped fresh chives
    2 tablespoons chopped fresh parsley
   ½ teaspoon salt
   ¼ teaspoon freshly ground black pepper

1. Place potato in a saucepan; cover with water. Bring to a boil;
cover, reduce heat, and simmer 10 minutes or until tender.
Drain. Return potato to pan. Add milk and remaining ingredients; mash with a potato masher to desired consistency. Yield:
6 servings (serving size: ¾ cup).

CALORIES 215 (30% from fat); FAT 7.1g (sat 4.5g, mono 1.8g, poly 0.3g); PROTEIN 4.5g;
CARB 34.5g; FIBER 2.4g; CHOL 20mg; IRON 0.7mg; SODIUM 280mg; CALC 51mg

Bacon and Cheddar Mashed Potatoes

You'll make this recipe time and again. Tailor the flavors to suit your
preferences by using Swiss cheese instead of Cheddar or prosciutto
instead of bacon.

 2½ pounds cubed peeled baking potato
    1 cup (4 ounces) shredded extrasharp
      Cheddar cheese
    1 cup 2% reduced-fat milk
   ½ cup chopped green onions
    2 tablespoons reduced-fat sour cream
   ½ teaspoon salt
   ½ teaspoon freshly ground black pepper
    4 bacon slices, cooked and crumbled
      (drained)

1. Place potato in a saucepan, and cover with water. Bring to a
boil. Reduce heat; simmer 15 minutes or until tender.
2. Drain and return potato to pan. Add cheese and milk; mash
to desired consistency. Cook 2 minutes or until thoroughly
heated, stirring constantly. Add onions and remaining ingredients, stirring to combine. Yield: 8 servings (serving size: ¾ cup).

CALORIES 214 (30% from fat); FAT 7.1g (sat 4.1g, mono 2.1g, poly 0.4g); PROTEIN 8.9g;
CARB 29.6g; FIBER 2.6g; CHOL 22mg; IRON 1.4mg; SODIUM 330mg; CALC 157mg

test kitchen tips for holiday spuds

Potatoes are considered by most to be the ultimate comfort food. What Sunday dinner or holiday spread would be complete without fluffy mashed potatoes? Here are some of our best tips for preparing America's number-one side:

- Our mashed potato recipes direct you to cube the potatoes before you cook them. You can cook them whole, if you prefer; it just takes longer.

- After you drain the potatoes, take a moment to place the pan over low heat, and then shake the potatoes in the pan to dry them before mashing. If your pan is stainless, mash the potatoes right in the pan over low heat to keep them warm.

- Russet and thin-skinned white potatoes have a fluffy, dry texture and often require slightly more liquid for creamy results. If you have a potato ricer, use it with these spuds.

- Waxy red potatoes and Yukon golds make good chunky mashed potatoes. Peel them before or after cooking, or leave the skin on for rustic appeal.

- If your menu includes gravy or jus, keep your mashed potatoes simple.

Sformato

Sformato

This dish is baked in a springform pan to make a mashed-potato "cake." Substitute it for traditional mashed potatoes on your holiday buffet.

```
 3  (1-ounce) slices white bread
 7  cups peeled baking potato, cut into 2-inch pieces
    (about 3 pounds)
 2  tablespoons butter
 6  cups (¼-inch-thick) sliced onion (about 1¼ pounds)
 8  garlic cloves, crushed
 ¾  cup 2% reduced-fat milk
1½  teaspoons salt
 ½  teaspoon black pepper
 ¼  cup chopped fresh parsley, divided
 2  large eggs, lightly beaten
Cooking spray
Fresh parsley sprigs (optional)
```

1. Preheat oven to 350°.
2. Place bread in a food processor; pulse 2 times or until crumbly. Sprinkle crumbs on a baking sheet; bake at 350° for 5 minutes or until golden (breadcrumbs should measure 1½ cups). Set aside. Increase oven temperature to 375°.
3. Place potato in a Dutch oven; cover with water. Bring to a boil. Reduce heat; simmer 15 minutes or until tender. Drain.
4. Melt butter in pan over medium-high heat. Add onion and garlic, and sauté 10 minutes or until browned. Add milk, salt, and pepper; bring to a simmer over medium heat, stirring frequently. Reduce heat; simmer 3 minutes. Place onion mixture in a food processor in batches, and process until smooth. Add potato; process until smooth. Add 2 tablespoons chopped parsley and eggs; pulse 10 times or until combined.
5. Combine 1¼ cups breadcrumbs and 2 tablespoons chopped parsley; spread breadcrumb mixture in bottom of a 10-inch springform pan coated with cooking spray. Spread potato mixture over breadcrumb mixture; sprinkle with ¼ cup breadcrumbs. Bake at 375° for 45 minutes or until golden brown. Run a knife around outside edge; cool 10 minutes. Garnish with parsley sprigs, if desired. Yield: 10 servings (serving size: 1 wedge).

CALORIES 217 (18% from fat); FAT 4.3g (sat 2.1g, mono 1.3g, poly 0.4g); PROTEIN 6g; CARB 39.5g; FIBER 3.9g; CHOL 50mg; IRON 1.2mg; SODIUM 456mg; CALC 67mg

Roasted Potatoes with
Tangy Watercress
Sauce

Roasted Potatoes with Tangy Watercress Sauce

Add watercress, basil, and mint to a yogurt base for a fragrant, fresh-tasting sauce you can make up to 2 days ahead. Serve with chicken, beef, or lamb. You can also use the sauce as a dip for vegetables.

Sauce:
1½ cups plain fat-free yogurt
1 cup trimmed watercress
⅓ cup light mayonnaise
¼ cup chopped green onions
3 tablespoons chopped fresh basil
1 tablespoon chopped fresh mint
1 teaspoon balsamic vinegar
¼ teaspoon salt
⅛ teaspoon freshly ground black pepper
Potatoes:
3 pounds small red potatoes, quartered
1½ tablespoons olive oil
1 teaspoon freshly ground black pepper
½ teaspoon salt
Cooking spray

1. Preheat oven to 450°.
2. To prepare sauce, place first 9 ingredients in a food processor or blender; process until smooth, scraping sides. Cover and chill.
3. To prepare potatoes, combine potatoes and next 3 ingredients in a jelly-roll pan or shallow roasting pan coated with cooking spray, tossing to coat. Bake at 450° for 35 minutes or until tender, stirring occasionally. Serve with sauce. Yield: 8 servings (serving size: 1 cup potatoes and 2 tablespoons sauce).

CALORIES 210 (26% from fat); FAT 6.1g (sat 0.9g, mono 1.9g, poly 0.3g); PROTEIN 6.6g; CARB 33.2g; FIBER 3.1g; CHOL 4mg; IRON 2.6mg; SODIUM 347mg; CALC 123mg

Two-Cheese Scalloped Potatoes

This casserole is perfect when served with baked ham or cold roast beef. It comes from the oven hot and bubbly and retains most of its heat until the last bite has been served.

1½ cups fat-free milk
1½ cups (6 ounces) shredded reduced-fat extrasharp Cheddar cheese, divided
1 cup (4 ounces) shredded reduced-fat Monterey Jack cheese, divided
¼ cup ketchup
2 teaspoons Worcestershire sauce
¼ teaspoon black pepper
2½ pounds peeled baking potatoes, cut into ¼-inch-thick slices
2 cups vertically sliced onion
Cooking spray
2 tablespoons chopped fresh parsley

1. Preheat oven to 350°.
2. Combine milk, ¾ cup Cheddar, ½ cup Monterey Jack, and next 3 ingredients. Set aside.
3. Arrange half of potatoes and half of onion in bottom of a 13 x 9-inch baking dish coated with cooking spray. Top with half of milk mixture. Repeat layers; top with remaining ¾ cup Cheddar, ½ cup Monterey Jack, and parsley. Cover and bake at 350° for 1 hour and 15 minutes. Uncover; bake an additional 20 minutes or until potatoes are tender and cheese is browned. Yield: 8 servings (serving size: ¾ cup).

CALORIES 233 (27% from fat); FAT 7.1g (sat 4g, mono 1.9g, poly 0.3g); PROTEIN 14.8g; CARB 28.5g; FIBER 2.5g; CHOL 25mg; IRON 1.2mg; SODIUM 377mg; CALC 377mg

Potato-Gorgonzola Gratin

The traditional potatoes au gratin will take a backseat to this cheesy potato dish at Christmas dinner. And your holiday company will be glad for the change—especially cheese lovers. Substitute fontina or Monterey Jack for the blue cheese, if you like.

  2 tablespoons butter
2½ tablespoons all-purpose flour
  1 teaspoon chopped fresh thyme
2½ cups fat-free milk
 ¾ cup (3 ounces) crumbled Gorgonzola or other blue cheese
1½ teaspoons salt
 ¼ teaspoon freshly ground black pepper
  3 pounds baking potatoes, peeled and cut into ⅛-inch-thick slices
    Cooking spray
 ⅓ cup (1½ ounces) grated Parmigiano-Reggiano cheese

1. Preheat oven to 375°.
2. Melt butter in a small saucepan over medium-high heat. Add flour, and cook 2 minutes, stirring constantly with a whisk. Stir in thyme. Gradually add milk, stirring with a whisk; cook over medium heat until slightly thick (about 3 minutes), stirring constantly. Stir in Gorgonzola; cook 3 minutes or until cheese melts, stirring constantly. Stir in salt and pepper. Remove from heat.
3. Arrange one-fourth of potatoes in bottom of a 13 x 9-inch baking dish coated with cooking spray; spoon about ¾ cup sauce over potatoes. Repeat layers twice; arrange remaining potatoes over sauce. Sprinkle with Parmigiano-Reggiano. Cover and bake at 375° for 30 minutes. Uncover and bake 40 minutes or until potatoes are tender. Remove from oven; let stand 10 minutes before serving. Yield: 8 servings (serving size: about 1 cup).

CALORIES 254 (28% from fat); FAT 7.9g (sat 5g, mono 2g, poly 0.2g); PROTEIN 10.6g; CARB 36.8g; FIBER 2.8g; CHOL 22mg; IRON 1.5mg; SODIUM 751mg; CALC 228mg

Potato, Ham, and Spinach Gratin

Here's a recipe to help use up leftover Christmas ham. For best results, peel and slice the potatoes just before assembling the gratin. Using a "V" slicer or mandoline really helps make uniformly thin slices.

  2 teaspoons olive oil
 ½ cup thinly sliced shallots
  2 garlic cloves, minced
  1 cup chopped reduced-fat ham (about 4 ounces)
  1 teaspoon salt, divided
 ¾ teaspoon freshly ground black pepper, divided
 ⅛ teaspoon grated whole nutmeg
  1 (10-ounce) package frozen chopped spinach, thawed, drained, and squeezed dry
  2 cups 1% low-fat milk
 ⅓ cup all-purpose flour
  7 cups (⅛-inch-thick) slices peeled Yukon gold potato (about 2½ pounds)
    Cooking spray
 ¾ cup (3 ounces) shredded Gruyère cheese

1. Preheat oven to 375°.
2. Heat oil in a small nonstick skillet over medium-high heat. Add shallots and garlic, and sauté 2 minutes or until tender. Remove from heat; stir in ham, ¼ teaspoon salt, ¼ teaspoon pepper, nutmeg, and spinach. Combine milk, flour, ¼ teaspoon salt, and ½ teaspoon pepper, stirring with a whisk.
3. Arrange half of potato slices in an 8-inch square baking pan coated with cooking spray; sprinkle with ¼ teaspoon salt. Spread spinach mixture over potato slices. Arrange remaining potato slices over spinach mixture; pour milk mixture over top. Sprinkle with ¼ teaspoon salt. Cover with foil coated with cooking spray. Bake at 375° for 1 hour and 15 minutes or until potato is tender. Uncover and sprinkle with cheese; bake an additional 15 minutes.
4. Preheat broiler.
5. Broil gratin 2 minutes or until cheese is lightly browned. Yield: 8 servings.

CALORIES 240 (24% from fat); FAT 6.3g (sat 2.9g, mono 2.5g, poly 0.5g); PROTEIN 12.8g; CARB 34g; FIBER 3g; CHOL 22mg; IRON 1.7mg; SODIUM 581mg; CALC 235mg

Potato-Gorgonzola Gratin

Leek, Potato, and Caraway Latkes with Spiced Sour Cream

Latkes remain a staple for Hanukkah, and they're a nice addition to any other festive holiday dinner. Aromatic caraway seeds add a nutty licorice flavor that's a little like fennel. The spicy sour cream sauce cools and adds heat at the same time.

Latkes:
- 1/4 cup all-purpose flour
- 4 cups shredded peeled baking potato (about 2 pounds)
- 2 cups chopped leek
- 1 teaspoon caraway seeds
- 1/2 teaspoon salt
- 1/4 teaspoon black pepper
- 1 large egg
- 1 large egg white
- 4 teaspoons vegetable oil, divided
- Cooking spray

Sauce:
- 1/4 teaspoon ground cumin
- 1/8 teaspoon ground red pepper
- 1/8 teaspoon garlic powder
- 1 (8-ounce) carton reduced-fat sour cream

1. Preheat oven to 350°.
2. To prepare latkes, lightly spoon flour into a dry measuring cup; level with a knife. Combine flour and next 7 ingredients in a large bowl; stir well.
3. Heat 1 teaspoon oil in a large nonstick skillet over medium-high heat. Spoon 1/4 cup batter for each of 4 pancakes into pan; cook 3 minutes on each side or until browned. Repeat procedure with remaining oil and batter.
4. Place pancakes on a baking sheet coated with cooking spray. Bake at 350° for 12 minutes or until crisp.
5. To prepare sauce, combine cumin and next 3 ingredients, and stir well. Serve sauce over latkes. Yield: 16 servings (serving size: 1 latke and 1 tablespoon sauce).

CALORIES 105 (28% from fat); FAT 3.3g (sat 1.4g, mono 0.4g, poly 0.8g); PROTEIN 2.8g; CARB 16.4g; FIBER 1.2g; CHOL 20mg; IRON 0.6mg; SODIUM 94mg; CALC 36mg

Maple-Orange Sweet Potatoes

What's a holiday meal without sweet potatoes? We turned to the microwave for this casserole to free up the oven.

- 2 1/2 pounds peeled sweet potatoes, cut into 1/4-inch-thick slices
- 1/3 cup fresh orange juice
- 1/4 cup maple syrup
- 2 tablespoons brown sugar
- 1 tablespoon butter, melted
- 1/2 teaspoon salt
- 1/8 teaspoon ground cloves
- 1/4 cup chopped pecans, toasted

1. Place potato slices in a 2-quart casserole. Combine juice and next 5 ingredients; pour mixture over potatoes. Cover loosely with plastic wrap; microwave at HIGH 10 minutes, stirring after 5 minutes. Uncover and microwave at HIGH 5 minutes or until potato is tender. Sprinkle with pecans. Yield: 10 servings (serving size: 1/2 cup).

CALORIES 152 (21% from fat); FAT 3.5g (sat 1g, mono 1.5g, poly 0.8g); PROTEIN 1.9g; CARB 29.4g; FIBER 3.2g; CHOL 3mg; IRON 1.1mg; SODIUM 157mg; CALC 42mg

Oven-Roasted Sweet Potatoes and Onions

Five ingredients come together to make one fabulous side dish. It only dirties one dish, and it's pretty much hands-off cooking. Try serving alongside roasted chicken, pork loin, or ham at holiday gatherings.

- 4 peeled sweet potatoes, cut into 2-inch pieces (about 2 1/4 pounds)
- 2 Oso Sweet or other sweet onions, cut into 1-inch pieces (about 1 pound)
- 2 tablespoons extravirgin olive oil
- 3/4 teaspoon garlic-pepper blend (such as McCormick)
- 1/2 teaspoon salt

1. Preheat oven to 425°.
2. Combine all ingredients in a 13 x 9-inch baking dish, tossing to coat.
3. Bake at 425° for 35 minutes or until tender, stirring occasionally. Yield: 6 servings (serving size: 1 cup).

CALORIES 247 (19% from fat); FAT 5.1g (sat 0.7g, mono 3.4g, poly 0.6g); PROTEIN 3.6g; CARB 47.8g; FIBER 6.5g; CHOL 0mg; IRON 1.2mg; SODIUM 255mg; CALC 53mg

Cranberry-and-Sweet Potato Bake

2 (15-ounce) cans sweet potatoes, drained
1 (8-ounce) can crushed pineapple in juice, drained
2 tablespoons butter, melted
¼ teaspoon salt
⅛ teaspoon ground nutmeg
Dash of black pepper
1 large egg
1 (16-ounce) can whole-berry cranberry sauce, divided
Cooking spray

1. Preheat oven to 350°.
2. Combine sweet potatoes and pineapple in a large bowl; mash with a potato masher. Stir in butter, salt, nutmeg, pepper, and egg. Swirl in 1 cup cranberry sauce. Spoon ⅓ cup sweet potato mixture into each of 8 (4-ounce) ramekins coated with cooking spray. Top each with 1 tablespoon cranberry sauce. Bake at 350° for 40 minutes. Yield: 8 servings.
Note: You may substitute a 1-quart casserole for ramekins, if desired. Bake at 350° for 40 minutes.

CALORIES 212 (17% from fat); FAT 3.9g (sat 2g, mono 1.1g, poly 0.4g); PROTEIN 2.6g; CARB 43.2g; FIBER 1.7g; CHOL 35mg; IRON 1.3mg; SODIUM 186mg; CALC 32mg

Brûléed Mashed Sweet Potatoes

Borrowing from the classic dessert crème brûlée, this sweet holiday dish has a hard candy topping—a crunchy contrast to the creamy sweet potatoes.

6 cups hot mashed sweet potatoes (about 4 pounds)
¾ cup whole milk
3 tablespoons butter, softened
½ teaspoon salt
¼ teaspoon ground cinnamon
⅛ teaspoon ground nutmeg
Cooking spray
½ cup packed brown sugar

1. Preheat broiler.
2. Combine first 6 ingredients in a bowl. Spoon potato mixture into an 11 x 7-inch baking dish coated with cooking spray. Sprinkle brown sugar evenly over top. Broil 2 minutes or until sugar melts. Let stand until melted sugar hardens (about 5 minutes). Yield: 14 servings (serving size: about ½ cup).

CALORIES 207 (14% from fat); FAT 3.3g (sat 1.9g, mono 0.9g, poly 0.3g); PROTEIN 2.8g; CARB 42.4g; FIBER 2.6g; CHOL 8mg; IRON 1mg; SODIUM 137mg; CALC 53mg

Cranberry-and-Sweet Potato Bake

Squash-Rice Casserole

Easy to prepare and rich in flavor, this casserole pairs fabulously with roasted chicken, ham, or pork chops. This simple dish has become a staff favorite, and we believe it will be popular in your home, too.

    8   cups sliced zucchini (about 2½ pounds)
    1   cup chopped onion
    ½   cup fat-free, less-sodium chicken broth
    2   cups cooked rice
    1   cup (4 ounces) shredded reduced-fat sharp Cheddar
        cheese
    1   cup fat-free sour cream
    ¼   cup (1 ounce) grated fresh Parmesan cheese, divided
    ¼   cup Italian-seasoned breadcrumbs
    1   teaspoon salt
    ¼   teaspoon black pepper
    2   large eggs, lightly beaten
    Cooking spray

1. Preheat oven to 350°.
2. Combine first 3 ingredients in a Dutch oven; bring to a boil. Cover, reduce heat, and simmer 20 minutes or until tender. Drain; partially mash with a potato masher.
3. Combine zucchini mixture, rice, Cheddar cheese, sour cream, 2 tablespoons Parmesan cheese, breadcrumbs, salt, pepper, and eggs in a bowl; stir gently. Spoon mixture into a 13 x 9-inch baking dish coated with cooking spray; sprinkle with 2 tablespoons Parmesan cheese. Bake at 350° for 30 minutes or until bubbly.

4. Broil 1 minute or until lightly browned. Yield: 8 servings (serving size: 1 cup).

CALORIES 197 (25% from fat); FAT 5.5g (sat 2.7g, mono 1.5g, poly 0.4g); PROTEIN 12.7g; CARB 24g; FIBER 1.4g; CHOL 65mg; IRON 1.5mg; SODIUM 623mg; CALC 209mg

Roasted Butternut Squash with Herbes de Provence

Herbes de Provence is a combination of dried herbs, including rosemary, lavender, thyme, marjoram, and sage. If you're roasting in a stainless pan, use a metal spatula to turn the butternut squash so you scrape up all of the flavorful browned edges.

    6   cups (1½-inch) cubed peeled butternut squash (about
        2½ pounds)
    1   tablespoon olive oil
    1½ teaspoons dried herbes de Provence
    ¾   teaspoon kosher salt
    ½   teaspoon freshly ground black pepper
    2   medium onions, each cut into 8 wedges (about ¾ pound)
    Cooking spray

1. Preheat oven to 425°.
2. Place first 6 ingredients in a shallow roasting pan coated with cooking spray; toss well. Bake at 425° for 30 minutes or until tender and lightly browned, stirring occasionally. Yield: 4 servings (serving size: 1 cup).

CALORIES 125 (27% from fat); FAT 3.8g (sat 0.5g, mono 2.5g, poly 0.5g); PROTEIN 3.6g; CARB 22.5g; FIBER 4.2g; CHOL 0mg; IRON 1.3mg; SODIUM 362mg; CALC 75mg

Squash-Rice Casserole

Spinach and Gruyère Soufflé

Gruyère, which has a nutty, slightly sweet flavor, is an aged Swiss cheese that's commonly made in France. Substitute Swiss, Jarlsberg, or Asiago if you can't find Gruyère.

Cooking spray
3 tablespoons dry breadcrumbs, divided
¼ cup finely chopped onion
2 tablespoons all-purpose flour
¼ teaspoon salt
¼ teaspoon freshly ground black pepper
⅛ teaspoon ground red pepper
Dash of ground nutmeg
1 cup fat-free milk, divided
1 large egg yolk, lightly beaten
⅓ cup (1½ ounces) finely grated Gruyère cheese
1 (10-ounce) package frozen chopped spinach, thawed, drained, and squeezed dry
6 large egg whites, lightly beaten
¼ teaspoon cream of tartar

1. Preheat oven to 400°.
2. Coat a 1-quart soufflé dish with cooking spray; sprinkle with 1 tablespoon breadcrumbs.
3. Heat a medium saucepan coated with cooking spray over medium-high heat. Add onion; sauté 2 minutes or until tender. Remove from heat. Add flour, salt, peppers, and nutmeg, stirring well. Gradually add ½ cup milk, stirring with a whisk until well blended. Stir in ½ cup milk. Cook over medium heat 2 minutes or until thick and bubbly, stirring constantly with a whisk. Remove from heat.
4. Place egg yolk in a bowl. Gradually add milk mixture to egg yolk, stirring constantly with a whisk. Return mixture to pan. Cook 1 minute or until thick. Remove from heat; stir in cheese and spinach. Cool 5 minutes.
5. Place egg whites and cream of tartar in a large bowl; beat with a mixer at high speed until stiff peaks form. Gently stir one-fourth of egg white mixture into milk mixture; gently fold in remaining egg white mixture and 2 tablespoons breadcrumbs. Spoon into prepared dish. Bake at 400° for 30 minutes or until soufflé is puffy and set. Serve immediately. Yield: 6 servings.

CALORIES 109 (29% from fat); FAT 3.5g (sat 1.6g, mono 1.1g, poly 0.3g); PROTEIN 9.8g; CARB 9.6g; FIBER 1.8g; CHOL 44mg; IRON 1.4mg; SODIUM 261mg; CALC 187mg

Puree of Roasted Garlic and White Vegetables

Turnips and celeriac turn ordinary mashed potatoes into a dish that can stand up to lamb and venison.

1 whole garlic head
3¼ cups chopped peeled baking potato (about 1¾ pounds)
3 cups chopped peeled turnip
2½ cups chopped peeled celeriac (celery root; about ¾ pound)
1 cup chopped onion
2 tablespoons butter
¼ cup whipping cream
1½ tablespoons white wine vinegar
1 teaspoon salt
½ teaspoon freshly ground black pepper

1. Preheat oven to 350°.
2. Remove white, papery skin from garlic head (do not peel or separate cloves). Wrap garlic head in foil. Bake at 350° for 1 hour; cool 10 minutes. Separate garlic cloves; squeeze to extract garlic pulp. Discard skins.
3. Place potato, turnip, celeriac, and onion in a large Dutch oven; cover with water. Bring to a boil, reduce heat, and simmer 15 minutes or until vegetables are tender. Drain. Place half of vegetables in a food processor; process until smooth. Pour pureed vegetables into a bowl. Repeat procedure with remaining vegetables.
4. Melt butter in pan over medium heat. Stir in garlic pulp, pureed vegetables, and cream; cook 5 minutes or until thoroughly heated, stirring frequently. Stir in vinegar, salt, and pepper. Yield: 8 servings (serving size: ¾ cup).

CALORIES 181 (29% from fat); FAT 5.9g (sat 3.6g, mono 1.7g, poly 0.4g); PROTEIN 3.5g; CARB 30.1g; FIBER 3.9g; CHOL 18mg; IRON 0.9mg; SODIUM 406mg; CALC 58mg

how to: SQUEEZE GARLIC

Once garlic is roasted, its pulp comes out of the skin with a simple squeeze.

Caramelized Onion,
Green Bean, and
Cherry Tomato Tian

Caramelized Onion, Green Bean, and Cherry Tomato Tian

This slightly sweet vegetable dish takes its name from the French term *tian* (tee-AHN), which refers to
mixed vegetables prepared gratin-style. The colors alone make it the perfect addition to a Christmas meal.

 5 cups (1-inch) cut green beans (about 1 pound)
Cooking spray
 3 cups thinly sliced onion
 6 garlic cloves, minced
 2 teaspoons sugar
 ½ teaspoon salt
 ¼ teaspoon black pepper
 2 tablespoons balsamic vinegar
 1 teaspoon dried basil
 ½ teaspoon dried oregano
 4 cups cherry tomatoes, halved
 ¼ cup (1 ounce) grated fresh Parmesan cheese

1. Preheat oven to 400°.

2. Cook beans in boiling water 3 minutes. Drain and rinse with cold water; set aside.

3. Heat a nonstick skillet coated with cooking spray over medium-high heat. Add onion and next 4 ingredients; sauté 8 minutes or until lightly browned, stirring frequently. Stir in vinegar, basil, and oregano, and cook 2 minutes. Remove from heat.

4. Arrange beans in an 11 x 7-inch baking dish coated with cooking spray. Top with onion mixture. Arrange tomatoes on top of onion mixture, and sprinkle with cheese. Bake at 400° for 35 minutes or until cheese is lightly browned. Yield: 6 servings (serving size: 1 cup).

CALORIES 75 (16% from fat); FAT 1.3g (sat 0.6g, mono 0.3g, poly 0.2g); PROTEIN 3.7g; CARB 14g; FIBER 3.7g; CHOL 2mg; IRON 1.3mg; SODIUM 216mg; CALC 86mg

The key to perfecting holiday dressing is experimentation. For example, if you prefer moist dressing, add more broth; if you like a drier recipe, try cutting back a little on the broth or baking the dressing a little longer.

Blue Corn Bread Dressing

Cooking spray
1   tablespoon all-purpose flour
⅓   cup sugar
5   tablespoons butter, softened
5   large eggs
½   cup fat-free buttermilk
1   cup all-purpose flour
1   cup blue cornmeal
2   teaspoons baking powder
1   teaspoon baking soda
1   teaspoon salt
5   (14-ounce) cans fat-free, less-sodium chicken broth
1   teaspoon olive oil
1   cup finely chopped onion
1   cup frozen corn kernels, thawed
1   (7-ounce) bottle roasted red bell peppers, drained and chopped
8   cups (1-inch) cubed French bread (about 8 ounces)
¾   cup chopped green onions

1. Preheat oven to 450°.
2. Coat a 13 x 9-inch baking pan with cooking spray, and dust with 1 tablespoon flour.
3. Place sugar and butter in a bowl; beat with mixer at medium speed until well blended. Add eggs, 1 at a time, beating well after each addition. Stir in buttermilk. Lightly spoon 1 cup flour into a dry measuring cup; level with a knife. Combine flour, cornmeal, baking powder, baking soda, and salt, stirring well with a whisk. Add flour mixture to buttermilk mixture, stirring until moist.
4. Pour batter into prepared baking pan. Bake at 450° for 20 minutes or until a wooden pick inserted in center comes out clean. Cool completely. Cut corn bread into 1-inch cubes.
5. Reduce oven temperature to 350°.
6. Bring broth to a boil in a large saucepan; cook until reduced to 5 cups (about 30 minutes). Heat oil in a large nonstick skillet over medium-high heat. Add 1 cup onion; sauté 3 minutes. Add corn and bell pepper; sauté 3 minutes.
7. Combine onion mixture, corn bread, French bread, and green onions in a large bowl, stirring to combine. Add broth,

tossing to coat. Spoon mixture into a 13 x 9-inch baking pan coated with cooking spray. Bake at 350° for 40 minutes or until set. Yield: 8 servings.

CALORIES 216 (30% from fat); FAT 7.2g (sat 3.5g, mono 2.1g, poly 0.6g); PROTEIN 7.6g; CARB 30.7g; FIBER 1.5g; CHOL 79mg; IRON 1.5mg; SODIUM 534mg; CALC 62mg

Oyster Dressing

1½   cups corn bread stuffing mix (such as Pepperidge Farm)
1   (16-ounce) container standard oysters, undrained
4   hard-cooked large eggs
Cooking spray
½   cup chopped onion
½   cup chopped fresh parsley
½   cup chopped green bell pepper
3   cups cooked wild rice
½   cup fat-free, less-sodium chicken broth
½   cup sliced green onions
½   teaspoon salt
¼   teaspoon black pepper

1. Preheat oven to 350°.
2. Prepare stuffing according to package directions, omitting fat. Set aside.
3. Drain oysters in a colander over a bowl, reserving ⅓ cup oyster liquid.
4. Slice eggs in half lengthwise; discard yolks. Finely chop egg whites.
5. Heat a large nonstick skillet coated with cooking spray over medium heat. Add chopped onion, parsley, and bell pepper, and cook 3 minutes or until tender, stirring frequently. Stir in oysters, and cook 2 minutes. Stir in prepared stuffing, ⅓ cup oyster liquid, egg whites, wild rice, and remaining ingredients. Spread dressing in an 8-inch square baking dish coated with cooking spray. Bake dressing at 350° for 30 minutes or until thoroughly heated. Yield: 10 servings (serving size: about ¾ cup).

CALORIES 140 (13% from fat); FAT 2g (sat 0.4g, mono 0.3g, poly 0.8g); PROTEIN 8.2g; CARB 22.3g; FIBER 1.8g; CHOL 25mg; IRON 4.1mg; SODIUM 313mg; CALC 43mg

Mama's Corn Bread Dressing

"These days, whenever I cook for my guests, I'm conscious that many folks don't eat meat, so I will also include plenty of meat-free side dishes that can be enjoyed by everyone," Curtis Aikens, produce expert, cookbook author, and Food Network host, says. Aikens's savory corn bread dressing, a recipe that originated with his mother, fits the bill.

     5 cups Mama's Corn Bread, crumbled
     3 cups (1-inch) cubed, toasted white bread (about
        5 [1-ounce] slices)
     1 cup crushed saltine crackers (about 20 crackers)
     3 cups vegetable broth
     2 cups chopped celery
     2 cups chopped onion
    ¼ cup butter
    1½ teaspoons dried rubbed sage
    ¼ teaspoon salt
    ¼ teaspoon black pepper
     2 large eggs
     1 large egg white
        Cooking spray

1. Preheat oven to 375°.
2. Combine first 3 ingredients in a large bowl. Combine broth, celery, onion, and butter in a large saucepan; bring to a boil. Reduce heat; simmer 10 minutes. Add broth mixture to corn bread mixture, stirring well. Add sage and next 4 ingredients; stir well to combine.
3. Pour mixture into an 11 x 7-inch baking dish coated with cooking spray. Bake at 375° for 45 minutes; cover and bake an additional 30 minutes or until golden. Yield: 12 servings.

CALORIES 243 (39% from fat); FAT 10.5g (sat 3.7g, mono 3g, poly 2.5g); PROTEIN 7.1g; CARB 30.4g; FIBER 2.6g; CHOL 65mg; IRON 1.9mg; SODIUM 622mg; CALC 68mg

Mama's Corn Bread

    1¾ cups yellow cornmeal
    ¼ teaspoon baking powder
    ¼ teaspoon baking soda
    ¼ teaspoon salt
     1 cup 1% low-fat buttermilk
     1 cup water
     1 large egg
     1 large egg white
        Cooking spray
     3 tablespoons vegetable oil

1. Preheat oven to 375°.
2. Combine first 8 ingredients in a large bowl; stir well. Coat a 9-inch cast-iron skillet with cooking spray; add oil, and place in oven 5 minutes. Remove from oven; stir oil into batter. Pour batter into pan. Bake at 375° for 35 minutes or until golden. Yield: 9 servings (serving size: 1 wedge).

CALORIES 161 (32% from fat); FAT 5.8g (sat 1.1g, mono 1.4g, poly 2.9g); PROTEIN 4.4g; CARB 22.4g; FIBER 2g; CHOL 25mg; IRON 1.2mg; SODIUM 157mg; CALC 42mg

Sourdough-Sausage Stuffing

If you're looking for a stuffing that is reminiscent of what you grew up with, this is an excellent choice to round out your Thanksgiving menu. It's just like the stuffing Mom used to make—only better! If you have only one oven, make the stuffing first, and keep it warm; then pop it back into the oven for a quick reheat before serving the Thanksgiving meal.

     3 turkey Italian sausage links (about 11 ounces)
     1 teaspoon olive oil
     2 cups chopped onion
     2 cups chopped celery
     2 tablespoons chopped fresh parsley
     2 teaspoons dried rubbed sage
     1 teaspoon dried thyme
    ½ teaspoon salt
    ½ teaspoon dried marjoram
    ½ teaspoon black pepper
    12 cups (½-inch) cubed sourdough bread (about
        1 pound)
     2 cups can fat-free, less-sodium chicken broth
        Cooking spray

1. Preheat oven to 350°.
2. Remove casings from sausage. Heat oil in a large nonstick skillet over medium-high heat; add sausage, and sauté 5 minutes or until browned, stirring to crumble. Add onion and celery; sauté 3 minutes. Stir in parsley and next 5 ingredients. Place sausage mixture in a large bowl; stir in bread and broth. Spoon stuffing into an 11 x 7-inch baking dish coated with cooking spray. Cover and bake at 350° for 15 minutes. Uncover; bake an additional 20 minutes or until golden brown. Yield: 9 servings (serving size: 1 cup).

CALORIES 208 (21% from fat); FAT 5g (sat 1.7g, mono 1.9g, poly 2.4g); PROTEIN 11.9g; CARB 28.9g; FIBER 2.1g; CHOL 30mg; IRON 2.3mg; SODIUM 699mg; CALC 76mg

Creamy Polenta with Warm Tomato Compote

You can keep the polenta warm over very low heat for up to 30 minutes; stir in a little water or milk if it gets too thick. This side dish makes a great accompaniment to lamb.

    6   cups cherry tomatoes (about 2 pounds)
        Cooking spray
    1   tablespoon olive oil
    ¼   cup sliced shallots (about 3 medium)
    1½ tablespoons sugar
    ¾   cup dry white wine
    1½ teaspoons salt, divided
    ¼   teaspoon black pepper
    2   cups 1% low-fat milk
    2   cups water
    1   cup dry polenta
    ½   cup (2 ounces) shaved fresh Parmesan cheese

1. Preheat oven to 425°.
2. Cut several slits in bottom of each tomato; place, stem sides down, in a shallow roasting pan coated with cooking spray. Bake at 425° for 20 minutes. Reduce oven temperature to 375° (do not remove tomatoes from oven); bake 45 minutes or until browned. Cover and let stand 10 minutes.
3. Heat oil in a large nonstick skillet over medium-high heat. Add shallots; sauté 5 minutes or until browned. Add sugar; sauté 5 minutes. Add wine; reduce heat, and simmer 5 minutes. Add ½ teaspoon salt and pepper. Remove from heat; stir in tomatoes. Cover; set aside.
4. Combine milk and water in a large saucepan; bring to a boil. Remove from heat; gradually add polenta, stirring constantly with a whisk. Cover; cook over medium-low heat 2 minutes. Add 1 teaspoon salt; cover and let stand 5 minutes or until thick, stirring occasionally. Top polenta with tomato compote and Parmesan cheese. Yield: 8 servings (serving size: ½ cup polenta, ⅓ cup tomato compote, and 1 tablespoon Parmesan cheese).

CALORIES 153 (28% from fat); FAT 4.8g (sat 1.9g, mono 2g, poly 0.4g); PROTEIN 6.8g; CARB 21.6g; FIBER 1.7g; CHOL 7mg; IRON 0.9mg; SODIUM 597mg; CALC 169mg

Pumpkin-Sage Polenta

Serve this alongside pan-sautéed ham steaks. Polenta thickens if you make it ahead; just thin it with water or chicken broth. Rewarm it over medium-low heat, stirring with a whisk.

    2½ cups 1% low-fat milk
    2   cups water
    ¾   cup canned pumpkin
    1¼ teaspoons salt
    1¼ cups instant dry polenta
    ¾   cup (3 ounces) grated fresh Parmesan cheese
    2   tablespoons ⅓-less-fat cream cheese, softened
    1   tablespoon chopped fresh sage
    ¼   cup (1 ounce) shaved fresh Parmesan

1. Bring milk and water to a boil in a large saucepan over medium heat. Add pumpkin and salt; stir with a whisk. Reduce heat to low, and gradually whisk in polenta; cook 1 minute or until thick. Remove from heat. Add ¾ cup grated Parmesan, cream cheese, and sage; stir until cheeses melt. Top with shaved Parmesan. Serve immediately. Yield: 8 servings (serving size: ¾ cup).

CALORIES 197 (21% from fat); FAT 4.7g (sat 3g, mono 1.4g, poly 0.1g); PROTEIN 10.1g; CARB 28.7g; FIBER 3.2g; CHOL 14mg; IRON 1mg; SODIUM 614mg; CALC 253mg

Pumpkin-Sage
Polenta

Butternut Squash Risotto

This creamy Italian side dish makes a great first course for Thanksgiving.
(Recipe adapted from *Every Night Italian,* by Giuliano Hazan; Scribner, 2000.)

2   cups water, divided

2   (14-ounce) cans less-sodium beef broth

2   teaspoons olive oil

½   cup finely chopped yellow onion

3   cups (¾-inch) cubed peeled butternut squash
    (about 1 pound)

½   teaspoon salt

¼   teaspoon freshly ground black pepper

1½ cups Arborio rice or other
    short-grain rice

½   cup (2 ounces) grated Parmigiano-Reggiano
    cheese

3   tablespoons unsalted butter

2   tablespoons finely chopped fresh parsley

1. Bring 1½ cups water and broth to a simmer in a large saucepan (do not boil). Keep warm over low heat.

2. Heat oil in a Dutch oven over medium heat. Add onion; cook 8 minutes or until golden, stirring frequently. Add ½ cup water, squash, salt, and pepper; cook 10 minutes or until squash is tender and water has almost evaporated. Add rice; stir until combined. Stir in ½ cup broth mixture; cook until liquid is nearly absorbed, stirring constantly. Add remaining broth mixture, ½ cup at a time, stirring constantly until each portion of broth is absorbed before adding next (about 30 minutes total). Stir in cheese, butter, and parsley. Serve immediately. Yield: 8 servings (serving size: ⅔ cup).

CALORIES 272 (25% from fat); FAT 7.6g (sat 4g, mono 2.8g, poly 0.5g); PROTEIN 7.9g; CARB 41.4g; FIBER 2.8g; CHOL 15mg; IRON 1mg; SODIUM 275mg; CALC 119mg

Butternut Squash Risotto

Risotto with Mushrooms and Parmesan

    2 cups water
    1 (14-ounce) can vegetable broth
    4 teaspoons olive oil, divided
    2 cups chopped cremini mushrooms (about 6 ounces)
  ½ cup chopped onion
1 ½ cups Arborio rice or other short-grain rice
    1 cup dry white wine
  ½ cup (2 ounces) grated fresh Parmesan cheese
  ¼ cup chopped fresh parsley
    2 tablespoons chopped fresh basil
  ¼ to ½ teaspoon crushed red pepper
  ¼ teaspoon salt
  ¼ teaspoon black pepper

1. Bring water and broth to a simmer in a saucepan (do not boil). Keep warm over low heat. Heat 2 teaspoons oil in a medium saucepan over medium-high heat. Add mushrooms; sauté 5 minutes or until tender. Remove mushrooms from pan. Heat 2 teaspoons oil in pan over medium-high heat. Add onion; sauté 2 minutes. Add rice; cook 1 minute, stirring constantly. Stir in wine; cook 2 minutes or until liquid is nearly absorbed, stirring constantly.
2. Add broth mixture, ½ cup at a time, stirring constantly until each portion of broth mixture is absorbed before adding the next (about 20 minutes total). Stir in mushrooms, cheese, and remaining ingredients. Yield: 7 servings (serving size: about ¾ cup).

CALORIES 276 (16% from fat); FAT 5g (sat 1.7g, mono 2.5g, poly 0.3g); PROTEIN 8.2g; CARB 41.9g; FIBER 1.7g; CHOL 5mg; IRON 0.9mg; SODIUM 475mg; CALC 123mg

Minnesota Wild Rice Pilaf

1 ¼ cups water
    4 cups fat-free, less-sodium chicken broth
1 ½ cups uncooked wild rice (Gourmet House Minnesota Cultivated Wild Rice)
    1 tablespoon butter
    3 cups sliced mushrooms
    1 cup chopped onion
  ½ cup finely chopped fresh parsley
  ⅓ cup chopped pecans, toasted
  ¾ teaspoon poultry seasoning
  ½ teaspoon salt
  ¼ teaspoon black pepper
Cooking spray

1. Bring water and broth to a boil in a medium saucepan. Add wild rice; cover, reduce heat, and simmer 1 hour or until rice is tender. Drain.
2. Preheat oven to 325°.
3. Melt butter in a large nonstick skillet over medium-high heat. Add mushrooms and onion; sauté 6 minutes. Remove from heat; stir in parsley and next 4 ingredients. Combine rice and mushroom mixture in a 2-quart casserole coated with cooking spray. Cover and bake at 325° for 25 minutes. Yield: 8 servings (serving size: 1 cup).

CALORIES 177 (27% from fat); FAT 5.4g (sat 1.2g, mono 2.6g, poly 1.1g); PROTEIN 6.9g; CARB 27.2g; FIBER 2.8g; CHOL 4mg; IRON 1.4mg; SODIUM 347mg; CALC 21mg

Barley, Wild Rice, and Currant Pilaf

    1 cup uncooked pearl barley
  ½ cup uncooked wild rice
    2 teaspoons vegetable oil
1 ½ cups finely chopped onion
1 ⅓ cups finely chopped celery
    1 cup finely chopped carrot
    2 garlic cloves, minced
  ⅔ cup currants
    2 teaspoons dried rubbed sage
    1 teaspoon salt
    1 teaspoon dried thyme
  ½ teaspoon black pepper
5 ¼ cups fat-free, less-sodium chicken broth
    2 bay leaves

1. Place barley and rice in a large skillet over medium heat. Cook 7 minutes or until lightly browned, stirring frequently. Place in a bowl; set aside.
2. Heat oil in skillet until hot. Add onion, celery, carrot, and garlic; stir well. Cover and cook over medium-low heat 8 minutes or until vegetables are tender.
3. Add barley mixture, currants, and remaining ingredients, and bring to a boil. Cover, reduce heat, and simmer mixture 50 minutes or until liquid is absorbed, stirring occasionally. Discard bay leaves. Yield: 8 servings (serving size: 1 cup.)

CALORIES 217 (11% from fat); FAT 2.7g (sat 0.5g, mono 1g, poly 1g); PROTEIN 8.2g; CARB 43.4g; FIBER 6.7g; CHOL 0mg; IRON 1.9mg; SODIUM 370mg; CALC 53mg

desserts

From crème brûlée to classic cakes, these sweet indulgences will crown a variety of holiday meals with festive finishes.

Espresso Crème Brûlée

Espresso Crème Brûlée

We prefer the convenience of a small butane kitchen torch to melt and caramelize the sugar, but the stovetop method works fine, too. Cold custards stand up well to the heat of the torch, so you can make them 1 to 2 days ahead.

 2 cups 2% reduced-fat milk
 1 cup whole espresso coffee beans
 ¾ cup nonfat dry milk
 3 tablespoons sugar, divided
 1 teaspoon vanilla extract
Dash of salt
 4 large egg yolks, lightly beaten
 ¼ cup sugar

1. Combine 2% milk, espresso beans, dry milk, and 2 tablespoons sugar in a medium saucepan. Cook mixture over medium heat to 180° or until tiny bubbles form around edge (do not boil), stirring occasionally. Remove milk mixture from heat. Cover and steep 30 minutes.

2. Preheat oven to 300°.

3. Strain milk mixture through a sieve into a bowl; discard solids. Stir in vanilla.

4. Combine 1 tablespoon sugar, salt, and egg yolks in a medium bowl, stirring well with a whisk.

5. Gradually add milk mixture to egg mixture, stirring constantly with a whisk. Divide the mixture evenly among 4 (4-ounce) ramekins, custard cups, or shallow baking dishes. Place ramekins in a 13 x 9-inch baking pan, and add hot water to pan to a depth of 1 inch.

6. Bake at 300° for 25 minutes or until center barely moves when ramekin is touched. Remove ramekins from pan; cool completely on a wire rack. Cover; chill at least 4 hours or overnight.

7. Sift 1 tablespoon sugar evenly over each custard. Holding a kitchen torch about 2 inches from top of each custard, heat sugar, moving torch back and forth, until sugar is completely melted and caramelized (about 1 minute). Serve immediately or within 1 hour. Yield: 4 servings.

Note: If you don't have a kitchen torch, you can make the sugar topping on the stovetop. Place ¼ cup sugar and 1 tablespoon water in a small, heavy saucepan. Cook over medium heat 5 to 8 minutes or until golden (resist the urge to stir, since doing so may cause the sugar to crystallize). Immediately pour the sugar mixture evenly over cold custards, spreading to form a thin layer.

CALORIES 262 (26% from fat); FAT 7.7g (sat 3.2g, mono 2.7g, poly 0.7g); PROTEIN 11.3g; CARB 36g; FIBER 0g; CHOL 225mg; IRON 0.6mg; SODIUM 215mg; CALC 315mg

how to: MAKE CRÈME BRÛLÉE

with a kitchen torch

1. Carefully sift sugar, using a small sieve, over each custard. This disperses sugar evenly.

2. Torch sugar immediately after it's sifted onto custards, or it will dissolve into custards. Hold torch about 2 inches away, and work from side to side until all sugar is melted and caramelized.

on the stovetop

1. In a small saucepan or skillet, cook sugar over medium heat until golden (about 5 to 8 minutes). Resist the urge to stir since doing so may cause the sugar to crystallize.

2. Working quickly, evenly drizzle sugar topping over cold custards. Using a rubber spatula coated with cooking spray, spread caramel evenly to form a thin layer. Work quickly or caramel will set.

Expect a crowd in the kitchen when you crown these custards with their burnt-sugar shells.

Persimmon Flan

Persimmons are a winter fruit with a short season, generally October through December.
We prefer to use the Fuyu variety, a nonastringent persimmon shaped like a tomato.
They're firm when ripe and have a sweet-spicy flavor, with notes of banana, plum, and winter squash.

1½ cups sugar, divided
¼   cup water
2   ripe persimmons, peeled and quartered
2   tablespoons all-purpose flour
1   (8-ounce) block ⅓-less-fat cream cheese
3   large egg whites
2   large eggs
2   cups 2% reduced-fat milk
½   cup pomegranate seeds
24 thin slices peeled ripe persimmon (about 4 persimmons)

1. Combine 1 cup sugar and water in a small, heavy saucepan; cook over medium-high heat until sugar dissolves, stirring frequently. Continue cooking 9 minutes or until golden. Immediately pour into a 9-inch round cake pan, tipping quickly until sugar coats bottom of pan.

2. Place persimmon quarters in a food processor; process until smooth, scraping sides of bowl once.

3. Preheat oven to 350°.

4. Combine ½ cup sugar and flour. Beat cream cheese with a mixer at medium speed until smooth. Add flour mixture; beat until well blended. Add egg whites and eggs; beat well. Gradually add milk and ½ cup persimmon puree; beat well. Pour batter into prepared cake pan. Place cake pan in a broiler pan; add hot water to broiler pan to a depth of 1 inch. Bake at 350° for 1½ hours or until a knife inserted in center comes out clean. Remove cake pan from broiler pan; cool completely on a wire rack. Cover and chill 8 hours.

5. Loosen edges of flan with a knife or rubber spatula. Place a serving plate, upside down, on top of pan, and invert the flan onto the plate. Drizzle any remaining caramelized syrup over the flan. Sprinkle flan with pomegranate seeds, and garnish with persimmon slices. Yield: 10 servings (serving size: 1 wedge).

CALORIES 282 (24% from fat); FAT 7.4g (sat 4.2g, mono 2.2g, poly 0.3g); PROTEIN 6.8g; CARB 49.2g; FIBER 1.1g; CHOL 65mg; IRON 0.5mg; SODIUM 145mg; CALC 89mg

Persimmon Flan

If you're short on time during the holidays—like most of us—here's a list of items you can pick up at the market and have on hand for unexpected guests.

- Use leftover caramel syrup from Cinnamon Bread Puddings with Caramel Syrup (recipe below right) over ice cream, toasted pound cake slices, waffles, or plain store-bought cheesecake.
- Slightly warmed chocolate sauce is ideal for serving as fondue. Strawberries, pineapple chunks, marshmallows, and graham crackers make delightful dippers.
- Blend a few tablespoons of fudge sauce into softened vanilla ice cream for a rich, thick milk shake.
- Melt vanilla ice cream in the microwave as a quick sauce for fresh fruit.

Outrageous Warm Double-Chocolate Pudding

Custard Layer:
- ¼ cup sugar
- ¼ cup egg substitute
- 1 cup plus 2 tablespoons evaporated fat-free milk
- 1½ ounces semisweet baking chocolate (such as Hershey's), chopped
- Cooking spray

Cake Layer:
- 3 ounces dark-chocolate candy bar (such as Hershey's), chopped
- ⅓ cup sugar
- ⅓ cup egg substitute
- ¼ cup applesauce
- 6 tablespoons frozen fat-free whipped topping, thawed

1. Preheat oven to 325°.

2. To prepare custard layer, combine ¼ cup sugar and ¼ cup egg substitute, stirring well with a whisk. Cook milk in a small, heavy saucepan over medium-high heat to 180° or until tiny bubbles form around edge (do not boil). Remove from heat; add semisweet chocolate, stirring until chocolate melts. Gradually add hot milk mixture to sugar mixture, stirring constantly with a whisk.

3. Pour hot milk mixture into 6 (4-ounce) ramekins or custard cups coated with cooking spray. Place ramekins in a baking pan, and add hot water to pan to a depth of 1 inch. Bake at 325° for 30 minutes or until almost set. Remove ramekins from oven, and cool in pan 30 minutes. Remove the ramekins from pan, and drain water.

4. To prepare cake layer, place dark chocolate in a small glass bowl. Microwave at HIGH 2 minutes or until almost melted; stir after 1 minute. Set aside. Beat ⅓ cup sugar and ⅓ cup egg substitute with a mixer at medium speed until well blended (about 5 minutes). Add dark chocolate and applesauce; beat until well blended. Pour evenly over custard layer. Place ramekins in baking pan; add hot water to pan to a depth of 1 inch. Bake at 325° for 20 minutes. Remove ramekins from pan. Top each serving with 1 tablespoon whipped topping. Yield: 6 servings.

CALORIES 257 (26% from fat); FAT 7.5g (sat 4.3g, mono 1.8g, poly 0.5g); PROTEIN 6.9g; CARB 41.1g; FIBER 1.8g; CHOL 4mg; IRON 1.1mg; SODIUM 104mg; CALC 131mg

Cinnamon Bread Puddings with Caramel Syrup

This recipe starts with cinnamon-swirl bread, reducing the need to add other flavorings. Commercial caramel syrup saves time, too. Baking the pudding in muffin cups creates individual servings.

- 1⅓ cups 2% reduced-fat milk
- ½ cup sugar
- 3 large eggs, lightly beaten
- 1 (1-pound) loaf cinnamon-swirl bread, cut into 1-inch cubes
- Cooking spray
- ⅔ cup fat-free caramel sundae syrup

1. Combine first 3 ingredients in a large bowl, stirring well with a whisk. Add bread, tossing gently to coat. Cover and chill 30 minutes or up to 4 hours.

2. Preheat oven to 350°.

3. Divide bread mixture evenly among 11 muffin cups coated with cooking spray. Bake at 350° for 30 minutes or until a knife inserted in center comes out clean. Serve warm with syrup. Yield: 11 servings (serving size: 1 bread pudding and about 1 tablespoon syrup).

CALORIES 251 (20% from fat); FAT 5.6g (sat 1.5g, mono 2.9g, poly 0.2g); PROTEIN 7.1g; CARB 46.3g; FIBER 3g; CHOL 60mg; IRON 1.3mg; SODIUM 255mg; CALC 52mg

New Orleans Bread
Pudding with Bourbon
Sauce

New Orleans Bread Pudding with Bourbon Sauce

Raisin-studded bread pudding and buttery, bourbon-spiked sauce combine in this time-honored dessert. It's
elegant enough for a formal holiday dinner party, yet casual enough for a December supper club.

Pudding:

¼   cup raisins

2   tablespoons bourbon

1¼ cups 2% reduced-fat
    milk

½   cup sugar

1   tablespoon vanilla extract

½   teaspoon ground cinnamon

¼   teaspoon ground nutmeg

Dash of salt

3   large eggs, lightly beaten

4½ cups (½-inch) cubed French
    bread (about 8 ounces)

Cooking spray

Sauce:

½   cup sugar

¼   cup light-colored corn
    syrup

¼   cup butter

¼   cup bourbon

1. To prepare pudding, combine raisins and 2 tablespoons
bourbon in a bowl. Let stand 30 minutes. Drain mixture in a
sieve over a bowl, reserving liquid.

2. Combine reserved liquid, milk, and next 6 ingredients in a
large bowl; stir well with a whisk. Add bread; toss gently to coat.
Spoon mixture into an 8-inch square baking dish coated with
cooking spray. Sprinkle evenly with raisins; press gently into
bread mixture. Cover with foil; chill 30 minutes or up to 4 hours.

3. Preheat oven to 350°.

4. Place dish in a 13 x 9-inch baking pan; add hot water to
pan to a depth of 1 inch. Bake, covered, at 350° for 20 minutes.
Uncover and bake an additional 10 minutes or until a knife
inserted in center comes out clean.

5. To prepare sauce, combine ½ cup sugar, corn syrup, and
butter in a small saucepan over medium heat. Bring to a
simmer; cook 1 minute, stirring constantly. Remove from heat;
stir in ¼ cup bourbon. Serve each bread pudding piece warm
with about 1 tablespoon sauce. Yield: 9 servings.

CALORIES 309 (24% from fat); FAT 8.2g (sat 4.3g, mono 2.7g, poly 0.6g); PROTEIN 5.6g;
CARB 47.6g; FIBER 1g; CHOL 87mg; IRON 1.1mg; SODIUM 272mg; CALC 74mg

Hot Maple Soufflés

This dessert has become a holiday favorite at *Cooking Light*. The ingredients are simple, but the technique elevates it—literally and figuratively.

1 tablespoon butter, softened
2 tablespoons granulated sugar
3 tablespoons bourbon
3 tablespoons maple syrup
1 cup maple syrup
4 large egg whites
1/8 teaspoon salt
1 teaspoon baking powder
1 tablespoon sifted powdered sugar

1. Preheat oven to 425°.

2. Coat 6 (10-ounce) ramekins with butter; sprinkle evenly with granulated sugar. Combine bourbon and 3 tablespoons syrup in a small microwave-safe bowl; microwave at HIGH 1½ minutes or until mixture boils. Pour about 1 tablespoon bourbon mixture into each prepared ramekin.

3. Cook 1 cup syrup in a medium, heavy saucepan over medium-high heat 8 minutes or until a candy thermometer registers 250°.

4. Beat egg whites and salt with a mixer at medium speed until foamy. Pour hot maple syrup in a thin stream over egg whites, beating at medium speed, then at high speed, until stiff peaks form. Add baking powder; beat well.

5. Spoon evenly into ramekins; place on a jelly-roll pan. Bake at 425° for 13 minutes or until puffy and set. Sprinkle with powdered sugar. Serve immediately. Yield: 6 servings.

CALORIES 212 (8% from fat); FAT 2g (sat 0.4g, mono 0.8g, poly 0.6g); PROTEIN 2.3g; CARB 47.8g; FIBER 0g; CHOL 0mg; IRON 0.8mg; SODIUM 193mg; CALC 89mg

Rich Chocolate Soufflé Cakes with Crème Anglaise

These don't need to be served to your dinner guests immediately (although they can be). We loved their fudgy, dense texture when chilled. The crème anglaise is good warmed or chilled.

Soufflé Cakes:

Cooking spray
8 teaspoons sugar
⅔ cup sugar
½ cup water
2 ounces semisweet chocolate, chopped
1 ounce unsweetened chocolate, chopped
½ cup Dutch process cocoa
3 tablespoons cornstarch
⅛ teaspoon salt
2 large egg yolks
1 teaspoon vanilla extract
4 large egg whites
¼ teaspoon cream of tartar
3 tablespoons sugar

Crème Anglaise:

3 large egg yolks, lightly beaten
⅛ teaspoon salt
⅓ cup sugar
1 cup 1% low-fat milk
2 teaspoons vanilla extract

Rich Chocolate
Soufflé Cakes with
Crème Anglaise

1. Preheat oven to 350°.

2. To prepare soufflé cakes, lightly coat 8 (4-ounce) ramekins with cooking spray. Sprinkle each with 1 teaspoon sugar.

3. Combine ⅔ cup sugar and ½ cup water in a medium, heavy saucepan. Bring to a boil over medium heat, stirring to dissolve sugar. Remove from heat. Add chopped chocolates, stirring with a whisk until chocolates melt. Combine cocoa, cornstarch, and ⅛ teaspoon salt. Add cocoa mixture to chocolate mixture, stirring with a whisk. Whisk in 2 egg yolks and 1 teaspoon vanilla extract.

4. Place egg whites and cream of tartar in a large bowl; beat with a mixer at medium speed until soft peaks form. Gradually add 3 tablespoons sugar, 1 tablespoon at a time, beating at high speed until stiff peaks form. Gently stir one-fourth of egg white mixture into chocolate mixture; fold in the remaining egg white mixture. Spoon chocolate mixture into prepared ramekins. Place ramekins in a large baking dish; add hot water to dish to a depth of ¾ inch.

5. Bake at 350° for 15 minutes or until puffy and slightly cracked. Remove ramekins from dish.

6. To prepare crème anglaise, combine 3 egg yolks and ⅛ teaspoon salt in a medium bowl. Gradually add ⅓ cup sugar, whisking until thick and pale yellow (about 3 minutes).

7. Cook milk in a heavy saucepan over medium heat to 180° or until tiny bubbles form around edge (do not boil). Remove from heat.

8. Gradually add hot milk to egg yolk mixture, stirring with a whisk. Return egg yolk mixture to pan; cook over medium-low heat 5 minutes or until slightly thick and mixture coats back of a spoon, stirring constantly (do not boil). Remove from heat. Stir in 2 teaspoons vanilla. Serve with soufflé cakes. Yield: 8 servings (serving size: 1 soufflé cake and about 1 tablespoon sauce).

CALORIES 271 (27% from fat); FAT 8.2g (sat 4g, mono 2.2g, poly 0.5g); PROTEIN 6.4g; CARB 47.1g; FIBER 2.7g; CHOL 134mg; IRON 1.4mg; SODIUM 123mg; CALC 63mg

Chocolate Decadence

Christmas is the best time of the year for your favorite indulgences, particularly for dark chocolate pudding cakes with warm fudgy centers! While this is a lightened version, we guarantee it has the fudgy burst of flavor you are craving.

Cooking spray
½ cup plus 3 tablespoons sugar, divided
¼ cup 2% reduced-fat milk
8 teaspoons unsweetened cocoa
1½ tablespoons butter
½ ounce unsweetened chocolate, chopped
5 tablespoons all-purpose flour
½ teaspoon vanilla extract
⅛ teaspoon salt
1 large egg white, lightly beaten
8 teaspoons semisweet chocolate chips

1. Preheat oven to 350°.

2. Lightly coat 4 (2-ounce) ramekins with cooking spray, and sprinkle ¾ teaspoon sugar into each, shaking and turning to coat. Set prepared ramekins aside.

3. Combine ½ cup plus 2 tablespoons sugar, milk, and cocoa in a small saucepan, stirring well with a whisk. Bring to a boil over medium heat. Cook 30 seconds or until sugar dissolves, stirring constantly. Remove from heat; add butter and unsweetened chocolate. Stir until chocolate melts and mixture is smooth. Cool chocolate mixture 10 minutes.

4. Add flour, vanilla, salt, and egg white to chocolate mixture, stirring with a whisk just until blended. Spoon 2 tablespoons chocolate mixture into each prepared ramekin, and top with 2 teaspoons chocolate chips. Divide remaining chocolate mixture evenly among ramekins, spreading to cover chocolate chips. Place on a baking sheet. Bake at 350° for 20 minutes or until barely set. Cool 10 minutes. Invert onto dessert plates. Serve warm. Yield: 4 servings.

CALORIES 315 (31% from fat); FAT 11g (sat 5.7g, mono 2.8g, poly 0.8g); PROTEIN 4.1g; CARB 52.1g; FIBER 1.6g; CHOL 13mg; IRON 2.2mg; SODIUM 140mg; CALC 27mg

Chocolate
Decadence

German-Chocolate Cake with Coconut-Pecan Sauce

This is the perfect dessert to take to a holiday office party, since it serves a crowd. Warm the Coconut-Pecan Sauce in the microwave before serving.

⅓   cup butter
1   (4-ounce) bar sweet baking chocolate, chopped
1¼   cups sugar
½   cup water
1½   teaspoons vanilla extract
2   large egg whites
1   large egg
2   cups all-purpose flour
2   teaspoons baking powder
⅛   teaspoon salt
    Cooking spray
    Coconut-Pecan Sauce

1. Preheat oven to 350°.
2. Place butter and chocolate in a microwave-safe bowl; microwave at HIGH 1 minute or until melted, stirring until smooth. Stir in sugar, water, and vanilla. Add egg whites and egg; stir with a whisk. Lightly spoon flour into dry measuring cups; level with a knife. Combine flour, baking powder, and salt; add to chocolate mixture, stirring with a whisk until smooth. Coat bottom of a 13 x 9-inch baking pan with cooking spray; pour batter into pan. Bake at 350° for 30 minutes or until a wooden pick inserted in center comes out clean. Cool in pan on a wire rack. Serve with Coconut-Pecan Sauce. Yield: 20 servings (serving size: 1 cake piece and 2 tablespoons sauce).

(Totals include Coconut-Pecan Sauce) CALORIES 267 (30% from fat); FAT 8.9g (sat 4.7g, mono 3g, poly 0.7g); PROTEIN 3.7g; CARB 44.5g; FIBER 0.6g; CHOL 25mg; IRON 0.9mg; SODIUM 144mg; CALC 84mg

Coconut-Pecan Sauce

1½   cups sugar
2½   tablespoons cornstarch
1   (12-ounce) can evaporated low-fat milk
3   tablespoons butter
⅓   cup chopped pecans
¼   cup flaked sweetened coconut
1½   teaspoons vanilla extract

1. Combine sugar and cornstarch in a medium, heavy saucepan. Add milk, and stir with a whisk. Add butter. Bring mixture to a boil over medium heat, and cook 1 minute, stirring constantly. Remove from heat; stir in pecans, coconut, and vanilla. Serve warm. Yield: 2⅔ cups (serving size: about 2 tablespoons).

CALORIES 110 (29% from fat); FAT 3.5g (sat 1.6g, mono 1.4g, poly 0.4g); PROTEIN 1.5g; CARB 18.8g; FIBER 0.2g; CHOL 5mg; IRON 0.1mg; SODIUM 40mg; CALC 51mg

Molasses Cake with Lemon Cream Cheese Frosting

Cake:
    Cooking spray
2   cups sifted cake flour
1   teaspoon baking soda
1   teaspoon ground cinnamon
½   teaspoon salt
1   cup fat-free buttermilk
¾   cup molasses
½   cup granulated sugar
6   tablespoons butter, melted
1   tablespoon minced peeled fresh ginger
1   large egg, lightly beaten

Frosting:
½   cup powdered sugar
1   tablespoon grated lemon rind
1   (8-ounce) block ⅓-less-fat cream cheese, softened

1. Preheat oven to 350°.
2. To prepare cake, coat a 9-inch square baking pan with cooking spray; line bottom of pan with wax paper. Coat wax paper with cooking spray.
3. Sift together flour, baking soda, cinnamon, and salt.
4. Place buttermilk and the next 5 ingredients in a large bowl, and beat with a mixer at medium speed until mixture is well blended. Add flour mixture to buttermilk mixture, stirring just until combined.
5. Spoon batter into prepared pan. Bake at 350° for 35 minutes or until a wooden pick inserted in center comes out clean. Cool in pan 10 minutes on a wire rack. Loosen cake from sides of pan with a narrow metal spatula; remove from pan. Peel off wax paper; cool completely on a wire rack.
6. To prepare frosting, place powdered sugar, lemon rind, and cream cheese in a bowl; beat with a mixer at medium speed until smooth. Spread frosting over top of cake. Cut into squares. Yield: 12 servings.

CALORIES 253 (29% from fat); FAT 8.2g (sat 4.9g, mono 1.9g, poly 0.3g); PROTEIN 4.6g; CARB 41.7g; FIBER 0.4g; CHOL 41mg; IRON 4mg; SODIUM 369mg; CALC 147mg

Warm Gingerbread with Lemon Glaze

When family and friends open your door and get a whiff of this bread baking, they'll know the holiday season has begun!

⅓ cup butter, cut into small pieces
⅔ cup hot water
1 cup light or dark molasses
1 large egg
2¾ cups all-purpose flour
1½ teaspoons baking soda
1½ teaspoons ground ginger
1 teaspoon ground cinnamon
½ teaspoon salt
¼ teaspoon ground cloves
Cooking spray
1½ cups powdered sugar
6 tablespoons fresh lemon juice
1 cup frozen reduced-fat whipped topping, thawed
Ground cinnamon (optional)
Lemon slices (optional)

1. Preheat oven to 350°.

2. Combine butter and hot water in a large bowl, stirring with a whisk until butter melts. Add the molasses and egg, and stir with a whisk until blended. Lightly spoon flour into dry measuring cups, and level with a knife. Combine flour, baking soda, ginger, cinnamon, salt, and cloves. Add flour mixture to molasses mixture, stirring just until moist.

3. Spoon batter into a 9-inch cake pan coated with cooking spray. Bake at 350° for 30 minutes or until a wooden pick inserted in center comes out clean.

4. Combine sugar and lemon juice, stirring until well blended. Pierce top of gingerbread liberally with a wooden pick. Pour glaze over gingerbread.

5. Top each serving with whipped topping. Sprinkle gingerbread with cinnamon, and garnish with lemon slices, if desired. Yield: 12 servings (serving size: 1 gingerbread slice and about 1½ tablespoons whipped topping).

CALORIES 296 (20% from fat); FAT 6.5g (sat 3.7g, mono 1.7g, poly 0.4g); PROTEIN 3.6g; CARB 57.3g; FIBER 1g; CHOL 35mg; IRON 2.8mg; SODIUM 322mg; CALC 68mg

Warm Gingerbread with
Lemon Glaze

Cranberry Upside-Down
Cake with Cognac Cream

Cranberry Upside-Down Cake with Cognac Cream

Everyone will love the great flavor of tart cranberries and crunchy pecans embedded in a moist cake crowned with cognac cream.

2   tablespoons butter, melted
Cooking spray
½   cup packed brown sugar
¼   cup chopped pecans, toasted
1   (12-ounce) package fresh cranberries
1⅓   cups all-purpose flour
1½   teaspoons baking powder
⅛   teaspoon salt
¾   cup granulated sugar
3   tablespoons butter, softened
2   large egg yolks
1   teaspoon vanilla extract
½   cup fat-free milk
2   large egg whites
1   cup frozen fat-free whipped topping, thawed
1   tablespoon cognac

1. Preheat oven to 350°.

2. Pour melted butter into an 8-inch square baking pan coated with cooking spray; sprinkle with brown sugar. Bake at 350° for 2 minutes. Remove from oven; top with pecans and cranberries.

3. Lightly spoon flour into dry measuring cups; level with a knife. Combine flour, baking powder, and salt in a bowl; stir with a whisk.

4. Place granulated sugar and softened butter in a large bowl, and beat with a mixer at medium speed until well blended. Add egg yolks, 1 at a time, beating well after each addition. Stir in vanilla extract.

5. Add the flour mixture and milk alternately to butter mixture, beginning and ending with flour mixture, and mix after each addition. Beat egg whites with a mixer at high speed until stiff peaks form using clean, dry beaters, and fold beaten egg whites into batter.

6. Spread batter over cranberries. Bake at 350° for 45 minutes. Cool in pan 5 minutes on a wire rack. Loosen edges of cake with a sharp knife. Place a plate upside down on top of cake pan; invert cake onto plate.

7. Combine whipped topping and cognac, and serve with warm cake. Yield: 9 servings (serving size: 1 cake piece and about 2 tablespoons cognac cream).

CALORIES 316 (29% from fat); FAT 10.2g (sat 4.6g, mono 3.7g, poly 1.2g); PROTEIN 4.3g; CARB 51.7g; FIBER 2.4g; CHOL 65mg; IRON 1.5mg; SODIUM 210mg; CALC 88mg

Angel Food Cake with Fall Fruit Compote

Cake:

- 1 cup sifted cake flour
- 1½ cups sugar, divided
- 12 large egg whites
- 1 teaspoon cream of tartar
- ¼ teaspoon salt
- 1 tablespoon vanilla extract

Compote:

- 3 cups water
- ¼ cup sugar
- 1 vanilla bean, split lengthwise
- ½ cup dried cranberries
- 8 dried figs, halved (about 4 ounces)
- 2 (7-ounce) packages dried mixed fruit

Remaining Ingredient:

- ¾ cup crème fraîche

1. Preheat oven to 325°.

2. Combine cake flour and ¾ cup sugar. Beat egg whites with a mixer at high speed until foamy. Add cream of tartar and salt; beat until soft peaks form. Add ¾ cup sugar, 2 tablespoons at a time; beat until stiff peaks form. Fold in vanilla. Sift flour mixture over egg white mixture, 3 tablespoons at a time; fold in.

3. Spoon batter into an ungreased 10-inch tube pan, spreading evenly. Break air pockets by cutting through batter with a knife. Bake at 325° for 50 minutes or until cake springs back when lightly touched. Invert pan, and cool completely. Loosen cake from sides of pan using a narrow metal spatula. Invert cake onto plate. Cut cake into 12 slices.

4. Combine water, ¼ cup sugar, and vanilla bean in a medium saucepan. Bring to a boil over medium heat; stir until sugar dissolves. Cover and reduce heat; simmer 15 minutes. Add dried fruits; cover and simmer 25 minutes or until fruit is tender, stirring once. Remove from heat. Remove vanilla bean; let stand 5 minutes. Scrape seeds from bean; stir seeds into fruit mixture. Discard bean. Cool compote to room temperature. Spoon compote over cake slices; top with crème fraîche. Yield: 12 servings (serving size: 1 cake slice, ⅓ cup compote, and 1 tablespoon crème fraîche).

CALORIES 346 (15% from fat); FAT 5.9g (sat 3.5g, mono 1.7g, poly 0.3g); PROTEIN 5.9g; CARB 70g; FIBER 4.3g; CHOL 20mg; IRON 2mg; SODIUM 117mg; CALC 41mg

Chocolate Pound Cake with Chocolate-Pistachio Glaze

Cake:

- 3 cups all-purpose flour
- ½ cup unsweetened cocoa
- 1 teaspoon baking powder
- ¼ teaspoon salt
- 2¼ cups granulated sugar
- ¾ cup butter, softened
- 3 large eggs
- 2 teaspoons vanilla extract
- 1¼ cups fat-free milk
- Cooking spray

Glaze:

- ¾ cup powdered sugar
- 3 tablespoons unsweetened cocoa
- 2 tablespoons fat-free milk
- ½ teaspoon vanilla extract
- 2 tablespoons chopped pistachios

1. Preheat oven to 325°.

2. To prepare cake, lightly spoon flour into dry measuring cups; level with a knife. Combine flour, ½ cup cocoa, baking powder, and salt in a small bowl, stirring with a whisk.

3. Place granulated sugar and butter in a large bowl; beat with a mixer at medium speed until well blended (about 5 minutes). Add eggs, 1 at a time, beating well after each addition. Beat in 2 teaspoons vanilla. Add flour mixture and 1¼ cups milk alternately to sugar mixture, beginning and ending with flour mixture.

4. Spoon batter into a 12-cup Bundt pan coated with cooking spray. Bake at 325° for 40 minutes or until a wooden pick inserted in center comes out clean. Cool in pan 10 minutes on a wire rack; remove from pan. Cool completely on wire rack.

5. To prepare glaze, combine powdered sugar and 3 tablespoons cocoa. Add 2 tablespoons milk and ½ teaspoon vanilla; stir with a whisk until smooth. Drizzle over cooled cake; sprinkle with pistachios. Yield: 18 servings (serving size: 1 slice).

CALORIES 290 (30% from fat); FAT 9.6g (sat 5.4g, mono 3g, poly 0.6g); PROTEIN 4.7g; CARB 48.2g; FIBER 1.8g; CHOL 56mg; IRON 1.7mg; SODIUM 159mg; CALC 53mg

Keep your menu simple. Offer your guests one decadent made-from-scratch dessert along with another simple option, such as store-bought specialty cookies.

Darjeeling-Chocolate
Layer Cake

Darjeeling-Chocolate Layer Cake

Cake:

Cooking spray

⅔ cup boiling water

6 tablespoons loose Darjeeling tea

2 cups sifted cake flour

1 teaspoon baking soda

¼ teaspoon salt

⅔ cup unsweetened cocoa

⅔ cup boiling water

¼ cup plain fat-free yogurt

2 teaspoons vanilla extract

1¼ cups granulated sugar

¾ cup packed brown sugar

¼ cup butter, softened

3 large egg whites

1 large egg

Icing:

½ cup boiling water

5 tablespoons loose Darjeeling tea

⅔ cup (6 ounces) ⅓-less-fat cream cheese, softened

2½ cups powdered sugar

½ cup unsweetened cocoa

Remaining Ingredient:

2 tablespoons chopped hazelnuts, toasted

1. Preheat oven to 350°.

2. To prepare cake, coat 2 (9-inch) round cake pans with cooking spray; line bottoms of pans with wax paper. Coat wax paper with cooking spray; set aside.

3. Pour ⅔ cup boiling water over 6 tablespoons Darjeeling tea leaves in a bowl, and steep for 5 minutes. Strain tea through a

fine sieve into a bowl, and cool to room temperature.

4. Combine flour, baking soda, and salt, stirring with a whisk; set aside.

5. Combine ⅔ cup cocoa and ⅔ cup boiling water; stir with a whisk. Cool in freezer 10 minutes; stir in brewed tea, yogurt, and vanilla.

6. Place granulated sugar, brown sugar, and butter in a large bowl, and beat with a mixer at medium speed until well blended (about 5 minutes). Add egg whites and egg, 1 at a time, beating well after each addition. Add flour mixture and brewed tea mixture alternately to sugar mixture, beginning and ending with flour mixture. Pour batter into prepared cake pans; sharply tap pans once on counter to remove air bubbles. Bake at 350° for 30 minutes or until a wooden pick inserted in center comes out clean. Cool in pans 10 minutes on a wire rack; remove from pans. Carefully remove and discard wax paper. Cool completely on wire rack.

7. To prepare icing, pour ½ cup boiling water over 5 tablespoons tea leaves in a bowl; steep 5 minutes. Strain through a fine sieve into a bowl; cool to room temperature. Place cream cheese in a large bowl, and beat with a mixer at medium speed until fluffy (about 1 minute). Sift together powdered sugar and ½ cup cocoa. Gradually add cocoa mixture and 2½ to 3 tablespoons brewed tea to cream cheese. Beat just until smooth (do not overbeat or icing will be too thin). Discard any remaining tea.

8. Place 1 cake layer on a plate and spread with ½ cup icing. Top with remaining cake layer. Spread remaining icing over top and sides of cake. Sprinkle with hazelnuts. Store loosely covered in refrigerator. Yield: 16 servings (serving size: 1 slice).

CALORIES 305 (21% from fat); FAT 7.1g (sat 3.9g, mono 2.3g, poly 0.4g); PROTEIN 4.7g; CARB 60.3g; FIBER 2.5g; CHOL 29mg; IRON 1.9mg; SODIUM 212mg; CALC 33mg

Old-Fashioned Caramel Layer Cake

Cake:

	Cooking spray
1	tablespoon all-purpose flour
1½	cups granulated sugar
½	cup butter, softened
2	large eggs
1	large egg white
2¼	cups all-purpose flour
2½	teaspoons baking powder
½	teaspoon salt
1¼	cups fat-free milk
2	teaspoons vanilla extract

Frosting:

1	cup packed dark brown sugar
½	cup evaporated fat-free milk
2½	tablespoons butter
2	teaspoons light-colored corn syrup
	Dash of salt
2	cups powdered sugar
2½	teaspoons vanilla extract

1. Preheat oven to 350°.

2. To prepare cake, coat 2 (9-inch) round cake pans with cooking spray; line bottoms of pans with wax paper. Coat wax paper with cooking spray; dust with 1 tablespoon flour.

3. Beat granulated sugar and ½ cup butter with a mixer at medium speed until well blended (about 5 minutes). Add eggs and egg white, 1 at a time, beating well after each addition. Lightly spoon 2¼ cups flour into dry measuring cups; level with a knife. Combine 2¼ cups flour, baking powder, and salt; stir well with a whisk. Add flour mixture to sugar mixture alternately with 1¼ cups milk, beginning and ending with flour mixture. Stir in 2 teaspoons vanilla.

4. Pour batter into pans; sharply tap pans once on counter to remove air bubbles. Bake at 350° for 30 minutes or until a wooden pick inserted in center comes out clean. Cool in pans 10 minutes on a wire rack; remove from pans. Peel off wax paper; cool completely on wire rack.

5. To prepare frosting, combine brown sugar and next 4 ingredients in a saucepan. Bring to a boil over medium-high heat, stirring constantly. Reduce heat, and simmer until thick (about 5 minutes), stirring occasionally. Remove from heat. Add powdered sugar and 2½ teaspoons vanilla, and beat at medium speed until mixture is smooth and slightly warm. Cool 2 to 3 minutes (frosting will be thin but will thicken as it cools).

6. Place 1 cake layer on a plate; spread with ½ cup frosting. Top with remaining cake layer. Spread remaining frosting over top and sides of cake. Store loosely covered in refrigerator. Yield: 18 servings (serving size: 1 slice).

CALORIES 307 (22% from fat); FAT 7.5g (sat 4.4g, mono 2.2g, poly 0.4g); PROTEIN 3.8g; CARB 56.7g; FIBER 0.4g; CHOL 43mg; IRON 1.2mg; SODIUM 251mg; CALC 97mg

Old-Fashioned Caramel
Layer Cake

Double-Coconut Cake
with Fluffy Coconut
Frosting

Your cake becomes all the more stunning when presented on a cake stand, so take a few extra minutes to locate the stand you inherited from your grandmother. You'll give your guests a feast for the eyes as well as the palate.

Double-Coconut Cake with Fluffy Coconut Frosting

Cooking spray
1   tablespoon sifted cake flour
2¼ cups sifted cake flour
2¼ teaspoons baking powder
½   teaspoon salt
1⅔ cups sugar
⅓   cup butter, softened
2   large eggs
1   (14-ounce) can light coconut milk
1   tablespoon vanilla extract
    Fluffy Coconut Frosting
⅔   cup flaked sweetened coconut, divided

1. Preheat oven to 350°.
2. Coat 2 (9-inch) round cake pans with cooking spray; dust with 1 tablespoon flour.
3. Combine 2¼ cups flour, baking powder, and salt, stirring with a whisk. Place sugar and butter in a large bowl, and beat with a mixer at medium speed until well blended (about 5 minutes). Add eggs, 1 at a time, beating well after each addition. Add flour mixture and coconut milk alternately to sugar mixture, beginning and ending with flour mixture. Stir in vanilla.
4. Pour batter into prepared pans. Sharply tap pans once on counter to remove air bubbles. Bake at 350° for 30 minutes or until a wooden pick inserted in center comes out clean. Cool 10 minutes on wire racks; remove from pans. Cool completely on wire racks.
5. Place 1 cake layer on a plate; spread with 1 cup Fluffy Coconut Frosting. Sprinkle with ⅓ cup coconut. Top with remaining cake layer; spread remaining frosting over top and sides of cake. Sprinkle ⅓ cup coconut over top of cake. Yield: 14 servings (serving size: 1 slice).

(Totals include Fluffy Coconut Frosting) CALORIES 298 (24% from fat); FAT 7.9g (sat 5g, mono 1.7g, poly 0.3g); PROTEIN 3.4g; CARB 53.8g; FIBER 0.4g; CHOL 42mg; IRON 1.6mg; SODIUM 273mg; CALC 52mg

Fluffy Coconut Frosting

4   large egg whites
½   teaspoon cream of tartar
    Dash of salt
1   cup sugar
¼   cup water
½   teaspoon vanilla extract
¼   teaspoon coconut extract

1. Place egg whites, cream of tartar, and salt in a large bowl; beat with a mixer at high speed until stiff peaks form. Combine sugar and water in a saucepan; bring to a boil. Cook, without stirring, until a candy thermometer registers 238°. Pour hot sugar syrup in a thin stream over egg whites, beating at high speed. Stir in extracts. Yield: about 4 cups (serving size: about ¼ cup).

CALORIES 54 (0% from fat); FAT 0g; PROTEIN 0.9g; CARB 12.7g; FIBER 0g; CHOL 0mg; IRON 0mg; SODIUM 32mg; CALC 1mg

how to: MAKE THE FROSTING

Slowly beating the hot sugar syrup into stiff egg whites creates what's called an Italian meringue, yielding a dense, glossy, smooth frosting. Heating the sugar syrup to 238° cooks the egg whites.

Espresso Layer Cake

If the intense aroma of freshly ground coffee causes you to swoon, make this dessert. It's a big, impressive two-layer cake.

Cake:

- Cooking spray
- ¼ cup hot water
- 2 tablespoons finely ground espresso
- 2¼ cups all-purpose flour
- 1 teaspoon baking soda
- ½ teaspoon salt
- 1 cup granulated sugar
- ¼ cup packed brown sugar
- ½ cup vegetable shortening
- 1 teaspoon vanilla extract
- 3 large eggs
- 1 cup low-fat buttermilk

Frosting:

- ¼ cup butter
- ½ cup packed brown sugar
- 7 tablespoons evaporated fat-free milk
- 2 teaspoons finely ground espresso
- 1½ teaspoons vanilla extract
- 3 cups powdered sugar
- Whole coffee beans (optional)

1. Preheat oven to 350°.

2. To prepare cake, coat 2 (9-inch) round cake pans with cooking spray; line bottom of pans with wax paper. Coat wax paper with cooking spray; set aside.

3. Combine hot water and 2 tablespoons espresso in a small bowl; stir to dissolve. Set aside. Lightly spoon flour into dry measuring cups; level with a knife. Sift together flour, baking soda, and salt; set aside.

4. Combine granulated sugar and ¼ cup brown sugar. Place ¼ cup sugar mixture, shortening, and 1 teaspoon vanilla in a large bowl; beat with a mixer at low speed 30 seconds or until well combined. Increase speed to medium; add remaining sugar mixture, ¼ cup at a time, beating 15 seconds after each addition. Scrape sides of bowl; beat 5 minutes. Add eggs, 1 at a time, beating 1 minute after each addition. Add espresso mixture, beating until well combined. Add flour mixture and buttermilk alternately to egg mixture, beginning and ending with flour mixture. Pour batter into prepared pans. Bake at 350° for 30 minutes or until a wooden pick inserted in center comes out clean. Cool in pans 10 minutes on a wire rack; remove from pans. Cool completely on wire rack. Discard wax paper.

5. To prepare frosting, melt butter in a medium, heavy saucepan over medium heat. Add ½ cup brown sugar; cook 3 minutes or until mixture is smooth, stirring frequently with a whisk. Stir in evaporated milk, 1 tablespoon at a time; cook 3 minutes or until mixture resembles caramel sauce. Remove from heat; stir in 2 teaspoons espresso. Cool to room temperature. Stir in 1½ teaspoons vanilla. Gradually add powdered sugar, stirring with a whisk until smooth.

6. Place 1 cake layer on a plate; spread with ½ cup frosting. Top with remaining cake layer; spread remaining frosting over top and sides of cake. Arrange coffee beans around top edge of cake, if desired. Let stand 1 hour or until frosting is set. Yield: 18 servings (serving size: 1 slice).

CALORIES 309 (26% from fat); FAT 9g (sat 3.3g, mono 2.9g, poly 1.6g); PROTEIN 3.7g; CARB 53.4g; FIBER 0.4g; CHOL 43mg; IRON 1.1mg; SODIUM 197mg; CALC 50mg

Orange Marmalade Layer Cake

This old-fashioned cake is just like Grandma used to make. After the cake layers are drenched with fresh orange syrup, they become moist and delicate. Store the cake in the refrigerator.

- Cooking spray
- 3 cups sifted cake flour
- 1½ teaspoons baking soda
- ¾ teaspoon salt
- 9 tablespoons butter, softened
- 2 cups sugar, divided
- 1 tablespoon grated orange rind
- 1 tablespoon vanilla extract
- 4 large egg whites
- 1¼ cups low-fat buttermilk
- 1 cup fat-free milk
- ½ cup fresh orange juice
- 1 (12-ounce) jar orange marmalade, melted and cooled
- ¼ cup low-fat sour cream
- 1½ cups frozen reduced-calorie whipped topping, thawed

1. Preheat oven to 350°.

2. Coat 2 (9-inch) round cake pans with cooking spray, and line bottoms of pans with wax paper; set aside.

3. Combine flour, baking soda, and salt, stirring with a whisk. Place butter in a large bowl, and beat with a mixer at medium speed until light and fluffy (about 2 minutes). Gradually add 1¾ cups sugar, 1 tablespoon at a time, beating until well blended. Beat in orange rind and vanilla. Add egg whites, 1 at a time, beating well after each addition.

4. Combine the buttermilk and fat-free milk. Add the flour mixture and buttermilk mixture alternately to the butter mixture, beginning and ending with the flour mixture. Pour batter into prepared pans, and sharply tap pans once on counter to remove air bubbles. Bake at 350° for 25 minutes or until a wooden pick inserted in center comes out clean. Cool in pans 20 minutes on a wire rack, and remove from pans. Cool completely on wire rack. Remove wax paper.

5. Combine juice and ¼ cup sugar; stir until sugar dissolves.

Pierce cake layers liberally with a wooden pick. Slowly drizzle juice mixture over cake layers.

6. Carefully place 1 layer on a plate; spread with ⅓ cup marmalade. Top with remaining cake layer; spread remaining marmalade on top of cake. Fold sour cream into whipped topping; spread over sides of cake. Cover and chill at least 2 hours. Yield: 16 servings (serving size: 1 slice).

CALORIES 309 (23% from fat); FAT 7.8g (sat 4.7g, mono 1.9g, poly 0.3g); PROTEIN 3.9g; CARB 57.7g; FIBER 0.4g; CHOL 23mg; IRON 1.5mg; SODIUM 350mg; CALC 61mg

Orange Marmalade Layer Cake

Blood Orange Layer Cake

Get a jump start on the holidays and make the cake layers ahead; keep them frozen for up to 2 months. Thaw at room temperature and then assemble. This cake is best served within 2 hours of assembling.

Cake:
  Cooking spray
  4 large eggs
  ¼ teaspoon vanilla extract
  ⅛ teaspoon salt
  ½ cup granulated sugar
  1 cup all-purpose flour

Filling:
  1 (16-ounce) carton plain yogurt
  2 tablespoons honey
  ½ teaspoon vanilla extract
  ⅓ cup whipping cream
  ¼ cup sifted powdered sugar
  5 cups blood orange sections (about 3 blood oranges)
  2 tablespoons chopped fresh mint

Syrup:
  1 cup blood orange juice (about 2 blood oranges)
  ¼ cup granulated sugar

Garnish:
  Mint sprigs (optional)

1. Preheat oven to 375°.
2. To prepare cake, coat an 8-inch round cake pan with cooking spray; line bottom of pan with wax paper. Coat wax paper with cooking spray; set aside.
3. Combine eggs, ¼ teaspoon vanilla, and salt in a large bowl, and beat with a mixer at high speed 2 minutes. Gradually add ½ cup granulated sugar, beating until egg mixture is thick and pale (about 3 minutes). Lightly spoon flour into dry measuring cup; level with a knife. Gently fold flour into egg mixture, ¼ cup at a time. Spoon batter into prepared pan.
4. Bake at 375° for 20 minutes or until cake springs back when touched lightly in center. Cool in pan 10 minutes on a wire rack; remove from pan. Cool completely on wire rack.
5. To prepare filling, place a colander in a 2-quart glass measure or bowl. Line colander with 4 layers of cheesecloth, allowing cheesecloth to extend over outside edges. Spoon yogurt into colander. Cover loosely with plastic wrap; refrigerate 12 hours.
6. Spoon yogurt cheese into a large bowl; discard liquid. Add honey and ½ teaspoon vanilla to yogurt, stirring well with a whisk.
7. Combine cream and powdered sugar in a medium bowl, and beat with a mixer at high speed until soft peaks form. Gently stir one-fourth of cream mixture into yogurt mixture; gently fold in remaining cream mixture. Cover mixture, and chill 15 minutes.
8. Arrange orange sections in a single layer on several layers of paper towels, and let stand 5 minutes. Reserve half of sections; roughly chop remaining sections. Combine chopped orange sections and chopped mint. Cover and chill.
9. To prepare syrup, combine juice and ¼ cup granulated sugar in a small saucepan; bring to a boil over medium-high heat, stirring constantly with a whisk. Reduce heat; simmer until reduced to ¼ cup (about 15 minutes). Remove from heat; cool.
10. Split cake in half horizontally using a serrated knife; place bottom layer, cut side up, on a plate. Brush with 2 tablespoons syrup. Spread with half of yogurt mixture, leaving a ¼-inch border. Sprinkle chopped orange mixture evenly over yogurt mixture.
11. Top with remaining cake layer, cut side down. Brush top layer with remaining syrup; spread with remaining yogurt mixture. Top cake with reserved whole orange sections; garnish with mint sprigs, if desired. Yield: 12 servings (serving size: 1 slice).

CALORIES 240 (25% from fat); FAT 6.7g (sat 3.4g, mono 2g, poly 0.3g); PROTEIN 6.1g; CARB 41.9g; FIBER 0.4g; CHOL 101mg; IRON 1.1mg; SODIUM 77mg; CALC 101mg

Cranberry-Speckled White Chocolate Cheesecake

Yogurt Cheese:
  1 (32-ounce) container plain fat-free yogurt
Crust:
  2 cups graham cracker crumbs (about 9 cookie sheets)
  2 tablespoons butter, melted
  Cooking spray
Cranberry Jam:
  1 cup dried cranberries
  ½ cup sugar
  ⅓ cup water
  3 tablespoons fresh lemon juice
Filling:
  1 (3.5-ounce) bar premium white chocolate, chopped
  2 tablespoons fat-free milk
  1 tablespoon vanilla extract
  1 cup sugar
  ¼ cup cornstarch
  ¼ teaspoon salt
  1 (8-ounce) block ⅓-less-fat cream cheese
  1 (8-ounce) carton reduced-fat sour cream
  2 large eggs

Cranberry-Speckled White
Chocolate Cheesecake

1. To prepare yogurt cheese, place a colander in a medium bowl. Line colander with 2 layers of cheesecloth, allowing cheesecloth to extend over outside edges. Spoon yogurt into colander. Cover loosely with plastic wrap; refrigerate 12 hours. Spoon yogurt cheese into a bowl; discard liquid. Cover and refrigerate.

2. Preheat oven to 350°.

3. To prepare crust, combine cracker crumbs and butter, tossing with a fork until moist. Press into bottom of a 9-inch springform pan coated with cooking spray. Bake at 350° for 10 minutes; cool on a wire rack. Reduce oven temperature to 300°.

4. To prepare cranberry jam, combine cranberries and next 3 ingredients in a medium, heavy saucepan. Bring to a boil over medium-high heat. Cover, reduce heat to medium-low, and simmer 10 minutes or until cranberries are soft. Remove from heat; cool slightly. Place cranberry mixture in a food processor; process 2 minutes or until almost smooth. Set aside.

5. To prepare filling, place chocolate and milk in top of a double boiler. Cook over simmering water 5 minutes or until chocolate melts and mixture is smooth, stirring constantly. Remove from heat; stir in vanilla. Set aside.

6. Place yogurt cheese, 1 cup sugar, and next 4 ingredients in a large bowl; beat with a mixer at low speed 1 minute. Beat at medium-high speed 2 minutes or until smooth, scraping bowl occasionally. Beat in chocolate mixture. Add eggs, 1 at a time, beating well after each addition. Scrape bowl; beat 30 seconds. Fold in cranberry jam. Pour over crust, and smooth top. Loosely cover with aluminum foil.

7. Bake at 300° for 1 hour and 10 minutes. Turn oven off; remove foil. Cool cheesecake in closed oven 1 hour and 15 minutes. Remove cheesecake from oven; run a knife around outside edge. Cool to room temperature. Cover and chill at least 8 hours. Yield: 16 servings (serving size: 1 wedge).

CALORIES 310 (31% from fat); FAT 10.8g (sat 5.4g, mono 3.2g, poly 0.4g); PROTEIN 6.7g; CARB 48.2g; FIBER 0.6g; CHOL 49mg; IRON 0.8mg; SODIUM 286mg; CALC 49mg

Vanilla Cheesecake with
Rum Raisin Syrup

Vanilla Cheesecake with Rum Raisin Syrup

Pureed cottage cheese gives this cheesecake a silky, creamy texture. The rum raisin syrup is good on ice cream, too.

Crust:

⅔ cup reduced-fat vanilla wafer crumbs (about 20 cookies)

1 large egg white, lightly beaten

Cooking spray

Filling:

1 (12-ounce) carton 1% low-fat cottage cheese

1 (8-ounce) block ⅓-less-fat cream cheese, softened

⅔ cup sugar

2 tablespoons cornstarch

1 teaspoon vanilla extract

1 large egg

Syrup:

¾ cup dark rum

½ cup raisins

¼ cup sugar

2 tablespoons water, divided

1 teaspoon cornstarch

1. Preheat oven to 325°.

2. To prepare crust, combine crumbs and egg white, tossing with a fork until moist. Press into bottom of an 8-inch spring-form pan coated with cooking spray. Bake at 325° for 5 minutes or until lightly browned; cool on a wire rack.

3. To prepare filling, place cottage cheese in a food processor; process until smooth (about 2 minutes), scraping sides of bowl once. Add cream cheese, and process until smooth. Add ⅔ cup sugar, 2 tablespoons cornstarch, vanilla, and egg; pulse just until combined. Pour batter into prepared crust.

4. Bake at 325° for 30 minutes. Reduce temperature to 300° (do not remove cheesecake from oven); bake 20 minutes or until center barely moves when pan is touched. Remove cheesecake from oven; run a knife around outside edge. Cool to room temperature. Cover and chill at least 8 hours.

5. To prepare syrup, combine rum and raisins in a microwave-safe bowl; microwave at HIGH 2 minutes. Cover with plastic wrap; let stand 10 minutes.

6. Combine ¼ cup sugar and 1 tablespoon water in a small saucepan over medium heat; cook, without stirring, 5 minutes or until golden. Combine 1 teaspoon cornstarch and 1 table-spoon water, stirring with a whisk. Stir rum mixture and corn-starch mixture into sugar mixture; bring to a boil. Cook 1 minute. Serve syrup chilled or at room temperature with cheesecake. Yield: 12 servings (serving size: 1 cheesecake wedge and about 1½ tablespoons syrup).

CALORIES 203 (25% from fat); FAT 5.6g (sat 3.1g, mono 1.6g, poly 0.2g); PROTEIN 6.6g; CARB 27.9g; FIBER 0.3g; CHOL 33mg; IRON 0.5mg; SODIUM 223mg; CALC 41mg

Cheesecake with Cranberry-Maple Topping

Prepare and refrigerate topping and cheesecake up to 3 days ahead.

Topping:

1 cup maple syrup

2 (8-ounce) packages fresh cranberries

Cheesecake:

15 gingersnaps

24 cinnamon graham crackers (6 cookie sheets)

2 tablespoons butter, melted

Cooking spray

1¼ cups sugar

1½ teaspoons vanilla extract

2 (8-ounce) blocks ⅓-less-fat cream cheese, softened

1 (8-ounce) block fat-free cream cheese, softened

4 large egg whites

1. To prepare topping, combine syrup and cranberries in a saucepan; bring to a boil. Reduce heat; simmer 15 minutes, stirring occasionally. Cover and chill.

2. Preheat oven to 375°.

3. To prepare cheesecake, place gingersnaps and graham crackers in a food processor; process until fine crumbs measure 1¾ cups. Drizzle with butter; pulse 2 times or until moist. Firmly press mixture into bottom and 1 inch up sides of a 9-inch springform pan coated with cooking spray.

4. Place sugar, vanilla, and cheeses in a large bowl. Beat with a mixer at high speed until smooth. Add egg whites, 1 at a time, beating well after each addition. Pour into prepared pan. Bake at 375° for 35 minutes or until center barely moves when pan is touched. Remove from oven; run a knife around outside edge. Cool. Cover; chill at least 8 hours. Serve with topping. Yield: 16 servings (serving size: 1 wedge and 2½ tablespoons topping).

CALORIES 283 (30% from fat); FAT 9.3g (sat 5.3g, mono 2.9g, poly 0.6g); PROTEIN 6.6g; CARB 43.7g; FIBER 1.5g; CHOL 28mg; IRON 1mg; SODIUM 288mg; CALC 84mg

Eggnog Semifreddo

Semifreddo, Italian for "half cold," refers to a dessert that's chilled or partially frozen. Christmas eggnog is transformed from a beverage into a slushy treat. If you don't like rum, substitute vanilla or hazelnut syrup.

⅔ cup sugar
1 teaspoon ground nutmeg
2 large eggs
2 cups 1% low-fat milk
⅔ cup plain low-fat yogurt
2 tablespoons dark rum
2 teaspoons vanilla extract

1. Combine first 3 ingredients in a medium bowl, and stir with a whisk.

2. Cook milk in a heavy saucepan over medium-high heat to 180° or until tiny bubbles form around edge (do not boil). Gradually add hot milk to egg mixture, stirring constantly with a whisk. Return milk mixture to pan; cook over medium heat until thick (about 8 minutes), stirring constantly. Remove from heat.

3. Place pan in a large ice-filled bowl until custard cools to room temperature (about 15 minutes), stirring frequently. Stir in yogurt, rum, and vanilla; pour mixture into a glass bowl. Cover; place in freezer 8 hours. Remove mixture from freezer; let stand 15 minutes. Place in a food processor; process until smooth. Serve immediately. Yield: 6 servings (serving size: ½ cup).

CALORIES 181 (15% from fat); FAT 3.1g (sat 1.4g, mono 1g, poly 0.3g); PROTEIN 6.2g; CARB 28.6g; FIBER 0.1g; CHOL 76mg; IRON 0.3mg; SODIUM 82mg; CALC 159mg

Honey-Roasted Pears with Sweet Yogurt Cream

Pears for roasting—and elegant holiday entertaining—are best if they're slightly firm. Because the skins take on a beautiful deep amber glaze when roasted, we left them on.

8 firm Bosc pears, cored and quartered
Cooking spray
3 tablespoons chilled butter, cut into small pieces
¾ cup apple cider
½ cup honey
1 tablespoon fresh lemon juice
2 teaspoons vanilla extract
Sweet Yogurt Cream

1. Preheat oven to 400°.

2. Place pears in a 13 x 9-inch baking dish coated with cooking spray; dot with butter.

3. Combine cider, honey, juice, and vanilla in a small saucepan. Bring to a boil; pour over pear mixture. Cover; bake mixture at 400° for 20 minutes. Uncover; bake an additional 30 minutes or until pears are tender, basting occasionally. Remove from oven, and let stand 10 minutes. Serve warm with Sweet Yogurt Cream. Yield: 8 servings (serving size: 4 pear quarters, 2 tablespoons basting liquid, and 2 tablespoons Sweet Yogurt Cream).

(Totals include Sweet Yogurt Cream) CALORIES 263 (20% from fat); FAT 5.9g (sat 3.3g, mono 1.7g, poly 0.4g); PROTEIN 3.8g; CARB 52.8g; FIBER 4.1g; CHOL 15mg; IRON 0.7mg; SODIUM 86mg; CALC 127mg

Sweet Yogurt Cream

1 (16-ounce) container plain low-fat yogurt
4½ teaspoons honey
¼ teaspoon vanilla extract

1. Place a colander in a 2-quart glass measure or medium bowl. Line colander with 4 layers of cheesecloth, allowing cheesecloth to extend over outside edges. Spoon yogurt into colander. Cover loosely with plastic wrap; refrigerate 24 hours. Spoon yogurt cheese into a bowl; discard liquid. Stir in honey and vanilla. Yield: 1 cup (serving size: 2 tablespoons).

CALORIES 48 (17% from fat); FAT 0.9g (sat 0.6g, mono 0.2g, poly 0g); PROTEIN 3g; CARB 7.3g; FIBER 0g; CHOL 4mg; IRON 0.1mg; SODIUM 40mg; CALC 104mg

Peppermint
Ice Cream

*Ice cream aficionados adore cold desserts, even in
the winter. Perhaps you do, too, and will serve one of these
delicious frozen desserts at your next gathering.*

Peppermint Ice Cream

This is a great make-ahead dessert; if it's frozen solid, remove it from the freezer 30 minutes before serving so it can soften.

2½ cups 2% reduced-fat milk, divided
2 large egg yolks
2 teaspoons vanilla extract
1 (14-ounce) can fat-free sweetened condensed milk
⅔ cup crushed peppermint candies (about 25 candies)

1. Combine 1¼ cups 2% milk and 2 large egg yolks in a heavy saucepan over medium heat. Cook until egg mixture is slightly thick and coats the back of a spoon (about 8 minutes), stirring constantly (do not boil). Cool egg mixture slightly.
2. Combine egg mixture, 1¼ cups 2% milk, vanilla, and condensed milk in a large bowl. Cover and chill completely. Stir in crushed candies. Pour mixture into the freezer can of an ice-cream freezer; freeze according to manufacturer's instructions. Spoon ice cream into a freezer-safe container; cover and freeze 1 hour or until firm. Yield: 8 servings (serving size: ½ cup).

CALORIES 268 (10% from fat); FAT 2.9g (sat 1.3g, mono 0.9g, poly 0.2g); PROTEIN 7.6g; CARB 52.2g; FIBER 0g; CHOL 62mg; IRON 0.3mg; SODIUM 99mg; CALC 238mg

Frozen Yogurt with Rum-Raisin Sauce

The sauce can be made in advance and reheated in the microwave. Place it in a 2-cup glass measure; microwave at HIGH 1 minute or until heated, stirring every 30 seconds.

⅓ cup packed brown sugar
2 tablespoons water
1 tablespoon butter
1½ tablespoons all-purpose flour
1¼ cups 2% low-fat milk
⅓ cup raisins
½ teaspoon rum flavoring
3 cups low-fat vanilla frozen yogurt

1. Combine first 3 ingredients in a small saucepan over medium heat; cook 3 minutes or until butter melts, stirring occasionally. Combine flour and milk in a small bowl; stir with a whisk. Add milk mixture and raisins to pan; stir well. Cook, stirring constantly, 5 minutes or until thick. Remove from heat; stir in rum flavoring. Serve over frozen yogurt. Yield: 6 servings (serving size: ½ cup frozen yogurt and ¼ cup sauce).

CALORIES 216 (22% from fat); FAT 4.8g (sat 2.4g, mono 1.1g, poly 1.2g); PROTEIN 5g; CARB 39.4g; FIBER 0.5g; CHOL 14mg; IRON 0.5mg; SODIUM 87mg; CALC 173mg

Frozen White Chocolate and Hazelnut Mousse

2 large egg yolks, lightly beaten
3 tablespoons water
1 teaspoon butter
2 ounces premium white baking chocolate, finely chopped
¼ cup Frangelico (hazelnut-flavored liqueur)
½ teaspoon cream of tartar
Dash of salt
6 large egg whites
¾ cup sugar
⅔ cup water
1½ cups frozen fat-free whipped topping, thawed
3 tablespoons chopped hazelnuts, toasted

1. Place egg yolks in a medium bowl. Combine 3 tablespoons water, butter, and chocolate in a large, heavy saucepan over medium heat, stirring constantly until chocolate melts. Gradually add chocolate mixture to egg yolks, stirring constantly with a whisk. Return chocolate mixture to pan; cook over medium heat until thick (about 3 minutes), stirring constantly. Remove from heat; stir in liqueur. Cool slightly.
2. Place cream of tartar, salt, and egg whites in a large bowl; beat with a mixer at high speed until foamy. Combine sugar and ⅔ cup water in a saucepan; bring to a boil. Cook, without stirring, until a candy thermometer registers 238°. Gradually pour hot sugar syrup in a thin stream into egg white mixture, beating at high speed until stiff peaks form (5 to 7 minutes).
3. Gently stir one-fourth of egg white mixture into chocolate mixture; gently fold in remaining egg white mixture. Fold in whipped topping and hazelnuts. Spoon mixture into a chilled freezer-safe container; freeze 8 hours or overnight. Yield: 8 servings (serving size: about ¾ cup).

CALORIES 207 (25% from fat); FAT 5.7g (sat 2.2g, mono 2.5g, poly 0.5g); PROTEIN 4.2g; CARB 30g; FIBER 0.3g; CHOL 56mg; IRON 0.3mg; SODIUM 81mg; CALC 25mg

Buttery Apple Crumble

Whole wheat flour adds an unexpected nutty flavor to the oatmeal topping. Removing the foil halfway through baking allows the topping to become crisp and browned. Serve as a fall harvest dessert or with Thanksgiving dinner.

¾ cup whole wheat flour

1¼ cups regular oats

½ cup packed brown sugar

1 teaspoon ground cinnamon

½ teaspoon salt

½ cup butter, melted

2 teaspoons vanilla extract, divided

½ cup apple cider

¼ cup granulated sugar

1½ teaspoons cornstarch

Dash of salt

10 cups sliced peeled baking apples

Cooking spray

1. Preheat oven to 375°.

2. Lightly spoon flour into a dry measuring cup, and level with a knife. Combine flour, oats, brown sugar, cinnamon, and ½ teaspoon salt in a small bowl. Add butter and 1 teaspoon vanilla; stir with a fork until moist and crumbly.

3. Combine 1 teaspoon vanilla, cider, granulated sugar, cornstarch, and dash of salt in a large bowl; stir with a whisk until sugar dissolves and mixture is smooth. Add apples; toss to coat. Spoon apple mixture into a 13 x 9-inch baking dish coated with cooking spray. Sprinkle with oat mixture. Cover with foil; bake at 375° for 30 minutes. Uncover and bake 30 minutes or until browned and bubbly. Yield: 9 servings (serving size: ⅔ cup).

CALORIES 356 (31% from fat); FAT 12.2g (sat 6.6g, mono 3.4g, poly 1.1g); PROTEIN 5.3g; CARB 59.6g; FIBER 6g; CHOL 27mg; IRON 1.8mg; SODIUM 257mg; CALC 36mg

Streusel Apple Pie

1　(4-inch) piece vanilla bean, split lengthwise, or
　　1½ teaspoons vanilla extract
¼　cup packed brown sugar
1½　tablespoons all-purpose flour
½　teaspoon ground cinnamon
2½　pounds Rome or other cooking apples, peeled, cored,
　　and thinly sliced
1　cup all-purpose flour, divided
3　tablespoons ice water
1　teaspoon granulated sugar
¼　teaspoon salt
3　tablespoons vegetable shortening
　Cooking spray
¼　cup all-purpose flour
½　cup packed brown sugar
¼　cup regular oats
¼　teaspoon ground cinnamon
3　tablespoons chilled butter

1. Scrape seeds from vanilla bean into a large bowl, and
discard bean. Add ¼ cup brown sugar, 1½ tablespoons flour,
and ½ teaspoon cinnamon to bowl, and stir well. Add apple
slices; toss well to coat. Set aside.
2. Lightly spoon 1 cup flour into a dry measuring cup; level
with a knife. Combine ¼ cup flour and ice water, stirring with
a whisk until well blended; set aside. Combine ¾ cup flour,
granulated sugar, and salt in a bowl; cut in shortening with a
pastry blender or 2 knives until mixture resembles coarse meal.
Add ice water mixture; stir with a fork until flour mixture is
moist. Gently press into a 4-inch circle on heavy-duty plastic
wrap; cover with additional plastic wrap.
3. Preheat oven to 350°. Roll pastry, still covered, into an
11-inch circle. Freeze 10 minutes. Remove 1 sheet of plastic
wrap from pastry; fit pastry into a 9-inch pie plate coated with
cooking spray, and remove top sheet of plastic wrap. Flute
edges of pastry decoratively. Spoon apple mixture into prepared crust. Cover with foil; bake at 350° for 45 minutes or
until apple mixture is crisp-tender.
4. Lightly spoon ¼ cup flour into a dry measuring cup; level with a
knife. Combine ½ cup brown sugar, ¼ cup flour, oats, and ¼ teaspoon cinnamon; cut in butter until mixture is crumbly. Uncover
pie; sprinkle streusel over apple mixture. Bake, uncovered, an additional 25 minutes. Yield: 8 servings (serving size: 1 wedge).

CALORIES 303 (28% from fat); FAT 9.3g (sat 3.9g, mono 1.2g, poly 0.4g); PROTEIN 3g;
CARB 53.8g; FIBER 2.5g; CHOL 12mg; IRON 1.6mg; SODIUM 112mg; CALC 32mg

Chocolate Cream Pie

Think this doesn't sound like a pie to serve at Thanksgiving? Set it out,
and watch it go.

Crust:
40　graham crackers (10 cookie sheets)
2　tablespoons sugar
2　tablespoons butter, melted
1　large egg white
　Cooking spray
Filling:
2　cups fat-free milk, divided
⅔　cup sugar
⅓　cup unsweetened cocoa
3　tablespoons cornstarch
⅛　teaspoon salt
1　large egg
2　ounces semisweet chocolate, chopped
1　teaspoon vanilla extract
1½　cups frozen reduced-calorie whipped topping, thawed
¾　teaspoon grated semisweet chocolate

1. Preheat oven to 350°.
2. To prepare crust, place crackers in a food processor; process
until crumbly. Add 2 tablespoons sugar, butter, and egg white;
pulse 6 times or just until moist. Press crumb mixture into a
9-inch pie plate coated with cooking spray. Bake at 350° for
8 minutes; cool on a wire rack 15 minutes.
3. To prepare filling, combine ½ cup milk, ⅔ cup sugar, and
next 4 ingredients in a bowl, stirring with a whisk.
4. Cook 1½ cups milk in a heavy saucepan over medium-high
heat to 180° or until tiny bubbles form around edge (do not
boil). Remove from heat. Gradually add hot milk to sugar
mixture, stirring constantly with a whisk. Return milk mixture
to pan. Add chopped chocolate; cook over medium heat
until thick and bubbly (about 5 minutes), stirring constantly.
Reduce heat to low; cook 2 minutes, stirring constantly.
Remove from heat; stir in vanilla. Pour into prepared crust;
cover surface of filling with plastic wrap. Chill 3 hours or until
cold. Remove plastic wrap; spread whipped topping evenly
over filling. Sprinkle with grated chocolate. Yield: 10 servings
(serving size: 1 wedge).

CALORIES 242 (30% from fat); FAT 8g (sat 4.6g, mono 2.1g, poly 0.8g); PROTEIN 5g;
CARB 38.5g; FIBER 0.1g; CHOL 30mg; IRON 1.4mg; SODIUM 189mg; CALC 83mg

Key Lime Pie

Key Lime Pie

A simple garnish can transform your family's favorite pie into the perfect dessert for your holiday table.
Sugared Cranberries (recipe on page 103) makes an excellent garnish for this pie.

1   teaspoon unflavored gelatin
2   tablespoons cold water
½   cup fresh lime juice
2   large egg yolks
1   (14-ounce) can fat-free sweetened condensed milk
Graham Cracker Crust
3   egg whites
¼   teaspoon cream of tartar
⅛   teaspoon salt
⅓   cup sugar
Lime rind strips (optional)
Sugared Cranberries (optional; recipe on page 103)

1. Preheat oven to 325°.
2. Sprinkle gelatin over cold water in a small bowl; set aside.
Combine lime juice and egg yolks in a small, heavy saucepan;
cook over medium-low heat 10 minutes or until slightly thick
and very hot (180°), stirring constantly (do not boil). Add softened gelatin to lime juice mixture; cook 1 minute, stirring until
gelatin dissolves. Place pan in a large ice-filled bowl; stir gelatin
mixture 3 minutes or until mixture reaches room temperature
(do not allow gelatin mixture to set). Strain gelatin mixture in a
sieve over a medium bowl; discard any solids. Gradually add milk,
stirring with a whisk until blended (mixture will be very thick).
Spoon mixture into Graham Cracker Crust; spread evenly.
3. Beat egg whites, cream of tartar, and salt with a mixer at high

speed until foamy. Gradually add sugar, 1 tablespoon at a time;
beat until stiff peaks form. Spread evenly over filling.
4. Bake at 325° for 25 minutes; cool 1 hour on a wire rack. Chill
3 hours or until set. Cut with a sharp knife dipped in hot water.
Garnish with lime rind strips and Sugared Cranberries, if desired.
Yield: 8 servings (serving size: 1 wedge).

Note: You may substitute a commercial reduced-fat graham
cracker pie shell for the Graham Cracker Crust, if desired.

(Totals include Graham Cracker Crust) CALORIES 279 (13% from fat); FAT 4g (sat 1.5g,
mono 1.4g, poly 0.7g); PROTEIN 8.1g; CARB 53.3g; FIBER 0.6g; CHOL 58mg; IRON 0.7mg;
SODIUM 209mg; CALC 154mg

Graham Cracker Crust

2   tablespoons sugar
1   tablespoon chilled butter
1   large egg white
1¼ cups graham cracker crumbs (about 5 cookie sheets)
1   teaspoon ground cinnamon
Cooking spray

1. Preheat oven to 325°. Combine first 3 ingredients in a
bowl; beat with a mixer at medium speed until blended. Add
crumbs and cinnamon; stir with a fork until moist. Press
crumb mixture into a 9-inch pie plate coated with cooking
spray. Bake at 325° for 20 minutes or until lightly browned;
cool on a wire rack. Yield: 1 (9-inch) crust.

Classic Sweet Potato Pie

 1 (9-inch) unbaked Cream Cheese Piecrust
 2 cups mashed cooked sweet potato (about 1¼ pounds)
 1 cup evaporated fat-free milk
 ¾ cup sugar
 1 teaspoon vanilla extract
 ½ teaspoon grated lemon rind
 ½ teaspoon ground cinnamon
 ¼ teaspoon salt
 ¼ teaspoon ground nutmeg
 2 large eggs
 1¼ cups frozen reduced-calorie whipped topping, thawed

1. Prepare Cream Cheese Piecrust in a 9-inch pie plate; set aside.
2. Preheat oven to 350°.
3. Combine sweet potato and next 8 ingredients in a food processor; process until smooth. Spoon mixture into prepared crust. Bake at 350° for 45 minutes or until set; shield edges of piecrust with foil after 20 minutes. Cool completely on a wire rack. Top each serving with whipped topping. Yield: 10 servings (serving size: 1 wedge and 2 tablespoons topping).

(Totals include Cream Cheese Piecrust) CALORIES 274 (20% from fat); FAT 6.1g (sat 3.5g, mono 1.5g, poly 0.5g); PROTEIN 6.5g; CARB 48.4g; FIBER 2.3g; CHOL 76mg; IRON 1.3mg; SODIUM 223mg; CALC 117mg

Cream Cheese Piecrust

 2 tablespoons butter
 2 tablespoons (1 ounce) ⅓-less-fat cream cheese
 2 tablespoons sugar
 1 teaspoon vanilla extract
 1 tablespoon 1% low-fat milk
 1 large egg yolk
 1 cup all-purpose flour
 ¼ teaspoon baking powder
 ¼ teaspoon salt
    Cooking spray

1. Combine first 4 ingredients in a large bowl; beat with a mixer at medium speed until smooth. Add milk and egg yolk; beat until well blended. Lightly spoon flour into a dry measuring cup; level with a knife. Add flour, baking powder, and salt to milk mixture, stirring until well blended.
2. Gently press mixture into a 4-inch circle on heavy-duty plastic wrap; cover with additional plastic wrap. Chill 15 minutes. Roll, still covered, into an 11-inch circle. Place in freezer 5 minutes or until plastic wrap can be easily removed.

3. Remove 1 sheet of plastic wrap; fit dough into a 9-inch pie plate coated with cooking spray. Remove top sheet of plastic wrap. Press dough against bottom and sides of pan. Fold edges under; flute. Fill and bake crust according to recipe directions. Yield: 1 (9-inch) crust.

(Totals include 1 [9-inch] crust) CALORIES 916 (36% from fat); FAT 37g (sat 20.5g, mono 10.7g, poly 2.3g); PROTEIN 19.3g; CARB 123.1g; FIBER 3.4g; CHOL 302mg; IRON 6.7mg; SODIUM 1,074mg; CALC 158mg

Maple-Bourbon Pumpkin Pie

Maple syrup and brown sugar give this pumpkin pie a rich molasses-like flavor. Serve at an informal weeknight dinner or make it the highlight of your Thanksgiving meal.

 ½ (15-ounce) package refrigerated pie dough (such as Pillsbury)
 ¾ cup evaporated fat-free milk
 ½ cup maple syrup
 ⅓ cup packed dark brown sugar
 3 tablespoons bourbon
 2 teaspoons pumpkin pie spice
 1 teaspoon vanilla extract
 ¼ teaspoon salt
 2 large eggs
 1 large egg white
 1 (15-ounce) can unsweetened pumpkin
 ¼ cup (2 ounces) ⅓-less-fat cream cheese, softened
 1 tablespoon maple syrup

1. Preheat oven to 350°.
2. Fit dough into a 9-inch pie plate. Fold edges under; flute. Place pie plate in freezer until ready to use.
3. Combine milk and next 9 ingredients in a large bowl. Stir well with a whisk. Combine cheese and 1 tablespoon syrup in a small bowl; stir with a whisk until smooth. Pour pumpkin mixture into crust. Drop cream cheese mixture by small spoonfuls onto filling; swirl with a knife. Bake at 350° for 55 minutes or until a knife inserted in center comes out clean; cool completely on a wire rack. Yield: 8 servings (serving size: 1 wedge).

CALORIES 297 (30% from fat); FAT 10g (sat 4.3g, mono 4.1g, poly 1g); PROTEIN 5.8g; CARB 44.3g; FIBER 2.3g; CHOL 64mg; IRON 1.1mg; SODIUM 258mg; CALC 125mg

Gingered Pumpkin Pie

A gingersnap streusel topping adds crunch to traditional pumpkin pie. Refrigerated pie dough speeds preparation.

- ½ (15-ounce) package refrigerated pie dough (such as Pillsbury)
- 10 gingersnap cookies
- 2 tablespoons sugar
- 1 tablespoon all-purpose flour
- 2 tablespoons chilled butter, cut into small pieces
- ¾ cup sugar
- 1½ teaspoons ground cinnamon
- ½ teaspoon ground ginger
- ¼ teaspoon salt
- ¼ teaspoon ground nutmeg
- 1 (15-ounce) can unsweetened pumpkin
- 1 (12-ounce) can evaporated fat-free milk
- 1 large egg
- 3 large egg whites

1. Roll dough into a 12-inch circle; fit into a 10-inch deep-dish pie plate. Fold edges under, and flute. Freeze 30 minutes.
2. Place cookies, 2 tablespoons sugar, and flour in a food processor; process until cookies are ground. Add butter; pulse until crumbly.
3. Preheat oven to 350°.
4. Combine ¾ cup sugar and next 8 ingredients; pour into prepared crust. Bake at 350° for 35 minutes. Sprinkle crumb mixture over pie; bake an additional 20 minutes or until center is set. Cool to room temperature on a wire rack. Yield: 8 servings (serving size: 1 wedge).

CALORIES 338 (31% from fat); FAT 11.5g (sat 5.1g, mono 4.7g, poly 1.1g); PROTEIN 7.2g; CARB 51.7g; FIBER 2.6g; CHOL 41mg; IRON 1.2mg; SODIUM 340mg; CALC 157mg

Gingered Pumpkin Pie

Lemon-Buttermilk Chess Pie

Crust:
- 1 cup all-purpose flour
- 2 tablespoons sugar
- ⅛ teaspoon salt
- ¼ cup chilled butter, cut into small pieces
- 3½ tablespoons ice water
  Cooking spray

Filling:
- 1 cup sugar
- 2 tablespoons all-purpose flour
- 2 teaspoons lemon rind
- 2 tablespoons fresh lemon juice
- 1 teaspoon vanilla extract
- 2 large eggs
- 2 large egg whites
- 1 cup low-fat buttermilk

1. Preheat oven to 425°.
2. To prepare crust, lightly spoon 1 cup flour into a dry measuring cup; level with a knife. Combine 1 cup flour, 2 tablespoons sugar, and salt in a bowl; cut in butter with a pastry blender or 2 knives until mixture resembles coarse meal. Sprinkle surface with ice water, 1 tablespoon at a time; toss with a fork until moist and crumbly (do not form a ball).
3. Press mixture gently into a 4-inch circle on heavy-duty plastic wrap; cover dough with additional plastic wrap. Roll dough, still covered, into a 12-inch circle. Freeze 10 minutes or until plastic wrap can be easily removed.
4. Remove 1 sheet of plastic wrap; fit dough into a 9-inch pie plate coated with cooking spray. Remove top sheet of plastic wrap. Fold edges under; flute. Line dough with a piece of foil; arrange pie weights (or dried beans) on foil. Bake at 425° for 10 minutes or until edge is lightly browned. Remove pie weights and foil; reduce oven temperature to 350°. Bake crust an additional 5 minutes; cool on a wire rack.
5. To prepare filling, combine 1 cup sugar and next 6 ingredients in a bowl; stir with a whisk until well blended. Gradually stir in buttermilk. Pour into prepared crust. Bake at 350° for 40 minutes or until set, shielding crust with foil after 30 minutes, if necessary. Cool pie on a wire rack. Yield: 8 servings (serving size: 1 wedge).

CALORIES 265 (26% from fat); FAT 7.8g (sat 4.3g, mono 2.3g, poly 0.5g); PROTEIN 5.5g; CARB 43.7g; FIBER 0.5g; CHOL 71mg; IRON 1mg; SODIUM 141mg; CALC 50mg

Peanut Butter Pie

This pie tastes like a peanut butter and chocolate candy bar.

1   cup powdered sugar
1   (8-ounce) block ⅓-less-fat cream cheese, softened
1   cup natural-style, reduced-fat creamy peanut butter (such as Smucker's)
1   (14-ounce) can fat-free sweetened condensed milk
1   (12-ounce) container frozen fat-free whipped topping, thawed
2   (9-inch) commercial reduced-fat graham cracker pie shells
4   teaspoons fat-free chocolate sundae syrup

1. Combine first 3 ingredients in a large bowl; beat with a mixer at medium speed until smooth. Add condensed milk, and beat until combined. Stir in whipped topping. Divide mixture evenly between shells; chill 8 hours or until set (pies will have a soft, fluffy texture). Cut into wedges, and drizzle with chocolate syrup. Yield: 20 servings (serving size: 1 wedge).

CALORIES 264 (28% from fat); FAT 8.2g (sat 1.8g, mono 2.2g, poly 1.3g); PROTEIN 7.3g; CARB 40.3g; FIBER 0.8g; CHOL 5mg; IRON 0.6mg; SODIUM 213mg; CALC 69mg

Life is short; eat dessert first. You'll have few regrets when you invite friends to your home for a holiday dessert party.

Pecan Pie with
Spiked Cream

Pecan Pie with Spiked Cream

You can make and freeze the unbaked crust up to 1 week ahead; bake the pie up to
1 day in advance, and refrigerate. Remove from the refrigerator about 1 hour before serving.

Crust:

    1   cup all-purpose flour, divided
    3   tablespoons ice water
    1   teaspoon fresh lemon juice
    2   tablespoons powdered sugar
    ¼   teaspoon salt
    3   tablespoons vegetable shortening

Filling:

    1   cup brown rice syrup or dark corn syrup
    ¼   cup maple syrup
    2   tablespoons all-purpose flour
    ¼   teaspoon salt
    2   large eggs
    1   large egg white
    ½   cup pecan halves
    1   teaspoon vanilla extract

Topping:

    ⅔   cup frozen fat-free whipped topping, thawed
    1   tablespoon bourbon

1. Preheat oven to 350°.

2. To prepare crust, lightly spoon 1 cup flour into a dry measuring cup, and level with a knife. Combine ¼ cup flour, ice water, and lemon juice, stirring with a whisk until well blended to form a slurry. Combine ¾ cup flour, powdered sugar, and ¼ teaspoon salt in a large bowl; cut in shortening with a pastry blender or 2 knives until mixture resembles coarse meal. Add slurry; toss with a fork until flour mixture is moist.

3. Gently press mixture into a 4-inch circle on 2 sheets of overlapping heavy-duty plastic wrap; cover with 2 additional sheets of overlapping plastic wrap. Roll dough, still covered, into a 12-inch circle. Freeze dough 10 minutes or until plastic wrap can be easily removed.

4. Remove dough from freezer. Remove top 2 sheets of plastic wrap; let dough stand 1 minute or until pliable. Fit dough, plastic wrap side up, into a 9-inch pie plate, allowing dough to extend over edge. Remove remaining plastic wrap. Press dough into bottom and up sides of pie plate. Fold edges under; flute. Bake at 350° for 8 minutes. Cool on a wire rack.

5. To prepare filling, place rice syrup and next 5 ingredients in a large bowl; beat with a mixer at medium speed until well blended. Stir in pecans and vanilla. Pour filling into prepared crust. Bake at 350° for 50 minutes or until edges puff and center is set (shield edges of piecrust with foil if crust gets too brown). Cool on wire rack.

6. To prepare topping, combine whipped topping and bourbon until blended. Serve with pie. Yield: 10 servings (serving size: 1 wedge and about 1 tablespoon topping).

CALORIES 295 (27% from fat); FAT 8.8g (sat 1.6g, mono 3.9g, poly 2.3g); PROTEIN 3.9g; CARB 48.8g; FIBER 0.8g; CHOL 43mg; IRON 1.1mg; SODIUM 194mg; CALC 21mg

Kentucky Derby Pie

Crust:
Cooking spray
7 sheets phyllo dough, thawed
2 tablespoons dry breadcrumbs

Filling:
⅔ cup light- or dark-colored corn syrup
½ cup packed dark brown sugar
⅓ cup bourbon
¼ teaspoon salt
3 large egg whites
2 large eggs
½ cup chopped pecans
¼ cup semisweet chocolate chips
1 teaspoon vanilla extract

1. Preheat oven to 350°.
2. To prepare crust, coat a 9-inch pie plate with cooking spray. Working with 1 phyllo sheet at a time (cover remaining dough to keep from drying), place phyllo sheet in pie plate with edge overlapping plate rim. Lightly coat phyllo with cooking spray; sprinkle with 1 teaspoon breadcrumbs. Place another sheet of phyllo over first sheet in a crisscross design, and lightly coat with cooking spray. Sprinkle with 1 teaspoon breadcrumbs. Repeat process with 4 phyllo sheets, cooking spray, and 4 teaspoons breadcrumbs. Top with remaining phyllo sheet, and coat with cooking spray; fold edges over. Set pie plate aside.
3. To prepare filling, combine corn syrup and next 5 ingredients in a large bowl, stirring with a whisk until mixture is well blended. Stir in pecans, chocolate chips, and vanilla. Pour mixture into prepared crust. Bake at 350° for 25 minutes or until lightly browned; cover with foil, and bake an additional 20 minutes or until a knife inserted 1 inch from edge comes out clean. Cool pie on a wire rack. Yield: 8 servings (serving size: 1 wedge).

CALORIES 303 (28% from fat); FAT 9.3g (sat 2g, mono 4.6g, poly 2g); PROTEIN 5.2g; CARB 49g; FIBER 1.4g; CHOL 53mg; IRON 1.5mg; SODIUM 244mg; CALC 32mg

Strawberry-Almond Cream Tart

1½ cups shortbread cookie crumbs (such as Lorna Doone; about 25 cookies)
3 tablespoons honey
Cooking spray
¼ cup sugar
3 tablespoons cornstarch
1½ cups fat-free milk
1 large egg, lightly beaten
1½ teaspoons lemon juice
1 teaspoon vanilla extract
¼ teaspoon almond extract
3½ cups small strawberries, halved
⅓ cup red currant jelly
1 tablespoon water
Mint sprigs (optional)

1. Place cookie crumbs and honey in a food processor; pulse 4 times or until blended.
2. Preheat oven to 350°. Coat a 10½-inch round removable-bottom tart pan with cooking spray. Place crumb mixture in pan, pressing mixture in bottom and ¾ inch up sides of pan. Bake at 350° for 8 minutes or until crust is lightly browned. Cool crust completely on a wire rack.
3. Combine sugar and cornstarch in a saucepan. Gradually add milk to sugar mixture; stir with a whisk until well blended. Bring milk mixture to a boil over medium heat. Cook 1 minute; stir constantly.
4. Stir about one-fourth of hot milk mixture into beaten egg, and add to remaining hot milk mixture, stirring constantly. Cook an additional 2 minutes or until thick and bubbly, stirring constantly. Remove from heat, and stir in lemon juice and extracts. Pour mixture into a bowl, and cool 20 minutes, stirring occasionally. Pour mixture into prepared crust, and arrange strawberries on top of filling.
5. Combine red currant jelly and water in a small saucepan, and cook mixture over medium heat until jelly melts, stirring occasionally. Drizzle melted jelly over strawberries. Garnish tart with mint sprigs, if desired. Yield: 8 servings (serving size: 1 wedge).

CALORIES 250 (23% from fat); FAT 6.3g (sat 1.4g, mono 2.2g, poly 0.6g); PROTEIN 4.4g; CARB 46.6g; FIBER 1.4g; CHOL 31mg; IRON 1.6mg; SODIUM 135mg; CALC 73mg

Cranberry-Orange
Tart

Cranberry-Orange Tart

Crust:

1½ cups all-purpose flour

2 tablespoons sugar

⅛ teaspoon salt

6 tablespoons chilled butter, cut into small pieces

⅓ cup ice water

Cooking spray

Filling:

⅓ cup orange juice

2½ tablespoons cornstarch

1 cup sugar

¼ cup orange marmalade

2 tablespoons chopped walnuts, toasted

1 tablespoon grated orange rind

1 (12-ounce) package fresh cranberries

1. Preheat oven to 425°.

2. To prepare crust, lightly spoon flour into dry measuring cups; level with a knife. Combine flour, 2 tablespoons sugar, and salt in a bowl; cut in butter with a pastry blender or 2 knives until mixture resembles coarse meal.

3. Sprinkle surface with ice water, 1 tablespoon at a time, and toss with a fork until moist and crumbly (do not form a ball). Gently press mixture into a 4-inch circle on plastic wrap. Cover and chill 15 minutes.

4. Slightly overlap 2 lengths of plastic wrap on slightly damp surface. Unwrap chilled dough; place on plastic wrap. Cover dough with 2 additional lengths of overlapping plastic wrap. Roll dough, still covered, into a 14-inch circle. Place dough in freezer 5 minutes or until plastic wrap can be easily removed.

5. Remove plastic wrap; fit dough into a 10-inch round removable-bottom tart pan coated with cooking spray. Fold edges under or flute decoratively.

6. To prepare filling, combine juice and cornstarch in a large bowl; stir well with a whisk. Stir in 1 cup sugar and remaining 4 ingredients. Pour mixture into prepared pan.

7. Bake at 425° for 20 minutes. Reduce oven temperature to 350° (do not remove tart from oven); bake an additional 35 minutes or until crust is lightly browned. Cool completely on a wire rack. Yield: 10 servings (serving size: 1 wedge).

CALORIES 274 (27% from fat); FAT 8.2g (sat 4.4g, mono 2.2g, poly 1.1g); PROTEIN 2.5g; CARB 49.4g; FIBER 2.2g; CHOL 19mg; IRON 1.1mg; SODIUM 105mg; CALC 14mg

Sweet Potato Tart with Pecan Crust

Crust:
- 1 cup whole wheat pastry flour
- ¼ cup pecans
- ⅛ teaspoon salt
- 3½ tablespoons chilled butter, cut into small pieces
- 2 tablespoons maple syrup
- Cooking spray

Filling:
- ½ cup maple syrup
- 2 tablespoons cornstarch
- 1½ cups mashed cooked sweet potatoes
- ¾ cup soft tofu, drained
- 1½ teaspoons finely chopped peeled fresh ginger
- 1½ teaspoons grated orange rind
- ¾ teaspoon vanilla extract
- ¼ teaspoon ground cinnamon
- ⅛ teaspoon ground nutmeg

Syrup:
- ½ cup maple syrup

1. Preheat oven to 350°.

2. To prepare crust, lightly spoon flour into a dry measuring cup; level with a knife. Place flour, pecans, and salt in a food processor; process until pecans are finely ground. Add butter; pulse 4 times or until mixture resembles coarse meal.

3. With processor on, slowly add 2 tablespoons syrup through food chute, processing just until combined (do not form a ball). Place dough on a lightly floured surface; knead lightly 4 or 5 times (dough will be sticky).

4. Place dough in a 9-inch round removable-bottom tart pan lightly coated with cooking spray. Place a sheet of plastic wrap over dough; press dough into bottom and up sides of pan. Discard plastic wrap. Pierce bottom and sides of dough with a fork; bake at 350° for 15 minutes or until lightly browned. Cool on a wire rack.

5. To prepare filling, combine ½ cup syrup and cornstarch. Place syrup mixture, sweet potato, and next 6 ingredients in a food processor; process until smooth, scraping sides. Spoon mixture into prepared crust, spreading evenly. Bake at 350° for 50 minutes or until set. Cool on a wire rack.

6. Place ½ cup syrup in a heavy saucepan; bring to a boil. Cook until reduced to ⅓ cup; remove from heat. Cool and drizzle about 1½ teaspoons over each serving. Yield: 10 servings (serving size: 1 wedge).

CALORIES 264 (25% from fat); FAT 7.3g (sat 2.8g, mono 2.5g, poly 1.2g); PROTEIN 4g; CARB 46.6g; FIBER 3.4g; CHOL 11mg; IRON 1.6mg; SODIUM 81mg; CALC 45mg

Lemon-Macaroon Tartlets

Macaroon Tart Shells
- 1 large egg, lightly beaten
- ¾ cup sugar
- 5 teaspoons cornstarch
- ½ teaspoon grated lemon rind
- ⅓ cup water
- ⅓ cup fresh lemon juice
- 2 drops yellow food coloring (optional)
- ½ cup frozen reduced-calorie whipped topping, thawed
- 2 tablespoons flaked sweetened coconut, toasted

1. Prepare Macaroon Tart shells, and set aside.

2. Place egg in a small bowl, and set aside. Combine sugar, cornstarch, and lemon rind in a saucepan. Gradually add water and lemon juice, and stir with a whisk until blended. Bring to a boil over medium heat, and cook 1 minute, stirring constantly. Gradually stir one-fourth of hot lemon mixture into egg, and add to remaining lemon mixture, stirring constantly. Cook over medium heat 1 minute or until thick, stirring constantly. Pour mixture into a bowl, and stir in food coloring, if desired. Place plastic wrap on surface, and chill.

3. Spoon 1 tablespoon lemon mixture into each tart shell. Top with 2 teaspoons whipped topping; sprinkle each with ½ teaspoon toasted coconut. Yield: 1 dozen (serving size: 1 tartlet).

Note: If lemon mixture is held overnight before placing in tart shells, increase cornstarch to 2 tablespoons.

CALORIES 180 (25% from fat); FAT 5g (sat 4.2g, mono 0.3g, poly 0.1g); PROTEIN 2g; CARB 32.5g; FIBER 0.7g; CHOL 18mg; IRON 0.5mg; SODIUM 49mg; CALC 6mg

Macaroon Tart Shells

- 2 cups flaked sweetened coconut
- ½ cup sugar
- 6 tablespoons all-purpose flour
- 1 teaspoon vanilla extract
- 2 large egg whites
- Cooking spray

1. Preheat oven to 400°. Combine all ingredients except cooking spray in a bowl; divide mixture evenly among 12 muffin cups coated with cooking spray, pressing mixture into bottom and up sides of muffin cups. Bake at 400° for 15 minutes or until edges are browned. Cool in pan on a wire rack 2 minutes. Remove from pan; cool completely on a wire rack. Yield: 1 dozen (serving size: 1 shell).

CALORIES 109 (33% from fat); FAT 4g (sat 3.5g, mono 0.2g, poly 0.1g); PROTEIN 1.4g; CARB 17.3g; FIBER 0.6g; CHOL 0mg; IRON 0.4mg; SODIUM 41mg; CALC 3mg

Sweet Potato Streusel Tarts

These tarts feature a topping made with hazelnuts, although pecans and walnuts will work, too. Keep these little treats on hand to serve to drop-in guests or as a reward for yourself after a long day of shopping.

Crust:

- 1 cup all-purpose flour
- 2 tablespoons granulated sugar
- ⅛ teaspoon salt
- 2 tablespoons chilled butter, cut into small pieces
- 2 tablespoons vegetable shortening
- 3 tablespoons ice water

Cooking spray

Filling:

- ¼ cup maple syrup
- 2 tablespoons brown sugar
- ¾ teaspoon ground cinnamon
- ½ teaspoon ground allspice
- ¼ teaspoon salt
- 1 large egg
- 1 cup mashed cooked sweet potato
- ¼ cup evaporated fat-free milk

Streusel:

- 2 tablespoons finely chopped hazelnuts
- 2 tablespoons brown sugar
- 1½ teaspoons chilled butter, cut into small pieces

1. To prepare crust, lightly spoon flour into a dry measuring cup, and level with a knife. Place flour, granulated sugar, and ⅛ teaspoon salt in a food processor; pulse 2 times or until combined. Add 2 tablespoons butter and shortening; pulse 4 times or until mixture resembles coarse meal. With processor on, add ice water through food chute, 1 tablespoon at a time, processing until combined (do not form a ball). Shape mixture into a 6-inch log; wrap in plastic wrap coated with cooking spray. Freeze 30 minutes.

2. Preheat oven to 425°.

3. Cut log evenly into into 24 slices; place 1 slice in each of 24 miniature muffin cups coated with cooking spray. Press dough into bottoms and up sides of muffin cups.

4. To prepare filling, place syrup and next 5 ingredients in a bowl; beat with a mixer at medium speed 1 minute or until well blended. Add sweet potato and milk; beat until well blended. Spoon about 4 teaspoons filling into each muffin cup.

5. To prepare streusel, combine hazelnuts and 2 tablespoons brown sugar in a small bowl; cut in 1½ teaspoons butter with a pastry blender or 2 knives until mixture resembles coarse meal. Sprinkle streusel evenly over tarts; bake at 425° for 10 minutes. Reduce heat to 350° (do not remove tarts from oven), and bake for 12 minutes or until filling is set. Cool for 5 minutes on a wire rack. Run a knife around outside edges. Remove tarts, and cool completely on wire rack. Yield: 2 dozen (serving size: 1 tart).

CALORIES 81 (32% from fat); FAT 2.9g (sat 1.1g, mono 1.2g, poly 0.4g); PROTEIN 1.3g; CARB 12.6g; FIBER 0.5g; CHOL 12mg; IRON 0.5mg; SODIUM 57mg; CALC 18mg

Sweet Potato
Streusel Tarts

Pecan Tassies in Cream Cheese Pastry

One way to serve these tassies (miniature tarts) during the holidays is on a dessert bar alongside an assortment of winter fruits and hot drinks.

Pastry:
  1 cup all-purpose flour
  1 tablespoon granulated sugar
  Dash of salt
  ¼ cup (2 ounces) ⅓-less-fat cream cheese, softened
  2 tablespoons butter, softened
  2 tablespoons fat-free milk
  Cooking spray

Filling:
  ⅓ cup finely chopped pecans
  ½ cup packed brown sugar
  ⅓ cup light-colored corn syrup
  1 teaspoon vanilla extract
  ⅛ teaspoon salt
  1 large egg, lightly beaten
  1 large egg white

1. Preheat oven to 350°.
2. To prepare pastry, lightly spoon flour into a dry measuring cup; level with a knife. Combine flour, 1 tablespoon granulated sugar, and dash of salt in a small bowl. Combine cream cheese, butter, and milk in a large bowl; beat with a mixer at medium speed until well blended. Add flour mixture; beat at low speed just until blended (mixture will be crumbly). Press flour mixture into a ball.
3. Turn dough out onto a lightly floured surface, and knead lightly 3 or 4 times. Divide dough into 24 portions. Place 1 dough portion into each of 24 miniature muffin cups coated with cooking spray. Press dough into bottom and up sides of muffin cups, using lightly floured fingers.
4. To prepare filling, divide pecans evenly among muffin cups. Combine brown sugar and next 5 ingredients; spoon about 2 teaspoons filling over pecans in each muffin cup.
5. Bake at 350° for 20 minutes or until pastry is lightly browned and filling is puffy. Cool in cups 10 minutes on a wire rack. Run a knife around outside edge of each tassie; remove from pan. Cool completely on wire rack. Yield: 2 dozen tassies (serving size: 1 tassie).

CALORIES 77 (35% from fat); FAT 3g (sat 1.1g, mono 1.2g, poly 0.4g); PROTEIN 1.4g; CARB 11.3g; FIBER 0.2g; CHOL 14mg; IRON 0.4mg; SODIUM 50mg; CALC 9mg

Peanut Butter-Fudge Cups

Crust:
  ¼ cup chunky peanut butter
  3 tablespoons brown sugar
  2 tablespoons chilled butter, cut into small pieces
  1½ tablespoons corn syrup
  1 cup all-purpose flour
  ⅛ teaspoon salt
  3 tablespoons cold water
  Cooking spray

Filling:
  ⅔ cup packed brown sugar
  2 tablespoons unsweetened cocoa
  2 tablespoons semisweet chocolate chips
  3 tablespoons 1% low-fat milk
  1 tablespoon butter
  2 tablespoons all-purpose flour
  1 large egg
  2 teaspoons powdered sugar

1. Preheat oven to 350°.
2. To prepare crust, place first 4 ingredients in a large bowl; beat with a mixer at medium speed until smooth. Lightly spoon 1 cup flour into a dry measuring cup, and level with a knife. Add 1 cup flour and salt to peanut butter mixture; cut in flour with a pastry blender or 2 knives until mixture resembles coarse meal. Sprinkle surface with cold water, 1 tablespoon at a time; toss with a fork until combined.
3. Shape flour mixture into 24 balls. Place 1 ball in each of 24 miniature muffin cups coated with cooking spray. Press dough into bottoms and up sides of muffin cups.
4. To prepare filling, combine ⅔ cup brown sugar and next 4 ingredients in a small saucepan over medium-low heat. Cook 3 to 4 minutes or until smooth, stirring frequently. Remove from heat; stir in 2 tablespoons flour and egg until well blended. Divide chocolate mixture evenly among muffin cups. Bake at 350° for 10 minutes or until pastry is lightly browned; cool in pan on a wire rack 5 minutes. Run a knife around outside edges of cups. Remove cups from pan; cool completely on wire rack. Sprinkle with powdered sugar. Yield: 2 dozen (serving size: 1 cup).

CALORIES 92 (33% from fat); FAT 3.4g (sat 1.4g, mono 1.3g, poly 0.5g); PROTEIN 1.7g; CARB 14.6g; FIBER 0.5g; CHOL 13mg; IRON 0.6mg; SODIUM 48mg; CALC 13mg

Mini Peppermint and Chocolate Chip Cheesecakes

These mini cheesecakes are ideal because you can make them ahead of your party, giving you more time to make sure the house is clean and decorated. Just cover and store them in the refrigerator. Add the topping just before serving them to your guests.

Crust:
    1   cup chocolate wafer crumbs (such as Nabisco's Famous
        Chocolate Wafers; about 22 cookies)
    2   tablespoons sugar
    2   tablespoons butter, melted
    Cooking spray
Filling:
   12   hard peppermint candies, divided
   ⅔   cup (5 ounces) block-style fat-free cream cheese,
        softened
   ½   cup (4 ounces) ⅓-less-fat cream cheese, softened
   ¼   cup sugar
    2   tablespoons flour
    2   large egg whites
    1   large egg
    1   (8-ounce) carton low-fat sour cream
   ¼   cup semisweet chocolate minichips
   ¼   teaspoon peppermint extract
    1   cup frozen fat-free whipped topping, thawed
    2   tablespoons chocolate sprinkles

1. Preheat oven to 325°.
2. To prepare crust, combine first 3 ingredients in a small bowl. Press about 1½ teaspoons crumb mixture into bottom of each of 48 miniature muffin cups coated with cooking spray. Bake at 325° for 5 minutes.
3. To prepare filling, place 6 candies, fat-free cream cheese, and next 6 ingredients in a food processor; process until smooth. Stir in minichips and peppermint extract. Divide filling evenly among prepared crusts. Bake at 325° for 12 minutes or until done. Cool in pans on a wire rack 30 minutes. Remove cheesecakes from pans; cool completely. Top each mini cheesecake with 1 teaspoon whipped topping. Crush 6 candies; sprinkle crushed candies and chocolate sprinkles over cheesecakes. Yield: 4 dozen (serving size: 1 cheesecake).

CALORIES 54 (37% from fat); FAT 2.2g (sat 1.3g, mono 0.6g, poly 0.1g); PROTEIN 1.6g; CARB 6.9g; FIBER 0.2g; CHOL 10mg; IRON 0.2mg; SODIUM 62mg; CALC 15mg

Apple and Cream Cheese Roll-Ups

Filled with fruit and cream cheese, these desserts resemble small strudels. They're a great addition to any holiday brunch.

Filling:
    1   cup dried apples, chopped
   ⅓   cup thawed apple juice concentrate, undiluted
   ¼   teaspoon ground cinnamon
    Dash of ground nutmeg
   ¼   cup sugar
   ¼   cup (2 ounces) ⅓-less-fat cream cheese
    1   large egg
Pastry:
   12   sheets frozen phyllo dough, thawed
    Cooking spray
   ½   cup graham cracker crumbs, divided
   ¼   cup sugar, divided
Topping:
   1½   teaspoons sugar
   ½   teaspoon ground cinnamon

1. To prepare filling, combine first 4 ingredients in a small saucepan over medium-high heat. Bring apple mixture to a boil; cover, reduce heat, and simmer 5 minutes or until most of liquid is absorbed. Cool to room temperature. Combine ¼ cup sugar and cream cheese; beat with a mixer at low speed until blended. Add egg; beat until blended. Fold in apple mixture; cover and set aside.
2. Preheat oven to 350°.
3. To prepare pastry, place 1 phyllo sheet on a large cutting board or work surface (cover remaining dough to keep from drying), and lightly coat with cooking spray. Sprinkle phyllo with 2 teaspoons graham cracker crumbs and 1 teaspoon sugar. Repeat layers twice, ending with crumbs and sugar. Cut phyllo stack lengthwise into 6 (2¾-inch-wide) strips using a sharp knife. Spoon 1 rounded teaspoon apple mixture ½ inch from end of each phyllo strip. Roll up each strip, beginning with apple mixture end; place strips, seam sides down, on a baking sheet coated with cooking spray, and lightly coat each roll with cooking spray. Repeat procedure 3 times.
4. To prepare topping, combine 1½ teaspoons sugar and ½ teaspoon cinnamon; sprinkle evenly over phyllo rolls. Bake at 350° for 10 minutes, and cool on a wire rack. Yield: 24 servings (serving size: 1 roll-up).

CALORIES 81 (18% from fat); FAT 1.6g (sat 0.6g, mono 0.6g, poly 0.2g); PROTEIN 1.4g; CARB 15.4g; FIBER 0.6g; CHOL 11mg; IRON 0.5mg; SODIUM 77mg; CALC 6mg

Cream
Puffs

Cream Puffs

Bake the shells up to a month in advance, and freeze in an airtight container. Several hours before serving,
cut top third off puffs. Fill puffs with the custard filling, replace tops, and refrigerate.

Filling:

1½ cups 2% low-fat milk, divided
¼ cup granulated sugar
3 tablespoons cornstarch
⅛ teaspoon salt
2 large eggs, lightly beaten
1 teaspoon chilled butter, cut into small pieces
2 teaspoons vanilla extract
1 cup frozen fat-free whipped topping, thawed

Shells:

1 cup water
3 tablespoons butter
2 teaspoons granulated sugar
¼ teaspoon salt
1 cup all-purpose flour
2 large eggs
2 large egg whites
1 teaspoon powdered sugar

1. To prepare filling, heat 1¼ cups milk in a medium, heavy saucepan to 180° or until tiny bubbles form around edge (do not boil). Combine ¼ cup milk, ¼ cup granulated sugar, cornstarch, ⅛ teaspoon salt, and 2 eggs in a medium bowl, stirring well with a whisk. Gradually add hot milk to sugar mixture, stirring constantly. Pour milk mixture into pan. Add 1 teaspoon butter; cook over medium heat until thick and bubbly (about 3 minutes), stirring constantly. Reduce heat to low; cook

2 minutes, stirring constantly. Strain mixture through a sieve into a bowl; stir in vanilla. Place plastic wrap directly on surface of custard; refrigerate 2 hours or until chilled. Fold in whipped topping. Cover; chill.

2. Preheat oven to 425°.

3. To prepare shells, cover a large, heavy baking sheet with parchment paper. Combine water, 3 tablespoons butter, 2 teaspoons granulated sugar, and ¼ teaspoon salt in a large, heavy saucepan over medium-high heat, stirring occasionally with a wooden spoon. Bring to a boil; remove from heat. Lightly spoon flour into a dry measuring cup; level with a knife. Add flour to water mixture, stirring well until smooth and mixture pulls away from sides of pan. Return pan to heat; cook 30 seconds, stirring constantly. Remove from heat. Add eggs and egg whites, 1 at a time, beating with a mixer at medium speed just until combined. Beat 1 minute at medium speed.

4. Drop dough into 10 mounds (about ¼ cup each), 2 inches apart, onto prepared baking sheet. Bake at 425° for 20 minutes; reduce oven temperature to 350° (do not open oven door). Bake an additional 20 minutes. Turn oven off; partially open oven door. Pierce top of each puff with a knife; cool puffs in oven 20 minutes. Remove from oven; cool completely on a wire rack.

5. Cut top third off puffs, and fill each puff with about 1 tablespoon filling. Replace tops, and sprinkle with powdered sugar. Yield: 10 servings (serving size: 1 cream puff).

CALORIES 177 (33% from fat); FAT 6.6g (sat 3.4g, mono 2.1g, poly 0.5g); PROTEIN 5.8g; CARB 22.4g; FIBER 0.4g; CHOL 98mg; IRON 0.9mg; SODIUM 185mg; CALC 58mg

Gingerbread
People Cookies

Gingerbread People Cookies

These classic cookies make great holiday ornaments. Prior to baking, make a hole in the top of each
using a wooden pick; string baked, cooled cookies with yarn, and hang them on the tree or mantel.

2 ¼   cups all-purpose flour

1 ½   teaspoons ground ginger

  1   teaspoon ground cinnamon

 ½   teaspoon baking powder

 ¼   teaspoon baking soda

 ¼   teaspoon salt

 ¼   teaspoon ground nutmeg

 ¼   teaspoon ground cloves

  6   tablespoons granulated sugar

 ¼   cup butter, softened

 ½   cup molasses

  1   large egg white

Cooking spray

  2   tablespoons dried currants

1 ¼   cups powdered sugar

  2   tablespoons lemon juice

 ¼   teaspoon vanilla extract

1. Lightly spoon flour into dry measuring cups; level with a knife. Combine flour and next 7 ingredients in a bowl. Combine granulated sugar and butter in a large bowl; beat with a mixer at medium speed 5 minutes. Add molasses and egg white; beat well. Add flour mixture to sugar mixture; beat at low speed until well blended. Divide dough in half. Shape each half into a ball; wrap in plastic wrap. Chill 1 hour.

2. Preheat oven to 350°.

3. Working with 1 portion of dough at a time (keep remaining half chilled until ready to use), roll dough to ⅛-inch thickness on a heavily floured surface; cut with a 2½-inch boy or girl cookie cutter. Place gingerbread cookies 1 inch apart on baking sheets coated with cooking spray. Arrange currants on cookies as eyes. Bake at 350° for 8 minutes. Remove from pans; cool on wire racks.

4. Combine powdered sugar, lemon juice, and vanilla in a bowl. Spoon into a decorating bag or a heavy-duty zip-top plastic bag with a tiny hole snipped in 1 corner of bag, and decorate as desired. Yield: 4 dozen (serving size: 1 cookie).

CALORIES 59 (15% from fat); FAT 1g (sat 0.2g, mono 0.4g, poly 0.3g); PROTEIN 0.7g; CARB 11.9g; FIBER 0.2g; CHOL 0mg; IRON 0.5mg; SODIUM 38mg; CALC 13mg

6 tips for great low-fat cookies

1. Lightly spoon flour into dry measuring cups; level with a knife. Too much flour will make the cookies tough.

2. Use the exact ingredient measurements called for in the recipe.

3. Don't give in to the temptation to add more liquid, even if the batter seems dry.

4. Preheat oven for 15 minutes before baking cookies.

5. Bake cookies on the second rack from the bottom of the oven.

6. Make cookies about the same size so they'll bake more evenly.

Share the sweet spirit of the season with a beautiful box of cookies. Layer the treats, or stack and tie them; then fill your own designer box to offer loved ones. For other cookie recipes and gift ideas, see page 106.

Basic Icebox Sugar Cookies

1	cup all-purpose flour
¼	teaspoon baking soda
⅛	teaspoon salt
¼	cup butter, softened
⅔	cup sugar
1	teaspoon vanilla extract
1	large egg white

Cooking spray

1. Lightly spoon flour into a dry measuring cup; level with a knife. Combine flour, baking soda, and salt in a bowl, and set aside.
2. Beat butter with a mixer at medium speed until light and fluffy. Gradually add sugar, beating until well blended. Add vanilla and egg white; beat well. Add flour mixture; stir until well blended. Turn dough out onto wax paper; shape into a 6-inch log. Wrap log in wax paper; freeze 3 hours or until very firm.
3. Preheat oven to 350°.
4. Cut log into 24 (¼-inch) slices; place slices 1 inch apart on a baking sheet coated with cooking spray. Bake at 350° for 8 to 10 minutes. Remove from pan; cool on wire racks. Yield: 2 dozen (serving size: 1 cookie).

CALORIES 59 (31% from fat); FAT 2g (sat 0.4g, mono 0.8g, poly 0.6g); PROTEIN 0.7g; CARB 9.6g; FIBER 0.1g; CHOL 0mg; IRON 0.2mg; SODIUM 50mg; CALC 2mg

Brown Sugar Icebox Cookies: Substitute ⅔ cup packed brown sugar for granulated sugar in Basic Icebox Sugar Cookies recipe.

CALORIES 60 (30% from fat); FAT 2g (sat 0.4g, mono 0.8g, poly 0.6g); PROTEIN 0.7g; CARB 10g; FIBER 0.1g; CHOL 0mg; IRON 0.4mg; SODIUM 52mg; CALC 7mg

Giant Oatmeal-Raisin Cookies

1	cup sugar
¼	cup butter, softened
2	large eggs
¾	cup applesauce
1	teaspoon vanilla extract
2	cups all-purpose flour
½	teaspoon baking soda
½	teaspoon pumpkin-pie spice
¼	teaspoon salt
1	cup regular oats
1	cup golden raisins
½	cup chopped pecans

Cooking spray

1. Preheat oven to 375°.
2. Beat sugar and butter in a large bowl with a mixer at medium speed until well blended (about 4 minutes). Add eggs, 1 at a time, beating well after each addition. Add applesauce and vanilla; beat well.
3. Lightly spoon flour into dry measuring cups; level with a knife. Combine flour and next 3 ingredients in a bowl. Add to sugar mixture; beat well. Stir in oats, raisins, and pecans.
4. Drop dough into 24 mounds 2 inches apart onto baking sheets coated with cooking spray. Bake at 375° for 14 minutes or until golden brown. Remove from pans; cool on wire racks. Yield: 2 dozen (serving size: 1 cookie).

CALORIES 148 (27% from fat); FAT 4.4g (sat 0.7g, mono 2.1g, poly 1.2g); PROTEIN 2.6g; CARB 25.4g; FIBER 1.3g; CHOL 18mg; IRON 0.9mg; SODIUM 80mg; CALC 11mg

Ginger Cookies

Cookies can be one of the toughest foods to lighten, but these cookies received
our Test Kitchens staff's highest rating for flavor and appearance.

⅔ cup plus 3 tablespoons sugar, divided
¼ cup plus 2 tablespoons butter, softened
¼ cup molasses
1 large egg
2 cups all-purpose flour
2 teaspoons baking soda
1 teaspoon ground ginger
1 teaspoon ground cinnamon
½ teaspoon ground mace
Cooking spray

1. Beat ⅔ cup sugar and butter with a mixer at medium speed until well blended. Add molasses and egg; beat well.

2. Lightly spoon flour into dry measuring cups; level with a knife. Combine flour and next 4 ingredients; gradually add to sugar mixture. Stir until well blended. Divide in half. Wrap each portion in plastic wrap; freeze 30 minutes.

3. Preheat oven to 350°.

4. Shape each portion of dough into 26 (1-inch) balls; roll in 3 tablespoons sugar. Place cookies 2 inches apart on baking sheets coated with cooking spray. Bake at 350° for 12 minutes or until lightly browned. Remove from pans; cool on wire racks. Store in an airtight container. Yield: 52 cookies (serving size: 1 cookie).

CALORIES 46 (29% from fat); FAT 1.5g (sat 0.3g, mono 0.6g, poly 0.4g); PROTEIN 0.6g; CARB 7.7g; FIBER 0.1g; CHOL 4mg; IRON 0.3mg; SODIUM 49mg; CALC 13mg

Ginger
Cookies

Chewy Chocolate Chip Cookies

2¼ cups all-purpose flour
 1 teaspoon baking soda
 ¼ teaspoon salt
 ¾ cup packed brown sugar
 2 tablespoons light butter
 1 teaspoon vanilla extract
 4 large egg whites
 ½ cup granulated sugar
 ⅓ cup light-colored corn syrup
1¼ cups semisweet chocolate chips
    Cooking spray

1. Preheat oven to 375°.
2. Lightly spoon flour into dry measuring cups; level with a knife. Combine flour, baking soda, and salt. Beat brown sugar, butter, and vanilla with a mixer at medium speed until well blended (about 5 minutes).
3. Beat egg whites until foamy using clean, dry beaters. Gradually add granulated sugar, 1 tablespoon at a time; beat until soft peaks form. Add corn syrup; beat until stiff peaks form. Fold brown sugar mixture into egg white mixture. Add flour mixture; stir in chocolate chips.
4. Drop by level tablespoons 1 inch apart onto baking sheets coated with cooking spray. Bake at 375° for 10 minutes or until golden. Remove from oven, and let stand 5 minutes. Remove from pans; cool on wire racks. Store loosely covered. Yield: 4 dozen (serving size: 1 cookie).

CALORIES 71 (24% from fat); FAT 1.9g (sat 0.9g, mono 0.5g, poly 0.1g); PROTEIN 1.1g; CARB 13.1g; FIBER 0.2g; CHOL 0.8mg; IRON 0.4mg; SODIUM 40mg; CALC 5mg

Peanut Butter-Chocolate Chip Brownies

    Cooking spray
 1 cup all-purpose flour
 ¼ cup semisweet chocolate minichips
 ¼ teaspoon baking soda
 ⅛ teaspoon salt
 ¾ cup granulated sugar
 ¼ cup packed dark brown sugar
 ¼ cup creamy peanut butter
 1 tablespoon vegetable oil
 1 teaspoon vanilla extract
 1 large egg
 1 large egg white

1. Preheat oven to 350°.
2. Coat bottom of an 8-inch square baking pan with cooking spray (do not coat sides of pan).
3. Lightly spoon flour into a dry measuring cup, and level with a knife. Combine flour, chocolate chips, baking soda, and salt in a bowl.
4. Combine sugars and next 5 ingredients in a bowl; stir until well blended. Add flour mixture; stir just until blended. Spread batter in bottom of prepared pan. Bake at 350° for 25 minutes or until a wooden pick inserted in center comes out almost clean. Cool on a wire rack. Yield: 16 servings (serving size: 1 brownie).

CALORIES 125 (30% from fat); FAT 4.2g (sat 1.1g, mono 1.7g, poly 1.1g); PROTEIN 2.7g; CARB 19.8g; FIBER 0.5g; CHOL 14mg; IRON 0.6mg; SODIUM 66mg; CALC 7mg

Fudgy Chocolate Brownies

 ¼ cup plus 1 tablespoon butter
 1 ounce unsweetened chocolate
 ⅔ cup Dutch process or unsweetened cocoa
1½ cups sugar
 3 large egg whites, lightly beaten
 1 large egg, lightly beaten
 1 cup all-purpose flour
 ½ teaspoon baking powder
    Cooking spray

1. Preheat oven to 325°.
2. Melt butter and chocolate in a large saucepan over medium heat. Stir in cocoa; cook 1 minute. Stir in sugar, and cook 1 minute (mixture will almost form a ball and will be difficult to stir). Remove pan from heat; cool slightly. Combine egg whites and egg. Gradually add warm chocolate mixture to egg mixture; stir with a whisk until well blended. Lightly spoon flour into a dry measuring cup; level with a knife. Combine flour and baking powder. Add flour mixture to chocolate mixture, stirring well.
3. Spoon batter into a 9-inch square baking pan coated with cooking spray. Bake at 325° for 30 minutes (do not overbake). Cool on a wire rack. Yield: 20 servings (serving size: 1 brownie).

CALORIES 132 (29% from fat); FAT 4.3g (sat 1.3g, mono 1.6g, poly 1g); PROTEIN 2.5g; CARB 21.7g; FIBER 0.2g; CHOL 11mg; IRON 0.9mg; SODIUM 46mg; CALC 16mg

Raspberry-Cream Cheese Brownies

Filling:

⅓ cup sugar

⅓ cup (3 ounces) ⅓-less-fat cream cheese, softened

2 teaspoons all-purpose flour

½ teaspoon vanilla extract

1 large egg white

Brownies:

Cooking spray

¾ cup all-purpose flour

¼ teaspoon baking powder

¼ teaspoon baking soda

⅛ teaspoon salt

1 cup sugar

⅔ cup unsweetened cocoa

¼ cup butter, melted

1 tablespoon water

1 teaspoon vanilla extract

1 large egg

2 large egg whites

3 tablespoons raspberry preserves

1. Preheat oven to 350°.

2. To prepare filling, beat first 5 ingredients with a mixer at medium speed until well blended, and set aside.

3. To prepare brownies, coat bottom of an 8-inch square baking pan with cooking spray (do not coat sides of pan). Lightly spoon ¾ cup flour into dry measuring cups, and level with a knife. Combine flour, baking powder, baking soda, and salt in a medium bowl. Combine 1 cup sugar and next 6 ingredients, stirring well with a whisk. Add to flour mixture, stirring just until moist. Spread two-thirds of batter in bottom of prepared pan. Pour filling over batter, spreading evenly. Carefully drop remaining batter and preserves by spoonfuls over filling; swirl together using tip of a knife to marble. Bake at 350° for 40 minutes or until a wooden pick inserted in center comes out almost clean. Cool on a wire rack. Yield: 16 servings (serving size: 1 brownie).

CALORIES 161 (28% from fat); FAT 5g (sat 3g, mono 1.4g, poly 0.2g); PROTEIN 3.3g; CARB 25.9g; FIBER 0.2g; CHOL 26mg; IRON 1mg; SODIUM 113mg; CALC 18mg

Raspberry-Cream Cheese Brownies

Instead of placing bar cookies in your holiday cookie jar, store them in the pan in which they were baked, sealed tightly with aluminum foil.

Orange Fig Bars

Dough:

    6   tablespoons butter, softened
    ¼   cup sugar
    ¼   cup honey
    1   teaspoon vanilla extract
    1   large egg
    1¾ cups all-purpose flour
    1   teaspoon baking powder
    ¼   teaspoon salt

Filling:

    2   cups dried figs (about 12 ounces)
    1   tablespoon grated orange rind
    ¼   cup boiling water
    2   tablespoons sugar
    2   tablespoons honey
    2   tablespoons fresh orange juice

Remaining Ingredients:

    Cooking spray
    1   teaspoon fat-free milk
    1   large egg yolk, lightly beaten

1. To prepare dough, beat butter with a mixer at medium speed until smooth. Add ¼ cup sugar; beat 2 minutes. Add ¼ cup honey, vanilla, and egg; beat until well blended. Lightly spoon flour into dry measuring cups; level with a knife. Combine flour, baking powder, and salt in medium bowl. Add flour mixture to egg mixture, stirring just until moist. Divide dough in half; gently press each half of dough into a square on plastic wrap. Cover with additional plastic wrap; chill 8 hours.
2. Preheat oven to 375°.
3. To prepare filling, place figs and orange rind in a food processor; process until minced. Combine boiling water, 2 tablespoons sugar, and 2 tablespoons honey, stirring until sugar dissolves. Stir in orange juice. With processor on, slowly add orange juice mixture to fig mixture through food chute. Process until well blended, scraping sides of bowl occasionally; set aside.
4. Working with 1 portion of dough at a time (keep remaining dough covered), roll each portion to a 9-inch square on a heavily floured surface. Fit 1 portion of dough into a 9-inch square baking pan coated with cooking spray. Spread fig mixture evenly over dough in pan. Place remaining square of dough on top of filling. Combine milk and egg yolk in a small bowl, stirring with a whisk; brush over top of dough.
5. Bake at 375° for 30 minutes or until top is golden. Cool 30 minutes on a wire rack. Remove from pan; cool completely. Transfer to a flat surface or cutting board, and cut into bars using a sharp, heavy knife. Yield: 20 servings (serving size: 1 bar).

CALORIES 147 (25% from fat); FAT 4.1g (sat 1.9g, mono 1.6g, poly 0.2g); PROTEIN 2.2g; CARB 25.5g; FIBER 2.4g; CHOL 30mg; IRON 1.1mg; SODIUM 85mg; CALC 42mg

Two-Layer Caramel-Pecan Bars

These bars have a crunchy brown-sugar base and a gooey caramel top. Try cutting the panful into four equal strips with a large, heavy knife, using firm pressure. After removing the strips, cut each crosswise into five pieces.

    ⅓   cup packed brown sugar
    ¼   cup butter, softened
    1   teaspoon vanilla extract
    ¼   teaspoon salt
    ¾   cup all-purpose flour
    Cooking spray
    2   tablespoons fat-free milk
    40 small soft caramel candies
    1   teaspoon vanilla extract
    ¼   cup finely chopped pecans

1. Preheat oven to 375°.
2. Beat first 4 ingredients with a mixer at medium speed until well blended. Lightly spoon flour into dry measuring cups; level with a knife. Add flour to sugar mixture, stirring until well blended (mixture will be crumbly). Firmly press mixture into bottom of an 8-inch square baking pan coated with cooking spray. Bake at 375° for 15 minutes.
3. While crust is baking, combine milk and caramel candies in a medium saucepan. Place over low heat; cook until candies melt, stirring occasionally. Stir in 1 teaspoon vanilla; remove from heat. Remove crust from oven. Pour caramel mixture evenly over hot crust. Sprinkle with pecans. Bake at 375° for 3 additional minutes. Cool completely on a wire rack. Yield: 20 servings (serving size: 1 bar).

CALORIES 123 (34% from fat); FAT 4.7g (sat 2.6g, mono 1.5g, poly 0.4g); PROTEIN 1.4g; CARB 19.6g; FIBER 0.4g; CHOL 7mg; IRON 0.3mg; SODIUM 94mg; CALC 29mg

holiday helpers

Consult this "go-to" guide for answers to all of your holiday entertaining questions.

Countdown to Party Time

Ask any great host or hostess for his or her secret to successful entertaining, and you'll find that success all comes down to planning. Use the following checklist to organize your holiday party. You'll be refreshed and relaxed and able to enjoy your party every bit as much as your guests.

Planning Ahead

Four to Six Weeks Ahead

• Set a date and time.

• Make out your guest list.

• Decide which menu you'll use. Consult make-ahead recipe notes. On your calendar, write when you'll prepare or assemble each dish. Order any food you decide to have catered.

• Select invitations if you plan to send them for your party.

Three Weeks Ahead

• Mail your invitations three weeks ahead—holiday schedules fill quickly.

Two Weeks to Go

• Check your supply of chairs, serving dishes, flatware, and glassware.

• Check your supply of linens and tableware, including serving dishes of different sizes and shapes (which make a more interesting buffet table). If you come up short, ask a friend or relative to lend you a few pieces. If convenience is most important to you, buy paper napkins and plastic wineglasses, plates, and utensils.

• Make a grocery list.

• Give some thought to your home's exterior. Plant seasonal flowers in a planter on the front porch, hang a festive wreath, or wash front-facing windows—anything to give your place a lift.

Only One More Week

• Select holiday music to play.

• Grocery shop for nonperishable items.

• Plan a timetable of the recipes you can prepare ahead.

One or Two Days Before

• Clean the house. If you're too busy, think about hiring a cleaning crew. Or delegate specific chores to family members.

• Buy fresh flowers or greenery to put in vases, or set out a few pots of seasonal bulbs in bloom. An arrangement of candles can also look lovely, and candles won't wilt like a floral centerpiece.

• Get out china, serving dishes, and utensils. Polish silver. Make sure that each dish has its serving utensil.

• Arrange furniture to maximize seating.

• Grocery shop for perishable items.

• Prepare dishes that can be made ahead.

• Chill beverages. Make extra ice.

• Make place cards.

The Day of the Party

• Finish preparing food, and arrange it on serving dishes. Fill additional trays so that you can replenish the table by exchanging a full tray for an empty one.

• Think about coat storage and traffic flow—not only around the buffet table but also throughout your house.

• Set the table.

• Reserve some time for rest.

Setting the Table

Keep in mind the order in which dishes, glasses, and flatware will be used when setting the table. Use the tips below as a guide.

- Lay place mats flush with the table edge or about 1 inch from the edge.
- Fold the napkins, and lay them on the place mat to the left of the forks.
- Aim to keep the amount of flatware that will be used to a minimum. Generally, there should be no more than three pieces of flatware on each side of the plate.
- Put knives and spoons to the right of the plate, with each knife's cutting edge facing the plate. Forks go to the left of the plate.
- As a general rule, start from the outside and work your way in. That is, the flatware for the first course is on the outside, farthest from the plate.
- Place water glasses above the knife. Position additional glasses in order of use.
- Place bread-and-butter plates near the tip of the fork. If there is no bread-and-butter plate, place the salad plate there.
- If there is a bread-and-butter plate, place the salad plate to the left and a little below the bread-and-butter plate.

Setting Up the Buffet

Set the buffet on a surface, such as a dining table, chest, kitchen counter, or sideboard, that will accommodate a stack of dinner plates and serving dishes of food. Arrange the buffet using these tips.

- Place serving dishes in an arrangement that allows for easy circulation and traffic flow.
- Set the buffet near the kitchen so that it's easy to refill serving dishes, or fill additional trays to replace empty ones.
- If a dish is to be served over rice, locate the rice first in line.
- Place dressings and sauces close to the dish they complement.
- Serve desserts at one end of the buffet, or place them on a serving cart.
- Arrange beverages on a side table, or serve them from a tray after guests are seated.

Mix and match china, glassware, and flatware to reflect your personal style.

Add a warm glow to the table with small accent candles.

Wrap silverware in colorful napkins for display on the buffet.

Selecting and Serving Wine

Half the fun of entertaining is the planning, even if it's just a small dinner with friends. And planning which wines to serve, how much to serve, and how to serve them can be exciting, too. Following these six wine solutions will help you entertain with ease at your next party.

Which Wines to Serve There's something wonderful about a dinner where the food and wine work seamlessly together. One easy way to achieve a delicious food and wine marriage is to choose a wine that mirrors the dish you're making. So if your dish is light and fresh with lots of herbal flavors, ask your wine merchant for a wine with similar qualities. Or make a pairing based on the wine guide on page 347. Remember: Pairing wine and food isn't a science, and there are no absolutely right or absolutely wrong answers.

How to Store Wine Until Serving If you plan to offer red wines, leave them where it's relatively cool. Warm places (like on top of the refrigerator or beside the stove) can make red wine taste flat and dull. White wines need to be served quite cool, but it's hard to find extra space in the refrigerator when entertaining. Chill whites in a big galvanized metal bucket. Fill it with a slushy mix of ice and cold water, and put the wine in an hour before your guests arrive; by then, the wine will be perfectly chilled.

Rent Wineglasses There are several advantages to renting glasses—even for a relatively small party. First, you won't have to worry about having enough matching glasses for everyone. Second, the glasses will be delivered to you clean and ready for use. Third, you can return the glasses dirty, since the rental company washes them when you're done. Most party rental companies rent wineglasses, and the service is usually inexpensive (starting at less than $1 per glass). Rent large balloon-shaped glasses, and ask for the highest quality available.

How Much Wine You Need It's always better to overestimate since unopened bottles can be saved and enjoyed later. Figure on a half-bottle of wine per person as a minimum. While this may seem like a lot—it really isn't because a half-bottle of wine yields about two and a half glasses—remember that your guests will probably be sipping wine over the course of many hours.

How to Save Opened Bottles Whether the wine is red or white, recork opened bottles, and put them in the refrigerator to preserve freshness. White wine will be ready to enjoy the following night straight from the refrigerator. For red wine, you'll want to let it warm to room temperature.

And how long can you keep an opened bottle of wine? That depends on the varietal (some—like Cabernet Sauvignon—are more sturdy than others) and a host of complex factors like the amount of air in the bottle, how quickly you recorked it after it was opened, and so on. But as a general rule of thumb, most opened wines remain in good condition for up to three days.

Cooking with Wine Wine used as an ingredient in a dish should always be high quality, just like any other ingredient in the recipe. So when buying a wine for the recipe, choose one that you plan on serving as well. It's not only smart shopping—your dish will taste better, too.

quick tips

- Don't cook with a wine that you wouldn't drink.
- When recipes call for a small amount of wine, small bottles—called splits—are the best buy.
- Store open bottles of wine corked and refrigerated up to three days.
- Don't throw out leftover wine. Freeze i plastic bags for use in soups, stews, sauces, and casseroles.
- You may substitute broth or fruit juice for wine in some recipes, but you may lose the full-bodied flavor of the dish.

A successful food-and-wine pairing must result in both the wine and the food tasting better.

All About Wine Pairing

Wine Type	Herbs & Spices	Vegetables	Fish & Shellfish	Meats	Cheeses	Good Bridges
SAUVIGNON BLANC	Basil, bay leaf, cilantro, dill, fennel, lemongrass, marjoram, mint, parsley, savory, thyme	Carrots; eggplant; most green vegetables (lettuces, snow peas, zucchini); tomatoes	Sea bass, snapper, sole, swordfish, trout, tuna, clams, mussels, oysters, shrimp, scallops	Chicken, game birds, turkey	Buffalo mozzarella, feta, fontina, goat, Parmigiano-Reggiano, ricotta, Swiss	Bell peppers (fresh, roasted); capers; citrus (lemon, lime, orange); fennel; garlic; green figs; leeks; olives; sour cream; tomatoes (fresh, sun-dried)
CHARDONNAY	Basil, clove, tarragon, thyme	Corn, mushrooms, potatoes, pumpkin, squash	Grouper, halibut, monkfish, salmon, swordfish, tuna, crab, lobster, scallops, shrimp	Chicken, pork, turkey, veal	Brie, Camembert, Monterey Jack, Swiss	Apples; avocado; bacon; butter; citrus (lemon juice, lemon zest); coconut milk; cream; Dijon mustard; milk; nuts (toasted hazelnuts, cashews, pine nuts, almonds); pancetta; pears; polenta; tropical fruits (mango, papaya, pineapple); vanilla
RIESLING	Chile pepper, cilantro, dill, five-spice, ginger, lemongrass, nutmeg, parsley	Carrots; corn; onions (roasted, sautéed); parsnips	Sole; smoked fish (salmon, trout); snapper; trout; crab; scallops	Chicken, game birds, pork	Emmenthaler, Gouda	Apricots (fresh, dried); citrus (lime, orange, citrus zest); dried fruits (plums, figs, raisins); peaches; tropical fruits (mango, papaya)
PINOT NOIR	Basil, black pepper, cinnamon, clove, fennel, five-spice, oregano, rosemary, star anise, thyme	Beets, eggplant, mushrooms	Salmon (baked, grilled, sautéed); tuna	Beef, chicken, game birds, lamb, liver, rabbit, squab, turkey, veal	Aged Cheddar, Brie	Beets; butter; Dijon mustard; dried fruits (plums, cherries, raisins, cranberries); shallots; mushrooms; onions (roasted, sautéed); pomegranates; tea; pomegranate molasses; cooked tomatoes; truffles
SYRAH|SHIRAZ	Allspice, chile pepper, coriander, cumin, five-spice, pepper, rosemary, sage	Eggplant; onions (roasted, sautéed); root vegetables	Blackened "meaty" fish (salmon, tuna)	Bacon, duck, lamb, pancetta, pheasant, quail, sausage, short ribs, squab, venison	Cheddar, goat, Gouda, Gruyère	Black figs; black licorice; black olives; black pepper; cherries (fresh, dried); chocolate/cocoa
CABERNET SAUVIGNON	Juniper, oregano, rosemary, sage, savory, thyme	Mushrooms, potatoes, root vegetables	None	Beef (roasts, grilled steak); duck; lamb; venison	Camembert, Cantal, Carmody, aged Jack, aged Gouda	Balsamic vinegar; blackberries; black olives; black pepper; butter; cassis; cherries (fresh, dried); cream; currants; roasted red pepper; toasted nuts (walnuts, pecans)

Choosing Seasonal Produce

		Fruit		
FRUIT	**AVAILABILITY**	**WHY WE LIKE IT**	**STORING**	**PUTTING IT TO USE**
Blood Orange (Moro)	December - March	Smaller, sweeter, and less acidic than traditional oranges, this somewhat expensive fruit with a slight berry flavor is prized for its bright color and flavor. The fruit's skin may be pitted or smooth, and the color of the skin does not indicate the internal color or flavor.	Keep refrigerated for 2 to 4 weeks.	Consider different ways to highlight its brilliant color. Squeeze fresh juice, or use the peeled sections as a garnish.
Bosc Pears	September - May	This pear is as attractive as it is sweet and richly flavored. It's excellent eaten fresh, but also holds its shape when poached, boiled, or baked.	Keep ripe pears cold in the refrigerator. Do not refrigerate unripe pears.	The firm texture of a Bosc pear is best for cooking in desserts and meat dishes. Its dramatic appearance makes it ideal for a fruit bowl.
Clementine	December - January	This juicy-sweet, seedless member of the mandarin family peels effortlessly and breaks easily into sections.	Keep refrigerated for a week.	Save yourself a lot of work by substituting these oranges in recipes calling for orange sections. Or simply peel and eat.
Cranberries	October - December	These berries absorb sugar well, so they are delicious used in sauces, breads, and desserts. Look for round, plump, firm berries with a rich crimson color and smooth skin.	Keep refrigerated for 1 month, or freeze for up to 9 months.	Don't wash cranberries until you are ready to use them. Chop them in a food processor rather than with a knife.
Kumquat	December - April	Because of their sweet skin and tart flesh, these 2-inch oblong fruits can be chopped or eaten whole, seeds included. Use them whole and uncooked to garnish holiday platters and ornamental fruit bowls, and buy only firm fruit.	Store at room temperature if eating soon. Otherwise, keep refrigerated for 2 weeks.	The intense sour-orange flavor makes this citrus fruit a nice addition to chutneys and marmalades paired with beef, pork, or chicken.
Persimmon (Fuyus)	October - December	Fuyus, the nonastringent variety of persimmons, are firm when ripe and have a sweet-spicy flavor with notes of banana, plum, and winter squash.	Keep Fuyus refrigerated for up to a month.	Fuyus should be crisp, smooth, and hard, like apples. Shaped like a tomato, this fruit is ideal for salads and good served with roasted pork or chicken.
Pomegranate	August - December	Hundreds of seeds are surrounded by glistening, luminescent ruby red pulp, which has an intense sweet-tart flavor. Look for heavy, large, and richly colored fruit. The skin should be uniform, free of blemishes, thin, and tough.	Refrigerate whole pomegranates, or freeze seeds in an airtight container for 3 months.	Although the flesh is inedible and bitter, the seeds add a sweet-tart flavor to salads, roasts, and desserts. The juice makes a wonderful, vibrant syrup.

Fruit

FRUIT	AVAILABILITY	WHY WE LIKE IT	STORING	PUTTING IT TO USE
Quince	September - December	The scent of this firm-textured fruit is heavenly. In fact, a noticeable perfume is the best indicator of ripeness. It tastes like a cross between an apple and a pear, with a slight pineapple flavor.	Refrigerate whole quince for as long as 2 to 3 months. They bruise easily, so handle them with care.	Because of its luminescent color and sweet-tart flavor, the quince is excellent in recipes that need to cook long and slow, such as stews, roasts, and jams.

Vegetables

VEGETABLE	AVAILABILITY	WHY WE LIKE IT	STORING	PUTTING IT TO USE
Broccoli	yearlong but peak season is October - April	The entire vegetable is edible raw or cooked. Look for broccoli with a deep green color or a greenish purple color on the florets. Revive limp broccoli by trimming $1/2$ inch from the base of the stalk and then setting the head in a glass of water in the refrigerator overnight.	Store unwashed broccoli in the vegetable crisper of the refrigerator for 3 to 5 days.	Although the florets are most commonly used in recipes, we also chop the stalks and use them in stir-fries. We also add the leaves to salads.
Brussels Sprouts	late fall - early winter	Brussels sprouts have a distinct flavor, but take care in cooking because overcooking can make them bitter. There's no difference between small and large Brussels sprouts, but if they're larger than $1/2$ inch wide, you may need to halve them or quarter them so they'll cook quickly. Buying them on the stalk is a sign of freshness.	Refrigerate in a paper bag for up to 3 days. If refrigerated longer, the flavor may be too strong.	Remove discolored leaves, and cut off stem ends. Brussels sprouts are best when lightly cooked 5 to 10 minutes.
Roots (Beets, Celeriac, Fennel, Parsnips, Turnips, Rutabagas)	yearlong but best in the winter months	These vegetables are the cornerstone of healthy eating, and because of their various textures, they also lend themselves to a variety of cooking methods. Avoid roots that have soft spots or hairy rootlets, which indicate age.	Roots will last for months if stored in a cool, dry place, such as the refrigerator.	Roots are best for roasting, pureeing, or tossing into soups and stews.
Sweet Potatoes	late fall - early winter	Sweet potatoes can be left whole for baking or peeled, if desired, and sliced or cut into chunks.	Store in a cool, dry, dark place for about 3 to 4 weeks. Do not refrigerate.	Mash sweet potatoes, or try tossing them into soups and stews.
Winter Greens (Endive, Escarole, Kale, Spinach, Turnip Greens)	yearlong but best in the winter months	Although greens are available throughout the year, they become sweeter and more tender during the winter, allowing some to be eaten raw. Others are cooked to mellow their slight bitterness.	Store leafy greens unwashed in plastic bags in the refrigerator.	Soak greens, and then wash them leaf by leaf. Winter greens are most often used in salads with various other greens.
Winter Squash (Acorn, Butternut, Hubbard, Pumpkin, Spaghetti)	yearlong but best fall - winter	The best winter squash have thick skins with no soft spots and are slightly heavy. They're picked in the fall and stored until spring.	Store whole in a cool, dry place for 1 month or in the refrigerator for up to 3 months.	These squash have large seeds that need to be removed.

Turkey Tips

Simple Ways to Use Your Turkey Leftovers

Quesadillas: Shred turkey breast; sandwich between flour tortillas with cheese and refried beans. Cook a few minutes per side in a nonstick skillet.

Salad: Grill turkey breast; top a salad of romaine lettuce, kalamata olives, pepperoncini peppers, and feta cheese.

Blackened turkey sandwiches: Season turkey with blackening seasoning, grill, and arrange on hoagie rolls with coleslaw.

Barbecue pizza: Shred turkey, toss with barbecue sauce, and arrange on pizza dough with smoked Cheddar cheese and chopped green onions.

Skewers: Dip turkey in low-fat Italian dressing, cut into bite-sized pieces, skewer with olives and artichoke hearts, and grill.

Fried rice: Sauté chopped turkey, garlic, green onions, and rice.

Pesto focaccia sandwiches: Grill turkey breast; serve with roasted red bell peppers on focaccia spread with pesto.

Stuffed breasts: Cut a horizontal slit into turkey breast to form a pocket; stuff with ham and reduced-fat Swiss cheese. Sauté. Try other combinations like spinach and feta cheese or goat cheese and chutney.

Stuffed potatoes: Chop turkey, season with cumin and chili powder, and sauté. Toss with thawed frozen corn, chopped green onions, lime juice, and chopped cilantro. Spoon over baked potatoes.

Turkey saté: Pound breast into long, thin strips; toss with commercial peanut sauce, skewer, and grill.

poultry safety

Storing: Refrigerate raw poultry (chicken, Cornish hens, duck, and turkey) for up to 2 days and cooked poultry for up to 3 days. Raw skinless, boneless poultry can marinate in the refrigerator for up to 8 hours; raw poultry pieces with skin and bone can marinate for up to 1 day. Freeze uncooked poultry for up to 6 months and cooked poultry for up to 3 months.

Thawing: To thaw poultry in the refrigerator, allow 5 hours thawing time per pound. For the cold-water method, submerge poultry—still in its wrapping—in a sink or pot of cold water; change the water every 30 minutes until thawed. If using the microwave for thawing poultry, follow your microwave's directions.

Handling: Wash your hands with hot water and soap before and after handling poultry. Use hot water and soap to wash the cutting board and any utensils that come in contact with the meat. Be careful when you rinse poultry; you may splash water from the poultry onto a clean area.

Cooking: To prevent food-borne illnesses, poultry must be cooked to 180°. For whole birds, use an instant-read thermometer inserted in the thickest part of the thigh to confirm the temperature. Pierce poultry parts with the tip of a knife—the flesh should be opaque and the juices clear when the poultry is done. We do not recommend stuffing the whole bird because the stuffing may prevent the inside of the bird from reaching a safe temperature, and then the bacteria from the uncooked bird might cross-contaminate the stuffing.

For more guidance on poultry, call the USDA Meat and Poultry Hotline (888-674-6854).

Freezer Facts

Here are some guidelines about how to freeze leftovers and the length of time you can keep foods in the freezer without a compromise in quality.

• Don't overcook food items that are intended for the freezer, and be particularly careful to slightly undercook pasta, rice, and vegetables.

• Cool foods completely by setting them in the refrigerator for at least an hour before freezing.

• Allow time for your frozen foods to thaw before reheating. About 24 to 48 hours in the refrigerator will completely thaw most freezer items.

• Label (we use a permanent ink marker) with reheating instructions before freezing. Include the name of the recipe, date frozen, number of servings, temperature and length of time it bakes, and any other necessary information.

• Thaw casseroles (unless directed otherwise in the recipe) before baking. Going straight from freezer to oven with frozen unbaked dishes causes uneven baking. The outer edges tend to overcook, while the middle is uncooked.

Freezer No-No's

Air and moisture can cause freezer burn. That's why moistureproof, airtight containers and packaging are a must. Just say no to the temptation to use any of the following items for freezer storage—you'll be glad you did.

• Milk or juice cartons, or plastic jugs

• Ricotta, cottage cheese, or yogurt containers or butter/margarine tubs

• Glass jars that don't have "Ball" or "Kerr" on them or glass jars with narrow mouths (even if they're Ball or Kerr jars)

• Plastic zip-top storage bags (as opposed to plastic zip-top freezer bags)

• Plastic sandwich, produce, or bread bags

Freezer Storage Guide

TYPE OF FOOD	STORAGE TIME
Eggs and Cheeses	
cheese	4 months
egg whites or egg substitute	6 months
egg yolks	8 months
Fruits and Vegetables	
commercial frozen fruits	1 year
commercial frozen veggies	8 months
Meats and Poultry	
ground meat	3 to 4 months
beef	6 months to 1 year
veal, lamb	6 to 9 months
pork	3 to 6 months
cooked meats	3 months
turkey	6 months
chicken pieces	3 months
whole chicken	3 to 6 months
cooked chicken	1 month
Breads and Desserts	
muffins, baked	1 month
quick breads, baked	1 month
yeast bread, baked	1 month
layer cakes, baked	1 month
pound cakes, baked	1 month
cookies, baked	1 month
Nuts	6 to 12 months
Soups and Stews (without potatoes)	1 month

Ingredient Substitutions

If you're right in the middle of cooking and realize you don't have a particular ingredient, use the substitutions from these lists.

	INGREDIENT	SUBSTITUTION
BAKING PRODUCTS	Arrowroot, 1 teaspoon	1 tablespoon all-purpose flour or 1 1/2 teaspoons cornstarch
	Baking Powder, 1 teaspoon	1/2 teaspoon cream of tartar and 1/4 teaspoon baking soda
	Chocolate Semisweet, 1 ounce	1 ounce unsweetened chocolate and 1 tablespoon sugar
	Unsweetened, 1 ounce	3 tablespoons cocoa and 1 tablespoon butter
	Cocoa, 1/4 cup	1 ounce unsweetened chocolate (decrease fat in recipe by 1/2 tablespoon)
	Coconut, grated fresh, 1 1/2 tablespoons	1 tablespoon flaked coconut
	Corn Syrup, light, 1 cup	1 cup sugar and 1/4 cup water or 1 cup honey
	Cornstarch, 1 tablespoon	2 tablespoons all-purpose flour or granular tapioca
	Flour All-purpose, 1 tablespoon	1 1/2 teaspoons cornstarch, potato starch, or rice starch
	Cake, 1 cup sifted	1 cup minus 2 tablespoons all-purpose flour
	Self-rising, 1 cup	1 cup all-purpose flour, 1 teaspoon baking powder, and 1/2 teaspoon salt
	Shortening Melted, 1 cup	1 cup vegetable oil (do not use oil if recipe does not call for melted shortening)
	Solid, 1 cup	1 1/8 cups butter (decrease salt in recipe by 1/2 teaspoon)
	Sugar Brown, 1 cup, firmly packed	1 cup granulated white sugar
	Powdered, 1 cup	1 cup sugar and 1 tablespoon cornstarch (processed in food processor)
	Honey, 1/2 cup	1/2 cup molasses or maple syrup
DAIRY PRODUCTS	Eggs 1 large	2 egg yolks for custards and cream fillings or 2 egg yolks and 1 tablespoon water for cookies
	1 large	1/4 cup egg substitute
	2 large	3 small eggs
	1 egg white (2 tablespoons)	2 tablespoons egg substitute
	1 egg yolk (1 1/2 tablespoons)	2 tablespoons sifted dry egg yolk powder and 2 teaspoons water or 1 1/2 tablespoons thawed frozen egg yolk
	Milk Fat-free, 1 cup	4 to 5 tablespoons fat-free dry milk powder and enough cold water to make 1 cup
	Buttermilk, low-fat or fat-free, 1 cup	1 tablespoon lemon juice or vinegar and 1 cup low-fat or fat-free milk (let stand 10 minutes)
	Sour Cream, 1 cup	1 cup plain yogurt
FRUITS & VEGETABLES	Lemon, 1 medium	2 to 3 tablespoons lemon juice and 2 teaspoons grated rind
	Juice, 1 teaspoon	1/2 teaspoon vinegar
	Peel, dried	2 teaspoons freshly grated lemon rind
	Orange, 1 medium	1/2 cup orange juice and 2 tablespoons grated rind
	Tomatoes Fresh, chopped, 2 cups	1 (16-ounce) can (may need to drain)
	Juice, 1 cup	1/2 cup tomato sauce and 1/2 cup water
	Tomato Sauce, 2 cups	3/4 cup tomato paste and 1 cup water
MISC.	Broth, beef or chicken, canned, 1 cup	1 bouillon cube dissolved in 1 cup boiling water
	Capers, 1 tablespoon	1 tablespoon chopped dill pickles or green olives
	Chili Paste, 1 teaspoon	1/4 teaspoon hot red pepper flakes

INGREDIENT	SUBSTITUTION
Chili Sauce, 1 cup	1 cup tomato sauce, $\frac{1}{4}$ cup brown sugar, 2 tablespoons vinegar, $\frac{1}{4}$ teaspoon ground cinnamon, dash of ground cloves, and dash of ground allspice
Gelatin, flavored, 3-ounce package	1 tablespoon unflavored gelatin and 2 cups fruit juice
Ketchup, 1 cup	1 cup tomato sauce, $\frac{1}{2}$ cup sugar, and 2 tablespoons vinegar (for cooking, not to be used as a condiment)
Tahini (sesame-seed paste), 1 cup	$\frac{3}{4}$ cup creamy peanut butter and $\frac{1}{4}$ cup sesame oil
Vinegar, cider, 1 teaspoon	2 teaspoons lemon juice mixed with a pinch of sugar
Wasabi, 1 teaspoon	1 teaspoon horseradish or hot dry mustard
Allspice, ground, 1 teaspoon	$\frac{1}{2}$ teaspoon ground cinnamon and $\frac{1}{2}$ teaspoon ground cloves
Apple Pie Spice, 1 teaspoon	$\frac{1}{2}$ teaspoon ground cinnamon, $\frac{1}{4}$ teaspoon ground nutmeg, and $\frac{1}{8}$ teaspoon ground cardamom
Bay Leaf, 1 whole	$\frac{1}{4}$ teaspoon crushed bay leaf
Chives, chopped, 1 tablespoon	1 tablespoon chopped green onion tops
Garlic, 1 clove	1 teaspoon bottled minced garlic
Ginger Crystallized, 1 tablespoon	$\frac{1}{8}$ teaspoon ground ginger
Fresh, grated, 1 tablespoon	$\frac{1}{8}$ teaspoon ground ginger
Herbs, fresh, 1 tablespoon	1 teaspoon dried herbs or $\frac{1}{4}$ teaspoon ground herbs (except rosemary)
Horseradish, fresh, grated, 1 tablespoon	2 tablespoons prepared horseradish
Lemongrass, 1 stalk, chopped	1 teaspoon grated lemon zest
Mint, fresh, chopped, 3 tablespoons	1 tablespoon dried spearmint or peppermint
Mustard, dried, 1 teaspoon	1 tablespoon prepared mustard
Parsley, chopped fresh, 1 tablespoon	1 teaspoon dried parsley
Vanilla Bean, 6-inch bean	1 tablespoon vanilla extract

Liqueurs, spirits, and wines add special flavors that are difficult to replace. Alcohol itself evaporates at 172°, leaving only its flavor behind. However, this chart gives ideas for substitution of alcoholic ingredients, should you choose to change the recipe.

INGREDIENT	SUBSTITUTION
Amaretto (2 tablespoons)	$\frac{1}{4}$ to $\frac{1}{2}$ teaspoon almond extract
Grand Marnier or other orange-flavored liqueur (2 tablespoons)	2 tablespoons orange juice concentrate or 2 tablespoons orange juice and $\frac{1}{2}$ teaspoon orange extract
Kahlúa, coffee- or chocolate-flavored liqueur (2 tablespoons)	2 tablespoons strong brewed coffee and 1 teaspoon sugar
Rum or Brandy (2 tablespoons)	$\frac{1}{2}$ to 1 teaspoon rum or brandy extract for recipes in which liquid amount is not crucial (add water if necessary to have a specified amount of liquid)
Sherry or Bourbon (2 tablespoons)	1 to 2 teaspoons vanilla extract
Port, Sherry, Rum, Brandy, or fruit-flavored liqueur ($\frac{1}{4}$ cup or more)	equal measure of orange juice or apple juice and 1 teaspoon of corresponding flavored extract or vanilla extract
White Wine ($\frac{1}{4}$ cup or more)	equal measure of white grape juice or apple juice for dessert recipes; equal measure of fat-free, less-sodium chicken broth for savory recipes
Red Wine ($\frac{1}{4}$ cup or more)	equal measure of red grape juice or cranberry juice for dessert recipes; for soups, stews, and other savory dishes, sometimes may substitute an equal measure of beef broth

Metric Equivalents

The information in the following charts is provided to help cooks outside the United States successfully use the recipes in this book. All equivalents are approximate.

Equivalents for Different Types of Ingredients

Standard Cup	Fine Powder (ex. flour)	Grain (ex. rice)	Granular (ex. sugar)	Liquid Solids (ex. butter)	Liquid (ex. milk)
1	140 g	150 g	190 g	200 g	240 ml
3/4	105 g	113 g	143 g	150 g	180 ml
2/3	93 g	100 g	125 g	133 g	160 ml
1/2	70 g	75 g	95 g	100 g	120 ml
1/3	47 g	50 g	63 g	67 g	80 ml
1/4	35 g	38 g	48 g	50 g	60 ml
1/8	18 g	19 g	24 g	25 g	30 ml

Liquid Ingredients by Volume

1/4 tsp					=	1	ml
1/2 tsp					=	2	ml
1 tsp					=	5	ml
3 tsp	=	1 tbl		= 1/2 fl oz	=	15	ml
		2 tbls	= 1/8 cup	= 1 fl oz	=	30	ml
		4 tbls	= 1/4 cup	= 2 fl oz	=	60	ml
		5 1/3 tbls	= 1/3 cup	= 3 fl oz	=	80	ml
		8 tbls	= 1/2 cup	= 4 fl oz	=	120	ml
		10 2/3 tbls	= 2/3 cup	= 5 fl oz	=	160	ml
		12 tbls	= 3/4 cup	= 6 fl oz	=	180	ml
		16 tbls	= 1 cup	= 8 fl oz	=	240	ml
		1 pt	= 2 cups	= 16 fl oz	=	480	ml
		1 qt	= 4 cups	= 32 fl oz	=	960	ml
				33 fl oz	= 1000	ml	= 1 l

Dry Ingredients by Weight

(To convert ounces to grams, multiply the number of ounces by 30.)

1 oz	=	1/16 lb	=	30 g
4 oz	=	1/4 lb	=	120 g
8 oz	=	1/2 lb	=	240 g
12 oz	=	3/4 lb	=	360 g
16 oz	=	1 lb	=	480 g

Length

(To convert inches to centimeters, multiply the number of inches by 2.5.)

1 in =			2.5 cm
6 in = 1/2 ft		=	15 cm
12 in = 1 ft		=	30 cm
36 in = 3 ft	= 1 yd	=	90 cm
40 in =			100 cm = 1 m

Cooking/Oven Temperatures

	Fahrenheit	Celsius	Gas Mark
Freeze Water	32° F	0° C	
Room Temperature	68° F	20° C	
Boil Water	212° F	100° C	
Bake	325° F	160° C	3
	350° F	180° C	4
	375° F	190° C	5
	400° F	200° C	6
	425° F	220° C	7
	450° F	230° C	8
Broil			Grill

Recipe Index

Subject Index

Red Onion Marmalade;
Spicy Thyme and Garlic
Oil (recipes on page 102)

how to use it and why

Glance at the end of any *Cooking Light* recipe, and you'll see how committed we are to helping you make the best of today's light cooking. With six chefs, two registered dietitians, three home economists, and a computer system that analyzes every ingredient we use, *Cooking Light* gives you authoritative dietary detail like no other magazine. We go to such lengths so you can see how our recipes fit into your healthful eating plan. If you're trying to lose weight, the calorie and fat figures will probably help most. But if you're keeping a close eye on the sodium, cholesterol, and saturated fat in your diet, we provide those numbers, too. And because many women don't get enough iron

or calcium, we can also help there, as well. Finally, there's a fiber analysis for those of us who don't get enough roughage.

Here's a helpful guide to put our nutrition analysis numbers into perspective. Remember, one size doesn't fit all, so take your lifestyle, age, and circumstances into consideration when determining your nutrition needs. For example, women who are pregnant or breast-feeding need more protein, calories, and calcium. And men over 50 need 1,200mg of calcium daily, 200mg more than the amount recommended for younger men.

in our nutritional analysis, we use these abbreviations:

sat	saturated fat	**CHOL**	cholesterol
mono	monounsaturated fat	**CALC**	calcium
poly	polyunsaturated fat	**g**	gram
CARB	carbohydrates	**mg**	milligram

Daily Nutrition Guide

	women ages 25 to 50	women over 50	men over 24
Calories	2,000	2,000 or less	2,700
Protein	50g	50g or less	63g
Fat	65g or less	65g or less	88g or less
Saturated Fat	20g or less	20g or less	27g or less
Carbohydrates	304g	304g	410g
Fiber	25g to 35g	25g to 35g	25g to 35g
Cholesterol	300mg or less	300mg or less	300mg or less
Iron	18mg	8mg	8mg
Sodium	2,400mg or less	1,300mg or less	1,500mg or less
Calcium	1,000mg	1,200mg	1,000mg

The nutritional values used in our calculations either come from The Food Processor, Version 7.5 (ESHA Research), or are provided by food manufacturers.